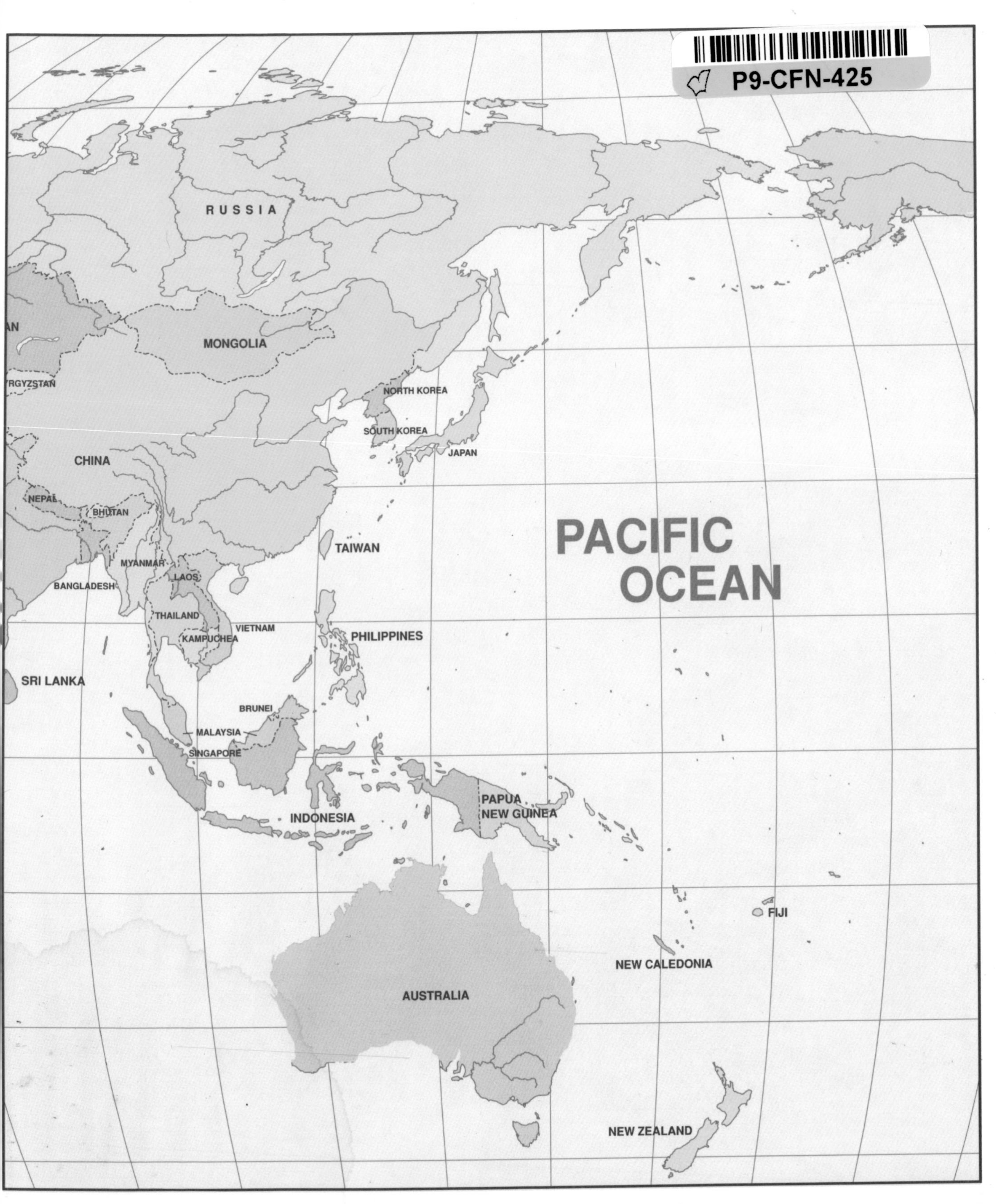

P9-CFN-425
RUSSIA
AN
MONGOLIA
RGYZSTAN
NORTH KOREA
SOUTH KOREA
JAPAN
CHINA
NEPAL
BHUTAN
TAIWAN
MYANMAR
LAOS
BANGLADESH
THAILAND
VIETNAM
KAMPUCHEA
PHILIPPINES
PACIFIC
OCEAN
SRI LANKA
BRUNEI
MALAYSIA
SINGAPORE
PAPUA
NEW GUINEA
INDONESIA
FIJI
NEW CALEDONIA
AUSTRALIA
NEW ZEALAND

Global Economic Issues and Policies

Joseph P. Daniels, Marquette University

David D. VanHoose, Baylor University

Australia · Canada · Mexico · Singapore · Spain · United Kingdom · United States

Global Economic Issues and Policies

Joseph P. Daniels and David D. VanHoose

Editor-in-Chief:
Jack W. Calhoun

Vice President, Team Director:
Michael P. Roche

Publisher of Economics:
Michael B. Mercier

Acquisitions Editor:
Michael W. Worls

Senior Developmental Editor:
Jan Lamar

Senior Marketing Manager:
Janet Hennies

Production Editor:
Daniel C. Plofchan

Manufacturing Coordinator:
Sandee Milewski

Senior Media Technology Editor:
Vicky True

Media Developmental Editor:
Peggy Buskey

Media Production Editor:
Pam Wallace

Compositor:
Shepherd, Inc.

Design Project Manager:
Rik Moore

Internal Designer:
John W. Robb,
JWR Design Interaction

Cover Designer:
Rik Moore

Cover Photographer/Illustration:
PhotoDisc, Inc.
Cartesia Software

Printer:
Phoenix Color
Hagerstown, MD

Printed in the United States of America
1 2 3 4 5 05 04 03 02

For more information contact South-Western, 5191 Natorp Boulevard, Mason, Ohio 45040.
Or you can visit our Internet site at: http://www.swlearning.com

Library of Congress Control Number: 2002111174

Package ISBN: 0-324-07188-4

Book ISBN: 0-324-26908-0

Brief Contents

Contents

Preface

To the Instructor

Instructors we know typically spend considerable time and effort trying to find accessible textbooks addressing the full range of topics that they wish to discuss in a survey course covering global economic issues and policies. There are a number of good texts in international economics from which to choose. Virtually all of them, however, presume a relatively sophisticated audience composed of students who have completed courses in principles of economics or, in many cases, even intermediate economics. In the past, this was sensible because most of the students interested in taking courses in international economics were economics students.

Increasingly, however, students in business and public policy programs are excited about studying the economic issues confronting the global economy. Students enrolling in a global economics course today, therefore, have a much more diverse academic background than in years past. Fewer students are interested in being immersed in economic theory. Our key objective in writing *Global Economic Issues and Policies* was to develop a book suitable for this group of students. This led us to write a book accomplishing the following:

- Covering the wide range of economic issues and policies generated by globalization
- Emphasizing *facts,* as well as theories
- Providing a general student with only the *essential* theoretical concepts required to understand the various economic issues associated with globalization
- Relying only on *principles* of economics to acquaint students with the fundamentals of issues and policies in international trade and finance
- Communicating key economic concepts *verbally* and using diagrams only as an additional—and optional—means of reinforcing student understanding

In an effort to achieve these goals, this text has the following features:

- The text addresses a full set of topics relating to globalization:
  Why nations trade
  How governments regulate international trade
  Regionalism and multilateralism in trade policies
  The role of foreign exchange markets and exchange-rate arrangements
  Public policy issues in international money and finance
  Effects of globalization on both the developed nations and emerging economies
  Industrial and public sector policies in the global economy
  Policy credibility and rules versus discretion
  Policies regarding financial crises and the international financial architecture
- All chapters emphasize factual information about the global economy
- Every new economic concept is introduced and explained within the text, without requiring an instructor to rely on economic diagrams to teach the material
- All topics are discussed at a principles level, so that even students who have not taken a course in economics principles can develop the tools they require to understand how to apply economic concepts to global economic issues and policies
- All theoretical diagrams appear in self-contained *Visualizing Global Economic Issues* features. These features are designed to *reinforce* economic concepts, which are introduced and explained within the text without reliance on the diagrams. Thus, an instructor can choose to cover all, some, or none of the theoretical diagrams.

Features That Teach and Reinforce

To further motivate student learning, we have included examples drawn from nations throughout the world. In addition, four types of application features are incorporated throughout the text:

POLICY NOTEBOOKS

Events relating to global economic policymaking dominate the news. Hence, features covering a wide range of important policy issues appear at appropriate locations. Topics covered include:

- Should the United States Expand Trade with Africa?
- Bananas and Carousels: Is This the Way to Fair Trade?
- Gravity, Trade, and the Euro
- The International Monetary Fund—Dismantle or Reform?

- Monetary Policy Goes Multilingual in Europe
- That Price Is Too Low!—Wal-Mart Meets German Antitrust Policy
- Can Unemployment Insurance Substitute for a Conservative Central Banker?
- Is Capital Market Liberalization the Right Policy?

MANAGEMENT NOTEBOOKS

To acquaint students with the variety of issues faced by business managers in a globalized economy, we have included features on topics such as the following:

- *Anoplophora Glabripennis*—Unwanted Imports
- Do Manufacturers Really Need a Factory?
- Just How Widespread Is the Use of Derivatives by U.S. Businesses?
- Sandwiching Currency Values in a Sesame Seed Bun—The Big Mac Index
- Is the United States Importing Gender Earnings Equality?
- Is Production Sharing Making Mexico a "Trampoline" for U.S. Products?
- The U.S. Drug-Import Ban—Protecting Consumers from Inferior Medicines or Pharmaceuticals Firms from Foreign Competition?
- Do Financial Markets Predict Financial Crises?

ONLINE GLOBALIZATION

The Internet has emerged as an important factor in international trade and finance. Students can learn more about the role of global electronic commerce in features such as the following:

- Is the U.S. "First-Mover Advantage" in E-Commerce Unassailable?
- India's Online Business Services Industry
- Online Foreign Exchange Services
- Increasing the Scope for International Arbitrage via Multicurrency Payment Processing
- The Global Digital Divide
- Are Privacy Protection and Online Protectionism Synonyms in the European Union?
- A French Judge Combats an International Externality

VISUALIZING GLOBAL ECONOMIC ISSUES

Economic diagrams often help students gain a deeper understanding of how economists apply essential concepts and theories to better understand global economic issues and policies. Topics covered in features containing diagrammatical explanations of key issues include the following:

- The Demand and Supply Curves
- Production Possibilities Frontiers and Comparative Advantage

- The Factor Price Equalization Theorem
- A Tariff in a Small-Country Setting
- Trade Creation versus Trade Diversion in a Three-Country World
- The Dollar Demand-Euro Supply Relationship
- Why Covered Interest Parity Is Often Satisfied
- The Wage and Employment Effects of Increased Competition from Abroad
- International Trade and Economies of Scale
- Foreign Monopoly and Dumping in a Domestic Market—Who Gains, and Who Loses?

CRITICAL THINKING EXERCISES

Critical thinking is an important aspect of every college student's education. We make sure that students are introduced to critical-thinking activities by ending each applications feature with critical-thinking questions called "For Critical Analysis." The suggested answers to these critical-thinking questions are included in the *Instructor's Manual.*

Connecting to Global Economic Issues and Policies on the Web

Today, students around the world know how to use the Internet. We provide two very useful features for them:

1) **Margin URLs:** A feature entitled "On the Web" appears in the margins throughout the text. At appropriate locations relative to text discussions, a URL is presented that relates to the topic at hand.
2) **Chapter-Ending Online Applications:** Each chapter concludes with an extensive Internet exercise, which guides the student to a particular URL and provides application questions. Each on-line application concludes with a group exercise called "For Group Study and Analysis."

Special Note on the Graphs

We have spent considerable effort in developing more than 80 charts and graphs for this textbook. All lines and curves are shaded in a consistent manner to assist students in understanding the relationships depicted in the figures. In addition, we have provided full explanations in captions that appear below or alongside each graph or set of graphs.

Key Pedagogy

Student learning must be an active process. We have included an ample number of pedagogical devices to help students master the material.

FUNDAMENTAL ISSUES AND ANSWERS WITHIN THE TEXT OF EACH CHAPTER

A key feature of *Global Economic Issues and Policies* is the inclusion of five to seven fundamental issues at the opening of each chapter. At appropriate locations within the chapter, these fundamental issues are repeated, and appropriate answers are provided. This allows the student to immediately see the relationship between the text materials and the fundamental issues while reading the chapter.

VOCABULARY IS EMPHASIZED

Vocabulary is often a stumbling block in economics courses, and this can be a particular difficulty for students in a course in international economics. Consequently, we have **boldfaced** all important vocabulary terms within the text. Immediately in the margin these boldfaced terms are defined. They are further defined in the end-of-text glossary.

CHAPTER SUMMARY

The chapter summary is a numbered point-by-point formatting that corresponds to the chapter-opening fundamental issues, further reinforcing the full circular nature of the learning process for each chapter.

QUESTIONS AND PROBLEMS

Each chapter ends with several questions and problems. Suggested answers are provided in the *Instructor's Manual.*

REFERENCES AND RECOMMENDED READINGS

Appropriate references for materials in the chapter are given in this section.

Instructor's Manual/Test Bank

The *Instructor's Manual/Test Bank,* which was written by Tim Manuel, University of Montana, is designed to simplify the teaching tasks faced by instructors of courses in international money and finance. It includes an outline of each chapter, possible response(s) to the Critical Thinking questions that conclude the pedagogical features, answers to the end-of-chapter questions (provided by the text authors), and a variety of true/false and multiple-choice test questions for each chapter.

ExamView®

ExamView Computerized Testing Software contains all of the questions in the printed test bank. This program is an easy-to-use test creation software compatible with Microsoft® Windows. Instructors can add or edit questions, instructions, and answers; and select questions by previewing them on the screen, selecting them randomly, or selecting them by number. Instructors can also create and administer quizzes online, whether over the Internet, a local area network (LAN), or a wide area network (WAN).

Study Guide

The *Study Guide,* which was written by Norman Miller, Miami University of Ohio, includes a chapter overview, key terms and concepts, and multiple-choice and short-answer questions to aid the student in their study.

Text Web Site with PowerPoint® Lecture Slides

Students and instructors can address questions and provide commentary directly to the authors and/or South-Western through the text Web page http://daniels.swlearning.com. Instructors can also download PowerPoint Lecture Slides from this site for use in enhancing lectures and incorporating technology into the classroom.

TextChoice: Economic Issues and Activities

TextChoice is the home of Thomson Learning's online digital content. TextChoice provides the fastest, easiest way for you to create your own learning materials. South-Western's Economic Issues and Activities content database includes a wide variety of high-interest, current event/policy applications as well as classroom activities designed specifically to enhance economics courses. Choose just one reading, or many—even add your own material—to create an accompaniment to the textbook that is perfectly customized to your course. Contact your South-Western/Thomson Learning sales representative for more information.

InfoTrac College Edition

An InfoTrac College Edition 4-month subscription card is automatically packaged **free** with new copies of this text. With InfoTrac College Edition, journals like *Business Week, Fortune,* and *Forbes* are just a click away! InfoTrac College Edition provides students with anytime, anywhere access to 20 years' worth of full-text articles (***more than 10 million!***) from nearly **4,000** scholarly and popular sources! In addition to receiving the latest business news as reported in the popular business press, students also have access to many other journals, among them those that are particularly valuable to the economics discipline—including the *Economist (US), American Economist, Economic Review,* and *Quarterly Journal of Economics.* For more information on InfoTrac College Edition, visit http://infotrac/thomsonlearning.com/index.html

Economic Applications (e-con@apps) Web Site (http://econapps.swlearning.com)

Complimentary access to South-Western's e-con@apps Web site is included with every new copy of this textbook.* This site includes a suite of highly-acclaimed and content-rich dynamic Web features developed specifically for economics classrooms: EconNews Online, EconDebate Online, and EconData Online. Organized and searchable by key economic topic for easy integration into your course, these regularly-updated features are pedagogically designed to deepen students' understanding of theoretical concepts through hands-on exploration and analysis of the latest economic news stories, policy debates, and data.

*Students buying a used book can purchase access to the site at http://econapps.swlearning.com.

Acknowledgments

We benefited from an extremely active and conscientious group of reviewers of the manuscript for this first edition of *Global Economic Issues and Policies.* Several of the reviewers went above and beyond the call of duty, and our rewrites of the manuscript improved accordingly. To the following reviewers, we extend our sincere appreciation for the critical nature of your comments that we think helped make this a better text.

Burton A. Abrams
University of Delaware

Rose-Marie Avin
University of Wisconsin–Eau Claire

Moshin Bahmani
University of Wisconsin–Milwaukee

Christopher B. Barrett
Cornell University

Don P. Clark
University of Tennessee

Alan Deardoff
University of Michigan–Ann Arbor

Lewis R. Gale
University of Louisiana at Lafayette

Mary H. Lesser
Iona College

Donald G. Richards
Indiana State University

George Samuels
Sam Houston State University

Henry Thompson
Auburn University

Evridiki Tsounta
University of Minnesota

Abu N. M. Wahid
Tennessee State University

Gary J. Wells
Clemson University

Of course, no textbook project is completed by the authors alone. We wish to thank the economics editor, Michael Worls, and the developmental editor, Jan Lamar, for their assistance. Our production editor, Dan Plofchan, put together an excellent design and provided consistent guidance throughout the project. The copy editor, Cheryl Ferguson, masterfully rearranged our manuscript to make the book read more smoothly.

We anticipate revising this text for years to come and therefore welcome all comments and criticism from students and instructors alike.

J. P. D.
D. D. V.

To Bill, Leigh, and Wesley, for their patience.

J. P. D.

To Chuck Bass.

D. D. V.

UNIT ONE

Introduction to the Global Economy

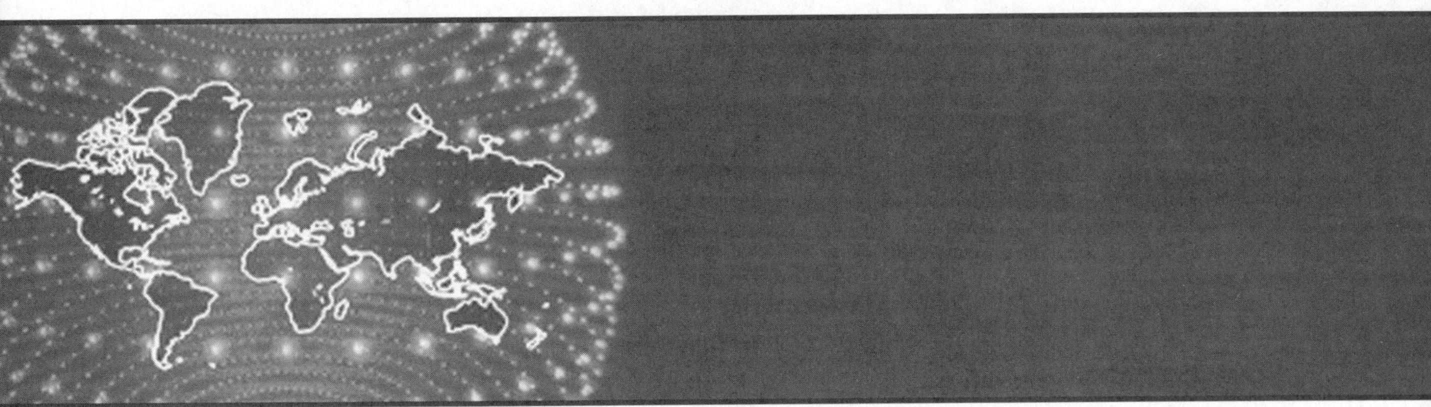

CHAPTER ONE

Understanding the Global Economy

Fundamental Issues

1. **Why study global economic issues and policies?**
2. **How important is the global market for goods and services?**
3. **How important are the international monetary and financial markets?**
4. **What are market supply and demand?**
5. **What are consumer surplus and producer surplus?**
6. **How are market prices determined?**

Quebec City, Prague, Davos, Seattle, Washington, D.C., and Genoa are cities that recently hosted gatherings of the world's policymakers, diplomats, leading business executives, and prominent academics. The agendas of these meetings varied, but they all centered on the expansion of global trade and capital flows and the roles of international organizations. The common rationale for these conferences has been that expanding global markets will promote global prosperity, a "lifting of all boats," and democracy.

Demonstrators are also common at these gatherings. Some activist organizations, through persistent and unified campaigns, have effected positive change. Jubilee 2000—a worldwide movement to cancel the debt of impoverished nations—helped maintain public pressure on officials of the leading industrialized nations to implement genuine reductions in the debt burdens of the world's poorest nations.

Nevertheless, some activists see globalization as the root cause of many social injustices. These groups claim that, rather than promoting democracy, globalization erodes democratic processes and national sovereignty. They contend that labor and environmental standards are eroding and the distribution of global and domestic income is becoming more inequitable. Their position is that globalization and free trade contribute to these social injustices.

Finally, there are those who simply attempt to disrupt the meetings for the purpose of chaos. They challenge security gates and barricades, creating an unruly situation that drowns out the voices of individuals and organizations with legitimate positions. Inevitably, the demonstrations have led to clashes with police and the destruction of millions of dollars in private and public property.

What is globalization? What is the extent of global trade in goods and services? How important are the international capital markets? What concepts do economists use to examine international economic issues and policies? In this chapter you will begin your investigation of international economic issues and policies by addressing these questions.

Global Economic Policy and Issues

The process of globalization and its impact on societies and peoples everywhere are topics of great importance today. In general, **globalization** is defined as the increasing interconnectedness of people and societies and the increasing interdependence of economies, governments, and environments. Despite all the attention paid to globalization, there is no clear-cut method for measuring the extent of globalization. Researchers have employed a number of measures, including the number of minutes of international phone calls, the number of international travelers, the volume of trade in goods, services, and capital, the number of Internet servers per person, and the comovement of prices and interest rates.

Globalization
The increasing interconnectedness of peoples and societies and the interdependence of economies, governments, and environments.

THE MOST GLOBALIZED NATIONS

Foreign Policy, a bimonthly magazine, combined a number of these measures in an attempt to rank individual nations according to their degree of globalization. Table 1-1 on the next page shows the ranking of the top twenty nations that *Foreign Policy* surveyed. As the table indicates, only one of the seven largest advanced economies—the United States, France, Germany, Japan, the United Kingdom, Canada, and Italy—ranks among the top seven globalized nations. Instead, it is the smaller advanced economies with relatively unrestricted financial markets that occupy these positions.

The authors of this study also attempted to determine if globalization is associated with civil liberties, political rights, levels of perceived corruption, and income patterns. There appears to be a clear direct relationship among greater civil liberties,

Table 1-1 The Top Twenty Globalized Nations

Using several measures of global integration, authors for the magazine *Foreign Policy* ranked the top twenty globalized nations. The smaller advanced economies tend to be the most globalized countries.

Source: *Foreign Policy* http://www.foreignpolicy.com.

Rank	Nation
1	Ireland
2	Switzerland
3	Singapore
4	Netherlands
5	Sweden
6	Finland
7	Canada
8	Denmark
9	Austria
10	United Kingdom
11	Norway
12	United States
13	France
14	Germany
15	Portugal
16	Czech Republic
17	Spain
18	Israel
19	New Zealand
20	Malaysia

more political rights, lower levels of corruption, and the level of globalization, but there is no clear pattern between the inequality of income patterns and globalization. Based on this information, it appears that increasing globalization brings real benefits to the citizens of globalizing nations. Why, then, is globalization such a contentious topic of debate? (To consider some of the arguments for and against engaging in trade with other nations, see *Policy Notebook: Should the United States Expand Trade with Africa?*)

ON THE WEB

For timely articles on international issues and policies, visit *Foreign Policy's* home page at http://www.foreignpolicy.com.

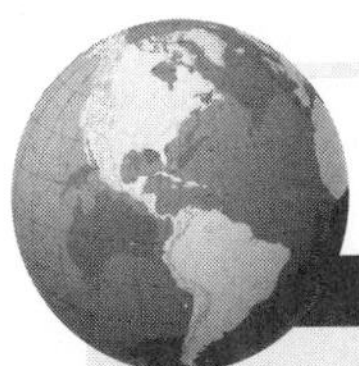

POLICY *Notebook*

POLICY MANAGEMENT

Should the United States Expand Trade with Africa?

In 2000, the U.S. Congress passed the African Growth and Opportunity Act. This legislation eliminated the duties on nearly all goods produced by the nations of sub-Saharan Africa. The stated purpose of the law was to offer these nations access to the global market for goods and services, thereby promoting economic growth and development.

Although the stated intentions of the act were laudable, it faced considerable criticism. Detractors contended that expanded trade with Africa, where labor costs are much lower than in the United States, would disrupt U.S. industries and result in job losses. In addition, they argued that U.S. businesses would use the opportunity to exploit African workers and harm the environment.

A year after the passage of the act, Robert Zoellick, the U.S. trade representative, revisited the issue. Zoellick argued that early evidence on the impact of expanded trade between the nations is positive. African exports to the United States remain a small percentage of overall trade and, therefore, have had little impact on U.S. importing industries. U.S. exports to Africa—such as aircraft, wheat, and automobiles, however, increased by more than 20 percent.

The early evidence also contradicts the arguments that U.S. businesses would exploit workers and the environment. Every sub-Saharan African nation endorsed the law, noting that when U.S. businesses locate in their region, they pay higher wages and promote better labor and environmental standards than do domestic firms.

Zoellick admits that trade alone will not solve all of the region's problems with growth and development. Nonetheless, the African Growth and Opportunity Act may well represent a significant step toward improving economic conditions. The Act may also complement other programs and promote further action on other important issues, such as debt relief and combating AIDS and tuberculosis.

For Critical Analysis:

Why might U.S. business promote higher labor and environmental standards? How would this affect their ability to compete in the region relative to firms already located there?

IMPORTANT ISSUES ADVANCED IN THIS TEXT

Economic integration *The extent and strength of real-sector and financial-sector linkages among national economies.*

In this text you will consider many of the issues underlying globalization and assess the policies intended to manage global commerce. The next two sections of this chapter narrow the scope of analysis and focus on the economic components of globalization. We will concentrate on **economic integration,** which refers to the extent and strength of commercial linkages—international transactions in goods and services and exchanges of financial assets—among national economies.

Economic integration is arguably the most important and most contentious element of globalization. Hence, the economic aspects of globalization represent a dynamic and interesting area of study. Your study of international economic issues and policies will lead you to consider these topics:

- The benefits and risks of international trade in good and services, and the global exchange of national currencies and financial assets
- The efficiency gains from increased trade in goods and services and unrestricted capital flows
- The distribution of gains and losses stemming from economic integration, and the regulation of international commerce
- The advantages and disadvantages of joining regional trade blocs that establish common rules governing the international trade of member nations
- The extent to which globalization benefits workers of developing and industrialized nations
- The implications of increased trade and capital flows for the world's environment
- The effects of globalization on the ability of national governments to finance public expenditures and social service programs
- The pros and cons of the international coordination of economic policies
- Whether international organizations rob nations of policy sovereignty, and the role of international organizations in expanding and managing world trade and global capital flows

1 **Fundamental Issue**

Why study global economic issues and policies?

The process of economic integration is shaping political and social institutions, affecting the way that nations approach policymaking and changing the incomes and purchasing patterns of households. With its far-reaching impact, economic integration is one of the most hotly contested issues of today. Hence, a thorough understanding of global economic issues and policies is important to students of all academic disciplines.

The Global Market for Goods and Services

In order to measure domestic and international economic activity, economists typically separate the production of goods and services from the exchange of financial assets. This is not to say that these two types of activities are independent. They, indeed, are not. Nonetheless, these activities are distinct.

THE REAL SECTOR

The **real sector** of an economy refers to the domestic and international production and exchange of goods and services. The **financial sector** refers to domestic and international transactions of financial assets. The most common measures of economic integration focus on three aspects:

1) The volume of international trade in the real sector
2) The global market for goods and services
3) The volume of trade in the international monetary, and financial markets.

After the end of World War II, the global market for goods and services experienced reductions in trade barriers, advances in telecommunications, and declines in transportation costs. As a result, global trade in goods and services steadily increased. (To learn how the Internet is being used to promote global trade in traditional industries such as steel, see *Online Globalization: Smokestack Industries Turn to the Web to Promote Global Business.*)

Real sector
A designation for the portion of the economy engaged in the production and sale of goods and services.

Financial sector
A designation for the portion of the economy in which people trade financial assets.

Online Globalization

Smokestack Industries Turn to the Web to Promote Global Business

The steel industry has long relied on informal networks and face-to-face or telephone negotiations to complete transactions. Business-to-business Web sites, however, are bringing new methods of attracting global business for participating firms.

Two recent e-commerce sites, MetalSite and e-Steel, offer Web-based services to the global steel industry. These sites allow buyers and sellers of primary and secondary steel products to negotiate transactions in a virtual global market. MetalSite, for example, offers an online catalog of products with both list price and auction options. The company reports that it averages more than four thousand transactions a month, averaging $20,000 per transaction. These e-commerce services generate revenue by charging participation fees and/or transaction-based fees.

Although many e-commerce services have failed to live up to expectations, steel e-commerce recently took a giant step forward when U.S. Steel Group, the United States' largest steelmaker, assumed a minority position in e-Steel. This strategic alliance positions e-Steel to guarantee the delivery of large-scale transactions and positions it to attract more business.

For Critical Analysis:
Would it be better for e-commerce sites to be independent of the steel firms, thereby promoting price competition, or to be partly owned by the firms to guarantee the availability of materials?

Figure 1-1

Growth of Global Trade in Goods and Services

World trade in goods and services has increased at an average annual rate of nearly 6 percent since 1970. The cumulative effect of this growth is a more than fivefold increase in the volume of world trade.

Source: International Monetary Fund, *World Economic Outlook*, various issues.

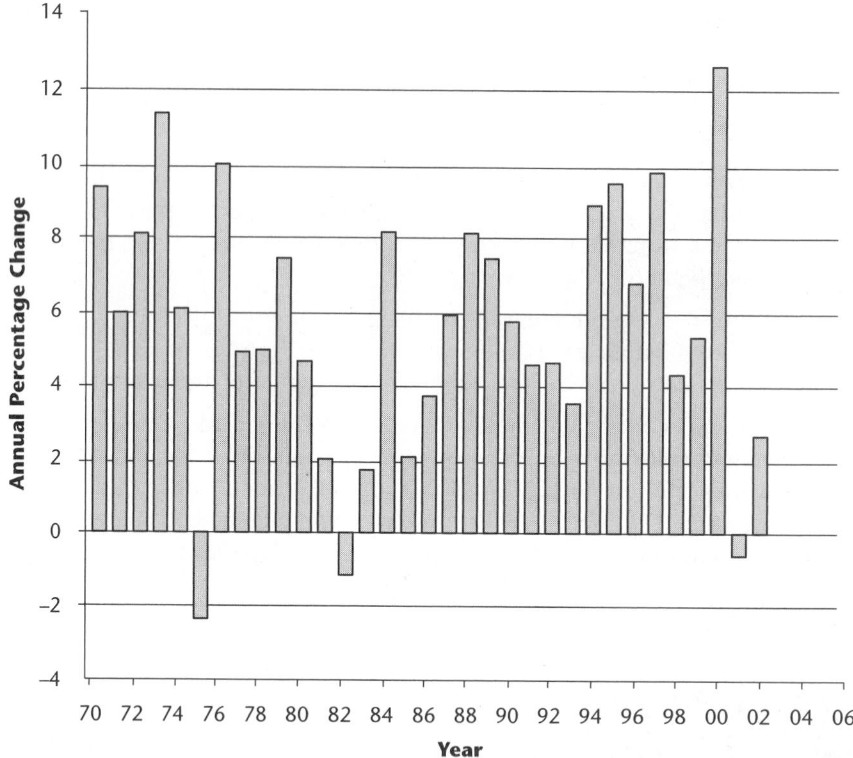

Figure 1-1 displays the annual percentage change in the global trade in goods and services since 1970. World trade of goods and services expanded in all but three of those years. For the entire period shown in the figure, the growth of world trade increased at an average annual rate of more than 6 percent. The cumulative effect of these annual increases resulted in more than a five-fold increase in the volume of world trade.

THE IMPORTANCE OF GLOBAL TRADE

The global market for goods and services has become increasingly important for most nations. To measure the importance of global trade to individual countries, economists typically divide the volume of a nation's global trade—that is, its exports plus its imports—by the total volume of its domestic output. The resulting measure estimates the nation's global trade as a share of the total amount of economic activity in its real sector.

Figure 1-2 displays this measure of global trade for 1970 and 2000 for ten nations. As the figure demonstrates, among the selected nations the importance of

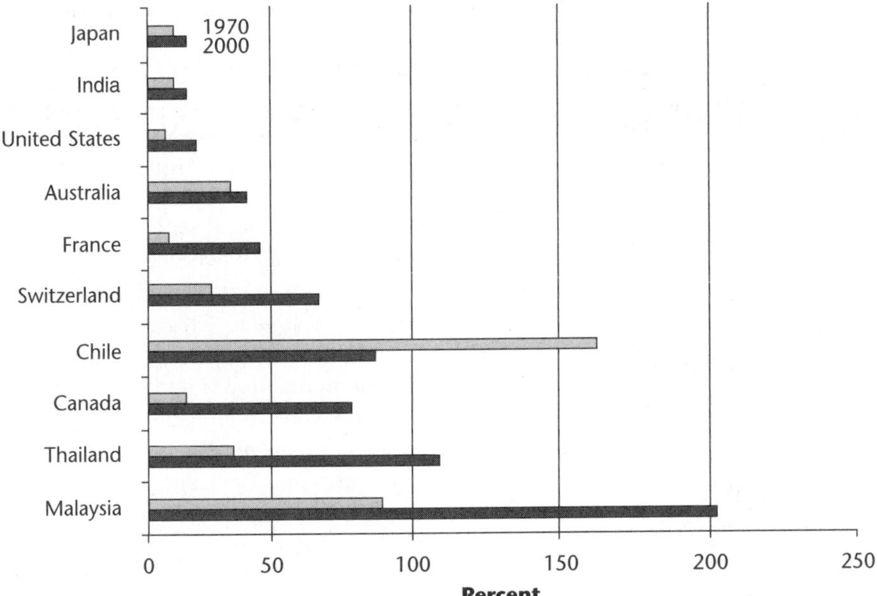

Figure 1-2

Selected Individual Nations' Trade in Goods and Services

The global market for goods and services has become increasingly important for individual nations. The figure plots the sum of each nation's exports and imports as a percentage of the nation's volume of economic output for the years 1970 and 2000. This percentage measures the nation's trade as a share of the total economic activity in its real sector. This percentage increased for every nation listed except Chile since 1970.

Source: International Monetary Fund, *International Financial Statistics,* various issues.

global trade in goods and services increased significantly for all but Chile. Generally, the economies of larger nations, such as the United States and Japan, tend to depend less on the global market for goods and services and more on their domestic markets. The economies of smaller nations, such as Thailand and Malaysia, rely much more on the global market for goods and services. Regardless, all of the nations graphed in Figure 1-2 except Chile experienced increases in the share of international trade, by amounts ranging from 100 percent to 800 percent. (Growth of global trade in goods and services often results in unexpected and unintended consequences, however; see on page 10 *Management Notebook:* Anoplophora glabripennis—*Unwanted Imports.*)

Fundamental Issue

How important is the global market for goods and services?

Since the 1950s, the volume of global trade in goods and services has grown at an average annual rate of more than 6 percent per year. The cumulative effect of this growth has been more than a five-fold expansion of the global market for goods and services. As measured by the trade in goods and services as a share of domestic output, the global market for goods and services has become more important for the world's nations.

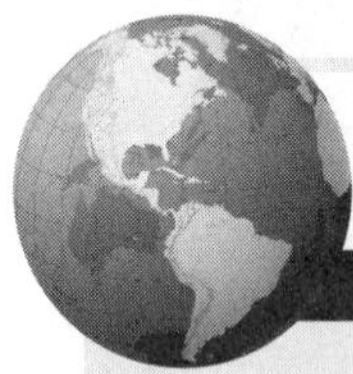

MANAGEMENT *Notebook*

POLICY MANAGEMENT

Anoplophora Glabripennis—Unwanted Imports

Sometimes imports have hidden surprises. Such is the case with the *Anoplophora glabripennis,* or the Asian long-horned beetle. This pesky insect was inadvertently exported to the United States in 1996 within wooden crates and pallets used to ship goods from China. The beetle made its presence known in twelve different states and became a serious problem in Chicago and New York.

The beetle is extremely damaging. It bores into hardwood trees and eventually kills them. The insect has proved to be impervious to pesticides. The only way to rid an area of the pest is to cut down trees and burn them. Estimates of the potential damage to U.S. forests are in the neighborhood of $140 billion. Already 5 percent of the Chicago area is under quarantine, and trees are being cut down and removed.

To address the problem, the U.S. Secretary of Agriculture required that all solid-wood packing materials used by the Chinese to export to the United States be chemically or heat treated. Chinese officials have countered that U.S. officials are being irrational and that the rule will harm the flow of trade between the two nations at a time when Asian nations desperately seeking export markets. The United States is the largest export market for China, and the rule could increase packing and transportation costs of Asian exporters by nearly $80 billion.

For Critical Analysis:
How would the restrictions imposed by the U.S. Secretary of Agriculture affect the competitiveness of Chinese manufacturers relative to other Asian manufacturers?

The International Monetary and Financial Markets

Although the growth of the global market for goods and services is remarkable, it pales in comparison to developments in the international monetary and financial markets.

THE FOREIGN EXCHANGE MARKETS

Foreign exchange market
A system of private banks, foreign exchange brokers, and central banks through which households, firms, and governments buy and sell national currencies.

Table 1-2 displays estimates of the annual turnover in **foreign exchange markets**—that is, the markets for national currencies—and the growth of world exports. The first column of the table provides estimates of the turnover, or value of transactions, of foreign currencies. The second column displays the volume of world exports of goods. Using this table, we can calculate that the value of world exports has increased by more than 400 percent since 1979. The first column, however, shows that turnover in the foreign exchange markets has increased by

Table 1-2 Annual Turnover in Foreign Exchange Markets

World exports have grown at an impressive rate since 1979. The turnover of foreign exchange, however, has increased from twelve times the volume of world exports of goods to nearly forty-five times.

Source: Held, David, Anthony McGrew, David Goldblatt, and Jonathan Perraton, *Global Transformations*, p. 209; Bank for International Settlements, *Central Bank Survey of Foreign Exchange and Derivatives Market Activity*, 1998, International Monetary Fund, *World Economic Outlook*, 1998, 2001.

	Foreign Exchange Turnover (in $ trillions)	World Exports of Goods (in $ trillions)	Ratio
1979	$17.5	$1.5	12:1
1986	75.0	2.0	38:1
1989	190.0	3.1	61:1
1992	252.0	4.7	54:1
1995	297.5	5.0	60:1
1998	372.5	5.4	69:1
2001	300.0	6.6	45:1

more than 1600 percent over this same period. The final value in the first column reveals that the *annual* turnover in the foreign exchange markets is estimated at $300 trillion. This means that the *daily* turnover in the foreign exchange markets exceeds $1.0 trillion.

The third column of Table 1-2 provides the ratio of the turnover in foreign exchange instruments to the volume of world exports, which is a measure of the value of foreign exchange transactions to world exports. The computed ratios show that foreign exchange turnover has grown from approximately twelve times the value of world exports to nearly seventy times the value of world exports in 1998 before declining to forty-five times the value of world exports in 2001.

FOREIGN DIRECT INVESTMENT

A second significant trend in the international monetary and financial markets is the growth of foreign direct investment. **Foreign direct investment** (FDI) is an investment that involves a long-term relationship and represents a controlling interest in an enterprise located in another economy. Since the 1970s, there has been a gradual deregulation of long-term capital markets and a harmonization of

Foreign direct investment
The acquisition of assets that involves a long-term relationship and controlling interest of 10 percent or greater in an enterprise located in another economy.

Table 1-3 Global Foreign Direct Investment Flows

A gradual deregulation of long-term capital markets and a harmonization of tax policies has led to remarkable increases in FDI flows. Following a worldwide recession in the early 1980s, the rates of growth of FDI flows surpassed the rates of change in world exports.

Source: UNCTAD, *Handbook of Statistics,* various issues and author's estimates.

	FDI Inflows (Percentage Change)	FDI Outflows (Percentage Change)	World Exports (Percentage Change)
1971–1975	19.8	17.3	24.0
1976–1980	18.5	17.4	18.1
1981–1985	2.1	2.4	–0.5
1986–1990	24.0	27.6	15.0
1991–1995	20.0	15.7	9.5
1996–2000	32.2	27.0	3.5

national tax policies and accounting rules. Table 1-3 shows the remarkable increase in FDI flows that resulted. After a worldwide recession and a debt crisis in the Latin American economies during the early 1980s, the rates of growth of FDI easily surpassed the growth rates of world exports.

ON THE WEB

For definitions and data relating to foreign direct investment, visit the home page of the United Nations Conference on Trade and Development at http://www.unctad.org.

CAPITAL FLOWS TO EMERGING ECONOMIES

A recent development concerning the international monetary and financial markets is the sizable increase in private (non-governmental) capital flows to the emerging economies. Figure 1-3 illustrates the most recent data on these flows. The figure separates capital flows into foreign direct investment, shorter-term capital, and other capital—consisting primarily of bank loans. As shown in the figure, capital flows have averaged $150 billion annually since 1990. Although there was a decline in private capital flows following the 1997–1998 financial crises in East Asia and Russia, long-term private capital flows continued with some strength.

As you can see, during the last few decades the global market for goods and services has grown considerably. Nonetheless, the rates of growth of the international monetary and financial markets dwarf those of the global market for goods and services. Now that you know about the real and financial sectors and their global expansions, you will embark on a more detailed study of each sector. The remainder of this chapter develops a conceptual framework that will be employed in a substantial portion of this text.

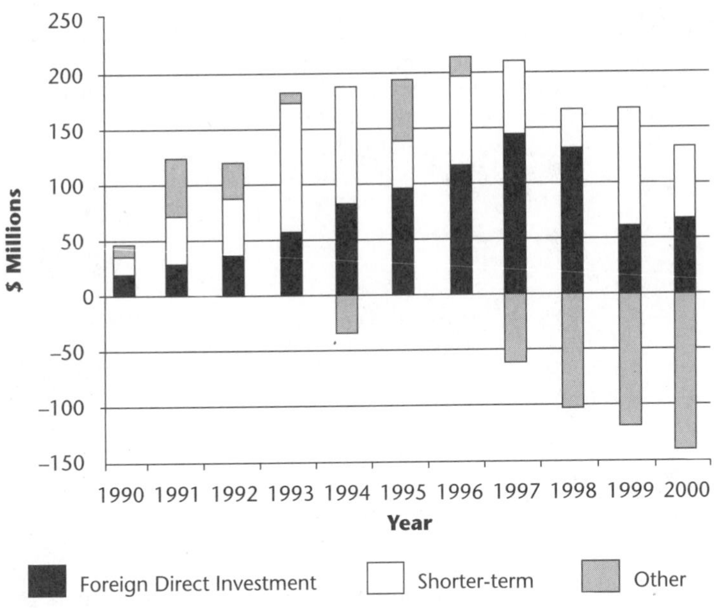

Figure 1-3

Private Capital Flows to the Emerging Economies

Private capital flows to the emerging economies have grown at an impressive rate since 1990. Despite the 1994 Mexican financial crisis and the East Asian crises of 1997 and 1998, foreign direct investment and shorter-term investment continued to flow to the emerging economies.

Source: International Monetary Fund, *Annual Report*, and *International Capital Markets*, various issues.

Fundamental Issue 3

How important are the international monetary and financial markets?

The international monetary and financial markets have experienced substantial growth, greatly surpassing the volume of trade in goods and services. Foreign exchange turnover has grown to more than 70 times the volume of exports of goods and services. Foreign direct investment continues to expand, in spite of worldwide recessions and debt crises. After rebounding from the 1997–1998 financial crises, private capital continues to flow to emerging economies.

Understanding Global Markets: Supply and Demand

For the remainder of this chapter you will consider a framework of basic economic concepts that will be used in several instances to quantify and evaluate the impact of global issues and policies. You will learn about the concepts of supply, demand, consumer surplus, and producer surplus, and you will understand how to apply these tools to a number of domestic and international examples.

DEMAND AND SUPPLY

How much are consumers willing and able to pay for a given quantity of a product or service? That is, what is the demand for the product or service? Economists

Table 1-4 An Individual Consumer's Demand Schedule

A demand schedule tabulates possible prices and the quantities that a consumer demands of a good or service at those prices. Quantity demanded and price are negatively related. As the price of gasoline falls, quantity demanded rises.

Price	Quantity
$1.95	1
$1.90	2
$1.85	3
$1.80	4
$1.75	5

Demand
The relationship between the prices that consumers are willing and able to pay for various quantities of a good or service for a given time period, all other things constant.

Law of demand
An economic law that states that there is an inverse, or negative, relationship between the price that consumers are willing and able to pay and the quantities that they desire to purchase.

Supply
The relationship between the prices of a good or service and the quantities supplied to the market by producers within a given time period, all other things constant.

Law of supply
An economic law that states that there is a positive or direct relationship between the prices producers receive and the quantities that they are willing to supply to the market.

define **demand** as the relation displaying the prices that consumers are willing and able to pay for various quantities demanded during a specified time period, holding all other things constant. The relation between price and quantity demanded follows an economic law. This **law of demand** states that there is an inverse, or negative, relationship between price and quantity demanded. Hence, as price rises, an individual's quantity demanded declines.

The Demand Schedule

An individual's *demand schedule* tabulates the price the consumer is willing and able to pay for various quantities of a good or service during a specified time period, all other things held constant. Table 1-4 displays an individual consumer's demand schedule for gasoline.

As the table shows, the demand schedule lists possible prices and the quantities demanded at each of these prices. At a price of $1.90, for example, the consumer's quantity demanded is 2 gallons per week, while at a price of $1.85 quantity demanded is 3 gallons per week. As you can see, the demand schedule displays a negative relationship between price and quantity demanded; as the price of gasoline falls, quantity demanded rises.

Supply

Economists define **supply** as the relation displaying the prices that a producer is willing to accept for various quantities supplied during a given time period, holding all other things constant. This relation between price and quantity supplied follows an economic law. The **law of supply** states that price and quantity supplied are positively related. When price rises, for example, the higher price induces a greater quantity supplied.

Table 1-5 An Individual Firm's Supply Schedule

A supply schedule tabulates possible prices and the quantities that a producer supplies of a good or service at those prices. Quantity supplied and price are positively related. As the price of gasoline falls, quantity supplied declines.

Price	Quantity
$1.95	250
$1.90	200
$1.85	150
$1.80	100
$1.75	50

The Supply Schedule

A *supply schedule* tabulates the minimum price a supplier is willing to accept for various quantities supplied of a good or service. Table 1-5 displays an individual firm's weekly supply of transportation gasoline.

The supply schedule illustrates possible prices and the weekly quantity supplied by the firm at each of the possible prices. At the price of $1.90, for example, the quantity supplied by the firm is 200 gallons per week. At a price of $1.85, however, the quantity supplied falls to 150 gallons per week. As you can see, the supply schedule displays a positive relationship between price and quantity supplied; as the price falls, the quantity supplied declines. (To observe how to depict the demand and supply curves in graphs, see on pages 16–17 *Visualizing Global Economic Issues: The Demand and Supply Curves.*)

CHANGES IN DEMAND AND SUPPLY

As shown in the previous section, quantity demanded and quantity supplied depend on the price of the good or service. The demand for and supply of a particular good or service depend on a number of other factors, however. Because these factors are things other than the price of the item, we refer to them as *factors that influence demand and supply.*

Factors Influencing Demand

We say that demand increases when there is a greater quantity demanded at any given price. Demand decreases when there is a lower quantity demanded at any given price.

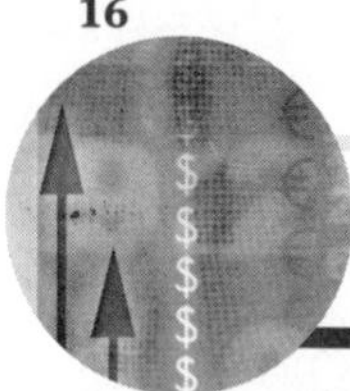

Visualizing Global Economic Issues

The Demand and Supply Curves

To see how to graph demand and supply schedules, consider the demand schedule for transportation gasoline in Table 1-4, and the individual producer's supply schedule in Table 1-5. The demand curve labeled *D* in panel (a) of Figure 1-4 plots the weekly quantities of gasoline demanded by the individual at various prices. The curve slopes downward, illustrating the law of demand, or a negative relationship between price and quantity demanded.

The supply curve labeled *S* in panel (b) in Figure 1-4 plots the weekly quantities supplied by the individual firm at various prices. The supply curve is upward sloping, or has a positive slope, because of the positive relation between price and quantity supplied.

When using graphs of demand and supply, it is very important to differentiate between demand and quantity demanded and between supply and quantity supplied. As already stated, the demand curve is the overall relationship between price and quantity demanded. Hence, the demand for gasoline is represented by the position of the entire demand curve in the graph. Quantity demanded is represented by an individual point on the demand curve, such as the point labeled *A* in panel (a) of Figure 1-4, which indicates that at a price of $1.90 a gallon, the quantity demanded is 2 gallons.

Likewise, the supply of gasoline is the overall relationship between price and quantity supplied. The entire supply curve and its position in the graph represents supply, whereas an individual point on the supply curve, such as point *A* in panel (b) of Figure 1-4, represents the quantity supplied.

To further understand the difference between demand and quantity demanded and supply and quantity supplied, consider a change in the price of gasoline. Suppose that the price of gasoline falls from $1.90 per gallon to $1.85 per gallon. As shown in panel (a) of Figure 1-4, as the price declines from $1.90 to $1.85, there is a movement down and along the demand curve as quantity demanded rises from 2 to 3 gallons. In panel (b), this price reduction causes a movement down and along the supply curve as quantity supplied falls from 200 gallons of gasoline to 150 gallons. A movement along the demand curve,

---

Although there are numerous factors that affect demand, we can group them into a small number of general categories, summarized in Table 1-6 on page 18.

Consumer tastes and preferences are perhaps the most important factors influencing demand. For example, when European scientists discovered that *bovine spongiform encephalopathy*—mad-cow disease—could be transmitted to humans as new variant Creutzfeld–Jakob disease, there was an immediate drop in the demand for beef and an increase in demand for substitute food items, such as veggie burgers. At any given price of beef, therefore, the quantity of beef demanded decreased. At any given price of veggie burgers, there was an increase in the quantity of veggie burgers demanded.

As incomes change, consumers' ability to purchase an item changes. If an increase in income results in a decrease in the demand for a particular good, that good is considered an *inferior good.* A *normal good,* on the other hand, is a good for

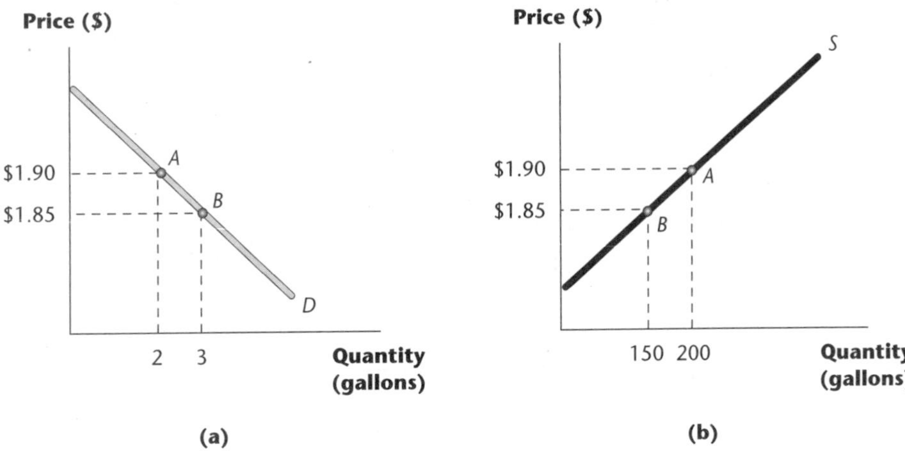

Figure 1-4

The Demand for and Supply of Gasoline

Panel (a) illustrates an individual consumer's weekly demand curve for transportation gasoline. Each point on the demand curve represents the maximum price the consumer is willing and able to pay for a specific quantity of gasoline. Panel (b) illustrates an individual firm's weekly supply curve for transportation gasoline. Each point on the supply curve represents the quantity the producer is willing to offer for a specific price.

therefore, is a change in *quantity demanded* induced by a price change, while a movement along the supply curve is a change in *quantity supplied*. The demand and supply curves remained in their original position, so demand and supply have not changed.

For Critical Analysis:
What might cause a change in the demand for gasoline? What might cause a change in the supply of gasoline? Can you think of a single event that might shift both the demand curve and the supply curve?

which consumer demand rises with an increase in income. Most goods are normal goods, so that when incomes increase, people demand a larger quantity at any given price.

Consumers purchase a broad range of goods and services. When the price of one good changes, consumers must reallocate their budgets. They may increase their purchases of some goods while decreasing purchases of others. Goods that are consumed together, such as coffee and cream, are called *complement goods*. Goods that substitute for each other, such as coffee and tea, are called *substitute goods*.

Factors Influencing Supply

As with demand, supply depends on a number of factors other than the price of the particular good or service supplied. These are *factors influencing supply*. That is, the quantity of the good supplied changes at any given price. When there is an

Table 1-6 Factors Influencing Demand

A number of factors influence demand. Economists typically group these factors into categories. The most important categories of factors influencing demand are tastes and preferences, changes in income, changes in the price of related goods, and changes in the number of consumers in the market.

Factor	How It Affects Demand
Changes in consumer preferences	An increase in consumer tastes or preferences for an item increases the demand for that item. A decrease in consumer tastes or preferences for an item decreases the demand for that item.
Changes in income	An increase (decrease) in a consumer's income increases (decreases) the consumer's demand for *normal goods* and decreases (increases) the consumer's demand for *inferior goods.*
Changes in the prices of related goods	An increase (decrease) in the price of a *complement good* decreases (increases) a consumer's demand for a related good. An increase (decrease) in the price of a *substitute good* increases (decreases) a consumer's demand for a related good.
Changes in the number of consumers	An increase (decrease) in the number of consumers in a market increases (decreases) the demand for a good or service.

increase in supply, the quantity supplied at each of the various prices increases. When there is a decrease in supply, the quantity supplied at each of the various prices declines.

There are many factors that affect supply, summarized in Table 1-7 and grouped into a small number of categories.

A change in the cost and availability of inputs or resources is perhaps the most important factor influencing supply. When inputs become less expensive, production costs fall and producers are willing to offer a larger quantity of the good or service at a given price. Hence, supply increases when input costs decrease.

A change in technology affects supply in the same way as a change in the price of inputs. A technological advance allows a firm to produce more units of a good or service with the same amount of resources. A technological advance, therefore, results in an increase in supply. At any given price, the firm can produce more units than it could previously.

A change in the price of related goods may also affect supply. An increase in the price of a *substitute good in production*—a good that substitutes for another good in the production process—results in a decrease in the supply of the other good. An increase in the price of a *complement good in production*—a good that is

Table 1-7 Factors Influencing Supply

A number of factors influence supply. Economists typically group these factors into categories. The most important categories of factors influencing supply are the cost and availability of inputs, changes in technology, changes in the prices of related goods or services, taxes and producer subsidies, and the number of producers in the market.

Factor	How It Affects Supply
Changes in the cost and availability of inputs	Supply increases when input costs decrease. Supply decreases when input costs rise.
Advances in technology	An advance in technology allows a firm to produce more units of a good or service with the same amount of resources. Hence, at any given price, the firm can produce more units than it could previously.
Changes in the prices of related goods or services	An increase (decrease) in the price of a *substitute good in production* results in a decrease (increase) in the supply of the related good. An increase (decrease) in the price of a *complement good in production* results in an increase (decrease) in the supply of the related good.
Taxes and producer subsidies	A production tax causes supply to decrease, while a production subsidy increases supply.
Change in the number of producers	An increase (decrease) in the number of producers in a market increases (decreases) the supply of a good or service.

produced in conjunction with another good—results in an increase in the supply of the other good.

Taxes and producer subsidies are also factors that influence supply. Taxes and subsidies affect the prices that producers are willing to receive for a particular quantity of a good and, therefore, change supply. Taxes and subsidies are covered in greater detail in later chapters.

We shall consider other factors that influence demand and supply later in this chapter. These additional categories, however, are best understood after considering the *market demand* and *market supply,* as opposed to an individual's demand or supply.

MARKET DEMAND AND SUPPLY

Now that you understand individual demand and supply, let's consider *market* demand and supply. **Market demand** is the sum of the quantities demanded by *all* consumers at various prices during a specific time period, all other things constant. From this point onward, when we refer to demand in this text, we shall be speaking of market demand unless otherwise specified.

Market demand
A curve that illustrates the prices that consumers are willing and able to pay for various quantities of a good or service for a given time period, all other things constant. Because of the negative relationship between price and quantity demanded, the demand curve slopes downward.

To better understand market demand, suppose that in a particular market there are 1,000 identical consumers, each having the same demand schedule for gasoline as that given in Table 1-4 on page 14. At each price, therefore, there is 1,000 times the quantity demanded in the individual consumer's demand schedule.

Now consider an additional factor affecting a change in demand, the number of consumers in the market. As just explained, market demand is the sum of all consumers' quantity demanded at various prices. Hence, if there is an increase in the number of consumers, the total quantity demanded at each of the various prices is greater. Conversely, if the number of consumers decreases, demand declines.

Market supply
A curve that illustrates the prices that producers are willing to accept for various quantities of a good or service they supply to the market for a given time period, all other things constant. Because of the positive relationship between price and quantity supplied, the supply curve slopes upward.

Market supply is the sum of the quantities supplied by all producers at various prices during a specific time period, all other things constant. When we refer to supply in this text we shall be speaking of the market supply, unless otherwise indicated.

Suppose that in a particular market there are twenty identical producers, each having the same supply schedule of gasoline as that given in Table 1-5 on page 15. At each price, therefore, there is twenty times the quantity supplied by the individual producer.

Now we can consider another factor influencing supply, the number of producers. As explained above, market supply is the sum of all producers' quantity supplied at various prices. If there is an increase in the number of producers, the total quantity supplied at each of the various prices is greater. Consequently, supply increases. By way of comparison, if the number of producers decreases, supply declines.

4 Fundamental Issue

What are market supply and demand?

Demand is the relationship between prices and quantities consumers are willing and able to purchase, while supply is the relationship between prices and the quantities producers are willing to supply.

Consumer and Producer Surplus

The previous section introduced you to the concepts of supply and demand. Next we will build on these concepts by considering *consumer surplus* and *producer surplus*. Consumer and producer surplus are two important tools that we will apply in this text to gauge the impact of domestic and international events and policies on the welfare of consumers, producers, taxpayers, and governments.

CONSUMER SURPLUS

As described earlier, demand is the relationship between prices and the quantities that consumers are willing and able to purchase. Table 1-4, which displays an individual consumer's demand schedule for gasoline, showed that the consumer is willing and able to pay $1.95 for one gallon of gasoline. It follows that the value of the first gallon to this consumer is $1.95.

What if, however, the **market price** of gasoline, the price determined by the interaction of *all* consumers and producers in the market, is only $1.85 per gallon? Because consumers can purchase a gallon of gasoline for the market price of $1.85, and yet each consumer values the first gallon of gasoline at $1.95, each consumer receives a benefit, or surplus. The difference between what consumers are willing to pay for a particular quantity of a good or service and the market price they must pay to purchase that quantity of the good or services is called **consumer surplus.**

Market price
The price determined by the interactions of all consumers and producers in the marketplace.

Consumer surplus
The benefit that consumers receive from the existence of a market price. Consumer surplus is measured as the difference between what consumers are willing and able to pay for a good or service and the market price.

PRODUCER SURPLUS

As you learned earlier, supply is the relationship between prices and the quantities that producers are willing to provide. Table 1-5 displays an individual firm's supply schedule of gasoline. The table shows that at a price of $1.80 a gallon, the producer is willing to supply 100 gallons. It follows that the producer must receive $1.80 to be motivated to offer the first 100 gallons for sale.

What if the market price for gasoline is $1.85? The producer can sell 150 gallons of gasoline at the market price even though it is willing to accept $1.80 for the first 100 gallons of gasoline. Hence, producers receive a benefit, or surplus. **Producer surplus** is the difference between the market price that producers can charge for a particular quantity of a good or service and the minimum price they are willing to receive for that quantity. (To gain a further understanding of consumer and producer surplus, see on pages 22–23 *Visualizing Global Economic Issues: Measuring Consumer and Producer Surplus.*)

Producer surplus
The benefit that producers receive from the existence of a market price. Producer surplus is measured as the difference between the price that producers are willing to accept to supply a particular quantity and the market price.

Fundamental Issue 5

What are consumer surplus and producer surplus?

Consumer and producer surplus are concepts that economists use to gauge the benefits that consumers and producers receive from the existence of a market price. Consumer surplus is the difference between what consumers are willing to pay for a given quantity and the price they must pay. Producer surplus is the difference between what producers are willing to accept for a given quantity and the price they are able to receive for that quantity.

How Market Prices Are Determined

How is the market price introduced in the previous section determined? To answer this question, we bring together the concepts of supply and demand.

Together the laws of supply and demand demonstrate the different price perspectives of producers and consumers. On one hand, as the price of a good or service rises, the quantity supplied rises. On the other hand, as the price rises, the quantity demanded falls. These different price perspectives are resolved through a market process in which the quantity demanded and the quantities supplied eventually are equalized.

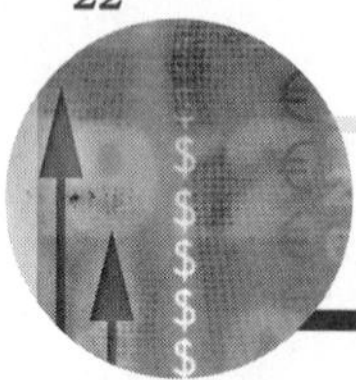

Visualizing Global Economic Issues

Measuring Consumer and Producer Surplus

To visualize consumer and producer surplus, let's consider the market demand and supply curves that were discussed earlier. Panel (a) of Figure 1-5 illustrates the demand curve that results if there are a thousand identical consumers, each with the same demand as that illustrated in panel (a) of Figure 1-4. Likewise, panel (b) illustrates the supply curve that results if there are twenty identical producers, each with the same supply of gasoline as that shown in panel (b) of Figure 1-4.

The demand curve in panel (a) of Figure 1-5 shows that consumers value the first gallon of gasoline at \$1.95, but the market price is only \$1.85. Consumers, therefore, receive a surplus. This surplus is the difference between the price that consumers are willing and able to pay and the market price, or, in our example, \$0.10 per gallon. Likewise, for the second thousand gallons of gasoline consumers are willing and able to pay \$1.90. For the third thousand gallons of gasoline, the market price is equal to what consumers are willing and able to pay. Hence, there is no additional surplus associated with the third thousand gallons of gasoline.

As with other goods and services, gasoline can be bought in much smaller units than thousand gallons. If we were to consider all the possible quantities in the figure that consumers are willing and able to purchase at a price of \$1.85, consumer surplus equals the triangle formed by points *A, B,* and *C* in panel (a) of Figure 1-5. Hence, we can say that consumer surplus is the area below the demand curve and above the market price.

We can quantify consumer surplus by simply calculating the area of the triangle in panel (a) in Figure 1-5. Recall that the area of a triangle is the value of the base times the height, divided by two. In this example, therefore, consumer surplus is \$300:

$$[(\$2.05 - \$1.85) \times 3{,}000]/2 = \$300$$

We can determine producer surplus in a similar manner. Panel (b) of Figure 1-5 shows that producers are willing to accept no less than \$1.75 for the first thousand gallons of gasoline, and yet the market price is \$1.85. Likewise, producers are willing to accept \$1.80 for the second 1,000 gallons of gasoline. For the third 1,000 gallons of gasoline, producers are willing to accept a price of \$1.85, which equals the market price. Hence, there is no additional surplus associated with the third thousand gallons.

If we consider all the possible quantities in panel (b) of Figure 1-5 that producers are willing and able to supply at a price of \$1.85 per gallon, then producer surplus is given by the triangle formed by points *A, B,*

EXCESS QUANTITY SUPPLIED AND EXCESS QUANTITY DEMANDED

Excess quantity supplied
The amount by which quantity supplied exceeds quantity demanded at a given price.

Consider, for example, what happens if at a given market price the quantity supplied is greater than the quantity demanded. At this price, there is an **excess quantity supplied,** which is the amount by which quantity supplied exceeds quantity demanded at a specific price. Because of the excess quantity supplied, there is downward pressure on the market price, as producers will want to eliminate their excess inventories. Hence, the market price will fall, spurring an increase in quantity demanded and a decrease in quantity supplied. The price will

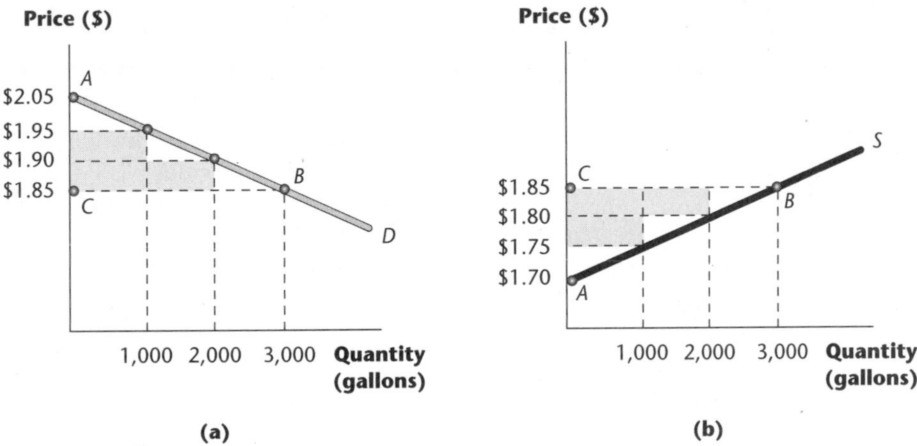

Figure 1-5

Consumer and Producer Surplus

Panel (a) illustrates the weekly demand curve for transportation gasoline for 1,000 identical consumers. In this figure, the market price is $1.85 per gallon. The quantities demanded at the prices given are taken from Table 1-4 (e.g., at $1.95/gallon, 1,000 identical consumers would buy a total of 1,000 gallons). Consumer surplus is illustrated by the triangle denoted by points A, B, *and* C*—the area above the market price and below the demand curve. Panel (b) illustrates a weekly supply curve for 20 identical producers. Price and quantity supplied are taken from Table 1-5. At the market price of $1.85 per gallon, producer surplus is illustrated by the triangle formed by points* A, B, *and* C*—the area below the market price and above the supply curve.*

and C. Hence, we can say that producer surplus is the area below price and above the supply curve. We can quantify producer surplus by calculating the area of triangle *ABC* in panel (b) of Figure 1-5. In this example, producer surplus is $225 :

$$[(\$1.85 - \$1.70) \times 3{,}000]/2 = \$225$$

For Critical Analysis:

OPEC, the Organization of Petroleum Exporting Countries, seeks to protect the interests of its members. Explain, using the concepts of consumer and producer surplus, how OPEC might achieve this objective.

continue to fall until an excess quantity supplied no longer exists, or until the quantity demanded equals the quantity supplied.

Next, consider what happens if the market price is at a level where quantity demanded is greater than quantity supplied. At this price, there is an **excess quantity demanded,** which is the amount by which quantity demanded exceeds quantity supplied. Because of the excess quantity demanded, there is pressure for the market price to rise. In turn, the price increase spurs an increase in the quantity supplied and a decrease in the quantity demanded. The price will

Excess quantity demanded
The amount by which quantity demanded exceeds quantity supplied at a given price.

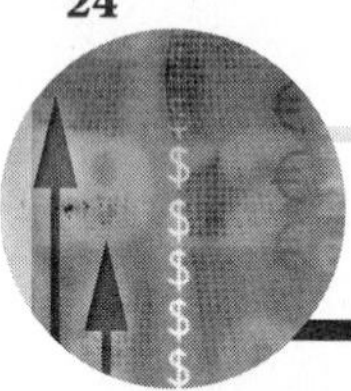

Visualizing Global Economic Issues

The Equilibrium Market Price

To visualize the determination of the equilibrium price, view panel (a) of Figure 1-6, which combines the supply and demand curves of Figure 1-5. Using the data in Figure 1-5, consider what happens if the price of transportation gasoline is $1.90 per gallon. At this price, quantity supplied is 4,000 gallons while the quantity demanded is 2,000 gallons. Hence, there is an excess quantity supplied. Producers will offer to supply gasoline at a lower price to induce greater sales, and the price will begin to fall in the marketplace.

Next, consider what happens if the market price is $1.80 per gallon. At this price, quantity demanded is 4,000 gallons while the quantity supplied is 2,000 gallons. Hence, there is an excess quantity demanded. Consumers will offer to purchase gasoline at a higher price, and the price will begin to rise in the marketplace.

At a price of $1.85, quantity supplied equals quantity demanded and there is neither an excess quantity supplied nor an excess quantity demanded. Hence, $1.85 is the market equilibrium price.

Now let's consider what happens if there is a change in the price of crude oil. In the early 2000s, for example, the price of crude oil rose considerably. Because gasoline is refined from crude oil, the price of an essential input increased. This caused a decrease in supply, illustrated by a leftward shift of the supply curve to *S′* in panel (b) of Figure 1-6.

At a price of $1.85, there is now an excess demand for gasoline, as quantity demanded exceeds quantity supplied by 2,000 gallons. Because of the excess quantity demanded, the market price rises, generating an increase in the quantity supplied and a decrease in the quantity demanded. Price will continue to rise until it reaches $1.90 per gallon, where quantity supplied equals quantity demanded. All other things constant, 2,000 gallons of gasoline will continue to be exchanged at the equilibrium price of $1.90 per gallon.

For Critical Analysis:
Suppose that, as the supply of gasoline falls, while consumers turn to more fuel-efficient automobiles. How would these two events together affect the equilibrium price of gasoline and the quantity transacted in the market?

continue to rise until the excess quantity demanded is eliminated, or when the quantity demanded equals the quantity supplied.

THE EQUILIBRIUM PRICE

Market clearing or equilibrium price
The price at which quantity supplied equals quantity demanded. The equilibrium price is referred to as a market-clearing price, because neither an excess quantity demanded nor an excess quantity supplied exists at this price.

When quantity demanded and quantity supplied are equal, there is neither an excess quantity demanded nor an excess quantity supplied, and the market is said to have *cleared.* The price at which quantity demanded equals quantity supplied is called the **market clearing or equilibrium price.** Because there is neither an excess quantity demanded nor an excess quantity supplied, there is no pressure on price to change. All other things constant, the good or service will continue to be exchanged at the market-clearing price. (To understand the equilibrium price and how changes in supply and demand effect the equilibrium price, see *Visualizing Global Economic Issues: The Equilibrium Market Price.*)

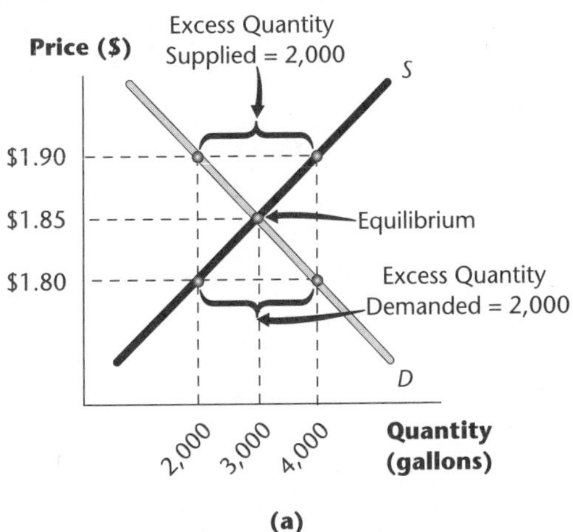

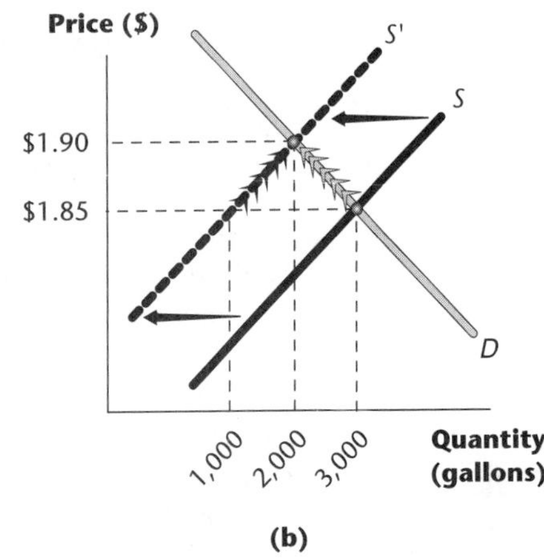

Figure 1-6

The Equilibrium Market Price

Panel (a) illustrates the weekly demand curve for, and weekly supply curve of transportation gasoline. A price of $1.85 is a market equilibrium price because, at this price, there is neither an excess quantity demanded nor an excess quantity supplied. Panel (b) shows that a decrease in supply, illustrated by a leftward shift of the supply curve, results in a higher equilibrium price and a lower quantity transacted.

THE GLOBAL MARKET

The market supply and demand framework can be extended to consider the global market for goods and services. What is required is to bring together the forces of supply and demand of all participants in the global market. As you learned in the previous sections, the equilibrium price is the price at which quantity demanded equals quantity supplied. This remains true in a global setting, as well. Excess quantities supplied and excess quantities demanded, however, take on a special significance in a global market framework.

Exports

Suppose that the global equilibrium price of personal computers is higher than the equilibrium price that would prevail in the domestic economy if international trade did not take place. If the domestic nation's government were to open the country's borders to international trade, the price of personal computers would rise, spurring an increase in the quantity supplied and a decrease in the quantity demanded. At the global price, therefore, the domestic nation experiences an excess quantity supplied of computers.

Residents of the domestic nation could use the excess quantity supplied of personal computers to purchase, or import, other goods and services not available to it prior to international trade. That is, domestic residents could export the personal computers so as to import other items. In this way an excess quantity supplied is equivalent to a nation's exports of the good or service.

Imports

Suppose, on the other hand, that the global price of personal computers is below the equilibrium price that would prevail in the domestic economy if international trade did not take place. If the domestic nation's government were to open the country's borders to international trade, the price of personal computers would fall, spurring a decrease in the quantity supplied and an increase in the quantity demanded. At the global price, therefore, the domestic nation experiences an excess quantity demanded of computers. Residents of the domestic nation could satisfy the excess quantity demanded of personal computers by purchasing them on the global market, or importing computers. It is in this way that an excess quantity demanded is equivalent to a nation's imports of the good or service.

The equilibrium global market price is one at which all excess quantities demanded equal all excess quantities supplied. In other words, equilibrium is reached when the quantity of exports supplied equals the quantity of imports demanded.

An Example: The Global Coffee Market

As an example of the global market process, let's examine the international supply of and demand for coffee. The coffee producers of Latin American nations such as Brazil and Columbia account for a large share of the supply of coffee in the international market. Other nations, such as the United States and Canada, are large importers of raw coffee beans and major producers of processed coffee.

Suppose the international price of unprocessed coffee is $0.65 a pound and that 3 million metric tons are sold each year. Consider what happens if an unexpected frost occurs in Brazil, damaging a large portion of the coffee crop. Undoubtedly, the frost would cause a precipitous drop in the supply of coffee.

At a price of $0.65, the quantity demanded of coffee by residents of importing nations would now exceed the quantity supplied by producers in exporting nations. In other words, the excess quantity demanded by residents of importing nations will not be met by the excess quantity supplied of producers of exporting nations. As a result, the global price of coffee will rise. In turn, the price increase induces an increase in the quantity supplied and a decrease in the quantity demanded. The price of coffee continues to rise until the market eventually clears.

ON THE WEB

For information on the global market for coffee and tea, access the Tea and Coffee Trade Journal at http://www.teaandcoffee.net.

CONSUMER AND PRODUCER SURPLUS AND THE GLOBAL MARKET

As you learned in the previous section, when a nation opens its borders to international trade, it might face different prices than those that prevail in the domestic economy if trade did not take place. When prices change, consumer and producer surplus also change. Recall that the area below the demand curve and above price measures consumer surplus, while the area above the supply curve and below price measures producer surplus. Hence, when the price increases, all other things constant, consumer surplus falls and producer surplus rises. In a more general sense, some groups are better off and some are not. (To better understand the determination of the global equilibrium price and change in consumer and producer surplus see on pages 28–29 *Visualizing Global Economic Issues: A Global Coffee Market.*)

As you can see, the change in consumer and producer surplus gives us insight as to the groups that may benefit from trade and those who may suffer. In the next several chapters, you will learn about the sources of nations' global price advantages and disadvantages. You will also contemplate the distribution of gains and losses of international trade and international policies.

Fundamental Issue 6

How are market prices determined?

The forces of supply and demand determine the market price. For an individual nation, the market-clearing price, or equilibrium price, occurs when there is neither an excess quantity demanded nor an excess quantity supplied. If nations engage in international trade, however, the *global* equilibrium market price arises when excess quantities demanded, or imports, equal excess quantities supplied, or exports.

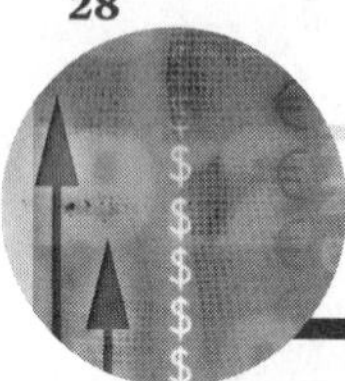

Visualizing Global Economic Issues

A Global Coffee Market

To visualize the determination of the global equilibrium price and the effects of trade on consumer and producer surplus, consider the supply of and demand for coffee for two hypothetical nations, Coffeeland and Creamerland. Panel (a) of Figure 1-7 shows the supply and demand conditions for Coffeeland, which has land well suited to growing coffee, while panel (b) of Figure 1-7 shows the supply and demand conditions for Creamerland, which does not have land well suited for growing coffee. Creamerland, consequently, has only a small domestic coffee industry.

As illustrated in Figure 1-7, if the two countries do not trade, the equilibrium price of coffee in Coffeeland is $0.35 per pound. The equilibrium price of coffee is $1.00 per pound in Creamerland. Consumer surplus in each nation is given by the triangle formed by the points *A, B,* and *C.* Producer surplus is given by the triangle formed by the points *C, B,* and *D.*

Now suppose the two nations begin to trade. At a price of $1.00, there is an excess quantity supplied of 20 tons of coffee in Coffeeland, whose producers would seek to export this amount. Residents of Coffeeland would not be able to export any coffee, however, because Creamerland has neither an excess quantity supplied nor an excess quantity demanded. Hence, the price of coffee would fall below $1.00 per pound. At a coffee price of $0.35, however, there is an excess quantity of coffee demanded in Creamerland, whose residents would seek to import 20 tons of coffee. Creamerland would be unable to import coffee, however, as Coffeeland has neither an excess quantity demanded nor an excess quantity supplied. Hence, the price of coffee would rise above $0.35 per pound.

What is the global equilibrium price? The global equilibrium price arises where the excess quantity demanded, or imports, of coffee by Creamerland residents exactly matches the excess quantity supplied, or exports, of coffee by Coffeeland producers. The equilibrium price in this example is $0.65. Exports of Coffeeland, 10 tons, equal coffee imports of Creamerland.

We can also see what happens to consumer and producer surplus when there is international trade. Before the two nations were opened to trade, consumer surplus was equal to the triangle formed by points *A, B,* and *C,* while producer surplus was equal to the triangle shaped by points *C, B,* and *D.* After trade, consumer surplus in Coffeeland equals the triangle *A, F,* and *E,* in panel (a), and consumer surplus in

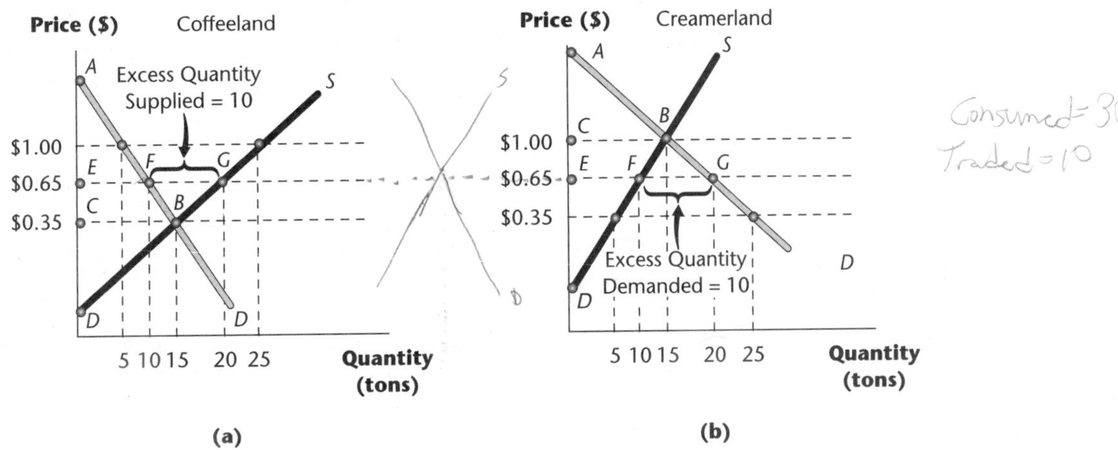

Figure 1-7

The Global Coffee Market

Panel (a) illustrates the supply of and demand for coffee in Coffeeland. Panel (b) illustrates the supply of and demand for coffee in Creamerland. At a price of $0.65 per pound, producers in Coffeeland supply 20 tons of coffee and consumers demand 10 tons of coffee. Hence, Coffeeland has an excess quantity supplied of 10 tons. At a price of $0.65 per pound, producers in Creamerland supply 10 tons of coffee and consumers demand 20 tons of coffee. Creamerland, therefore, has an excess quantity demanded of 10 tons. Under free trade, the global equilibrium price is $0.65 because, at this price, Coffeeland's excess quantity supplied equals Creamerland's excess quantity demanded.

Creamerland equals the triangle *A, G,* and *E,* in panel (b). After trade, producer surplus in Coffeeland equals the triangle shaped by points *E, G,* and *D,* in panel (a), and producer surplus in Creamerland equals the triangle formed by points *E, F,* and *D,* in panel (b).

For Critical Analysis:
Suppose that a frost damages a major portion of Coffeeland's crop. Show what would happen to the global price of coffee and to consumer and producer surplus in both nations.

CHAPTER SUMMARY

1) **Why the Study of Global Economic Issues and Policies Is Important:** Global economic integration affects many aspects of our day-to-day lives, as well as important business and government policy decisions. In turn, business and government policy decisions affect the pace and breadth of the process of economic integration. Global economic issues and policies, therefore, have become an important area of study for all disciplines.
2) **The Importance of the Global Market for Goods and Services:** During the past several years, global trade in goods and services has increased dramatically. This year-to-year growth resulted in more than a five-fold expansion of the global market for goods and services since 1979. As measured by the sum of exports and imports as a share of overall economic activity, global trade in goods and services today is more important for nearly all nations relative to a few decades ago.
3) **The Importance of the International Monetary and Financial Markets:** Although the growth of global trade in goods and services is impressive, it is greatly surpassed by the growth of the international monetary and financial markets. The value of all transactions in the foreign exchange markets grew from twelve times the volume of global exports in 1979 to more than forty-five times the value of global exports. Foreign direct investment among the leading industrialized nations and private capital flows to emerging and developed nations has grown in spite of worldwide recessions and sudden and severe financial crises.
4) **Market Supply and Demand:** Demand is the relationship between prices that consumers are willing and able to pay for various quantities of a good or service during a given time period. The law of demand states that there is a negative relationship between price and the quantity demanded. A demand schedule tabulates possible prices and the quantities demanded at the possible prices. Supply is the relationship between prices that producers are willing to accept for various quantities supplied during a given time period. The law of supply states that there is a positive relationship between price and quantity supplied. A supply schedule tabulates possible prices and the quantities supplied at those prices.
5) **Consumer and Producer Surplus:** Consumer and producer surplus are concepts that economists find useful in evaluating the welfare effects of global issues and policies. Consumer surplus is the difference between what consumers are willing to pay for a given quantity of a good or service and the market price. Producer surplus is the difference between the price that producers are willing to receive to supply a particular quantity and the market price.
6) **How Market Prices Are Determined:** The forces of supply and demand determine market prices. For an individual nation, the market-clearing price, or equilibrium price, arises when the quantity demanded equals quantity supplied. The equilibrium price in a global market arises when excess quantity

demanded, or imports, equals excess quantities supplied, or exports. An increase in demand results in a higher equilibrium price. An increase in supply results in a lower equilibrium price.

QUESTIONS AND PROBLEMS

1) Economists often use the sum of a nation's exports and imports divided by its overall economic activity as a measure of the nation's degree of *openness.* Explain why a large value for this measure may not always be a good indicator of openness.
2) Some researchers use the number of Internet sites per person in a given nation as a measure of that nation's degree of globalization. Explain why this may or may not be a good measure of globalization.
3) Suppose that advances in genetically modified crop technology enable farmers to produce greater amounts of agricultural products on the same amount of land. Explain how this event would affect demand, supply, price, quantity demanded, and quantity supplied in the global market.
4) Suppose that consumers in a region whose residents import large quantities of agricultural products become fearful about the health consequences associated with consuming genetically modified agricultural produce. Explain how this event would affect demand, supply, price, quantity demanded, and quantity supplied in the global market.
5) Suppose the events described in questions 3 and 4 above occur simultaneously. Explain the effects on demand, supply, price, quantity demanded, and quantity supplied in the global market.
6) Suppose U.S. government officials are concerned about importing beef that might be contaminated with hoof-and-mouth disease and they react by restricting imported beef from Argentina. Explain the impact of this action on price, quantity, consumer surplus, and producer surplus in both the United States and Argentina.
7) Consider Figure 1-7 on page 29. Calculate the value of consumer surplus in both nations. Calculate the value of producer surplus in both nations when residents of the two nations do not trade.
8) Consider Figure 1-7 on page 29 once more. Calculate the value of consumer surplus and producer surplus for both nations after the nations engage in trade. How has consumer surplus changed in both nations? How has producer surplus changed in both nations?
9) Suppose that the government of a nation whose producers export coffee burns one-third of all the coffee fields before they can be harvested. Explain the impact of this action on the global price and quantity of coffee.
10) Consider the event described in question 9. Can you explain, in economic terms, why the government would be motivated to do such a thing?

ONLINE APPLICATION

Internet URL: http://www.imd.ch/wcy/ranking

Title: **The Institute for International Management Development**

Navigation: To obtain national competitiveness rankings, go to the home page of the Institute for International Management Development (http://www02.imd.ch). Then click on "World Competitiveness Yearbook." Click on "Ranking 2002." Click on "WCY Overall Scoreboard." Print this document.

Application: Use the printed report and Table 1-1 on page 4. Answer the following questions.

1) Compare the top-ten nations that appear in the competitiveness ranking and the top-ten nations in the globalization ranking of Table 1-1. How many of the top ten nations in Table 1-1 appear in the top ten of the competitiveness ranking?
2) What do the nations that are in the top ten of both rankings have in common? What is different about them?
3) Why do you think that these nations appear in each list? In other words, does the extent of a nation's globalization have an effect on its competitiveness, or does its competitiveness have an effect on its degree of globalization?

For Group Study and Analysis: Assign this exercise to different groups, giving them specific nations that appear on the competitiveness list. Have them independently come up with answers to the questions above. Discuss and debate the different hypotheses that are put forward.

REFERENCES AND RECOMMENDED READINGS

Bordo, Michael D., Barry Eichengreen, and Douglas A. Irwin. "Is Globalization Really Different than Globalization a Hundred Years Ago?" National Bureau of Economic Research, Working Paper No. 7195 (June 1999).

Burtless, Gary, Robert Lawrence, Robert Litan, and Robert Shapiro. *Globalphobia: Confronting Fears About Open Trade.* Washington DC: Brookings Institution, 1998.

Daniels, Joseph P., and John D. Davis. "Corporations and Structural Linkages in World Commerce." In Alan Rugman and Gavin Boyd, eds., *The World Trade Organization in the New Global Economy.* Cheltenham, U.K.: Edward Elgar Publishing Ltd., 2001.

Held, David, Anthony McGrew, David Goldblatt, and Jonathan Perraton. *Global Transformations.* Stanford University Press, 1999.

Irwin, Douglas A. *Against the Tide: An Intellectual History of Free Trade.* Princeton, N.J.: Princeton University Press, 1996.

Lewis, Howard III, and J. David Richardson. *Why Global Commitment Really Matters.* Washington, D.C.: Institute for International Economics, 2001.

Obstfeld, Maurice. "The Global Capital Market: Benefactor or Menace?" *Journal of Economic Perspectives* 12 (4) (1998): 9–30.

Rodrick, Dani. "How Far Will International Economic Integration Go?" *Journal of Economic Perspectives* 14 (1) (Winter 2000): 177–186.

Rodrick, Dani. *Has Globalization Gone Too Far?* Washington, D.C.: Institute for International Economics, 1997.

United Nations Conference on Trade and Development. *World Investment Report.* New York: United Nations, 1999.

CHAPTER TWO

Comparative Advantage—How Nations Can Gain from International Trade

Fundamental Issues

1. **What are a nation's production possibilities, and what do they tell us about the costs of producing goods and services within that nation?**
2. **What is absolute advantage, and how can it help explain why nations engage in international trade?**
3. **Why is absolute advantage alone insufficient to account for trade among nations?**
4. **What is comparative advantage, and how does it allow countries to experience gains from trade?**
5. **Why, in spite of its benefits, does international trade ebb and flow and create so much controversy within the world's nations?**

For many generations, Hindu blacksmiths scratched out a living pounding copper into pots, jars, and jugs in the village of Setipokhari, located in the Himalayan foothills of Nepal. Then, the twentieth century arrived, and mass-produced aluminum and plastic containers crowded out their products in the world marketplace. Although the artisans of Setipokhari continued to teach their children the art of metalworking, many gave up their craft and moved to India to find gainful employment.

Enter the twenty-first century. At the beginning of 2000, copper items produced in Setipokhari began appearing alongside sweaters knitted by Peruvian villagers and pyramid candle holders handcrafted in Morocco on the Web site uncommongoods.com. This site is the retail marketing arm of world2market.com, which provides an infrastructure for skilled workers in developing countries to access the global electronic marketplace. It is one of a growing number of Web sites that sell home furnishings, gifts, accessories, and toys made by traditional craftspeople around the world. Most of the buyers of these various wares are Web surfers in the United States.

There is not a single telephone in Setipokhari, but the Internet has dramatically improved the lives of its inhabitants. Copper workers can now earn 150 to 300 rupees per day, or about $2.30 to $4.60. This may not seem like much, but it is about twice the average daily wage of a typical blue-collar worker in Nepal. The metal crafters' families now cook on gas stoves instead of over open fires, and they receive child-education and retirement benefits—employment benefits previously unknown to residents of Seipokhari.

Nepal is one of the world's poorest countries. The dollar value of the goods and services produced by a typical resident of Nepal is less than 1 percent of the value of the goods and services produced by a typical U.S. resident. This reflects the fact that the productive capabilities of the United States dwarf those of Nepal. Yet a number of U.S. Web surfers are buying copper goods produced by Nepalese artisans instead of those made by blacksmiths based in the United States. What lies behind this flow of trade from one of the world's smallest economies to its largest economy? After you read this chapter, you will know the answer to this question.

The Economics of "Going It Alone"

To think about why residents of rich nations with large economies might wish to trade with residents of poor nations that have small economies—and *vice versa*—let's begin by thinking about a country that does not trade with any other nations.

PRODUCTION POSSIBILITIES

The residents of any nation normally produce and consume a number of different goods and services. To keep things simple so that we can emphasize fundamental concepts, however, let's imagine a situation in which a country produces only two goods.

A Nation's Production Possibilities

Let's consider a particular nation called Northland, which engages in no international trade. Furthermore, let's suppose that Northland's residents currently produce and consume food and computers. Given its current technology and resources—people, machines, and so on—Northland has a fixed capability to produce food

Table 2-1 Northland's Production Possibilities

Thousands of Computers	Thousands of Baskets of Food
0	700
400	600
500	550
600	490
700	410
800	310
900	190
1,000	0

and computers. Its overall production capabilities for a given year, which economists call a nation's **production possibilities,** are displayed in Table 2-1.

Production possibilities
All possible combinations of total output of goods and services that residents of a nation can produce given currently available technology and resources.

The maximum amount of food, measured in baskets (which might include a certain amount of drinks, fruit, pasta, and so on) that the people of Northland can produce within the year, is 700,000. To produce this amount of food, Northland's residents must devote all of their resources to food production, which means that the nation cannot produce any computers during that year.

If Northland's residents are willing to forgo all food production during the year, however, they can produce 1,000,000 (1 million) computers. Nevertheless, producing this quantity of computers entails devoting all of the nation's resources to computer production, so this is the maximum number of computers that Northland's residents can produce, given its current technology and resources.

Table 2-1 illustrates a fundamental economic rule: With a given technology and fixed amounts of fully employed resources, increasing production of one good requires reducing production of another good. That is, a nation faces a *production possibilities trade-off.* In the case of Northland, Table 2-1 indicates that if Northland's residents initially were producing nothing but 700,000 baskets of food but then decided to develop a completely "high-tech" economy producing 1 million computers per year, then they would have to halt all food production.

Production Possibilities and Opportunity Cost

Opportunity cost
The highest-valued, next-best alternative that must be sacrificed to obtain an item.

A fundamental economic concept is **opportunity cost,** which is the highest-valued, next-best alternative that must be sacrificed to obtain an item. For Northland, any production decision entails an opportunity cost. As already noted, Northland's residents must give up producing 700,000 baskets of food to produce

1 million computers instead. This means that in Northland, the *opportunity cost* of producing 1 million computers is the 700,000 baskets of food that it could have otherwise produced with its current technology and all its resources.

Let's suppose that Northland has chosen not to be purely a food producer or a computer producer. Currently, it produces 400,000 computers. Table 2-1 indicates that, given current production possibilities, this means that Northland also produces 600,000 baskets of food. If Northland's residents decide to become a little more high-tech-oriented by producing 100,000 more computers, thereby yielding a total of 500,000 new computers this year, then they must reallocate to computer production tasks some of the resources that they previously had devoted to food production. This means that they must cut back on food production. According to Table 2-1, Northland's residents can raise their computer production to from 400,000 to 500,000 only if they reduce food production from 600,000 baskets to 550,000 baskets. Thus, producing 100,000 more computers entails incurring an *opportunity cost* equal to 50,000 baskets of food.

Now suppose that Northland's residents decide to aim for an even more high-tech production mix by raising their computer production by 100,000 more units, to 600,000 computers. This requires reducing food production from 550,000 baskets to 490,000 baskets. Consequently, producing another 100,000 computers requires Northland's residents to incur an opportunity cost equal to 60,000 baskets of food.

If Northland's residents raise computer production by yet another 100,000-unit increment, from 600,000 computers to 700,000 computers, then Table 2-1 indicates that food production must decline from 490,000 baskets to 410,000 baskets. The opportunity cost of producing the next 100,000 computers, therefore, is 80,000 baskets of food.

Note that each 100,000-unit increase in computer production requires a successively larger—50,000, then 60,000, and then 80,000—reduction in the quantity of baskets of food that Northland can produce. This illustrates a fundamental characteristic of the production possibilities tradeoffs that countries normally face: The opportunity cost of producing additional units of a particular good increases as more of that good is produced.

If you think about this for a minute, it will become clear to you that it makes a lot of sense. If the residents of a country such as Northland start transferring resources from food production to computer production, initially they will transfer over those people who are best at designing and manufacturing microprocessors, modems, DVD drives, operating systems, and so on. Initially they will also shift resources that are best suited to computer production—silicon, precious metals, materials useful for making plastics, and the like. As they continue to increase their production of computers, however, Northland's residents will discover that fewer resources readily lend themselves to producing computers. Some people transferred from food production to computer production may know a lot about botany, farming, or agricultural machinery but relatively little about computer manufacturing or programming. Iron, steel, and other resources that are useful for farming will also be less readily applied to computer production. Thus, each

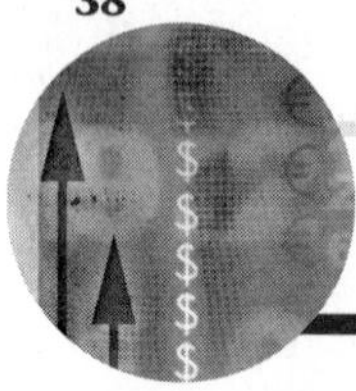

Visualizing Global Economic Issues

The Production Possibilities Frontier

The production possibilities for Northland can be displayed on a diagram, as shown in Figure 2-1. This figure plots the combinations of food and computer production from Table 2-1 on page 36, with the amount of food measured along the vertical axis and the amount of computers measured along the horizontal axis. These production combinations, plus all other feasible combinations of production of goods and services given technology and available resources, lie along a curve that economists call the production possibilities frontier. Northland's residents can produce combinations of food or computers that lie on or inside the frontier, but they cannot produce combinations that lie beyond the frontier.

Point *A* in Figure 2-1 corresponds to the second line of Table 2-1, and at this point Northland's residents can produce 400,000 computers and 600,000 baskets of food in a year's time. Point *B* corresponds to the fifth line of Table 2-1, which indicates that Northland's residents are able to raise their computer production to 700,000 computers if they reduce their production of food to 410,000 baskets.

Thus, we can calculate the opportunity cost of moving from one point to another along the production possibilities frontier. Let's consider a different question, however. What is the opportunity cost of increasing computer production by *one single unit* if Northland's residents currently are producing at point *A*? We can determine the answer by looking at the *slope* of a line tangent to the production possibilities frontier at point *A*. Recall that the slope of a line is the "rise" divided by the "run." A one-unit increase in computer production is a one-unit horizontal movement, or *run,* along the line. The accompanying vertical movement back down along the line is the *rise,* which is negative because it tells us the opportunity cost of the one-unit increase in computer production, which is measured in baskets of food.

Likewise, we can find the opportunity cost of a one-unit increase in computer production at point *B* by considering the slope of the line tangent to the production possibilities frontier at that point. Note that the *rise* accompanying a one-unit run along this tangent line is a larger negative amount. Thus, the opportunity cost of computer production is higher at point *B* than at point *A.* That is, when more resources are already devoted to computer production, shifting sufficient resources from food production to computer production to achieve a one-unit increase in computer production entails a higher opportunity cost measured in baskets of food.

For Critical Analysis:
If the opportunity cost of producing one additional computer was always the same no matter how many computers Northland produced, what would be the shape of its production possibilities frontier?

successive 100,000-unit increase in production of computers requires transferring successively larger numbers of resources away from food production. The result is a successively larger reduction in production of food due to each incremental increase in computer production, and hence a higher opportunity cost of producing computers. (To see how to examine opportunity costs on a graph of Northland's production possibilities, see *Visualizing Global Economic Issues: The Production Possibilities Frontier.*)

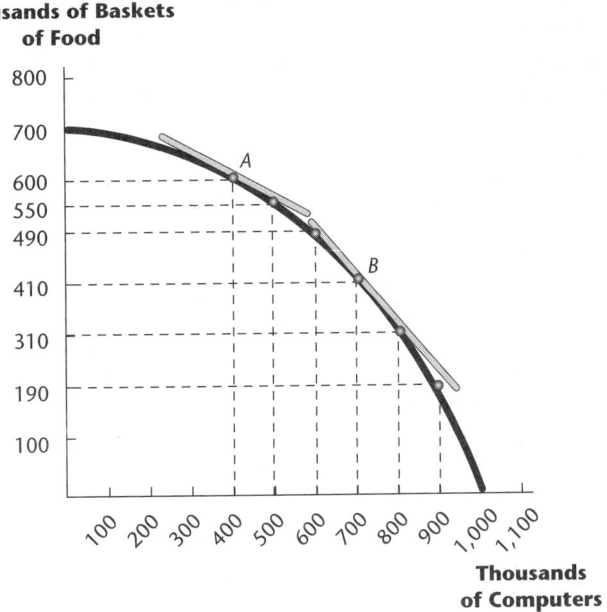

Figure 2-1

Northland's Production Possibilities Frontier

This diagram displays the combinations of food and computer production listed in Table 2-1 on page 36, which together with all other feasible combinations of production of goods and services is Northland's production possibilities frontier. Given technology and available resources, Northland's residents can produce combinations of food or computers that lie on or inside this frontier but cannot produce combinations that lie beyond the frontier. To increase production of computers from 400,000 at point A to 700,000 at point B, Northland's residents must reduce their food production from 600,000 baskets to 410,000 baskets, so the opportunity cost of 300,000 computers is 190,000 baskets of food. At point A the opportunity cost of producing one additional computer is the slope of the line tangent to point A. Likewise, at point B the opportunity cost of producing one more computer is the slope of the line tangent to that point. The absolute slope of the tangent line at point B is greater than the absolute slope of the tangent line at point A, which indicates that increasing total computer production generates a rise in the opportunity cost of producing computers.

CONSUMPTION POSSIBILITIES AND CHOICES

By assumption, residents of Northland engage in no international trade. Hence, whatever combination of food and computers that Northland's residents produce stays within the nation's borders for domestic consumption.

This means that Northland's **consumption possibilities,** or the amounts of goods and services that its residents are able to consume, are exactly the same as

Consumption possibilities
All possible combinations of goods and services that a nation's residents can consume.

its production possibilities. The production possibilities depicted in Table 2-1, therefore, are also Northland's consumption possibilities.

How much will the residents of Northland choose to produce and consume? This will depend on their preferences. If they have a taste for baskets of food, then they will choose a combination toward the upper part of Table 2-1. By way of contrast, if they enjoy playing computer games and surfing the Internet, then they will choose a production mix toward the lower part of Table 2-1.

Fundamental Issue

What are a nation's production possibilities, and what do they tell us about the costs of producing goods and services within that nation?

The production possibilities of a nation are combinations of goods and services that its residents are capable of producing given currently available technology and resources. When the nation's residents raise their production of one item, they must forgo producing some amount of another good or service, thereby incurring an opportunity cost. This opportunity cost increases as the nation's residents produce more of the particular item.

Absolute Advantage—Do Big Countries Have an Upper Hand?

ON THE WEB

For data on U.S. trade with all other nations of the world, go to http://www.census.gov/foreign-trade/balance/index.html.

As noted at the beginning of this chapter, it is not uncommon for residents of countries with relatively highly productive capabilities to engage in trade with people residing in nations with relatively low production capabilities. To many people, such trade flows seem counterintuitive; indeed, some observers of trade flows between large countries and small countries jump to the conclusion that such flows imply exploitation of the small country (say, Nepal) by the large country (say, the United States)—and possibly some of the workers in the large country.

Before you can begin to think through why trade might be beneficial for both types of countries, you must first understand the concept of absolute advantage. As you will see, this concept can help explain why international trade takes place, but it cannot provide a complete justification for real-world trade patterns.

ABSOLUTE ADVANTAGE AS A RATIONALE FOR TRADE

Absolute advantage *The ability of a nation's residents to produce a good or service at lower cost, measured in resources required to produce the good or service, or, alternatively, the ability to produce more output from given inputs of resources, as compared with other nations.*

For a variety of reasons, such as differing terrains, climates, and technologies, countries of the world differ in their ability to produce various goods. At one time, international trade was thought to arise from the ability of some countries to produce goods or services at a lower production cost, in terms of units of labor or other resource inputs required to produce each unit of a good or service.

Absolute Advantage

Because of this emphasis on production costs, early thinking about why countries trade focused on the possibility that one country might have an **absolute**

Table 2-2 Weekly Production in Northland and Westcoast without Specialization

	Northland		Westcoast		Combined Weekly Output
Product	Workers	Weekly Output	Workers	Weekly Output	
Computers	100	30	100	40	70
Food	100	50	100	25	75

advantage arising from its ability to produce more output, as compared with other nations, from given inputs of resources. As an example, consider Table 2-2. If a representative set of 100 workers from Northland is assigned to manufacture computers, given a fixed set of additional productive resources, then in a week's time they can produce 30 computers. Alternatively, if a set of 100 Northland residents is put to work producing food, the result is 50 baskets of output in a week's time. By way of contrast, in a neighboring country called Westcoast, during a given week one set of 100 workers can, using an identical set of additional resources, produce 40 computers, while another group of 100 workers can produce 25 baskets of food. Thus, if the two countries engage in no trade, the combined weekly output by the 200 workers is 70 computers and 75 baskets of food.

Because 100 workers in Northland can produce more baskets of food than the same number of workers can produce each week in Westcoast, we can conclude that Northland has an absolute advantage in producing food. Westcoast, however, has an absolute advantage in computer production, because 100 workers in that nation can produce more computers than the same number of workers in Northland are able to produce during a given week.

Absolute Advantage as a Basis for Trade

Absolute advantage can provide a rationale for cross-border trade between Northland and Westcoast. The reason is that, in principle, both countries can gain from specializing in producing the goods for which they have an absolute advantage. To see why this is so, take a look at Table 2-3 on the next page. Northland has an absolute advantage in producing food, and if both groups of workers in Northland produce food, then the 200 workers together can produce 100 baskets of food each week. At the same time, if the 200 workers in Westcoast manufacture computers, the good that Westcoast has an absolute advantage in producing, then their weekly output is 80 computers.

If you look back at Table 2-2, you will see that specialization increases the total output of both nations. The 100 baskets of food that the 200 workers in Northland can produce each week exceeds the 75 baskets that the same number of workers in both nations can produce when the countries do not specialize. Likewise, the 80 computers that the 200 workers in Westcoast are able to manufacture

Table 2-3 Weekly Production in Northland and Westcoast with Specialization

	Northland		Westcoast		Combined
Product	**Workers**	**Weekly Output**	**Workers**	**Weekly Output**	**Weekly Output**
Computers	0	0	200	80	80
Food	200	100	0	0	100

in a week's time is greater than the 70 computers that a total of 200 laborers in both countries can make without specialization.

This means that both countries have an incentive to specialize in production and engage in trade. To see why, suppose that the countries' residents agree to trade one basket of food for one computer. Suppose further that the residents of Northland exchange 35 baskets of food for 35 of Westcoast's computers each week. From Table 2-3, you can see that Northland's residents will still have 65 baskets of food available for domestic consumption each week, which is greater than the 50 baskets that Table 2-2 indicates they would have been able to consume without specialization and trade.

At the same time, the 35 baskets of food that Westcoast's residents are able to obtain through specialization and trade exceed the 25 baskets that they could consume in the absence of trade. Furthermore, the 35 computers that residents of Northland can obtain via trade exceeds the 30 that Table 2-2 indicates that they could have produced on their own, while the 45 computers that Westcoast residents can retain after trading away 35 each week to Northland exceeds the 40 that they would have available for domestic use in the absence of specialization and trade.

2 Fundamental Issue

What is absolute advantage, and how can it help explain why nations engage in international trade?

A nation has an absolute advantage in producing an item if its residents can produce more of that good or service with a given amount of resources, as compared with other nations. This can give the nation's residents an incentive to specialize in producing goods and services for which their nation has an absolute advantage and to trade those goods and services for items produced in nations that have an absolute advantage in producing those items.

Table 2-4 Production Possibilities in Northland and Westcoast

Northland		Westcoast	
Thousands of Computers	Thousands of Baskets of Food	Thousands of Computers	Thousands of Baskets of Food
0	700	0	600
400	600	350	585
500	550	500	550
600	490	650	495
700	410	800	425
800	310	950	335
900	190	1,100	120
1,000	0	1,250	0

WHAT ABSOLUTE ADVANTAGE IMPLIES—AND WHAT IT DOESN'T

The previous example shows that absolute advantage can provide a rationale for trade among nations. By specializing in producing goods or services for which they have an absolute advantage in production and then trading these goods and services, countries potentially can consume more goods and services than they could otherwise.

Production Possibilities and Absolute Advantage

Another way to illustrate how countries can gain from specialization and trade is by examining their overall production possibilities. Take a look at Table 2-4, which displays Northland's production possibilities from Table 2-1 alongside the overall production possibilities available to Westcoast.

Table 2-4 indicates that Northland has an absolute advantage over Westcoast in producing food, in the sense that if the residents of both countries produce nothing but food, Northland can produce 700,000 baskets, whereas Westcoast can produce only 600,000. Westcoast has an absolute advantage in producing computers, because if residents of both Northland and Westcoast produce only computers, those in Westcoast can produce 1.25 million computers, as compared with the 1 million computers that residents of Northland can manufacture.

Table 2-5 Weekly Production in Northland and Southsea without Specialization

	Northland		Southsea		Combined
Product	Workers	Weekly Output	Workers	Weekly Output	Weekly Output
Computers	100	30	100	15	45
Food	100	50	100	10	60

It is not obvious from the table, however, that this absolute advantage will necessarily induce the two countries to trade. For instance, each country might happen to produce 500,000 computers and 550,000 baskets of food (see the third line of Table 2-4). If both countries choose this identical production mix, it is unclear why they might want to trade—at least from the standpoint of any argument based on the idea of absolute advantage.

Absolute Advantage Cannot Fully Explain International Trade

In general, it turns out that absolute advantage has limited usefulness in helping us to understand why many countries trade. Consider, for instance, weekly computer and food production capabilities of two groups of 100 residents in Northland versus two other groups of 100 residents in Southsea, a neighboring island archipelago nation. As you can see from Table 2-5, Northland has an absolute advantage over Southsea in producing *both* goods. From the perspective of absolute advantage, therefore, Northland has no incentive to specialize and engage in trade with Southsea.

Nevertheless, there are good reasons to think that both countries would gain from trading. Table 2-5 indicates that to produce 30 more computers in a given day, Northland must reallocate 100 workers from food production and give up 50 baskets of food. Thus, the opportunity cost of a computer in Northland is 50 baskets of food divided by 30 computers, or 5/3 baskets of food per computer. In Southsea, producing 15 more computers would require giving up only 10 baskets of food, so the opportunity cost of a computer in Southsea is 10 baskets of food divided by 15 computers, or 2/3 basket of food per computer. Even though Northland has an absolute advantage in producing computers, the *opportunity cost* of producing computers is lower in Southsea.

Table 2-5 also indicates that to produce 50 more baskets of food on a given day, Northland's residents must give up 30 computers, so that the opportunity cost of producing food in Northland is 30 computers divided by 50 baskets of food, or 3/5 computer per basket of food. In Southsea, producing 10 more baskets of food on a given day requires forgoing the production of 15 computers. Consequently, the opportunity cost of producing a basket of food in Southsea is 15 computers divided by 10 baskets of food, or 1½ computers per basket of food. Hence, the opportunity cost of producing a basket of food is lower in Northland than in Southsea.

Now, for the sake of argument, let's suppose that residents of Northland and Southsea are willing to exchange 1 basket of food for 1 computer, and *vice versa.* Trading goods at this rate of exchange is beneficial for Northland residents, because giving up 1 basket of food to Southsea residents in exchange for a computer is a better deal than sacrificing 5/3 baskets of food to obtain a computer within its own borders. Likewise, giving 1 computer for 1 basket of food from Northland is advantageous for residents of Southsea, because this is a better deal than giving up 1½ computers to obtain a basket of food within its own borders.

Clearly, absolute advantage alone cannot fully explain why many countries engage in international trade. Differences in internal opportunity costs are likely to be fundamental determinants of whether countries can gain from trading goods and services with other nations. We turn next to this fundamental explanation for why countries trade with one another.

Fundamental Issue 3

Why is absolute advantage alone insufficient to account for trade among nations?

Absolute advantage by itself cannot fully explain why countries trade, because residents of a nation can benefit from trade with another country even when their nation has an absolute advantage in producing all goods and services. The reason is that the opportunity cost of producing an item within their nation may exceed the amount of goods and services required to obtain that item from residents of another country.

Comparative Advantage—Why Trade Benefits Nearly Everyone

As the previous example indicates, two countries may have an incentive to trade goods or services even if one has an absolute advantage over the other in producing the goods or services. The reason is that *opportunity costs* of producing goods and services vary from country to country. If the opportunity cost of producing a good or service in even a very small country with meager production of goods and services is low relative to the opportunity cost of producing the same good or service in a large nation capable of producing massive quantities of output, trade may still take place.

COMPARATIVE ADVANTAGE

Comparative advantage *The ability of a nation's residents to produce an additional unit of a good or service at a lower opportunity cost relative to other nations.*

When residents of a country are able to produce a good or service at a lower opportunity cost compared with other nations, then that country is said to have a **comparative advantage.** Even if a country is at an absolute disadvantage in producing goods or services, that country may still have a comparative advantage

Online Globalization

Will Other Languages Stand a Chance Against English?

International trade typically involves goods that can only be consumed by one person at a time. Some goods, however, can be jointly consumed by many individuals. A good example is a language, because everyone who uses a language owns it and cannot be excluded from using it. Of course, sometimes we may use language for communicating only with ourselves, such as when we save notes in a computer file for future reference. Mostly, however, we use language to communicate with others.

English and the Net

The Internet has emerged as one of the world's primary modes of communication. Nevertheless, the bulk of Internet hosts and users are located in the United States, where English is the predominant language. Estimates are that English accounts for about 80 percent of the *stock* of all information stored in the world's computers. English also is used in roughly the same percentage of the *flow* of Internet information transmissions—e-mail messages, file transfers, and so on. Undoubtedly, this has provided many of the world's non–English speakers with a powerful incentive to learn English. Berlitz International, the world's largest language school, reports that more than two-thirds of the 5 million language lessons it provides each year are for people who wish to become more proficient in English. Spanish is the fastest-growing spoken language in the world, but it is used by far fewer of the world's people than English.

Many language specialists and even some politicians fret that English so dominates the global communications network that it might endanger the future of other languages and damage traditional cultural identities. A former president of France contemplating the growing use of English by French residents once called the Internet "a major risk for humanity."

Comparative Advantage Applies to Languages, Too

There are, nonetheless, some strong arguments favoring the view that growing use of the Internet will

in producing one or more goods or services, which can induce other nations to engage in trade with that country. (The principle of comparative advantage can also help us contemplate the likelihood that online globalization will gradually cause languages other than English to fall into disuse; see *Online Globalization: Will Other Languages Stand a Chance Against English?*)

Production Possibilities and Comparative Advantage

For another perspective on why comparative advantage is such a crucial factor influencing international trade, consider Table 2-6 on page 48, which gives overall production possibilities for Northland and Southsea. The feasible combinations of food and computer production for Northland are again the same as in Table 2-1 on page 36. Note that Southsea is capable of producing both fewer computers and actually *reduce* the likelihood that languages other than English will fall into disuse. Before the Internet, media that relied solely on one-way transmissions, such as radio and television, helped bring about head-on competition among languages. European broadcasters, for instance, often determined that the time allocated to transmission of a recent Hollywood movie blockbuster dubbed in Danish could more effectively reach a target advertising audience in the original English version that more people could understand. By way of contrast, on the Internet e-mail transmissions and Web sites in various languages do not directly compete. Promoters of a Danish historical exhibit can post Web advertisements for a festival in English, German, or French, but they can also post them in Danish.

Applying economic analysis to languages indicates that the key factor determining which ones are most likely to remain in use is the principle of comparative advantage. People will use a particular language when there is a lower opportunity cost of using that language relative to alternative languages. A non–English-speaking individual will use her native tongue when the cost of doing so is lower as compared with trying to use another language, whether the conversation takes place on a street corner, on the editorial page of a local newspaper, or in an Internet chat room. She will tend to choose a nonnative tongue, such as English, for formal communications with others around the globe who have a shared knowledge of that language.

Some who study languages argue that the widespread use of English on the Internet eventually could pose greater problems for English than for other languages. If a "techie" version of English begins to develop on the Internet, then someday to get by in both the real world and the virtual world, English speakers may have to know two languages to get by: the version of English that they read and speak at home and the offshoot of English that they use in their Web-based communications.

For Critical Analysis:

Does English currently have an absolute advantage over other languages?

fewer baskets of food than Northland. Thus, Northland has an *absolute advantage* in producing both goods.

Now suppose that in the absence of trade both nations choose to produce combinations of computers and food listed in the fifth row of Table 2-6. Hence, Northland currently produces 700,000 computers and 410,000 baskets of food during the year, while Southsea produces 250,000 computers and 240,000 baskets of food. The table indicates that if Northland were to increase its production of computers by 100,000, to 800,000, it would have to give up 100,000 baskets of food, which implies an *average* opportunity cost of 1 basket of food per computer. In Southsea, however, increasing computer production by 100,000 units, to 350,000 computers, would entail reducing the amount of food production to 150,000 baskets, or by 90,000 baskets. This means that the *average* opportunity cost of increasing computer

Table 2-6 Production Possibilities in Northland and Southsea

Northland		Southsea	
Thousands of Computers	Thousands of Baskets of Food	Thousands of Computers	Thousands of Baskets of Food
0	700	0	300
400	600	100	295
500	550	150	285
600	490	200	270
700	410	250	240
800	310	300	200
900	190	350	150
1,000	0	400	0

production in Southsea is 0.9 basket of food per computer. Over these ranges along the two nations' production possibilities, therefore, Southsea has a comparative advantage in producing computers.

Over the same ranges, however, Northland has a comparative advantage in producing food. Increasing food production from 310,000 baskets to 410,000 baskets in Northland requires giving up producing 100,000 computers, or an *average* opportunity cost of 1 computer per basket of food. In Southsea, however, raising food production from 150,000 baskets to 240,000 baskets, or by 90,000 baskets, entails forgoing the production of 100,000 computers, which implies an *average* opportunity cost of approximately 1.11 computers per basket of food (100,000 computers divided by 90,000 baskets of food). Thus, the opportunity cost of producing food over these ranges of production possibilities is lower in Northland, so that Northland has a comparative advantage in food production over these ranges of production possibilities.

Production Possibilities and Trade

We have determined that Northland has a comparative advantage in food production while producing 700,000 computers and 410,000 baskets of food and that Southsea has a comparative advantage in computer production while producing 250,000 computers and 240,000 baskets of food. Does this mean that there may be incentive for Northland's residents to specialize in producing food to trade for computers that Southsea's residents specialize in producing?

To answer this question, note that based on our calculations, if Northland's residents wish to obtain more computers than the 700,000 they currently produce, on average it would cost 1 basket of food to obtain each computer. This means that Northland's residents will be willing to obtain more computers through trade with Southsea's residents if Southsea's residents will be willing to accept less than 1 basket of food in exchange.

At the same time, if Southsea's residents desire to consume more than the 240 thousand baskets of food they currently produce, then on average it would cost 1.11 computers to obtain each basket of food. Southsea's residents, therefore, will be willing to offer to trade their computers for food produced in Northland as long as they can trade less than 1.11 computers for each basket of Northland's food. A rate of exchange of 1.11 computers per basket of food is the same as a rate of exchange of 0.9 basket of food per computer. Thus, as long as the rate of exchange of food for computers is higher than 0.9 basket of food per computer, Southsea residents will be willing to trade their computers for food produced in Northland.

We can conclude that in this example, as long as the rate of exchange of food for computers is *between* 0.9 basket of food per computer and 1 basket of food per computer, Northland's residents are willing to consider trading some of their food for Southsea's computers, and Southsea's residents are willing to consider trading some of their computers for Northland's food. The reason is that as long as the food–computer exchange rate is within this range, both can come out ahead if they can agree about how many baskets of food and computers to trade. (To see how to examine comparative advantage and incentives to trade on a diagram, see on pages 50–51 *Visualizing Global Economic Issues: Production Possibilities Frontiers and Comparative Advantage*.)

ON THE WEB

View the most recent overall trade statistics for the United States at http://www.census.gov/indicator/www/ustrade.html.

GAINS FROM TRADE

Let's suppose that residents of Northland and Southsea agree to exchange food and computers at a rate of exchange of 0.95 basket of food per computer (which is approximately the same as 1.053 computer per basket of food). Let's further suppose that at this exchange rate, Northland trades 100,000 baskets of food to Southsea in exchange for 105,300 computers.

We can use Table 2-6 to determine that each country will experience **gains from trade**, or additional goods and services over and above the amounts that it could have produced on its own, as a result of this transaction. According to Table 2-6, if Northland's residents had given up 100,000 computers, they could have increased their own production of computers by 100,000. Hence, the trade with Southsea entails a gain from trade equal to 5,300 computers for Northland.

Gains from trade
Additional goods and services that a nation's residents can consume, over and above the amounts that they could have produced within their own borders, as a consequence of trade with residents of other nations.

For Southsea, recall that the average opportunity cost of food was equal to 1.11 computers per basket of food. Hence, obtaining 100,000 baskets of food (at least, in the production possibilities range that we considered) would have cost Southsea residents about 110,000 computers if they had produced them on their own. Because they are able to trade only 105,300 computers for 100,000 baskets of

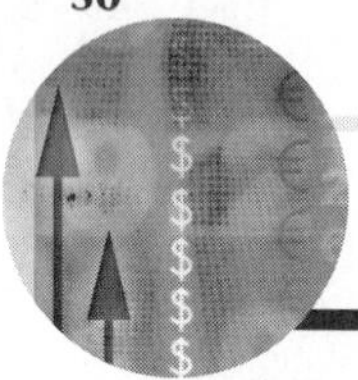

Visualizing Global Economic Issues

Production Possibilities Frontiers and Comparative Advantage

Figure 2-2 shows the production possibilities frontiers for Northland and Southsea, based on the information in Table 2-6 on page 48. Because Northland has an absolute advantage in producing both food and computers, the production possibilities frontier for Southsea lies completely inside Northland's production possibilities frontier. Hence, absolute advantage cannot provide a rationale for trade between Northland and Southsea.

In our example, we examined *average* opportunity costs for Northland and Southsea in a range containing the fifth row of Table 2-6, where initially Northland produces 700,000 computers and 410,000 baskets of food and Southsea produces 250,000 computers and 240,000 baskets of food. These are denoted as points *N* and *S* in the figure.

Recall that the opportunity cost of increasing computer production by a *single* unit is equal to the slope of the production possibilities frontier at the current production combination. Consequently, the *exact* opportunity cost of higher computer production in Northland equals the slope of the line tangent to point *N*. Likewise, the *exact* opportunity cost of higher computer production in Southsea equals the slope of the line tangent to point *S*. The line tangent to point *S* is slightly less steeply sloped than the line tangent to point *N*, thereby indicating that at point *S* Southsea can produce an additional computer at less cost than Northland can produce at point *N*. As long as the rate of exchange of food for computers is between the values of these two slopes, there is an incentive for both nations to consider engaging in trade.

For Critical Analysis:
Would the incentives for residents of Northland and Southsea change if points *N* and *S* were in different locations along the nations' production possibilities frontiers?

Northland's food production, however, Southsea's residents experience a gain from trade equal to 4,700 computers.

Finally, note that this trade adds to Northland's trade balance in food while subtracting from its trade balance in computers, and it adds to Southsea's trade balance in computers while subtracting from its trade balance in food. If these two nations have similar comparative advantages *vis-à-vis* other countries, then Northland is likely to have an overall trade surplus in food and an overall trade deficit in computers, and Southsea is likely to have an overall trade deficit in food and an overall trade surplus in computers. Hence, a nation's trade balances in categories for specific goods or services are likely to be related in large part to comparative advantage. (This means that the current leadership that the United States has in selling products over the Internet will not necessarily last if other countries can develop comparative advantages in various aspects of electronic

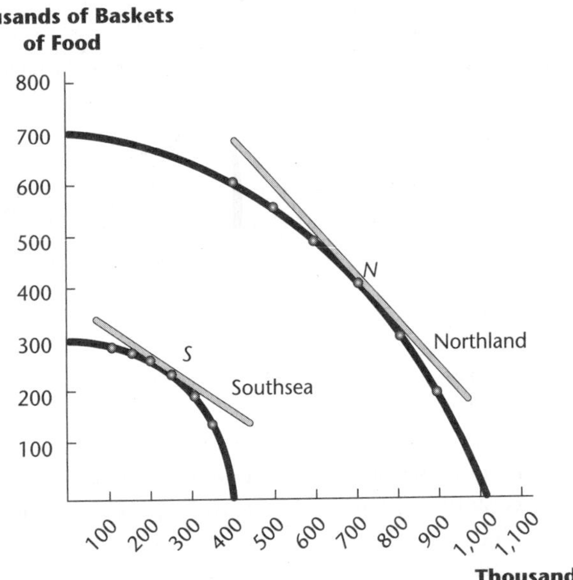

Figure 2-2

Production Possibilities Frontiers for Northland and Southsea

This graph uses the data from Table 2-6 on page 48 to display the production possibilities frontiers for Northland and Southsea. Northland has an absolute advantage in producing both food and computers. Consequently, Southsea's production possibilities frontier lies inside Northland's production possibilities frontier, and absolute advantage cannot explain trade between the nations. The residents of the countries currently produce at points S and N. Because the line tangent to point S is slightly less steeply sloped than the line tangent to point N, Southsea presently produces an additional computer at lower cost. At the same time, Northland produces an additional basket of food at lower cost. Hence, there is an incentive for both nations to consider trading.

commerce; see on the next page *Online Globalization: Is the U.S. "First-Mover Advantage" in E-Commerce Unassailable?*)

Fundamental Issue 4

What is comparative advantage, and how does it allow countries to experience gains from trade?

A nation has a comparative advantage when its residents can produce additional units of a good or service at a lower cost than in other countries. This gives residents of a country with higher costs of producing additional units of the good or service, an incentive to trade with the nation that has a comparative advantage. Residents of the country with higher opportunity costs can reap gains from trade, because through trade they can obtain more units of the good or service at a lower cost than the domestic cost of producing the good or service.

Online Globalization

Is the U.S. "First-Mover Advantage" in E-Commerce Unassailable?

Amazon.com, eBay, and other Web-based businesses have benefited from the so-called *first-mover advantage*—jumping into the electronic marketplace ahead of the pack, carving out a big market share. They hold onto customer loyalty via consumers' bookmarks on their Internet browsers, e-mail updates to consumers about new products that past purchases have revealed they might like to buy, patented one-click shopping technologies, and the like. According to some commentators, the United States exults in a dominance of the emerging economy. Being first in embracing the Internet has made the United States such a global leader in electronic commerce, they say, that the American lead will do nothing but grow, with the United States benefiting from a long-term trade surplus from sales of information technology hardware, computer data processing, and software design.

As the principle of comparative advantage makes clear, however, being first and biggest will not necessarily translate into a trade advantage for the United States. Decades ago, after all, any economic pundit would have assured you that the U.S. dominance of a number of manufacturing industries, such as the oil and steel industries in which top U.S. producers had a first-mover advantage, was also unassailable. It took a few decades, but ultimately other countries caught up. Now the U.S. imports much of its oil, and its steel industry is a shadow of its former self.

Beyond a doubt, the United States currently has an absolute advantage in information technology products and services. In many areas, it also has a comparative advantage. Nevertheless, within just a few years Ireland has developed into a European center for processing information for firms throughout Europe. India and Russia have already become net exporters of software code, and U.S. firms are their primary customers. Comparative advantage ultimately will determine what countries are net exporters or net importers in the virtual marketplace, just as it has in the physical markets for goods such as oil and steel.

For Critical Analysis:
What factors are likely to determine whether the United States achieves a long-lasting comparative advantage in information technology products and services?

Why Trade Is Not a Clear-Cut Issue

You have learned that absolute advantage gives nations an incentive to specialize in production and engage in international trade. Furthermore, comparative advantage promises gains from trade, even in situations when absolute advantage fails to provide a motivation for trade.

Why, then, do the volumes of trade among nations tend to ebb and flow over time? In addition, why does international trade often generate so much controversy and debate within nations around the world? Let's consider each of these questions in turn.

GAINS FROM TRADE CAN BE FLEETING

Recall the earlier discussion of Nepalese village blacksmiths, who were able to export handcrafted copper containers to residents of other nations. During most of the twentieth century, cross-border trade in their wares dried up. Then the flow of trade recovered again at the beginning of this century. Undoubtedly, the ability to market their wares over the Internet helped Nepalese artisans establish a new foothold in the international marketplace for handcrafted goods. Nevertheless, changing opportunity costs likely played a role as well, as evidenced by the fact that other nations developed a comparative advantage in producing close substitutes for copper containers that tended to crowd out trade in Nepalese handicrafts during several decades of the twentieth century.

In our examples, we were careful to emphasize two key assumptions underlying our examinations of production possibilities and opportunity costs: (1) a *given* technology and (2) a *fixed* set of available resources. Of course, these assumptions only apply to a short-run time horizon. Countries' production possibilities do not remain unchanged over time. Technological improvements expand a nation's production possibilities, and the amounts of resources, such as labor, can increase over time. Furthermore, technological change and growth in available resources sometimes favor the production of one good over another.

This means that a nation's absolute advantage in producing a particular item often can dissipate with the passage of time as other countries develop greater capabilities to produce the same good or service. In addition, opportunity costs of producing particular goods or services can change as technological innovations and changes in resources tend to make one good or service less expensive to produce relative to another. As a result, a nation that once had a comparative advantage in, say, crafting copper containers may discover within a few years that this advantage has evaporated following changes in the opportunity costs of production in other nations.

In short, gains from trade can evaporate for one item for a time but then gradually reappear years later. Sometimes changes in nations' production possibilities can even result in reversing gains from trade, so that a country that once was a net exporter of a good for which it had a comparative advantage ultimately becomes a net importer when other nations develop a comparative advantage in producing that good.

THE REDISTRIBUTIVE EFFECTS OF TRADE

For Nepalese blacksmiths, change was painful. Before the mid-twentieth century, artisans of Nepal had a comparative advantage in producing inexpensive bowls, jars, and jugs, and they were able to earn a modest living producing these goods. When alternatives that could be produced at lower opportunity cost arrived on the scene, many felt obliged to move to India to find gainful employment producing goods or services in which that nation had an absolute or comparative advantage. When conditions changed a few years ago because of improved marketing opportunities, changed consumer preferences, and altered opportunity costs outside Nepal, good times returned for Nepalese blacksmiths as consumers in the United States and elsewhere began to buy their copper containers.

This boom-and-bust story of Nepalese copperware is just a small example of the sweeping *internal* changes that individual countries can witness as a result of ebbs and flows in absolute or comparative advantages among nations. Such changes illustrate the **redistributive effects of trade**, which are internal rearrangements of income flows among a nation's residents arising from variations in flows of international trade. Through such redistributive effects, technological change and other factors that affect nations' production possibilities and alter global absolute and comparative advantages have domestic as well as international impacts. Naturally, redistributive effects of trade have implications for domestic politics within each of the world's nations. More important, however, they affect the well being of people around the globe. We shall revisit this theme throughout the chapters that follow.

Redistributive effects of trade
Altered allocations of incomes among a nation's residents as a result of changes in international trade flows.

5 **Fundamental Issue**

Why, in spite of its benefits, does international trade ebb and flow and create so much controversy within the world's nations?

The potential for gains from specialization and trade arising from absolute and comparative advantage varies over time as changes in technology and available resources alter opportunity costs of production within nations. As a result, nations can develop or lose absolute and comparative advantages over time, and domestic income redistributions can thereby take place.

CHAPTER SUMMARY

1) **Production Possibilities and What They Indicate about a Nation's Costs of Producing Goods and Services:** A nation's production possibilities are combinations of goods and services that its residents can feasibly produce using currently available technology and fixed amounts of productive resources. Increasing production of one item entails reducing production of some amount of another good or service, which implies that the nation's residents must incur an opportunity cost. The opportunity cost of producing an item rises as the nation's residents produce more of that item.
2) **Absolute Advantage and How It Can Help Explain Why Nations Engage in International Trade:** A country has an absolute advantage in producing a good or service if those residing in that country can produce more of the item than residents of another nation. This can give the nation's residents an incentive to specialize in producing goods and services for which their nation has an absolute advantage. They can then trade these items for goods and services produced in countries with an absolute advantage in producing those items.
3) **Why Absolute Advantage Alone Is Insufficient to Account for Trade Among Nations:** By itself, absolute advantage is unable to completely explain why countries trade. Residents of a country can benefit from trading

with another nation even though their nation may have an absolute advantage, because the opportunity cost of producing an item within their country may exceed the amount of goods and services required to obtain that item from residents of another nation.

4) **Comparative Advantage and How It Enables Countries to Experience Gains from Trade:** A country has a comparative advantage when residents of that country can produce additional units of an item at a lower opportunity cost compared with other nations. Residents of another nation with a higher cost of producing that item thereby have an incentive to engage in trade with the nation that has a comparative advantage. Residents of the country with higher costs of producing the item can reap gains from trade. By trading, they can obtain more units of the item a lower cost relative to the cost of producing the item domestically.

5) **Why, in Spite of Its Benefits, International Trade Ebbs and Flows and Creates Controversy within Nations of the World:** Technological innovations and changes in the availability of resources within nations alter the extent to which countries experience absolute and comparative advantage by affecting relative opportunity costs of production across countries. As a result, the potential for gains from specialization and trade changes over time, and countries can develop or lose absolute and comparative advantages as time passes, resulting in redistributions of income within countries.

QUESTIONS AND PROBLEMS

1) Consider the following production possibilities for a country that produces computer modems and DVD drives, and then answer the questions that follow, assuming that currently residents of this nation produce 500,000 modems and 570,000 DVD drives.

Thousands of DVD Drives	Thousands of Modems
800	0
700	300
640	400
570	500
490	600
400	700
250	800
0	900

(a) What is the opportunity cost of producing 200,000 more modems?

(b) What is the opportunity cost of producing 70,000 more DVD drives?

(c) What is the opportunity cost of completely specializing in the production of modems? Why might residents of this nation consider specializing in modem production?

2) Consider the following table, which shows unspecialized productive capabilities of sets of workers in Northland and neighboring Eastshore, when answering the questions that follow:

	Northland		Eastshore		Combined
Product	**Workers**	**Output**	**Workers**	**Output**	**Output**
Modems	50	25	50	45	70
DVD drives	50	50	50	15	65

(a) Which country has an absolute advantage in producing modems? DVD drives?

(b) Which country has a comparative advantage in producing modems? DVD drives?

(c) Abstracting from any other factors, what is the range for rates of exchange of modems for DVD drives that will induce Northland and Eastshore to trade modems and DVD drives? If trade occurs, which country exports modems and imports DVD drives?

3) Refer to the table below when answering the following questions:

Northland		Eastshore	
Thousands of Modems	**Thousands of DVD drives**	**Thousands of Modems**	**Thousands of DVD drives**
0	800	0	500
300	700	100	485
400	640	150	455
500	570	200	400
600	490	250	330
700	400	300	250
800	250	350	160
900	0	400	0

(a) Which, if either, country has an absolute advantage in producing modems? DVD drives?

(b) Currently both nations produce the combinations displayed in the fourth line of the table. Based on the average opportunity costs that each nation would face if it were to produce 100,000 additional modems, is it possible that Northland could gain from trading with Eastshore if it desires to obtain more computer modems? Explain.

4) The following table displays the labor input requirements to produce identical quantities of two goods in two different nations, holding all other inputs unchanged. Use this information to answer the following questions.

	Cheese	Wine
Denmark	8	4
Portugal	10	4

(a) Which, if either, country has an absolute advantage in producing cheese? Wine?

(b) Which, if either, country has a comparative advantage in producing cheese? Wine?

(c) If Denmark imports one additional unit of its import good, how much labor does it save?

(d) If Portugal imports one additional unit of its import good, how much labor does it save?

(e) Explain why Denmark and Portugal can realize gains from trade if they import the good in which the other nation has a comparative advantage.

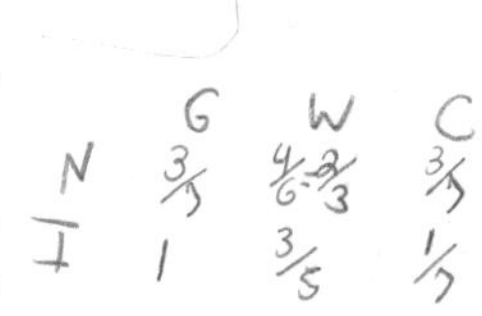

5) The following table displays the labor input requirements to produce identical quantities of three goods in two nations, holding all other inputs unchanged. Use this information to answer the following questions.

	Grains	Wine	Clothing
Nepal	3	4	3
India	4	3	1

(a) Arrange the goods in order of Nepal's comparative advantage, from greatest advantage to lowest advantage (or disadvantage).

(b) Which good or goods could Nepal gain from exporting to India? From importing from India?

6) Take a look back at the table in question 2, which applied to Northland and Eastshore ten years ago. After technological change has taken place in each nation, the following table now applies in the absence of specialization and trade:

Product	Northland Workers	Northland Output	Eastshore Workers	Eastshore Output	Combined Output
Modems	50	50	50	150	200
DVD drives	50	100	50	75	175

(a) Which country now has an absolute advantage in producing modems? DVD drives?

(b) Which country now has a comparative advantage in producing modems? DVD drives?

(c) Abstracting from any other factors, what is the range for rates of exchange of modems for DVD drives that will now induce Northland and Eastshore to trade modems and DVD drives? If trade occurs, which country currently exports modems and imports DVD drives?

ONLINE APPLICATION

Internet URL: http://www.census.gov/foreign-trade/www/press.html

Title: **U.S. International Trade in Goods and Services**

Navigation: Go to the home page of the Bureau of the Census (http://www.census.gov) and click on "Foreign Trade," and then click on "New Data."

Application: Perform the indicated operations, and answer the accompanying questions.

1) Click on "Exhibit 15: Exports and Imports of Goods by Principal SITC Commodity Groupings" and examine the data. During the most recent months displayed in the report, what are goods for which the United States experienced a trade surplus? A trade deficit? Are there any patterns among types of goods within surplus and deficit categories? If so, do these patterns provide any indication of whether the United States may have either an absolute or comparative advantage?
2) Back up and click on "Exhibits 3 and 4: U.S. Services by Major Category"—exports and imports—and examine the data in each exhibit. Does the United States tend to experience trade surpluses or deficits in services? Does this provide any indication of whether the United States may have either an absolute or comparative advantage in services?

For Group Study and Analysis: Divide the class into groups, and assign different product and service categories to each group. Ask each group to identify goods or services for which the United States appears to have an absolute or comparative advantage. For each category, discuss whether trade likely arises because the United States has an absolute or comparative advantage.

REFERENCES AND RECOMMENDED READINGS

Caves, Richard, Jeffrey Frankel, and Ronald Jones. 8th ed. *World Trade and Payments.* New York: Addison-Wesley, 1999.

Ethier, Wilfred. *Modern International Economics.* 4th ed., New York: Norton, 1997.

Micklethwait, John, and Adrian Wooldridge. *A Future Perfect: The Challenge and Hidden Promise of Globalization,* Time Books, 2000.

UNIT TWO

International Trade: Enduring Issues

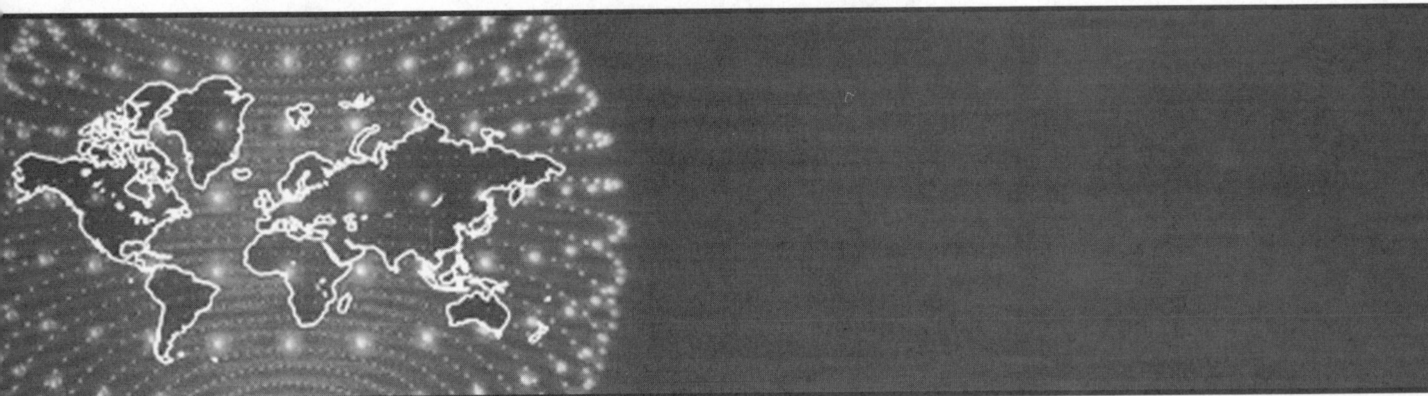

CHAPTER THREE

Sources of Comparative Advantage

Fundamental Issues

1. **What is the factor proportions explanation of comparative advantage?**
2. **What is the Heckscher–Ohlin theory of trade?**
3. **How well does the factor proportions approach explain trade patterns?**
4. **What is the relationship between trade and factor prices?**
5. **What is the relationship between trade and real income?**
6. **Is international production consistent with the concept of comparative advantage?**
7. **How does economic growth affect trade patterns?**

Passage of the North American Free Trade Agreement significantly reduced trade restrictions among Mexico, Canada, and the United States. Textile trade between the United States and Mexico is one of the most affected industries. Mexican garment assemblers were the primary beneficiaries, as they became the largest exporters of sewn garments to the United States. At the same time, U.S. textile mills became the largest exporters of fabric to Mexico, accounting for 40 percent of the total value of fabric exports to Mexico.

As a result, the textile industry has interesting and complex relationships involving Mexican and U.S. firms. Firms manufacture yarn in the southern United States for export to Mexico. Processors in Mexico then dye the yarn and export it back to the United States. U.S. textile firms mill the dyed yarn into cut pieces of fabric and export it back to Mexico. Garment firms in Mexico assemble the fabric pieces into garments and export them back to the United States for final sale.

Why do some stages of textile manufacturing occur in Mexico while others take place in the United States? In the case of dyeing yarn and assembling garments, certain regions in Mexico have two important resources: relatively inexpensive labor, which is required for garment assembly, and relatively inexpensive water, which is required for the dyeing process. The United States has firms with high levels of capital used to mill yarn and fabric concentrated in the southeastern region of the country.

Why do residents of nations export certain products and import others? In the previous chapter you found that a key basis of trade is comparative advantage. What, then, is the source of a nation's comparative advantage? In this chapter you will learn about the factor proportions explanation of comparative advantage. You will also develop an understanding of how to relate the factor proportions approach to issues such as factor prices, free trade's winners and losers, outsourcing, and economic growth.

The Factor Proportions Explanation of International Trade

As discussed in Chapter 2, the concept of comparative advantage can explain why residents of different nations trade. That is, by producing those goods in which a nation has a comparative advantage and trading them for goods in which it has a comparative disadvantage, the nation's residents may reap gains from trade. In this way, there are mutual benefits from trade. In this chapter we shall explore the basic theory that economists use to explain the *source* of a nation's comparative advantage.

THE FACTOR PROPORTIONS APPROACH

The basic theory of comparative advantage that you studied in Chapter 2 represents the main framework that economists used to discuss and analyze trade patterns for nearly one hundred years. In the early 1900s, however, two Swedish economists, Eli Heckscher and Nobel laureate Bertil Ohlin, developed a more general approach to explaining trade patterns called the *Heckscher–Ohlin theorem.*

In the mid-twentieth century, the work of Heckscher and Ohlin was expanded and articulated by another Nobel laureate, Paul Samuelson of MIT. Samuelson's contribution to this economic theory was so significant, it is often called the Heckscher–Ohlin–Samuelson model. As you will soon understand, this model highlights a nation's endowment of the various **factors of production**—the resources that firms utilize to produce goods and services—as a source of comparative advantage. Hence, we shall refer to the simple version of the model used here as the *factor proportions* model.

ON THE WEB

To find information on the Nobel laureates in economics, see the Bank of Sweden's Nobel e-museum at http://www.nobel.se/economics/laureates.

Factors of production
The resources firms utilize to produce goods and services.

The basic factor proportions approach examines two nations that produce two identical goods using two identical factors of production, or inputs, and the same production technology. The two inputs, **capital**—the physical equipment and buildings used to produce goods and services—and labor, can move freely from industry to industry, but cannot move from one nation to another. There are no restrictions on trade and no transportation costs, so the two goods move freely across nations. The residents of the two nations have identical tastes for each of the two goods.

Capital
The physical equipment and buildings used to produce goods and services.

Factor Endowments

As you can see, there is nothing at this point to distinguish one nation from the other. Where the nations differ is in the quantities of the two factors they possess. The two goods differ as well, because their relative requirements of the two inputs in the production process are distinct.

To understand the difference in factor endowments, let's use once again the example of the nation of Northland introduced in Chapter 2. Suppose that residents of Northland consider trade with residents of Eastisle, who have the same tastes and preferences for computers and food, the two goods in question, as the residents of Northland. Firms in these two nations combine labor and capital using the most current and identical technology to produce food and computers. Suppose that the residents of Northland have 800 units of labor and 1,000 units of capital, while the residents of Eastisle have 1,000 units of labor and 800 units of capital.

Using these figures for the factor endowments of both nations, we can calculate their respective labor-to-capital ratios. The labor-to-capital ratio for Eastisle is 1,000/800 = 1.25, while the ratio for Northland is 800/1,000 = 0.80. The labor-to-capital ratios show that Eastisle is the **relatively labor-abundant nation** because it is endowed with more labor units per capital unit than is Northland.

Relatively labor-abundant nation
In a two-country setting, the nation endowed with more labor units per capital unit than the other nation.

If we invert the labor-to-capital ratios calculated above, we can determine the capital-to-labor ratio and, therefore, the **relatively capital-abundant nation.** Doing so, we find that Eastisle's capital-to-labor ratio is 0.80 (800/100 = 0.80), while the capital-to-labor ratio for Northland is 1.25 (500/400 = 1.25). Hence, Northland is the *relatively capital-abundant nation* because it is endowed with more capital units per labor unit than is Eastisle.

Relatively capital-abundant nation
In a two-country setting, the nation endowed with more capital units per labor unit than the other nation.

Factor Intensities

Now let's consider the *factor intensities,* or input requirements to produce food and computers. Suppose that the current production technology for food always requires, in fixed proportions, more labor per capital unit than the labor-per-capital requirement for producing computers. Or, equivalently, the production technology for computers always requires more capital per labor unit than the capital-per-labor requirement of food. Hence, food is the **relatively labor-intensive good,** because production of food uses more labor units per capital unit than does the production process for computers. Likewise, we can say that computers are

Relatively labor-intensive good
In a two-good setting, the good with a production process requiring more labor per capital unit than the other good.

relatively capital-intensive goods, because production of computers requires more capital units per labor unit than does the production of food.

Relatively capital-intensive good
In a two-good setting, the good with a production process requiring more capital per labor unit than the other good.

Both countries employ the same production technology. Hence, the relative factor endowments of the two nations and the relative factor requirements of the two goods determine where comparative advantages lie. (To consider and compare the production possibilities of both nations, see on the next page *Visualizing Global Economic Issues: Factor Endowments and the Production Possibilities Frontier.*)

Fundamental Issue 1

What is the factor proportions explanation of comparative advantage?

According to the factor proportions approach, relative factor endowments of two nations and the relative factor requirements of two goods their residents trade determine where comparative advantage lies. The factor proportions model is a two-country, two-factor, two-good model that focuses on relative factor endowments of nations and relative factor intensities of goods. This model can be used to prove the factor proportions explanation of comparative advantage.

THE HECKSCHER–OHLIN THEOREM AND INTERNATIONAL TRADE

Using the factor proportions model, Heckscher and Ohlin developed one of the most fundamental, and perhaps one of the most tested, ideas in economics, known as the **Heckscher–Ohlin theorem.**

Heckscher–Ohlin theorem
A theorem stating that a relatively labor-abundant nation will export a relatively labor-intensive good, while a relatively capital-abundant nation will export a relatively capital-intensive good.

The Heckscher–Ohlin Explanation of Trade

According to this theorem, residents of a nation that is relatively labor abundant will export the relatively labor-intensive good, while residents of a nation that is relatively capital abundant will export the relatively capital-intensive good. We can restate this theorem in another way:

> **The nation that is relatively labor abundant will have a comparative advantage in the production of the relatively labor-intensive good, while the nation that is relatively capital abundant will have a comparative advantage in the production of the relatively capital-intensive good.**

Using the example of Northland and Eastisle, we can determine the trade pattern that results when residents of these two nations trade. Because Northland is the relatively capital-abundant nation, its residents will export computers, the relatively capital-intensive good, and will import food, the relatively labor-intensive good. Residents of Eastisle, the relatively labor-abundant nation, will export food, the relatively labor-intensive good, and will import computers, the relatively capital-intensive good. (To view the application of the theorem to the example of Northland and Eastisle, see on pages 68–69 *Visualizing Global Economic Issues: The Heckscher–Ohlin Theorem.*)

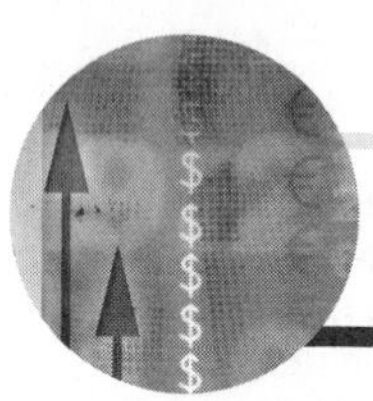

Visualizing Global Economic Issues

Factor Endowments and the Production Possibilities Frontier

To see how factor endowments affect the production possibilities frontier (PPF), consider the two PPFs in Figure 3-1. The figure illustrates the PPF for Northland, the relatively capital-abundant nation, and for Eastisle, the relatively labor-abundant nation. Next consider the relative factor intensities. Computers are relatively capital intensive in their production process, while food is relatively labor intensive in its production process.

Because Northland is the relatively capital-abundant nation and computers are the relatively capital-intensive good, residents of Northland have a greater relative capacity to produce computers than do residents of Eastisle. Hence, Northland's PPF is skewed toward computers, as compared with the shape of Eastisle's PPF. Likewise, because Eastisle is the relatively labor-abundant nation and food is the relatively labor-intensive good, residents of Eastisle have a greater relative capacity to produce food than do residents of Northland. Hence, Eastisle's PPF is skewed toward food, as compared to the shape of Northland's PPF.

As explained in Chapter 2, the slope of a line tangent line to the PPF reflects the opportunity cost of production at that particular bundle of goods. With this in mind, suppose that in **autarky,** or a no-trade situation, both nations produce and consume at point *A*. At this point, the absolute slope of the line tangent to Eastisle's PPF is much larger than that of Northland. Hence, residents of Northland have a lower opportunity cost in the production of computers than do residents of Eastisle. It is in this way that the relative factor endowments and relative factor intensities affect a nation's PPF.

For Critical Analysis:
Suppose Eastisle has many fewer residents and resources as compared with Northland. Do any of the points made above change?

Autarky
A no-trade situation.

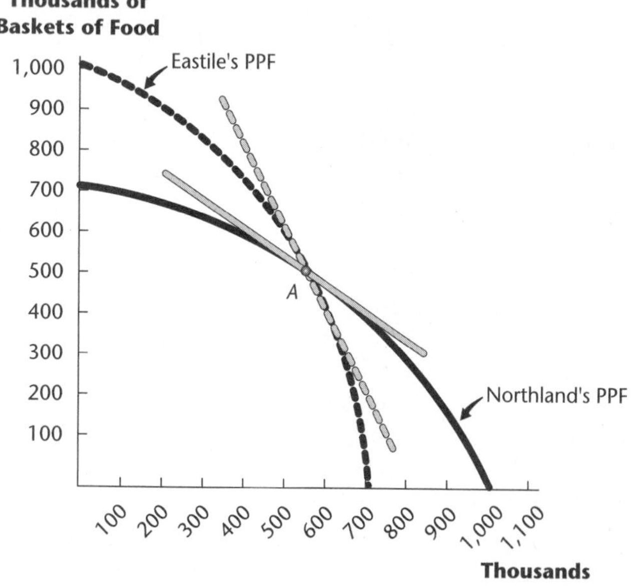

Figure 3-1

Factor Endowments and the Production Possibilities Frontier

Because Northland is relatively capital abundant, its PPF is skewed toward computers. Because Eastisle is relatively labor abundant, its PPF is skewed toward food. Suppose both nations produce and consumer the bundle indicated by point A. Because Northland has a lower opportunity cost of producing more computers at this point, the slope of the line tangent to Northland's PPF is shallower than the slope of the line tangent to Eastisle's PPF.

A General Application of the Heckscher–Ohlin Theorem

We can apply the Heckscher–Ohlin theorem to the real world and attempt to derive some conclusions about trade patterns among different nations if trade is truly free. Advanced economies tend to be relatively capital-abundant nations, whereas emerging and developing economies tend to be relatively labor-abundant. Based on these assumptions, the Heckscher–Ohlin theorem implies that the advanced economies will be net exporters of relatively capital-intensive goods such as chemicals, electrical equipment, and precision instruments, while the emerging and developing economies will be net exporters of labor-intensive goods such as clothing, toys, and sporting goods. (We would also expect the advanced economies to be net exporters of business services, a topic covered later in this chapter.)

Nations with large landmass are relatively abundant in land and natural resources. Based on the Heckscher–Ohlin theorem, we would expect large-landmass nations to be net exporters of agricultural and food products, and minerals.

Do our general conclusions correspond to the evidence on trade in goods? Table 3-1 on pages 70–71 shows the international trade of goods and services for selected nations during 2000. It presents exports, imports, and trade balances for nine categories. Using this information, we can draw some general conclusions.

As you can see, countries such as Argentina and Canada, which are endowed with a great deal of farmable and mineral-rich land, show a trade surplus in food items, agricultural raw materials, fuels, and ores and metals. Nations endowed with considerable high-technology capital, such as the United States, the United Kingdom, and Germany, experience surpluses in chemicals. The United States, Canada, the United Kingdom, and Germany are also endowed with populations that are highly educated, and they run surpluses in services as well. Nations with relatively large labor forces, such as Korea, run surpluses in machinery and transport equipment. Hence, a casual look at the data on global trade indicates that the Heckscher–Ohlin theorem does provide some insight on trade patterns. In the next section you will go beyond a casual look at trade data and consider the empirical evidence on the factor proportions approach in explaining trade patterns. (Highly educated workers allow India to offer information technology services globally; see on page 72 *Online Globalization: India's Online Business Services Industry*.)

Fundamental Issue 2

What is the Heckscher–Ohlin theory of trade?

Using the factor proportions model, Eli Heckscher and Bertil Ohlin developed the Heckscher–Ohlin theorem. This theorem asserts that a nation's residents will export goods and services that use relatively intensively the nation's relatively abundant factor. Likewise, the theorem claims that a nation's residents will import goods and services that use relatively intensively the nation's relatively scarce factor. The predictions of the Heckscher–Ohlin theorem relate, in an informal manner, to trade patterns in basic commodities and manufactured goods.

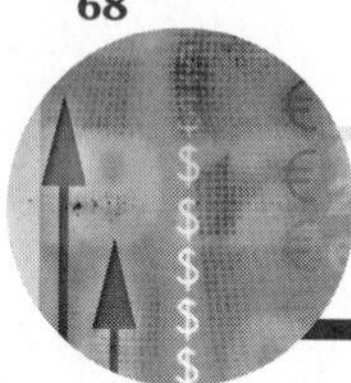

Visualizing Global Economic Issues

The Heckscher–Ohlin Theorem

To see an application of the Heckscher–Ohlin theorem, let's return to the earlier example of Eastisle and Northland. Consider Figure 3-2, which builds on Figure 3-1.

Suppose that, under autarky, residents of Eastisle and Northland produce and consume a bundle of computers and food indicated by point *A* on their respective production possibilities frontiers (PPF). As shown in Figure 3-2, at this combination of food and computers, residents of Northland face the lower opportunity cost of producing additional computers—equivalent to its domestic price ratio—given by the tangent line labeled P_A^N, while residents of Eastisle face the higher opportunity cost, given by the tangent line labeled P_A^E.

Now suppose that the residents of the two nations decide to engage in trade. Further, for the sake of simplicity, let's suppose that the residents of Eastisle and Northland are willing to exchange the two goods at a price ratio of 1.1 baskets of food for each computer. (Recall from Chapter 2 that there are constraints on the value of the rate of exchange if trade is to be mutually beneficial.) This price ratio is illustrated in the figure as a line tangent to both PPFs and labeled P_T. The absolute value of P_T equals 1.1. We calculate this slope using the points of tangency, P_T^E and P_T^N. Over this segment of the tangent line, the absolute value of the rise equals 440,000 baskets of food and the run equals 400,000 computers. Hence, the absolute value of the line is 440/400 = 1.1.

You can see that, when the residents of the two nations trade at price P_T, their production bundles adjust. Northland residents adjust their production bundles in response to the new and greater relative price for computers by moving down and along the PPF, producing more computers and less food. Residents of Eastisle adjust their production bundles in response to the new and lower relative price for computers by moving up and along its PPF, producing more food and fewer computers.

Finally, let's assume that residents of both nations consume the combination of food and computers given by point *C*. Note that point *C* lies beyond each nation's PPF, so that residents of both nations can now produce and consume more of both goods. This illustrates the benefits of specializing in the production of the good in which the nation has the comparative advantage, as discussed in Chapter 2.

Because Eastisle's residents now consume 600,000 computers but only produce 400,000, they must be importing 200,000 computers from residents of Northland. Likewise, because Eastisle's residents produce 750,000 baskets of food, but only consume 530,000 baskets, they must be exporting 220,000 baskets to residents of Northland. In the same manner, because Northland's residents consume 530,000 baskets of food, but only produce 310,000 baskets, they must be importing 220,000 baskets from residents of Eastisle. Because Northland's residents produce 800,000 computers but only consume 600,000 computers, they must be exporting 200,000 computers to residents of Eastisle.

Note that in this two-country example, exports of the residents of Eastisle are equivalent to imports of the

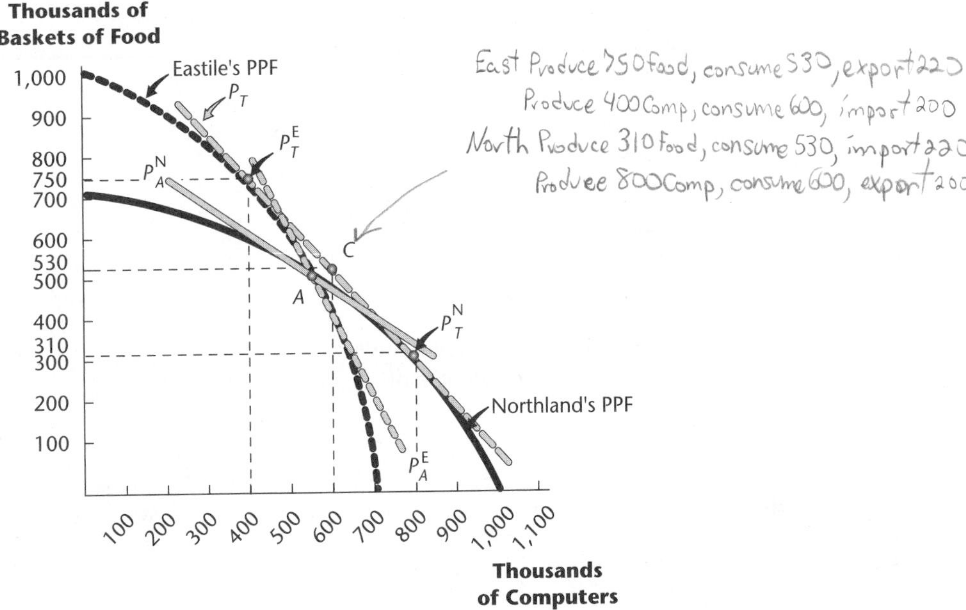

Figure 3-2

Illustrating the Heckscher–Ohlin Theorem

Suppose the residients of Northland and Eastisle are willing to trade at a rate of exchange of 1.1 baskets of food for each computer. Also suppose that at this rate of exchange, the residents of each country consume 530,000 baskets of food and 400,000 computers, illustrated by point C. At this rate of exchange, the residents of Northland export 200,000 computers and import 220,000 baskets of food, and the residents of Eastisle export 220,000 baskets of food and import 200,000 computers.

residents of Northland, and exports of the residents of Northland are equivalent to imports of the residents of Eastisle. Further note that the 220,000 baskets of food that are traded exchange for 200,000 computers, or at a ratio of 1.1 baskets of food per computer.

As you can see, under free trade, residents of Eastisle, the relatively labor-abundant nation, export the relatively labor-intensive good. Residents of Northland, the relatively capital abundant nation, export the relatively capital-intensive good.

For Critical Analysis:
Why, in Figure 3-2, do residents of Northland and Eastisle consume identical baskets of food and computers?

Table 3-1 Trade in Goods and Services of Selected Nations

($ millions)	Classification	Exports	Imports	Balance
Argentina	All food items	12,985,769	1,538,314	11,447,455
	Agricultural raw materials	478,298	467,909	10,389
	Fuels	1,937,690	817,923	1,119,767
	Ores and metals	699,007	646,950	52,057
	Manufactured goods	8,971,560	27,479,429	–18,507,869
	Chemical products	1,679,251	4,799,495	–3,120,244
	Other manufactured goods	3,232,370	7,230,936	–3,998,566
	Machinery and transport equipment	4,059,940	15,448,998	–11,389,058
	Total services	4,507	8,825	–4,318
Canada	All food items	15,614,998	11,158,694	4,456,304
	Agricultural raw materials	14,361,222	2,803,941	11,557,281
	Fuels	17,584,232	6,847,750	10,736,482
	Ores and metals	11,339,174	5,259,778	6,079,396
	Manufactured goods	141,008,059	169,580,304	–28,572,245
	Chemical products	11,792,789	16,363,071	–4,570,282
	Other manufactured goods	41,035,028	48,164,351	–7,129,323
	Machinery and transport equipment	88,180,241	105,052,882	–16,872,641
	Total services	30,281	35,249	–4,968
Germany	All food items	24,665,135	39,364,032	–14,698,897
	Agricultural raw materials	4,719,678	9,333,961	–4,614,283
	Fuels	5,988,530	25,455,974	–19,467,444
	Ores and metals	12,246,561	16,111,239	–3,864,678
	Manufactured goods	463,912,041	331,345,855	132,566,186
	Chemical products	67,137,669	40,097,422	27,040,247
	Other manufactured goods	12,525,236	122,972,861	2,322,375
	Machinery and transport equipment	275,478,552	168,275,572	107,202,980
	Total services	78,903	125,039	–46,136

Source: Data from UNCTAD, *Handbook of Statistics,* 2000.

How Well Does the Factor Proportions Approach Explain Trade?

Does the factor proportions approach explain a nation's trade? Do countries relatively well endowed with a particular resource export goods that use that resource relatively intensively in their production? Several decades passed before economists were able to rigorously evaluate the merits of the Heckscher–Ohlin theorem and the factor proportions approach explanations of trade.

THE LEONTIEF PARADOX

In 1954, Wassily Leontief completed the first empirical examination of the factor proportions approach. Leontief pioneered an approach that tracked the resources

Table 3-1 Tradė in Goods and Services of Selected Nations (Continued)

($ millions)	Classification	Exports	Imports	Balance
South Korea	All food items	2,635,193	5,643,591	–3,008,398
	Agricultural raw materials	1,377,694	3,580,652	–2,202,958
	Fuels	4,613,377	18,299,001	–13,685,624
	Ores and metals	2,204,453	6,289,355	–4,084,902
	Manufactured goods	114,239,901	54,478,029	59,761,872
	Chemical products	10,100,064	9,033,192	1,066,872
	Other manufactured goods	39,119,776	14,244,692	24,875,084
	Machinery and transport equipment	65,020,062	31,200,145	33,819,917
	Total services	132,302,370	93,280,939	39,021,431
United Kingdom	All food items	17,310,172	29,108,516	–11,798,344
	Agricultural raw materials	1,865,907	5,471,304	–3,605,397
	Fuels	11,324,504	7,814,228	3,510,276
	Ores and metals	5,728,622	9,481,125	–3,752,503
	Manufactured goods	229,307,161	257,052,402	–27,745,241
	Chemical products	34,678,835	28,886,201	5,792,634
	Other manufactured goods	65,776,270	88,274,304	–22,498,034
	Machinery and transport equipment	128,852,056	139,891,898	–11,039,842
	Total services	100,548	78,792	21,756
United States	All food items	52,790,068	45,995,883	6,794,185
	Agricultural raw materials	15,252,249	16,319,965	–1,067,716
	Fuels	10,297,089	62,224,053	–51,926,964
	Ores and metals	12,090,263	22,477,102	–10,386,839
	Manufactured goods	516,957,522	757,752,172	–240,794,650
	Chemical products	66,046,449	55,480,702	10,565,747
	Other manufactured goods	122,456,749	270,953,516	–148,496,767
	Machinery and transport equipment	328,454,327	431,317,951	–102,863,624
	Total services	239,957	165,827	74,130

used to produce a good from its first step of production until the good is in its final form. This approach, called *input–output analysis,* allowed him to determine the amount of capital and labor used in the production of various goods. The U.S. Bureau of Economic Analysis continues to use input-output analysis to track U.S. production.

ON THE WEB

To see U.S. input–output production data, visit the Web site of the Bureau of Economic Analysis at the U.S. Department of Commerce at: http://www.bea.doc.gov.

Leontief's Approach

At the time Leontief conducted his research, it was widely accepted that the United States was a relatively capital-abundant nation. The factor proportions approach, therefore, implies that U.S. residents would be net exporters of relatively capital-intensive goods and net importers of relatively labor-intensive goods. Using data on U.S. trade for 1947, Leontief tested this hypothesis.

Leontief's study was limited in a number of ways. First, his input–output analysis was confined to U.S. industries. This meant that the value of capital used

Online Globalization

India's Online Business Services Industry

Most U.S. business services companies find that they must conduct many activities to support their core services. A credit card company, for example, must collect from delinquent customers, handle customer inquiries, and analyze data to improve their operations. Airline companies must book reservations and manage frequent-flyer data. What these tasks have in common is that they require articulate English-speaking workers.

A sizable and highly educated English-speaking work force and advances in telecommunications and the Internet allow India to offer "IT-enabled services" to businesses in North America at a much lower cost. Other examples of the types of services that India can now offer U.S. firms include data processing of international money transfers, telemarketing and customer inquiries, legal and scientific research, and accounting services. India also excels in another important service, transcribing medical doctors' dictation into medical records. This particular service has grown to the point that India now boasts of 200 transcription firms and more than 10,000 transcribers.

Some estimates indicate that U.S. firms save as much as 50 percent on the cost of completing these tasks by transmitting them to India. Part of the savings is due to the salary gap between a college-educated U.S. worker and a college-educated Indian worker. U.S. firms find that they can use college-educated Indian workers for slightly more than they can employ high-school-educated domestic workers. By using college-educated workers, firms reduce data processing errors and overall costs.

Many of the Indian firms that offer IT-enabled services are less than a year old. Nonetheless, providing business services appears to be a vibrant and vital enterprise. Seeing the future, one Indian entrepreneur attempted to trade all of the firm's sewing machines for telephone headsets.

For Critical Analysis:
Advances in telecommunications and the Internet enable India to provide business services to firms in other nations. How might further advances, such as voice-recognition software, affect India's ability to remain cost competitive?

per worker in each U.S. industry, or the *capital-to-labor ratio,* was used to infer the capital-to-labor ratio of industries in other countries. In other words, he used the capital-to-labor ratio of U.S. automobile manufacturers, for example, to infer the capital-to-labor ratios of German and Japanese automobile manufacturers. Second, because he used U.S. production data, Leontief had to exclude industries in which there was no domestic production. Coffee, for example, is an industry in which the residents of the United States import substantial quantities but produce very little. Nonetheless, he was able to examine the production and trade data for approximately two hundred industries.

Leontief's Paradox

Leontief determined that the annual expenditures on capital per labor unit for industries in which U.S. residents were net exporters was more than $24,864 (in 2002 dollars). That is, annual expenditures on capital totaled more than $24,864 per worker. In net-import industries, by way of contrast, this value was slightly more than $31,968. Hence, Leontief's results indicated that the *imports* of residents of the United States were relatively *more capital intensive* that their exports. In other words, the results were in direct contradiction to the factor proportions approach explanation of international trade. Because of this contradiction, Leontief's result became known as the **Leontief paradox.**

Leontief paradox
A finding by Wassily Leontief that contradicted the Heckscher–Ohlin theorem, in that it indicated that imports of the United States, a relatively capital abundant nation, were relatively more capital intensive than the exports of the United States.

Leontief's research was controversial, because it directly contradicted a fundamental theory of trade, the Heckscher–Ohlin theorem. Hence, Leontief's work met with a great deal of criticism. One complaint was the period Leontief chose to examine. Many economists argued that 1947, being so close to the end of World War II, did not represent a "typical" trade year for the United States. In response, Leontief repeated his test using data for 1951. His general conclusion, that the net imports of residents of the United States are relatively more capital intensive than their net exports, still held true. This sparked a number of empirical studies, and the factor proportions approach is now one of the most tested propositions in the field of economics.

MORE RECENT TESTS OF THE FACTOR PROPORTIONS APPROACH

Much of the research conducted during the thirty years following Leontief's pathbreaking study confirmed his general results. The paradoxical result forced economists to consider generalizations to the factor proportions approach.

Generalizations of the Factor Proportions Approach

One such generalization is to allow for the residents of differing nations to have different tastes for goods and services. Residents of the United States, for example, may have much stronger preferences for relatively capital-intensive goods than the residents of other nations. If this is the case, it may explain why U.S. imports tend to be more capital intensive.

Another important generalization is to disaggregate labor and capital into more specific categories, thereby increasing the number of factors considered. Workers, for example, may be separated into the categories of *skilled* and *nonskilled* labor, based on their level of **human capital,** the amount of knowledge and skill that workers possess.

Human capital
The knowledge and skills that workers possess.

Yet another generalization is to allow that some factors (e.g., skilled labor) move from one nation to another. Other factors, however, may be unable to move from one industry to another within the domestic economy.

Performance of a More Generalized Approach

Adrian Wood of Sussex University provides one example of recent studies that use a generalized factor proportions approach. Wood argues that capital moves freely internationally and, therefore, does not explain trade patterns. He assumes that labor is heterogeneous—separating workers into skilled groups and unskilled groups—and does not move from one nation to another.

Allowing for these generalizations, Wood finds that the Heckscher–Ohlin theory explains trade in manufactured goods between residents of developed nations and residents of developing nations. Wood found that the developed nations are relatively well endowed with skilled workers, while developing nations are relatively well endowed with unskilled workers. Consistent with the factor proportions approach, residents of developed economies tend to export relatively skilled-labor-intensive goods and import relatively unskilled-labor-intensive goods from residents of the developing economies.

What years of studies show is that the traditional factor proportions approach is rather weak at explaining the direction of trade flows. A more generalized approach, however, does yield useful insights for particular types of trade flows such as primary commodities and manufactured goods.

3 **Fundamental Issue**

How well does the factor proportions approach explain trade patterns?

For several decades following the development of the Heckscher–Ohlin theorem, economists were unable to rigorously test the factor proportions approach to trade. In the mid-1950s, using input–output analysis, Wassily Leontief examined U.S. trade data and found that U.S. imports were relatively more capital intensive in their production than U.S. exports. This contradiction to the factor proportions approach sparked substantial research on the approach and its predictions. Most subsequent studies show that the factor proportions approach is rather weak at explaining a nation's trade pattern. As a result, a more generalized factor proportions approach emerged. Generalized approaches do predict trade patterns for particular sectors, such as primary commodities and manufacturing.

Trade, Factor Prices, and Real Income

As discussed in Chapter 2, international trade can result in redistributive effects, or changes in income flows among residents *within* a nation. Redistributive effects of international trade may also occur *between* nations. The size of these effects is often at the center of debates on international trade and globalization.

On one hand, opponents claim that trade has caused a gap in earnings, with upper-income groups within most nations getting richer and the lower income groups becoming poorer. Likewise, opponents claim that trade has caused a gap between nations, with the richer advanced economies becoming wealthier and the poorer developing economies becoming poorer. On the other hand, proponents of trade and globalization contend that international trade is the best hope to improve conditions and incomes in the poorest nations.

The relationship between trade, prices, and incomes, therefore, is an important issue. What insight does the factor proportions approach offer in this regard?

Factor price equalization theorem *A theorem indicating that under the assumptions of the factor proportions model, uninterrupted trade will bring about equalization of goods prices and factor prices across nations.*

FACTOR PRICE EQUALIZATION

Two important theorems on international trade, wages, and income resulted from the factor proportions model. The first, which is the **factor price equalization theorem,** asserts that, given the assumptions of the factor proportions model, uninterrupted trade will lead to the global equalization of all factor prices, such as wages paid to resource owners for their labor, interest paid to resource owners for use of their capital—also called the *rental rate of capital*—and rental payments to resource owners for the use of their land, across nations.

Role of the Global Market for Goods and Services

Recall that the factor proportions approach assumes that factors of production cannot move freely from one nation to another. Hence, there is no *global* market for factors of production and no supply and demand mechanism to equilibrate factor prices. Factor price equalization, therefore, results through the price adjustment that occurs in the global market for *goods and services*. In other words, the global market for goods and services provides the equilibrating mechanism for factor price adjustment.

The Equalization Process

To understand how the factor price equalization process occurs, consider the example of Northland and Eastisle once again. Recall that Northland is the relatively capital-abundant nation and Eastisle is the relatively labor-abundant nation. In autarky, therefore, we would expect the wage rate relative to the rental rate of capital to be higher in Northland than in Eastisle.

The Heckscher–Ohlin theorem tells us that, under free trade, residents of Northland will export computers, the relatively capital-intensive good, and import food, the relatively labor-intensive good. Because Northland has a comparative advantage in computers and a comparative disadvantage in food, the free-trade relative price of computers is higher than Northland's domestic relative price under autarky. The free-trade relative price of food is lower than Northland's domestic relative price of food under autarky.

As discussed earlier, under free trade, residents of Northland will adjust their level of production, producing more computers and less food. When they reduce the production of food, the residents of Northland free up more labor relative to the capital that they release. Hence, the supply of labor relative to the supply of capital increases. When Northland's residents increase the production of computers, they must hire more capital relative to labor, so the demand for labor declines relative to the demand for capital. Thus, the adjustment process increases the relative supply of labor and decreases the relative demand for labor, which lowers the value of the wage rate relative to the value of the rental rate of capital.

The residents of Eastisle, in a similar manner, adjust their production pattern, producing more food and fewer computers. As Eastisle's residents produce fewer computers, they reduce their utilization of capital relative to labor. As they produce more food, however, they require more labor relative to capital. Hence, the adjustment process in Eastisle bids up the wage rate relative to the rental rate of capital.

This process continues until prices are equal across both nations and there are no further gains from specialization. Or, in other words, the process continues until the wage rate relative to the rental rate of capital is the same in both nations. (For additional insight on the factor price adjustment process, see on pages 76–77 *Visualizing Global Economic Issues: The Factor Price EqualizationTheorem.*)

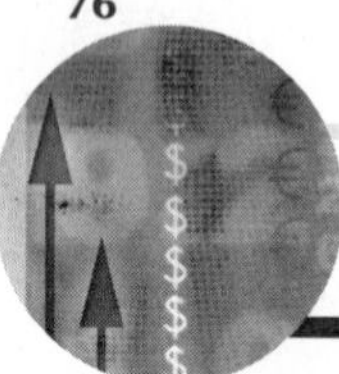

Visualizing Global Economic Issues

The Factor Price Equalization Theorem

To visualize the factor price adjustment process under free trade, consider again the example of Northland and Eastisle. Figure 3-3 plots the price of food, P_F, relative to the price of computers, P_C, on the vertical axis, labeled P_F/P_C. The figure relates P_F/P_C to the wage rate, W, relative to the rental rate of capital, R, which is plotted on the horizontal axis. Recall that Eastisle is the relatively labor-abundant nation, while Northland is the relatively labor-scarce nation. Hence, under autarky, the wage rate relative to the rental rate of capital in Northland, $(W/R)_N$, is greater than the wage rate relative to the rental rate of capital in Eastisle, $(W/R)_E$.

Also, recall that, according to the Heckscher–Ohlin theorem, Northland has a comparative advantage in computers and Eastisle has a comparative advantage in food. Hence, under autarky, the price of food relative to the price of computers in Northland, $(P_F/P_C)_N$, is greater than the price of food relative to the price of computers in Eastisle, $(P_F/P_C)_E$.

The Adjustment Process in Northland

Suppose that the combination of (P_F/P_C) and (W/R) under autarky is given by point N for Northland and by point E for Eastisle, as in Figure 3.3. Next consider what happens as the residents of the two nations begin to trade. As the residents of Northland reduce their production of food, they free up more labor relative to the capital they release. Hence, the supply of labor relative to the supply of capital increases. When the residents of Northland increase their production of computers, they must hire more capital relative to labor, so the demand for capital rises relative to the demand for labor. This adjustment process bids up the rental rate of capital relative to the wage rate, or a decline in $(W/R)_N$. As the residents of Northland begin to export computers and import food, the price of food relative to the price of computers declines. The change in goods prices and factor prices is shown by the movement down and along the dotted line, as indicated by the arrows.

The Adjustment Process in Eastisle

As the residents of Eastisle reduce their production of computers, they free up more capital relative to the labor they release. Hence, the supply of labor relative to the supply of capital decreases. When the residents of Eastisle increase their production of food, they must hire more labor relative to capital, so the demand for labor rises relative to the demand for capital. This adjustment process bids up the wage rate relative to the rental rate of capital, or an increase in $(W/R)_E$. As the residents of Eastisle begin to export food and import computers, the price of food relative to the price of computers rises. The movement up and along the dashed line indicated by the arrows shows the change in goods prices and factor prices.

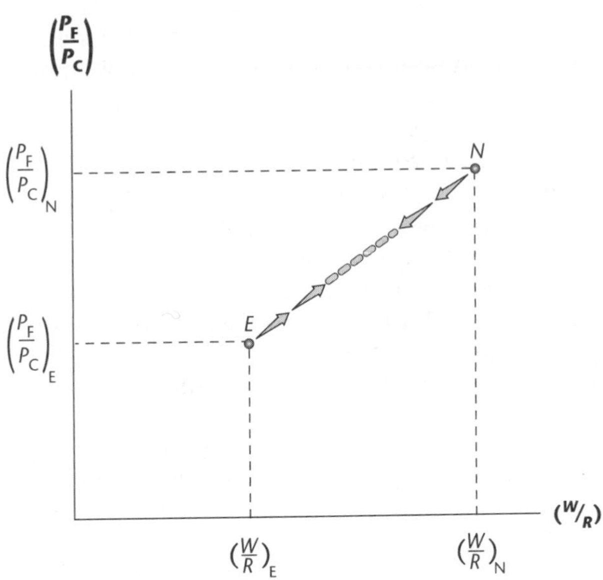

Figure 3-3

Illustrating the Factor Price Equalization Theorem

As the residents of Northland increase their production of computers and decrease their production of food, their demand for labor falls relative to their demand for capital, and the supply of labor relative to the supply of capital rises. The change in production causes the wage rate relative to the rental rate of capital and the price of food relative to computers to decline, shown by the movement down and along the dashed line. As the residents of Eastisle increase their production of food and decrease their production of computers, their demand for labor rises relative to their demand for capital, and the supply of labor relative to the supply of capital falls. The change in production causes the wage rate relative to the rental rate of capital and the price of food relative to computers to rise, shown by the movement up and along the dashed line. The movement along the dashed line illustrates that factor prices become more equal.

The Equalization Process

As you can see in the figure, the wage rate relative to the rental rate of capital in Eastisle and Northland becomes more equal. According to the factor price equalization theorem, if free trade continues to take place, factor prices eventually equalize.

For Critical Analysis:

Suppose both nations open their borders to trade but retain polices that constrain trade to a level lower than under free-trade conditions. How would this affect the adjustment of factor prices, and how would you illustrate this situation in Figure 3-3?

Evidence on Factor Price Convergence

Now that you understand the theory of factor price convergence, let's consider the evidence. Recall that the factor price equalization theorem asserts that unhindered trade will cause a convergence of commodity prices. As commodity prices converge, so will factor prices. In regard to the real-world evidence, factor price equalization is perhaps the most controversial theorem among economists.

Chapter 8 explains that trade has yet to cause a complete convergence of commodity prices. Hence, we should not expect a complete convergence of factor prices. Nonetheless, trade may be causing factor prices to become *more equal,* even though they have yet to equalize.

The process of factor price equalization should be recognized as a very long-run process. With this in mind, Jeffrey Williamson of Harvard University examined the behavior of wage rates relative to the rental rates of capital over a very long time period. Williamson considered three different periods, 1830 through 1853, 1854 through 1913, and post–World War II. For the early period, Williamson found no evidence of factor price convergence among the Atlantic economies of Brazil, France, Great Britain, Ireland, the Netherlands, Spain, Sweden, and the United States. The evidence is explained by the fact that this early period was one of restrictions on international trade and labor migration and was marked by an underdeveloped capital market.

The second period, however, is one of extensive relative wage convergence. Although much of the convergence can be explained by the mass migration that occurred during this period, the evidence also shows that wage convergence is greater among the most open economies and lower among the most closed economies. The post–World War data shows relative wage convergence along the lines of the previous period. Postwar restrictions on labor mobility, however, slowed the pace of wage convergence relative to that of the previous period.

4 Fundamental Issue

What is the relationship between trade and factor prices?

The factor proportions approach spurred the development of two very important ideas about factor prices and international trade. The factor price equalization theorem contends that unhindered trade brings about an equalization of goods prices and, therefore, an equalization of factor prices across nations. This equalization process results through the price adjustment that occurs in the global market for goods and services. Real-world evidence indicates that trade may be causing factor prices to become more equal, but they have yet to equalize.

TRADE AND REAL INCOME

The factor price equalization theorem is helpful for us to understand how factor prices might adjust across nations. But how does trade affect earnings of workers and owners of capital within nations? Arguably all major economic changes result in winners and losers. Who are the winners and losers when a nation engages in international trade?

The Stolper-Samuelson Theorem

The Stolper-Samuelson theorem, contributed by Wolfgang Stolper and Paul Samuelson in the early 1940s, is another important theorem resulting from the factor proportions model. The **Stolper–Samuelson theorem** asserts that, in the context of the factor proportions model, free trade raises the earnings of the nation's relatively abundant factor and lowers the earnings of the relatively scarce factor.

Stolper–Samuelson theorem
Theory that, in the context of the factor proportions model, free trade raises the earnings of the nation's relatively abundant factors and lowers the earnings of the relatively scarce factors.

Returning to our previous example, the Stolper–Samuelson theorem implies that as residents of Northland, the relatively capital-abundant nation, begin to trade with residents of Eastisle, the wage rate will fall and the rental rate of capital will rise. This occurs because as Northland opens its borders to trade, the price of computers will rise and the price of food will fall.

The Magnification Principle

A key proposition of the Stolper–Samuelson theorem is the **magnification principle,** which implies that the change in the price of the factor is greater than the change in the price of the good that uses the factor relatively intensively in its production process. Suppose that as the residents of Northland begin to trade, the price of computers rises by 5 percent and the price of food falls by 2 percent. According to the magnification principle, the rental rate of capital must rise by more than 5 percent, and the wage rate must fall by more than 2 percent. Hence, if the rental rate of capital rises by 7 percent, owners of capital are better off, because their ability to consume computers and food, that is, the *real income* of the owners of capital, is enhanced. Workers, however, because their ability to consume the two goods is reduced—the real income of workers—are worse off. Hence, in Northland, owners of capital are clearly better off with free trade, while workers are worse off.

Magnification principle
A position of the Stolper–Samuelson theorem which implies that the change in the price of a factor is greater than the change in the price of the good that uses the factor relatively intensively in its production process.

Implications of the Stolper–Samuelson Theorem

The Stolper–Samuelson theorem has very important policy implications. It shows that even though free trade may bring overall gains to a nation, there are winners and losers. Free trade, therefore, will certainly have supporters and detractors. The theorem also implies that those who support free trade are likely to be the owners of the nation's relatively abundant factors, and those who oppose free trade are the owners of the nation's relatively scarce factors. We might expect that in the advanced economies, which tend to be relatively capital abundant, owners of capital will support free trade, and workers will oppose free trade.

For data on wages in a large number of nations, visit the Web page of the International Labour Organization at http://www.ilo.org.

Fundamental Issue

What is the relationship between trade and real income?

The Stolper–Samuelson theorem is another important development of the factor proportions approach. This theorem asserts that free trade benefits owners of the nation's relatively abundant factor by increasing their real income, and harms owners of the nation's relatively scarce factor by decreasing their real income. An important implication is that the owners of the relatively abundant factor are likely to support free trade, while the owners of the relatively scarce factor are likely to oppose free trade.

International Production and Comparative Advantage

The production of a good involves many stages. Each stage involves combining resources and technology to produce a given output. Hence, the entire production process entails many separate activities. Take, for example, the computers that the residents of Northland and Eastisle produce. Each stage of production requires different components, different combinations of skilled and unskilled labor, and different types of capital. Suppose that the production of a computer can be broken down into four stages; manufacturing components, assembly of the computer, marketing the computer, and delivering the computer to the final user. It might be that Northland has a comparative advantage in some of the stages of production for example, manufacturing components and assembly of the computer, while Eastisle has a comparative advantage in marketing and delivery.

THE INTERNATIONALIZATION OF PRODUCTION

As described in Chapter 1, economic integration, the reduction of transportation costs, and advances in communications have generated remarkable gains in trade. At the same time, these advances change the way that firms approach the production of goods and services. Firms can now focus on the stage of production in which they have the greatest comparative advantage.

Outsourcing

Value added
The revenue received by a producer less the cost of the intermediate good it purchased.

Outsourcing
A strategy in which one organization hires another organization to complete a particular stage of the production process.

At each stage of production, a firm adds resources and technology, creating additional value. Economists refer to the difference between the value of a good or service and the cost of intermediate goods as the **value added** for that particular stage of production. Lower transportation costs and advances in communications allow firms to break down the production process and concentrate on the stages of production in which the firm has the greatest profit. The firm can then **outsource,** or hire other firms to complete other stages of production. Economists refer to this strategy as the *internationalization of production.* (To see how internationalization is changing production strategies, see *Management Notebook: Do Manufacturers Really Need a Factory?*)

Internationalizing and Outsourcing Barbie

Contract manufacturing
A production strategy in which one organization hires another organization to manufacture a good under the hiring firm's name and to the hiring firm's specifications.

Robert Feenstra of the University of California–Davis and the National Bureau of Economic Research offers the Barbie doll as an example of outsourcing and the internationalization of production processes. The raw materials for Barbie are plastic and high-tech hair, purchased from Taiwan and Japan, and cotton cloth, purchased from China. The molds for the doll and some paints used to decorate the doll come from the United States. Assembly occurs in Indonesia, Malaysia, and China. The dolls are shipped from Hong Kong to the United States. The export cost of each doll is roughly $2.00. Of this $2.00 value added, $0.35 derives from Chinese labor, $0.65 from material, and the remaining $1.00 goes to transportation

MANAGEMENT *Notebook*

POLICY MANAGEMENT

Do Manufacturers Really Need a Factory?

Globalization is bringing about fundamental changes for manufacturers, and a new type of organization is emerging as a result. In consumer electronics, the process began as early as the 1980s, when International Business Machines outsourced the manufacturing of its personal computers to a contract manufacturer. *Contract manufacturing* occurs when a firm designs a product to certain specifications and pays another firm to produce the tangible product to its specification and under its brand name.

Contract Manufacturing in Electronics

Flextronics, a contract manufacturer located in Guadalajara, Mexico, produces electronic devices for firms such as Philips and Sony. One device, Web television control boxes, is produced for both companies on side-by-side assembly lines. The devices are slightly different in specification, and carry the names of the two electronics firms. This relationship between the electronics firms and the contract manufacturer goes virtually unnoticed by the final consumer.

Currently, contract manufacturing accounts for more than $10 billion of electronics output per year, and is growing at an impressive rate of more than 20 percent a year. The recent spread of consolidation among contract manufacturing firms will most likely accelerate this trend.

Standardization of national communications requirements is one of the factors that lead to contract manufacturing. Standardization allows firms to separate the design and innovation of electronics equipment from the actual production of its components. Advances in the compactness of electronics components and the high-tech nature of production processes means that production is no longer as labor-intensive as in years past. Robots now do work that once was completed by low-skilled labor. This allows firms to specialize in high-tech production processes and reduce average costs of production. The electronics firms, in turn, can now focus on design, marketing, and distribution.

Contract Manufacturing in Other Sectors

Contract manufacturing is prevalent in other sectors as well. Producers of clothing, particularly of well-known, brand-name clothing, rely on contract manufacturing. (See the introduction to this chapter for an example of outsourcing in the textiles industry.) Firms such as Tommy Hilfiger and Ralph Lauren base their operations entirely on design, licensing, and marketing. Other firms are licensed to produce the clothing and sell the completed product to retailers. Most often, they pay royalties to the licensor.

The types of services that contract manufacturers provide are likely to expand. In electronics, for example, contract manufacturers are beginning to provide customer service support. Greater contact with the final consumer positions contract manufacturers to become more involved in the design and innovation stage, making contract manufacturers vital players in the industry.

For Critical Analysis:

The Internet plays a very important role in the relationship between electronics firms and contract manufacturers. How do you suppose the Internet facilitates the relationship between the firm that innovates and the firm that produces the actual product?

and overhead. When the Barbie doll is sold in the United States, it retails for about $10.00. Mattel Corporation earns about $1.00 of this. The rest covers transportation, advertising, wholesaling, and retailing within the United States. Most of the value added occurs through activity within the United States that takes place after the doll is actually manufactured. According to sales data for 1995, two Barbie dolls are purchased every second, totaling $1.4 billion in sales for Mattel Corporation.

KALEIDOSCOPIC COMPARATIVE ADVANTAGE

The fact that firms engage in internationalized production and specialize in specific stages of production reflects the competitive nature of the global marketplace. Increased competition forces firms to produce in the most efficient manner, which entails concentrating on their expertise or comparative advantage.

Intense competition and rivalry push firms to produce at the highest value-added stages of production in pursuit of maximum profits. This makes it difficult for firms to hold an edge in a particular stage of production. As we concluded in Chapter 2, comparative advantage can be fleeting.

As a firm internationalizes its production process and outsources various stages of production, specializing in but a part of the overall production process, it can gain or lose a competitive advantage very quickly. Jagdish Bhagwati and Vivek Dehejia of Columbia University have called the propensity for comparative advantage to suddenly shift from one country to another as *kaleidoscopic comparative advantage*. In an environment of kaleidoscopic comparative advantage, firms must be very concerned with the actions of their competitors. Rapid changes in comparative advantage can also cause workers to lose their jobs very quickly in one industry while bringing about a shortage of workers in another industry. Both effects lead to greater pressure on policymakers to enact barriers to trade, a subject of later chapters.

Is international production consistent with the concept of comparative advantage?

Economic integration and reduced transportation and communication costs allow firms to specialize in certain stages of production and outsource other stages to firms in other nations. This process of internationalized production is consistent with the concept of comparative advantage as applied to the specific stages of production, such as the design, marketing, and manufacturing of a good. As a firm internationalizes its production process and outsources various stages of production, it can gain or lose a comparative advantage very quickly. This property for comparative advantage to suddenly shift from one country to another is known as kaleidoscopic comparative advantage.

Economic Growth and International Trade

So far in this chapter, you have learned about three of the fundamental theorems on trade: the Heckscher–Ohlin theorem, the factor price equalization theorem, and the Stolper–Samuelson theorem. There is one remaining theorem, which deals with economic growth and a nation's trade pattern: the Rybczynski theorem. Together, these theorems represent the basic foundation of analysis employed by economists who study international trade.

ECONOMIC GROWTH

As discussed in Chapter 2, a nation's production possibilities are the various combinations of goods and services that it can produce, given its limited resources and fixed technology. **Economic growth** occurs when there is an increase in available resources or a technological advance, so that the nation's production possibilities expand.

Economic growth
Occurrence when a nation experiences an increase in available resources or a technological advance and the nation's production possibilities expands.

How Economic Growth Occurs

When there is an increase in a nation's endowment of resources, the new resources can be put to use in production and can increase the nation's set of production possibilities. Technological advance is similar to an increase in available resources. One view of technological advance is that it is resource saving. That is, with the same amount of resources, the nation can generate higher levels of output. Technological advance, therefore, has the same effect as an increase in the nation's endowment of resources. Economic growth, whether it is an increase in resources or a technological advance, expands a nation's set of production possibilities.

Industry-Specific Effects

In the framework of factor proportions, economic growth may well have different effects on two industries. To see why this is so, reconsider the earlier examples of food, a relatively labor-intensive good, and computers, a relatively capital-intensive good. Suppose that the residents of Northland, because of past savings, experience an increase in their capital endowments. Because of the increase in capital, Northland's residents could increase their production of either food or computers. The gains that occur in either industry would not be the same, however. Northland's residents could not increase the production of food as easily as computers, because food requires a larger amount of labor per capital unit than does the production of computers. Thus, even though an increase in the endowment of a particular factor causes Northland's production possibilities to expand, the expansion favors the good that uses the growing factor intensively in its production process.

Technological advance could generate differential effects, as well. If the advance occurs in both industries and saves the same amount of each factor, then production possibilities proportionately expand the same amount for each good. If technological advance occurs in only one industry, then that industry will experience the greatest growth. If technological advance occurs in both industries but saves on capital, then the capital-intensive industry, in this case the computer industry, will experience the greatest growth.

Regardless of how economic growth occurs, the nation effectively experiences an increase in its endowment of resources. As you learned earlier, in the factor proportions framework a nation's trade pattern is determined by factor endowments and factor intensities. Economic growth, therefore, will affect a nation's exports and imports.

THE RYBCZYNSKI THEOREM

Rybczynski theorem
The theory that if a nation experiences an increase in the amount of a resource, it will produce more of the good that uses the resource relatively intensively in its production process and produce less of the other good.

The Rybczynski theorem, developed by T. M. Rybczynski, addresses the way that economic growth affects a nation's trade. The **Rybczynski theorem** maintains that an expansion of a nation's endowment of a particular factor of production will, in the context of the factor proportions approach and at a given opportunity cost, lead to an increase in the production of the good that uses that factor intensively in its production process and a decrease in the production of the other good.

If the residents of Northwood, for example, were to experience an increase in their endowments of capital, then their output of computers would rise while their output of food would decline. (For an illustration of the Rybczynski theorem, see *Visualizing Global Economic Issues: The Rybczynski theorem.*)

GROWTH AND TRADE

The Rybczynski theorem helps us understand how a nation's production bundle changes. Now let's consider how a change in the production bundle resulting from economic growth affects the nation's trade pattern.

Consider the result of Northland's economic growth just described. An increase in capital led to an increase in the production of computers and a decrease in the production of food. Prior to economic growth, Northland's residents exported computers and imported food. Economic growth led residents of Northland to increase their production of the export good, computers, and decrease their production of the import good, food. This change in production will lead Northland's residents to increase both their imports and their exports. In other words, this particular type of economic growth had a pro-trade effect.

Not all production changes are pro-trade, however. Consider what happens if Northland's residents experience an increase in their relatively scarce factor, labor. According to the Rybczynski theorem, an increase in labor leads Northland's residents to produce more food and fewer computers. In other words, residents of Northland will increase their production of the import good and decrease the production of the export good. This change in the production bundle leads Northland's residents to engage less in trade. Thus, this type of economic growth had an anti-trade effect.

As you can see, the Rybczynski theorem is very useful in determining how economic growth might affect a nation's trade. In Chapter 1 you learned that the United States continues to experience very high levels of capital inflows. Based on the Rybczynski theorem, we would expect the United States to continue to expand in high-technology areas, while its labor-intensive industries contract further.

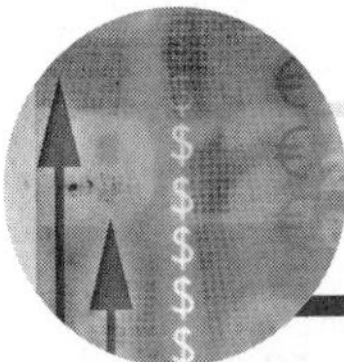

Visualizing Global Economic Issues

The Rybczynski Theorem

To see an illustration of the Rybczynski theorem, consider Northland's production possibilities frontier (PPF) in Figure 3-4. Suppose that prior to economic growth occurring, the residents of Northland produce F_1 baskets of food and C_1 computers, as indicated by point *P* in the figure. As discussed in Chapter 2, the slope of the line tangent to point *P*, labeled *OC*, indicates the opportunity cost of producing this combination of goods.

Now consider the effects of an increase in Northland's residents' capital endowments. Because computers are relatively capital intensive and food is relatively labor intensive, the increase in capital disproportionately affects the production of computers. The increase in capital causes the PPF to rotate outward as it shifts, reflecting the disproportional effect on the computer industry.

The Rybczynski theorem assumes that opportunity costs remain the same after economic growth occurs. To reflect this assumption, the line *OC* shifts outward, maintaining the same slope, until it is tangent to the new PPF at point *P′*. Point *P′* indicates that the residents of Northland now produce F_2 food and C_2 computers.

Note that the production of computers, the relatively capital-intensive good, increased from C_1 to C_2 while the production of food fell from F_1 baskets to F_2 baskets. This outcome illustrates the Rybczynski theorem, because an increase in capital leads to an increase in the production of the capital-intensive good, computers, and a decrease in the production of the labor-intensive good, food.

For Critical Analysis:
Does the increase in capital make Northland's residents more or less likely to trade? What if labor were to increase instead of capital?

Figure 3-4

Illustrating the Rybczynski Theorem

If the residents of Northwood experience an increase in their endowments of capital, Northwood's PPF rotates outward. At constant opportunity costs, this type of economic growth leads the residents of Northwood to increase their production of the good that uses capital intensively, computers, from C_1 to C_2, and decrease their production of the good that uses labor intensively, food, from F_1 to F_2.

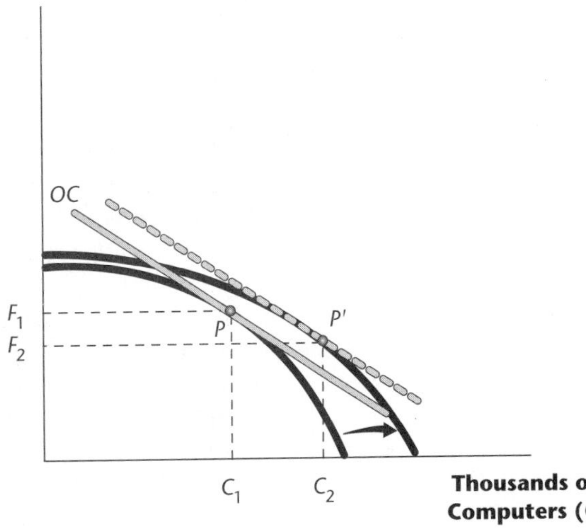

How does economic growth affect trade patterns?

The Rybczynski theorem asserts that an increase in the endowment of a particular factor will, with prices constant, lead to an increase in the production of the good that uses the factor relatively intensively in the production process and to a decrease in the production of the other good. The change in production that results from economic growth can generate more trade or less trade. An increase in the nation's relatively abundant factor will lead the nation's residents to produce more of the export good and less of the import good, spurring additional trade. An increase in the nation's relatively scarce factor will induce residents to trade less.

CHAPTER SUMMARY

1) **The Factor Proportions Explanation of Comparative Advantage:** The factor proportions approach focuses on the relative factor endowments of nations and the relative factor intensities of goods and services as explanations of comparative advantage. The factor proportions model is a two-country, two-factor, two-good model. Relative factor endowments and relative factor intensities are the central features of this model. The factor proportions model is often used to test the factor proportions explanation of comparative advantage.
2) **The Heckscher–Ohlin Theory of Trade:** The Heckscher–Ohlin theorem resulted from the factor proportions approach. This theory maintains that a nation's residents will export goods and services that use intensively the relatively abundant factor. Likewise, the nation's residents will import goods and services that use intensively the relatively scare factor.
3) **Evidence on the Factor Proportions Explanation of Trade Patterns:** In 1954, Wassily Leontief conducted the first rigorous examination of the factor proportions approach. Leontief found that U.S. trade data contradicted the predictions of the factor proportions approach. Economists refer to his findings as the Leontief paradox. His results sparked a great deal of research into the factor proportions approach. As a result, a more generalized factor proportions approach emerged.
4) **The Relationship Between Trade and Factor Prices:** The factor price equalization theorem asserts that unhindered international trade will bring about an equalization of factor prices among trading nations. The equalization process occurs through the price adjustments that take place in the global market for goods and services.
5) **The Relationship Between Trade and Real Income:** The Stolper–Samuelson theorem indicates that free trade increases the real income of a nation's relatively abundant factor and reduces the real income of a nation's relatively scarce factor. In other words, international trade benefits a nation's relatively abundant factor and harms a nation's relatively scare factor. An important implication of this theory is that the owners of a nation's relatively

abundant factor are likely to support free-trade policies while the owners of a nation's relatively scare factor are likely to oppose free-trade policies.

6) **International Production and Comparative Advantage:** In the current global environment of increased economic integration and lower transportation and communication costs, firms often engage in internationalized production. Internationalized production occurs when firms specialize in particular stages of production and outsource other stages to firms in other countries. As firms internationalize their production process, they can gain or lose their comparative advantage very quickly. This property of comparative advantages suddenly shifting from one nation to another is known as kaleidoscopic comparative advantage.

7) **Economic Growth and Trade Patterns:** The Rybczynski theorem indicates that an increase in a particular endowment will, with opportunity costs constant, lead a nation's residents to produce a greater quantity of the good that uses that factor intensively, and to produce less of the other good. The change in production that results from economic growth may induce a nation's residents to trade more or less. An increase in the relatively abundant factor leads a nation's residents to produce more of the export good and less of the import good, which generates greater levels of trade. An increase in the nation's relatively scarce factor leads it to trade less as the production of the export goods falls and the production of the import good rises.

QUESTIONS AND PROBLEMS

1) Utopia's residents are endowed with 100 labor units and 75 capital units. Idealand's residents are endowed with 75 labor units and 50 capital units. Which nation is relatively labor abundant and which is relatively capital abundant?

2) Suppose that, at the current level of production, sandwiches require 1 labor unit and 0.5 capital units to produce, while bicycles require 0.9 labor units and 0.9 capital units. Based on this information, which of the two goods is relatively capital intensive in its production process, and which is relatively labor intensive?

3) Answer the following using your answers to questions 1 and 2. Suppose Utopia's and Idealand's residents begin to trade. Which good will Utopia's residents export, and which good will Utopia's residents import? Explain your answer in the context of the Heckscher–Ohlin theorem.

4) Based on your answer to question 3, under autarky will Utopia or Idealand have the higher price of sandwiches relative to bicycles? Which has the higher price of bicycles relative to sandwiches? Under autarky, which nation has the higher wage rate relative to the rental rate of capital? Explain how the wage rate relative to the rental rate of capital adjusts when the residents of the two nations begin to trade.

5) Based on your answer to question 3, explain how free trade between the residents of Utopia and Idealand benefits or harms workers and the capital holders in the two nations.

6) Consider Figure 3-2. If the residents of the two nations, Northland and Eastisle, are able to expand their consumption possibilities by specializing in the production of the good in which they have their respective comparative advantages, why did they not completely specialize? In other words, why did they stop specializing at the points labeled P_T^N and P_T^E?

7) Suppose that the manufacturing process for personal computers involves five stages: design, manufacturing of components, assembly, marketing, and delivery. Consider a computer company, such as U.S.-based Hewlett Packard Computer Corporation. For which stages of production do you think HP has a comparative advantage relative to a firm in a developing economy? In other words, if HP were to restructure, what are the stages of production in which it has the greatest comparative advantages?

8) Emerging nations in East Asia experienced considerable inflows of capital during the early 1990s. According to the Rybczynski theorem, how would an increase in East Asia's residents' capital endowments affect their patterns of trade?

9) Consider your answer to question 8. Do you think the economic growth that took place in East Asia during the early 1990s made the residents of East Asian nations more or less likely to engage in trade with residents of other regions?

10) Explain how the migration of labor from Central America to the United States might affect production in the United States.

ONLINE APPLICATION

Internet URL: http://www.wto.org

Title: **World Trade Organization**

Navigation: Begin at the home page of the World Trade Organization (WTO). Click on "Resources." Next click on "Statistics." Scroll down to "International Trade Statistics." Click on and open the PDF file for the most recent trade statistics.

Application: Perform the following operations, and answer the following questions.

1) Before reviewing the statistics in the file you opened, answer the following questions. Which regions do you think the residents of the fifteen European Union nations collectively trade with the most: North America, Latin America, Western Europe, Africa, the Middle East, or Asia? Rank these regions from highest to lowest. Which of the product groups (agricultural, food, raw materials, mining, fuels, manufactures, iron, chemical, transport equipment, tex-

tiles, clothing, and other consumer goods) do you think are net exports of the residents of the European Union? Which of the product groups do you think are net imports of the residents of the European Union?

2) Return to the document you opened. Move down to the Appendix, Table A11. Based on the information you see there, answer question 1 again.

For Group Study and Analysis: Assign questions 1 and 2 to different groups, dividing the task between the two groups based on merchandise groups and regions. Have each group present its findings and explain how they compare with the Heckscher–Ohlin theorem.

REFERENCES AND RECOMMENDED READINGS

Bhagwati, Jagdish, and Vivek H. Dehejia. "Freer Trade and Wages of the Unskilled—Is Marx Striking Again?" In Jagdish Bhagwati and Marvin H. Kosters, eds., *Trade and Wages: Leveling Wages Down?* Washington, D.C.: American Enterprise Institute, 1994.

Bhagwati, Jagdish, and Marvin H. Kosters, eds. *Trade and Wages: Leveling Wages Down?* Washington, D.C.: American Enterprise Institute, 1994.

Borjas, George J. "The Internationalization of the U.S. Labor Market and the Wage Structure." *Federal Reserve Bank of New York Economic Policy Review* (January 1995): 3–8.

Davis, John. "Is Trade Liberalization an Important Cause of Increasing U.S. Wage Inequality? The Interaction of Theory and Policy." *Review of Social Economy* LVII (4) (December 1999): 488–506.

Feenstra, Robert C. "Integration of Trade and Disintegration of Production in the Global Economy." *Journal of Economic Perspectives* 12 (4) (Fall 1998): 31–50.

Rassekh, Farhad, and Henry Thompson. "Factor Price Equalization: Theory and Evidence." *Journal of Economic Integration* 8 (1) (Spring 1993): 1–32.

Trefler, Daniel. "The Case of the Missing Trade and Other Mysteries." *American Economic Review 85* (5) (December 1995): 1029–1046.

Williamson, Jeffrey G. "Globalization, Labor Markets and Policy Backlash in the Past." *Journal of Economic Literature* 12 (4) (Fall 1998): 51–72.

Wood, Adrián. "Give Heckscher and Ohlin a Chance!" *Weltwirtschaftliches Archiv* 130 (1) (1994): 20–49.

CHAPTER FOUR

Regulating International Trade—Trade Policies and Their Effects

Fundamental Issues

1. **How do taxes affect the market price, and what are the redistributive effects of taxes?**
2. **What are tariffs, and what are the economic effects of tariff barriers?**
3. **What are quotas, and how do they represent a direct approach to restricting trade?**
4. **What are voluntary export restraints?**
5. **What are the effects of export subsidies, and how do policymakers typically react to export promotion policies?**
6. **What are the advantages and disadvantages of trade barriers?**

For decades, representatives of U.S. textile firms and labor groups lobbied policymakers for protection from foreign competition. In response, lawmakers enacted a vast number of regulations and restrictions on imported textiles and created an elaborate system administered by U.S. trade agencies.

The body of regulations applied to imported textiles is so complex that its administration involves nearly 75 percent of U.S. International Trade Administration employees. The International Trade Administration, an office of the Department of Commerce, has the power to require an accounting of the entire trail of the production of a garment. Foreign manufacturers must complete extensive documentation of the locations where cutting, sewing, and assembly took place. Officials may perform surprise inspections of foreign manufacturing facilities to ensure that each piece of a garment is produced according to this documentation.

In Hong Kong, for example, manufacturers link computers to workers' desks to log the hours spent sewing shirts together. In this way, manufacturers can provide evidence to U.S. trade administrators that they assembled the shirt in Hong Kong instead of China, because U.S. restrictions on Chinese garments are much more draconian. Manufacturers report that paperwork requirements represent a sizable portion of overall production costs.

The protection afforded to U.S. textile and garment manufacturers drives up the price of clothing purchased by a typical U.S. consumer. In the course of government business overseas, however, U.S. trade and commerce representatives once purchased tailored shirts and suits in Hong Kong. Photographs of William Daley, former secretary of commerce, and Donald Johnson, chief textile negotiator for former U.S. President Clinton, hang on the walls of Sam's Tailor Shop in Kowloon, Hong Kong. When confronted by a writer for the Wall Street Journal, *Mr. Johnson stated that he paid the appropriate duties on a tailor-made suit upon entering the United States. Secretary Daley, however, had not. His spokesperson referred to the matter as a mere "oversight."*

In spite of the potential welfare-enhancing effects of international trade described in Chapters 2 and 3, policymakers continue to enact trade barriers that serve to restrict trade and protect specific domestic groups. What types of barriers do policymakers use? How do these trade barriers affect domestic and foreign households, firms, and governments? What are the economic consequences of trade restrictions? In this chapter you will learn about the most commons tools used to restrict trade and develop an understanding of the economic consequences of using such policies.

Taxes and Their Direct Effect on Price

Policymakers can use a wide variety of instruments to restrict or alter trade flows. To begin our examination of these tools, we shall start with one of the most commonly used international policy instruments, which is a *tariff* barrier. A **tariff** is a tax on an imported good or service. To understand how a tariff works, you must first understand how a tax affects the market for a good or service.

Tariff
A tax on imported goods and services.

TAXES AS A FACTOR INFLUENCING SUPPLY

As discussed in Chapter 1, taxes are among the various categories of factors that influence supply. Let's now evaluate how a tax influences supply and, in turn, how a tax influences market outcomes.

The Effect on the Supply Schedule

Consider the monthly supply schedule for a running shoe manufacturer given in Table 4-1. As the table shows, at a market price of $75.00 per pair, the manufacturer is willing to produce and offer for sale 1,000 pairs of a particular running shoe.

Now consider the effects of a tax on running shoes. (To make our example easy to track, we shall assume that the manufacturer sells its shoes directly to the customer over the Internet.)

Suppose that the government imposes a tax of $5.00 on each pair of running shoes the manufacturer sells and that the government requires the manufacturer to remit the tax to a designated tax agency.

Table 4-2 shows the original, or pre-tax, supply schedule, and the new combinations of price and quantity after the tax, or post-tax, supply schedule. After the government imposes the tax, the manufacturer now requires $80.00 for each pair of running shoes to be willing to manufacture and offer for sale 1,000 pairs of shoes a month. When the customer pays $80.00 per pair, the manufacturer col-

Table 4-1 The Supply Schedule of a Running Shoe Manufacturer

The supply schedule tabulates the quantity supplied at various prices.

Price (per pair)	Quantity (pairs)
$72.50	750
$75.00	1,000
$77.50	1,250
$80.00	1,500

Table 4-2 The After-Tax Supply Schedule

The imposition of a tax causes a decline in the quantity supplied at each of the various prices.

Price (per pair)	Pre-Tax Quantity	Post-Tax Quantity
$72.50	750	250
$75.00	1,000	500
$77.50	1,250	750
$80.00	1,500	1,000

lects $80.00, remits $5.00 to the government, and keeps $75.00. (We are ignoring any costs associated with recording sales and taxes, and reporting the taxes to the government. These "red tape" costs, however, may be quite sizable.) In a similar manner, the manufacturer now requires $75.00 to supply 500 pairs of shoes and $77.50 to supply 750 pairs. Thus, the price the manufacturer requires at each quantity rises by the amount of the tax.

There is another way we can view the difference between the pre-tax supply schedule and the post-tax supply schedule. Note that at each of the various prices, the quantity supplied is lower after the imposition of the tax. Hence, the *supply* of running shoes decreases.

The Effect on Price

As discussed in Chapter 1, because the supply of running shoes decreases, there is upward pressure on the market price. Does this mean that the market price of running shoes rises by $5.00 per pair? According to the law of demand, when price rises, quantity demanded falls. At a price of $80.00, therefore, fewer running shoes are sold. As a result of this relationship between price and quantity demanded, imposing a tax causes the market price to rise, but not by the full amount of the tax.

WHO REALLY PAYS A TAX?

Because a tax influences market outcomes, it has redistributive effects, meaning that it transfers purchasing power among consumers, producers, and the government. A tax is **forward shifted** if the consumer must pay the tax in the form of a higher price per unit. A tax is **backward shifted** if the producer must pay the tax in the form of lower revenue per unit.

Forward shifted
The portion of a tax that consumers pay in the form of a higher price per unit.

Backward shifted
The amount of a tax that producers pay in the form of lower revenue per unit.

As just discussed, imposing a tax typically causes an increase in the market price that is less than the full amount of the tax. This means that part of the tax is forward shifted and part of the tax is backward shifted. By definition, the amount of the tax that is forward shifted and the amount that is backward shifted is the amount the government receives in tax revenue.

To see how taxes are typically forward and backward shifted, suppose that after the tax is imposed, the market price of a pair of running shoes rises to $77.50, and the equilibrium quantity falls to 750 pairs. At the new equilibrium, the producer receives $77.50 per pair of running shoes sold to the consumer, pays $5.00 to the government, and keeps $72.50 per pair. The tax revenue that the government receives is $5.00 × 750 = $3,750.00. The portion of the tax that is forward shifted onto consumers—the portion of the $3,750.00 paid by consumers in the form of a higher price—is ($77.50 – $75.00) × 750 = $1,875.00. The portion of the tax that is backward shifted—the portion of the $3,750.00 paid by producers in the form of revenue per unit—is ($75.00 – $72.50) × 750 = $1,875.00.

If part of the tax is backward shifted and part is forward shifted, then both the consumer and the producer share in paying the tax. The degrees to which a tax is

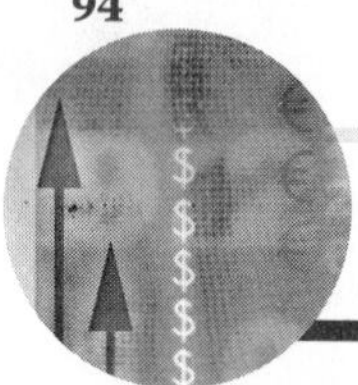

Visualizing Global Economic Issues

The Effects of a Tax

To see how a tax alters market outcomes, consider Figure 4-1. As shown in the figure, the market for running shoes is initially in equilibrium at point *A*, with a market price of $75.00 per pair of shoes and an equilibrium quantity of 1,000 pairs.

Now suppose the government imposes a $5.00 tax on each pair of shoes sold. The quantity supplied declines at each of the various prices, so the tax causes a decrease in supply. The decrease in supply is shown by the leftward and upward shift of the supply curve to *S′*. Note that at each of the various quantities, the supply curve shifts vertically by the amount of the tax.

Because of the decrease in supply, there is upward pressure on the price of running shoes. Consumers are resistant to this price increase and reduce their quantity demanded, as shown by a movement up and along the demand curve. A new equilibrium is reached at point *B*, at a price of $77.50 per shoe and a quantity of 750 pairs. As you can see in the figure, the tax causes the market price to rise above its initial level of $75.00, but not by the full amount of the tax.

In this example, the government's tax revenue equals $5.00 × 750 = $3,750. The total tax revenue is illustrated in Figure 4-1 by the rectangle formed by areas *C* and *P*. The base of this rectangle equals the equilibrium quantity sold, 750 units, and the height equals the per-unit tax, $77.50 – $72.50 = $5.00. Hence, the area of the rectangle is equal to the tax revenue.

Figure 4-1 also illustrates the portion of the tax that is forward shifted and the portion that is backward shifted. The amount of the tax that is forward shifted, which is shown by the rectangle labeled *C*, is $1,875 [($77.50 – $75.00) × 750]. The base of this rectangle is equal to the equilibrium quantity sold, and the height is equal to the difference between the equilibrium price after the tax and the equilibrium price before the tax, $77.25 – $75.00 = $2.50. Hence, the area of rectangle *C* equals the total amount of the tax forward shifted onto consumers.

The amount of the tax that is backward shifted, which is depicted by the rectangle labeled *P*, is $1,875 [($77.50 – $75.00) × 750]. The base of this rectangle is equal to the quantity transacted, and the height is equal to the difference between the equilibrium price

forward shifted and backward shifted depend on the responsiveness of consumers and producers to changes in price. (To further consider the redistributive effects of a tax, see *Visualizing Global Economic Issues: The Effects of a Tax*.) We reach the following conclusion:

> **Typically, imposing a tax causes the market price to rise, but not by the full amount of the tax. Forward shifting of a tax is the amount of the tax that the consumer pays in the form of a higher price. Backward shifting of a tax is the amount of the tax that is paid by the producer in the form of lower prices. Because the price typically does not rise by the full amount of the tax in most situations, part of the tax is forward shifted and part is backward shifted.**

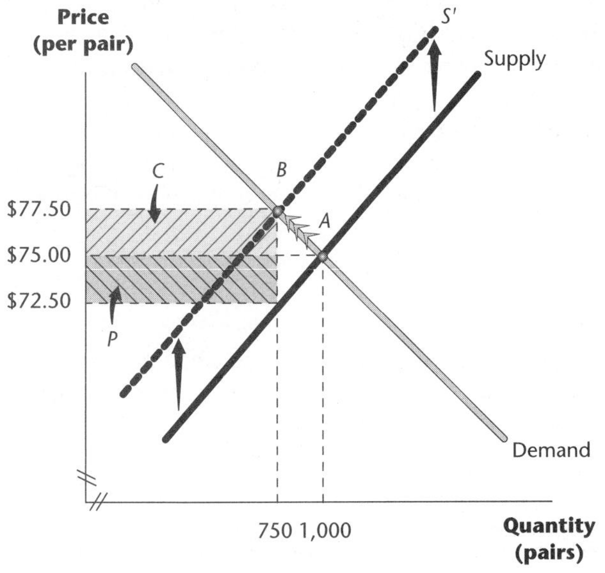

Figure 4-1

The Effects of a Tax

The imposition of a tax causes the supply curve to shift vertically an amount equal to the tax. The decrease in supply generates an increase in the market price. Although the market price rises, it typically does not rise by the full amount of the tax. The entire amount of tax revenue is given by the sum of areas C and P. Area C is the portion of the tax forward shifted onto consumers and area P is the amount of the tax backward shifted onto producers.

before the tax and the price the producer keeps after paying the tax to the government tax agency, $75.00 – $72.50 = $2.50. Hence, the area of rectangle *P* equals the total amount of the tax backward shifted onto shoe producers.

For Critical Analysis:
Suppose the tax was 5 percent of the price, as opposed to a fixed amount per unit. How would Figure 4-1 be different?

How do taxes affect the market price and what are the redistributive effects of taxes?

Fundamental Issue

The imposition of a tax causes the supply of the particular good or service to decrease. Although the decrease in supply generates an increase in the market price, it typically does not rise by the full amount of the tax in most situations. Because a tax influences market outcomes, it has redistributive effects. A tax is forward shifted if the consumer must pay the tax in the form of a higher price per unit. A tax is backward shifted if the producer must pay the tax in the form of lower revenue per unit.

The Economic Effects of a Tariff

As discussed earlier, a tariff is a tax on imported goods or services. A tariff, therefore, has many of the same effects on price and quantity in the example of a tax on running shoes. There is, however, an important difference. A tariff is a tax on imported goods and services and does not apply to the output of domestic producers. This means that the backward shifting of a tariff is different from the backward shifting of a tax on domestic output. Another aspect to consider is that a tariff has the potential to affect the global price by affecting the global supply, as discussed in Chapter 1. Before you can begin to analyze the economic effects of a tariff, you must first understand the basic types of tariffs and their strengths and weaknesses. Then we will consider economic effects in two possible environments: a *small-country* setting and a *large-country* setting.

Specific tariff
A tariff specified as an amount of money per unit of the good sold.

***Ad valorem* tariff**
A tariff calculated as a percentage of the value of the good or service.

Combination tariff
A tariff that combines an ad valorem *tariff and a specific tariff.*

TYPES OF TARIFFS

There are three basic kinds of tariffs. A **specific tariff** is a fixed tariff amount per unit imported. An ***ad valorem* tariff** is calculated as a percent of the value of the good or service imported. A **combination tariff** is a blend of a specific tariff and an *ad valorem* tariff. Table 4-3 lists tariff rates applied by the United States on

ON THE WEB

Obtain information on U.S. tariff rates from the International Trade Administration at the U.S. Department of Commerce at http://www.ita.doc.gov.

Table 4-3 Selected U.S. Tariff Rates

Source: Harmonized Tariff Schedule of the United States http://dataweb.usitc.gov/scripts.tariff.asp.

Item	*Ad Valorem* Tariff (percent)	Specific Tariff (dollar amount per unit)
Grass Shears and Parts Thereof	45	$0.20
Carpets and Other Textile Floor Coverings: Of Wool or Fine Animal Hair	6.2	0
Floor Coverings of Coconut Fibers	0	$1.29
Capers	8.0	0
Mushrooms	20	$0.088
Cigars	4.7	$1.89
Cigarettes	0.9	$0.417
Pre-Shave, Shaving, or After-Shave Preparations	4.9	0
Lawn Tennis Rackets, Strung	5.3	0
Bicycles	11.0	0

selected items. Grass shears, for example, are subject to a combination tariff consisting of a 45 percent *ad valorem* tariff and a $0.20 specific tariff.

Benefits and Weaknesses of Specific Tariffs

There are advantages and disadvantages of using specific tariffs and *ad valorem* tariffs. A specific tariff is easy to calculate, but it does not adjust to price changes. Consider, for example, a $1,000 specific tariff applied to Swedish automobiles. The tariff is easy to calculate, because the trade authorities must simply count the number of automobiles brought into the country and then multiply this number by $1,000. Suppose that the imported auto wholesales for $20,000, so that the $1,000 specific tariff represents 5 percent of the value of the automobile. The Swedish auto manufacturer, however, can export a more expensive model valued at $25,000. Then the $1,000 tariff represents only 4 percent of the value of the auto. The relative size of the tariff—as a percent of the value of the automobile—declines when the manufacturer simply substitutes a more expensive automobile.

Benefits and Weaknesses of *Ad Valorem* Tariffs

The benefit of an *ad valorem* tariff is that it always amounts to the same percentage of the value of the good or service. A 5 percent *ad valorem* tariff, for example, remains 5 percent of the value of the automobile regardless of the model the Swedish automobile manufacturer exports. The tariff amount generated by an *ad valorem* tariff, therefore, rises as the price of the good increases. An *ad valorem* tariff, however, is more difficult to calculate. The trade authorities can no longer simply count the number of autos. They must first determine the numbers of each type of imported auto and tabulate the market prices of all models.

As you can see, specific tariffs and *ad valorem* tariffs have their own individual strengths and weaknesses. To take advantage of the strengths of each type of tariff, trade authorities often find combination tariffs useful.

EFFECTS OF A TARIFF IN A SMALL-COUNTRY SETTING

A **small country** is one in which the consumption and production decisions of its domestic residents do not affect the international price in a particular market, so that the residents of a small country take the international price in that market as a given. Hence, in the small-country setting, the imposition of a tariff causes the domestic price of the good or service to change, but it does not affect the international price.

Small country
A country so small its consumption and production decisions do not affect the international price, so that its residents take the international price as a given.

The Price Effect of a Tariff in a Small-Country Setting

In any environment, the domestic price that consumers must pay equals the global price plus the amount of the tariff. In a small-country setting, however, the decisions of domestic producers and domestic consumers do not affect the global price. Consequently, the domestic price paid by domestic consumers and the revenue received by domestic producers rises by the full amount of a tariff. The increase in domestic price causes quantity demanded to decline and induces domestic producers to increase their quantity supplied.

Foreign producers must remit the tariff to the domestic government. The per-unit revenue they receive after the tariff, therefore, is still equal to the international price. Nonetheless, because quantity demanded declines and quantity supplied by domestic producers increases, the tariff causes the quantity of imports to shrink.

Forward and Backward Shifting of the Tariff in a Small-Country Setting

The forward- and backward-shifting aspects of a tariff are straightforward in a small-country setting. The revenue per unit that domestic producers receive increases, so none of the tariff is backward shifted to domestic producers. The revenue per unit that foreign producers receive after paying the tariff remains the same, so none of the tariff is backward shifted to foreign producers. Because the domestic price rises by the full amount of the tariff, all of the tariff revenue is forward shifted. Domestic consumers pay the entire tariff in the form of higher prices of foreign products they purchase.

Redistributive Effects of a Tariff in a Small-Country Setting

Now that you understand the forward and backward shifting of a tariff in a small-country setting, let's consider the redistributive effects of a tariff using the concepts of consumer and producer surplus. Recall from Chapter 1 that consumer surplus is the difference between what consumers are willing to pay for a particular quantity and the market price they must pay. Producer surplus is the difference between the market price that producers receive and the price needed to persuade them to supply a particular quantity. Consumer and producer surplus, therefore, are affected by a change in price, which, in turn, changes when a government imposes a tariff.

In the case of the tariff in the small-country setting, there is an increase in both the price that consumers must pay and the revenue per unit that domestic producers receive. Consumer surplus, therefore, falls and the surplus of domestic producers rises. Because the revenue per unit that foreign producers receive remains unchanged, foreign producer surplus remains unchanged.

Part of the loss of consumer surplus, the forward-shifted tariff revenue, is transferred to the domestic government as tariff revenue. Another part of the loss of consumer surplus is transferred to domestic producers as an increase in domestic producer surplus. Finally, part of the loss of consumer surplus is not transferred to any other party. Losses of consumer or producer surplus not transferred to any other party, or **deadweight losses,** result from a loss of economic efficiency. **Economic efficiency** requires that resources be allocated in the most cost-efficient manner. Because a tariff distorts the domestic price, scarce domestic resources are shifted into the tariff-protected industry and away from other, more efficient industries, resulting in a loss of economic efficiency.

Deadweight loss
A loss of consumer or producer surplus that is not transferred to any other party and that represents a decline in economic efficiency.

Economic efficiency
A condition when scarce resources are allocated in a most productive, least-cost pattern.

A tariff, therefore, redistributes consumer surplus to domestic producers and the domestic government. The loss of consumer surplus exceeds the amount transferred to domestic producers and the domestic government. Hence, a tariff in a small-country setting leads to a net welfare loss for domestic residents. (To further evaluate the effects of a tariff in a small country, see on pages 100–101 *Visualizing Global Economic Issues: A Tariff in a Small-Country Setting.*)

EFFECTS OF A TARIFF IN A LARGE-COUNTRY SETTING

The effects of a tariff in a *large-country setting* differ from those arising in a small-country setting in an important regard. A **large country's** market share is sufficiently large that the production and consumption decisions of domestic consumers and producers affect the global prices of good and services. A tariff applied in a large-country setting distorts the domestic price and induces changes in the domestic quantities demanded and supplied, thereby altering the global price.

Large country
A large country's market share is sufficiently large that the production and consumption decisions of its residents affect the global prices of goods and services.

The Price Effect of a Tariff in a Large-Country Setting

Consider the following example to understand the price effect of the imposition of a tariff in a large country. Suppose that at a global price of $200, U.S. manufacturers import 50 million tons of steel per month from Japanese steel producers, and suppose the respective market shares of Japan and the United States are sufficiently large to affect the global price of steel. Consider what happens when the U.S. government imposes a specific tariff of $50 per ton. Imposing the tariff causes the U.S. price of steel to rise, which reduces the domestic quantity demanded and increases the domestic quantity supplied, thereby reducing U.S. imports of steel from Japan.

If the global price of steel remains at $200, Japanese steel producers continue to supply 50 million tons of steel in the global market. Thus, an excess quantity supplied results in the global market. As explained in Chapter 1, an excess quantity supplied causes the price to fall until the quantity demanded equals the quantity supplied and a new equilibrium is reached. Hence, the global price of steel declines until the quantity supplied to the global market by Japanese steel producers equals the quantity demanded by U.S. steel consumers.

There are two prices that we must keep track of in this example: the U.S. price of steel (the global price of steel plus the $50 tariff), and the global price of steel. Let's suppose that after the U.S. government applies the tariff, the excess quantity of steel supplied in the global markets causes the global price of steel to decline to $180 per ton. The price of steel in the United States rises from the global price of $200 to $230 ($180 + $50).

Forward and Backward Shifting of a Tariff in a Large-Country Setting

As you can see in this example, applying the tariff causes the price of steel in the United States to rise, but not by the full $50 per ton. We can conclude that in a large-country setting, part, but not all, of a tariff is forward shifted to domestic consumers. The remaining portion of the tariff is backward shifted. But to whom is the tariff backward shifted?

The higher price of steel in the United States causes the surplus of U.S. steel producers to increase, so the tariff is not backward shifted to domestic producers.

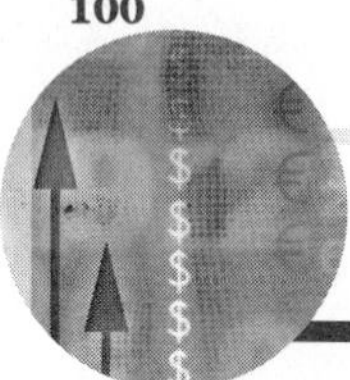

Visualizing Global Economic Issues

A Tariff in a Small-Country Setting

To visualize the impact of a tariff in a small-country setting, consider the market for steel depicted in Figure 4-2. In the figure, the demand curve labeled *D* is the domestic demand, and the curve labeled S_{DOM} is the supply of domestic steel producers. The global price is $200, and residents of the small country can purchase as much steel as they desire at the global price of $200 without driving up the global price. Hence, *from the perspective of the residents of the small country,* the global supply curve—representing the supply curve of all foreign producers—is horizontal at the global price.

At the global price of $200, domestic producers supply 75 tons of steel to the domestic market and the total quantity demanded is 150 tons of steel. Steel imports, or the difference between domestic quantity demanded and the quantity supplied by domestic producers, equal 75 tons.

Suppose that the domestic government imposes a specific tariff of $50 per ton. Because the tariff is on imported steel only, the global supply curve faced by domestic residents shifts upward by $50 to S'_{Global}, while the domestic supply curve remains at its original position. As shown in Figure 4-2, the domestic price of steel rises by the full amount of the tariff, to a new equilibrium price of $250 per ton. As the domestic price of steel rises, the quantity supplied by domestic producers rises from 75 tons to 85 tons. Domestic quantity demanded, however, falls to 135 tons and imports shrink to 50 tons.

Redistributive Effects of the Tariff

Because the domestic price rises by the full amount of the tariff, the entire tariff is forward shifted onto the consumer. The areas labeled *C, E, F,* and *G* in Figure 4-2 represent the total loss of consumer surplus. Of this total, the rectangle labeled *C* illustrates the amount of the tariff revenue and, therefore, the amount that is forward shifted onto steel consumers. The base of this rectangle equals the quantity imported, 50 tons, and the height equals the amount of the tariff, $50. Hence, the area *C*, $50 \times \$50 = \$250$, equals tariff revenue.

The area *E* represents a loss of consumer surplus that is transferred to domestic producers in the form of higher revenue per ton of steel sold in the domestic market. In other words, domestic producers' surplus rises as the revenue per unit increases. The value of this transfer is determined by calculating the area of the rectangle and the triangle that together form the area *E*, or $(75 \times \$50) + (10 \times \$50)/2 = \$4{,}000$.

Deadweight Losses

As shown in Figure 4-2, the loss of consumer surplus exceeds the amounts transferred to the domestic

---

At the same time, the surplus of Japanese steel producers falls because of the decline in the global price of steel. Consequently, part of the tariff is backward shifted to Japanese steel producers.

Beggar-thy-neighbor policy
A policy action that benefits one nation's economy but worsens economic performance in another nation.

Backward shifting a portion of the tariff results in a gain for the country applying the tariff because the domestic government captures foreign producer surplus as tariff revenue. This constitutes a loss for foreign producers. Economists call a tariff applied by a large country a **beggar-thy-neighbor policy:** it benefits agents in one nation at the expense of agents in another nation.

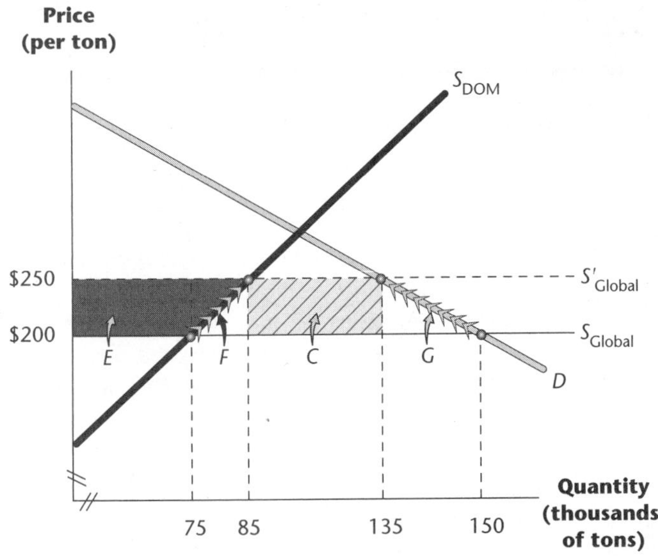

Figure 4-2

The Small-Country Tariff

The imposition of a tariff by the government in a small country causes the market price in the small country to rise by the full amount of the tariff. The entire amount of the tariff is forward shifted onto consumers. The loss of consumer surplus equals the sum of areas E, F, C, *and* G. *Area* E *is transferred to domestic producers as an increase in producer surplus. Area* C *is transferred to the small-country government as tariff revenue. Areas* F *and* G *are deadweight losses.*

government and to domestic producers. Hence, there are deadweight losses resulting from the tariff. The two triangles labeled *F* and *G* represent the tariff deadweight losses. The triangle *F,* which has an area equal to (10 × $50)/2 = $250, represents a loss of economic efficiency that results when domestic producers shift scarce resources from unprotected, more efficient industries to domestic production within the protected industry. The triangle *G,* which has an area equal to (15 × $50)/2 = $375, represents a loss of steel consumers' satisfaction that results when they shift consumption from steel to less-desired substitutes. The total deadweight loss generated by the tariff equals $250 + $375 = $625.

For Critical Analysis:
Suppose the domestic government imposed a 25 percent *ad valorem* tariff as opposed to a specific tariff. Would the graphical analysis differ from that shown in Figure 4-2?

Redistributive Effects of a Tariff in a Large-Country Setting

Like a tariff in a small-country setting, a tariff in a large-country setting has redistributive effects. The increase in the domestic price generates a loss of consumer surplus. Part of this loss is transferred to domestic producers as higher revenue and a corresponding increase in producer surplus. Another part of the loss of consumer surplus is transferred to the domestic government as tariff revenue. As in the small-country setting, the loss of consumer surplus exceeds the amount of surplus transferred to other parties. Thus, deadweight losses arise from the same types of inefficiencies created by a tariff in a small-country setting.

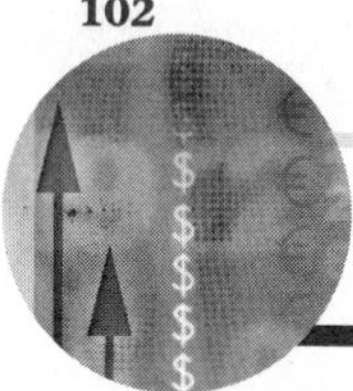

Visualizing Global Economic Issues

The Effects of a Tariff in a Large-Country Setting

A tariff applied by the government of a large country can affect the global price. To see the effects of a tariff in a large-country setting, consider a simplified example of related steel markets in only two nations, the United States and Japan.

Panel (a) in Figure 4-3 shows the U.S. market for steel, and panel (b) depicts the Japanese market for steel. The initial global price of steel is $200. Figure 4-3 shows that, at this price, Japanese steel producers export 50,000 tons of steel to the United States.

Now suppose the United States government imposes a specific tariff on steel imports equal to $50 per ton. As shown in Figure 4-3, the tariff causes the U.S. price of steel to rise to $230 per ton. The higher U.S. steel price spurs a decrease in the quantity demanded by U.S. residents to 135,000 tons and an increase in the quantity supplied by U.S. producers to 115,000 tons. Hence, U.S. imports of steel from Japan fall to 20,000 tons.

At the initial global price of $200, the decline in U.S. steel imports from Japan results in an excess quantity supplied of 30,000 tons of steel in the Japanese steel market. This excess quantity supplied causes the global price of steel to decline to $180. At this price, exports of Japanese steel producers equals the imports of U.S. steel consumers.

Redistributive Effects of the Tariff

The tariff applied to U.S. steel imports generates tariff revenue for the U.S. government totaling (20,000 × $50) = $1 million. The areas labeled *C* and *E* in panel (a) of Figure 4-3 illustrate the amount of the tariff revenue. The area *C*, which equals (20,000 × $30) = $600,000, depicts the amount forward shifted to U.S. steel consumers. The area *E*, which equals (20,000 × $20) = $400,000, shows the amount of the tariff backward shifted to Japanese steel producers.

The increase in the U.S. price of steel results in a loss of U.S. consumer surplus shown by the areas labeled *A*, *B*, *C*, and *D* in panel (a). Area *A* is a loss of consumer surplus that is transferred to U.S. steel producers in the form of higher revenue per ton of steel. This increase in U.S. producer surplus equals (100,000 × $30) + (15,000 × $30)/2 = $3,225,000. Areas *B* and *D* indicate the deadweight losses, and both areas equal (15,000 × $30)/2 = $225,000. Hence, the total loss of U.S. consumer surplus is $3,225,000 + $225,000 + $600,000 + $225,000 = $4,275,000.

The areas labeled *F*, *G*, *H*, and *I* in panel (b) illustrate the loss of producer surplus for Japanese steel producers. Area *F* illustrates the transfer of producer surplus to Japanese steel consumers in the form of a lower price per ton of steel. This increase in Japanese steel consumer surplus equals (75,000 × $20) + (15,000 × $20)/2 = $1,650,000. The area labeled *H* represents the transfer of Japanese steel producer surplus to the U.S. government in the form of tariff revenue. [Note that area *E* in panel (a) equals area *H* of panel (b), or $400,000.] Areas *G* and *I* illustrate the deadweight losses, and both equal (15,000 × $20)/2 = $150,000. Thus, the total decline in Japanese producer surplus equals $2,350,000.

Deadweight Losses

As you can now see, the U.S. tariff results in deadweight losses for both economies. The reason is

As explained earlier, there is also a loss of foreign producer surplus. Part of this loss is transferred to the domestic government in the form of tariff revenue. The entire loss of foreign producer surplus caused by the tariff, however, exceeds the total amount transferred to other parties in either the domestic economy or foreign economy. Hence, in contrast to the case of a small country, a tariff in the

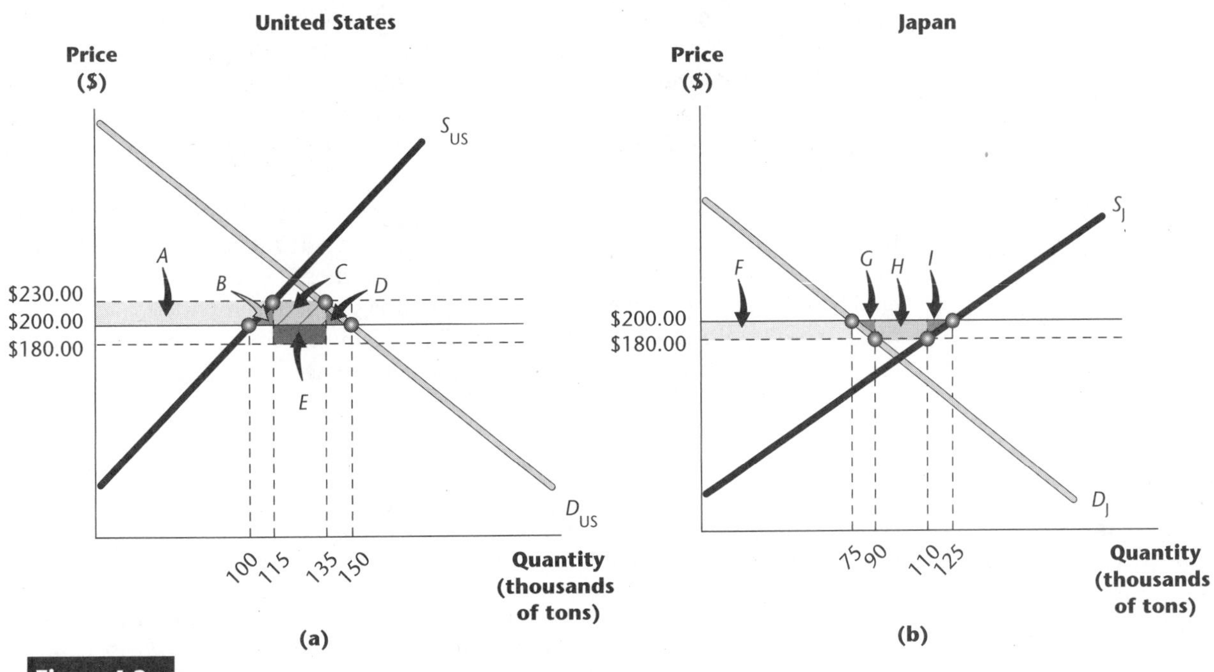

Figure 4-3

The Effects of a Tariff in a Large-Country Setting

The imposition of a tariff by the government of a large country, such as the United States, results in an increase in the market price of steel in the United States and a decrease in the market price of steel in the global market. The loss of U.S. consumers' surplus due to the higher price of steel in the United States equals the sum of areas A, B, C, *and* D. *Area* A *is transferred to U.S. steel producers, area* C *is transferred to the U.S. government as tariff revenue, and areas* B *and* D *are deadweight losses. The loss of Japanese steel producers' surplus due to the lower global price of steel equals the sum of areas* F, G, H, *and* I. *Area* F *is transferred to Japanese steel consumers, area* H, *which equals area* E, *is transferred to the U.S. government as tariff revenue. Areas* G *and* I *are deadweight losses.*

that economic inefficiencies are created as U.S. steel producers shift scarce resources into the U.S. steel industry and away from more efficient industries, and as U.S. steel consumers reduce their quantity demanded of steel and switch to less desirable substitutes. At the same time, Japanese producers move scarce resources out of the Japanese steel industry and Japanese steel consumers increase their quantity demanded and reduce their consumption of more desirable substitutes.

For Critical Analysis:
In Figure 4-3, the tariff transferred surplus away from Japanese steel producers to the U.S. government. On net is the U.S. economy better off because of the tariff?

large-country setting results in deadweight losses in the foreign economy as well as in the domestic economy. (To further understand the redistributive effects of a tariff in a large-country setting, see *Visualizing Global Economic Issues: The Effects of a Tariff in a Large-Country Setting*.)

Can Residents of a Large Country Benefit from the Imposition of a Tariff?
Because a tariff in a large-country setting results in deadweight losses in the domestic economy and a transfer of surplus from foreign producers to the domestic government, the amount of foreign producer surplus transferred to the domestic government could be greater than the amount of deadweight losses in the domestic economy. If so, domestic residents could, on net, *benefit* from the application of a tariff.

Although a tariff in the large-country setting may lead to a net gain for domestic residents, the loss of producer surplus incurred by foreign producers is likely to spur retaliatory actions by the foreign government. The foreign government could apply tariffs or other types of trade barriers to goods imported from the domestic country. In this case, the action of the domestic government and reaction of the foreign government most likely would lead to net losses for both economies.

Fundamental Issue

What are the economic effects of tariff barriers?

The redistributive effects of a tariff differ in a small-country setting as compared to a large-country setting. Because a tariff in a small-country setting does not affect the global price, the entire amount of the tariff is forward shifted to domestic consumers. The imposition of a tariff in a large country causes the global price to decline. Thus, part of the tariff is forward shifted to domestic consumers and part is backward shifted to foreign producers. A tariff always results in deadweight losses for both small and large countries.

Quotas: A Direct Approach to Restricting Trade

Non-tariff barriers *Instruments other than import tariffs that restrict international trade.*

Import quota *A policy that restricts the quantity of imports.*

Absolute quota *A quantitative restriction that limits the amount of a product that can enter a country during a specified time period.*

Tariff-rate quota *A quota that allows a specified quantity of a good to enter the country at a reduced tariff rate. Any quantity above that amount is subject to a higher tariff rate.*

There are a number of policy instruments other than tariffs, called **non-tariff barriers,** which policymakers can use to restrict global trade. Policymakers often use an **import quota,** which restricts the physical quantity of a product that can be imported. An **absolute quota** is a quantitative amount that may enter the country during a specified time period. A **tariff-rate quota** allows entry of a specified quantity at a reduced tariff rate. Quantities above the specified amount are subject to a higher tariff.

Table 4-4 provides information on quotas applied by the U.S. International Trade Administration's Office of Textiles and Apparel to specific countries for gloves and mittens, dresses, and men's and boy's shirts. (To understand how the phase-out of these quotas might affect U.S. firms, see on page 106 *Online Globalization: Will the Internet Save the U.S. Textile Industry from Falling Trade Barriers?*)

ECONOMIC EFFECTS OF A QUOTA

Because an import quota limits the amount of a product that can be imported, it has a *direct* effect on the quantity sold in the domestic market. A tariff, by way of contrast, directly influences the price of an imported good, and thereby *indirectly* affects the quantity sold in the domestic market. Nevertheless, in spite of this dif-

Table 4-4 Selected U.S. Import Quotas

The United States has an extensive quota system in the textile industry. The table lists only a small sample of goods and countries.

Source: The U.S. Office of Textiles and Apparel, http://www.otexa.ita.doc.gov.

Country	Cotton Gloves and Mittens (pairs)	Cotton Dresses	Men's and Boy's Knit Shirts
Philippines	7,398,029	847,690	2,611,936
Hong Kong	4,171,166	240,854	2,798,767
Malaysia	2,799,960	623,415	1,545,593
Taiwan	514,862	122,400	818,999
Brazil	0	119,455	2,150,160
Pakistan	3,261,497	639,065	6,044,496

ference between tariffs and quotas, their price, quantity, and redistributive effects are comparable. Because of the similarities, we shall restrict our analysis of quotas to an absolute quota in a small-country setting, and then generalize the results to a large-country setting.

A Quota's Effect on Quantity and Price

An absolute quota affects the quantity of a product consumed and sold by restricting the amount that may enter the country. To understand the effects of a quota on the price of a product, consider an example. Suppose that at the global price of $30 a blouse, domestic consumers in a small country import 1 million women's cotton blouses over the course of a year and purchase an additional 500,000 from domestic manufacturers. In addition, suppose that domestic policymakers succumb to pressure applied by domestic garment manufacturers and enact a quota that limits the quantity of imported cotton blouses to 500,000 units a year.

At the current domestic price of $30, the quantity of cotton blouses demanded remains at 1.5 million blouses while the quantity supplied falls to 1 million blouses (500,000 by domestic producers and 500,000 imported under the quota), so the quota creates an excess quantity demanded. This excess quantity demanded causes the domestic price of blouses to rise above the global price. Thus, a quota directly affects the quantity of imports and indirectly affects the domestic price.

As the domestic price rises, the quantity demanded by domestic consumers declines, and the quantity supplied by domestic producers rises. At a new equilibrium, the quantity demanded by domestic consumers exactly equals the total

ON THE WEB

For information on U.S. quotas on textiles, visit the home page of the U.S. Customs Service at http://www.customs.ustreas.gov or the U.S. International Trade Administration's Office of Textiles and Apparel at http://www.otexa.ita.doc.gov. For information on U.S. quotas on dairy and sugar products, visit the home page of the U.S. Department of Agriculture's Foreign Agriculture Service at http://www.fas.usda.gov.

Online Globalization

Will the Internet Save the U.S. Textile Industry from Falling Trade Barriers?

Since the 1970s, the U.S. textile industry has had a special arrangement known as CITA—the Committee for the Implementation of Textile Agreements. CITA comprises appointees from the U.S. Departments of Commerce, Labor, State, and Treasury, along with the chief textile negotiator of the Office of the President. CITA holds no open meetings, but during the late 1990s CITA reduced or threatened to reduce quota limitations on specific types of textile imports, including men's underwear from the Dominican Republic, cotton nightwear from Jamaica, and wool coats from Honduras. These CITA quotas, as pointed out in the introduction to this chapter, are but one of the many types of instruments used to protect the U.S. textile industry. Nevertheless, in recent years the annual benefit of CITA quotas for U.S. textile firms has been estimated to be as high as $12 billion in additional profits.

The End of U.S. Textile Dominance?

A gradual phase-out of U.S. textile quotas has begun, however. By 2005, the United States has pledged to be in full compliance with various international treaties ending quotas in its domestic textile industries.

Initially, voices of gloom and doom predominated in the U.S. textile industry, as the 1990s ended with news of numerous domestic factory shutdowns as fabric-making jobs "followed the needle" to mills in Mexico and Asia. Some observers even predicted the ultimate demise of the U.S. textile industry. Even though the United States produces more cotton than any other country except China, it ultimately would be shipping most of that cotton elsewhere to be woven into under- and outerwear for shipment back to U.S. retailers.

In fact, although U.S. textile imports continued to rise in the early 2000s, textile employment dropped by a lower-than-expected 7 percent before stabilizing and even showing signs of recovery in 2000 and 2001. U.S. textile producers' share of the global market dipped slightly before leveling off at about 25 percent of world textile sales, and some textile experts even predicted that the U.S. share might begin to grow once again.

A key factor contributing to strengthening U.S. textile exports has been that there is more to garment manufacturing and marketing than the ability to produce boatloads of inexpensive T-shirts. The demand for high-fashion clothing made by U.S. producers tends to be price-insensitive. In markets for the latest clothing fads, speed to market usually counts more than rock-bottom prices offered by low-cost textile firms based in Latin American or Asia.

Many U.S. textile manufacturers have taken advantage of the lead the United States enjoys in business-to-business commerce on the Internet. By cutting distribution costs and speeding up deliveries, they have been able to retain, and in some cases enhance, their shares in the global textile marketplace. Today, many Latin American and Asian textile manufacturers are complaining that U.S. firms' ready access to business-to-business e-commerce constitutes a type of barrier to free and open international trade.

For Critical Analysis:
Do Latin American and Asian textile companies have a legitimate complaint?

quantity of cotton blouses supplied by domestic producers plus the quota-restricted quantity supplied by foreign producers.

Let's suppose that after the quota is in place, the new equilibrium price is $35, at which the quantity of cotton blouses demanded is 1.2 million blouses and the quantity of cotton blouses supplied by domestic producers is 700,000. Hence, the quantity supplied by foreign producers, 500,000, and quantity supplied by domestic producers, 700,000, exactly equals the quantity demanded. By restricting imports, the quota increases the domestic price and expands the market share of domestic producers.

Redistributive Effects of a Quota

This example shows that the price and quantity effects of a quota are similar to the price and quantity effects of a tariff. The redistributive effects differ because the domestic government does not receive tariff revenue, however.

Like a tariff, a quota causes the domestic price to rise and thereby generates a decline in consumer surplus. Part of this loss of consumer surplus is transferred to domestic producers in the form of higher revenues. Another part of this loss of consumer surplus is transferred to the foreign producers who fill the quota and receive a higher price per unit. In addition, the increase in price generates a rise in domestic quantity supplied and a decline in domestic quantity demanded. These changes in price and quantity result in the same type of deadweight losses that tariffs create, as domestic producers shift scarce resources away from production in more efficient industries into the quota-protected industry and consumers substitute away from the quota-protected good to less desirable substitutes.

QUOTA RENT

In our example of a quota on women's blouses, domestic consumers pay $5 more for each imported blouse after the quota is in place. With the imposition of a tariff, this higher price per unit on imported blouses would be transferred to the domestic government as tariff revenue. With a quota, however, this amount is transferred to another party, such as foreign producers, as an increase in surplus.

Calculating the Quota Rent

Economists call this transfer of consumer surplus a **quota rent.** A quota rent is calculated by multiplying the number of units of the product imported under the quota by the higher price per unit generated by the quota. In our example, the quota rent is (500,000 × $5) = $2.5 million. If the government imposed a tariff that generated a $5 increase in price, the tariff revenue would exactly equal the quota rent.

Quota rent
A portion of the loss of consumer surplus caused by an import quota that is transferred to the foreign supplier as additional profits.

Allocating the Quota Rent

Because governments can determine what foreign firms may fill the quota, they also have the ability to determine who receives, or has the rights to, the quota rent. The way in which an agency allocates the right to supply imports up to the

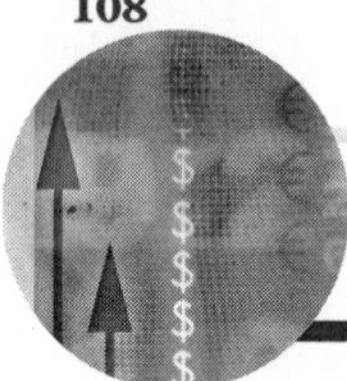

Visualizing Global Economic Issues

The Effects of an Import Quota

To understand in greater detail the effects of an import quota, consider the market for women's cotton blouses illustrated in Figure 4-4. At a global price of \$30, the quantity of cotton blouses demanded by domestic consumers equals 1.5 million and the quantity of cotton blouses supplied by domestic producers is 500,000. Imports, therefore, equal 1 million units.

Suppose the domestic government establishes an import quota that restricts the quantity of cotton blouses imported each year to 500,000 units. At the global price of \$30, the quantity demanded is 1.5 million blouses and the total quantity supplied by domestic and foreign producers is 1 million, so the quota creates an excess quantity demanded.

The Effects on Price and Quantity

To evaluate the resulting price increase, we add the amount of the quota, 500,000 units, to the quantity supplied by domestic producers at each of the various prices above the global price of \$30. This results in a new supply curve, labeled S_{Dom+Q}, which lies 500,000 units to the right of the supply curve of domestic producers at each of the various prices.

As you can see, the figure indicates that the import quota results in a new domestic equilibrium at a price of \$35 per blouse. Moreover, you will note that the equilibrium price is no longer equal to the global market price because of the quota restricting the quantity of imports. The increase in the domestic price generates a decrease in quantity demanded to 1.2 million units and an increase in domestic quantity supplied to 700,000 units. Hence, the total quantity of cotton blouses supplied by domestic and foreign producers again equals the quantity demanded.

The Redistributive Effects of the Quota

Because the domestic price of blouses increases, there is a decline in domestic consumer surplus. The sum of the areas labeled *A, B, C,* and *D* depict the total loss of consumer surplus. Area *A* represents a transfer of $[(500{,}000 \times \$5) + (200{,}000 \times \$5)/2] = \$3$ million from domestic consumers to domestic producers. Area *B,* which equals $[(200{,}000 \times \$5)/2] = \$500{,}000$, is a deadweight loss arising when domestic producers shift scarce resources out of more productive industries to increase production within the less-efficient quota-

quota limit determines the allocation of the quota rent. One way a government could allow the quota to be filled is on a first-come basis. In this case, the quota revenue is allocated to those firms who get their goods and services to the nation's customs agency first.

A second way the government can allocate the quota rent is to allow the quota to be filled by the firms of nations receiving preferential treatment. A developed nation, for example, might let the firms in a developing nation fill the quota and receive the quota rent.

A third way to allocate the quota rent is for the domestic government to charge for licenses that authorize foreign firms to fill the quota. By charging for a license, the government receives some or all of the quota rent as revenue in a manner similar to a tariff. If the government charges a per-unit license fee that is

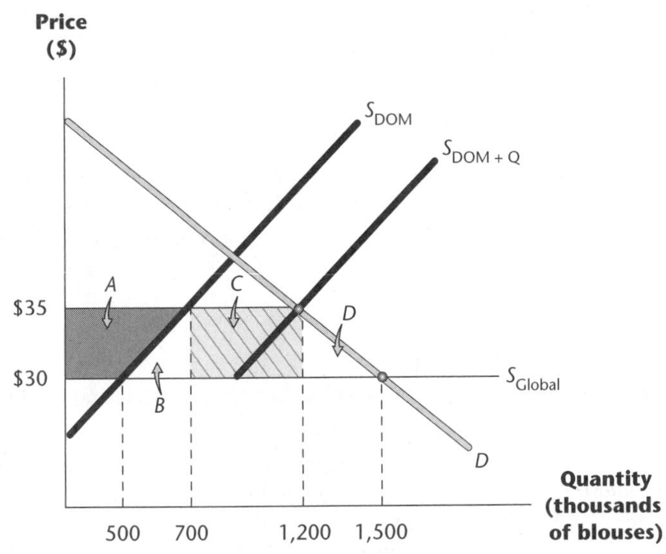

Figure 4-4

The Effects of an Import Quota

The imposition of an import quota results in an excess quantity demanded, thereby generating an increase in the market price. Because of the increase in the market price, consumer surplus falls by an amount equal to the sum of the areas A, B, C, *and* D. *Area* A *is transferred to domestic producers as an increase in producer surplus. Area* C *is a quota rent, whose distribution is determined by the government imposing the import quota. Areas* B *and* D *are deadweight losses.*

protected industry. Area *D,* which equals [(300,000 × $5)/2] = $750,000, is a deadweight loss that results when domestic consumers switch away from the quota-protected good to less desirable substitutes.

Area *C,* which equals (500,000 × $5) = $2.5 million, is a quota rent that is transferred from domestic consumers to another party designated by the domestic government. The domestic government can allocate the quota rent to foreign firms or sell licenses to supply the import good and capture some or the entire quota rent as government quota revenue.

For Critical Analysis:
In which industries do you suppose policymakers are more likely to impose import quotas, goods, or services? Why?

exactly equal to the per-unit quota rent, then all of the quota rent is transferred to the domestic government as revenue. In this case, the redistributive effects of the quota are identical to a tariff. (To further analyze the effects of a quota, see *Visualizing Global Economic Issues: The Effects of an Import Quota.*)

EFFECTS OF A QUOTA IN A LARGE COUNTRY

As you can now see, other than the allocation of the quota rent, tariffs and quotas have similar effects on the market. Earlier you learned that a tariff in a large-country setting can influence the global price of a good or service. A quota applied by the government of a large country can also affect the global price of a product.

At the global price, a quota levied by a large country, like a tariff, creates an excess quantity supplied of a product in the global market. This excess quantity supplied causes the global price of the good or service to decline. As a result, producer surplus of foreign firms falls. Some of the loss of foreign producer surplus is transferred to foreign consumers due to a decline in the price per unit that they must pay.

A quota rent is another portion of the loss of foreign producer surplus. Foreign producers may be able to recapture this, depending on how the government of the large country allocates the rights to sell under the quota. The remainder of the loss of foreign producer surplus represents the deadweight losses created by a large-country government imposition of the quota.

3 Fundamental Issue

What are quotas, and how do they represent a direct approach to restricting trade?

An import quota is a restriction on the amount of a particular good or service that domestic residents can import during a specific time period. A quota directly affects the quantity of imports, whereas a tariff indirectly influences quantity by altering the product price. A domestic government may allocate the quota rent to foreign firms or charge for licenses that authorize foreign firms to fill the quota. Hence, the welfare effects of a quota and a tariff may differ, depending on how the quota rent is distributed.

Voluntary Export Restraints

Voluntary export restraint (VER) *An agreement between policymakers and producers in two nations to restrict the exports of a good from one nation to the other.*

Voluntary export restraints are another type of nontariff barrier. They have become more popular among policymakers during the past few decades. A **voluntary export restraint (VER)** is an informal agreement between policymakers in one nation and policymakers and producers in another nation to restrict exports within a particular sector of the economy.

THE APPEAL OF VERs

Because a VER restricts the quantity of imports, it is, in effect, an absolute quota. Why, then, would policymakers in either nation choose to enact a VER as opposed to a formal import quota? One reason is that formal trade legislation can take a long time to finally pass through the necessary government channels. As a result, by the time trade legislation is enacted, it is often much broader than originally intended. In addition, once governments enact formal trade barriers, such barriers are often difficult to repeal. Hence, exporters may find it preferable to restrict their activities on their own instead of submitting themselves to the whims of foreign policymakers. Perhaps the most important motivating factor behind the increased use of VERs is that these agreements are voluntary. Consequently, VERs do not come under the jurisdiction of regulatory bodies that monitor the type of regional and multilateral trade agreements you will learn about in Chapter 5.

U.S. AUTOMOBILES AND JAPANESE VERs

Because of its large consumer market, the United States is the destination of many nations' exports. U.S. policymakers often leverage the size of its lucrative consumer market to pressure foreign governments and exporters to agree to implement VERs.

VERs as a Bilateral Agreement

In the early 1980s, U.S. automobile producers faced both stiff competition from imported Japanese-made economy cars and a downturn in the demand for larger and less fuel-efficient U.S.-produced autos. U.S. automobile producers and labor representatives of U.S. automobile workers responded by lobbying the U.S. government for protection.

U.S. and Japanese policymakers, and Japanese automobile manufacturers, reacted by negotiating a VER on Japanese autos. The agreement called for a physical limit to the number of automobiles that Japanese manufacturers would export to the United States. The VER did not limit, however, automobiles manufactured in *other* nations for export to the United States or by Japanese producers operating within the United States.

VERs and Prices

A VER, like an import quota, causes the domestic price to rise. Hence, a VER is a bilateral agreement that only indirectly affects imports from producers in another nation through its effect on price. An unintended consequence of the Japanese VER with the United States is that it helped European automobile manufacturers who exported automobiles to the United States.

In the case of the Japanese automobile manufacturers, the price effect of the VER had a significant effect on the *type* of car exported. Because there was an agreement on quantity, but not on price, Japanese automobile manufacturers switched from exporting economy cars to more luxurious automobiles, which proved to be lucrative. In the late 1980s, the U.S. government ended its request for export restraints. Because Japanese automobile manufacturers were experiencing higher revenues producing luxury cars for export to the United States, they were slow to increase their exports of ordinary automobiles.

EFFECTS OF VERs

A VER establishes an informal quota on exports, so its economic effects are similar to the effects of a quota. Because the domestic price rises, there is a loss of domestic consumer surplus. Part of this surplus is transferred to domestic producers in the form of higher revenue per unit. Deadweight losses are another portion of the loss of consumer surplus. A rent, similar to a quota rent, is also part of the loss of domestic consumer surplus. Unlike a quota, however, the rent accrues to the foreign producers that agree to the VER.

Because VERs are a bilateral agreement, third-country effects are an important difference between a VER and a quota. By agreeing to restrict automobile exports to the United States, for example, the Japanese VER offered protection to automobile manufacturers in other nations who exported their autos to the United States. Hence, part of the loss of domestic consumer surplus was transferred to third-country automobile manufacturers in the form of higher revenues on automobiles exported to the U.S. market.

What are voluntary export restraints?

Voluntary export restraints (VERs) are informal agreements between policymakers in an importing country and policymakers and producers in another country to restrict the quantity of a product exported for a specified time period. VERs are similar to quotas in the way that they affect price, quantity, and their redistributive effects. One important difference, however, is that the quota rent is always transferred to foreign producers. Because they are voluntary agreements, VERs typically do not come under the jurisdiction of regional and multilateral trade regulators.

Export Subsidies and Countervailing Duties

Domestic industry and worker advocacy groups often argue to policymakers that they face "unfair" competition from abroad. Frequently, they claim that foreign governments subsidize firms, enabling foreign firms to sell their products abroad at lower prices than they do in their own markets or below the cost of production.

Export subsidy
A payment by a government to a domestic firm for exporting its goods or services.

An **export subsidy** is a payment by a domestic government to a domestic firm for exporting goods or services. A government can provide an export subsidy either as a specific amount per unit exported or as a percent of the value of the exported goods or services. Governments specifically design export subsidies to promote exports and increase revenues of domestic firms.

EFFECTS OF AN EXPORT SUBSIDY

As with a tariff, a quota, and a VER, an export subsidy influences the market price and the quantity consumed. Because of this influence on price and quantity, an export subsidy also has redistributive effects.

Price and Quantity Effects of a Subsidy

For ease of analysis, let's consider a two-country setting in which the foreign government provides an export subsidy to firms in the foreign country. Foreign firms receive a payment for every unit exported, which induces them to increase the amount they export, thereby increasing the supply of the product in the global market. Because global supply increases, the global market price declines. The price that residents in the domestic nation must pay for imports of the product declines as well. As the domestic price falls, the quantity demanded by domestic consumers rises and the quantity supplied by domestic firms falls. Hence, the imposition of the subsidy by the foreign government generates an increase in the amount imported by domestic residents.

Redistributive Effects of a Subsidy

The redistributive effects of an export subsidy also mirror those of a tariff. Suppose that, in our two-country setting, the foreign government subsidizes steel exports. Because the foreign subsidy causes the domestic price of steel to fall, domestic consumer surplus increases. Domestic manufacturers, for example, can now purchase steel at a lower price, reducing their overall costs of production. The decline in the domestic price of steel, however, reduces domestic steel producers' surplus.

DUMPING

By promoting exports, the subsidy induces foreign firms to place more attention on exporting their output as opposed to selling it in their home market. Dumping can be defined two ways. The definition used most often by economists is that **dumping** occurs when a firm charges foreign consumers a price that is lower than the price it charges its domestic consumers. The second is that dumping occurs when a firm prices its exports below their cost of production.

Dumping
A situation in which a firm sells its output to foreign consumers at a price that is less than what the firm charges its domestic consumers, or when a foreign firm prices its exports below their cost of product.

Is Dumping Harmful to Domestic Firms?

As you will learn in more detail in Chapter 11, domestic firms typically claim that dumping by foreign firms costs domestic firms revenues they would otherwise earn if global trade were "fair." The lost revenues, they claim, are a combination of the decline in the revenue per unit on quantities that domestic firms continue to sell to domestic consumers and the previous domestic price times the reduction in the quantity they sell. Note, however, that firms that use the *dumped* good as an input in their production process receive a benefit. Foreign governments, in effect, subsidize production for these domestic firms.

Countervailing Duties

Sometimes domestic workers and firms in an industry are successful in arguing that, through the use of production subsidies, foreign governments support foreign firms and harm the domestic industry. If the domestic government is able to determine that the foreign industry is subsidized by its government and that it inflicted harm on domestic producers, then by the rules of most regional and multilateral trade arrangements (described in more detail in Chapters 5 and 11), the domestic government is allowed to impose a countervailing duty.

A **countervailing duty (CVD)** is a tax on imported goods—a tariff—designed to offset the domestic price effect of foreign export subsidies. By taxing imports and raising the domestic price, domestic producers' revenue per unit rises and domestic producer surplus increases. If the CVD is equal to the subsidy, the gain in surplus that domestic consumers previously experienced from the foreign subsidy is lost.

Countervailing duty (CVD)
A tax on imported goods and services designed to offset the domestic price effect of foreign export policies.

In 2000, the U.S. government and U.S. firms initiated nearly 40 investigations of foreign subsidies to industries, of which 80 percent were in the steel industry. Other industries where claims of foreign subsidies and subsequent dumping are being investigated include chemicals and plastics, mechanical appliances, textiles, food and agricultural products, and paper and wood.

As you can imagine, foreign subsidies, dumping investigations, and retaliatory duties result in considerable losses of economic efficiency. As you will learn in the next section, the costs of protection can be very high. (To get a glimpse of how trade policies can multiply, see on the next page *Policy Notebook: Bananas and Carousels: Is This the Way to Fair Trade?*)

What are the effects of export subsidies, and how do policymakers typically react to export promotion policies?

An export subsidy is a payment to firms for selling abroad. Providing an export subsidy increases global supply and drives down the global price and the price in the domestic market. The lower price per unit reduces domestic producer surplus and increases domestic consumer surplus. Governments often react to the claims of dumping and unfair trade by firms and labor groups by imposing a countervailing duty (CVD). A CVD is designed to offset the effect the subsidy has on the domestic price.

Trade Barriers and Their Costs

In this chapter you have learned that tariff and non-tariff trade barriers have redistributive effects and, in most cases, cause a net loss of welfare. Why then, do policymakers continue to use these instruments?

One common explanation is that those who benefit from trade barriers—firms and workers in protected industries—share a common objective, are relatively few in number (thereby benefiting considerably from protection), and therefore are easy to organize. Those who pay the costs of protection—domestic consumers, in particular—do not share a common view on trade, are relatively large in number (thereby the individual costs of protection are rather small), and are therefore not easily organized. Hence, those who benefit from protection are able to lobby policymakers much more effectively than those who pay the costs.

Many other arguments for trade barriers are covered in later chapters. What we are concerned with here is whether trade barriers are the "best" policy approach.

First-best trade policy *A trade policy that deals directly with the problem that policymakers seek to remedy.*

Second-best trade policy *A trade policy that deals indirectly with a problem that policymakers seek to remedy.*

FIRST- AND SECOND-BEST POLICIES

To gauge the appropriateness of a particular policy, economists often consider whether the policy is a first- or second-best response. A **first-best trade policy** is a policy that deals directly with the problem that the policy is designed to remedy. A **second-best trade policy** is a policy that attempts to remedy a problem through indirect means.

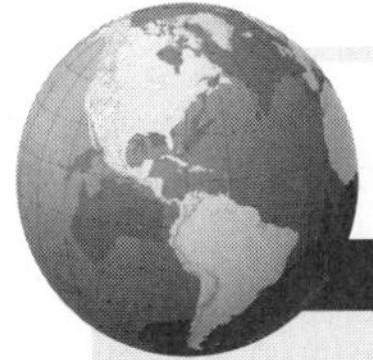

POLICY *Notebook*

POLICY MANAGEMENT

Bananas and Carousels: Is This the Way to Fair Trade?

During the 1990s, trade representatives from the United States and the European Union were locked in a heated dispute over the EU practice of giving preferential treatment to banana producers in the former French and United Kingdom colonies of Africa, the Caribbean, and the Pacific. U.S. officials claimed that the EU's preferential treatment harmed Latin American growers. Not by coincidence, the U.S. firms Dole Foods and Chiquita Brands International are the principal distributors of Latin American–grown bananas.

The United States took its case to the World Trade Organization, an international trade governing body, which ruled in favor of the United States. The ruling gave the United States the authorization to impose duties on European products. In 1999, the United States imposed duties, most at a rate of 100 percent, on more than $190 million worth of European goods such as *Louis Vuitton* handbags, Roquefort cheese, and sausage casings. The U.S. government intended for the duties to force the European Union to abandon the banana regime.

Carousel Tariffs

The U.S. government viewed the concessionary changes to the EU regime to be unsatisfactory, and in 2000 the U.S. Congress recommended to the office of the U.S. Trade Representative to enforce a *carousel tariff policy,* in which the trade representative periodically changes the list of goods subject to the duties. The idea behind a carousel tariff approach is to spread the pain of duties to a large number of EU industries. The hope was that EU policymakers will receive more complaints and drop the banana regime.

Congress expanded the list of goods to more than $3 million worth of European products. A few items, such as Roquefort cheese remained on the list. New products included sweet biscuits and wafers from the United Kingdom, Italian Pecorino cheese, and Spanish paprika.

Veto Power to U.S. Firms?

In response to the U.S. Trade Representative's inaction on Congress's recommendations, Senator Trent Lott, a Republican from Mississippi, attempted to force through the U.S. Congress a bill that would give Chiquita the right to veto any proposed settlement to the banana regime. European policymakers were outraged by the unprecedented power that Chiquita would have if the bill were passed, further inflaming the dispute between the two powers.

For Critical Analysis:

Should firms have the right to approve bilateral trade agreements? Should firms receive the revenue generated by countervailing duties imposed to offset export promotion policies?

Suppose, for example, that firms and workers in a particular industry seek protection from foreign competition because foreign producers are more efficient and able to produce at a lower cost. A first-best policy deals directly with the inefficiency of the domestic industry. A trade barrier is a second-best policy because it indirectly deals with the problem of less-efficient domestic firms by raising the domestic price of the good or service to compensate for the inefficiency.

THE COSTS OF PROTECTION

Because trade barriers are second-best policy responses, they create additional economic inefficiencies. These deadweight losses make trade protection a very costly policy action.

During the last few years, the Institute for International Economics in Washington, D.C., has commissioned several studies in an attempt to measure the costs of protection in various nations. The authors of these studies examined protected sectors and determined the benefits to consumers, costs to domestic producers, and the gains in economic efficiencies that would result from removing existing trade barriers. The authors also considered the cost of protecting a job in the domestic industry.

Table 4-5 illustrates these costs for four nations, China, Japan, Korea, and the United States. (Note that some of the figures are in terms of the U.S. dollar and others are not. Some data for European industries are provided in Chapter 5.) Column 1 identifies the nations, and column 2 identifies the particular industry.

Table 4-5 The Costs of Protection

Source: Data from Shuguang, Yansheng and Zhongxin (1998), Sazanami, Urato and Hiroki (1995), Kim (1996), Hufbauer and Elliot (1994).

Product	Change in Consumer Surplus	Change in Producer Surplus	Deadweight Loss	Cost of Preserving Job To Consumers	Cost of Preserving Job In Loss of Efficiency
China		($ millions)		($)	($)
Sugar	1,497	543	285	5,059	964
Plywood	685	104	58	23,338	1,968
Motorcycles	1,746	635	137	56,721	4,460
Color Televisions	227	139	4	15,859	305
Japan		(¥ billions)		(¥ millions)	(¥ millions)
Clothing	878.9	221.6	234.9	63.7	17.0
Pharmaceuticals	182.9	151.0	0.9	153.5	0.8
Cosmetics	500.6	102.1	351.0	213.3	149.5
Semiconductor Devices	1,046.6	538.3	332.4	44.9	13.9
Korea		(won billions)		(won millions)	(won millions)
Beef	771	453	82	30	5
Milled Rice	3,469	3,102	367	15	3
Dairy Products	1,289	1,066	94	241	49
Cosmetics	29	24	1	139	24
United States		($ millions)		($ thousands)	($ thousands)
Women's Handbags	148	16	13	191,462	16,818
Canned Tuna	73	31	4	187,179	25,641
Sugar	1,357	776	185	600,177	256,966
Peanuts	54	32	22	136,020	55,416

Column 3 provides the increase in consumer surplus that would result from removing the barriers, column 4 provides the decrease in producer surplus, and column 5 the deadweight loss that would be transferred back to domestic consumers. Columns 6 and 7 show the costs of protecting the average job in the industry in terms of consumer costs and losses of economic efficiency.

As you can see in the table, the costs of protecting these domestic industries are very high. More importantly, the loss of economic efficiency makes the cost of preserving a single domestic job very expensive—more expensive than the income that each worker would typically receive. In the United States, for example, the annual cost to consumers from preserving a job in the women's handbag industry is nearly $200,000, which is considerably more than what the average worker receives in the industry.

In the case of the United States, the study found that the average annual cost to consumers of preserving a job across all industries was $170,000. It would actually be cheaper to buy the imported goods and pay idle workers their salaries than to protect the domestic industry.

Fundamental Issue 6

What are the advantages and disadvantages of trade barriers?

There are many explanations for why policymakers resort to trade barriers. One commonly held view is that domestic firms and workers that benefit from trade protection are better organized than the consumers who pay the costs of protection. Because they are well organized, firms and workers can lobby policymakers more effectively. A first-best policy is a policy that deals directly with the problem the policy is designed to remedy. Trade barriers are second-best policies because they only indirectly deal with the problems that policymakers seek to remedy. As second-best policies, trade barriers are costly to domestic consumers and entail considerable losses of economic efficiency.

CHAPTER SUMMARY

1) **The Effect of Taxes on Domestic Price, and the Redistributive Effects of Taxes:** The imposition of a tax causes the supply of a good or service to decrease. This decline in supply generates an increase in the market price. Although the market price rises, it typically does not rise by the full amount of the tax. Because the tax influences market outcomes, it has redistributive effects. A tax is forward shifted if the consumer must pay the tax in the form of a higher price per unit. A tax is backward shifted if producers must pay the tax in the form of a lower price per unit.
2) **Economic Effects of Tariff Barriers:** A specific tariff is calculated as a fixed tariff amount per unit, whereas an *ad valorem* tariff is calculated as a percent of the value of the good or service. A combination tariff consists of a specific tariff component and an *ad valorem* component. A tariff imposed by policymakers in a small country does not affect the global price. As a result, the domestic price rises by the full amount of the tariff, and the entire tariff is

forward shifted to domestic consumers. A tariff imposed by policymakers in a large country may cause the global price to decline. In this setting, part of the tariff is forward shifted to domestic consumers and part is backward shifted to foreign producers. It is in this sense that a large-country tariff is a beggar-thy-neighbor policy. For both small and large countries, a tariff results in net welfare losses, either at home or abroad.

3) **Quotas as a Direct Approach to Restricting Trade:** An import quota is a policy limiting the amount of a good or service that can enter a country during a specified time period. A quota directly affects the quantity of imports, whereas a tariff indirectly affects the quantity of imports by first affecting the price. An absolute quota establishes a quantitative limit. A tariff-rate quota allows a specific quantity to enter the country at a reduced tariff rate. If the government collects the quota rent in the form of an import license, then a quota and an equivalent tariff have identical redistributive effects.
4) **Voluntary Export Restraints:** A voluntary export restraint (VER) is an informal agreement between policymakers and producers in two nations to restrict the quantity of a product exported from one nation to the other. Because they are voluntary agreements, VERs typically do not come under the scrutiny of regional and multilateral trade agreements. The price, quantity, and distributive effects of VERs are similar to those of a quota. One important difference between a quota and a VER is that the quota rent is always transferred to foreign producers.
5) **Effects of an Export Subsidy, and the Reaction of Policymakers to Export Promotion Policies:** An export subsidy is a payment to a firm for exporting their output as opposed to selling it in the domestic market. Governments design export subsidies to increase the revenue of domestic firms. From the perspective of firms and consumers in the importing country, export subsidies have effects similar to the removal of a tariff, because they increase supply in the global market and drive down the domestic price. The decrease in domestic price results in an increase in domestic consumer surplus and a decrease in domestic producer surplus. Often policymakers will answer the claims of dumping and unfair trade by domestic industry and labor groups by imposing a countervailing duty (CVD). A CVD is intended to offset the effect that an export subsidy has on domestic price.
6) **Advantages and Disadvantages of Trade Barriers:** One explanation for why policymakers continue to use trade barriers in spite of their high costs is that the groups that benefit from trade protection are highly organized, while those that pay the costs of protection are not. Because they are highly organized, firms and labor groups can effectively lobby for protection. A first-best policy deals directly with the problem the policy is designed to remedy. Trade barriers are second-best policies that deal indirectly with the problem that policymakers seek to remedy. Hence, trade barriers entail greater economic inefficiencies and are costly. Recent studies of the costs of protection show that, on average, the cost of preserving a job in a protected industry typically is much greater than the income received by the worker whose job is saved.

QUESTIONS AND PROBLEMS

1) Suppose that policymakers *eliminate* tariffs on imported pharmaceuticals. For a specific drug, the tariff originally was $0.60 per unit, and the domestic price with the tariff in place was $2.90. Now, under free trade, the domestic price is $2.50. With the tariff, the domestic quantity demanded was 14 million units, and domestic quantity supplied was 6 million. Now under free trade, the domestic quantity demanded is 20 million, and the domestic quantity supplied is 4 million.
   (a) Is the country in question a large country or a small country? Explain your answer.
   (b) Illustrate this example in a supply and demand framework for the home country *and* the international market.
2) Using the diagram you constructed in question 1, answer the following questions.
   (a) What is the value of the gain to the domestic consumers due to the removal of the tariff?
   (b) What is the value of the loss to the domestic producers due to the removal of the tariff?
   (c) What is the value of the loss of tariff revenue due to the removal of the tariff?
3) In questions 1 and 2, does the home country experience a net welfare gain or loss from the removal of the tariff?
4) Is the statement, "A tariff on imports *always* leads to a reduction of domestic welfare," true, false, or uncertain? Explain your answer.
5) Consider the following situation for a nation in a small-country setting that has an import quota on men's shirts.

	With Quota	**Free Trade**
Price	$45	$30
Quantity Purchased	1 million	1.2 million
Domestic Quantity Supplied	400,000	300,000
Quota	600,000	None

   (a) Illustrate the effects of the quota in a supply and demand framework.
   (b) Indicate in your diagram and calculate:
      i. The loss of consumer surplus
      ii. The gain in domestic producer surplus
      iii. The deadweight losses
      iv. The quota rent

6) Suppose that policymakers in the nation depicted in question 5 would like to switch from a quota to a tariff. What is the equivalent tariff rate for a specific tariff? For an *ad valorem* tariff? What benefits would there be to switching from a quota to a tariff?
7) Suppose that, to protect domestic producers from "unfair" competition, policymakers impose a countervailing duty on imported automobiles. Should domestic automakers receive the duty? Why or why not?
8) Suppose that under free trade, the global price of automobiles is $20,000. At this price, the quantity supplied in a small country, Country 1, is 750,000. Producers in Country 2 supply 500,000 autos to consumers in country 1 and producers in Country 3 supply 2.25 million autos to consumers in Country 1. Now suppose that policymakers in Country 1 and Country 3 agree to a VER that restricts the quantity of automobiles exported from Country 3 to Country 1 to 1 million. Because of the VER, the price in Country 1 rises to $25,000, the quantity supplied by producers in Country 1 rises to 1.25 million, and the quantity supplied by producers in Country 2 rises to 550,000.
   (a) Diagram the situation described above in a supply and demand framework for Country 1.
   (b) Who benefits from the VER? Who is harmed?
9) Each year consumers of a small country purchase 1 million pounds of sugar at the global price of $1.50 per pound. Domestic firms produce 500,000 pounds and domestic consumers import the remainder. Policymakers of the world's major supplier of sugar begin an export subsidy program that rewards firms for exporting sugar. This program causes the global price of sugar to drop to $1 per pound. The domestic quantity demanded in the small country climbs to 1.3 million pounds, and the domestic quantity supplied falls to 300,000 pounds.
   (a) Diagram the small-country market for sugar under free trade and with the export subsidy in place.
   (b) Calculate the loss of domestic producer surplus and the increase in domestic consumer surplus.
   (c) What is the total value of the subsidy in the small-country market?
   (d) Can you identify any deadweight losses?
10) Based on the information in question 9, what is the *ad valorem* countervailing duty rate that would restore the domestic price in the small country to its free trade level? Who do you think is entitled to the revenue generated by the countervailing duty?

ONLINE APPLICATION

Internet URL: http://dataweb.usitc.gov

Title: **U.S. International Trade Commission Interactive Tariff and Trade Data Web**

Navigation: Start at the home page for the U.S. International Trade Commission's Interactive Tariff and Trade Date Web (http://dataweb.usitc.gov). Scroll down to "Current Tariffs" and click on the most recent annual "Tariff Database." Click on "Yes, go to USITC Tariff Database."

Application: Suppose that, before enrolling in a course on international economics, you purchased a notebook that cost $3.00, a mechanical pencil that cost $5.00, and a backpack that cost $30.00, and that all three items were imported. Perform the following operations, and answer the following questions.

1) At the query window of the USITC Database enter *notebook* or 48201020. Click on detail. Record the "NTR Duty Rate" for a notebook.
2) Click your browser's *back* button twice. Enter *pencils* in the query window. Click on the first category, numbers 96084040. Record the "NTR Duty Rate" for a mechanical pencil.
3) Click your browser's *back* button twice. Enter 42029230 in the query window. Click on "Detail." Record the "NTR Duty Rate."
4) Based on the tariff rates you retrieved, what is the total amount that you paid in tariffs?

For Group Study and Analysis: Calculate the total amount of tariffs paid by the class. (In other words, multiply your answer to 4 above by the number of students in the class.) Divide into three smaller groups. One group should represent consumers, another should represent domestic producers, and the third should represent foreign producers. Debate the costs and benefits of the tariffs on these three items.

REFERENCES AND RECOMMENDED READINGS

Bagwell, Kyle, and Robert W. Staiger. "Strategic Export Subsidies and Reciprocal Trade Agreements: The Natural Monopoly Case." National Bureau of Economic Research, Working Paper No. 5574 (1996).

Baier, Scott L., and Jeffrey H. Bergstrand. "The Growth of World Trade: Tariffs, Transport Costs, and Income Similarity." *Journal of International Economics* 53 (1) (February 2001): 1–27.

Batra, Ravi. "Are Tariffs Inflationary?" *Review of International Economics* 9 (3) (August 2001): 378–382.

Bergsten, Fred. "Globalizing Free Trade." *Foreign Affairs* 75 (3) (May–June 1996): 105–120.

Berry, Steven, James Levinsohn, and Ariel Pakes. "Voluntary Export Restraints on Automobiles: Evaluating a Trade Policy." *American Economic Review* 89 (3) (June 1999): 400–430.

Collie, David R. "A Rationale for the WTO Prohibition of Export Subsidies: Strategic Export Subsidies and World Welfare." *Open Economics Review* 11 (3) (July 2000): 229–249.

Daly, Michael, and Sergios Stamnas. "Tariff and Non-tariff Barriers to Trade in Korea." *Journal of Economic Integration* 16 (4) (December 2001): 500–525.

Ethier, Wilfred J. "Unilateralism in a Multilateral World." *Economic Journal* 112 (479) (April 2002): 266–292.

Gould, David M., and William C. Gruben. "Will Fair Trade Diminish Free Trade?" *Business Economics* 32 (2) (April 1997): 7–13.

Hickson, Charles. "The WTO, the IMF, and the Impact of Their Free-Trade Policies on Developing Nations." *Global Business and Economics Review* 3 (2) (December 2001): 175–185.

Hufbauer, Gary Clyde, and Kimberly Ann Elliott. *Measuring the Costs of Protection in the United States.* Washington, D.C.: The Institute for International Economics, 1994.

Irwin, Douglas. "Changes in U.S. Tariffs: The Role of Import Prices and Commercial Policies." *American Economic Review* 88 (4) (1998): 1015–1026.

Kim, Namdoo. *Measuring the Costs of Visible Protection in Korea.* Washington, D.C.: The Institute for International Economics, 1996.

Lahiri, Sajal et al. "Optimal Foreign Aid and Tariffs." *Journal of Development Economics* 67 (1) (February 2002): 79–99.

Mastel, Greg. "The U.S. Steel Industry and Antidumping Law." *Challenge* 42 (3) (May–June 1999): 84–94.

McCorriston, Steve, and Ian M. Sheldon. "Selling Import Quota Licenses: The U.S. Cheese Case." *America Journal of Agricultural Economics* 76 (4) (November 1994): 818–827.

Paarlberg, Robert. The Political Economy of U.S. Export Subsidies for Wheat: Comment. *The Political Economy of American Trade Policy* (1996): 332–334.

Sazanami, Yoko, Shujiro Urato, and Kawai Hiroki. *Measuring the Costs of Protection in Japan.* Washington, D.C.: The Institute for International Economics, 1995.

Shivakumar, Ram. "Strategic Trade Policy: Choosing between Export Subsidies and Export Quotas under Uncertainty." *Journal of International Economics* 35 (1–2) (August 1993): 169–183.

Shuguang, Zhang, Zhang Yansheng, and Wan Zhongxin. *Measuring the Costs of Protection in China.* Washington, D.C.: The Institute for International Economics, 1998.

Tokarick, Stephen. "Export Promotion: The Role of Transportation Subsidies." *Journal of Economic Studies* 23 (4) (1996): 50–63.

Watts, Julie R. "Immigration policy and the challenge of globalization: Unions and employers in unlikely alliance." Ithaca and London: Cornell University, ILR Press, 2002.

Xiangqun, Chen. "Competition and the Equivalence of Tariffs and Quotas." *American Economist* 38 (2) (Fall 1994): 36–39.

CHAPTER FIVE

Regionalism and Multilateralism

Fundamental Issues

1. **What are the main types of regional trade agreements, and how do economists measure trade within regional trading groups?**
2. **How is a free trade area such as the North American Free Trade Agreement different from other types of preferential trade arrangements?**
3. **What distinguishes customs unions such as the European Economic Community of the 1970s and the current Andean Community from common markets such as the European Union and Mercosur?**
4. **How can regional trading arrangements lead to both trade creation and trade diversion?**
5. **What is trade deflection, and how do rules of origin help to limit the extent to which trade deflection occurs?**
6. **How do multilateral trade agreements contrast with regional trade arrangements?**

To its proponents, the time was right to seriously consider a proposal whose time they believed had come. To its opponents, the time had finally arrived to reject an especially zany idea. At the request of the Senate Finance Committee, the U.S. International Trade Commission, a federal agency that makes trade recommendations to both the president and Congress, held special hearings in 2000 to consider the proposal to allow another nation to join the United States, Canada, and Mexico within the North American Free Trade Agreement (NAFTA). This island nation once fought two wars against the United States. Nevertheless, it has for some time had a particularly close political and economic relationship with Canada, and its relationship with the United States is also very close. The nation is the United Kingdom.

The United Kingdom was not the first country from outside North America to be considered for membership in NAFTA. Just a few years earlier, there had been serious discussion of admitting Chile into the free-trade area. That idea has never completely been ruled out, but it failed to attract sufficient interest to advance beyond the "consideration" stage. Proponents of NAFTA membership for the United Kingdom were hopeful that they could push their idea much further.

Even as the International Trade Commission's hearings commenced, officials within the U.S. and U.K. governments were casting cold water on the idea, and so far, the idea has not progressed to the stage of a formal proposal. Nevertheless, a few important leaders in the U.S. Congress and the U.K. Parliament have continued to push for formal consideration of U.K membership in NAFTA. To British enthusiasts, NAFTA membership would make it easier for the United Kingdom to avoid becoming politically entangled in the European Union (EU) while reaping benefits of broadened trade with both continental Europe and North America. U.S. proponents also have broad strategies in mind: They believe that bringing the United Kingdom under the NAFTA umbrella would help to restrain alleged protectionist leanings of the EU. British entry into NAFTA, they argue, would force the EU to drop rules giving its central body, the European Commission, sole power to negotiate trade deals on behalf of its members.

Would it make sense for European or South American nations to be part of the North American Free Trade Agreement? To evaluate this question, you must first understand the issues raised by regional trading agreements such as NAFTA. As you will learn, such trading arrangements can potentially either encourage or discourage international trade.

Regional Trade Blocs

During recent years there has been a proliferation of special trade deals among nations granting trade preferences in the form of reduced or eliminated tariffs, duties, or quotas. There are currently more than 130 bilateral or regional trade agreements in effect around the globe.

REGIONAL TRADE AGREEMENTS

Nearly half of the current regional trade agreements were adopted after 1990, and a number of these establish *regional trade blocs,* or countries that have granted preferential trade status to one or more nations.

Preferential trade arrangement
A trading arrangement in which a nation grants partial trade preferences to one or more trading partners.

Free trade area
A trading arrangement that removes all barriers to trade among participating nations but that allows each nation to retain its own restrictions on trade with countries outside the free trade area.

Customs union
A trading arrangement that entails eliminating barriers to trade among participating nations and common barriers to trade with other countries outside the group.

Common market
A trading arrangement under which member nations remove all barriers to trade among their group, erect common barriers to trade with other countries outside the group, and permit unhindered movements of factors of production within the group.

Economic union
A trading arrangement that commits participating nations to remove all barriers to trade among their group, to abide by common restrictions on trade with other countries outside the group, to allow unhindered movements of factors of production within the group, and to closely coordinate all economic policies with other participants.

Regionalism
Establishment of trading agreements among geographic groupings of nations.

There are five basic types of regional trade agreements.

1) **Preferential trade arrangements:** The least restrictive sort of regional trade agreement is a **preferential trade arrangement,** under which a nation grants partial trade preferences to a set of trading partners. Often a preferential trade arrangement is one-sided. In some cases, however, nations can form *reciprocal* arrangements. These entail the establishment of equal trade preferences among two or more trading partners.
2) **Free trade area:** One type of reciprocal trade arrangement is a regional trade agreement that establishes a **free trade area.** Within a free trade area, participating nations agree to remove all trade barriers. Each nation, however, retains its own barriers to trade with countries outside the free trade area.
3) **Customs union:** When nations participating in a regional trade agreement go beyond removing trade barriers among themselves and adopt common barriers to trade with other countries, then they have established a **customs union.** To ensure equivalent trade policies, members of a customs union must establish elaborate coordination schemes. In principle, therefore, a customs union entails a more significant commitment as compared with a free trade area.
4) **Common market:** Preferential trade arrangements, free trade areas, and customs unions establish rules breaking down barriers to cross-border trade in goods and services. When countries also agree to remove barriers to free movement of factors of production, they have created a **common market.** Thus, nations that form a common market agree to open cross-border flows of both final outputs of goods and services and inputs used in production.
5) **Economic union:** The next step beyond freeing up cross-border flows of goods, services, and factors of production is to coordinate uniform national economic policies. Countries that take this next step have established an **economic union.** Political union is not technically a prerequisite to economic union, but successful implementation often requires considerable political coordination among participating nations.

Economists are divided about whether this trend toward **regionalism**—the formation of trading agreements among geographic groupings of countries—promotes or discourages trade. Before you can understand why this is an issue, you must first understand how economists measure trade among regional trade blocs. You must also have a broader background on how the various types of regional trading groups function.

MEASURING HOW MUCH REGIONALISM MATTERS FOR TRADE

How much trade takes place among members of regional trading groups? Trying to answer this question first requires considering how to measure the extent of a nation's trade with the rest of the world.

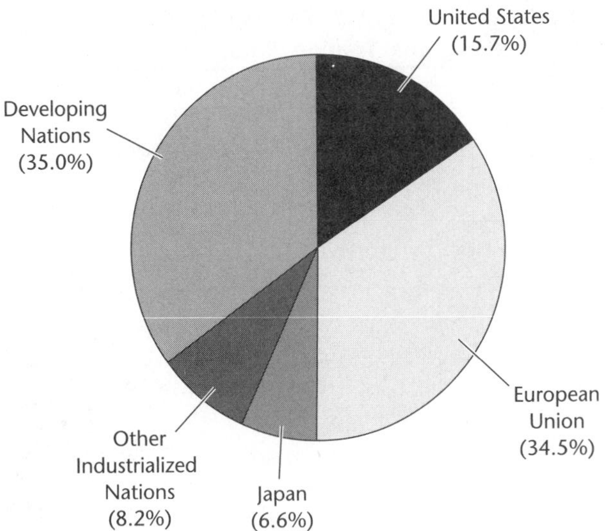

Figure 5-1

World Trade Shares

Industrialized countries account for about two-thirds of total international trade. Together, the United States and the European account for more than half of cross-border trade flows.

Source: International Monetary Fund *Direction of Trade Statistics,* various issues.

Shares of Trade

The most commonly used measure of international trade is the total flow of trade across national borders, which is simply the sum of export and import flows within a given interval. Economists make nations' trade flows comparable by measuring all countries' exports and imports in terms of a common currency, such as the U.S. dollar. Then they often consider **trade shares,** which are a nation's trade flow as percentages of regional or world trade totals.

Trade share
One nation's flow of international trade as a percentage of a regional or global trade total.

Figure 5-1 displays trade shares for the European Union, the United States, Japan, other industrialized nations, and developing nations. These shares are U.S. dollar measures of nations' cross-border trade flows as percentages of the total dollar value of world trade. As the figure indicates, trade crossing the borders of industrialized countries accounts for about two-thirds of total world trade. International trade flowing across EU and U.S. borders alone accounts for more than half of global flows of international trade.

One way to try to determine how much nations within regional trading groups engage in trade with countries inside and outside their trading groups is to examine their shares of regional and world trade. Table 5-1 on the next page shows trade shares for nations within NAFTA, Mercosur, the Andean Community, the Association of Southeast Asian Nations (ASEAN), and the European Union. Note that each EU nation conducts at least half of its trade with other countries within the European Union. Furthermore, Canada and Mexico conduct at least three-fourths of their trade with their other NAFTA partner, the United States.

Figure 5-2 on page 129 displays the aggregate shares of world trade for each of the regional trading groups from Table 5-1. Based on trade-share data, the European Union and NAFTA clearly emerge as important regional trading groups.

Table 5-1 Regional and World Trade Shares of Nations in Selected Regional Trading Blocs

Source: *IMF Direction of Trade Statistics,* 2001.

	Share of Trade with Regional Trading Bloc	Share of World Trade
NAFTA		
United States	32.2	15.48
Canada	78.5	3.96
Mexico	82.9	2.63
Mercosur		
Argentina	26.6	0.47
Brazil	16.0	0.75
Paraguay	58.0	0.04
Uruguay	43.7	0.02
Andean Community		
Bolivia	16.6	0.02
Colombia	15.4	0.19
Ecuador	13.9	0.08
Peru	11.3	0.09
Venezuela	8.4	0.27
ASEAN		
Brunei	40.2	0.03
Indonesia	17.2	0.74
Malaysia	29.7	1.16
Philippines	15.1	0.55
Singapore	34.2	1.74
Thailand	20.9	0.84
European Union		
Austria	65.3	1.08
Belgium	71.6	2.75
Denmark	67.8	0.74
Finland	57.2	0.71
France	63.0	5.05
Germany	54.2	8.08
Greece	54.5	0.30
Ireland	58.3	0.98
Italy	55.6	3.64
Luxembourg	83.3	0.15
Netherlands	65.3	3.43
Portugal	76.1	0.47
Spain	66.6	1.95
Sweden	59.0	1.19
United Kingdom	53.0	4.76

All amounts are percentages.

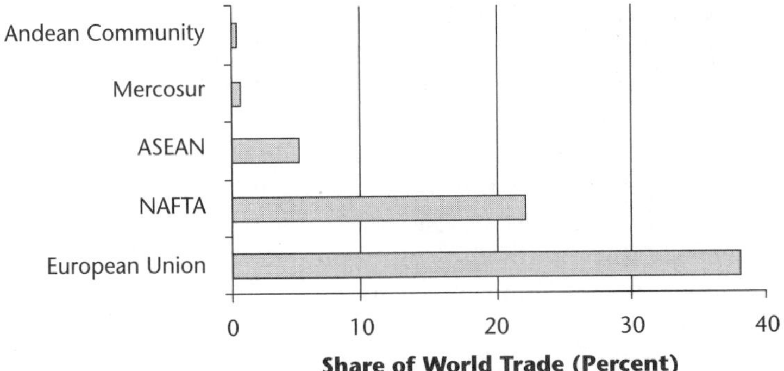

Figure 5-2

Trade Shares of Selected Regional Trade Blocs

The European Union and NAFTA together account for nearly 60 percent of global trade. World trade shares of ASEAN, the Andean Community, and Mercosur are much smaller.

Source: *IMF Direction of Trade Statistics,* 2001.

ASEAN and the two South American blocs, the Andean Community and Mercosur, appear to be much less significant regional trading arrangements.

The Pitfall of Using Trade Shares to Measure Regional Trade

Trade-share statistics must be interpreted with caution, however. It is hardly surprising that the European Union and NAFTA are regional trading groups with large shares of global trade, because nations within those groups engage in the bulk of the world's international trade. Nations within these regional blocs are among the most powerful players in global trade.

Looking back at Table 5-1 indicates that even the smallest EU nation, Luxembourg, engages in more than three times as much international trade as Mercosur's Paraguay. Does being a member of the European Union necessarily make it more likely that Luxembourg will engage in trade with other EU members than Paraguay does with other nations in Mercosur? Conceivably. Because Luxembourg already comprises a relatively larger share of the world economy than Paraguay, however, it is inevitable that Luxembourg trades more with EU nations than Paraguay does with nations within Mercosur.

Luxembourg, of course, is a relatively small country. More dramatically, NAFTA's largest member, the United States, engages in about 57 times more international trade than Venezuela, which conducts more international trade than any other member of the Andean Community. Canada conducts more than fourteen times as much international trade as Venezuela, and even Mexico engages in more than nine times as much trade as Venezuela. Hence, the size of NAFTA's share of world trade as compared with the trade share of the Andean Community at least partly reflects the relatively large trade volumes of NAFTA's members.

Determining how a regional trade arrangement affects trade patterns requires taking into account absolute size differences of nations within the regional trading group. That is, we must use a measure of the relative *intensity* of trade *within* the group. Trade-share measures are useful for indicating whether members of regional trade blocs are powerful players on the world scene, but they fail to indicate just how intensively international trade is concentrated within regional trading groups themselves.

Trade Concentration Ratios

Trade concentration ratio
The sum of bilateral trade shares within a regional trading bloc divided by the region's share of world trade.

To measure the intensity of trade within trading groups, economists have developed a trade measure called the **trade concentration ratio,** which equals the sum of bilateral trade shares within a regional trading bloc divided by the region's share of world trade. For instance, to calculate the trade concentration ratio for NAFTA, we first add together the trade flows between the United States and Canada, between the United States and Mexico, and between Canada and Mexico. Then we divide this sum by the combined trade flow of NAFTA to determine the portion of all three NAFTA members' trade that takes place with other NAFTA members. Finally, we divide this NAFTA trade share by NAFTA's total share of world trade to obtain the NAFTA trade concentration ratio. If NAFTA bilateral trade patterns are simply proportionate to the distribution of its member nations' overall trade with other nations of the world, then the NAFTA trade concentration ratio will equal 1.0. If the trade flows of NAFTA nations tend to be more concentrated within NAFTA, however, then the ratio will exceed 1.0. Hence, a relatively larger trade concentration ratio indicates a relatively greater intensity of trade within a regional trade bloc.

Figure 5-3 displays trade concentration ratios for the Andean Community, Mercosur, ASEAN, the European Union, and NAFTA. If you compare Figure 5-3 with Figure 5-2, you can readily see how important it is to take into account countries' relative importance in world trade. The NAFTA trade concentration ratio of about 1.4 certainly indicates that the United States, Canada, and Mexico trade somewhat more intensively with one another than they do with other countries. Nevertheless, the 17.2 value of the trade concentration ratio for the Andean Com-

Figure 5-3

Trade Concentration Ratios for Selected Regional Trade Blocs

Even though NAFTA and the European have greater shares of world trade, trade concentration ratios, or sums of bilateral trade shares within each regional trading bloc divided by the region's share of world trade, reveal that the intensity of trade is greater within Mercosur and the Andean Community.

Source: IMF *Direction of Trade Statistics.*

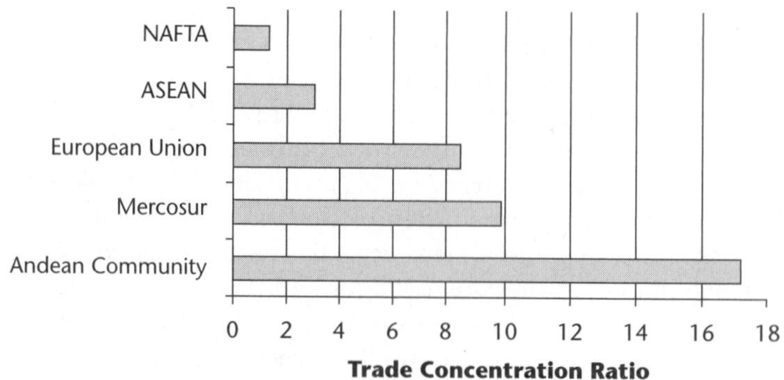

munity is more than 12 times greater than NAFTA's trade concentration ratio. Venezuela and the rest of the Andean Community account for less than 1 percent of global trade, compared with the just over 22 percent trade share of NAFTA. The much higher trade concentration ratio for the Andean Community reflects a significantly greater concentration of their relatively smaller trade volumes within their regional trading group.

The EU trade concentration ratio of about 8.4 implies that intra-EU trade flows are more important to Luxembourg and other EU members than intra-NAFTA flows are to the United States, Canada, and Mexico. Nevertheless, the 9.9 value of Mercosur's trade concentration ratio indicates that a similar trade intensiveness exists among Paraguay and other Mercosur members relative to nations within the European Union.

Fundamental Issue 1

What are the main types of regional trade agreements, and how do economists measure trade within regional trading groups?

The major forms of regional trade agreements are preferential trade arrangements, free trade areas, customs unions, common markets, and economic unions. Economists often measure the extent of trade—the sum of exports and imports—within regional trading groups using trade shares, which are percentages of a nation's trade flows relative to a regional or world total. A country's absolute importance in world trade can distort simple trade share measures, however. Thus, economists measure the intensity of trade within a group of nations using trade concentration ratios, which equal the sum of bilateral trade shares of nations within a regional trading group divided by the region's share of world trade.

Preferential Trade Arrangements and Free Trade Areas

What factors determine whether being part of a regional trading group causes trade with others in that group to increase mildly or dramatically? Before we can address this question, you must first understand in greater detail how each type of regional trade arrangement functions. Let's begin with the weakest trade arrangements, which are preferential trade arrangements and free trade areas.

PREFERENTIAL TRADE ARRANGEMENTS

Hollywood has produced innumerable movies called romantic comedies. Some romantic relationships that Hollywood depicts on the big screen start off very one-sided: One person becomes romantically attracted to another and tries to get him or her to pay attention. Some preferential trade arrangements have mirrored this story line. A country may, for instance, unilaterally lower trade barriers to inflows of goods or services from another nation. This has happened, for instance, when countries facing famine have sought to obtain lower prices on imports of grains and other foodstuffs by eliminating tariffs or duties.

There is also a standard romantic-comedy plot in which an attractive, outgoing, and popular young man or woman takes pity on an especially withdrawn, bashful, and neglected individual. The normal happy ending to such a tale entails two outcomes. First, the popular individual becomes less smug about his or her status. Second, the neglected person experiences a personality transformation and becomes attractive, outgoing, and popular.

A preferential trade arrangement usually is intended to achieve this sort of happy ending for specially selected nations. A good example is the *Caribbean Basin Initiative.* This is a preferential trade arrangement under which the United States gives numerous trade preferences, though only to a specific set of goods, to less-developed Caribbean nations. The United States grants these preferences partly so that its residents can aid their neighbors. It also does so in the hope that greater trade with the United States will enhance growth and development of Caribbean nations, thereby making them better neighbors.

Not all preferential trade arrangements are one-sided affairs. In principle, a group of countries can form a *preferential trade area,* in which they grant reciprocal, partial trade concessions to each member nation. When the concessions entail full elimination of tariffs, duties, and import restrictions, then the countries have established a free trade area.

FREE TRADE AREAS

Most romantic comedies released by Hollywood chronicle complications faced by pairs of fictional characters who meet and then proceed in fits and starts in the direction of perhaps ultimately "tying the knot." Typically, one of the individuals has trouble going beyond just having a relatively informal but steady relationship. A basis for a typical movie plot, therefore, hinges on the difficulties arising from the willingness of a person to "go steady" but his or her inability to "make a commitment."

"Going Steady"

A marriage between two people is more than just a publicly announced commitment. Marriage is also a legal arrangement that links the financial status of a couple. In the eyes of governments, therefore, a marriage is a legally binding *union* of two people. In a way, when two nations form a free trade area, it can be analogous to a couple "going steady": Both parties seek certain benefits of a relationship without entering into a formal union that neither feels certain is in its long-term interest. By granting reciprocal trade preferences, nations may seek to jump-start trade flows that both feel will yield significant gains from trade. Alternatively, they may have in mind deriving benefits from a longer-term relationship—as when some couples choose to live together without a formal marriage—but wish to avoid political entanglements that might arise if they were to enter into a broader and deeper commitment.

The Andean Community, which currently aims to become a common market by 2005, is an example of a free trade area. So is ASEAN, which in 2000 joined

China, Japan, and South Korea in establishing "ASEAN+3." This new organization is exploring the establishment of reciprocal trade preferences but so far has not made significant progress.

The European Free Trade Association (EFTA) is another example of a free trade area. The EFTA is composed of Iceland, Liechenstein, Norway, and Switzerland. It has also worked out preferential trade arrangements with more than twenty countries, including the European Union.

In addition, the Economic Community of West African States continues its efforts to develop a free trade area by harmonizing preferential trade arrangements. So does the recently ratified Community of East and Southern Africa, which includes South Africa and other nations that encompass 300 million people. Australia and New Zealand also constitute a free trade area. There is even an effort under way to establish an all-encompassing Western Hemisphere free trade area, tentatively called the Free Trade Area of the Americas, by an ambitious target date of 2005. In addition, twenty-one nations, including Japan and the United States, make up the Asia Pacific Economic Cooperation (APEC) forum that commits them to establishing a broad free trade area by no later than 2020. Several APEC nations are committed to achieving APEC free-trade goals by as soon as 2010.

ON THE WEB

Visit the APEC home page at http://www.apecsec.org.sg/.

Experience with the North American Free Trade Agreement

The North American Free Trade Agreement is a good example of nations "going steady" while avoiding a commitment to broader forms of trade liberalization. Before NAFTA's establishment in 1994, there was considerable controversy within the United States concerning its entry into the regional trading group. A major worry was that a number of U.S. producers might respond, possibly for some reasons we shall discuss, by shifting operations to Mexico. The result, U.S. NAFTA critics claimed, would be the loss of many U.S. jobs and an increase in U.S. imports from Mexico that would not be accompanied by a rise in U.S. exports to Mexico.

In fact, the U.S. employment picture brightened from the early 1990s, when many producers began developing more trading connections in anticipation of NAFTA's formation, through the early 2000s. As panel (a) in Figure 5-4 on the next page indicates, the Mexican share of U.S. imports did increase substantially between 1990 and 2000, from 6 percent to more than 11 percent. So did the share of exports to Mexico, however. As a share of total U.S. trade, exports to Mexico rose from about 7 percent in 1990 to more than 14 percent in 2000.

NAFTA critics voiced fewer concerns about possible adverse effects of U.S. links with Canada, perhaps because the two countries had already successfully implemented a bilateral free-trade agreement years earlier. Panel (b) shows that, in fact, the formation of NAFTA had little effect on the Canadian shares of U.S. exports and imports. Canadian trade shares barely changed between 1990 and 2000.

Canadian worries about the Mexican connection created by NAFTA were more muted. Most Canadian residents concluded that the potential gains from free trade with the United States would more than offset any complications created by increased trade with Mexico. As panel (a) of Figure 5-5 on page 135 shows, Mexico's shares of Canadian exports and imports have increased since

Figure 5-4

Canadian and Mexican Shares of U.S. Trade since 1980

Panel (a) shows that the 1994 establishment of NAFTA appeared to be associated with a noticeable increase in Mexican shares of U.S. trade, but panel (b) indicates that it did not have a significant effect on Canadian shares of U.S. trades.

Source: IMF *Direction of Trade Statistics.*

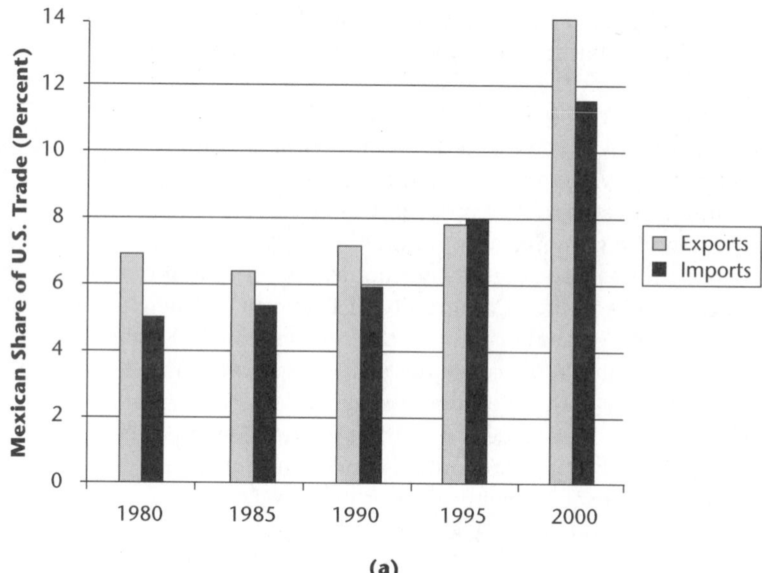

(a)

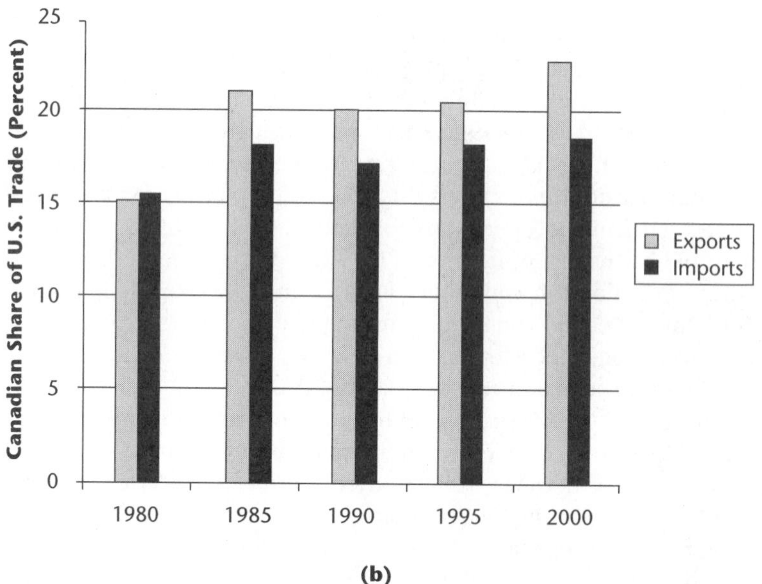

(b)

1990. Nevertheless, they remain relatively small. Canada's U.S. trade shares have risen as well, as shown in panel (b). The U.S. share of its exports has increased from 75 percent to more than 87 percent. The U.S. share of Canadian imports has remained more stable, at around 65 percent.

Figure 5-6 on page 136 displays U.S. and Canadian shares of Mexican trade. Mexico has expanded its trade with several nations, so the U.S. share of Mexican

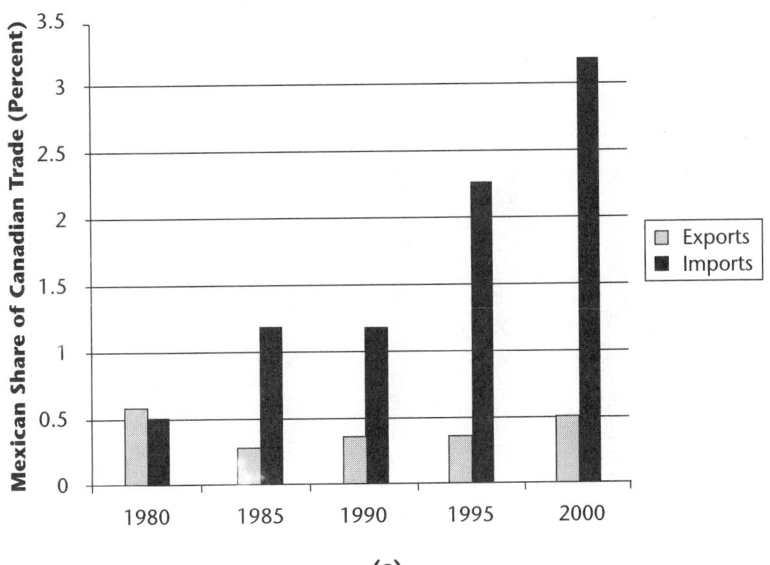

(a)

U.S. Share of Canadian Trade (Percent)

100 90 80 70 60 50 40 30 20 10 0

1980 1985 1990 1995 2000

Exports
Imports

(b)

Figure 5-5

Mexican and U.S. Shares of Canadian Trade since 1980

Panel (a) indicates that Mexico's share of Canadian trade jumped following the 1994 establishment of NAFTA. Panel (b) shows that NAFTA did not appear to result in a large rise in the U.S. share of Canadian trade.

Source: IMF *Direction of Trade Statistics.*

trade has not increased much since 1990. Consistent with the jump in the Mexican share of U.S. exports shown in panel (a) of Figure 5-4, there has been an increase in Mexican imports from the United States.

Panel (b) shows that from Mexico's perspective, NAFTA opened a new horizon in its trade relationship with Canada. Canadian exports and imports were miniscule shares of Mexican trade before the early 1990s. Now Canada is a more

ON THE WEB

Visit the home page of NAFTA at http://www.nafta-sec-alena.org.

Figure 5-6

U.S. and Canadian Shares of Mexico's Trade since 1980

Panel (a) indicates that the U.S. share of Mexico's trade did not noticeably change after the 1994 establishment of NAFTA, but panel (b) indicates that the Canadian share of Mexico's trade rose significantly.

Source: IMF *Direction of Trade Statistics.*

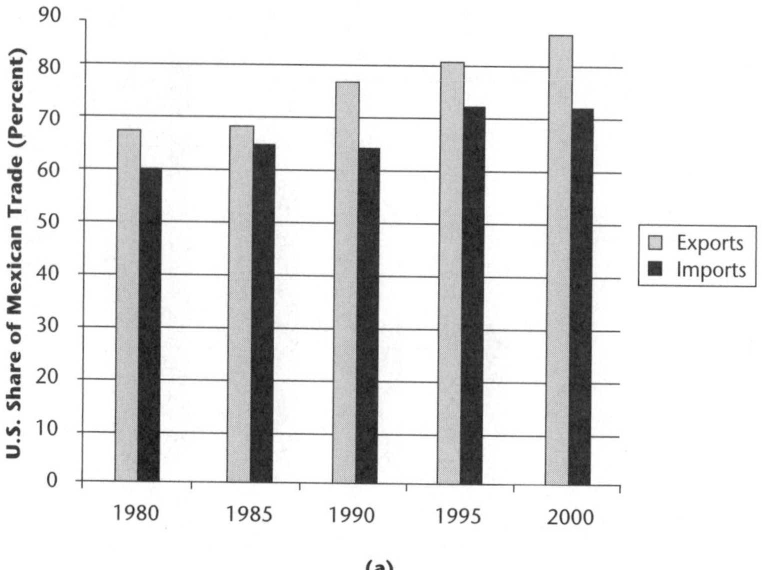

(a)

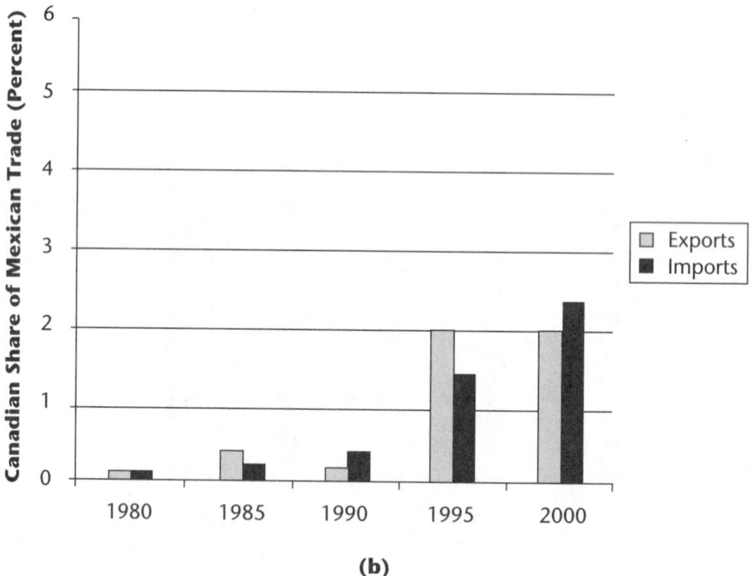

(b)

important export market for Mexican producers, as reflected by a Canadian export share above 2 percent. There has also been a noticeable increase in Mexican imports from Canada.

On net, therefore, the formation of NAFTA has had somewhat more significant effects on Canadian and Mexican trade than it has exerted on U.S. trade patterns. The United States engages in much larger volumes of international trade, so its relatively unchanged trade pattern dominates measures of the intensity of trade within NAFTA. This helps to explain why the NAFTA trade concentration ratio (see Figure 5-3 on page 130) is relatively low.

Fundamental Issue 2

How is a free trade area such as the North American Free Trade Agreement different from other types of preferential trade arrangements?

A preferential trade arrangement establishes trade preferences that apply to specific goods. In addition, it may be one-sided, so that only one nation or group of nations within the preferential trading arrangement benefits. By way of contrast, nations within a free trade area such as NAFTA establish reciprocal trade preferences that apply to all members of the regional trading group. Since the establishment of NAFTA, U.S. exports to Mexico and Mexican trade with Canada have increased notably, but U.S. imports from Mexico and Canadian trade with the United States have not changed dramatically.

Customs Unions and Common Markets

Some nations have been able to make a firmer commitment to longer-term, coordinated trade relationships. A few have formed customs unions, and some have taken a bigger step beyond just "going steady" by establishing common markets.

CUSTOMS UNIONS: TREATING OUTSIDERS EQUALLY

As we discussed earlier, a customs union differs from a free trade area in one fundamental way. Besides agreeing to treat themselves preferentially in trade, nations that are members of a customs union also commit themselves to adopting identical trade policies with respect to nations outside the customs union.

The Treaty of Rome and the European Economic Community

The most important customs union of the twentieth century existed in Europe from 1957 to 1968. It was important for two reasons. First, the major trading countries of Western Europe were members. Second, it blossomed into the European Economic Community, which established a common market and then a fledgling economic union.

In March 25, 1957, the governments of Belgium, France, then-West Germany, Italy, Luxembourg, and the Netherlands signed the Treaty of Rome. The road leading up to establishing a customs union composed of these nations was not a smooth one. Naturally, these nations had to overcome considerable political complications held over from the massive conflict of the Second World War.

Their economic objectives also were not always in complete harmony. For instance, on the one hand West Germany was anxious to increase trade flows with all nations to help stimulate an economy that had been devastated by the war. On the other hand, France was anxious to maintain restrictions on trade with countries outside Europe. Ultimately, the nations that signed the Treaty of Rome agreed to a compromise that entailed a gradual movement toward free trade among their group but imposed common restrictions on trade with other countries.

By 1969, trade among nations within the European customs union and between these countries and nations outside the customs union had expanded considerably. This induced other countries, most notably the United Kingdom, to consider joining the regional group, which became the European Economic Community. Negotiations during the early 1970s ultimately culminated with admittance of the United Kingdom and transformation of the customs union into a common market.

The Andean Community

At the same time that the European Common Market was launched, Bolivia, Chile, Colombia, Ecuador, and Peru were in the process of working out and signing the Cartagena Agreement establishing reciprocal trade preferences. Between 1973 and 1976, Chile withdrew from the agreement and was replaced with Venezuela. During the next two decades, this collection of South American nations gradually developed a free trade area, the Andean Community, which went into operation in January 1993. Peru gained full admittance to the group in 1997.

ON THE WEB

Find out how the Andean Community is pursuing further trade integration at http://www.comunidadandina.org.

As the trade concentration ratio in Figure 5-3 on page 130 indicates, there is considerable intensity of trade within the Andean Community. In addition, since 1998 the Andean Community has negotiated trade agreements with other countries, such as the United States and Canada, as a single entity. Thus, the Andean Community has become a customs union within just a few years.

Currently negotiations are underway to transform the Andean Community into a common market. Member nations have agreed to aim for achieving this goal by 2005.

COMMON MARKETS: FREEING UP RESOURCE FLOWS

The step from a free trade area to a customs union is a big one. When countries truly become serious about breaking down economic barriers, however, they typically reach the conclusion that they must take an even larger step by forming a common market. As we noted earlier, when a group of nations establish a common market, they remove most or even all barriers to cross-border flows of labor, capital, and other resources.

Mixed Messages from the European Union

In 1969 the European Economic Community became a common market. Since 1986 it has also styled itself as an economic union with highly coordinated policies regarding trade and resource flows.

Refer back to the concentration ratios depicted in Figure 5-3 (page 130), however, and you will see that concentration ratios indicate that trade among EU members is less intensive than trade within Mercosur and the Andean Community.

Economists disagree about exactly why free trade areas such as Mercosur experience more intensive regional trade than the European Union. One likely reason is that many EU nations historically had developed very broad trading relationships. After formation of the European Union, exporters and importers in these countries maintained these relationships. As we discuss later, it is also possible that countries in other regional trading blocs have adopted policies that do more to discourage trade from outside their own groups. That is, it is possible that trade increases within some regional blocs at the expense of trade between their members and nations outside the blocs. From this perspective, one might interpret the continuing trade between EU nations and other non-EU countries as indicative of a general movement toward freer trade—or at least no further movement toward protectionism—within the European Union.

Mercosur: Success and Strains

Argentina, Brazil, Paraguay, and Uruguay began moving toward a common market in 1991, when they initiated a *trade liberalization program* of gradual tariff reductions to zero for many goods and resources beginning in 1995. Mercosur does not yet have fully coordinated external tariffs, so it is not yet fully a customs union. Tariffs on some goods remained valid in Argentina, Brazil, and Uruguay until 2001, and certain of Paraguay's tariffs will remain in effect until 2006.

Nevertheless, the establishment of Mercosur was a major development in a region where nations have not always had harmonious relationships. At the beginning of the twentieth century, Argentina was one of the most prosperous nations in the world. Even after decades of economic decline that followed, many of Argentina's residents liked to think of themselves as South American Europeans, and they began to look down on their neighbors. This contributed to hard feelings, particularly with neighboring Brazil. Nevertheless, trade between Argentina and Brazil expanded by 400 percent between Mercosur's founding and the end of 1998, and a new spirit of cooperation emerged within the regional group.

Learn more about Mercosur at http://www.sice.oas.org/trade/mrcsr/mrcsrtoc.asp.

By the spring of 2000, however, things were not going so well in Mercosur. Groups of unemployed Argentine workers began trooping through the streets of Buenos Aires, the capital city of Argentina, carrying signs stating "Made in Brazil—No!" as part of a "Buy Argentine" campaign. Guests appearing on a public affairs program nearly came to blows after business leaders on the program complained that Brazil's investment climate was better than Argentina's. Talk-show hosts began branding Argentine consultants working with Brazilian companies as traitors.

What happened? In early 1999, Brazil reduced the value of its currency and then allowed its value to vary in foreign exchange markets. In the meantime, Argentina kept its currency equal to the U.S. dollar, as it had done consistently since 1991. Suddenly, wages and other business costs in Brazil fell nearly 30 percent below those of Argentina. Within a few months, multinational firms such as Philips Electronics and Goodyear and a number of Argentine companies shifted production from Argentina to Brazil, taking thousands of jobs along with them.

Mercosur's experience highlights an issue that common markets sometimes confront. Free flows of resources, including financial resources, can create instabilities within regional trading groups when significant exchange rate movements take place. This is a key factor that motivated the European Union to harmonize its monetary arrangements and move toward adoption of a single currency by most of its members. We shall return to this issue in greater detail in Chapter 8. (Some economists think that the adoption of a single currency by most EU nations is likely to increase the intensiveness of trade within the European Union. See *Policy Notebook: Gravity, Trade, and the Euro.*)

3 Fundamental Issue

What distinguishes customs unions such as the European Economic Community of the 1970s and the current Andean Community from common markets such as today's European Union and Mercosur?

Customs unions like the old European Economic Community and the Andean Community operate as free trade areas for their members and also establish common restrictions on trade with countries outside the customs union. Nevertheless, nations within a customs union often retain barriers to flows of factors of production, such as labor and capital. Within a common market such as the European Union and Mercosur, participating countries also remove restraints on the flows of factors of production.

Trade Creation, Diversion, or Deflection?

The rise of regional trade agreements has altered the landscape of the world trading system. As we noted earlier, there is some evidence that they have encouraged trade within regional trading groups. Economists who favor unhindered trade, however, are divided about whether the net effect of regional trade agreements is to enhance or to reduce *overall* international trade around the globe.

TRADE CREATION VERSUS TRADE DIVERSION

Figure 5-3 on page 130 shows that the intensity of trade, as revealed by trade concentration ratios, is greater within the Andean Community and Mercosur than within NAFTA and the European Union. There are two ways that one might interpret relatively high trade intensity within a regional trading bloc. On the one hand, intensive trade among members of a regional trading group could indicate that their regional trade agreement has contributed to **trade creation,** or a trade enhancement relative to trade flows that would have taken place without the agreement. On the other hand, intensive trade within a regional trading bloc might imply that a trade agreement among its members has induced **trade diversion.** Trade diversion occurs when an increase in a nation's imports from members of its regional trading group displace imports that otherwise would have come from nonmember countries.

Trade creation *An additional amount of international trade resulting from trade preferences that a nation grants to a trading partner.*

Trade diversion *A shift in international trade caused by one nation giving trade preferences to another, which can cause trade with a third country to decline.*

Why the Net Effect Matters

If regional trading blocs encourage trade creation, then on net the formation of these regional trading groups will contribute to larger volumes of *global* trade. As

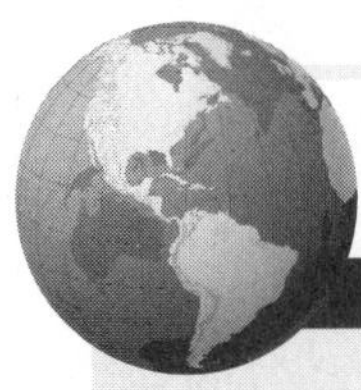

POLICY *Notebook*

POLICY MANAGEMENT

Gravity, Trade, and the Euro

When physicists and astronomers talk about gravity, they have in mind a fundamental attractive force that varies directly with the masses of two objects and inversely with the distance between the objects. Albert Einstein generalized physicists' views of gravity so that it works just about anywhere in our universe outside a black hole. Nevertheless, the basic view of gravity developed by Isaac Newton still works well for us on Earth and within our solar system. In the 1960s, economists got the idea of applying Newton's proposed relationship between gravity, sizes, and distance to international trade. They began testing whether flows of international trade vary directly with the sizes of two countries and inversely with the distance between the countries.

"Gravity Equations" and International Trade

Applying the theory of gravity to international trade makes intuitive sense. If two countries are relatively large, they are more likely to produce an array of goods and services that they might wish to trade. Furthermore, engaging in trade is likely to be a less costly undertaking if two countries are relatively close together.

It turns out that as long as economists take into account other factors affecting trade flows—population, cultural factors, language barriers, and the like—there is considerable evidence favoring using so-called *gravity equations* to measure determinants of international trade. These are statistical relationships that take into account the proposed direct relationship between countries' sizes and distances.

Could the Euro Exert a Gravitational Attraction?

In a 2000 study, Andrew Rose of the University of California at Berkeley examined data on 186 countries for 1970, 1975, 1980, 1985, and 1990, which amounted to 33,903 observations of bilateral trade flows. Rose added one additional explanatory factor to gravity equations of international trade: whether they shared the same currency. Although he found that entering into regional trade agreements had a positive effect on trade, sharing a common currency had a much bigger effect. On average, having the same currency led countries to trade three times as much with each other as countries with different currencies. Sharing a common currency also had a much larger effect—Rose estimated that it was more than 35 times bigger—than simply reducing the variability of the rate of exchange between two nations' currencies.

These conclusions, naturally, were received enthusiastically by European nations that had just established the euro as a common currency. If the results of Rose's study apply to participants in the European Monetary Union, then its members stand to reap considerable trade benefits from their decision to use a single currency.

Why does having the same currency do so much to encourage trade? In his study, Rose speculated that adopting a single currency might solidify governments' commitments to a common market, or perhaps even an economic union. As a result, residents might be more comfortable establishing long-term trading arrangements. In addition, he proposed that perhaps a common currency promotes more *financial* integration that helps promote trade. Furthermore, it is easier for residents of nations to compare domestic and foreign prices when they are quoted in the same currency. Finally, adopting a common currency eliminates exchange rate variability and saves traders the costs of engaging in costly risk-reduction strategies.

For Critical Analysis:

If sharing a single currency does so much to promote international trade, why don't nations agree to adopt a single world currency?

discussed in Chapter 3, the likely effect of trade creation will be that more nations will recognize existing absolute or comparative advantages. As a result, more of the world's people will experience gains from trade.

If the net effect of the widespread establishment of regional trade blocs is trade diversion, however, then global trade flows will not necessarily increase as a result of regional trade agreements. Equal-sized substitutions of regional trading partners' imports for the imports of countries outside regional trading groups will leave global trade flows unchanged. Furthermore, if members of regional trade blocs establish sufficiently protectionist policies against nonmember countries, it is possible that international trade flows could actually *decline*. For instance, consider what would happen if Mercosur were to place high tariffs on imports of computer products from countries outside Mercosur. Naturally, imports of computer products into Mercosur nations from the United States and other computer-exporting countries would decline. Undoubtedly, this would also cause a net decline in overall Mercosur trade in computer products, however, because there are few manufacturers of computer products in Argentina, Brazil, Paraguay, or Uruguay that could offer a full range of substitute computer products. Hence, trade diversion likely would lead to incomplete substitution of members' imports for the imports of nonmembers. (To see why both trade creation and trade diversion typically occur when members of regional trade blocs grant fellow members trade preferences, see on pages 144–145 *Visualizing Global Economic Issues: Trade Creation versus Trade Diversion in a Three-Country World.*)

Limiting Regional Trade Diversion

In light of the proliferation of regional trade blocs, economists who favor free trade have sought to determine how regional trading groups might limit tendencies to divert trade instead of fostering an environment of more open trade with all nations. Some have advanced a proposal that, on its surface, seems inconsistent with a free-trade philosophy: granting partial instead of complete reductions of trade barriers within a regional trade agreement. One basis of this argument is that complete removal of trade restrictions within a regional trade bloc that otherwise maintains restraints on trade with other nations provides a strong incentive for trade diversion. Another is that complete removal of tariffs that generate revenues for governments of nations in a regional trading group gives the governments an incentive to raise tariffs on countries outside the group, further increasing the incentive to divert trade.

Naturally, free-trade-oriented economists propose keeping all trade restrictions to a minimum. If regional trading groups insist on maintaining higher barriers for nonmembers than for members, then these economists promote keeping the differentials among tariffs, duties, and other barriers as low as possible.

Nearly all economists agree that a key way to encourage trade creation through regional trade agreements is to keep membership in such arrangements open to all. They argue that rules that effectively limit membership in more than one regional trading group at a time, such as EU rules preventing the United Kingdom from, say, belonging to the European Union and NAFTA simultaneously, can do little but drive wedges among regional trade blocs that contribute to trade diversion. (There is some evidence that trade diversion has occurred in Europe; see on pages 146–147 *Policy Notebook: The European Union—Fortress Europe?*)

Fundamental Issue 4

How can regional trading arrangements lead to both trade creation and trade diversion?

When one nation reduces trade restrictions previously imposed on another, there are two effects. One is a trade creation effect. The nation's residents substitute purchases of domestic goods with purchases of goods produced by the nation with which trade barriers have been reduced. In addition, however, they tend to reduce their purchases of goods from countries with which their nation retains barriers to trade, so there is also trade diversion.

TRADE DEFLECTION

Another complication that arises when assessing the overall trade effects of regional trade agreements is **trade deflection.** This takes place when a company located in a nation outside a regional trade bloc finds a way to move goods that are not quite fully assembled into a member country, complete assembly, and then export them to countries offering the trade preferences. A common way to engage in trade deflection is for a company to move a portion of its production facilities to nations participating in a regional trade agreement.

Trade deflection
The movement of goods or components of goods from a country outside a trading arrangement to one within such an arrangement so that the seller can benefit from trading preferences within the arrangement.

Rules of Origin

To try to reduce the extent to which trade deflection occurs, most regional trading agreements include **rules of origin.** These are regulations that carefully define categories of products that are eligible for trading preferences under the agreements.

Rules of origin
Regulations governing conditions under which products are eligible for trading preferences under trade agreements.

Some rules of origin require any products trading freely among members of a regional trading group to be entirely composed of materials produced within a member nation. For instance, if Mercosur applied such a stringent rule of origin, then an automobile assembled in, say, Argentina that contained a single component manufactured in a Mexican auto parts plant would not be eligible for free trade to Brazil.

Rules of origin typically are not so stringent, however. Most rules of origin instead mandate that goods eligible for preferred trade must have a certain percentage of value added by manufacturing within a country that is a member of the regional trading group.

Trade Deflection and Gains from Trade

Some economists favoring free trade applaud successful trade deflection. They argue that successful trade deflection circumvents trade restrictions and thereby allows residents of nations within regional trade blocs to experience gains from trade.

Other free-trade-oriented economists, however, worry that trade deflection can lead to welfare losses for residents of nations that fail to receive imports that are deflected when trading partners pursue favorable trade preferences offered by special

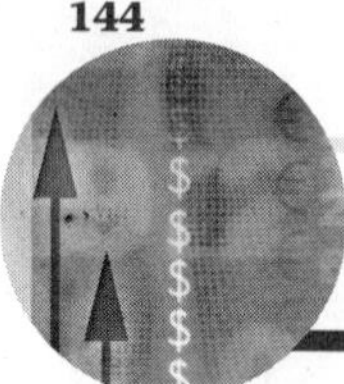

Visualizing Global Economic Issues

Trade Creation versus Trade Diversion in a Three-Country World

Let's apply basic demand–supply analysis to explain why it is that regional trading preferences typically produce *both* trade creation *and* trade diversion. Take a look at Figure 5-7. Panel (a) shows a nation's demand and supply curves for laptop computers manufactured domestically. Panel (b) shows the curves for laptops produced in another country that becomes a fellow member of a regional trade bloc. Panel (c) shows the nation's demand and supply for laptops made in another nation that is not a member of the regional trading group. The initial equilibrium dollar price of laptop computers in the home nation is $3,000.

Suppose that the initial foreign supply curves in panels (b) and (c) reflect a tariff on the nation's imports of laptop computers. After the country depicted in panel (b) joins the nation's regional trading group, however, the domestic country cuts the tariff on laptop computers imported from this new regional partner. Thus, as shown in panel (b), the supply of laptop computers from the regional partner increases. As the price of laptop computers imported from the regional partner declines toward $2,500, domestic residents substitute away from purchases of *both* domestically manufactured laptop computers *and* laptop computers manufactured in the nation that is not in the regional trading group and that still face a tariff. Hence, the demand curves shift leftward in panels (a) and (c). The new equilibrium dollar price of laptop computers in this nation is equal to $2,500.

Notice what happens to this nation's trade in laptop computers. To some extent, domestic residents shift some of their domestic purchases of laptop computers abroad, as illustrated by the decline in domestic purchases in panel (a) and the increase in purchases from the regional trading partner in panel (b). Thus, *trade creation* results from extending trade preferences to the new regional partner, as domestic purchases decline in favor of purchases from the member of the regional trading bloc. As panel (c) indicates, however, purchases of laptop computers from the foreign country that is not a member of the regional trade bloc decline. Thus, *trade diversion* also takes place.

For Critical Analysis:
In this example, would trade diversion occur if computer producers in both foreign nations were exempted from tariffs?

Figure 5-7

A Graphical Depiction of Trade Creation and Trade Diversion

Panel (a) shows a nation's demand and supply curves for laptop computers manufactured domestically, and panel (b) displays the domestic demand for and supply of laptop computers produced in another country that becomes a fellow member of a regional trade bloc. Panel (c) depicts the domestic demand and supply curves for laptop computers manufactured in another nation that is not a member of the regional trading group. The initial equilibrium U.S. dollar price of all laptop computers is $3,000. After the country depicted in panel (b) joins the nation's regional trading group, the domestic country cuts the tariff on laptop computers imported from this new regional partner, causing the supply of laptop computers from the regional partner to increase in panel (b). The decline in the price of laptop computers imported from the regional partner induces domestic residents to substitute its laptop computers for both domestically manufactured laptop computers and laptop computers manufactured in the nation outside the regional trading group that continues to still face a tariff, resulting in the declines in demands shown in panels (a) and (b). Trade creation occurs as domestic residents shift some of their domestic purchases of laptop computers abroad, as shown by the fall in domestic purchases in panel (a) and the rise in purchases from the regional trading partner in panel (b). At the same time, however, panel (c) shows that trade diversion occurs as domestic residents reduce their purchases of laptop computers from the foreign country that is not a member of the regional trade bloc decline.

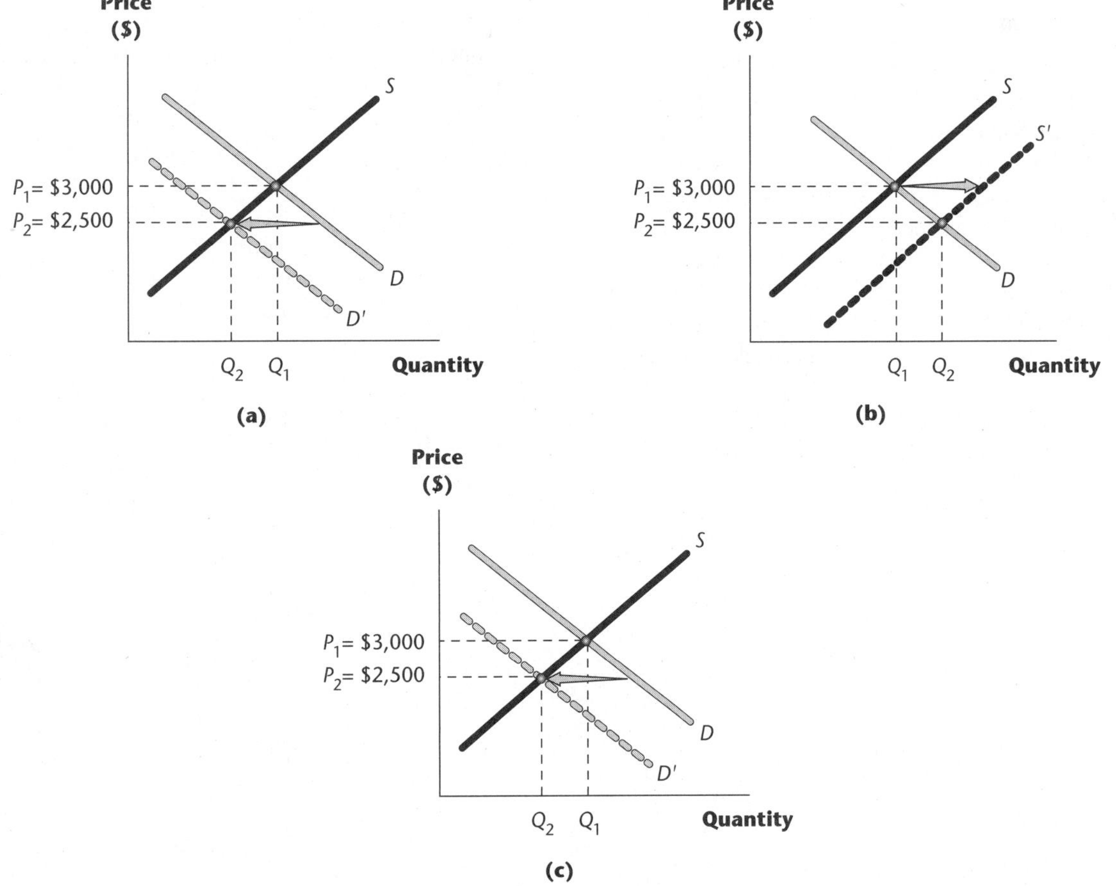

POLICY *Notebook*

POLICY MANAGEMENT

The European Union—Fortress Europe?

When the European Union (EU) was formed, participating nations agreed to reduce trade barriers with other EU nations. According to research by Patrick Messerlin of the Institute d'Etudes Politiques in France, however, European economies are nearly as protected from trade with nations outside Europe as they were at the time of the EU's establishment.

High Tariffs and Antidumping Duties

Officially, tariffs on imports into EU nations average only about 5 percent. This figure is a weighted average based on import volumes. Import volumes are depressed in markets that tariffs protect and in industrial sectors protected by other forms of import restrictions. Panel (a) of Figure 5-8 displays the average tariff rates actually applied to EU imports for selected products, including beef and lamb, cereals, and dairy products that clearly experience particularly high protection from non-EU competition.

In addition, officially published EU average tariff rates exclude antidumping duties that the EU imposes on so-called "unfairly cheap" imports of various products, such as those displayed in panel (b) of the figure. As you learned in Chapter 4, these antidumping duties essentially have the same effects as tariffs.

Assessing the Costs of EU Protectionism

The proposed benefit of these protectionist tariffs and antidumping duties is that they help protect jobs of European workers. Messerlin estimates that EU protectionism safeguards about 200,000 jobs.

How much does it cost to protect these jobs? According to Messerlin, the total cost to EU residents is about 7 percent of annual aggregate EU income, or about $43 billion per year. Hence, the cost of safeguarding the average job that would be threatened by eliminating protectionist tariffs, antidumping duties, and other import restrictions is about $215,000 per year. One can't help but wonder if the protected workers might prefer to receive annual cash payments from the rest of the EU's residents.

For Critical Analysis:
Who else, besides EU workers whose jobs are safeguarded, stands to benefit from EU protectionism?

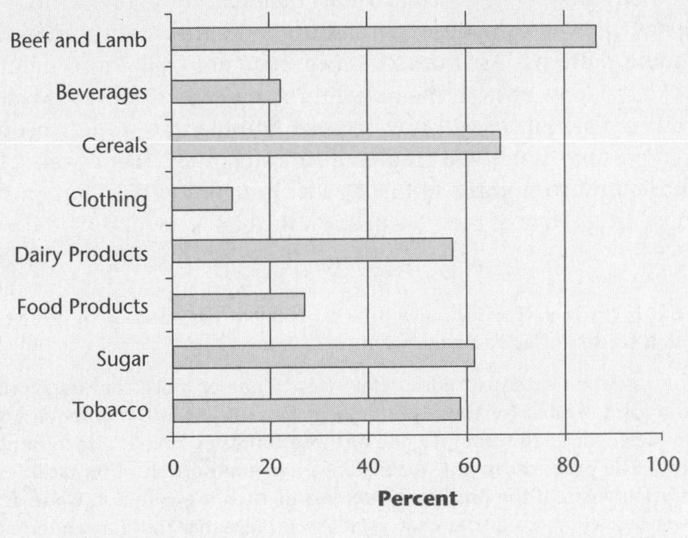

(a)

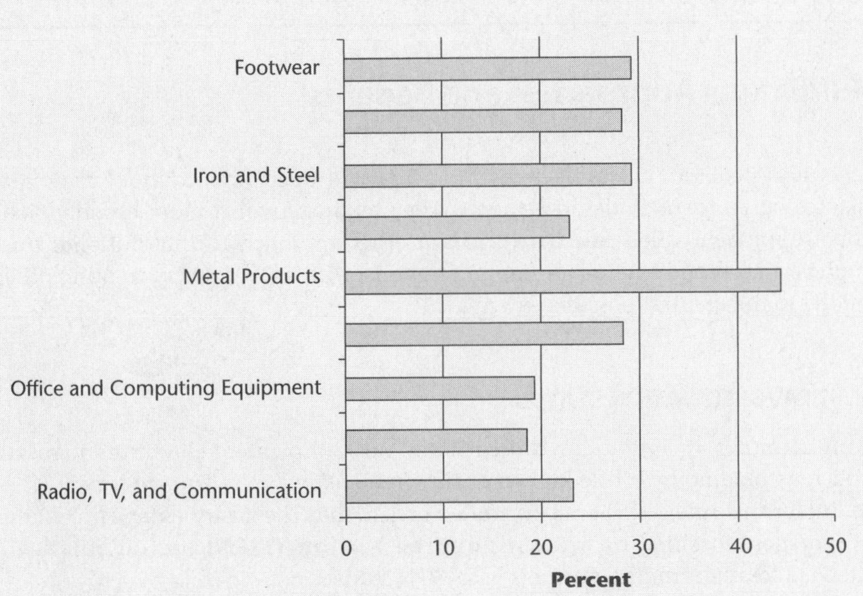

(b)

Figure 5-8

Average Tariff and Antidumping Rates in the European Union

Panel (a) shows average EU tariff rates for selected products, and panel (b) displays antidumping duties that the EU imposes on various goods and services.

Source: Patrick Messerlin, *Measuring the Costs of Protection in Europe,* Washington, D.C.: Institute for International Economics, 2000.

regional trade agreements. For instance, Mexican auto parts that are used as components in Argentine-manufactured automobiles to take advantage of Mercosur trade preferences might help prop up relatively inefficient Argentine auto producers that might be less able to compete with, say, Mexican producers in a truly open trading environment.

According to this second view, therefore, trade preferences established by regional trade agreements can introduce fundamental distortions into international trading patterns. As a consequence, regional trade agreements potentially can make residents of both member and nonmember nations worse off. In short, increased regionalism will not necessarily make the world's people better off. It is even possible that greater regionalism could make them worse off. This conclusion leads many economists to favor wider trade initiatives that encompass many nations, irrespective of their location on the globe.

5 Fundamental Issue

What is trade deflection, and how do rules of origin help to limit the extent to which trade deflection occurs?

When a nation extends trade preferences to one or more countries, producers located in a nation not eligible for these preferences have an incentive to move goods that are not in completely finished form into one of those countries in an effort to benefit from the preferences. The producer might, for instance, move a portion of its facilities to nations eligible for preferences. If the producer is successful, then it engages in trade deflection. To combat trade deflection, countries that establish preferential trade arrangements enforce rules of origin categorizing products that are eligible for preferential trade.

Multilateral Approaches and Benefits

Generally speaking, economists favoring free and open international trade look askance on regional trade agreements. They tend to favor a more broadly based global approach called **multilateralism.** This approach to international trade emphasizes a broad interaction among nations, with each country treating others equally to the greatest possible extent.

Multilateralism
An approach to achieving freer international trade via a wide interplay among many of the world's nations, with an aim toward inducing each country to treat others equally in trading arrangements.

MOST FAVORED NATION STATUS

Many countries, including the United States, have implemented a multilateral approach by abiding by a rule known as the *Unconditional Most Favored Nation Principle.* Under this rule, reductions in trade barriers that a country extends to a trading partner classified as a **most favored nation (MFN)** are automatically extended to other trading partners with MFN status.

Most favored nation (MFN)
A country that receives reductions in trade barriers to promote open international trade.

The motivation behind the MFN principle is that if a number of countries follow the principle, discrimination in international trade arrangements will become less common. Of course, the United States and other countries already discriminate through their membership in NAFTA and other regional trade blocs. Nevertheless, the overall hope of the nations that abide by the MFN principle is that if more and more countries abide by the principle, discriminatory trade arrangements will gradually die out.

To become a most favored nation, a country must show that it can credibly commit to patterns of conduct in international trade that other nations have also adopted. This raises an important question, however: Who is to decide whether a country has established a credible commitment to "acceptable" conduct? The answer that most of the world's nations have developed is to establish global trade agreements. More recently, nations have also agreed to have their trade conduct monitored by international organizations.

MULTILATERAL TRADE REGULATION

From 1947 until 1993, nations accounting for more than 85 percent of global international trade flows signed the **General Agreement on Tariffs and Trade (GATT).** Under the terms of this agreement, participating nations began to meet periodically to iron out disagreements about trade policies.

"Rounds" of GATT negotiations were named according to most clearly identified locations or individuals. The 1993 Uruguay Round of GATT, which 117 nations ratified, established the **World Trade Organization (WTO).** The WTO commenced formal operations on January 1, 1995, and today it has grown to encompass more than 140 member nations. A key factor contributing to the WTO's growth has been the growing importance of its functions as a global arbiter of trade rules and enforcement. Even nations that have had spotty records for "playing by the rules" in international trade have sought to join this multinational trade group. China successfully negotiated entry into the WTO in 2001.

General Agreement on Tariffs and Trade (GATT)
An international agreement among more than 140 nations about rules governing cross-border trade in goods.

World Trade Organization
A multinational organization that oversees multilateral trade negotiations and adjudicates trade disputes that arise under multilateral trade agreements formed under the GATT and the GATS.

General Agreement on Trade in Services (GATS)
An international agreement among more than 130 nations about rules under which services are traded internationally.

Functions of the World Trade Organization

The WTO has several basic functions. The WTO serves as a global forum for all multinational negotiations concerning international trade. It oversees rounds of trade negotiations and monitors compliance with trade agreements. In addition, it conducts periodic assessment of national trade policies and assists countries in developing these policies.

The WTO, which is based in Geneva, Switzerland, also administers the **General Agreement on Trade in Services (GATS),** another agreement reached in the Uruguay Round. This agreement covers most international service transactions and generally requires national treatment for services on the same terms as trade in goods. Nevertheless, services receive somewhat different treatment under the GATS than goods do under the GATT. (The growth of electronic commerce is complicating the WTO's task; see on the next page *Online Globalization: The WTO—"Wired Trade Organization?"*)

ON THE WEB
Learn more about the WTO at http://www.wto.org.

Addressing Allegations of Unfair Trading Practices

Another fundamental role of the World Trade Organization is to settle and adjudicate trade disputes. Under the terms of the WTO *Agreement on Subsidies and*

Online Globalization

The WTO—"Wired Trade Organization?"

Throughout human history, technological change has helped advance international trade. The development of faster transoceanic transport fed the growth of cross-border trade in the eighteenth and nineteenth centuries. Air transport played an important part in spurring trade among nations in the twentieth century.

E-Commerce in Goods and Services

The information technology revolution promises to help advance international trade in this century. Consumers have an easier time purchasing goods such as books and compact disks from afar using the Internet. Furthermore, the Internet also promises to be an avenue for increased trade in *services.* Anything that can be stored as digital information—such as architectural designs, information about new medical treatments and surgical techniques, and banking, insurance, and brokerage services—is fair game for international trade.

A Blurring Distinction

Electronic commerce is emerging as a big problem for the WTO, because WTO rules work differently for tariffs versus quotas. Most nations apply tariffs to goods. By way of contrast, many apply quotas to services by placing restrictions on access to national markets. Digital technology and the Internet are blurring the distinction between traded goods and traded services, however.

Currently, a recording by a top rock band that crosses a national border as a digital file on a CD is a good that is subject to tariffs. Is a digital recording sent over the Internet in digital form a service under WTO rules? Or is it no different from a CD and thus a good subject for the WTO's tariff guidelines? Likewise, if an architect ships drawings to a customer in another country, the drawings are treated as goods, and tariffs apply. But what if the firm sends the drawings to its client in the form of an e-mail attachment?

WTO rules concerning how to define goods and services are likely to influence choices between physical and digital methods of trade. National authorities already are having trouble keeping track of the proliferation of Internet-based service offerings. If quotas on cross-border Internet services are difficult for national authorities to enforce, then people will have a strong incentive to shift even more trade to the Internet.

For Critical Analysis:

Suppose that at some date in the future a U.S. software company were to charge that software firms based in Russia are unfairly allowing consumers around the world to download disk operating systems at very low prices. Could WTO antidumping rules be enforced in this situation?

Countervailing Measures, for example, the WTO has the power to discipline the use of subsidies that any country's government transmits to domestic firms to give them a trade advantage over firms located in other nations (see Chapter 4). A nation that feels it has been harmed by such subsidies can use the WTO's dispute-settlement procedure to press for the WTO to force a country that provides trade subsidies to withdraw them, or the nation experiencing the harm can seek WTO sanction to charge a countervailing duty. In recent years a key subject of WTO investigation of trade subsidies has been national tax laws, because to make their subsidies less overt many nations offer exporting firms tax breaks instead of direct payments. During the early 2000s, the European Union brought several successful charges against the United States for using tax laws to provide export subsidies.

Not all trade subsidies are unlawful under current WTO rules, and the WTO does not fully extend its powers to oversee countervailing duties. Until 2003 the WTO exempted most developing nations from restraints on trade subsidies, and it continues to extend exemptions to the least-developed nations of the world, which it defines to be those with per capita incomes of less than $1,000 per year. A number of developing nations also receive preferential treatment from the WTO in its enforcement of rules governing countervailing duties.

As noted in Chapter 4 (and see Chapter 11 for further discussion), when a firm sells a product in a nation at a price lower than it charges in its home country, it is said to be *dumping* the product. The WTO determines whether nations that claim to be recipients of dumped products can respond with antidumping policies, such as subsidies to companies affected by dumping or countervailing duties on the products of offending firms. (So-called "safeguard provisions" of U.S. trade-remedy laws are often touted as consistent with the U.S. government's commitment to WTO agreements, but they have increasingly become sources of international trade frictions; see on page 152 the *Policy Notebook: Section 201—Safeguard or Flashpoint?*)

WILL REGIONALISM ULTIMATELY EVOLVE INTO MULTILATERALISM?

The WTO has had to perform a careful balancing act to promote multilateralism and lower trade restrictions as regional trade agreements have proliferated. Economists continue to debate whether regionalism will add to or subtract from efforts to enhance free-trade efforts around the world.

Some Indications from Trade Shares

In an exhaustive study of world trade from the 1960s to the early 1990s, Jeffrey Frankel of Harvard University sought to address whether regionalism has improved or worsened prospects for freer trade. Like Andrew Rose (see the Policy Notebook on page 141), Frankel used "gravity equations" to try to estimate the effects of regional trade blocs on the general extent to which countries are open to trade. His conclusions generally favored a positive outlook for world trade as a result of regional trading agreements.

Specifically, Frankel found that ASEAN and other parts of East Asia have become highly open to trade. So has the EU portion of Europe (but not the rest of Europe) and the Mercosur portion of South America. In addition, Frankel concluded that the degree of trade openness of NAFTA countries, and in particular the United States, has tended to increase over time.

Frankel's study indicated that most countries with the greatest increase in openness to trade had also joined regional trade arrangements. These included Argentina, Brazil, and Paraguay of Mercosur, and Malaysia and Thailand of ASEAN. Frankel suggests that when countries go to the trouble to develop a political

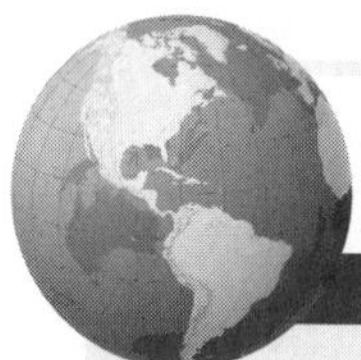

POLICY *Notebook*

POLICY MANAGEMENT

Section 201—Safeguard or Flashpoint?

The WTO *Agreement on Safeguards* permits a member nation to implement what are known as *safeguard measures,* or temporary restrictions on imports of foreign firms, when an industry within that nation is either "seriously injured" or "threatened with serious injury" resulting from an upsurge in imports. The WTO agreement provides criteria for determining when an industry has been injured and for how a nation can seek to protect the industry for four years or, with WTO approval, as many as eight years. Nevertheless, under the terms of the WTO agreement, countries with exporting firms affected by such safeguard measures are entitled to some form of compensation. In the absence of compensation, the exporting countries can retaliate by taking equivalent actions against that nation.

Section 201

In the United States, a key safeguard measure is Section 201 of the Trade Act of 1974 and its subsequent amendments. Under this law, U.S. industries that regard themselves as seriously injured or threatened can petition the International Trade Commission (ITC) for relief in the form of import quotas, other trade restraints, or direct financial assistance from the government. The ITC then makes recommendations to the president of the United States about whether relief is justifiable and, if so, what type of relief should be provided.

On its face, Section 201 is fully consistent with the WTO Agreement on Safeguards. Indeed, in 2000 the U.S. Congress amended the law in an attempt to bring it into full compliance with WTO rules. Nonetheless, critics of U.S. policy argue that in actual practice the U.S. government has used Section 201 as an instrument of protectionism.

Heavy Artillery in a Cold War on U.S. Imports?

According to critics of the U.S. government's use of Section 201, this portion of the 1974 Trade Act has been used to substitute for the Antidumping Act of 1916, which provided for U.S. industries injured by imports to seek treble damages and criminal fines from importers—and even imprisonment in certain cases. In 2000, the WTO found the 1916 legislation to be inconsistent with the GATT. Since then, companies have increasingly turned to Section 201 for relief from alleged dumping. Furthermore, the U.S. government itself has relied on Section 201 to justify countervailing duties imposed on foreign firms alleged to have benefited from subsidies, tax breaks, or other export-promoting policies in their home nations.

To date, the U.S. effort to use WTO safeguard measures to substitute for policies that are illegal under other WTO agreements has met little success. Time after time since the late 1990s, WTO panels have ruled against U.S. efforts to extend safeguard protections to a number of U.S. industries. To critics of Section 201, this indicates that the United States has been trying to pursue an inconsistent trade policy. The U.S. government has, the critics claim, publicly promoted the WTO and free global trade even as it has simultaneously tried to stretch the limits of laws intended to provide, in relatively rare situations, temporary safeguards for domestic firms.

For Critical Analysis:

In the near term, who would lose and who would gain in the event of a discontinuance of the WTO Agreement on Safeguards? What might be possible long-term consequences of scrapping this rule?

consensus favoring trade concessions to regional trading partners, it may become a shorter step to open borders to trade with other nations as well. Consequently, trade creation generally outweighs trade diversion within regional trade blocs. If Frankel is correct, regional trade arrangements may indeed act as a bridge to broader multilateral efforts to promote freer trade among the world's nations.

A Gradual Overlapping of Regional Trade Arrangements

One development that offers some support for Frankel's interpretation is that a number of regional trade agreements are beginning to overlap. For instance, the budding Asia and Pacific Economic Cooperation (APEC) forum includes countries that are members of NAFTA, ASEAN, Mercosur, and the Andean Community. Furthermore, these and other regional trade blocs have negotiated partial reciprocal trade preferences across their trading groups.

The European Free Trade Area Association has also developed into an overlapping set of reciprocal trade arrangements. Certainly, the EU remains a clearly separate bloc. Nevertheless, trade agreements linking EU and other EFTA nations to individual countries inside and outside Europe have blurred many of the trade borders that previously surrounded the European Union.

At present, therefore, at least some economists believe that regionalism has not necessarily emerged as a *substitute* for multilateralism. There is some indication, however, that regionalism has been *complementary* to multilateral efforts to enhance more open trade among nations.

Fundamental Issue 6

How do multilateral trade agreements contrast with regional trading arrangements?

Whereas regional trading arrangements establish trade agreements among limited sets of countries, multilateral trade agreements seek to involve most of the world's nations in efforts to free up flows of international trade. The fundamental multilateral trade agreements among more than 140 nations are the General Agreement on Tariffs and Trade (GATT) and the General Agreement on Trade in Services (GATS). Since 1995, the World Trade Organization has been responsible for monitoring compliance with these agreements. Recent evidence indicates that the proliferation of and gradual overlapping of regional trade agreements has reinforced multilateral trade arrangements.

CHAPTER SUMMARY

1) **The Main Types of Regional Trade Agreements, and How Economists Measure Trade within Regional Trading Groups:** The most important types of regional trade agreements are preferential trade arrangements, free trade areas, customs unions, common markets, and economic unions. Trade shares, or percentage of a country's flows of trade (the sum of its exports and imports) relative to a regional or world total, are commonly used to measure the extent of the country's trade. Because a country's

absolute importance in world trade can distort simple trade shares, economists measure the intensity of trade within a group of nations using a trade concentration ratio. This equals the sum of bilateral trade shares of nations within a regional trading group, divided by the region's share of world trade.

2) **How a Free Trade Area Such as the North American Free Trade Agreement Differs from Other Types of Preferential Trade Arrangements:** Preferential trade arrangements often create trade preferences for specific goods, and they are often one-sided agreements that benefit only one nation or group of nations. By way of contrast, countries within a free trade area such as NAFTA set up reciprocal trade preferences for all nations within the regional trading bloc. The establishment of NAFTA has so far led to rises in U.S. exports to Mexico and in Mexican trade with Canada, but U.S. imports from Mexico and Canadian trade with the United States have not changed notably.
3) **How Customs Unions Such as the European Economic Community of the 1970s and the Current Andean Community Are Distinguished from Common Markets Such as the European Union and Mercosur:** The European Economic Community and the Andean Community are examples of customs unions that function as free trade areas but also impose identical rules governing trade with countries outside the regional trading bloc. Today's European Union and Mercosur are common markets that additionally remove restraints on the flows of factors of production such as labor and capital.
4) **How Regional Trading Arrangements Can Lead to Simultaneous Trade Creation and Trade Diversion:** Reduction or elimination of trade barriers that a domestic nation had previously imposed on another induces the domestic nation's residents to reduce purchases of domestic goods in favor of buying goods produced by the country with which trade restrictions have been relaxed. This trade creation effect, however, is at least partly countered by a trade diversion effect. This second effect arises because the nation's residents also have an incentive to reduce their purchases of goods from countries with which their nation maintains barriers to trade.
5) **Trade Deflection and How Rules of Origin Limit Its Occurrence:** The establishment of preferential trade agreements or regional trading arrangements gives companies located in countries not covered by the trade preferences an incentive to move incompletely assembled goods into nations that are eligible. The companies can then complete production and take advantage of the trade preferences, thereby engaging in trade deflection. Nations often seek to reduce the extent of trade deflection by establishing and enforcing rules of origin regulating the eligibility of products for trade preferences.
6) **How Multilateral Trade Agreements Differ from Regional Trading Arrangements:** In contrast to regional trading arrangements that link relatively small groups of nations, the two main multilateral trade agreements, the General Agreement on Tariffs and Trade (GATT) and the General Agreement on Trade in Services (GATS), encompass more than 140 countries. Under the

auspices of these agreements, the World Trade Organization monitors compliance and adjudicates disputes. There is some evidence that the growing number of regional trade agreements that are now beginning to overlap complements a multilateral approach to freeing up trade among the world's nations.

QUESTIONS AND PROBLEMS

1) Consider the following data on flows of exports and imports among three nations, and suppose that the "world" is composed solely of these countries:
Country A exports to Country B: $35 million
Country A exports to Country C: $25 million
Country B exports to Country A: $30 million
Country B exports to Country C: $25 million
Country C exports to Country A: $20 million
Country C exports to Country B: $40 million
Calculate the following as a share of total world trade. Express your answers as percentages, and round to the nearest tenth of a percent.
(a) Country A's trade with Country B
(b) Country A's trade with Country C
(c) Country B's trade with Country C
2) Based on the information in question 1, which nation(s) has an overall trade deficit? Which has an overall trade surplus? Is world trade balanced?
3) Use the information in question 1 to calculate the following, and express your answers as percentages rounded to the nearest tenth of a percent:
(a) Country A's total share of world trade
(b) Country B's total share of world trade
(c) Country C's total share of world trade
4) Suppose that Country A and Country B in question 1 together constitute a regional trade bloc known as the A–B Trade Area. Use your answers to questions 1 and 2 to calculate the trade concentration ratio of this regional trade bloc.
5) In principle, why is the trade concentration ratio you calculated in question 4 a better measure of the intensiveness of trade within the A-B Trade Area than simply the combined share of world trade of Countries A and B? Give a verbal answer.
6) Suppose that a year passes, and the trade concentration ratio of the A-B Trade Area increases significantly. Does this observation necessarily imply that formation of the A-B Trade Area has enhanced overall world trade?
7) Another year passes, and the A-B Trade Area changes its name by inserting the word "Free" before "Trade Area." Under the agreement the two nations have reached, Country A will remove all remaining restrictions on trade with Country B this year. Both agree that another year will pass, however, before Country B will reciprocate by removing all remaining barriers to trade with

Country A. Draw diagrams to illustrate, from Country A's perspective, how this year's action by Country A is likely to generate both trade creation and trade diversion during the current year. Be sure to take into account Country A's trade with Country C as well.

8) It is now a year later, and Country B removes all remaining restraints on trade with Country A. Draw diagrams to show, from Country B's perspective, how this action is likely to generate both trade creation and trade diversion during the current year. Be sure to take into account Country B's trade with Country C as well.
9) One more year passes, and the A-B Free Trade Area negotiates a partial reduction in barriers to their trade with Country C. Without drawing any additional diagrams, is this action more likely on net to generate trade creation or trade diversion? Explain your reasoning.
10) Suppose that all three nations agree to remove remaining barriers to trade among the entire set, so that the "world" becomes a free trade area. Country C is twice as far from both County A and Country B as Country A and Country B are from each other. In addition, Country A and Country B are of equal size, but Country C is half as large. Are trade flows likely to be unequal even with unhindered trade? If so, how? (*Hint:* Take a look back at the discussion of the "gravity-equation" approach discussed on page 141.)

ONLINE APPLICATION

Internet URL: http://europa.eu.int/comm/trade/index_en.htm

Title: **The European Commission—EU Trade**

Navigation: Begin at the home page of the European Union (http://europe.eu.int), and click on "The European Union On-line." Go to "Institutions," and select "Commission." Then click on "Alphabetical Index," and then "Trade."

Application: Perform the indicated operations, and answer the questions that follow.

1) Click on "Trade Policy Instruments," and then click on "What's New?" Review recent EU trade policy actions. Is there a common theme to these recent actions? Do these actions appear to favor trade creation or trade diversion?
2) Back up to the EU trade menu and click on "Market Access Strategy." Does this strategy appear to be consistent with trade creation or trade diversion? Do you see any tension between your answer to this question and your answer to question 1? If so, what likely accounts for this tension?

For Group Study and Analysis: The EU trade menu at this Web site has buttons titled "Trade in Goods" and "Trade in Services" that provide links to various industry issues in the European Union. Assign industries to different groups, and evaluate whether EU policies regarding trade creation and trade diversion appear to be consistent across industry groups.

REFERENCES AND RECOMMENDED READINGS

Bhagwati, Jagdish, Arvind Panagariya, and Marvin Kosters. *The Economics of Preferential Trade Agreements.* Washington, D.C.: AEI Press, 1996.

Bergsten, C. Fred. *Whither APEC?* Washington, D.C.: Institute for International Economics, 1997.

Connolly, Michelle, and Jenessa Gunther. "Mercosur: Implications for Growth in Member Countries." *Current Issues in Economics and Finance* 5 (May 7, 1999).

Frankel, Jeffrey. *Regional Trade Blocs.* Washington, D.C.: Institute for International Economics, 1997.

Krueger, Anne. "Trade Creation and Trade Diversion under NAFTA." NBER Working Paper No. 7429, Cambridge, Mass.: National Bureau of Economic Research, December 1999.

Messerlin, Patrick. *Measuring the Costs of Protection in Europe.* Washington, D.C.: Institute for International Economics, 2000.

Rose, Andrew. "One Money, One Market: The Effect of Common Currencies on Trade." *Economic Policy* 30 (April 2000): 9–33.

World Bank. *Trade Blocs.* Oxford: Oxford University Press, 2000.

UNIT THREE

International Finance: Enduring Issues

CHAPTER SIX

Balance of Payments and Foreign Exchange Markets

Fundamental Issues

1. **What is a country's balance of payments, and what does this measure?**
2. **What is the role of foreign exchange markets in the global marketplace?**
3. **What is the spot foreign exchange market?**
4. **What is foreign exchange risk, and what is the role of forward foreign exchange markets?**
5. **What determines the value of a currency?**
6. **How are the spot and forward exchange markets related?**
7. **What other foreign exchange instruments are commonly traded?**

During the first two years following its introduction, the euro, the common currency of participating European nations, depreciated relative to the U.S. dollar by more than 30 percent. In spite of numerous policy moves by the European Central Bank designed to support the euro, demand for the euro sagged due to weak economic performance of the major European nations relative to U.S. economic performance.

During this same period, the decline in the value of the euro reduced the sales and profits of non–European firms that priced their exports in euros. For example, Manpower Inc., a temporary staffing agency based in the United States and operating in 54 nations, experienced euro-currency-denominated revenue gains of more than 25 percent in 2000. When the company translated these revenues to U.S. dollars, however, the gain shrank to 17 percent. In U.S. dollars, the translation of revenues represented a loss of more than $345 million. Likewise, Johnson Controls, a U.S. car battery manufacturer, reported a decline of $480 million in revenues after the translation *of European sales into dollars. Because of the significant impact on foreign sales revenues, many U.S. firms passed along the depreciation of the euro to their European customers by increasing prices quoted in euros. Microsoft, for example, twice increased the prices on its exports to Europe during 2000.*

The euro was not the only currency to lose value in the early 2000s. As Japan's economy continued to slump, the yen depreciated against the euro by more than 10 percent and against the dollar by more than 15 percent. The decline in the value of the yen inflated the value of foreign sales measured in yen. Profits for many Japanese auto producers improved, because the bulk of overseas sales are denominated in euros and dollars, while costs are denominated in yen. This improved analysts' ratings of Japanese companies' financial health and led to an increase in Japanese stock price forecasts.

In previous chapters of this text, you studied the global markets for goods and services. In this chapter, you will learn how economists measure a nation's international transactions of goods and services. You will also begin your study of the foreign exchange markets and will consider the role of foreign exchange markets in the global marketplace. You will also find out about exchange rates, foreign exchange risk, and factors that determine currency values.

Get current data on U.S. international transactions at the Bureau of Economic Analysis at: http://www.bea.doc.gov.

Balance of Payments

The **balance of payments** is a complete tabulation of the total market value of goods, services, and financial assets that domestic residents, firms, and governments exchange with residents of other nations during a given period. A nation's balance of payments is a system that accounts for flows of income and expenditures and the flow of financial assets. Table 6-1 on page 162 provides a summary statement of the U.S. balance of payments system that we shall refer to throughout the next several sections of this chapter.

Balance of payments
A system of accounts that measures transaction of goods, services, income, and financial assets between domestic residents, businesses, and governments and the rest of the world during a specific time period.

BALANCE OF PAYMENTS AS A DOUBLE-ENTRY BOOKKEEPING SYSTEM

A *double-entry bookkeeping system* records both sides of any two-party transaction with two separate and offsetting entries: a debit entry and a credit entry. The result is that the sum of all the debit entries, in absolute value, is equal to the sum of all the credit entries. The balance-of-payments system is like a typical double-entry accounting system in that every transaction results in two entries being

Table 6-1 **Summary Statement of the U.S. Balance of Payments**

Source: Bureau of Economic Analysis, International Accounts Data, U.S. Department of Commerce.

Line	(Credits +, Debits –) $ million	2001	Line	(Credits +, Debits –) $ million	2001
	Current Account			**Capital Account**	
1	**Exports of goods, services, and income**	**1,298,397**	13	U.S. private assets abroad, net [increase/financial outflow (–)]	–434,079
2	Goods	720,831	14	Foreign private assets in the United States, net [increase/ financial inflow (+)]	889,367
3	Services	283,758	15	Other capital account transactions, net	726
4	Income receipts	293,808	16	**Capital account (lines 13, 14 and 15)**	**456,014**
5	**Imports of goods, services, and income payments**	**–1,665,325**	17	U.S. official reserve assets and other U.S. government assets abroad, net	–5,484
6	Goods	–1,147,446	18	Foreign official assets in the United States, net	6,092
7	Services	–204,953	19	**Official settlement balance (lines 17 and 18)**	**608**
8	Income payments	–312,926	20	**Statistical discrepancy (lines 12, 16 and 19 with sign reversed)**	**–39,193**
9	**Unilateral current transfers, net**	**–50,501**	21	**Overall balance of payments (lines 12, 16, 19, and 20)**	**0**
10	**Balance on merchandise trade (lines 2 and 6)**	**–426,615**			
11	**Balance on goods, services, and income (lines 1 and 5)**	**–366,928**			
12	**Balance on current account (lines 1, 5, and 9)**	**–417,429**			

Table 6-2 Recording a U.S. Firm's Export in the Balance-of-Payments Accounts

Transaction	Offsetting Entries	Credit	Debit
Computer export	$2,000 computer exported by the U.S. firm	$2,000	
	$2,000 payment received by the U.S. firm		–$2,000

made in the balance-of-payments accounts. A **debit entry** records a transaction that results in a domestic resident making a payment abroad. A debit entry has a negative value in the balance-of-payments account. A **credit entry** records a transaction that results in a domestic resident receiving a payment from abroad. A credit entry has a positive value in the balance-of-payments account.

Debit entry
A negative entry in the balance of payments that records a transaction resulting in a payment abroad by a domestic resident.

Credit entry
A positive entry in the balance of payments that records a transaction resulting in a payment to a domestic resident from abroad.

In the balance-of-payments accounts, an international transaction that results in a credit entry also generates an offsetting debit entry, and an international transaction that results in a debit entry also generates an offsetting credit entry. In the balance-of-payments accounts, therefore, the sum of all the credit entries is equal in absolute value to the sum of all the debit entries.

To illustrate the double-entry nature of the balance-of-payments system, consider the following example. Suppose a U.S. manufacturer exports a computer to a Canadian firm in exchange for a payment of $2,000. Table 6-2 shows the transaction's effects on the U.S. balance-of-payments accounts. The export of the computer is a $2,000 credit, because it results in a $2,000 payment being made to the U.S. firm from the Canadian firm. Because of the double-entry nature of the system, there is an offsetting $2,000 debit entry made. Note that the sum of the debits, in absolute value, $2,000, is equal to the sum of the credits, $2,000.

BALANCE-OF-PAYMENTS ACCOUNTS

Countries exchange a vast array of goods, services, and financial assets. Economists group these transactions by type. There are different categories for each type of transaction, with various categories combined together to form accounts. Therefore, the balance-of-payments system consists of a number of different accounts. For most nations, the number of accounts can be quite large. We can easily understand the balance-of-payments system, however, by focusing on just three accounts; the current account, the private capital account, and the official settlements balance.

The Current Account

The **current account** measures the flow of goods, services, and income across national borders. It also includes transfers or gifts from the domestic government and residents to foreign residents and governments and foreign transfers to the domestic country. The four basic categories within the current account are goods, services, income, and unilateral transfers. Table 6-1 shows the exports and

Current account
Measures the flow of goods, services, income, and transfers or gifts between domestic residents, businesses, and governments and the rest of the world.

imports of goods, services, and income for the United States on lines 1 through 8. Line 9 is for the unilateral transfers category. Let's examine each of these four categories of the current account.

Goods

The goods category measures the imports and exports of tangible goods. This category includes trade in foods, industrial materials, capital goods (such as machinery), autos, and consumer goods. An export of any of these items is a credit in the goods category, because this would result in a payment from abroad. An import of any of these items is a debit in the goods category, because this would result in a payment made abroad.

Most economists consider the goods category to be the most accurately measured balance-of-payments category, because this category measures the trade of tangible items that, in many countries, must be registered with customs agents.

Services

The services category measures the imports and exports of services, tourism and travel, and military transactions. Payments, royalties, or fees received from abroad for providing consulting, insurance, banking, or accounting services, for example, are recorded as credits in the service category. Likewise, payments, royalties, or fees sent abroad for the import of these services is a debit in the service category. The service category also includes the import and export of military equipment, services, and aid.

To understand how travel and tourism services appear in the balance of payments, consider a domestic college student who traveled abroad during a semester break. Expenditures by this student on items such as a rail pass and hotel accommodations are imports, or debits, in the service category because these services are, in a sense, imported by the student.

The imports and exports of services are much more difficult to measure than exports and imports of goods. Because a tangible item is not registered at a customs point, it can be very difficult to estimate the amount of services provided internationally. Hence, economists refer to services as *invisibles*.

Income

The income category tabulates interest and dividend payments to foreign residents and governments who hold domestic financial assets. It also includes payments received by domestic residents and governments who hold financial assets abroad.

To illustrate how investment income appears in the balance of payments, suppose a U.K. resident receives an interest payment on a German treasury bill that she holds. The interest payment is an export, or credit, in the income category of the U.K. balance of payments because there is a receipt of a payment from abroad. Therefore, income payments received by domestic residents who hold financial assets abroad are credits, or exports, whereas income payments made to foreign residents who hold domestic financial assets are debits, or imports.

It is important to note that economists do not record the *purchase* of a financial asset in the service category. Only the income earned on the financial asset is included in the current account, because income earned on assets can be used for current consumption.

Unilateral Transfers

The unilateral transfers category measures international transfers, or gifts, between individuals and governments. This category, therefore, records the offsetting entries of exports or imports for which nothing except *goodwill* is expected in return. To illustrate how a gift appears in the unilateral transfers category, suppose the U.S. government sends $500,000 worth of rice as humanitarian aid to a country that had just experienced a flood. The export of the rice appears in the goods category as a credit. However, the U.S. government expects no payment for this export. A debit entry appears in the unilateral transfers category, indicating that the United States effectively has imported a $500,000 payment of goodwill from the foreign country.

The Capital Account

The private **capital account** measures the outflow of domestic assets abroad and the inflow of foreign assets into the domestic country that result from transactions involving private (nongovernmental) individuals and companies. The private capital account includes three categories of financial assets: financial assets of the domestic government, private domestic financial assets, and foreign financial assets. These financial assets include physical assets and financial assets such as bonds, bills, stocks, deposits, and currencies.

Capital account
A tabulation of the flows of financial assets between domestic private residents and businesses and foreign private residents and businesses.

The private capital account tabulates two types of asset *flows:* investment flows and changes in banks' and brokers' cash deposits that arise from foreign transactions. Investment flows include the following:

- Purchases of foreign securities by domestic residents and purchases of domestic securities by foreign residents
- Lending to foreign residents by domestic residents and borrowing by domestic residents from foreign residents
- Investment by domestic firms in their foreign affiliates and investment by foreign firms in their domestic affiliates

A debit entry in the capital account, for example, records the purchase of a foreign financial asset by a domestic private resident, because this transaction results in a payment made abroad. Likewise, a credit entry records the purchase of a domestic financial asset by a foreign private resident as this transaction generates a payment from abroad.

Table 6-1 (page 162) shows the categories of the private capital account for 2001 on lines 13 through 15. These categories tabulate private transactions of domestic assets and foreign assets. Changes in private U.S. assets abroad reflect an increase or decrease in private ownership of foreign assets. A net capital outflow means that the net purchases of foreign assets by domestic residents exceed the net purchases of domestic assets by private foreign residents. Changes in foreign assets in the United States reflect an increase or decrease in private foreign ownership of domestic assets. A net capital inflow means that the net purchases of domestic assets by private foreign residents exceeds the net purchases of foreign assets by domestic private residents.

The Official Settlements Balance

Official settlements balance
A balance-of-payments account that tabulates transactions of reserve assets by official government agencies.

The third and final account, the **official settlements balance,** measures the transactions of financial assets and deposits by official government agencies. Typically, the central banks and finance ministries, or treasuries, of national governments conduct these types of official transactions.

It is common for foreign central banks and government agencies to keep deposit accounts with other central banks. If, for example, the U.S. Treasury or Federal Reserve were to make a deposit with the Bank of England, the deposit appears as a capital outflow, or *debit,* in the U.S. balance of payments. If the Bank of England were to make a deposit with the Federal Reserve, however, the deposit is a capital inflow, or *credit*, in the U.S. balance of payments. In Table 6-1, line 17 shows the U.S. official assets, including gold and foreign currencies, Special Drawing Rights at the International Monetary Fund, and other U.S. government assets. Foreign official assets in the United States are shown on line 18 of Table 6-1. The official settlements balance, line 19, is the sum of lines 17 and 18.

DEFICITS AND SURPLUSES IN THE BALANCE OF PAYMENTS

If we sum all of the debits and credits that appear in the current account, private capital account, and official settlements balance, the total should be zero. However, this seldom happens in practice. A number of transactions are missed in the accounting process or hidden from the process intentionally. For example, illegal transactions are hidden from government agencies, and some legal transactions may be hidden from government agencies, such as customs officials, to avoid taxes. Furthermore, government statisticians make errors in their tabulation of credits and debits.

If the sum of the credits and debits in the current account, private capital account, and official settlements is not zero, then an offsetting entry appears in the balance of payments. Economists call this offsetting entry the *statistical discrepancy.* The statistical discrepancy can be very large. Line 20 of Table 6-1 shows that the statistical discrepancy for the United States for 2001 was more than $39 billion!

The *overall balance of payments* is the sum of the credits and debits in the current account, capital account, official settlements, and the statistical discrepancy. Because debit entries offset each and every credit entry, and the statistical discrepancy offsets any errors, the overall balance of payments necessarily is equal to zero.

It is common, and somewhat confusing, when economists and the media refer to balance-of-payments deficits or surpluses. As explained above, ignoring the statistical discrepancy, the overall balance of payments must sum to zero. Therefore, what economists and the media refer to is something other than the overall balance of payments.

A *balance-of-payments deficit* refers to a situation in which the official settlements balance is positive. Ignoring a statistical discrepancy, if the sum of the credits and debits in the current account and the private capital account is negative, private payments made to foreigners exceeds private payments received from foreigners. In this case, the official settlements balance must be positive, and is called a balance-of-payments deficit. A situation where the sum of the debits and credits in the current and private capital account is positive means that private payments received from foreigners exceed private payments made to foreigners. In this case, the official settlements balance is negative, and is called a *balance-of-payments surplus.* A *balance-of-payments equilibrium* refers to a situation where the sum of the debits and credits in the current account and the private capital account is zero, and thus the official settlements balance is zero. Therefore, we can conclude the following:

> **A balance of payments equilibrium, ignoring a statistical discrepancy, arises when the sum of the debits and credits in the current account and the private capital account equal zero, so that the official settlements balance is zero. A balance-of-payments deficit corresponds to a positive official settlements balance, and a balance-of-payments surplus corresponds to a negative official settlements balance.**

OTHER DEFICIT AND SURPLUS MEASURES

Economists use other deficit and surplus measures that are part of the balance-of-payments system. The *balance on merchandise trade* is the sum of the debit and credit entries in the merchandise or goods category. If the sum of the debit entries in this category exceeds the sum of the credit entries, then the balance on merchandise trade is negative, and there is a deficit in merchandise trade. If the sum of the debit entries is less than the sum of the credit entries, then the balance on merchandise trade is positive, and there is a merchandise trade surplus. Table 6-1 (page 162) lists merchandise or goods credits on line 2 and debits on line 6. The sum of the two amounts is the balance on merchandise trade, and this balance appears on line 10 of Table 6-1. Because the debits, or merchandise imports, exceed the credits, or merchandise exports, the total is a negative amount representing a merchandise deficit on line 10.

The *balance on goods, services, and income* is the sum of the debit and credit entries that appear in the merchandise, service, and income categories. If the total of the debit entries, or imports, exceeds the sum of the credit entries, or exports, then there is a deficit in goods, services, and income. If the total of the debit entries, or imports, is less than the sum of the credit entries, or exports, then there is a surplus in goods, services, and income. Table 6-1 provides the balance on goods, services, and income on line 11. This amount is negative, indicating that the United States experienced a negative balance, or deficit, on goods, services, and income in 2001.

As explained earlier, the current account includes the categories of goods, services, income, and unilateral transfers. Thus the *balance on the current account* is the sum of all the debit and credit entries in these categories. The current account balance is the most reported balance-of-payments measure. If the sum of the debit entries exceeds the sum of the credit entries, then there is a current account deficit. If the sum of the debit entries is less than the sum of the credit entries, then there is a current account surplus. Table 6-1 provides the balance on the current account on line 12. This balance is also negative, indicating that the United States experienced a negative balance, or deficit, on the current account for 2001.

The *balance on the capital account* reflects the net flow of financial assets purchased by private individuals. As explained earlier, purchases of foreign financial assets by private domestic residents represent a capital outflow, and appear as a debit. Purchases of domestic financial assets by private foreign residents represent a capital inflow, and appear as a credit. The balance on the capital account reflects the net inflow or outflow of capital. If the debit entries exceed the credit entries, there is a net capital outflow. If the debit entries are less than the credit entries, there is a net capital inflow. This balance appears on line 16 of Table 6-1. This positive balance indicates that the United States experienced a surplus on the capital account in 2001.

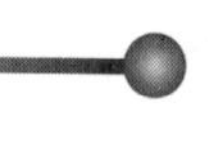

Fundamental Issue

What is a country's balance of payments, and what does this measure?

The balance of payments is an accounting system used to tabulate a nation's international transactions. The balance-of-payments system measures transactions of goods, services, income, unilateral transfers, private transactions of financial assets, and official reserves.

The Role of Foreign Exchange Markets in the Global Marketplace

In a sense, the *markets for foreign exchange* are the financial plumbing that facilitate the flow of goods and services. As you learned in Chapter 1, the *foreign exchange market* is a system of private banks, foreign exchange brokers, and central banks through which households, firms and governments buy and sell the currencies of other nations, or foreign exchange. Providing an arrangement for valuing transactions and delivering payments, the foreign exchange markets promote the flow of goods, services, and assets among nations. **Exchange rates,** which are the market prices of foreign exchange, are a critical element of this system.

Exchange rate
Expresses the value of one currency relative to another currency as the number of units of one currency required to purchase one unit of the other currency.

HOW FOREIGN EXCHANGE RATES AND FOREIGN EXCHANGE MARKETS FACILITATE GLOBAL TRANSACTIONS

As an example of the role of exchange rates, suppose you decide to purchase a new DVD player. After shopping at a local appliance store, you select a DVD player manufactured by a Japanese company with a dollar price of $300. Your decision to purchase this particular piece of equipment largely depends on its price. Conveniently, the price is denominated in your own currency, the currency you have in your billfold or handbag or in your bank account. Your payment to the appliance store for the DVD player is therefore a simple, straightforward transaction.

The Japanese residents who own the Japanese electronics company, however, must pay the company's workers and suppliers in Japanese yen. Japanese residents do not want to receive dollars. Therefore, after they receive a dollar-denominated bank deposit as payment from the appliance dealer for orders of additional electronic equipment, Japanese residents who own the electronics company deposit the payment with their bank, which converts the proceeds into yen. They can now make payments to their workers and suppliers from a yen-denominated bank account.

The Role of the Exchange Rate

How many yen is each dollar worth? That is, what is the value of the dollar relative to the yen? This is what an exchange rate tells us. An exchange rate expresses the value of one currency relative to another. It expresses the number of units of one currency required to purchase one unit of another currency, and thereby converts the value of this transaction into local currency terms.

The Role of the Foreign Exchange Market

What role does the foreign exchange market perform in the previous example involving the Japanese firm? The notion of a foreign exchange market may invoke the image of frantic traders in shirtsleeves and visors hustling money on a cluttered trading floor, with their actions determining the quotations for currencies that we see in daily newspapers such as the *Wall Street Journal* and the *Financial Times*. In our example, however, a foreign exchange market is not prominent. The Japanese company uses the services of its bank, not the foreign exchange market. Further, dollars and yen never crossed international borders. Only the DVD player did.

Indeed, the actual flow of currencies across national borders is an insignificant element of the foreign exchange market. The bulk of foreign exchange transactions occur in cyberspace via telephones and computers. Hard currency flows usually arise only as a result of activities such as tourism or illegal transactions. The financial assets that are typically traded in foreign exchange markets are **foreign-currency-denominated financial instruments,** which are financial assets such as bonds, stocks, and especially bank deposits denominated (valued) in terms of another nation's currency.

Foreign-currency-denominated financial instrument
A financial asset, such as a bond, a stock, or a bank deposit, whose value is denominated in the currency of another nation.

HOW A FOREIGN EXCHANGE TRANSACTION IS CONDUCTED

Let's return to the previous example and consider how a foreign exchange transaction might have been conducted. Suppose that Best Buy is the store from which you purchased the DVD player. After selling several DVD players, the managers of Best Buy decide to purchase more equipment from Toshiba, a Japanese electronics firm. As shown in Figure 6-1, Best Buy presents a \$1 million payment to Toshiba, which, in turn, presents the payment to its bank, Fuji Bank, for deposit.

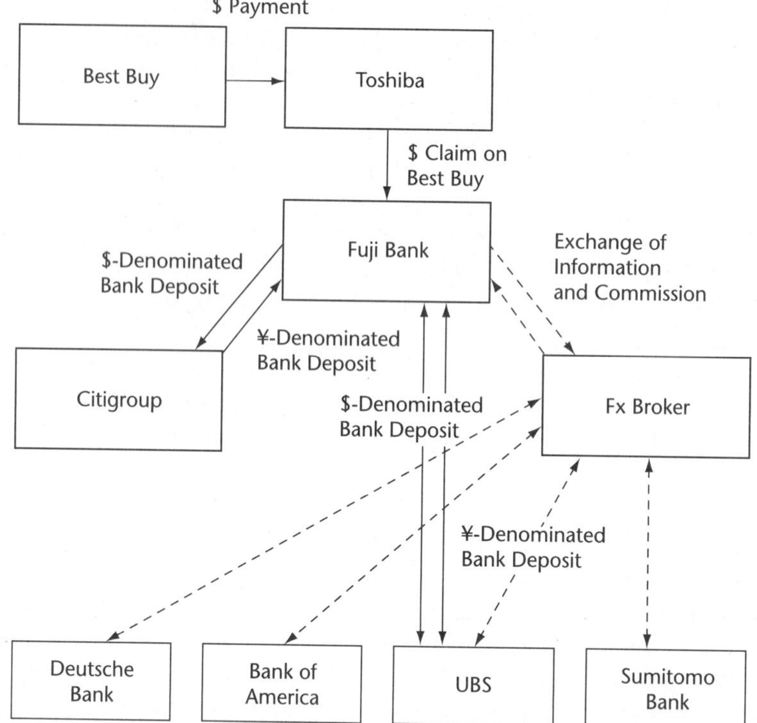

Figure 6-1

How a Foreign Exchange Transaction Is Conducted

Toshiba receives a dollar-denominated payment from Best Buy. Toshiba presents the payment to Fuji Bank. Fuji Bank, acting on behalf of Toshiba, must exchange the dollar-denominated payment for yen. Fuji Bank typically has two options. The first option is to contact another large bank such as Citigroup and negotiate an exchange of dollars for yen. The second option is to contact a foreign exchange broker. The foreign exchange broker connects an agent of Fuji Bank with an agent at United Bank of Switzerland, who then completes an electronic transfer of U.S. dollars for yen at an agreed rate of exchange.

As stated earlier, Toshiba must pay its workers and suppliers in yen. Hence, it prefers its deposit to be denominated in yen. Fuji Bank, acting on behalf of Toshiba, must exchange the $1 million payment for yen. Typically, Fuji Bank has two options. The first is to contact another large bank, say Citigroup, and negotiate an exchange of dollars for yen.

The second option is to contact a *foreign exchange broker.* A foreign exchange broker brings together buyers and sellers of currencies in return for a commission. Foreign exchange brokers constantly survey market participants to determine who is willing to buy or sell various currencies and at what exchange rates those parties are willing to trade. Because brokers collect and centralize this information, they typically have superior exchange rate information. On the one hand, the primary benefit of working with a broker is to reduce information costs that may result in a lower price for a particular currency. On the other hand, dealing directly with another bank eliminates the commission that a broker charges.

As shown in the figure, the foreign exchange broker may exchange information with Deutsche Bank, Bank of America, United Bank of Switzerland (UBS), and Sumitomo Bank. Let's suppose that Fuji Bank works with the broker, who has determined that UBS has the lowest price for yen. When the broker receives its commission, it connects an agent of Fuji Bank with an agent at UBS, who then completes an electronic transfer of U.S. dollars for yen at the agreed rate of exchange.

WHAT IS THE FOREIGN EXCHANGE MARKET?

The foreign exchange market is the oldest and largest financial market in the world. As discussed in Chapter 1, the average daily turnover in this market is more than $1 trillion. To make this number more relevant, consider that the average daily turnover in the foreign exchange market is nearly seven times the size of the market for U.S. government securities—the world's second largest financial market—and more than twenty-five times the combined volume of the world's ten largest stock markets.

A Global Market

Unlike stock or commodity markets, the foreign exchange market has no central trading floor where buyers and sellers meet. Foreign exchange traders conduct most foreign exchange trades by telephone or computer, so the foreign exchange market has evolved into a truly global market with transactions throughout the world. Nonetheless, most transactions are concentrated in a few major trading centers. The largest foreign exchange trading centers are, in rank order, the United Kingdom, the United States, Japan, Singapore, Germany, France, Hong Kong, and Switzerland.

A Twenty-Four-Hour Market

The foreign exchange market is open twenty-four hours a day, except for short gaps on weekends. Starting at the international dateline, trading first opens in Asian-Pacific markets. Before these markets close, trading opens in the Middle East and then in Europe. In the middle of the trading day in Europe, trading opens in New York. It then begins in the Western United States. Before North American markets close, trading begins once again in Asian-Pacific markets.

Market Participants and Instruments

Figure 6-1 illustrates a hypothetical foreign exchange transaction in which the primary options for Fuji Bank are to trade with another large bank or with a foreign exchange broker. These two types of financial institutions make up nearly 85 percent of all foreign exchange market transactions. Global banks account for approximately two-thirds of the market volume, while foreign exchange brokers and dealers account for approximately 20 percent. The remainder of foreign exchange volumes involve nonfinancial businesses. This last group is diverse and growing as more businesses and individuals find easier modes of access to the foreign exchange markets. (To understand how the Internet is affecting foreign exchange market transactions, see on the next page *Online Globalization: Online Foreign Exchange Services.*)

As you will discover in the remainder of this chapter, a wide array of financial instruments are traded on the foreign exchange market. It is not uncommon for the values of individual trades in these foreign exchange instruments to exceed $250 million. Studies show that foreign exchange market volumes are so large that transactions of this magnitude have little if any affect on currency values. In

Online Globalization

Online Foreign Exchange Services

The market for foreign exchange has long been a profitable line of business for large, money-center banks. Companies such as Chase Manhattan and Citigroup have invested billions of dollars upgrading their electronic foreign exchange network systems to handle the foreign exchange markets' large number of transactions more efficiently. Internet sites for foreign exchange, however, are slowly generating competition for the major banks. CFOWeb.com, for instance, claims to be the "first real, robust, truly independent portal for wholesale capital markets" and has over 2,000 corporate clients. This and other foreign exchange sites offer foreign exchange bidding and risk management services.

Survey evidence indicates that foreign exchange sites capture about 15 percent of the daily volume of foreign exchange. Forecasts indicate that this share will double in just five years. Online foreign exchange services claim that they simplify the bidding process, as compared with the traditional method of telephone bidding. The sites also appear to be an efficient means of settling large transactions among banks and corporate treasures. MasterCard already conducts 90 percent of its currency trades on the Web, and a number of financial institutions are moving in the direction of online trading of financial instruments such as fixed-income securities.

A growing number of medium-sized and small businesses are becoming involved in importing or exporting goods and services, so the portion of foreign exchange market trading associated with smaller currency transactions is likely to increase in future years. A company called GainCapital.com has sought to establish an electronic marketplace for pricing foreign exchange trades as low as $100,000 and no larger than $10 million and for selling market research to clients that typically execute foreign exchange trades within this range. Another Web site, called FXTrade.com, plans to allow traders to buy and sell the most popular currencies in amounts as low as $1. These and other companies are betting that smaller currency transactions will become more commonplace as e-commerce spreads across the globe.

For Critical Analysis:
Do you think that online foreign exchange services like those described above will have any impact on exchange rates prices and their volatility? Why or why not?

addition, quoted prices on instruments traded in the foreign exchange market change quickly, often more than twenty times per minute.

2 Fundamental Issue

What is the role of foreign exchange markets in the global marketplace?

The foreign exchange market is a system of private banks, brokers, and central banks through which households, firms, and governments buy and sell foreign exchange. These institutions develop market mechanisms for valuing transactions and delivering payments, thereby promoting the flows of goods and services among nations. The foreign exchange market is the oldest and largest financial market in the world. This market is truly a global market that is, for all practical purposes, open twenty-four hours a day.

The Spot Market for Foreign Exchange

In the previous example, we assumed that the managers at Fuji Bank wanted to convert its dollar holdings into yen immediately. The market in this example is the **spot market** for foreign exchange, which is a market for immediate purchase and delivery of currencies. Delivery in the spot market for foreign exchange usually occurs within two to three days. The media publish spot rates that pertain to the trading of foreign-currency-denominated deposits among major banks for $1,000,000 or more. You will examine other important foreign exchange markets and instruments later in this chapter.

Spot market
A market for immediate purchase and delivery of currencies.

Spot exchange rates are the market prices of foreign exchange in the spot market. Table 6-3 on page 174 displays spot exchange rates published on the Web sites or news outlets of business media such as the *Wall Street Journal* or the *Financial Times.*

The spot exchange rates in Table 6-3 are for foreign exchange transactions undertaken in the London market, and they represent the rate that a currency sold for at the close of the market. Notice in the text at the top of the Table 6-3 that the rates "apply to trading among banks in amounts of $1 million and more." This means that the quoted spot rates pertain to very large transactions. Smaller spot transactions, such as those involving individuals and small- to medium-sized businesses, incur less favorable exchange rates. Table 6-3 displays two versions of the spot rate: *U.S. dollar per currency* and *currency per U.S. dollar.* In the next section, we shall explain these two versions of the spot rate. In later sections you will find out about various ways that economists use spot rates to construct other useful measures of a currency's value.

EXCHANGE RATES AS RELATIVE PRICES

Because an exchange rate relates the values of two currencies, it is a relative price economists call a *bilateral exchange rate,* as bilateral means "two sides." Table 6-3 displays two columns for spot exchange rates. The first is the *U.S. dollar per currency,* or how many U.S. dollars it takes to purchase one unit of a foreign currency. For example, in Table 6-3 the exchange rate for the U.S. dollar relative to the British pound (£) is 1.4995 $/£, meaning that a trader must give 1.4995 U.S. dollars in exchange for one British pound.

The exchange rate also expresses how many foreign currency units it takes to purchase one dollar, or *currency per U.S. dollar.* This is the reciprocal of the U.S.-dollar-per-currency rate. Hence, the rate of exchange of the British pound for the U.S. dollar is 1/(1.4995 $/£), or 0.6669 £/$, so a trader must provide 0.6669 pounds in exchange for one U.S. dollar. Because there are two different ways to express an exchange rate, it is important to be sure whether an exchange rate is a U.S.-dollar-per-currency rate, or a currency-per-U.S.-dollar rate.

Currency Appreciation and Depreciation

As you can see in Table 6-3, the U.S.-dollar-per-currency rate for the British pound in Table 6-3 changed from 1.5033 $/£ to 1.4995 $/£. This means that the dollar

Table 6-3 Spot Rates for Currency Exchange

Values below are derived from data for the London closing rates and pertain to transactions among banks in the amount of $1 million or more.

Sources: http://www.ft.com, http://www.bankofengland.co.uk.

	U.S. Dollar per Currency[1]	Previous Close	Currency per U.S. Dollar[1]	Previous Close	Bank of England Index[2]
Argentina ($)	0.2703	0.2755	3.7000	3.6300	—
Australia (A$)	0.5741	0.5723	1.7419	1.7472	76.4832
Brazil (R$)	0.3570	0.3479	2.8010	2.8740	—
Canada (C$)	0.6553	0.6545	1.5260	1.5279	77.5296
Denmark (DKr)	0.1304	0.1314	7.6700	7.6085	102.349
Euro (€)	0.9691	0.9658	1.0319	1.0354	79.658
Hong Kong (HK$)	0.1282	0.1282	7.8000	7.8000	—
Japan (¥)	0.0082	0.0081	121.3900	123.3700	131.8623
Malaysia (M$)	0.2632	0.2632	3.8000	3.8000	—
Mexico (P)	0.1004	0.1010	9.9600	9.9025	—
Thailand (Bt)	0.0238	0.0238	42.0300	42.0650	—
United Kingdom (£)	1.4995	1.5033	0.6669	0.6652	107.5153
United States ($)	—	—	—	—	118.5031

1. Closing midpoint value
2. Bank of England nominal effective exchange rate index based on a basket of 21 currencies (1990 = 100).

appreciated against the pound, because the number of dollars required to purchase one pound decreased. In other words, the dollar price of the pound fell. Hence, we say that the pound *depreciated* relative to the dollar. Likewise, the currency-per-U.S.-dollar rate changed from 0.6652 £/$ to 0.6669 £/$, indicating that the number of pounds required to purchase one dollar increased, so that the pound price of the dollar rose.

We can determine the rate of appreciation or depreciation by calculating the percentage change in the exchange rate. We calculate the percentage change of an exchange rate by subtracting the previous value of the exchange rate from the new value, dividing this difference by the previous value, and multiplying by 100.

Using the U.S.-dollar-per-currency rates in Table 6-3, the percentage change in the spot exchange rate is $[(1.4995 - 1.5033)/1.5033] \times 100 \cong -0.25\%$. In words, the dollar appreciated relative to the pound by 0.25 percent. Using the currency-per-U.S.-dollar rate, the percentage change is $[(0.6669 - 0.6652)/0.6652] \times 100 \cong +0.25\%$.

The first percentage change calculation is negative, because the number of dollars required to purchase a pound decreased. The second percentage change calculation is positive, because the number of pounds required to purchase a dollar increased. As you can see, in order to determine whether a positive change or a negative change indicates an appreciation or depreciation, we must know whether the exchange rate is expressed as a U.S.-dollar-per-currency rate or as a currency-per-U.S.-dollar-rate.

Cross Rates

Table 6-3 indicates that, on this particular day, the U.S.-dollar-per-currency and currency-per-U.S.-dollar exchange rates for the euro (€) were equal to 0.9691 $/€ and 1.0319 €/$, respectively. Suppose, however, that our interest is in the rate of exchange between the British pound and the euro, not the rate of exchange between the dollar and the euro. To determine this rate of exchange, we can compute a *cross rate,* which is another bilateral exchange rate that we calculate from two bilateral rates.

In Table 6-3, the U.S.-dollar-per-currency rate for the British pound is 1.4995 $/£, and the U.S.-dollar-equivalent rate for the euro is 0.9691 $/€. Using these two bilateral rates, it is straightforward to calculate either the British-pound-per-euro exchange rate or the euro-per-British-pound exchange rate.

To calculate the British-pound-per-euro cross rate, we divide the dollar rate of exchange for the euro by the dollar exchange rate for the British pound. Thus, the pound-euro cross rate equals

$$\frac{0.9691\ \$/€}{1.4995\ \$/€}.$$

Dividing by a fraction is the same as multiplying by the reciprocal of the fraction. Therefore, we can express the cross rate as

$$\frac{0.9691}{1.4995} \times \frac{\$}{€} \times \frac{£}{\$}.$$

Notice in the calculation above, the dollar cancels out because it appears in the numerator of one fraction and the denominator of another. This yields the British-pound-per-euro cross rate, which is 0.6463 £/€.

If we wish to determine the euro-per-British-pound cross rate, we invert the British-pound-per-euro cross rate, which yields

$$\frac{1}{0.6463\ £/€} = 1.5473\ €/£.$$

Table 6-4 Cross-Rate Table Based on Rates in Table 6-3

The values are cross-rates of exchange between the currency listed in the row relative to the currency listed in the column. The first value listed in the column below the dollar, for example, is the U.S.-dollar-per-Canadian-dollar cross rate.

	U.S. Dollar	Canadian Dollar	Euro	British Pound
U.S. Dollar	—	1.5260	1.0319	0.6669
Canadian Dollar	0.6553	—	0.6762	0.4370
Euro	0.9691	1.4788	—	0.6463
British Pound	1.4995	1.2882	1.5473	—

ON THE WEB

For daily exchange rates, a currency converter for 164 currencies, and cross rates, visit the homepage of Oanda at: http://www.Oanda.com.

Using the U.S.-dollar-per-currency rates for the British pound and the euro, we have calculated a cross rate of exchange between the British pound and the euro.

The foreign exchange sections of major newspapers provide cross rates for many high-volume currencies in a *cross-rate table.* Table 6-4 is an example of such a table. The cross-rate table lists the currencies across the top row and the left-hand column. The cross rates in the table are the exchange rates between the currencies of the countries listed on the corresponding row and column. When the same country appears on both the row and the column, the entry is either blank or 1. The first column provides the U.S.-dollar-per-currency rate for each currency listed on the corresponding row. Therefore, the first row provides the currency-per-U.S.-dollar exchange rates.

REAL EXCHANGE RATES

Nominal exchange rate *A bilateral exchange rate that is unadjusted for changes in the two nations' price levels.*

So far we have discussed **nominal exchange rates.** These are exchange rates that do not reflect changes in nations' price levels. By measuring rates of depreciation and appreciation, the nominal exchange rate gauges changes in the market value of our own currency in exchange for a foreign currency.

Real exchange rate *A bilateral exchange rate that has been adjusted for price changes that occurred in the two nations.*

What if we are interested in the amount of foreign *goods and services* that we can buy with our domestic currency rather than how many units of the foreign currency we can purchase? The **real exchange rate** adjusts the nominal exchange rate for changes in both nations' price levels and thereby measures the *purchasing power of domestic goods and services in exchange for foreign goods and services.* Consequently, appraising how much of another country's goods and services individuals and firms can obtain by trading their own nation's goods and services, using their own currency as a medium of exchange in the transaction, requires knowing the value of the real exchange rate.

Nominal Exchange Rate Changes

To see why the real exchange rate matters, consider the bilateral exchange relationship between the United States and the nations participating in the European Monetary Union (EMU) between April 2000 and April 2002. This period provides an excellent example because of the euro's decline relative to the dollar that you learned about in the introduction to this chapter. In April 2000, the euro-per-U.S.-dollar spot rate was 1.058 €/$. By April 2002, the euro's value had fallen, and the exchange rate had climbed to 1.129 €/$.

Based on the values of these nominal exchange rates, the rate of appreciation of the dollar relative to the euro between April 2000 and April 2002 was equal to $[(1.129 - 1.058)/1.058] \times 100 = 6.71$ percent. This means that in April 2002 it required 6.7 percent more euros to buy a dollar in the foreign exchange market than was necessary in April 2000.

Measuring Price Changes: Consumer Price Indexes

To measure the purchasing power of a nation's currency, economists require measures of overall levels of prices. International economists typically find that a particularly useful measure of a nation's price level is the country's *consumer price index*. A **consumer price index** (CPI) is a measure of the economy-wide price level. Economists calculate a CPI by selecting fixed sets of domestic and foreign goods and services and tracking the prices of these specific goods and services from year to year.

Consumer price index (CPI)
A weighted sum of prices of goods and services that a typical consumer purchases each year.

To illustrate a CPI, let's make up a simple example. Let's call our example the "college consumer price index." Suppose that the "typical" college student spends one fourth of his or her available resources on tuition, one fourth on housing, one fourth on domestically manufactured food, clothing, and supplies, and one fourth on foreign-manufactured food, clothing and supplies. We could then collect information on the average prices of each of these components of the typical college consumer's expenses. Then we could multiply each one by one fourth. Summing the results would then yield a numerical value for our college consumer price index.

U.S., EMU, and other nations' government agencies compute the overall consumer price index in the same basic manner as in our fictitious example. The actual computation of an economy-wide CPI is much more complex than in our example, because it is a weighted sum of prices of a full set of goods and services that governments determine that their typical consumers purchase each year. Figure 6-2 on the next page displays the U.S. and EMU consumer price indexes since January 1995. Economists express the CPI in *index number* form, where a value of 100 applies to the *base year* for the index. This is a year selected to serve as a foundation for comparing changes in the aggregate price level over time. In the figure, the base year for both nations' consumer price indexes is 1996.

The Real Exchange Rate and Real Currency Appreciation or Depreciation

The immediate effects of the decline in the value of the euro relative to the dollar were that EMU goods and services effectively became cheaper for U.S. consumers

Figure 6-2

Consumer Price Indexes in the United States and the European Monetary Union

The consumer price index (CPI) is a weighted average of prices of a fixed group of goods and services. The base year for both nations' consumer price indexes is 1996 and, therefore, equals 100 in that year.

Sources: http://www.stls.frb.org and http://www.ecb.int.

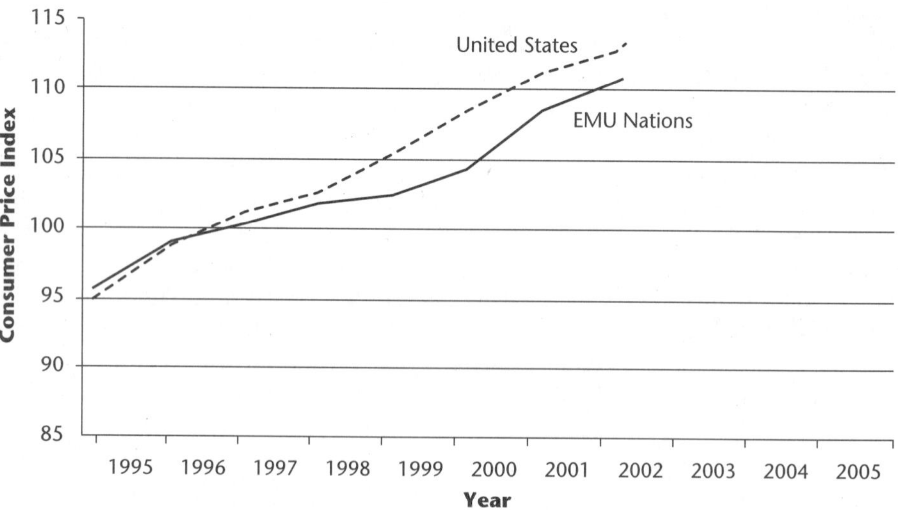

to purchase and that U.S. goods and services became more expensive from the perspective of EMU consumers. Something else that also happened between April 2000 and April 2002, however, was that the EMU had a higher inflation rate as compared with the United States.

In the EMU, the CPI for April 2000 was 105.7, while the CPI for April 2002 was 111.4. Economists use the percentage change in the CPI as a measure of the rate of consumer price inflation over a given time interval. Using these figures for the EMU, the rate of consumer price inflation from April 2000 to April 2002 was [(111.4 – 105.7)/105.7] × 100 = 5.4 percent. In the United States, the CPI for April 2000 was 109.0 and for April 2002, 114.4. This means that the rate of consumer price inflation in the United States over the same time period was [(114.4 – 109.0)/109.0] × 100 = 5.0 percent.

ON THE WEB

For historical data on the CPI in the United States, visit the production and prices section of the economic and financial database of the Federal Reserve Bank of Chicago at: http://www.chicagofed.org/economicresearchanddata/data/index.cfm.
For historical data on the CPI in the EMU, visit the Euro area statistical database of the European Central Bank at: http://www.ecb.int/stats/stats01.htm.

These relative inflation differences matter because changes in the prices of goods and services alter the effective prices that EMU residents pay for U.S. goods and services and that U.S. residents pay for EMU goods and services. To see how the inflation differences matter, let's measure the real exchange rates for April 2000 and April 2002.

To measure the real exchange rate between the European Monetary Union and the United States in April 2000, we multiply the nominal exchange rate at that time, 1.058 €/$, by the ratio of the U.S. consumer price index to the EMU price index, 109.0/105.7, to get 1.091

To calculate the real exchange rate for April 2002, we multiply the nominal exchange rate at the end of that year, 1.129 €/$, by the ratio of the U.S. consumer price index to the EMU price index, 114.4/111.4, which yields 1.159. Using these two real exchange rates implies that the *real rate of appreciation* for the dollar was equal to [(1.159 – 1.091)/1.091] × 100 = 6.23 percent. This calculated real rate of dollar appreciation was slightly lower for the April 2000 to April 2002 period than the nominal appreciation rate of 6.71 percent.

The relatively higher rate of consumer inflation in the EMU—or relatively lower rate of consumer inflation in the United States—implied that U.S. consumers' purchasing power of EMU goods and services decreased relative to their purchasing power of U.S. goods and services. Hence, the relatively higher consumer price inflation in the European Monetary Union mitigated the nominal appreciation in the dollar's value to produce a slightly smaller real appreciation in the dollar's value relative to the euro.

MEASURING THE OVERALL STRENGTH OR WEAKNESS OF A CURRENCY: EFFECTIVE EXCHANGE RATES

Bilateral exchange rates measure the value of a currency relative to *one* other currency. On any given day, a currency will strengthen, or appreciate, against some currencies and weaken, or depreciate, against others. On a given day, the dollar's value may have fallen against the British pound, Japanese yen, and Canadian dollar. Its value may have risen, however, against the euro, Swiss franc, and Mexican peso. So, some bilateral rates would have fallen and some would have risen. But overall is the dollar "stronger" or "weaker?" To answer this question, economists use an **effective exchange rate,** which is a weighted-average measure of the value of a currency relative to two or more other currencies.

Effective exchange rate
A weighted-average measure of the value of a currency relative to two or more currencies.

How Economists Construct Effective Exchange Rates

It is not practical to measure the value of a currency against every other currency in the world. Thus, in constructing an effective exchange rate, economists include only the currencies that they judge to be most important. What constitutes "important" currencies depends on the particular application. If a businessperson wants to know how changes in the value of the dollar affects U.S. imports and exports, then the individual will include the bilateral exchange rates of the largest trading partners of the United States. If a portfolio manager wants to know how changes in the value of the dollar affect the return on a portfolio of international assets, then the manager will want to include the bilateral exchange rates of the currencies that represent the largest shares of the portfolio. The currencies selected compose what economists call the currency basket.

Like the consumer price index, an effective exchange rate is expressed in an index number form, where a value of 100 applies to the base year, which serves as a reference point in time. Economists then measure changes in the value of the effective exchange rate from this base year. For example, if 2004 is the base year, then the value of the effective exchange rate for 2004 is 100. If the effective exchange rate is 125 for 2005, then we know there was a percentage increase in the effective exchange rate from 2004 to 2005 equal to $[(125 - 100)/100] \times 100 = 25$ percent.

Finally, because an effective exchange rate is a weighted average of bilateral exchange rates, economists select *weights* that place greater emphasis on the more important currencies in the currency basket and smaller emphasis on the less important currencies in the currency basket. Economists use these weights to calculate the weighted-average value of the currency relative to all of the currencies in the basket.

What an Effective Exchange Rate Tells Us

What does an effective exchange rate tell us? On any given day a currency may depreciate against some currencies and appreciate against others. The weighted-average value of the effective exchange rate tells us what happened, overall, to the value of the currency on that day.

A number of effective exchange rates are available from leading exchange rate sources. The Bank of England publishes effective exchange rates for a number of currencies, and Figure 6-3 illustrates these rates for the U.S. dollar, the U.K. pound, and the Japanese yen. The International Monetary Fund also publishes effective exchange rates in its monthly bulletin *International Financial Statistics*. The Federal Reserve board publishes several different effective exchange rates for the U.S. dollar in the *Federal Reserve Bulletin*. The *Financial Times* and the *Wall Street Journal* report the J.P. Morgan effective exchange rate index. Figure 6-3 displays effective exchange rates for the U.S. dollar, the U.K. pound, and the Japanese yen since 1980.

The figure shows that there was a dramatic increase in the average value of the dollar over the period 1980 through 1985 and a subsequent decline from 1985 through 1988. Following 1988, there was a steady, general decline in the average value of the dollar, until 1995 when the dollar began to gain value again. The figure shows that for the British pound, there was a decline in the average value over the period until 1995. The effective exchange rate for the British pound began the period at an index value of about 125 and finished at around 90 in 1994, indicating a 28 percent decline in average value. The Japanese yen rose from an index value of 60 in 1985 to an index value of 150 in 1994, which implied a 150 percent appreciation over the period. Between 1995 and 1996, however, the yen lost more than 13 percent of its overall value. In the early 2000s, the yen began to regain some of the value lost earlier.

Figure 6-3

Effective Exchange Rates Since 1980

Between 1985 and 1995, the average value of the U.S. dollar and the British pound declined, while the average value of the Japanese yen increased. This trend reversed in 1995.

Source: http://www.bankofengland.co.uk.

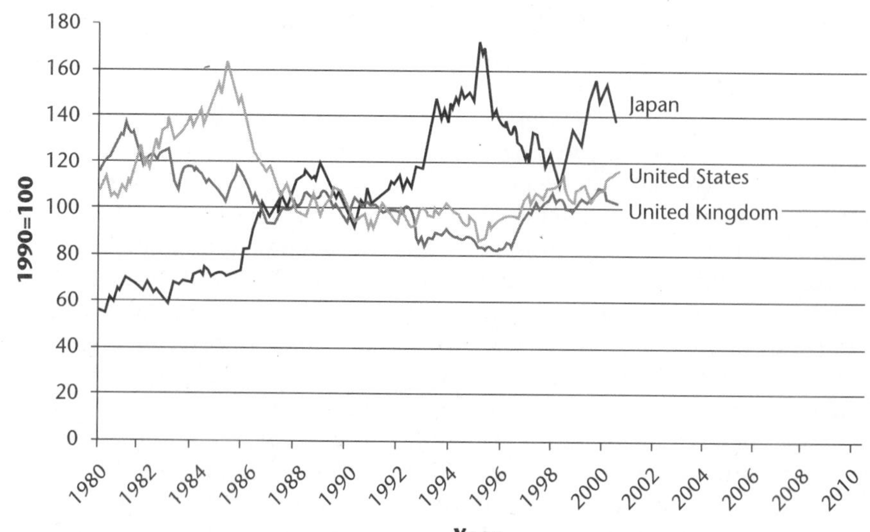

Real Effective Exchange Rates

Earlier in this chapter, you discovered that it is the real exchange rate that indicates changes in international purchasing power. It is possible to construct a *real effective exchange rate,* which is an effective exchange rate based on real exchange rates instead of nominal exchange rates. A real effective exchange rate is calculated in much the same way as a nominal effective exchange rate. In contrast to calculating effective nominal exchange rates, however, we use real exchange rates in computing the real effective exchange rate. Thus, constructing a real effective exchange rate also requires obtaining CPI data for all countries in the index, converting each nominal exchange rate to a real rate, and completing the remaining calculations as described earlier for nominal effective exchange rates.

Fundamental Issue 3

What is the spot foreign exchange market?

The spot market for foreign exchange is the market for contracts requiring immediate delivery of currencies. The spot market for foreign exchange is dominated by large-value transactions among commercial banks and foreign exchange brokers. Spot exchange rates are the prices of currency transactions that occur in this market. Economists use spot exchange rates to measure the appreciation and depreciation of currencies and to construct cross rates, real exchange rates, and effective exchange rates.

Foreign Exchange Risk and the Forward Market for Foreign Exchange

Exchange rates vary over time. Changes in exchange rates expose households, firms, and others who engage in international transactions to potential risk.

FOREIGN EXCHANGE RISK

Let's consider an example of how an international transaction may expose a firm to risk from exchange rate changes. Suppose you work for an international property developer based in the United States, and your firm has an interest in commercial real estate in the United Kingdom. The property agents will consider "substantial offers" on the property for a period of three months, at which time they will arrange sale of the property to the party submitting the highest offer. It will take approximately three more months for your employer to conclude the transaction and to assume possession of the property.

Based on an estimate of the property's income potential, your managers instruct you to submit a bid of £11 million. Suppose that the exchange rate is currently 1.4113 dollars per pound, so from your firm's perspective, the current price of the bid that you are submitting is $15,524,300, or the dollar price of the offer (£11 million × 1.4113 $/£ = $15,524,300). Your managers have indicated that they value the property at $15,524,300.

Suppose the sellers of the property accept your offer to pay £11 million six months from now. Your firm has a foreign-currency-denominated obligation that spans time and, therefore, creates a *foreign-exchange-risk exposure.* **Foreign exchange risk** is the prospect that the value of a foreign-currency-denominated liability or asset will change because of a variation in the exchange rate.

Foreign exchange risk
The risk that the value of a future receipt or obligation will change due to variations in foreign exchange rates.

Suppose that during the next six months the dollar depreciates against the British pound by 5 percent, to 1.4819 dollars per pound. The British pound price of the commercial estate is £11 million. The dollar price, however, changes because of the change in the spot exchange rate. The dollar price of the property rises to \$16,300,900 (£11 million × 1.4819 \$/£ = \$16,300,900). Because of the change in the exchange rate, the dollar price of the property increases by \$776,600, or by 5 percent. By agreeing to the future foreign-currency-denominated transaction, your firm incurs a 5 percent loss from foreign-exchange-risk exposure.

Types of Foreign Exchange Risk Exposure

There are three different ways that individuals or firms may expose themselves to foreign exchange risk. The first type of foreign exchange exposure, which the previous example illustrates, is *transaction exposure.* **Transaction exposure** is the risk that the revenues or costs of a transaction may change in terms of the domestic currency. A transaction exposure results when a firm agrees to complete a foreign-currency-denominated exchange some time in the future.

Transaction exposure
The risk that the revenues or costs associated with a transaction expressed in terms of the domestic currency may change due to variations in exchange rates.

The second type of foreign exchange risk is **translation exposure,** which arises when converting the values of foreign-currency-denominated assets and liabilities into a single currency value. It is easier to understand translation exposure by considering the balance sheet of a multinational corporation. The assets and liabilities of, say, a Swiss multinational corporation may be denominated in many different currencies. At the end of the year, the accountants at the Swiss corporation tabulate its balance sheet and value all its assets and liabilities in a common currency, the Swiss franc. As the exchange value of the Swiss franc changes, so does the value of assets and liabilities denominated in foreign currencies. The net worth of the company reported in the balance sheet also changes.

Translation exposure
Foreign exchange risk resulting from the conversion of a firm's foreign-currency-denominated assets and liabilities into the domestic currency value.

The final type of foreign exchange risk is **economic exposure,** which is the effect that exchange rate changes have on a firm's current valuation of future income streams. Economic exposure affects the ability of a firm to compete in a particular market over an extended period. Some economists believe that at least a portion of the foreign direct investment flows described in Chapter 1 results from firms' efforts to avoid economic exposure. Owning a plant or office in a foreign location of operation may help a firm avoid some of the foreign exchange risk that it would have incurred if all its plants and offices were in domestic locations only.

Economic exposure
The risk that changes in exchange values might alter today's value of a firm's future income streams.

Hedging Foreign Exchange Risk

When considering foreign exchange risk, it is important to understand that a change in the exchange rate may be positive or negative from the perspective of an individual or firm. Nonetheless, the possibility that the exchange rate may change introduces uncertainty that can make planning difficult. Individuals or firms can attempt to reduce or eliminate this uncertainty by cutting or removing the foreign exchange risk. **Hedging** is the act of offsetting exposure to risk. An exposure is **covered** if the hedging activity eliminates *all* of the exposure to risk.

Hedging
The act of offsetting or eliminating risk exposure.

There are a number of financial instruments available to offset foreign exchange risk. One such instrument is a *forward contract* for foreign exchange. You will consider other instruments, *derivative instruments,* used to offset foreign exchange risk later in this chapter.

Covered exposure
A foreign exchange risk that has been completely eliminated with a hedging instrument.

THE FORWARD MARKET FOR FOREIGN EXCHANGE

Let's assume again that you work for the U.S. property developer that has offered to buy a U.K. property. It is highly unlikely that your firm would want to purchase the British pound at the time of notification of acceptance of your company's offer. By immediately purchasing the pound, the firm would have more than $15 million of funds tied up in a foreign currency for six months. Your firm, therefore, desires the future delivery of the British pound.

The **forward exchange market** is a market for contracts ensuring the future delivery of a currency at a specified exchange rate. Most forward exchange trades are in the amount of $1 million or more and occur between large commercial banks. Forward exchange rates, which are the prices of contracts traded in the forward exchange market, are quoted in the foreign exchange tables of many business and financial publications. These publications typically provide prices for one-month, three-month, six-month, and one-year forward contracts.

Forward exchange market
A market for contracts that ensures the future delivery of and payment for a foreign currency at a specified exchange rate.

COVERING A TRANSACTION WITH A FORWARD CONTRACT

Because a forward contract guarantees a rate of exchange at a future date, it can eliminate foreign exchange risk, or *cover* an exposure. Following acceptance of the firm's offer on the commercial property, it has a *short position* in the pound, which is a future obligation denominated in a foreign currency, the pound. As explained earlier, the firm now has a foreign exchange risk exposure.

You could suggest to your superiors that the firm arrange a six-month forward contract on the pound, which would cover the transaction. Suppose that at the time the owner of the property accepts your firm's offer, the six-month forward rate on the pound is 1.4120 $/£. A six-month forward contract for £11 million guarantees that your firm can purchase the £11 million six months from now at an exchange rate of 1.4120 $/£. Entering into a forward contract thereby ensures that the final price of the commercial property will, six months from now, be $15,532,000 (£11 million × 1.4120 $/£ = $15,532,000). There is no uncertainty about the price of the property, so the transaction is covered.

A firm also can experience transaction exposures resulting from foreign-currency-denominated payments that it will receive in the future. In such a situation, a firm has a *long position* because it will receive future amounts denominated in foreign currencies. In this case, the firm can arrange a forward contract enabling it to sell foreign currencies at guaranteed exchange rates. The forward sell contracts will eliminate all of its foreign exchange risks and thus cover its receipts.

In both of these examples, firms eliminate positions with foreign exchange risk by entering into forward contracts that ensure the purchase or sale of a foreign currency at a guaranteed price. By assuming equal and offsetting positions in the forward market, firms can eliminate transaction risk and cover their risk positions. The elimination of uncertainty about the future value of foreign-currency-denominated assets and liabilities via forward exchange markets can generate additional international transactions of goods, services, and financial instruments.

Fundamental Issue

What is foreign exchange risk and the role of forward foreign exchange markets?

Foreign exchange risk is the prospect that the values of foreign-currency-denominated transactions change because of variations in the exchange rate. There are three types of foreign exchange risk exposures: transaction exposure, translation exposure, and economic exposure. The forward exchange market is a market for contracts ensuring the future delivery of a currency at a specified exchange rate. By guaranteeing a price for the future delivery of a currency, firms can cover their foreign exchange risk, thereby promoting greater flows of goods, services, and financial instruments across nations.

Demand for and Supply of Currencies

So far our discussion has focused on descriptions of the spot and forward exchange markets and the prices or exchange rates in these markets. Now let's consider the factors that determine the value of a nation's currency, using the concepts of supply and demand discussed in Chapter 1. In applying these concepts, we shall assume that there are no obstructions or controls on foreign exchange transactions. In addition, we shall assume that governments do not buy or sell currencies in order to manipulate their values. Under these assumptions, market forces of supply and demand determine the value of a currency.

DEMAND FOR A CURRENCY

The primary function of a currency is to facilitate transactions. Thus, the demand for a currency is a *derived demand,* meaning that the demand for a currency arises from the demand for the goods, services, and assets that people use the currency to purchase. The demand for the euro, for instance, stems from U.S. residents' demand for European goods, services, and euro-denominated assets. If U.S. consumers' demand for European goods were to increase, then, indirectly, there would be a rise in the demand for the euro to purchase the European goods. (For more analysis of the demand for a currency and changes in the demand for a currency see *Visualizing Global Economic Issues: The Demand for the Euro.*)

Quantity Demanded and the Exchange Rate

As with goods and services, the demand for a currency satisfies the law of demand. The intuition behind this relationship between the exchange rate and the

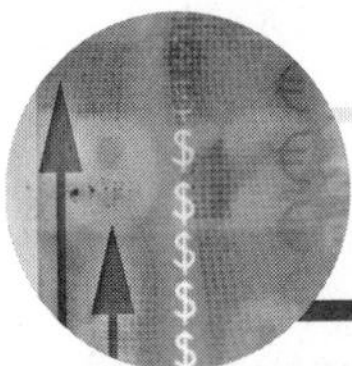

Visualizing Global Economic Issues

The Demand for the Euro

Figure 6-4 illustrates a hypothetical demand curve for the euro. Notice in panel (a) that the "price" on the vertical axis is the U.S.-dollar-per-euro exchange rate ($/€). Because the exchange rate between the dollar and the euro can be expressed as either the dollar-price of the euro ($/€) or the euro-price of the dollar (€/$), it is extremely important to keep in mind that the proper rate, the dollar price of the euro, appears on this vertical axis.

The downward sloping demand curve in panel (a) also illustrates the negative relationship between the exchange rate and the quantity of euros demanded. Suppose that the initial spot exchange rate is S_A, at which the quantity of euros demanded is Q_A. Now suppose that the dollar appreciates relative to the euro to S_B. At this new exchange rate, European goods are relatively less expensive to U.S. consumers. As a result, U.S. consumers would desire to purchase more European goods and require a greater amount of euros to do so. Hence, the quantity demanded of euros rises to Q_B, illustrated by a movement down and along the demand curve from point *A* to point *B*.

Now suppose that at the exchange rate S_A, illustrated in panel (b) of Figure 6-4, U.S. consumer tastes for European goods increases. In order to purchase a greater amount of European goods, U.S. consumers desire a greater quantity of euros at the given exchange rate. Hence, there is an increase in the demand for the euro, illustrated by a rightward shift of the demand curve from $D_€$ to $D_€'$ in panel (b) of Figure 6-4.

For Critical Analysis:
Would an appreciation of the dollar relative to the euro always result in a greater quantity demanded of euros? What role does the slope of the demand curve play in determining the answer to this question?

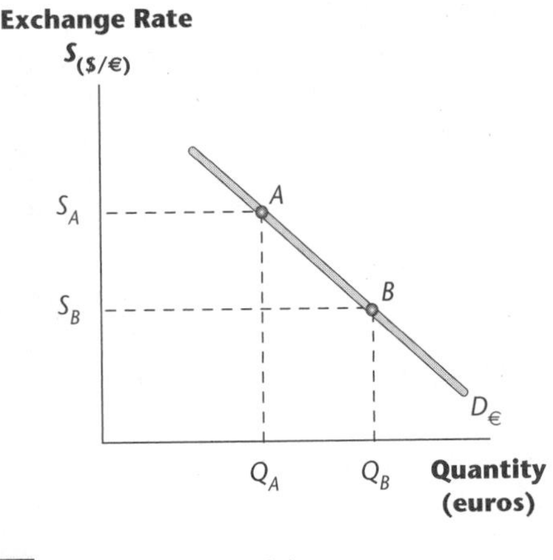

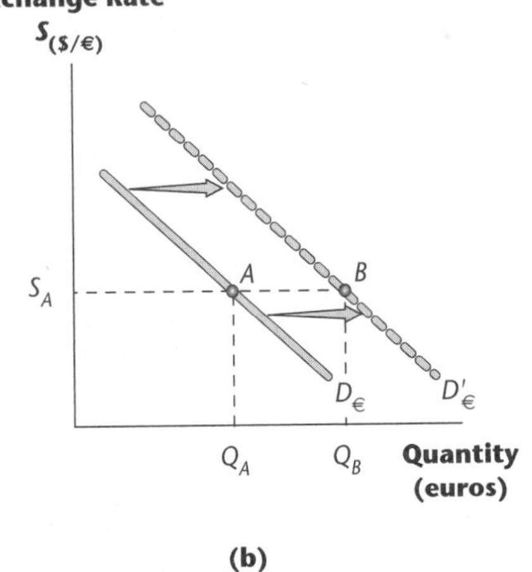

Figure 6-4

The Demand for the Euro

Panel (a) illustrates the demand curve for the euro. A decrease in the exchange rate from S_A *to* S_B *indicates that the U.S. dollar has appreciated relative to the euro. This makes European goods relatively less expensive to U.S. consumers. As a result, U.S. consumers increase their quantity of euros demanded to buy more European goods and services. An increase in U.S. consumers' demand for European goods and services leads to an increase in the demand for the euro. Panel (b) illustrates the increase in demand for the euro by a rightward shift of the demand curve from* $D_€$ *to* $D_€'$.

quantity is that as the dollar appreciates relative to the euro and the dollar price of the euro falls, European goods become relatively less expensive to U.S. consumers. As a result, U.S. consumers desire to purchase more European goods and require a greater amount of euros to facilitate these additional transactions. Consequently, there is a negative relationship between the price of the currency and the quantity demanded: a rise in the exchange rate causes a fall in the *quantity demanded* of a currency.

Changes in Currency Demand

Let's suppose that, at a given exchange rate, U.S. consumers' tastes and preferences for European goods increase. In this case, U.S. consumers desire a larger quantity of euros at the given exchange rate to purchase additional European goods. This is a *change in the demand* for the euro. Because the demand for a currency is a derived demand, the various factors that cause a change in the demand for a currency are all of the factors that cause a change in the foreign demand for that country's goods, services, and assets, such as a change in foreign residents' tastes and preferences for the nation's goods, services, and financial assets.

SUPPLY OF A CURRENCY

The supply of a currency is also derived from the demand for goods, services, and financial assets. The supply of a currency, however, is derived from *domestic* residents' demand for another nation's goods, services, and financial assets.

Quantity Supplied and the Exchange Rate

To understand the supply of a currency, consider a European consumer's demand for U.S. goods, services, and financial assets and, in turn, for the U.S. dollar. When the European consumer purchases U.S. dollars in order to buy U.S. goods, services, or financial assets, the European consumer exchanges euros for dollars. As a result, there is an increase in the quantity of euros supplied in the foreign exchange market. Thus, the European demand for the dollar also represents the supply of euros. It is in this way that the supply of the euro is derived from the demand for U.S. goods, services, and financial assets. (To understand how to derive the euro supply curve, see *Visualizing Global Economic Issues: The Dollar Demand-Euro Supply Relationship*.)

Changes in Currency Supply

If, at a given exchange rate, there is an increase in the demand for U.S. goods by European consumers, there is an increased demand for the dollar. As European consumers purchase dollars to facilitate additional purchases of U.S. goods, they exchange euros for dollars, increasing the quantity supplied of euros in the foreign exchange market, at the given rate. This is a *change in the supply* of euros. As you can now see, the various factors that cause a change in the supply of a currency are all of the factors that cause a change in the domestic demand for another nation's goods, services, and financial assets.

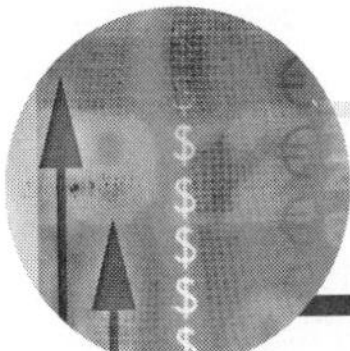

Visualizing Global Economic Issues

The Dollar Demand-Euro Supply Relationship

To see how the supply of a currency is derived from the demand of a nation's residents for another nation's goods, services, and financial assets, first consider European consumers' demand for the U.S. dollar. Panel (a) of Figure 6-5 illustrates the demand for the dollar. At an initial exchange rate of S_1^*, the quantity demanded of dollars equals Q_A^*. If the dollar were to depreciate—a decline in the €/$ exchange rate—U.S. goods become relatively cheaper to European consumers. As a result, European consumers desire more U.S. goods and, therefore, a greater amount of U.S. dollars to make these additional purchases. Hence, there is a movement down and along the demand curve from point A to point B, and the quantity demanded rises from Q_A^* to Q_B^*.

Panel (b) of Figure 6-5 shows an equivalent way of expressing this relationship. Note that panel (b) plots the quantity of euros on the horizontal and the dollar price of the euro ($/€) on the vertical axis. When the euro appreciates, the $/€ exchange rate rises from S_A to S_B. As European consumers purchase more dollars, they exchange euros for dollars. Hence, there is an increase in the quantity of euros supplied, shown by a movement up and along the supply curve from point *A* to point *B*. Thus, there is a positive relationship between the exchange rate and the supply of the euro, as depicted by the upward-sloping supply curve in panel (b).

For Critical Analysis:
How would you derive the supply curve for the U.S. dollar? What factors would influence the demand for the U.S. dollar?

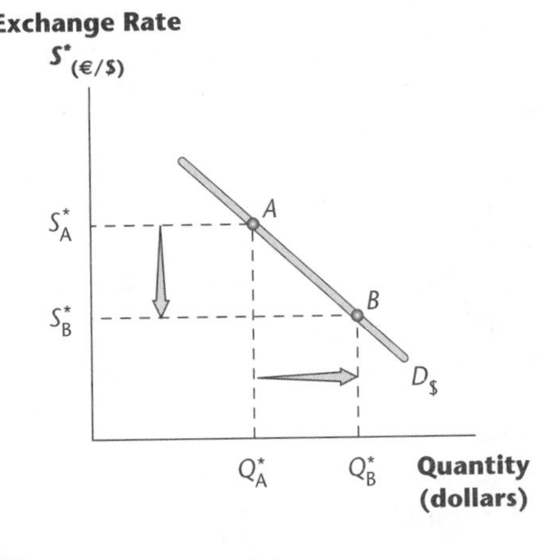

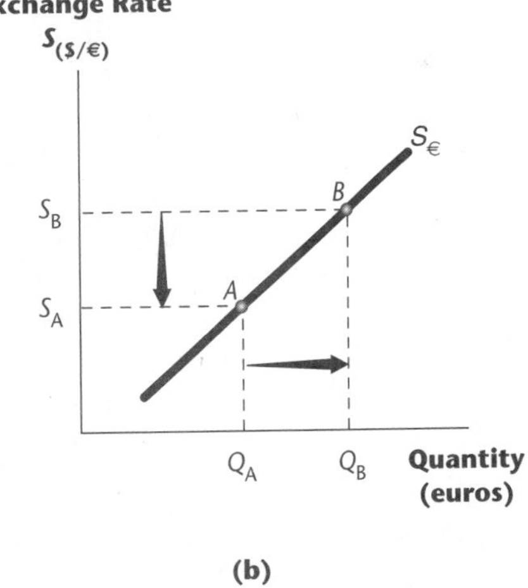

Figure 6-5

The Dollar Demand-Euro Supply Relationship

Panel (a) depicts the demand for the U.S. dollar. A decrease in the euro-per-dollar exchange rate leads to an increase in the quantity of dollars demanded. The quantity of euros supplied in the foreign exchange market increases as more U.S. dollars are purchased with the euro. Panel (b) illustrates the relationship between the dollar-per-euro exchange rate and the quantity of euros supplied. As the dollar-per-euro exchange rate rises, the quantity of euros supplied increases. The supply curve, $S_€$, illustrates the positive relationship between the dollar-per-euro exchange rate and the quantity of euros supplied.

THE EQUILIBRIUM EXCHANGE RATE

If currencies can flow freely across nations' borders and governments do not buy or sell currencies in order to manipulate their values, the forces of demand and supply determine equilibrium, or market clearing, exchange rates. The equilibrium exchange rate is the exchange rate at which the quantity of a currency demanded is equal to the quantity supplied. At the equilibrium exchange rate, the market *clears,* meaning that the quantity demanded of a currency is exactly equal to the quantity supplied. (To understand how the forces of supply and demand determine the equilibrium exchange rate in the supply and demand framework, see *Visualizing Global Economic Issues: The Equilibrium Exchange Rate.)*

A Change in Demand

Let's return to the first example of this chapter dealing with U.S. imports of Japanese electronics equipment. Suppose that there is an increase in U.S. consumers' demand for these types of Japanese-manufactured products. As U.S. consumers increase their purchases of these products, they desire a greater amount of yen to facilitate the additional transactions. Hence, the demand for yen rises. At the initial exchange rate, the increase in demand for the yen results in an excess quantity demanded of yen. As discussed in Chapter 1, an excess quantity demanded generates upward pressure on price. Hence, the dollar-per-yen exchange rate ($/¥) rises, indicating an appreciation of the yen relative to the dollar.

A Change in Supply

Now consider the effects of a change in Japanese residents' demand for U.S. financial instruments. Suppose that the returns on typical U.S. financial instruments rise above the returns on similar Japanese financial instruments, which causes Japanese residents to shift funds from Japan to the United States. In order to purchase the U.S. financial instruments, Japanese savers must obtain a larger amount of U.S. dollars. In doing so, Japanese residents exchange yen for dollars, thereby increasing the supply of yen. At the initial exchange rate, the increase in the supply of yen results in an excess quantity supplied yen. An excess quantity supplied puts downward pressure on price. Hence, the excess quantity supplied of yen causes the dollar-per-yen exchange rate to decline and depreciates the yen relative to the dollar.

5 **Fundamental Issue**

What determines the value of a currency?

The interaction between the demand for a currency and the supply of the currency determines the equilibrium exchange rate. If the exchange rate is free to change, then it adjusts to its equilibrium value through a market-clearing process. The equilibrium exchange rate is the exchange rate at which the quantity of the currency demanded equals the quantity of the currency supplied in the market.

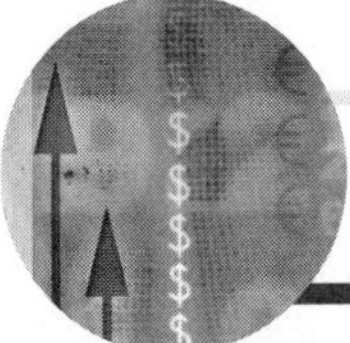

Visualizing Global Economic Issues

The Equilibrium Exchange Rate

To illustrate the determination of the equilibrium exchange rate, Figure 6-6 combines the demand and supply curves for the Japanese yen. Initially, S_A is the equilibrium dollar-per-yen exchange rate ($/¥). At this exchange rate, the quantity demanded of the yen exactly equals the quantity supplied, so there is neither an excess quantity demanded of the yen nor an excess quantity supplied.

Suppose that at exchange rate S_A, there is an increase in U.S. consumers' demand for Japanese electronic equipment. In order to purchase greater amounts of these Japanese goods, U.S. consumers wish to obtain a larger quantity of yen to facilitate their transactions. In other words, the demand for the yen rises, as shown by a shift of the demand curve from $D_¥$ to $D'_¥$.

At the initial exchange rate S_A, the increase in the demand for the yen results in an excess quantity demanded, which is the difference between quantity Q' and the initial quantity Q_A. The excess quantity of yen demanded generates upward pressure on the $/¥ exchange rate, indicating an appreciation of the yen relative to the dollar. As the exchange rate rises, there is a movement up and along the demand curve from point A' to point B. The yen continues to appreciate until the excess quantity demanded is eliminated and the market clears. A new equilibrium occurs at point B and spot exchange rate S_B.

For Critical Analysis:
What would happen to the equilibrium exchange rate of the yen if the demand for the yen and the supply of the yen were to increase simultaneously?

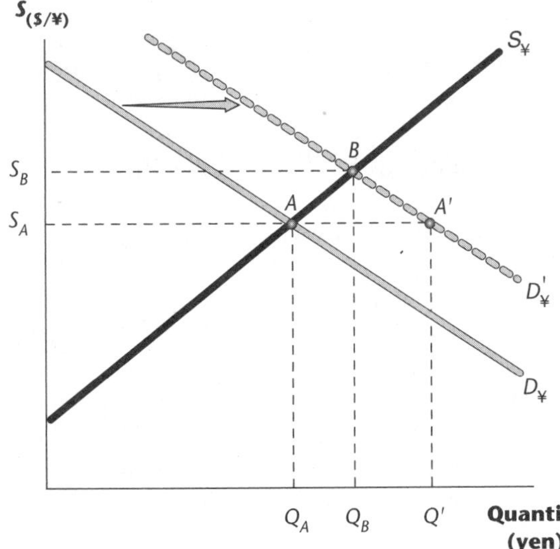

Figure 6-6

The Equilibrium Exchange Rate

At the equilibrium exchange rate S_A, the quantity of yen demanded equals the quantity of yen supplied. An increase in U.S. consumers' demand for Japanese goods results in an increase in demand for the yen. The shift in the demand curve from $D_¥$ to $D'_¥$ illustrates the increase in the demand for yen.

Relationship between the Spot Market and the Forward Market

You learned earlier that the forward exchange market is a market for contracts that ensure the future delivery of foreign exchange at a specified exchange rate, the *forward* rate. If exchange rates are free to adjust, the forces of supply and demand in the forward market for foreign exchange determine the forward exchange rate. Because the forward exchange rate reflects the supply and demand for a currency for future delivery, it is possible that the forward exchange rate provides information about the future spot exchange rate. That is, the forward exchange rate may be useful in forming expectations about future values of the spot rate. To begin to assess the relationship between the forward rate and the future spot rate, let's first explore the relationship between the forward rate and the *current* spot rate.

THE FORWARD PREMIUM AND DISCOUNT

Forward premium or discount
The difference between the forward exchange rate and the spot exchange rate expressed as a percentage of the spot exchange rate.

Suppose that the six-month forward rate on the British pound is 1.4255 dollars per pound and that the spot rate is 1.4113 dollars per pound. Because the dollar price of the pound in the forward market—that is, the forward exchange rate of the pound—is more than the dollar price of the pound in the spot market, the pound is said to trade at a **forward premium.** In a similar manner, if the forward exchange rate of a currency is less than the spot exchange rate, in contrast, the currency is said to trade at a **forward discount.**

THE STANDARD FORWARD PREMIUM

Economists usually state the forward premium or discount in a standardized manner by calculating *the standard forward premium or discount* as a percentage and expressing it in annual terms. To do this, they use the following formula:

$$\text{Standard forward premium/discount} = (F_N - S)/S \times 12/N \times 100,$$

where F_N is the forward rate, S is the spot rate, and N is the number of months of the forward contract.

This formula has three parts. The first part is the forward premium, which is the difference between the forward exchange rate and the spot exchange rate relative to the spot rate, $(F_N - S)/S$. The second part annualizes the forward premium by dividing by the number of months of the contract, expressing the forward premium on a monthly basis, and then multiplying by 12 to express the forward premium on an annual basis. The third part multiplies the annual forward premium by 100 to express it as a percentage. In our example, the standard forward premium is

$$(F_N - S)/S \times 12/N \times 100 = (1.4255 - 1.4113)/1.4113 \times 12/6 \times 100 = 2.0.$$

Hence, the standard forward premium is 2 percent.

THE FORWARD RATE AND THE EXPECTED FUTURE SPOT RATE

Now let's suppose that a foreign currency trader believes that the pound will appreciate against the dollar by 0.5 percent over the next six months (or 1 percent on an annual basis). The trader's expectation of future appreciation of the pound is different from the forward premium of the pound. Consequently, the trader may be able to profit from engaging in a forward currency transaction.

Suppose that the trader exchanges 1 million pounds for dollars in the forward market at a forward exchange rate of 1.4255 dollars per pound. In the assumed absence of transaction costs, six months from now the trader will pay £1 million to buy $1,425,500 forward [(£1 million × 1.4255 $/£) = $1,425,500]. Next, let's suppose that the trader's expectations are correct and the pound appreciates by 0.5 percent, from a rate of 1.4113 $/£ to 1.4184 $/£. The trader may use the proceeds from the forward contract to purchase the pound on the spot market. The $1,425,500 obtained with the forward contract exchanges for £1,005,006 on the spot market ($1,425,500/1.4184 $/£ = £1,005,006), yielding a profit of £5,006.

If other traders share the same expectation as this trader, then there is an increase in the total supply of pounds on the forward market. (Likewise, we could say that there is an increase in the total demand for dollars on the forward market.) Using what we now know about the interaction of the forces of supply and demand, an increase in the supply of pounds on the forward market places downward pressure on the equilibrium forward exchange rate. This reduces the amount of the forward premium and eliminates the difference between the forward premium and the expected rate of appreciation. Thus, the actions of savvy traders, such as the one in our example, eventually eliminate the opportunity to systematically profit from differences between the forward premium and actual changes in the spot rate. Hence, the following equilibrium condition must hold, on average:

$$\frac{F_N - S}{S} = \frac{S_N^e - S}{S}$$

where S_N^e is the spot exchange rate expected to prevail N months from now. This condition states that, in equilibrium, the forward premium must equal the expected appreciation of the currency, and the forward discount must equal the expected depreciation of the currency.

The condition can be simplified to yield

$$F_N = S_N^e.$$

This simplified version of the equilibrium condition implies that the forward exchange rate on a contract in N months must equal the spot exchange rate expected to prevail N months from now. If the forward rate systematically differs from the expected spot rate, then, like our previous example, a profit opportunity exists. If a profit opportunity exists, we can expect traders to take advantage of it. The actions of traders, in theory, generate changes in expected future spot exchange rates and forward exchange rates, eliminating the difference between the two.

Based on this equilibrium condition, we might expect a close relationship between the forward exchange rate and the realized future spot exchange rate. This is the reason that we might also expect the forward exchange rate to have some useful information for forecasting the future spot rate. Many empirical studies indicate that there is some co-movement between the forward exchange rate and the actual future spot exchange rate. The forward exchange rate sometimes overestimates the future spot exchange rate and sometimes underestimates it, however. Most economists conclude, therefore, that the forward premium has limited ability in forecasting the future spot exchange rate. In Chapter 8 you will explore the theories relating the spot rate, forward rate, and other economic variables.

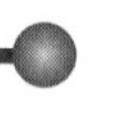
6 Fundamental Issue

How are the spot and forward markets related?

If exchange rates are free to adjust, the forces of supply and demand determine the forward exchange rate. A currency is said to trade at a forward premium if the forward exchange rate is greater than the spot exchange rate. If the forward exchange rate is less than the spot exchange rate, a currency is said to trade at a discount. The standard forward premium expresses the forward premium on an annual percentage basis. If the forward exchange rate systematically differs from the expected future spot rate, a profit opportunity exists. Thus, in theory, the actions of currency traders should eliminate this difference. Economists have studied the relationship between the forward rate and the spot rate quite extensively. The evidence indicates that the forward rate is limited in its use as a guide to future spot rate values.

Other Foreign Exchange Instruments

Forward exchange contracts are but one type of foreign exchange instrument that currency traders use to hedge against foreign exchange risk. During the last two decades, traders developed other *foreign exchange derivative instruments,* or *foreign exchange derivatives.*

FOREIGN EXCHANGE DERIVATIVES

Foreign exchange derivative instruments *Currency instruments with a return that is linked to, or derived from, the returns of other financial instruments.*

Foreign exchange derivative instruments are currency instruments with a return linked to, or derived from, the returns of other financial instruments. Forward exchange contracts fit the description of a derivative security because their payoff to traders depends upon spot exchange rates.

Hedging and Speculating with Foreign Exchange Derivatives

Earlier you learned how a forward contract was used to hedge a short position in the pound. The forward exchange contract allowed a property developer to cover a foreign-exchange exposure and remove all uncertainty about the cost to complete a pound-denominated transaction in the future. By locking in a rate of exchange for the pound, the firm relieves itself of the risk that the dollar cost of the property will rise above that guaranteed by the forward contract.

Although traders can use foreign exchange derivatives to protect against risks of loss, this does not mean that they do not use foreign exchange derivatives for purposes of risky speculation in the pursuit of profits. To see how foreign exchange derivatives may increase overall risk, let's slightly change the condition of the previous example. Suppose that a currency trader thinks that the spot exchange rate of the pound will not change during the next six months. His belief, however, is not consistent with the widespread views of other exchange market participants, who generally expect that the pound will appreciate. Nevertheless, the trader is so sure his expectation will turn out to be correct that he is willing to enter into a forward exchange contract with the managers of the U.S. property developer.

Recall that the current spot exchange rate between the dollar and the pound is 1.4113 $/£ and that the six-month forward rate is 1.4255 $/£. Let's suppose that the currency trader and the managers of the property development firm settle on a forward contract that calls for the currency trader to exchange £11 million for U.S. dollars with the managers at a forward rate of 1.4255 $/£. In other words, the managers exchange $15,680,500 for £11 million with the trader.

Let's suppose that the currency trader plans to buy the pound at the market rate that prevails in six months. If the trader's expectations hold true, his cost of purchasing the pound in the spot market six months from today is $15,524,300 [(£11 × 1.4113 $/£) = $15,524,300]. The trader then exchanges the £11 million with the managers of the property development firm for $15,680,500, netting a profit of $156,200. If the widespread expectation of a pound appreciation holds true, however, the trader's dollar cost of fulfilling the contract rises above what the trader currency *speculates* that it will be. Thus, to the extent that the consensus forecast of a pound appreciation indicates a strong likelihood that this actually will occur, the currency trader would have negotiated a speculative contract and added to his overall risk.

This example indicates that while foreign exchange market participants can use foreign exchange derivatives to hedge against risks, they also can use them to engage in speculative activities. Worldwide use of foreign exchange derivatives has increased dramatically since the early 1980s, as financial managers found ways to use derivatives in hedging strategies. At the same time, however, many traders determined that they could earn significant profits by speculating with foreign exchange derivatives.

Unfortunately, several traders found out that foreign exchange derivatives speculations can turn out badly. The results were sizable financial losses for a number of firms and individuals. The most notable losses resulting from foreign currency derivatives speculations were Volkswagen's $260 million loss, Procter & Gamble's $157 million loss, and PacifiCorp's $65 million loss in the 1990s. What is important to understand, however, is that for each loser in a derivatives speculation there is a winner. In the case of the three companies above, this means that these firms lost money because their managers' speculations about market outcomes were wrong, but that the losses resulted in profits for other firms and traders whose market expectations were correct.

COMMON FOREIGN EXCHANGE DERIVATIVES

There are many types of foreign exchange derivatives, yet they all share the same characteristic that their returns depend on prices of other financial instruments. In addition, traders may use foreign exchange derivatives in hedging strategies or in speculative strategies.

The most common types of foreign exchange derivative instruments, in addition to forward exchange contracts, are *currency futures, currency options,* and *currency swaps.* Table 6-5 summarizes the characteristics of these instruments. Let's consider each instrument in some detail.

Currency Futures

Currency futures *An agreement to deliver to another party a standardized quantity of a specific nation's currency at a designated future date.*

One type of foreign exchange derivative instrument that has grown in popularity among traders is a **currency futures** contract, which is an agreement by one party to deliver to another party a quantity of a national currency at a specific future date in exchange for a specified amount of another currency. In contrast to forward exchange contracts, currency futures contracts specify in advance *standardized* quantities of currencies and narrow guidelines for transactions. Because futures contracts are standardized, parties do not have to spend time negotiating contract terms. The world's largest currency futures market is the International Monetary Market of the Chicago Mercantile Exchange (CME) in which traders conduct futures transactions in the currencies of a large number of currencies.

Holders of currency futures experience profits or losses on the contracts at any time before the contract expires. This is because futures contracts require daily

Table 6-5 Basic Foreign Exchange Derivative Instruments

Foreign exchange derivatives are currency instruments whose return is linked to the returns of other financial instruments. The most common foreign exchange derivatives are forward exchange contracts, currency futures, currency options, and currency swaps.

Forward Exchange Contract	A contract that ensures the delivery of a foreign currency at a specified exchange rate.
Currency Futures Contract	An agreement to deliver to another party a standardized quantity of a specific nation's currency at a designated future date.
Currency Option Contract	A contract granting the right to buy or sell a given amount of a nation's currency at a certain price within a specific time period.
Currency Swap	A contract entailing an exchange of different payment flows denominated in different currencies.

cash-flow settlements. That is, profits or losses are settled daily. By way of contrast, profits or losses occur only at the expiration date of a forward contract, which requires settlements only at maturity. As a result, the market prices of currency futures contracts and forward exchange contracts usually differ.

Currency futures typically involve smaller currency denominations, as compared with forward exchange contracts. Large banking institutions and corporations that transmit large volumes of foreign currencies in their normal business operations are the primary users of forward contracts. Individuals and smaller firms that wish to undertake hedging or speculative strategies typically trade currency futures instead.

ON THE WEB

To learn more about the Chicago Mercantile Exchange and currency futures, visit the home page of the CME at http://www.cme.com.

Currency Options

Another type of foreign exchange derivative instrument is a **currency option,** which is a contract providing the holder the right to purchase or sell an amount of a national currency at a given price. This right does not require the holder to buy or sell. It gives the holder the *option* to do so. The given price at which the holder can exercise the right to purchase or sell an amount of currency is the option's **exercise price,** which traders also call the *strike price.*

Call options are options that allow the holder to *purchase* an amount of a currency at the exercise price. **Put options** are options that allow the buyer to *sell* an amount of a currency at the exercise price. Traders refer to an option granting the holder the right to exercise the right of purchase or sale at any time before or including the date at which the contract expires an **American option.** They call an option that allows the holder to exercise the right of purchase or sale *only* on the date that the contract expires a **European option.**

Multinational corporations can purchase currency options directly from banks via *over-the-counter* contracts, but they can also purchase them in organized exchanges. One of the largest options markets is the Philadelphia Stock Exchange.

Currency option
A contract granting the right to buy or sell a given amount of a nation's currency at a certain price within a given period or on a specific date.

Exercise price
The price at which the holder of an option has the right to buy or sell a financial instrument; also known as the strike price.

Call option
An options contract giving the owner the right to purchase an amount of a currency at a specific rate of exchange.

Put option
An options contract giving the owner the right to sell an amount of a currency at a specific rate of exchange.

American option
An option in which the holder may buy or sell an amount of a currency any time before or including the date at which the contract expires.

European option
An option in which the holder may buy or sell an amount of a currency only on the day that the contract expires.

Currency Swaps

A fourth type of foreign exchange derivative is a **currency swap,** which is an exchange of payment flows denominated in different currencies. Figure 6-7 illustrates a sample currency swap, in which we suppose that International Business Machines (IBM) Corporation earns a flow of yen-denominated revenues from computer sales in Japan, while Toshiba Corporation earns dollar revenues from selling computers in the United States. IBM pays dollar dividends and interest to its owners and bondholders, and Toshiba pays yen-denominated dividends and interest to its owners and bondholders. Therefore, IBM and Toshiba could, in principle, use a currency swap as a mechanism for trading their yen and dollar earnings for the purpose of paying income streams to their stockholders and bondholders.

In addition, firms often use currency swaps to lock in the domestic currency value of a debt payment or a future receipt. Sometimes swap partners are easier to find than counterparties to forward contracts, because swaps directly match traders that require flows denominated in currencies held by one another. (To consider how U.S. firms use these foreign exchange derivative instruments, see on page 197 *Management Notebook: Just How Widespread Is the Use of Derivatives by U.S. Businesses?*)

Currency swap
An exchange of payment flows denominated in different currencies.

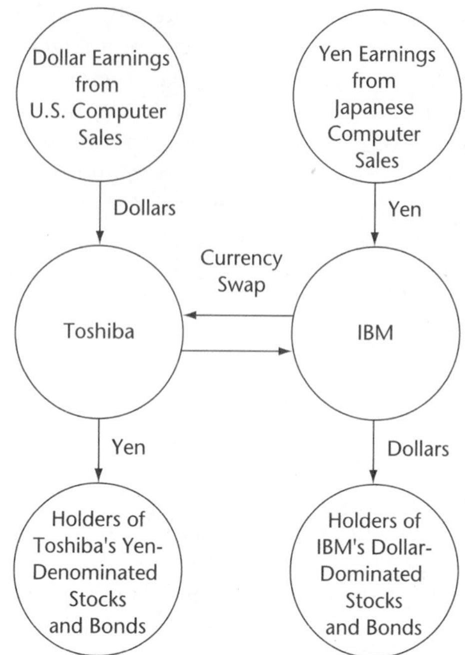

Figure 6-7

A Sample Currency Swap

IMB receives yen earnings from selling computers in Japan, and Toshiba receives dollar earnings from selling computers in the United States. The two companies could use a currency swap contract to trade their yen and dollar earnings to make payments to holders of the stocks and bonds.

7 Fundamental Issue

What other foreign exchange instruments are commonly traded?

In addition to foreign exchange forward contracts, other commonly traded foreign exchange instruments include currency futures, currency options, and currency swaps. Currency futures are an agreement to deliver to another party a standardized quantity of a specific nation's currency at a designated future date. Currency futures differ from forward contracts because traders exchange them in standardized quantities in organized markets in which flows of profits or losses take place daily, rather than only at maturity. A currency option is a contract granting the right to buy or sell an amount of a nation's currency at a certain rate of exchange within a specific period of time. A currency swap is an exchange of payment flows denominated in different currencies.

CHAPTER SUMMARY

1) **What the Balance of Payments Measures:** The balance of payments is a system of accounts used to record the international transactions of a nation. This system measures trade in goods, services, income, unilateral transfers, private transactions of financial assets, and official reserves. The current account comprises the goods, services, income, and unilateral transfers categories.
2) **The Role of the Foreign Exchange Markets in the Global Marketplace:** The foreign exchange market—a system of banks, brokers and central banks through which households, firms, and governments buy and sell

MANAGEMENT *Notebook*

POLICY MANAGEMENT

Just How Widespread Is the Use of Derivatives by U.S. Businesses?

Students often wonder just how much they are likely to apply what they learn in class to the "real world." In a recent study, Gordon Bodnar, Gregory Hart, and Richard Marston surveyed companies to try to determine just how commonplace derivatives are for nonfinancial firms. They found that exactly half of the firms they surveyed had used derivatives, and 42 percent of surveyed firms said that they had recently increased their use of these instruments. Among the largest firms surveyed, 83 percent reported that they used derivatives. This percentage dropped to 45 percent among medium-sized firms and to 12 percent among small firms. The portion of surveyed manufacturing companies that used derivatives was 48 percent, and 42 percent of service firms used these instruments.

Of those firms reporting that they use derivative instruments, 83 percent said that they did so to manage exposure to foreign exchange risks. The majority of these firms indicated that they hedge less than 25 percent of their perceived risk exposure. Only about a third reported hedging 75 percent or more of their total exposure to foreign exchange risk.

What are the common foreign exchange derivatives used by nonfinancial firms? According to this survey, more than 80 percent of currency derivatives used by companies are forward and futures contracts. Firms reported that they used currency swaps somewhat more frequently than currency options.

For Critical Analysis:
Why would larger firms be more likely to use foreign exchange derivative instruments than smaller firms? Why would firms that use foreign exchange derivatives hedges less than 100 percent of their perceived foreign exchange exposure?

foreign exchange—is the oldest and largest financial market in the world. The foreign exchange market is a global arrangement for valuing transactions and delivering payments, thereby facilitating the flow of goods and services among nations. The foreign exchange market functions twenty-four hours per day. There is a wide array of financial instruments traded in the foreign exchange market, in which exchange rates can change as often as twenty times a minute.

3) **The Spot Foreign Exchange Market:** The spot market for foreign exchange is the market for contracts that require the immediate delivery of foreign currencies. Large transactions of foreign-currency-denominated deposits of $1 million or more among commercial banks dominate this market. Economists use spot exchange rates to gauge an appreciation and depreciation of a currency and to construct cross rates, real exchange rates, and effective exchange rates.

4) **Foreign Exchange Risk and the Role of the Forward Foreign Exchange Markets:** Foreign exchange risk is the effect that uncertain future values of the exchange rate may have on the value of a foreign-currency-denominated obligation, receipt, asset, or liability. There are three types of exposure to foreign exchange risk: transaction exposure, translation exposure, and economic exposure. In principle, an individual or firm can use a forward exchange contract, which is a contract that obliges the future delivery of a foreign currency at a specified rate of exchange, to offset, or hedge, some or all of the exposure to foreign exchange risk. By eliminating uncertainty about the future value of a foreign-currency-denominated transaction, forward contracts spur additional international transactions of goods, services, and financial instruments.
5) **Determining the Value of a Currency:** The interaction between the demand for a currency and the supply of a currency determines the currency's market value. If the exchange rate is free to change, then a currency's value adjusts to its market equilibrium through a market clearing process. The equilibrium exchange rate is the value at which the quantity of a currency supplied equals the quantity of the currency demanded.
6) **The Relationship between the Spot and Forward Markets:** If exchange rates are free to adjust, the forces of supply and demand determine the forward exchange rate. The forward premium or discount is the difference between the forward exchange rate and the spot exchange rate, expressed as a percentage of the spot exchange rate. A currency is said to be trading at a premium if the forward exchange rate is greater than the spot exchange rate. A currency is said to be trading at discount if the forward exchange rate is less than the spot exchange rate. The standard forward premium expresses the forward premium on an annual basis.
7) **Other Commonly Traded Foreign Exchange Instruments:** In addition to forward exchange contracts, commonly traded foreign exchange derivative instruments, which are foreign exchange instruments whose returns are linked to the returns of other financial instruments, include currency futures, currency options, and currency swaps. A currency future is an agreement to deliver to another party a standardized quantity of a specific nation's currency at a designated date. A currency option is a contract guaranteeing the right to buy or sell a given amount of a nation's currency at a certain price within a specific time period. A currency swap is an exchange of payment flows denominated in different currencies.

QUESTIONS AND PROBLEMS

1) Using the following data (billions of dollars) for a given year, calculate the balance on merchandise trade, the balance on goods, services and income, and the current account balance. Indicate whether these balances are deficits or surpluses.

Exports of merchandise	106	Imports of services	28
Exports of services	34	Capital inflow	6
Net unilateral transfers	8	Imports of merchandise	119
Statistical discrepancy	0	Capital outflow	29
Official settlements balance	22		

2) Suppose the U.S.-dollar-per-euro exchange rate ($/€) was 0.9701 on Thursday and 0.9805 on Friday. Did the euro depreciate or appreciate relative to the dollar? How much was the appreciation or depreciation (in percentage change terms)?

3) Complete the following cross-rate table. (*Hint:* The first exchange rate is the £/$ exchange rate.)

	U.S. $	**U.K. £**	**Canadian $**	**Euro €**
U.S. $	—	0.7001	1.5433	1.0225
U.K. £				
Canadian $				
Euro €				

4) In January 2003, the spot exchange rate for the euro was 0.90 €/$, the euro-wide CPI was 105.3, and the U.S. CPI was 108.0. In July 2004, the spot exchange rate for the euro was 1.08 €/$, the euro-wide CPI was 108.8, and the U.S. CPI was 113.3.
   (a) Based on this information, in nominal terms did the euro appreciate or depreciate against the dollar? What was the rate of appreciation or depreciation of the euro relative to the dollar?
   (b) What were the rates of consumer price inflation in the United States and in the EMU?

5) Based on this information, did the euro experience a real appreciation or a real depreciation against the dollar? What was the rate of real appreciation or depreciation?

6) Suppose that an effective exchange rate for the euro was 130 in January 2004 and 125 in January 2005. At the same time, an effective exchange rate for the Japanese yen was 110 in January 2000 and 100 in January 2005. Overall, did the euro and the yen appreciate or depreciate between January 2000 and January 2005?

7) Based on the information in question 6, can you surmise whether the euro appreciated or depreciated against the yen from 2004 to 2005?

8) On a particular day, the spot exchange rate for the Thai baht was 45.80 (Bt/$). On the same day, the three-month forward exchange rate for the baht was 46.50. Was the Thai baht trading at a premium or discount? Given this information, what is the standard forward premium or discount for the Thai baht?

9) For each of the following examples, illustrate the demand for and supply of the Canadian dollar. Show how each event would affect the euro-per-Canadian-dollar (€/C$) equilibrium exchange rate.
   (a) European savers desire to shift funds from euro-denominated financial assets to Canadian-dollar-denominated financial assets.
   (b) European firms switch from buying minerals from Canadian firms to purchasing them from Russian firms.
10) Suppose that the two events described in question 8 (a) and 8 (b) occur at the same time. Illustrate the effect on the supply of and demand for the Canadian dollar and on the equilibrium exchange rate.
11) On Monday, the spot exchange rate for the Philippine peso was 53.20 P/$. On the same day, the one-year forward rate was 57.29 P/$. What would you expect the rate of appreciation or depreciation for the peso to be over the course of the year?

ONLINE APPLICATION

Internet URL: http://www.Oanda.com

Title: **Currency Investors**

Navigation: Go to the home page of Oanda at the above URL. Scroll down to "Forex Investors." Click on "Currency Trading." Scroll down to "Documentation and Help." Click on "Introduction to Currency Exchange."

Application: Read the document titled "Introduction to Currency Exchange" and answer the following questions.

1) What is a currency ISO code?
2) What is the "bid" price?
3) What is the "ask" price?
4) What is the "spread?"

For Group Study and Analysis: Divide into two groups. One group is to speculate that the U.S. dollar will depreciate relative to the euro, while the other group is to speculate that the U.S. dollar will appreciate relative to the euro. Based on the document "Introduction to Currency Exchange," each group is to describe how it would undertake a currency transaction to profit on movements of the dollar-euro spot exchange rate. Both groups should explain how hypothetical profits or losses are calculated.

REFERENCES AND RECOMMENDED READINGS

Bodnar, Gordon, Gregory Hart, and Richard Marston. "Wharton Survey of Derivative Usage by U.S. Non-Financial Firms." *Financial Management* 24 (2) (Summer 1995): 104–14.

Cohen, Benjamin J. *The Geography of Money*. Ithaca, N.Y.: Cornell University Press, 1998.

Cross, Sam Y. *All About the Foreign Exchange Market in the United States*. New York: Federal Reserve Bank of New York, http://www.ny.frb.org/pihome/addpub/usfxm, 1998.

Federal Reserve Bank of Chicago. *Strong Dollar Weak Dollar: Foreign Exchange Rates and the U.S. Economy*. Chicago: Federal Reserve Bank of Chicago, http://www.chicagofed.org/publications, 1997.

Fouquin, Michel. "The Impact of Fluctuation of the Dollar on European Industry." *The CEPII News Letter* 12 (Winter 1999–2000): 3–4.

Frankel, Jeffrey A. *On Exchange Rates*. Cambridge, Mass.: MIT Press, 1997.

Froot, Kenneth A., and Richard H. Thaler. "Anomalies: Foreign Exchange." *The Journal of Economic Perspectives* 4 (3) (Summer 1990): 179–192.

Goldberg, Linda S., and Keith Crockett. "The Dollar and U.S. Manufacturing." *Federal Reserve Bank of New York Current Issues in Economics and Finance* 4 (12) (November 1998).

Henning, C. Randall. *Currencies and Politics in the United States*. Germany, Japan, Washington, D.C.: Institute for International Economics, 1994.

Isard, Peter. *Exchange Rate Economics*. Cambridge, England: Cambridge University Press, 1995.

Kodres, Laura, E. "Foreign Exchange Markets: Structure and Systemic Risks." *Finance and Development*. http://www.imf.org/external/pubs/ft/fandd/fda.htm, 33 (4) (December 1996): 22–25.

Kraus, James. "Forex Trading Sites May Erode Bank Revenue." *American Banker* (May 4, 2000).

Rangan, Subramanian, and Robert Z. Lawrence. *A Prism on Globalization: Corporate Responses to the Dollar*. Washington, D.C.: Brookings Institution Press, 1999.

Taylor, Mark. "The Economics of Exchange Rates." *Journal of Economic Literature* 33 (March 1995): 13–47.

CHAPTER SEVEN

Exchange-Rate Systems, Past to Present

Fundamental Issues

1. **What is an exchange-rate system?**
2. **How does a gold standard constitute an exchange-rate system?**
3. **What was the Bretton Woods system of "pegged" exchange rates?**
4. **What post-Bretton Woods system of "flexible" exchange rates prevails today?**
5. **What are crawling-peg and basket-peg exchange-rate systems?**
6. **What is a currency board, and what is dollarization?**
7. **Which is best, a fixed or flexible exchange-rate system?**

In 1976, member nations amended the articles of agreement of the International Monetary Fund (IMF) to allow nations to select their own approach to exchange rate management. Since that time, policymakers have used a wide variety of exchange rate systems. Many systems prove successful in aiding economic stability and growth for a time but eventually face periods of stress. Sometimes they collapse and are abandoned for other types of systems.

A number of currency crises occurred in the late 1990s, leading many policymakers and economists to question whether exchange rates should be flexible or fixed. Because most emerging economies are highly dependent on exports, the exchange rate is an important variable, and its stability is crucial for sustained economic growth. For these nations, therefore, the choice of an exchange rate system is critical.

During the late 1990s and early 2000s, some Latin American countries considered abandoning their national currencies altogether, in favor of using the U.S. dollar as a medium of exchange. In September 2000, Ecuador, for example, adopted the U.S. dollar as its currency. El Salvador followed, adopting the U.S. dollar in January 2001.

Most recently, the trend among some emerging economies is to follow the policies of nations such as Canada, the United Kingdom, Australia, and New Zealand by allowing exchange rates to be flexible and currency values determined by market forces. Central banks, however, must meet mandated inflation targets. For Brazil, this practice temporarily resulted in lower inflation and a stable value for the domestic currency. In January 1999, however, the value of the Brazilian real declined by more than 25 percent relative to the U.S. dollar. It appears, at least for the time being, that fixed inflation targets and a flexible exchange rate may not provide the exchange rate stability that policymakers in emerging economies desire.

The determination of the international value of a nation's currency is a very important issue. Together with the way in which a nation conducts its macroeconomic policies, an exchange-rate system may promote a stable economic environment that promotes trade and investment, or an unstable environment that puts its industries at a competitive disadvantage. The history of exchange-rate management shows us that, even if adopted with the best intentions, few exchange-rate systems can avoid speculative and political pressures forever.

Exchange-Rate Systems

Before we can begin to understand the institutional framework that governs the value of a nation's currency, we must first understand a nation's monetary order. A **monetary order** is a set of laws and regulations that establishes the framework within which individuals conduct and settle transactions.

Monetary order
A set of laws and regulations that establishes the framework within which individuals conduct and settle transactions.

One decision a nation must make is whether its national money will be commodity money, commodity-backed money, or fiat money. *Commodity money* is a tangible good that individuals use as means of payment, or a medium of exchange, such as gold or silver coins. *Commodity-backed money* is a monetary unit that has a value relating to a specific commodity or commodities, such as silver or gold, and that national authorities will accept in exchange for the commodity. *Fiat money,* which is our money today, is a monetary unit not backed by any commodity. Its value is determined solely by the worth that people attach to it as a medium of exchange.

A nation's monetary order also sets forth the rules that form the nation's exchange-rate system, and, either formally or informally, the nation's participation

Exchange-rate system
A set of rules that determine the international value of a currency.

in an exchange rate system. An **exchange-rate system** is the set of rules governing the value of an individual nation's currency relative to other foreign currencies.

To better understand the relationships among a monetary order and an exchange-rate system, we will examine the history of three important exchange-rate systems: The gold standard, the Bretton Woods system, and the post–Bretton-Woods floating-rate system.

Fundamental Issue

What is an exchange-rate system?

An exchange-rate system is the set of rules established by a nation to govern the value of its currency relative to foreign currencies. The exchange-rate system evolves from the nation's monetary order, which is the set of laws and rules that establishes the monetary framework within which transactions are conducted.

The Gold Standard

By the mid-1870s, the major economies of the world had adopted a commodity-backed monetary order for their national currencies. Gold served as the underlying commodity, and the period until 1914 became known as the *gold standard era.* Under this framework, a nation would fix an official price of gold in terms of the national currency, known as the mint parity, and establish convertibility at that rate. **Convertibility** is the ability to freely exchange a currency for a commodity or another currency at a given rate of exchange. For example, between 1837 to 1933 (except for the suspension of convertibility during the Civil War), the U.S. mint parity of one fine ounce of gold was $20.646, with the dollar convertible at that rate. To maintain the mint parity, or the exchange value between gold and the national currency, a nation must condition its money stock on the level of its gold reserves.

Convertibility
The ability to freely exchange a currency for a reserve commodity or reserve currency.

THE GOLD STANDARD AS AN EXCHANGE-RATE SYSTEM

Other industrialized nations had adopted a commodity-backed order before or shortly after the same time that the United States reinstated convertibility following the Civil War, which ended in 1865. These decisions, though adopted unilaterally, also established each nations' exchange-rate system and informally led to an exchange-rate system among the nations. The gold standard established an exchange-rate system because it meant that people could exchange the dollar, both domestically and internationally, at the mint parity rate. Thus, the exchange value between gold and the dollar determined the international value of the dollar.

This also established an exchange-rate system among the countries that had adopted a gold standard. Because each country valued its currency relative to gold, this indirectly established an exchange value between the domestic currency and the currencies of all other countries on a gold standard.

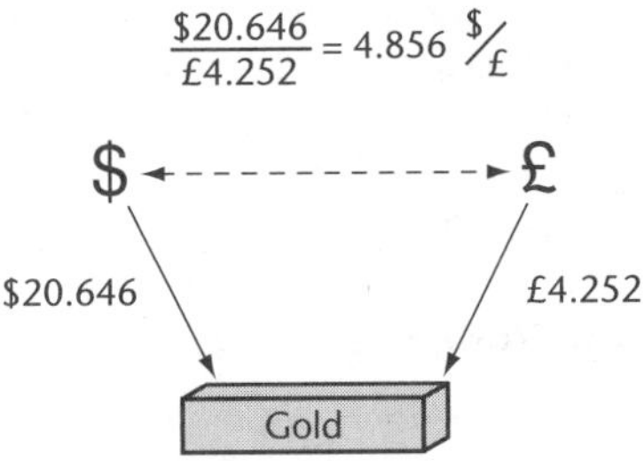

Figure 7-1

The Gold Standard as an Exchange-Rate System

Countries adopting a gold standard valued their currencies relative to gold. The gold parity rate for the British pound was £4.252 per troy ounce of gold and for the U.S. dollar $20.646 per troy ounce. The gold parity rates determined the rate of exchange between the two currencies.

As an example, under the gold standard, Britain's gold parity rate was, as shown in Figure 7-1, £4.252 per fine ounce. Using the gold parity rates of the U.S. dollar and the British pound, we can determine the rate of exchange that existed between the two currencies. The mint parity rate of the United States was $20.646 and the mint parity rate of the British pound was £4.252. As shown in Figure 7-1, the U.S.-dollar-per-currency rate of the British pound, $/£, was, therefore, $20.646/£4.252, or 4.856 $/£.

If the exchange rate deviated from this amount, ignoring transportation costs of gold, then an opportunity to profit from buying and selling the two currencies and gold would have existed. For example, suppose that, at the mint parity rates just given, the exchange rate between the U.S. dollar and the British pound was 5 $/£. One would have been able to take $20.646 and exchange it for one ounce of gold. The gold could then have been exported to Britain and exchanged for £4.252. The £4.252 would have exchanged on the foreign exchange market for £4.252 × 5 $/£, or $21.26, earning a profit of $0.614. If we consider the transportation costs of gold, the exchange rate between two currencies would remain in a range or band centered on the ratio of the mint parity values. These transportation and transaction costs of gold determine the width of the range, because they affect the profitability of exporting or importing gold.

Under the gold standard, all of the currencies of the nations adopting a gold standard were linked together, with their exchange values determined in the manner just described. Just as the mint parities established the exchange rate between the dollar and the pound, they also established the exchange values among the dollar, the French franc, and the German deutsche mark.

For example, under the gold standard the mint parity of the French franc was Ffr107.008, and the deutsche mark mint parity was DM86.672. The exchange rate between the dollar and the French franc, therefore, was 5.183 Ffr/$ (Ffr107.008/$20.646). The exchange rate between the dollar and the deutsche mark was 4.198 DM/$ (DM86.672/$20.646). The link to gold determined the cross rates between the various currencies as well. It is in this manner that the adoption of a commodity-backed monetary order by individual nations established the basis of an exchange-rate system.

How does a gold standard constitute an exchange-rate system?

A gold standard constitutes an exchange-rate system for an adopting nation because it establishes a domestic and international rate of exchange between the domestic currency and gold. A gold standard also links the exchange-rate systems between all of the nations adopting a gold standard. The exchange value between gold and a nation's currency indirectly establishes rates of exchange among all of the currencies.

PERFORMANCE OF THE GOLD STANDARD

Because the gold standard resulted from the decisions of individual nations made at different times, there is no single starting date for the system. Generally, however, economists consider the gold standard era to have begun in the 1870s. Though the system was temporarily suspended during World War I, and eventually collapsed in the early 1930s, some individuals still argue for a return to a gold standard. During recent U.S. political campaigns, conservatives such as Steve Forbes and Jack Kemp have recommended that a new president should stabilize the dollar value of the nation's gold reserves as a critical first step toward restoring "sound money" to America. What is the record of the gold standard, and why do individuals such as Mr. Forbes and Mr. Kemp long for its return?

Positive and Negative Aspects of a Gold Standard

As indicated earlier, an important element of a commodity-backed monetary order is that a nation's quantity of money, or its *money stock,* depends directly on the amount of commodity reserves the nation's monetary authority has. A given amount of commodity reserves may support a multiple number of units of money. As an example, between 1879 and 1913 the U.S. money stock was 8.5 times the amount of the monetary gold stock. Thus, *changes* in a nation's money stock depend only on *changes* in the mining and production of monetary gold.

If the supply of gold is rather constant, this particular aspect of a gold standard, therefore, promotes long-run stability of the nation's money stock and long-run stability of prices and exchange rates. Another important aspect of a commodity-backed monetary order is that it does not require a central bank: An official authority can maintain the ratio of money stock to gold reserves. Canada and the United States, for example, did not have a central bank during the late 1800s and early 1900s.

Nevertheless, a commodity-backed monetary order has some negative aspects. For example, a gold standard has significant resource costs, such as minting and transportation costs. It can be very costly for a nation to maintain and exchange a tangible commodity such as gold. If the supply of gold is not steady, it can result in inflation or a liquidity crisis. A major gold discovery, for example, would generate an increase in the amount of money in circulation and spur inflationary pressure. If the mining of gold fell behind, the amount of money in circulation would contract, potentially leading to a liquidity crisis. Arguably most important is the fact that a gold standard prevents policymakers from pursing discretionary monetary policy. In other words, the commitment to peg the value of the currency to gold prevents policymakers from setting monetary policy to achieve other policy objectives, a subject matter discussed in Chapter 9.

The Economic Environment of the Gold Standard Era

Now that you understand these important aspects of a gold standard, let's consider both the conditions that existed in the 1870–1913 period, and the contributions of the gold standard to the world economic environment. First, this period was peaceful, with no major wars among the participating nations. Second, there was virtually free capital mobility among nations. Finally, London was the center of the world's money and capital markets.

These latter two characteristics enabled the efficient and smooth functioning of the gold standard. Further, the Bank of England, at the center of the world's financial markets, maintained its gold parity values and established the credibility of the system. The apparent concentration of influence in the London market was so significant that economist J. M. Keynes stated that the Bank of England could almost have claimed to be the "conductor of the international orchestra." We can conclude, therefore, that the early gold standard period had some unique characteristics, at least two of which are not prevalent today.

During this period, most nations did indeed experience stable *long-run* real economic outputs, prices, and exchange rates. It is this long-run stability that proponents of a return to a gold standard praise. Because there were short-run random changes in the demand and supply of gold, however, there were also short-run random changes in the money stock and in the prices of goods and services. The short-run volatility of the money stock, in part, led to periodic financial and banking instability. Furthermore, the *short-run* volatility of prices was greater under the gold standard than the exchange-rate systems that followed.

THE COLLAPSE OF THE GOLD STANDARD

In 1914, after the beginning of World War I, many European nations suspended convertibility of their currencies into gold. For all practical purposes, the gold standard was no longer in effect, and exchange values between currencies did fluctuate. Many nations, therefore, restricted the types and amounts of international payments that their residents could make in hopes of maintaining the prewar values of their currencies.

Bank for International Settlements (BIS)
An institution based in Basle, Switzerland, which serves as an agent for central banks and a center of economic cooperation among the largest industrialized nations.

Early in the twentieth century, policymakers in the leading nations determined there was the need for an international organization to facilitate payments among nations. Following World War I, the **Bank for International Settlements** was founded as part of an effort to facilitate German reparations. Located in Basle, Switzerland, this organization assists central banks in the management of their external reserves, conducts economic research, and is a forum for international monetary policy cooperation. (For more on the Bank for International Settlements, see the Online Application on page 228.)

World War I formally ended with the signing of the Versailles treaty in 1919. There was a general desire among the leading nations to return to a gold standard. In 1925, the United Kingdom returned to a gold standard at the prewar parity, but other countries, such as France, returned at much lower values. As a result, many believed that the prewar parity rate would result in a market value for the pound that was higher than that predicted by economic models or theories, thereby making the pound an **overvalued currency.** To maintain the parity value, the United Kingdom had to endure high interest rates and high unemployment. The political costs of maintaining the value of the pound became too great, and the United Kingdom abandoned the gold standard in 1931 by suspending the convertibility of the pound to gold. The United States followed suit in 1933. By 1936, most of the industrialized nations had left the gold standard.

Overvalued currency
A currency in which the current market-determined value is higher than the value predicted by an economic theory or model.

What brought about the demise of the gold standard was a return to parity values that led to overvalued currencies, such as the case with the United Kingdom, or **undervalued currencies**—currencies whose market value is less than that predicted by economic models or theories—such as the case with the French franc. In addition, nations facing a worldwide depression decided to pursue objectives such as higher employment levels and real growth rates rather than to maintain the exchange value of their currencies.

Undervalued currency
A currency in which the current market-determined value is lower than that predicted by an economic theory or model.

The collapse of the gold standard, combined with the passage of protectionist trade polices such as the Smoot–Hawley Act in the United States, wreaked havoc on international trade flows. As a result, the volume of international trade in 1933 was less than one-third of its 1929 amount. This, in addition to other prevailing economic factors, contributed to the Great Depression, which began with an industrial depression in the United Kingdom in 1926 and the crash of the stock market in the United States in 1929. The Great Depression continued until the outbreak of World War II.

The Bretton Woods System

During World War II, the leaders of the United Kingdom and the United States recognized the importance of having a sound monetary order in place when the war ended. The economies of Europe and Japan would be in great need of rebuilding and would therefore require imports from nations with intact industrial bases, such as the United States. The nations' leaders, therefore, pressed for negotiations on an exchange-rate system that would facilitate international trade and payments.

Although forty-four nations participated in the conference that led to the postwar exchange-rate system, the primary architects of the system were Harry White of the U.S. Treasury and the renowned British economist John Maynard Keynes. Negotiations concluded with the ratification of a new system in 1944 at a small resort in Bretton Woods, New Hampshire. The conference, though officially called the International Monetary and Financial Conference of the United and Associated Nations, became known as the Bretton Woods Conference. Thus, the agreement reached there became known as the Bretton Woods agreement.

THE BRETTON WOODS AGREEMENT

One significant outcome of the Bretton Woods agreement was the creation of the **International Monetary Fund,** or IMF. The IMF's principle function was to lend to member nations experiencing a shortage of foreign exchange reserves. Nations could become members of the IMF by subscribing, or paying a quota or fee. The size and economic resources of a nation determined the initial quota, with 25 percent of the quota paid in gold and 75 percent in the nation's currency. Two other important institutions that arose at the end of the war were the International Bank for Reconstruction and Development (IBRD), known as the *World Bank,* and the *General Agreement on Tariffs and Trade (GATT).* The **World Bank** initially financed postwar reconstruction. It now focuses on making loans to developing nations to promote long-term development and economic growth. GATT promoted the reduction of trade barriers and settled trade disputes. The World Trade Organization (WTO) eventually replaced GATT.

International Monetary Fund
A supranational organization whose major responsibility is to lend reserves to member nations experiencing a shortage.

World Bank
A sister institution of the International Monetary Fund that is more narrowly specialized in making loans to about 100 developing nations in an effort to promote their long-term development and growth.

The exchange-rate system that emerged from the agreement was one of pegged, but adjustable, exchange rates. Under a **pegged exchange-rate system,** nations fix the value of their currencies to something other than a commodity, such as another nation's currency. As under a gold standard, each nation pegged its exchange rate. In contrast to a gold standard, the U.S. dollar was the anchor of the system. The Bretton Woods system, therefore, was a **dollar-standard exchange-rate system,** which is a system in which nations peg the value of their currency to the dollar and freely exchange their currency for the dollar at the pegged value.

Pegged exchange-rate system
An exchange rate system in which a country pegs the international value of the domestic currency to the currency of another nation.

Dollar-standard exchange-rate system
An exchange rate system in which a country pegs the value of its currency to the U.S. dollar and freely exchanges the domestic currency for the dollar at the pegged rate.

Under the Bretton Woods agreement, each country could choose to state the par value of its currency in terms of gold or to establish a par value for its currency relative to the U.S. dollar. Every participating country related the value of its currencies to the dollar, making the dollar the common unit of value in the system. Each country would then stand ready to buy and sell U.S. dollars in the foreign exchange market to maintain the exchange value of its currency within 1 percent, on either side, of the par value, commonly referred to as the *parity band.*

The United States, by way of contrast, fixed the value of the U.S. dollar to gold at a mint parity of $35 per troy ounce. The United States agreed to buy and sell gold with other official monetary agencies in settlement of transactions. Because other countries pegged the values of their currencies to the U.S. dollar and the U.S. maintained the value of the dollar relative to gold, each nondollar currency was indirectly linked to gold.

Figure 7-2 illustrates the system and the relationships among gold, the U.S. dollar, the British pound, and the German deutsche mark. The figure shows the dollar with a mint parity value of $35 per troy ounce of gold. The British pound

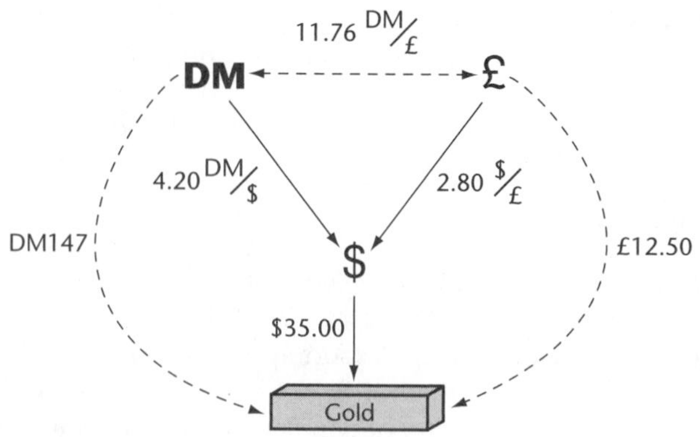

Figure 7-2

The Bretton Woods Exchange-Rate System

In practice, the Bretton Woods system linked all currencies, other than the U.S. dollar, to gold and to each other through the U.S. dollar. The United States pegged the dollar to gold at a parity rate of $35 per troy ounce. Other nations, such as the United Kingdom and West Germany, pegged their currencies to the dollar. This indirectly established exchange values among the British pound and the deutsche mark, and among the pound and the deutsche mark and gold.

Devalue
A situation in which a nation with a pegged exchange rate arrangement changes the pegged, or parity, value of its currency so that it takes a greater *number of domestic currency units to purchase one unit of the foreign currency.*

Revalue
A situation in which a nation with a pegged exchange-rate system changes the pegged, or parity, value of its currency so that it takes a smaller *number of domestic currency units to purchase one unit of the foreign currency.*

Reserve currency
The currency commonly used to settle international debts and to express the exchange value of other nation's currencies.

was pegged to the dollar at an exchange rate of 2.80 $/£ and the deutsche mark was pegged to the dollar at an exchange rate of 4.20 DM/$. This system established the link among the British pound and gold, the British pound and the deutsche mark, and the deutsche mark and gold.

Although each country pegged its currency, under the Bretton Woods agreement any nation could change the par value with the approval of the IMF. A nation **devalues** its currency when it raises the par value, meaning that a person must offer more units of the currency to purchase a unit of the commodity or foreign currency. A nation **revalues** its currency when it lowers the mint parity value or par value, meaning that one may offer fewer units of the currency to purchase a unit of the commodity or foreign currency. Thus, the Bretton Woods system was an adjustable-peg system, rather than a system of fixed exchange rates.

Under the Bretton Woods system, nations used the U.S. dollar to settle international transactions. This made the dollar the primary **reserve currency** of the system, or the currency accepted as a means of settling international transactions.

One problem encountered during the late 1940s and 1950s was that participating nations did not have sufficient U.S. dollar reserves. The Marshall Plan and the European Payments Union alleviated this dollar shortage problem. The purpose of the *Marshall Plan,* officially titled the European Recovery Program, was to help rebuild the European economies by supplying financial capital. The inflow of capital funds yielded dollars that the nations could use to conduct current account transactions.

The *European Payments Union* was a system among European nations to help settle cross-country deficits and surpluses. Under this system, member nations would track their net monthly deficit or surplus balances with each other. At the end of the month, the nations would settle, in U.S. dollars, only the net balance they had with each other.

What was the Bretton Woods system of "pegged" exchange rates?

Fundamental Issue 3

The Bretton Woods system was a system of adjustable pegged exchange rates whose parity values could be changed when warranted. Each country established and maintained a parity value of its currency, or peg, relative to gold or the U.S. dollar. All chose the U.S. dollar, making the system a dollar-standard system. Nations could change their parity values, either revaluing or devaluing, with approval of the IMF.

PERFORMANCE OF THE BRETTON WOODS SYSTEM

ON THE WEB

Learn more about the existing Bretton Woods Organizations at the International Monetary Fund Web site, http://www.imf.org, and the World Bank Web site, http://www.worldbank.org.

Because the United States stated the par value of the dollar in terms of gold and most other participating countries stated their par values in terms of the U.S. dollar, the system had two sets of rules: One for the United States and one for all other countries. Accordingly, the United States had to follow an independent and anti-inflationary monetary policy while standing ready to exchange the dollar for gold at the par value. All other nations had to buy or sell U.S. dollar reserves to keep their domestic currency exchange values against the dollar within the 1-percent parity band.

For most of the period between 1945 and 1968, the world economy experienced growth in output and a rapid increase in world trade. Nations did not undergo the type of liquidity crises that were prevalent during the gold standard. Consequently, short-run prices were more stable as well. The Bretton Woods system was not without its shortcomings, however.

Because the United States was the only country committed to converting its domestic currency for gold, the system had an inadvertent weakness. Even if the United States followed an anti-inflationary monetary policy, the possibility of a *run on the dollar,* in which traders and official foreign agencies seek to convert the dollar for gold *en masse,* existed. Because there was a limit to the U.S. gold stock, the dollar would not increase in value relative to gold, but it could always decrease in value. This situation made the dollar the target of foreign exchange speculators, as well as nationalistic politicians who opposed the dollar as the standard of the world's exchange-rate system.

The Gold Pool

In 1960, the United States and many of the European economies collectively began to intervene in the gold market. The purpose of these interventions was to maintain the dollar price of gold and to ensure the stability of the exchange-rate system. This coordinated arrangement became known as the *gold pool.*

Beginning in 1964, the U.S. government increased federal spending under heightened military involvement in Vietnam and the social programs termed the Great Society. The United States experienced a considerable economic expansion accompanied by rising inflation. The United States ran sizable balance-of-payments deficits with Germany and Japan in particular, and as a result, there was a considerable increase in the amount of dollars abroad. What had once been a dollar shortage on the world market was now a dollar glut.

The increase in the volume of dollars on the world market led many traders to believe that the United States would devalue the dollar relative to gold. That is, they anticipated that the dollar's parity value would increase, meaning that they would have to offer more dollars in exchange for a troy ounce of gold. If the parity value of the dollar increased, any individual or government holding dollar reserves would experience a capital loss on those dollar holdings.

In 1967, a devaluation of the British pound, which caused individuals and monetary agencies holding the pound to experience a 14.3 percent capital loss, increased speculation that the United States would devalue the dollar. Because of the speculation that a dollar devaluation was imminent, the demand for gold increased in the London commodities market. To meet the increase in demand and maintain the dollar parity value, the United States had to increase the supply of gold to the market. At one point, U.S. gold sales were so great that the weight of an emergency air shipment from Fort Knox to London collapsed the weighing room floor of the Bank of England.

The participating nations eventually abandoned the gold pool in 1968. Following the end of the gold pool, there was considerable pressure on the central banks of France and Germany to maintain their par values. Eventually, the crisis forced France to devalue the franc relative to the dollar by more than 11 percent. The day after the German elections of September 28, 1969, the German central bank, the *Bundesbank,* sought to maintain the parity value by purchasing $245 million in dollar reserves in the first hour and a half that the market was open. Eventually, the deutsche mark was revalued by over 9 percent. Although these two nations did change their parity values, other European nations did not, so pressure on the system continued.

In early 1971, the U.S. balance on goods and services, illustrated in Figure 7-3, swung from a surplus to a surprisingly large deficit, further confirming the perception of an overvalued dollar. In May 1971, as the U.S. trade deficit continued to expand, pressure to maintain the parity values between the European currencies, particularly the German mark, and the U.S. dollar climaxed. On May 4, 1971, in order to prevent an appreciation of the deutsche mark relative to the dollar, the Bundesbank bought $1 billion on the exchange market. During the first hour of trading on the following day, the Bundesbank bought an additional $1 billion. The Bundesbank then announced that it was abandoning official exchange operations to maintain the parity value. Austria, Belgium, the Netherlands, and Switzerland followed suit.

President Nixon Closes the Gold Window

On August 8, 1971, newspapers reported that the French were about to present $191 million of reserves to the United States in exchange for gold so that the

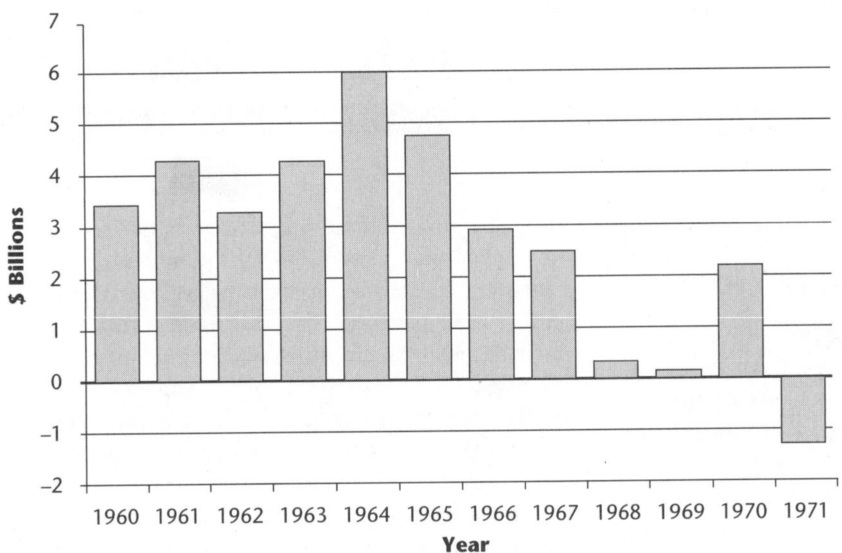

Figure 7-3

The U.S. Balance on Goods, Services, and Income: 1960 through 1971

The U.S. balance on goods, services, and income changed from a surplus in 1970 to a surprisingly large deficit in 1971. The deficits that emerged early in 1971 reinforced market participants' views that the dollar was overvalued relative to the other major currencies.

Source: Bureau of Economic Analysis, U.S. Department of Commerce.

French government could make a loan repayment to the IMF. This amount was far short of being a major concern to the United States. In this regard, economist Peter Kenen said, "No one country was large enough to blackmail Washington by demanding gold for dollars, but each was large enough to fear its actions could undermine the monetary system." Nonetheless, speculation against the dollar further increased, and the media reported gold outflows on a daily basis. Eventually, on August 15, 1971, during a televised address, U.S. President Richard Nixon announced that the United States would temporarily suspend the convertibility of the dollar into gold or other reserve assets. (Some argue for suspending the IMF: See on page 214 the *Policy Notebook: The International Monetary Fund—Dismantle or Reform?*)

By abandoning the convertibility of the U.S. dollar into gold for foreign central banks, the United States eliminated the anchor of the Bretton Woods system. The incompatibility of U.S. and European macroeconomic policies and the unwillingness of the U.S. government to devalue the dollar or of European governments to revalue their currencies brought about the end of the system. Once again, the world's exchange system was in disarray. Consequently, international trade between nations fell into a more chaotic state.

THE SMITHSONIAN AGREEMENT AND THE SNAKE IN THE TUNNEL

In an effort to restore order to the exchange-rate system, the ten nations with the largest share of reserves of the IMF met on December 16 and 17, 1971, at the Smithsonian Institution in Washington, D.C. These ten nations—West Germany, France, Japan, the United Kingdom, the United States, Italy, Canada, Belgium, the Netherlands, and Sweden—which together compose the **Group of Ten (G10),**

Group of Ten (G10)
The nations of France, Germany, Japan, the United Kingdom, the United States, Canada, Italy, Belgium, the Netherlands, and Sweden.

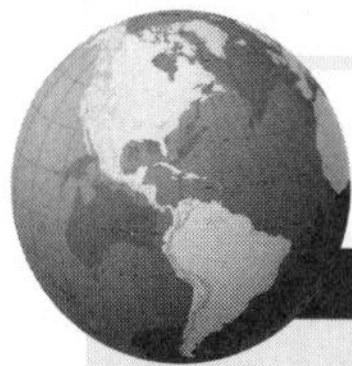

POLICY *Notebook*

POLICY MANAGEMENT

The International Monetary Fund—Dismantle or Reform?

The International Monetary Fund had a clear role under the Bretton Woods system: The IMF temporarily loaned reserves to nations experiencing external payments problems. In consultation with the IMF, a nation might devalue its currency and rebuild its reserves. For the most part, the system was stable, and the IMF served its function well.

With the collapse of the Bretton Woods system in 1971, pegged exchange-rate arrangements were no longer required, and capital markets became more predominant. The IMF found itself recreating and expanding its role. During the 1980s, a number of developing economies experienced debt crises. The IMF was one of the international institutions that lent funds to these nations. Hence, the IMF's activities expanded from short-term lending to longer-term loans, to which the IMF attached policy conditions that many critics now see as counterproductive. Additional expansion occurred during the 1990s, when the IMF played a pivotal role in providing development assistance to transitional economies of central Europe and Russia and engineered massive rescue packages for crisis-stricken economies such as Mexico and Thailand.

Criticism of the IMF escalated in the late 1990s. Its performance in bailing out East Asian economies, the misplacement of IMF funds loaned to Russia, and difficulties in selecting a new managing director put the IMF under great scrutiny. The U.S. Congress, in particular, questioned whether the IMF was worth its cost to U.S. taxpayers. The U.S. Congress created the International Financial Advisory Commission to investigate this very issue. Congress appointed Alan Meltzer of Carnegie Mellon University to head the Commission and charged it with advising Congress about how to reform both the IMF and the World Bank.

In early 2000, the Commission issued its final report. It recommended neither abolishing the IMF nor maintaining the status quo. Instead, it recommended that the IMF return to its principal function under the Bretton Woods system—providing short-term loans to nations experiencing external payments problems—and to leave long-term lending to its sister institution, the World Bank. If these reforms were instituted, the IMF would lend only to a small number of nations instead of the fifty or so it typically lends to at any given time. Members of the commission concluded that the IMF was simply "cracking under the strain of trying to do to much," and that serious restructure was desirable.

For Critical Analysis:
Currently there is only one International Monetary Fund. Is financial market stability best served by one single institution or by a number of institutions spread out over the globe?

negotiated the Smithsonian agreement. This established a new exchange-rate system that was similar in many respects to the Bretton Woods system. The agreement established new par values, most representing a revaluation of European currencies relative to the dollar, but with a wider band of 2.25 percent on either side of the parity value. The U.S. dollar, though devalued relative to gold, would not be convertible into gold. Following the conference, President Nixon characterized the agreement to the media as "the most significant monetary agreement in the history of the world."

Shortly after the Smithsonian agreement, on March 7, 1972, the six member nations of the European Economic Community (EEC) (France, West Germany, Italy, Belgium, the Netherlands, and Luxembourg), announced a plan to move toward greater monetary union. The member countries intended to maintain the exchange values of their currencies relative to each other within 2.25 percent. This system became known as the *snake in the tunnel.* Participating nations would maintain exchange values by selling or buying each other's currencies. Collectively, the EEC currencies represented the snake. Whenever the snake would move to the allowable edge of the Smithsonian exchange value—the tunnel—the EEC nations would buy and sell U.S. dollars as needed.

By the middle of 1972, the exchange markets were in turmoil once again. Britain took action first, abandoning the snake in the tunnel in June, only two months after joining. Early in 1973, failure of the Smithsonian agreement was on the horizon. Despite enormous diplomatic efforts and a 10 percent devaluation of the dollar against gold by the U.S. Treasury, the European nations participating in the snake announced that they would no longer maintain their parity values relative to outside nations, such as the United States. Thus ended the "most significant monetary agreement in the history of the world," just fifteen months after it began.

The Flexible Exchange-Rate System

Although there were attempts to return to some form of an adjustable pegged system, a *de facto* system of flexible exchange rates emerged. A *floating,* or **flexible exchange-rate system,** is one in which the forces of supply and demand determine a currency's exchange value in the private market. Leading U.S. economists, such as Milton Friedman, had argued in favor of a flexible-exchange-rate system since the early 1950s.

Flexible exchange-rate system
An exchange rate system whereby a nation allows market forces to determine the international value of its currency.

ECONOMIC SUMMITS AND A NEW ORDER

Although the world was operating under a floating-rate system, it was not an official system, because the constitution of the IMF forbade floating rates. In 1975, French President Valery Giscard d'Estaing decided to host an informal gathering of the leaders of the major industrialized nations, France, the United States, Germany, Japan, Italy, and the United Kingdom.

Discussions on the exchange-rate system continued between the representatives of the United States and France. On the eve on the summit, the two agreed to a system of flexible exchange rates with coordinated interventions in the foreign exchange market whenever they felt such interventions were required to ensure stability of exchange rates. President Giscard d'Estaing announced the breakthrough at the summit and received immediate endorsement for it from the other participating leaders.

With the leaders of the major industrialized countries endorsing the system envisioned in the French–United States negotiations, the members of the IMF rapidly went about completing the details and revising the constitution of the IMF. Member nations completed the negotiations, known as the **Jamaica Accords,** in Jamaica in 1976.

Jamaica Accords
A meeting of the member nations of the IMF, occurring in January 1976, amending the constitution of the IMF to allow, among other things, each member nation to determine its own exchange-rate system.

Within six months of the first economic summit, U.S. president Gerald Ford decided to host an economic summit of his own. President Ford, to the disapproval of President Giscard d'Estaing, also invited Canada to participate. With this action, President Ford institutionalized the summits, now held during the summer of each year and known as the Economic Summit. In 1997, summit host U.S. President William Clinton invited Russian President Boris Yeltsin to attend the summit from beginning to end, although he was excused from the economic meetings. At the 1998 Birmingham summit, British Prime Minister Tony Blair invited President Yeltsin to participate in all the summit meetings, formally expanding the participating nations to eight, or the **Group of Eight (G8).**

Group of Eight (G8)
The nations of France, Germany, Japan, the United Kingdom, the United States, Canada, Italy, and Russia.

ON THE WEB

Learn more about the annual economic summits from the University of Toronto G8 Research Group at: http://www.g8.utoronto.ca.

PERFORMANCE OF THE FLOATING-RATE SYSTEM

The flexibility of the current exchange-rate system allowed the major economies to endure some tumultuous economic conditions. Since 1973, which economists recognize as the beginning of the floating exchange-rate period, the major economies have experienced divergent macroeconomic policies, major internal and external economic shocks, and unprecedented fiscal and current account deficits. By allowing its currency's exchange value to be determined by market forces, a floating-rate country is also able to focus monetary policies on domestic objectives. Most nations, however, have experienced periods of dramatic increases and decreases in the exchange values of their currencies.

Arguably the greatest challenges to the leading industrialized economies and the exchange rate system occurred between 1973 and 1974 and in 1979. The outbreak of the Yom Kipper War in the Middle East and an oil embargo imposed in October 1973 resulted in oil price increases and subsequent inflation in oil-importing countries. In 1979, the Organization of Petroleum and Oil Exporting Countries (OPEC) undertook a series of actions that eventually tripled the price of crude oil on the world market. Already struggling with inflation, the oil-importing economies were hit hard by the increase in oil prices. At the end of the 1970s and early 1980s, Canada, France, Italy, the United Kingdom, and the United States were experiencing double-digit, or near double-digit, rates of inflation.

Also in 1979, U.S. President Jimmy Carter appointed Paul Volcker as chairman of the Federal Reserve. Volcker made it publicly known that the Federal Reserve would pursue a single objective of reducing inflation. The Fed's policy actions resulted in a U.S. recession in 1981 and 1982. More important to our discussion, monetary and fiscal policy actions resulted in very high interest rates and put upward pressure on the value of the dollar relative to other major currencies. (Chapter 8 examines the relationship between interest rates and exchange rates.) As a result, the dollar began an appreciation that continued until early 1985.

Figure 7-4

The U.S. Nominal Effective Exchange Rate since 1973

Between 1981 and 1985, the U.S. dollar experienced a considerable appreciation in average value relative to seven major currencies. Within two years, the appreciation had been reversed.

Source: U.S. Federal Reserve Board.

Figure 7-4 illustrates the Federal Reserve's nominal effective exchange value of the dollar relative to seven major currencies. The rise of the dollar's value from 1981 through 1985 is one prominent feature of the diagram. The other is the dramatic decline in the dollar's value from 1985 through 1987. We have explained why the dollar appreciated from 1981 through 1985, but why did it peak in 1985 and reverse direction until 1987?

THE PLAZA AGREEMENT AND THE LOUVRE ACCORD

For some time, the central bankers and finance ministers of a subset of the G10 nations have been meeting to discuss macroeconomic conditions and policies. This subgroup included the United States, the United Kingdom, Germany, Japan, and France, and is known as the **Group of Five,** or **G5.** The content, conclusions, and policy outcomes of these meetings had always been secret. In September 1985, the G5 met at the Plaza Hotel in New York to discuss, primarily, the status of the dollar. In an unprecedented move, the participants issued a statement to the media following the meeting. In what is now known as the **Plaza Agreement,** the G5 announced that it was its belief that the dollar was at a level inconsistent with underlying economic conditions. The G5 said that it would intervene *collectively* to drive down the value of the dollar.

The purpose of the press statement was to convince currency traders that the G5 meant business. The statement and periodic surprise interventions by the G5 appeared to have convinced currency traders. As shown in Figure 7-4, the dollar reversed its prior four-year appreciation within the subsequent two years.

Over the next two years, the G5 increased in ranks to include Italy and Canada (becoming consistent with the membership of the annual economic summits at that time). This expanded group is the **Group of Seven (G7).** In February of 1987, the G7 met at the Louvre in France. Once again, the dollar was the focus

Group of Five (G5)
The nations of France, Germany, Japan, the United Kingdom, the United States.

Plaza Agreement
A meeting of the central bankers and finance ministers of the G5 nations that took place at the Plaza Hotel in New York in September 1985. The participants announced that the exchange value of the dollar was too strong and that the nations would coordinate their intervention actions in order to drive down the value of the dollar.

Group of Seven (G7)
The nations of France, Germany, Japan, the United Kingdom, the United States, Canada and Italy.

Louvre Accord
A meeting of the central bankers and finance ministers of the G7 nations, less Italy, that took place in February 1987. The participants announced that the exchange value of the dollar had fallen to a level consistent with "economic fundamentals" and that the central banks would intervene in the foreign exchange market only to ensure stability of exchange rates.

Managed or dirty float
An exchange rate system in which a nation allows the international value of its currency to be primarily determined by market forces but intervenes from time to time to stabilize its currency.

of discussion. Following the meeting, known as the **Louvre Accord,** the finance ministers and central bankers announced that the dollar had reached a level now consistent with underlying economic conditions. The G7, therefore, would only intervene in the foreign exchange market as needed to ensure stability.

This meeting defined the exchange-rate management approach of the G7 and G10 economies from 1987 through the early 1990s. These nations intervene, usually on a collective and unannounced basis, only when a currency or currencies have reached a critical threshold. What is the critical threshold? This is unknown to traders, who are always trying to anticipate the actions of the finance ministers and central bankers.

Under the Louvre Accord, nations will intervene on behalf of their currencies from time to time. Consequently, the system is not a true flexible exchange-rate system. This type of exchange-rate system is a **managed float (or dirty float),** which is a system of flexible exchange rates but with periodic intervention by official agencies.

For the international monetary and financial markets, the 1990s proved no less interesting than the previous two decades. In December 1994, a devaluation of the Mexican peso sparked a financial crisis that caused a collapse in the value of the peso and rattled the economies of Latin America. In 1997, financial crisis triggered in Thailand affected several economies in East Asia, including Indonesia, Malaysia, and South Korea. In 1998, financial crises occurred in Russia and in Brazil. Some of these economies rebounded quickly. Others, such as Indonesia, are still suffering the economic consequences.

During 1998, eleven nations of the European Union irrevocably locked their exchange rates, and in January 1999 they created the European Central Bank and launched the euro. They converted banking and financial statements to euros during the next two and a half years. In January 2002, they began circulating euro notes and coins and halted the circulation of national currencies.

4 **Fundamental Issue**

What post–Bretton Woods system of "flexible" exchange rates prevails today?

Economists typically characterize the post–Bretton Woods exchange-rate system as one of floating exchange rates. Individual nations, however, have adopted a wide variety of exchange-rate systems, ranging from pegged to fully flexible exchange rates. Furthermore, the leading industrialized nations periodically intervene in the foreign exchange markets to stabilize their currencies, making the system a managed float instead of a truly flexible exchange-rate system.

Other Forms of Exchange-Rate Systems Today

In the previous sections of this chapter, we used an earlier period of the exchange system to illustrate the workings of a gold standard, the Bretton Woods system to illustrate an adjustable-peg dollar standard, and the post–Bretton Woods system

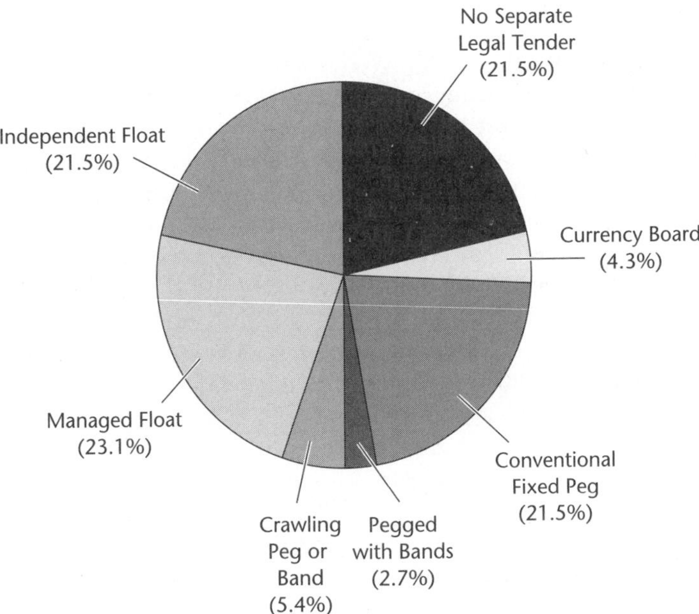

Figure 7-5

Current Foreign Exchange-Rate Systems

Currently, more than 44 percent of the member nations of the IMF report to have an independent float or managed float exchange-rate system. For those countries that peg their currency in some fashion, the U.S. dollar is the most common currency for a peg and a currency basket is the second most common.

Source: International Monetary Fund, *International Financial Statistics* (June 2002).

to illustrate a floating-exchange-rate system. Since the breakup of the Bretton Woods system, nations have adopted a wide variety of exchange rate systems.

Figure 7-5 illustrates the general types of exchange-rate systems that IMF member nations claim to have adopted. The figure shows the percent of those nations that use the currency of another nation or entity as their legal tender, conventional and non-conventional pegs, limited flexibility systems, and floating systems. The pie chart shows that more than 44 percent of the nations have a managed-float or an independently floating exchange-rate system, while slightly less than 44 percent peg their currencies in some fashion.

Although 21.5 percent of IMF-member nations claim to have an independently floating exchange-rate system, work by Guillermo Calvo and Carmen Reinhart of the University of Maryland indicates otherwise. Calvo and Reinhart's research shows that the variability of many emerging economies' exchange rates is less than that of "true floaters" such as the United States. These economists conclude that many policymakers in emerging nations still have a fear of floating and that they continue to intervene in the foreign exchange markets to support their national currencies.

Figure 7-5 illustrates that nations have adopted a wide variety of exchange rate systems. The figure, however, does not provide detail on the operation of these systems. As the 1997–1998 Southeast Asian currency crises painfully showed, the operation of a nation's currency system is of vital importance. Hence, we shall now consider four specific types of systems: a crawling peg, a currency-basket peg, a currency board (or independent currency authority), and dollarization.

CRAWLING PEGS

Even after the collapse of the Bretton Woods system, some nations have decided to peg their currencies to the currency of other nations. There are a number of reasons why a nation may chose to do this. The most common argument for pegged exchange rates is that reducing exchange rate volatility and uncertainty may yield gains in economic efficiency. Thus, a nation that has a large volume of trade with another nation, but a less stable currency, may choose to peg its currency. Pegging to another nation's currency and reducing exchange rate volatility, therefore, may promote price stability and greater trade and capital flows between the two nations.

The economic conditions of the two nations, however, may be quite different. When the economic conditions of the two nations differ, it is difficult, if not impossible, to maintain a pegged exchange rate. In this situation, nations that peg the value of their currencies to the currencies of other nations might allow the parity value to change continuously. This type of exchange-rate system is a **crawling peg.**

Crawling peg
An exchange rate system in which a country pegs its currency to the currency of another nation but allows the parity value to change at regular time intervals.

Nicaragua's Crawling-Peg Arrangement

Nicaragua's exchange arrangement is a good example of a crawling peg. To promote exchange-rate stability and facilitate exports, Nicaragua pegged the value of its domestic currency, the córdoba, to the U.S. dollar. U.S. and Nicaraguan macroeconomic conditions were very different, however. Inflation in the United States averaged about 2 to 3 percent, but inflation in Nicaragua remained between 10 to 20 percent a year. Because of this large inflation difference, Nicaraguan officials realized that there would be a general tendency for the córdoba to depreciate against the U.S. dollar. Hence, Nicaragua adopted a crawling peg.

During the late 1990s and early 2000s Nicaraguan officials reduced the parity value of the córdoba by a small percentage each week. As shown in Figure 7-6, the córdoba depreciated steadily against the U.S. dollar during this period. After cutting inflation substantially by late 1999 and consulting with the International Monetary Fund, Nicaragua reduced the rate of crawl. As Figure 7-6 shows, since the last half of 1999 the value of the córdoba has depreciated against the dollar at a very steady pace.

Exchange-rate band
A range of exchange values, with an upper and lower limit within which the exchange value of the domestic currency can fluctuate.

Crawling band
A range of exchange values that combines features of a crawling peg with the flexibility of an exchange-rate band.

The Parity Band

As in the gold standard and the Bretton Woods system, nations that peg their currencies usually allow the exchange rate to deviate from the parity value by a certain amount, typically expressed as a percentage, on either side of the parity value. The exchange rate, therefore, is not a fixed value, but can fluctuate within a band, known as an **exchange-rate band.**

Some countries, such as Columbia and Chile, have combined features of a crawling peg with the additional flexibility allowed by an exchange-rate band. This type of arrangement is a **crawling band.** Like an exchange-rate band, a crawling band features an upper and lower parity limit. The central parity,

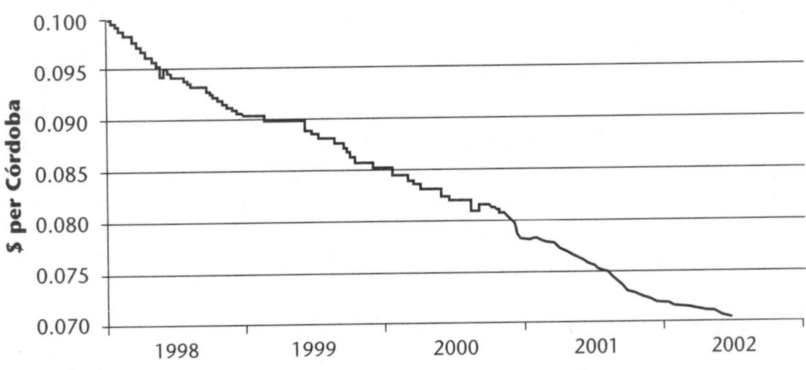

Figure 7-6

Nicaragua's Crawling-Peg System: Since 1998

Nicaragua's crawling-peg exchange-rate system allows for a small weekly rate of crawl, or depreciation, of the córdoba relative to the U.S. dollar. The weekly crawl is illustrated by the stairstep appearance of the exchange rate.

Source: Data from http://www.Oanda.com.

however, is adjusted on a regular basis. The upper and lower parity limits, therefore, change on a regular basis, usually allowing for a steady rate of depreciation.

ON THE WEB

To obtain IMF Reviews of member nations, see the Public Information Notices posted at http://www.imf.org.

CURRENCY BASKETS

The previous section outlined the most common argument for pegging the value of a nation's currency, which is that reducing exchange-rate volatility and uncertainty may yield gains in economic efficiency. For this same reason, a nation might choose to peg its currency to a weighted average of a number of foreign currencies. This is known as a **currency-basket peg.** The additional motivation for pegging to a currency basket is that the weighted average of a basket of currencies is likely to be less variable than the exchange rate of a single currency.

Currency-basket peg
An exchange-rate system in which a country pegs its currency to the weighted average value of a basket, or selected number of currencies.

To better understand what a currency basket is, imagine that you have six different coins in your hand, each from a different country. Next imagine that you place all of the coins in a basket. Let's allow the sum of the coins in the basket to equal one unit of your own fictitious currency. The value of the coins in the basket is the value at which you would try to maintain your own currency under a currency-basket system.

Selecting a Currency Basket

Typically, a nation that adopts a currency-basket peg will include a relatively small number of currencies in the basket, because as the number of currencies to which the nation pegs increases, managing the basket peg becomes more difficult. Most nations using a currency-basket system peg to six or fewer currencies.

The choice of currencies to be included in the basket is similar to the choice made in constructing an effective exchange rate (see Chapter 6). A basket typically includes selected currencies most prominent in the nation's international trade, capital flows, or international debt settlement. As in the construction of an effective exchange rate, the basket assigns a weight to each currency. The weights for a currency basket sum to unity, as well. The choice of weights reflects the relative importance of each currency in the nation's international transactions.

Managing the Currency Basket

Under a pegged exchange-rate system, the nation's monetary authority maintains the exchange rate between the domestic currency and the currency to which the nations pegs its currency. A currency-basket system introduces an interesting wrinkle. The authority must concentrate on the exchange rate between the domestic currency and the currencies included in the currency basket *and* the cross rates between the currencies in the basket. If these cross rates change, the monetary authorities must take action, either depreciating or appreciating their currency so as to maintain the currency-basket value. The weights determine the amount of appreciation or depreciation.

5 **Fundamental Issue**

What are crawling-peg and basket-peg exchange-rate systems?

Crawling-peg and basket-peg exchange-rate systems are types of pegged exchange-rate systems. Under a crawling peg, the parity value and the exchange rate bands are allowed to change at regular intervals, providing more flexibility in the system than a true pegged exchange-rate system. Under a basket-peg system, officials peg the domestic currency to a weighted-average value of a small number of currencies. A weighted-average value of currencies tends to be less volatile than the exchange value of a single currency.

INDEPENDENT CURRENCY AUTHORITIES

Earlier in this chapter, we explained that a gold standard does not require a central bank. Changes in a nation's official gold reserves govern changes in the nation's money stock. A gold standard only requires an official monetary agency that will increase or decrease the money in circulation as required. Some nations today do not have a central bank. Instead, they have an *independent currency authority* or *currency board.*

Currency board
An independent monetary authority that substitutes for a central bank. The currency board pegs the value of the domestic currency, and changes in the foreign reserve holdings of the currency board determine the level of the domestic money stock.

A **currency board,** or independent monetary authority, is an independent monetary agency that links the growth of the money stock to the foreign exchange holdings of the currency board. It does this by issuing domestic money in exchange for foreign currency at a fixed exchange rate.

The British Empire established the first currency board in Mauritius in 1849. The currency board was a means of providing Mauritius and other British colonies with a stable and convertible currency. The colony issued its monetary instruments—at a fixed rate of exchange—against the pound sterling assets that the currency board held in London. The colony's money, therefore, was convertible at a fixed rate and was as stable as the pound sterling. The colonies saved considerable resources because they did not need to hold and handle sterling coins and notes. Popularity of the currency-board system peaked in the 1940s and virtually disappeared during the 1960s.

As practiced today, a currency board pegs the value of its nation's currency to the currency of another nation and buys or sells foreign-currency reserves as appropriate to maintain the parity value. When the monetary authority buys or sells foreign reserves, it changes the amount of domestic money in circulation. This, and this alone, governs changes in the nation's money stock.

Currency boards have very limited responsibilities. They do not hold notes or bills issued by the domestic government, do not set reserve requirements on the nation's banks, and do not serve as a lender of last resort to the nation's banks, as a central bank typically does.

Because of these limited responsibilities, currency boards cannot engage in discretionary monetary policy and, therefore, are shielded from political influence. For this reason, there has been an increased interest in currency boards during the last few years. Some economists see currency boards as the best means for some nations to establish a credible approach to price stability.

There are several currency boards today. Some have been established recently. Bulgaria, Estonia, Lithuania, and Hong Kong, have currency board systems. Some currency boards have been very successful, while others have failed. Most recently, Argentinean policymakers abandoned the currency board system in favor of a floating exchange rate.

DOLLARIZATION

Some nations take an even more dramatic approach to exchange-rate management by allowing the currency of another nation to serve as legal tender. As shown in Figure 7-5 on page 219, 21.5 percent of the member nations of the International Monetary Fund use the currency of another nation. Additional nations also are considering abandoning their domestic currency altogether. This practice is referred to as **dollarization,** but it actually means the use of any other nation's currency, not just the dollar, as legal tender.

Dollarization
A system in which the currency of another nation circulates as the sole legal tender.

Recently Ecuador and El Salvador dollarized their economies. Other Latin American economies already are partially dollarized, and various Central and South American nations, such as Nicaragua and Guatemala, have debated dollarization since the late 1990s. (See on the next page *Policy Notebook: Should Argentina Dollarize?*)

Proponents of dollarization argue that policymakers of small nations bordering large economies with strong currencies should dollarize their economies so as to achieve economic growth and stability. If policymakers give up the national currency and adopt the currency of another nation, the argument goes, they will no longer be able to mismanage their currency. In turn, interest rates and inflation rates should mirror those of the countries whose currency these nations adopted. After examining the economic record of the small group of dollarized nations, Sebastian Edwards of the National Bureau of Economic Research

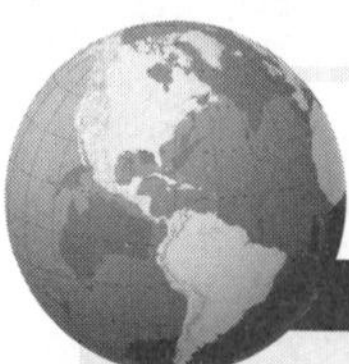

POLICY *Notebook*

POLICY MANAGEMENT

Should Argentina Dollarize?

In early 1990, dismal economic performance crippled Argentina. At one point, prices had risen a whopping 20,266 percent over twelve months, while GDP declined 23 percent for the year. In 1991, policymakers passed a set of economic reforms, which included the *Convertibility Law* that established a unique type of currency-board arrangement. Argentinean leaders hoped that the currency-board system would lend credibility to government policies and reduce inflation by separating politics from exchange-rate management. These reform measures reduced inflation to roughly 1 percent a year by 1998.

Argentina's Unique System

Argentina's currency-board system was unique because it allowed for a small degree of discretion not found in a typical currency board. The central bank had to back the domestic monetary base with U.S. dollar reserves. The central bank held most of these reserves in the form of interest-bearing instruments such as dollar-denominated deposits or short-term U.S. government debt. The central bank could, however, hold up to one-third of its reserves in the form of dollar-denominated Argentinean government debt. Although the bank did not exercise this option, it would permit some discretionary monetary policymaking.

In 1996, policymakers created the *Contingent Repurchase Facility,* which allowed the central bank to lend funds to illiquid banks. The lender of last resort is another feature not found in a currency-board system. This facility was funded by holding reserves in excess of those required under the currency-board arrangement. In late 1990, Argentina's foreign exchange reserves were nearly twice the amount required under the currency-board system.

Dollarization Options

Even though Argentina reduced its inflation rate to the levels the United States experienced in the late 1990s, interest rates in Argentina remained much higher than those in the United States. Economists viewed this interest rate gap as a sign that the government of Argentina has not gained full credibility. Because the government already held large U.S. dollar reserves and Argentina is already 75 percent dollarized, the Argentinean government considered fully dollarizing the Argentinean economy. By allowing the dollar to replace the Argentinean peso, there could be no question of the government's commitment to price stability. Interest rates might then fall to U.S. levels, spurring additional economic growth in Argentina.

One crucial argument against dollarization is the loss of the limited flexibility that the Argentine central bank now enjoys. David Altig and Owen Humpage of the Federal Reserve Bank of Cleveland argued that the central bank could continue to serve as the lender-of-last resort by holding U.S. dollar reserves in the *Contingent Repurchase Facility.* Their argument, therefore, is that "dollarization would impose no cost on Argentine monetary policy beyond those resulting from its currency board arrangements."

In spite of these arguments, Argentina continued with a currency-board arrangement until a financial crisis crippled the government in 2001. In January 2002, a new government finally abandoned the currency board and allowed the peso to float.

For Critical Analysis:
Can you still identify some benefits of dollarization, now that the forces of supply and demand determine the exchange value of the peso? Can you argue in favor of another type of exchange-rate arrangement?

concluded that dollarized economies have lower rates of inflation than similar nondollarized economies. A cost of this lower inflation rate appears to be a slower rate of economic growth, however.

Fundamental Issue 6

What is a currency board, and what is dollarization?

A currency board (or independent currency authority) supplants a central bank. The responsibilities of a currency board, however, are much more limited than those of a typical central bank. A currency board pegs the value of the domestic currency and buys and sells foreign reserves in order to maintain the pegged value. Changes in the stock of foreign reserves solely determine the domestic money stock. Currency boards, therefore, better isolate monetary policy from domestic political pressures. Dollarization is the adoption of another nation's currency as the sole legal tender. Recently policymakers in Ecuador and El Salvador dollarized their economies. Policymakers in other nations such as Nicaragua and Argentina continue to debate the benefits and costs of dollarization.

Fixed or Floating Exchange Rates?

Now that we have examined a number of exchange-rate systems, an obvious question is which one is best? Unfortunately, there is no clear-cut answer to this question, and the debate over the benefits of fixed versus flexible exchange rates is one of the oldest in economics. This is precisely the reason there are so many different types of systems in existence today.

On one hand, fixed exchange rates may promote sound macroeconomic policy, helping to reduce inflation and leading to a stable economic environment. This, in turn, can boost an economy's real economic growth. Under a fixed nominal exchange-rate system, however, real exchange rates may appreciate and reduce the competitiveness of the nation's exporters.

Flexible exchange rates, on the other hand, may help a country overcome external shocks such as an unusual inflow of capital from abroad or a sudden increase in the price of an imported resource. Nevertheless, flexible exchange rates introduce an additional element of uncertainty and additional volatility. This is the common criticism of flexible rates. In industrialized nations, there is no clear evidence that volatility of nominal exchange rates dampens foreign trade or investment.

What is more important than the type of exchange-rate system is sound economic policymaking. This is perhaps the most overlooked reality in the debate over fixed versus flexible exchange rates. Furthermore, the debate often contrasts the current and imperfect regime with a utopian version of another regime in which governments always conduct policymaking such that it is consistent with the exchange-rate system. As discussed in this chapter, that is not always the case.

Which is best, a fixed or flexible exchange-rate system?

Whether it is better to peg the value of the domestic currency or allow it to be flexible and market determined is one of the longest-running debates in economics. There is no clear-cut answer, because each system has it own advantages and disadvantages. Sound economic policymaking is more important in creating a stable economic environment than the choice of an exchange-rate system.

CHAPTER SUMMARY

1) **Exchange-Rate Systems:** An exchange-rate system is a nation's set of rules that determine the international exchange value of the domestic currency and link a nation's currency value to the currencies of other nations.
2) **A Gold Standard as an Exchange-Rate System:** A gold standard constitutes an exchange-rate system for a nation. With a rule of pegging the value of its currency to gold, a nation establishes the international value of its currency in terms of gold. A gold standard constitutes an exchange-rate system among participating nations. By establishing the value of each currency relative to gold, a gold standard establishes the exchange values among currencies.
3) **The Bretton Woods System of Pegged Exchange Rates:** Under the Bretton Woods system, nations pegged the values of their currencies relative to the U.S. dollar, which was linked to gold. Nations could change the parity values, and thus devalue or revalue their currencies, with the permission of the IMF. The Bretton Woods system was, therefore, a system of adjustable-pegged exchange rates.
4) **Post–Bretton Woods System of Flexible Exchange Rates:** In today's world economy, a number of exchange-rate systems are in place, ranging from flexible exchange-rate arrangements to fixed- or pegged-exchange-rate arrangements. The leading industrialized nations intervene from time to time in the foreign exchange markets. The overall system, therefore, is primarily one of managed, floating exchange rates.
5) **Crawling-Peg and Basket-Peg Exchange-Rate Systems:** Some nations desire the stability of a fixed exchange rate but find it difficult to maintain a rigid parity value. As a result, some nations have adopted either a crawling-peg or a basket-peg exchange-rate system. Under a crawling-peg exchange-rate system, a nation pegs the value of its currency, but it adjusts the parity rate at given time intervals. Under a basket-peg exchange-rate system, a nation pegs the value of its currency to the value of a basket of selected currencies.
6) **A Currency Board or Independent Currency Authority and Dollarization:** A currency board substitutes for a central bank. The responsibilities of the currency board, however, are much more limited. Under a currency board system, the currency board pegs the value of the nation's currency to another nation's currency. The currency board is responsible for maintaining the pegged value of the domestic currency by conditioning the nation's out-

standing stock of money on the amount of foreign reserves that the currency board has. Dollarization is the adoption of another nation's currency as the sole legal tender. Recently, the nations of Ecuador and El Salvador dollarized by adopting the U.S. dollar as the sole legal currency. A principle argument for dollarization is that it will reduce inflation and interest rates to mirror those of the nation whose currency is adopted. Although comparative empirical evidence on the economic performance of dollarized economies is limited, this evidence indicates that dollarized economies have lower rates of inflation and economic growth than similar nondollarized economies.

7) **Fixed Versus Flexible Exchange-Rate Arrangements:** There is no clear-cut answer about whether it is better to peg the value of a nation's currency or to allow the value of the currency to be determined in the market for foreign exchange. Each type of exchange-rate system has its benefits and its costs. Sound economic policymaking is actually more important in creating a sound and stable economic environment than is the choice of exchange-rate system.

QUESTIONS AND PROBLEMS

1) List all of the various types of exchange rate arrangements described in this chapter. (*Hint:* There are seven described in this chapter.) Order the list of exchange rate arrangements from fixed to most flexible.
2) Describe two primary functions of the International Monetary Fund.
3) Suppose the value of the U.S. dollar is pegged to gold at a rate of $50 per ounce. Next suppose that the value of the British pound is pegged to the U.S. dollar at a rate of 1.5 dollars per pound, and the value of the Canadian dollar is pegged to the U.S. dollar at a rate of 1.38 Canadian dollars per U.S. dollar. Calculate the value of the Canadian dollar and the British pound relative to gold.
4) Using the information in question 3, calculate the exchange rate between the Canadian dollar and the British pound.
5) Suppose Argentina decides to peg the value of its currency, the peso, to a basket consisting of 0.50 U.S. dollars and 0.50 euros. Further suppose the exchange rate between the U.S. dollar and the euro is 0.90 $/€. If the basket constitutes one peso, what is the appropriate exchange value between the peso and the dollar, and between the peso and the pound?
6) Explain the main difference between the exchange-rate systems of the Smithsonian agreement and the Bretton Woods system. Based on this difference, why do you think the Smithsonian agreement was so short lived?
7) What is the principle responsibility of a currency board? What are the three main restrictions on a currency board that make it different from a typical central bank?

8) Explain how the Louvre Accord represented a type of exchange-rate system.
9) What factors do you think should be considered when determining the rate of crawl for a crawling-peg exchange-rate system?
10) What, in your opinion, is the chief difference between a currency-board system and dollarization?

ONLINE APPLICATION

Along with the IMF and the World Bank, the Bank for International Settlements (BIS) is an important international financial institution. The BIS, however, is perhaps the least known and understood of the three institutions.

Internet URL: http://www.bis.org

Title: **The Bank for International Settlements**

Navigation: Begin at the home page for the BIS located at the Internet URL provided above. Click on the "About BIS" link. Next click on "BIS Profile" in the general information window.

Application: After reading the document titled "Profile of the Bank for International Settlements" and all its parts, answer the following questions.

1) When was the BIS founded, and what were the nations involved in its foundation?
2) What are the four primary functions of the BIS?
3) Approximately how many central banks and financial institutions have deposits with the BIS? What is the approximate total value of these deposits?

REFERENCES AND RECOMMENDED READINGS

Agénor, Pierre-Richard. "Parallel Currency Markets in Developing Countries: Theory, Evidence, and Policy Implications." *Essays in International Finance,* Princeton University, No. 188, (November 1992).

Altig, David, and Owen Humpage. "Dollarization and Monetary Sovereignty: The Case of Argentina." *Federal Reserve Bank of Cleveland Economic Commentary* (September 15, 1999), http:/www.clev.frb.org/research.

Berg, Andrew, and Eduardo Borensztein. "Full Dollarization: The Pros and Cons," International Monetary Fund, *Economic Issues,* No. 24.

Calvo, Guillermo A., and Carmen M. Reinhart. "Fear of Floating." *Quarterly Journal of Economics* 117 (May 2002): 379–408.

Craig, Ben, and Christopher Waller. "Dual-Currency Economies as Multiple-Payments Systems." *Federal Reserve Bank of Cleveland Economic Review* 36 (1), (Quarter 1, 2000): 2–13.

Edwards, Sebastian. "Dollarization and Economic Performance: An Empirical Investigation." *NBER Working Paper Number W8274* (May, 2001).

Grabbe, Orlin J. *International Financial Markets. 2nd ed.* New York: Elsevier, 1991, Chapter 1.

Humpage, Owen F. and Jean M. McIntire. "An Introduction to Currency Boards." *Federal Reserve Bank of Cleveland Economic Review* (Second Quarter 1995): 1–11.

International Monetary Fund. *Annual Report on Exchange Arrangements and Exchange Restrictions:* Washington, D.C., 2002.

Jordan, Jerry. "The Evolving Global Monetary Order." *Federal Reserve Bank of Cleveland Economic Commentary* (January 1, 2000),

Kasa, Kenneth. "Why Attack a Currency Board?" *Federal Reserve Bank of San Francisco Economic Letter,* Number 99-36 (November 26, 1999).

Kenen, Peter B. "Ways to Reform Exchange Rate Arrangements." *Reprints in International Finance,* No. 28, Princeton University, International Economics Section (November 1994).

Meltzer, Allan, and Jeffrey D. Sachs. "A Blueprint for IMF Reform." *The Wall Street Journal* (March 8, 2000): A22.

Solomon, Robert. *The International Monetary System, 1945–1976: An Insider's View.* New York: Harper and Row Publishers, 1977.

von Furstenberg, George M. "Can Small Countries Keep Their Own Money and Floating Exchange Rates?" in K. Kaiser, J. Kirton, and J. Daniels, eds. *Shaping a New International Financial System: Challenges of Governance in a Globalizing World.* Aldershot, United Kingdom: Ashgate Publishing, 2000: 187–202.

Williamson, John. *What Role for Currency Boards?* Washington, D.C.: Institute for International Economics, 1995.

CHAPTER EIGHT

The Power of Arbitrage—Purchasing Power and Interest Rate Parities

Fundamental Issues

1. **What does the concept of absolute purchasing power parity imply about the value of the real exchange rate?**
2. **What is relative purchasing power parity, and is it useful as a guide to movements in exchange rates?**
3. **What are the covered and uncovered interest parity conditions?**
4. **What is the distinction between adaptive and rational expectations?**
5. **What is foreign exchange market efficiency?**
6. **Under what conditions does real interest parity hold, and why is it a useful indicator of international integration?**

In January 1999, the initial eleven member nations of the European Monetary Union (EMU) introduced their new currency, the euro. At the time it was introduced, a European resident could obtain about US$1.12 with a euro. By late 2000, however, the euro had depreciated by more than 20 percent relative to the U.S. dollar. The euro appreciated slightly during 2001, but its dollar value remained well below what it had been at the time the European Monetary Union introduced the currency to the world.

As the euro's value relative to the dollar declined during 1999 and 2000, many economic commentators were critical of the performance of the EMU agency charged with regulating the quantity of euros in circulation, the European Central Bank (ECB). Critics complained that the ECB was not doing enough to restrain the euro's steady depreciation. Officials of the ECB, however, argued that the euro was somewhat "undervalued" relative to the U.S. dollar. Various factors, including the Asian crisis that lasted from 1997 to

1999, had caused the dollar to be "overvalued" in the world marketplace. Eventually, the ECB contended, market forces would push the euro's value back up relative to the dollar. In fact, by 2002 the euro had regained its value relative to the dollar.

As you learned in Chapter 6, when people say that a currency is *undervalued,* or *overvalued,* it is important for them to be clear about what theory they have in mind when judging the present market valuation of a currency. As a benchmark hypothesis for evaluating whether a currency is undervalued or overvalued in the marketplace, most economists consider the theory of *purchasing power parity.* Before you can learn about this theory and about international parity relationships involving interest rates, however, you must first understand real exchange rates and implications that a concept called the *law of one price* has for the values of real rates of exchange.

Law of One Price and Absolute Purchasing Power Parity

In its most basic form, the idea of **purchasing power parity (PPP)** presumes the absence of factors such as costs of transportation, cross-country tax differentials, and trade restrictions. Under these conditions, according to the PPP hypothesis, essentially identical goods and services that are traded across national borders should have the same price in two countries after converting their prices into a common currency.

Purchasing power parity (PPP)
A proposition that the price of a good or service in one nation should be the same as the exchange-rate-adjusted price of the same good or service in another nation.

ARBITRAGE AND THE LAW OF ONE PRICE

Economists often refer to the basic concept of purchasing power parity as the law of one price. To illustrate the law of one price, suppose that the market price of a high-quality orange is US$0.50 in Seattle, Washington. The market price of the same quality and type of orange in Victoria, British Columbia, is C$0.75. Thus, PPP would imply that the dollar equivalent exchange rate should be US$0.50/C$0.75 = 0.667 U.S. dollar per Canadian dollar. Using this rate, we can convert the Canadian dollar price of the orange in Victoria to a U.S. dollar price of US$0.50 (C$0.75 × 0.67 US$/C$ = $0.50). Therefore, the orange has the same price in Victoria as it does in Seattle after adjusting for the exchange rate.

If, however, the exchange rate were not 0.67 US$/C$, then there would be an opportunity to profitably engage in **arbitrage**—buying an item in one market to sell at a higher price in another market. Suppose the exchange rate is equal to 0.72 US$/C$. Then the U.S. dollar price of an orange in Victoria would be

Arbitrage
Buying an item in one market to sell at a higher price in another market.

C$0.75 × 0.72 US$/C$ = US$0.54. A Canadian resident who can buy many oranges in Seattle for US$0.50 per orange and haul them a short distance to Victoria to sell for C$0.75 each (US$0.54 in U.S. dollars at the 0.72 US$/C$ exchange rate) will earn a profit of US$0.04 per orange. Thus, if this individual can move 10,000 oranges from Seattle to Victoria to sell in Canada, the profit will be US$400, ignoring the relatively small transportation costs.

If a sufficient number of people engage in these sorts of arbitrage activity, then the result will be a flow of oranges from Seattle to Victoria. Canadian residents must exchange Canadian dollars for U.S. dollars in order to purchase the U.S. oranges. The exchange of the Canadian dollars for U.S. dollars on the foreign exchange market will cause an increase in the demand for U.S. dollars relative to Canadian dollars. The three markets (Seattle orange market, Victorian orange market, and foreign exchange market) will experience adjustments. The outflow of oranges from Seattle will generate an increase in the price of oranges in Seattle. The inflow of oranges to Victoria will cause a decrease in price of oranges in Victoria.

If a number of oranges and other goods and services are arbitraged in response to the misaligned exchange rate, then there will be an increase in the demand for U.S. dollars relative to Canadian dollars. This will cause the value of the U.S. dollar to appreciate relative to Canadian dollar. All of these adjustments, which result from the arbitrage activity, will tend to equalize the prices of traded goods and services, measured in terms of the same currency, thereby removing any further scope for profiting from cross-border arbitrage. (Recent developments in multicurrency payments may make cross-country arbitrage feasible on the Internet; see *Online Globalization: Increasing the Scope for International Arbitrage via Multicurrency Payment Processing.*)

ABSOLUTE PURCHASING POWER PARITY

This analysis of the relationship between prices and exchange rates implies the condition of *absolute purchasing power parity,* which we can formalize in the following manner. Let's define S to be the U.S.-dollar-equivalent exchange rate of the Canadian dollar (US$/C$), P to be the price of oranges in the United States, and P^* *to be the price of oranges in Canada. Then we can express absolute PPP as:*

$$P = S \times P^*.$$

In words, the U.S. price of oranges should equal the Canadian price times the spot exchange rate. Thus, in our example, if the U.S. dollar–Canadian dollar exchange rate is 0.667 US$/C$ and the Canadian price of oranges is C$0.75 per orange, then the U.S. dollar price of oranges should equal US$0.50.

Applying Absolute Purchasing Power Parity to All Goods and Services: A Theory of Exchange Rates

If *all* goods and services are fully and freely tradable across U.S. and Canadian borders, then absolute PPP will hold for all goods. In this instance, we can interpret

Online Globalization

Increasing the Scope for International Arbitrage via Multicurrency Payment Processing

Consider the following scenario. The year is 2013. Widespread Internet commerce stretches from Norway to South Africa and from Greenland to Chile, and managers of small businesses around the globe have set up shop on the Web. A New York jewelry retailer specializing in high-quality, handcrafted jewelry is searching for handmade necklaces to market within his physical establishment and on his company's Web site. At the Web sites of jewelry distributors in various nations, he can click a button that automatically translates product descriptions into English and converts necklace prices to dollars. After comparing handcrafted necklaces manufactured in Bolivia, Egypt, and West Virginia, the retailer settles on a necklace produced in a far-flung village in northern India. He enters his commercial credit card number and submits his order. The credit card transaction is automatically processed in dollars, but payment is made to the seller's bank in the Indian currency, the rupee.

After receiving the shipment of Indian necklaces, the retailer takes a look at prices that competing jewelry retailers in various nations have posted on the Web. After consulting current exchange-rate tables, he realizes that he can sell the necklaces in major nations at lower prices than those posted by his main international competitors. Quickly, he adds information about the necklaces and his own, lower dollar prices to his company's Web site. Within a few days, orders have arrived from consumers located in Tokyo, Berlin, and Mexico City, who, as he had expected, have been able to convert his company's dollar prices to yen, euros, and pesos to determine that in their local currencies, his company's prices beat the competition.

This scenario could prove feasible much earlier than 2013. One company, Planet Payment, has already signed up about 300 merchants in 30 countries to develop multilingual versions of their Web sites. The company also offers software that automatically converts prices in local currencies to other countries' currencies at the exchange rate prevailing at the moment the customer submits an Internet order. Thus, a buyer truly will be able to compare the dollar price of a handcrafted necklace marketed by a New York retailer to the price of a similar item sold by retailers located in other nations.

Planet Payment also offers a facility for multicurrency processing of credit card transactions conducted over the Internet. Payments are automatically routed among a network of international banks that translate payment debits to buyers' accounts and payment credits to sellers' accounts. Both debits and credits take place in local currency terms, however, so a transaction that once required an advance exchange of foreign currencies to take place can now bundle together both a purchase and an exchange of currencies.

For Critical Analysis:
If the yen value of the U.S. dollar rises considerably just before a Japanese customer is about to submit an order on a site using system such as the one operated by Planet Payment, thereby changing the terms of the transaction with a U.S. seller, will the Japanese customer be more or less likely to click on the "order submit" button?

P as the overall price level of U.S. goods and services and P^* as the overall price level of Canadian goods and services. Note that in this instance, we can rearrange the absolute PPP relationship to solve for the spot exchange rate:

$$S = P / P^*.$$

That is, when absolute purchasing power parity holds for all goods and services, the spot exchange rate equals the U.S. price level divided by the Canadian price level.

Thus, absolute PPP is a theory of exchange rates: If absolute PPP holds, then the bilateral spot exchange rate should equal the ratio of the price levels of the two nations. Hence, the demand and supply schedules in foreign exchange markets should move to positions yielding this bilateral exchange rate. Until they do, however, one could say that, based on absolute purchasing power parity, one nation's currency is overvalued or undervalued relative to the currency of the other nation.

Problems with Absolute Purchasing Power Parity

It is a big jump from oranges to all goods and services, however. To apply the concept of absolute PPP to exchange rates, our simplifying assumptions of no transportation costs, no tax differentials, and no trade restrictions that we used in our orange-exchange example must be met in the real world. This is highly unlikely to be true. After all, loading 10,000 or more oranges into a truck is a costly endeavor, orange sales might be subject to different tax rates in Canada and the United States, or one of the two nations could have legal restraints on orange trade. Certainly we might expect transportation expenses, different tax treatment, or trade restrictions to apply for a number of other goods, even if they do not have significant effects in the national markets for oranges.

Furthermore, even if transportation costs, tax differences, and trade restrictions are insignificant, we still would anticipate problems in applying absolute PPP to all goods and services of two nations. The reason is that people in two nations may consume different sets of goods and services. As an extreme example, imagine that the typical U.S. consumer buys oranges and apples, but the typical Canadian consumer buys oranges and pears. If these are the only goods people in each nation consume, then using overall price levels for the two nations to make predictions about exchange rates would be a mistake. The price levels for the two nations would be based on the prices of different goods, meaning that the arbitrage argument that lies behind the absolute PPP condition could not apply. Arbitrage could not really relate the prices of both sets of goods, so we would be mistaken to infer an exchange rate from the absolute PPP relationship.

Another way to see why absolute PPP is unlikely to hold in the real world is to recall how we calculate a real exchange rate. As you learned earlier, we multiply the spot exchange rate by the ratio of the price levels for two countries. That is, we multiply the exchange rate S by the price-level ratio P / P^*, which tells us that we can write the real exchange rate as $S \times (P^* / P)$.

If absolute PPP holds, however, then $S = P / P^*$, so that the real exchange rate is equal to

$$S \times (P^* / P) = (P / P^*) \times (P^* / P) = 1.$$

When the real exchange rate is equal to 1, this means that one unit of goods and services in a country, such as the United States, always exchanges one-for-one with a unit of goods and services in another country, such as Canada. Thus, absolute PPP implies that the real exchange rate is always equal to 1. If people in different countries consume goods and services in different proportions, however, it is highly unlikely that this will be so.

By the mid-1980s, the purchasing power parity doctrine was in such doubt that *The Economist* magazine developed an initially satirical measure of PPP called the *Big Mac index*. The idea was that the McDonald's Big Mac sandwich has the same basket of ingredients in all world locations, so if the law of one price holds the exchange-rate adjusted price of a Big Mac should be the same everywhere. In fact, from year to year the Big Mac guide to exchange rates does relatively poorly, though its longer-term performance is better. (See on the next page *Management Notebook: Sandwiching Currency Values in a Sesame Seed Bun—The Big Mac Index.*)

Fundamental Issue 1

What does the concept of absolute purchasing power parity imply about the value of the real exchange rate?

The concept of absolute purchasing power parity is based on the law of one price, which indicates that the price of a traded good or service in one nation should equal the exchange-rate-adjusted price of that same good or service in another country. If absolute PPP holds true, then the price level in one country equals the nominal exchange rate times the price level of another nation. This means that under absolute PPP, the real exchange rate always equals 1, which is rarely likely to be the case.

Relative Purchasing Power Parity

Because real exchange rates often differ from unity, absolute PPP is not a very useful theory of exchange rates. For this reason, economists often use a different benchmark for how exchange rates are determined, which is known as *relative purchasing power parity*.

PROPORTIONATE PRICE CHANGES AND RELATIVE PURCHASING POWER PARITY

The problem with absolute purchasing power parity is that people in different countries often consume distinctive baskets of goods and services. This means that simply applying the law of one price across prices of goods and services used to calculate measures of the price level such as consumer price indexes is inappropriate. To avoid this pitfall, economists often use the concept of relative purchasing power parity, which relates *relative changes* in exchange rates to *relative changes* in countries' price levels.

We can use the expression for absolute PPP to derive the relative version of PPP. Let's denote the percentage change of a variable by placing the characters "$\%\Delta$" in front of the variable. Then, for example, $\%\Delta P$ would represent the proportionate change in a county's price level over a period, which is the nation's inflation rate.

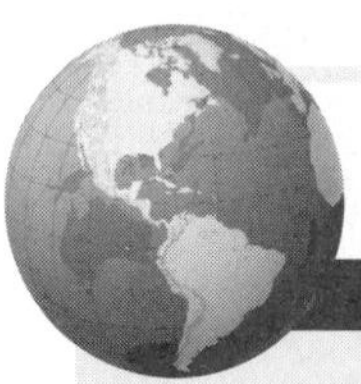

MANAGEMENT *Notebook*

POLICY MANAGEMENT

Sandwiching Currency Values in a Sesame Seed Bun—The Big Mac Index

Among businesspeople, the most popular version of PPP is the Big Mac index from *The Economist* magazine. The 2002 version of the Big Mac index appears in Table 8-1.

Table 8-1 shows that the price of a Big Mac in the United States is $2.49, whereas the price of a Big Mac in Switzerland is 6.30 Swiss francs (SFr). Using the equation for absolute PPP, $S = P / P^*$, the implied exchange rate is 2.53 SFr/$, which is shown in the second column of the table. The third column gives the actual value of the Swiss franc–dollar exchange rate at the time, 1.66 SFr/$. The true, market-determined value of the Swiss franc relative to the dollar is lower than the value implied by absolute PPP. The Big Mac index, therefore, indicates that the Swiss franc is overvalued relative to the dollar. We can express this overvaluation as the percentage difference between the implied value of the dollar according to the Big Mac PPP measure and the market value. This works out to be +53 percent for the Swiss franc. Hence, according to the Big Mac measure of PPP, the Swiss franc is overvalued and should depreciate relative to the dollar.

How does the Big Mac perform as a guide to exchange rate movements? In the short run, the index certainly is not an accurate predictor of exchange rates. The index performs better in the long run, but most of the adjustment to PPP occurs through price changes.

For Critical Analysis:
Studies have found that the Big Mac index is closely related to several other more elaborate measures of purchasing power parities, so some economists have concluded that the Big Mac index is a surprisingly good longer-term indicator of PPP valuations of exchange rates. What does the predictive performance of the Big Mac index imply about the likely usefulness of absolute PPP as a shorter-term *measure of currency under- or overvaluation?*

Table 8-1 The Hamburger Standard

	Big Mac Prices in Local Currency	Implied PPP Exchange Rate	Actual Exchange Rate	Local Currency Under (–) / Over (+) Valuation, %
United States	$2.49	—	—	—
Brazil	Real 3.60	1.45 Real/$	2.34 Real/$	–38
Canada	C$3.33	1.34 C$/$	1.57 C$/$	–15
Sweden	SKr 26.00	10.4 SKr/$	10.3 SKr/$	+1
Switzerland	SFr 6.30	2.53 SFr/$	1.66 SFr/$	+53
Thailand	Baht 70.00	22.1 Baht/$	43.3 Baht/$	–49

Source: Data from http://www.economist.com, April 2002.

By calculating the change of each variable in the equation for absolute PPP, we can express relative PPP as

$$\%\Delta S = \%\Delta P - \%\Delta P^*.$$

Thus, relative PPP implies that the percentage change in a rate of exchange for two countries' currencies equals the difference between the two nations' inflation rates.

In contrast to absolute PPP, the theory of relative PPP does not require the real exchange rate to equal a value of 1. All that is required for relative PPP to hold true is that the real exchange rate for two countries must be stable over time. This is still a tall order, however, because the purchasing power of goods and services in one country relative to goods and services in another nation can shift over time.

How does relative PPP do as a theoretical predictor of actual exchange-rate changes? Most studies indicate that relative PPP performs better than absolute PPP. Nevertheless, real exchange rates can vary considerably over relatively short-run intervals. Consequently, factors other than relative price levels or inflation rates can have significant effects on exchange rates. Relative PPP, therefore, typically is not a very good theory for predicting exchange-rate movements for periods of less than a few years. Our earlier example of the nearly 21 percent nominal depreciation of the euro relative to the U.S. dollar between late 1999 and late 2000, even though the U.S. inflation rate actually slightly exceeded the EMU inflation rate, is a case in point. Relative PPP often performs better over short-run intervals for countries that experience episodes of very high inflation. This is true because during such episodes, price changes typically are the dominant influence on the value of the domestic currency.

PURCHASING POWER PARITY AS A LONG-RUN DETERMINANT OF EXCHANGE RATES

Economists have long recognized the factors that limit their ability to use purchasing power parity as a complete theory of exchange rates. Nevertheless, the logic of the law of one price has led most economists to believe that, given sufficient passage of time, exchange rates should *eventually* adjust to values consistent with purchasing power parity, at least in its relative form.

In the 1970s and 1980s, however, study after study found that it was difficult to rule out the possibility that real exchange rates follow a *random walk.* This meant that if some factor, such as an abrupt, temporary change in the price level in one nation, were to occur, the real exchange rate would move to a new level. Then the real exchange rate would tend to stay at this new level until the next unexpected, short-lived event took place to "bump" the real exchange rate to another level. As we already noted, absolute PPP implies that the real exchange rate should tend toward the value of 1. Relative PPP is less restrictive, but if relative PPP holds, it turns out that the real exchange rate should tend toward a *constant* value (but not necessarily a value of 1). If the real exchange rate were to move in a random walk, however, then as time passes it would not necessarily settle down to a constant value. Thus, random-walk behavior of real exchange rates was strong evidence against purchasing power parity.

In the 1990s and early 2000s, new rounds of research on real exchange rates evaluated the possibility that earlier studies were biased because they only considered a few countries or relatively short spans of time. Looking at insufficient observations of the real exchange rate might make short-term variations in the real exchange rate look like random-walk movements, when, in fact, they were simply movements of real exchange rates toward levels consistent with purchasing power parity. One set of studies, therefore, examined large numbers of countries' real exchange rates simultaneously, thereby evaluating PPP with massive amounts of cross-country data. These studies consistently found little evidence of random-walk behavior of exchange rates. Recently, however, a debate has arisen about whether this "cross-country approach" to evaluating PPP suffers from its own special difficulties.

This has led other researchers to concentrate their attention on real-exchange-rate behavior over long time periods, spanning from six decades to as long as nearly seven centuries. The idea is that if PPP holds, it must hold on average over such long intervals. Indeed, these studies find strong evidence that, if given sufficient time, real exchange rates tend to settle down at constant long-term levels predicted by the purchasing power parity doctrine. These studies conclude that a reason that there is so little evidence in favor of PPP over shorter-term periods is that departures from PPP take so long to disappear. For example, if some temporary factor causes the real exchange rate to move above the level consistent with PPP, these studies of long-run horizons indicate that it typically takes between three and seven years for the real exchange rate to get halfway back to its PPP level. If these more recent studies are correct, PPP is truly a long-run determinant of exchange rates. This may help explain why *The Economist's* Big Mac index has shown signs of performing better when evaluated over intervals of several years, even though it consistently fails to fit exchange rates on a year-to-year basis.

2 Fundamental Issue

What is relative purchasing power parity, and is it useful as a guide to movements in exchange rates?

Relative purchasing power parity relates exchange rate appreciation or depreciation to national inflation rates. It states that the proportionate change in the nominal rate of exchange of two nations' currencies should equal the difference between the two countries' inflation rates. Because people in different countries consume differing baskets of goods and services, most economists view relative PPP as superior to absolute PPP when contemplating the relationship between prices and exchange rates. Nevertheless, most evidence indicates that even relative PPP is at best a long-run guide to understanding how exchange rates are determined.

International Interest Rate Parity

Complications such as transportation costs and trade restrictions limit the extent to which unhindered cross-border arbitrage activities can take place in markets for goods and services, thereby undermining the usefulness of purchasing power parity as a theory of exchange rates. By way of contrast, it is much easier to engage in international exchanges of financial assets, such as bonds, shares of stock, and national currencies. There are few costs of transferring shares of ownership across national borders. Indeed, nowadays many parties to exchange of financial assets make ownership transfers electronically. In addition, an increasing number of the world's nations permit nearly unhindered trade of financial assets across their borders.

Consequently, there is considerable scope for arbitrage activities in global financial markets. It turns out that this means that in today's world, exchange rates and interest rates on financial assets must be related.

THE FORWARD EXCHANGE MARKET AND COVERED INTEREST PARITY

The concepts of absolute and relative purchasing power parity discussed earlier arise from arbitrage across national markets for goods and services. Arbitrage can also take place across national financial markets, as traders attempt to earn profits by buying and selling bonds issued by individuals, companies, or governments of various nations.

For example, suppose the interest rate on a U.S. bond is 6.6 percent. At the same time, the interest rate on a British bond with all the same riskiness, liquidity, tax treatment, and term to maturity is 7.2 percent. Could a U.S. saver profit from shifting funds from the United States to the United Kingdom? The answer to this question depends on whether the realized return on the British bond is greater than the realized return on the U.S. bond. Comparing the realized returns, in turn, requires taking into account how covered interest returns (returns completely hedged against foreign-exchange risk) on the British bond depend on forward and spot exchange rates. Thus, forward exchange rates, spot exchange rates, and national interest rates must ultimately be taken into account by anyone who seeks arbitrage profits from trading bonds internationally.

ON THE WEB

Where on the Internet can one find daily updates concerning euro and yen forward exchange rates relative to the U.S. dollar? One place to check for these forward exchange rates is the Federal Reserve Bank of New York's daily 10 A.M. foreign exchange statistical release, located at http://www.ny.frb.org/pihome/statistics/forex10.shtml.

Covered Interest Parity

Now let's suppose that a U.S. resident has two alternatives. One is to purchase a one-period, dollar-denominated bond that has a market interest yield of R_{US}. After one year, the U.S. resident will have accumulated $1 + R_{US}$ dollars for each dollar saved.

The other saving option is to use each dollar to buy British pounds at the spot exchange rate of S dollars per pound, to obtain $1/S$ pounds with each dollar. Then the U.S. resident could use the $1/S$ pounds to buy a one-year British (U.K.) bond that pays the rate R_{UK}. After a year, the person would have accumulated $(1/S)(1 + R_{UK})$ *pounds*. When the U.S. resident buys the U.K. bond, however, we assume that at the same time the individual sells this quantity of pounds in the forward market at the forward exchange rate of F dollars per pound. This "covers" the individual against risk of exchange-rate changes by insuring that the effective gross return on the U.K. bond will be $(F/S)(1 + R_{UK})$.

When no profitable arbitrage opportunities exist, the realized returns on the two bonds will be the same. That is, there is no incentive for U.S. savers to arbitrage across the U.S. and British financial markets if the gross returns are equal:

$$1 + R_{US} = (F/S)(1 + R_{UK}).$$

Now we can use the algebraic fact that

$$F/S = (S/S) + (F - S)/S = 1 + (F - S)/S$$

to rewrite the condition as

$$1 + R_{US} = [1 + (F - S)/S](1 + R_{UK}).$$

Now we can cross-multiply the right-hand side to get

$$1 + R_{US} = 1 + (F - S)/S + R_{UK} + [R_{UK} \times (F - S)/S].$$

Because R_{UK} and $(F - S)/S$ are both typically small fractions, their product is approximately equal to zero. (For example, if R_{UK} is 0.062 and $(F - S)/S$ is –0.047, then their product is equal to –0.0029, which is very close to zero.) Making this approximation and subtracting 1 from both sides of the equation yields

$$R_{US} = R_{UK} + (F - S)/S.$$

Covered interest parity
A prediction that the interest rate on one nation's bond should approximately equal the interest rate on a similar bond in another nation plus the forward premium, or the difference between forward exchange rate and the spot exchange rate divided by the forward exchange rate.

This last equation is called the **covered interest parity** condition. As we noted earlier, the quantity $(F - S)/S$ is the forward premium or discount, so the condition of covered interest parity says that the interest rate on a U.S. bond should approximately equal the interest rate on the foreign (U.K.) bond plus the forward premium or discount for the pound. (Forces of supply and demand ensure that covered interest parity holds; see on pages 242–243 *Visualizing Global Economic Issues: Why Covered Interest Parity Is Often Satisfied.*)

UNCOVERED INTEREST ARBITRAGE

As we have discussed, covered interest arbitrage—covering the foreign exchange risk associated with bond transactions across national borders—leads to the covered interest parity condition. Under covered interest parity, the interest rate on a bond in one nation equals the interest rate on the equivalent bond in another country plus the forward discount. What happens, however, if people do not cover foreign exchange risk exposures?

A good reason why someone might choose not to use a forward currency contract to hedge against foreign exchange risks is that the transaction is too small to warrant going to the trouble to set up a forward contract. Indeed, a typical forward currency contract has a denomination of at least $1 million. Hence, the individual might decide to use a different hedging instrument (see Chapter 6), or the individual might choose not to hedge the transaction at all.

Uncovered Interest Parity

In our example, we considered a U.S. saver with a choice between a U.S. bond and a U.K. bond with equivalent riskiness, tax treatment, liquidity, and term to maturity. Let's consider the same example, but now let's consider a situation in which the U.S. saver does not purchase a forward exchange contract or hedge the foreign exchange risk in any other way, so that the transaction is *uncovered.*

In this case, the U.S. saver again anticipates a *dollar*-denominated interest return of R_{US} by holding a U.S. bond to maturity or a *pound*-denominated interest return of R_{UK} by holding an equivalent British bond to maturity. To the U.S. saver, however, what matters in choosing between the two bonds is the anticipated *dollar* value of the return on the British bond. This is equal to $R_{UK} + \%\Delta S^e$, where $\%\Delta S^e$ is the rate at which people expect the dollar to depreciate (or, if $\%\Delta S^e$ is negative, to appreciate) relative to the pound. If $\%\Delta S^e$ is positive, then the U.S. saver anticipates that the dollar will depreciate in value relative to the pound and will wish for the U.S. bond's interest rate to be higher than the rate on the British bond to compensate for this expected depreciation of the dollar.

Thus, this U.S. saver will be indifferent between holding U.S. or British bonds only if the anticipated returns are equal. This will be true when

$$R_{US} = R_{UK} + \%\Delta S^e,$$

or when the U.S. interest rate equals the U.K interest rate plus the expected rate of depreciation of the dollar relative to the pound. If the U.S. interest rate is less than the U.K. interest rate plus the expected rate of dollar depreciation, then U.S. savers who do not cover their transactions will allocate more savings to U.K. bonds. If the U.S. interest rate is greater than the U.K. rate plus the anticipated depreciation rate of the dollar, then U.S. savers will allocate fewer savings to U.S. bonds. In theory, shifts of funds in this pursuit of *uncovered arbitrage* profits will tend to push both interest rates to levels consistent with equality between the U.S. interest rate and the sum of the U.K. interest rate and the expected rate of dollar depreciation.

The equality between the interest rate in one nation and the sum of the interest rate and expected currency depreciation for another nation is called **uncovered interest parity.** It is called "uncovered" interest parity because it does not arise from foreign-exchange transactions that cover risks. The uncovered interest

Uncovered interest parity
A relationship between interest rates on bonds that are similar in all respects other than the fact that they are denominated in different nations' currencies. According to this condition, which applies to a situation in which an individual engages in unhedged currency trades to fund bond purchases abroad, the interest rate on the bond denominated in the currency that holders anticipate will depreciate must exceed the interest rate on the other bond by the rate at which the currency is expected to depreciate.

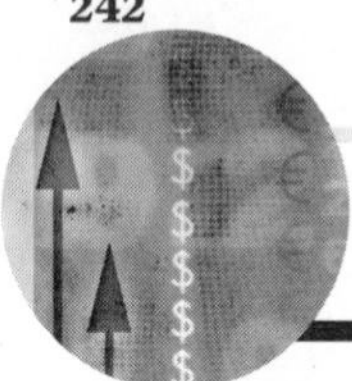

Visualizing Global Economic Issues

Why Covered Interest Parity Is Often Satisfied

There is considerable evidence that covered interest parity normally holds true in developed nations with borders that are open to international bond exchanges and to flows of funds in spot and forward exchange markets. To see why this is so, consider what would happened if covered interest parity failed to hold.

In Figure 8-1, panel (a) depicts the spot exchange market for the British pound, and panel (b) shows the forward market for the British pound. Panel (c) illustrates the determination of the U.S. interest rate, which arises where the quantity of *loanable funds* supplied by savers equals the quantity of loanable funds demanded by borrowers within the United States. Likewise, in panel (d), the equilibrium U.K. interest rate arises when the quantity of loanable funds supplied equals the quantity of loanable funds demanded within the United Kingdom.

Suppose that the interest rate on a U.S. bond is less than the sum of the rate on an equivalent British bond and a forward premium. This induces U.S. savers to move loanable funds to the United Kingdom, so the supply of loanable funds in the United States declines, as illustrated by the leftward shift of the supply schedule in panel (c), while the supply of loanable funds in the United Kingdom increases, as depicted by the rightward shift of the supply schedule in panel (d).

To purchase British financial instruments, U.S. savers must exchange dollars for British pounds in the spot exchange market, so the demand for pounds rises in panel (a), causing a rise in the equilibrium spot exchange rate, or a *spot depreciation* of the dollar relative to the pound, shown by the movement from S_1 to S_2. If, as in our example above, U.S. savers cover their exposures to foreign exchange risk, then they also purchase dollars (for future delivery with pounds earned by holding the British financial instruments) using forward currency contracts. As a result, there is an increase in the supply of pounds in the forward exchange market, shown by a rightward shift in the pound supply schedule in panel (b). The increase in the supply of pounds in the forward exchange market results in a *forward depreciation* of the pound relative to the dollar, as shown by the decrease in the equilibrium forward exchange rate from F_1 to F_2.

Thus, market forces tend to push national interest rates toward equilibrium values consistent with covered interest parity. The effort of U.S. savers to earn higher returns in the United Kingdom when the U.S. interest rate exceeds the sum of the U.K. rate and the forward premium tends to push up the equilibrium U.S. interest rate and to push down the equilibrium U.K. interest rate. Their effort to cover their foreign exchange risks also tends to push up the spot exchange rate and to push down the forward exchange rate, thereby reducing the forward premium. Normally, these market adjustments quickly bring about equality between the U.S. interest rate and the sum of the U.K. interest rate and the forward premium. This is why covered interest parity typically holds.

For Critical Analysis:
Under what circumstances could persistent deviations from covered interest parity take place?

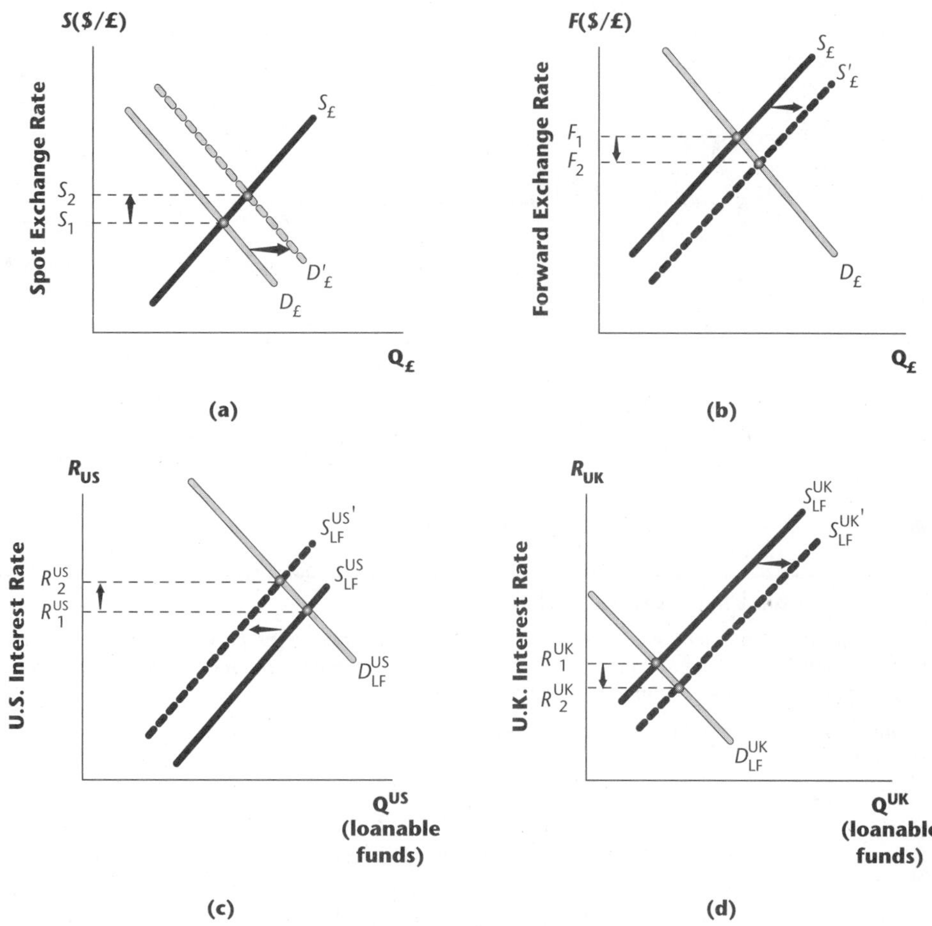

Figure 8-1

Covered Interest Arbitrage and Interest- and Exchange-Rate Adjustments

If the interest rate on a U.S. bond is less than the sum of the rate on an equivalent British bond and a forward premium, then the covered interest parity condition does not hold. This induces U.S. savers to move loanable funds into the United Kingdom. Thus, the supply of loanable funds declines in the United States, as shown in panel (c), and the supply of loanable funds in the United Kingdom increases, as depicted in panel (d). To purchase additional British bonds, U.S. Savers exchange dollars for pounds in the spot exchange market, which causes a rise in the demand for pound and a resulting increase in the equilibrium spot exchange rate. If U.S. savers cover their foreign-exchange-risk exposure by contracting for future delivery of dollars in exchange for pounds in the forward exchange market, then there is an increase in the supply of pounds in the forward exchange market, which causes a reduction in the equilibrium forward exchange rate.

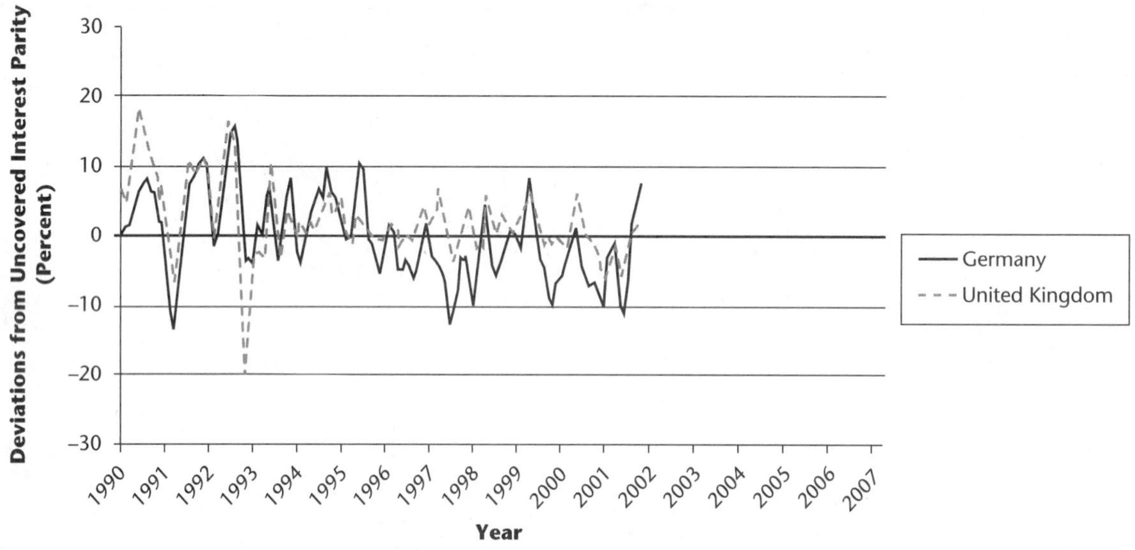

Figure 8-2

Approximate Deviations from Uncovered Interest Parity

This figure displays the deviations from uncovered interest parity for U.S. and German three-month treasury bills, and U.S. and U.K. three-month treasury bills, which are plotted by subtracting the three-month change in the spot exchange rate from the interest differential. Deviations from uncovered interest parity can persist for extended periods.

Source: *International Financial Statistics,* International Monetary Fund.

parity condition is more likely to hold for interest rates of nations that are most open to cross-border flows of funds. Figure 8-2 plots differences between interest differentials on three-month Treasury bills and the actual percentage change in the spot rate over the maturity period of the bonds of the United Kingdom and Germany relative to the United States. These are *approximate* deviations from the uncovered interest parity, because the true uncovered interest parity condition relates interest rates to *expected,* not actual, percentage changes in the spot rate. Nevertheless, the figure tends to indicate the possibility for persistent deviations from uncovered interest parity even among the most developed nations. These deviations are not large, however. The average absolute value of the deviations is about 0.75 percent.

Risk and Uncovered Interest Parity

The uncovered purchase of a foreign bond exposes a U.S. saver to foreign exchange risk. This is so because the saver's expectation about currency depreciation or appreciation during the term to maturity might turn out to be incorrect. In this instance, the realized return on the foreign bond would differ from the anticipated return.

If the value of a nation's currency is highly variable, then predicting its future value is difficult. This makes allocating a portion of one's wealth to holdings of a foreign bond a much riskier proposition. Consequently, borrowers located in nations with volatile currency values may have to offer higher interest returns to induce savers to purchase the bonds they issue. In this instance, it may be appropriate to include a risk premium in the uncovered interest parity condition. The risk premium is the increase in the return offered on a bond to compensate individuals for the additional foreign exchange risk they undertake in uncovered transactions.

For instance, if the U.S. dollar's exchange value becomes more volatile and less predictable, then the uncovered interest parity condition may be expressed as

$$R_{US} = R_{UK} + \%\Delta S^{e} + RP,$$

where RP is the risk premium that compensates savers for holding U.S. bonds instead of equivalent U.K. bonds. In this situation, the differential between the U.S. interest rate and the U.K. interest rate should equal the expected depreciation of the dollar relative to the pound plus the risk premium.

If volatility in relative currency values varies over time, then the risk premium can vary from period to period. Thus, the existence of *time-varying risk premiums* could help to account for the existence of deviations from uncovered interest parity indicated in Figure 8-2. Whether foreign exchange markets are efficient depends in part on how one interprets the contribution of risk premiums to deviations from uncovered interest parity.

What are the covered and uncovered interest parity conditions?

Fundamental Issue 3

Covered interest parity is a condition that arises if individuals hedge international financial transactions using forward currency contracts. It states that the interest rate in one nation equals the sum of another nation's interest rate and the forward premium or discount, which is the difference between the forward exchange rate and the spot exchange rate divided by the spot exchange rate. If individuals do not hedge exchange-rate risks associated with purchases of bonds with identical risks but which are denominated in different currencies, then another interest parity condition called uncovered interest parity may apply. According to the uncovered interest parity condition, the interest rate for the bond denominated in the currency that is expected to depreciate must be the greater of the two interest rates. The yield of the bond denominated in the currency that is expected to depreciate must exceed the other bond's yield by the rate at which the currency is expected to depreciate.

Are Foreign Exchange Markets Efficient?

Those who wish to trade currencies examine past and current market exchange rates in an effort to determine likely future values of exchange rates. They do this using their understanding of how exchange rates are determined. Therefore, *current* exchange rates should reflect how currency traders form their expectations of future exchange rates. This has led economists to develop a theory of the determination of exchange rates that explains how people use current information and forecasts of future exchange rates when they decide about how to adjust their holdings of currencies and other financial assets. This theory is called the *efficient-markets hypothesis.* This hypothesis provides an explanation of how expectations about the future relate to current market realities. Consequently, let's first consider alternative ways of looking at how people form expectations of future events.

ADAPTIVE VERSUS RATIONAL EXPECTATIONS

Clearly, to make any decisions that have future consequences, you must act on forecasts that you make based on whatever information you currently possess. There are two fundamental theories for how you might go about doing this.

Adaptive Expectations

One way to make an inference about a likely future value of an exchange rate or of a future return on a bond is to do so "adaptively." The easiest way to understand what this means is to consider an example. Imagine that a friend, or perhaps even a pollster, were to ask you for your forecast of the exchange value of the euro for U.S. dollars a year from now. How would you come up with an answer?

One approach might be to collect data on the euro–dollar exchange rate during recent weeks or months. You then could plot these data on a chart and make a rough drawing of the "trend line" along these points and beyond. The point on your trend line one year out from the present date would then give your forecast of the euro–dollar exchange rate a year from now.

If you have completed a statistics course, then you might adopt a more sophisticated approach. You could use statistical techniques to determine the specific equation for the trend line that best fits the euro-dollar exchange rate data that you have collected. This equation would enable you to give a predicted value, or forecast, of the exchange rate for a given time, including a year from now.

Either of these forecasting methods would require you to sacrifice time and effort to collect a considerable amount of data. If you do not wish to incur this opportunity cost to make a sophisticated forecast of the rate of exchange between the euro and the dollar a year from now, then you could choose a simpler method. For instance, you might just guess that next year's exchange rate will turn out to be an average of its value over the past three years. Even simpler, you might guess that next year's exchange rate will turn out not to be much different than it has been during the past year.

Adaptive expectations *Expectations that are based only on information from the past.*

Each of these forecasting methods is an example of an **adaptive expectation** process, meaning that each method entails using only *past information.* Drawing a rough trend line, using statistical techniques to calculate an exact trend line, computing a three-year average, or just extrapolating from the current inflation rate all share the common feature that past data formed the sole basis for the rate-of-return forecast. Relying only on past data makes the forecast an *adaptive forecast.*

Drawbacks of Adaptive Expectations

One of these examples may relate closely to how you think you make your own forecasts. Nevertheless, many economists reject the idea of adaptive expectations. One reason for this negative judgment is that if people really were to use adaptive expectations, then they often would make forecasts that they realize in advance should turn out to be wrong.

Suppose for instance, that a person's adaptive method for forecasting next year's rate of exchange of the euro for the dollar is to calculate an average of exchange rates for the past three years. If this average exchange rate is equal to, say, 0.982 euros per dollar, then that would be the individual's forecast of the exchange rate for next year. Now suppose that the person reads in the newspaper that the European Central Bank is likely to buy or sell large amounts of dollars within the next few days in an effort to influence the euro's market value. A person who stuck with the three-year-averaging procedure for calculating the exchange rate would consciously ignore this new information, even though the individual reasonably should recognize that actions by the European Central Bank in foreign exchange markets might alter the euro's value relative to the dollar.

This means that an economic theory based on the hypothesis of adaptive expectations would yield forecasts of market exchange rates that consistently ignored information relevant to the actual determination of exchange rates in the future. Thus, any economic theory based on adaptive expectations will be internally inconsistent, because the people whose behavior the model attempts to mimic would behave inconsistently.

Another troublesome aspect of the hypothesis of adaptive expectations is that there is no way to say, in advance, what adaptive expectations process is "best." For example, one individual might draw a chart of six months of past exchange rate data to plot a rough trend line to guide her exchange rate forecasts, another person might use the same technique using data from the previous twelve months, and yet another might use three years of data. Someone else might calculate a weighted average of exchange rates over the past five years. Indeed, there is an infinite number of possible adaptive expectations schemes. Which one should we include in a theory of the determination of exchange rates? There is no good way to answer this question.

Rational Expectations

These problems with adaptive expectations led economists to develop an alternative theory of how people make forecasts, which is called the **rational expectations hypothesis.** According to this hypothesis, an individual makes the best possible forecast of a market price or return using all available past *and current* information *and* drawing on an understanding of what factors affect the price or return. In contrast to an adaptive forecast, which only looks backward because it is

Rational expectations hypothesis
The idea that individuals form expectations based on all available past and current information and on a basic understanding of how markets function.

based on past information, a rational forecast also looks forward while taking into account past information.

Consider, for instance, the earlier example in which someone initially made an exchange rate forecast using an average of exchange rates over the past three years but then learned of imminent central bank actions to influence exchange rates. If that person's goal is to best predict the exchange rate, then sticking with her original, adaptive forecast clearly would not be in her best interest. The *rational* way for her to respond to the new information would be to use her own understanding concerning how central bank actions in foreign exchange markets would likely influence the exchange rate. Then she would update her exchange rate forecast for the coming year accordingly.

Thus, the distinction between adaptive and rational expectations can be summarized in the following manner:

An *adaptive* expectation is based only on past information. In contrast, a *rational* expectation takes into account both past and current information, plus an understanding of how the economy functions.

Advantages of the Rational Expectations Hypothesis

Because the rational expectations hypothesis does not impose artificial constraints on how people use information, it is a more general theory of expectations formation than adaptive expectations. Whereas an adaptive expectations process imposes the use of only past information, the rational expectations hypothesis states that if an individual can improve on an adaptive forecast, then that is what the individual will do.

This does not deny that a person's rationally formed expectation cannot look like an adaptive expectation from time to time. If a person has only past information and no special insight into how a market functions, then an adaptive forecast might be the best that person can do. In such a circumstance, an adaptive expectation would be that individual's rational expectation.

It seems most likely, nevertheless, that people would use all available current information plus all conceptions about how markets work when they try to infer market prices and returns. Consequently, a rationally formed expectation should, under most circumstances, differ from a purely adaptive expectation.

It is important to recognize that even though rational expectations generally will be better than adaptive expectations, forecasts based on all current information and an understanding of how markets operate will not always be correct. For example, the National Weather Service's adoption of Doppler radar has improved the ability of weather forecasters to predict where tornadoes may form. This only means that tornado forecasts are better than before. It does not mean that such forecasts always are on the mark. Indeed, during turbulent weather conditions very damaging and life-threatening tornadoes can form quickly in locations that Doppler radar previously indicated to be low-probability locales for such storms.

In like manner, rationally formed forecasts of the market prices and returns are better, on average, than adaptive forecasts. *Actual* prices and returns, however, can still turn out to be much higher or lower than people had rationally predicted.

Are There Limits on Rationality?

The rational expectations hypothesis poses a couple of conceptual problems of its own. One of these is that the hypothesis is very broad—so broad that incorporating it fully into a theory can prove challenging. For instance, each individual has his or her own perspective on how financial markets operate. In addition, at any given instant each person is informed to a somewhat different extent about current market developments. Does this indicate that economists should try to model every individual's expectations formation procedure?

A related difficulty is that the rational expectations hypothesis indicates that each person acts on his or her rationally formed expectation of market prices and returns. This means that *realized* market prices and returns will depend on how all individuals form their expectations. If each person realizes that the expectations of others thereby will play a role in affecting actual market prices and returns, does this mean that each person should attempt to forecast others' forecasts?

To get around these problems, economists often use two simplifying assumptions when they construct theories that include rational expectations. The first of these is the presumption that each person in the marketplace has access to the same information and has the same conception of how the market works. This assumption gets around the issue of different expectations across individuals in the market. It also dodges the problem of individuals worrying about others' forecasts, because by assumption each person's forecast is the same.

The second common assumption used in economic models with rational expectations is that people in the marketplace understand how the market functions. That is, an economist using the rational expectations hypothesis typically assumes that the people whose behavior their models try to describe behave *as if* they understand that the economy works according to the economists' own theory. This assumption boils down to presuming that the people in an economic model *know the model.*

Let's think about how we might apply the rational expectations hypothesis to this more realistic view on how exchange rates are determined. Under the rational expectations hypothesis, an optimal forecast reflects all available past *and* current information, as well as an understanding of how the relevant variable is determined. In the case of international interest returns, therefore, the rational expectations hypothesis indicates that exchange rate expectations that can influence market interest rates are rational forecasts of future exchange rates by those who trade foreign currencies.

What is the distinction between adaptive and rational expectations?

An adaptive expectation is one that is formed using only past information. In contrast, a rationally formed expectation is based on past and current information and on an understanding of how market prices and returns are determined.

The Efficient-Markets Hypothesis

Efficient-markets hypothesis *A theory that stems from application of the rational expectations hypothesis to financial markets, which states that equilibrium prices of and returns on bonds should reflect all past and current information plus traders' understanding of how market prices and returns are determined.*

The reasoning of the rational expectations hypothesis forms the basis for the **efficient-markets hypothesis.** This hypothesis states that prices of or returns on financial assets should reflect all available information, including bond traders' understanding of how financial markets determine asset prices.

More generally, the efficient markets theory says that the return on or price of *any* asset should reflect the rational forecast of the asset's returns. Consequently, the rate of exchange for a nation's currency should reflect knowledge of all available information by those who trade the currency. If the market exchange rate were to fail to reflect all such information, then the implication would be that foreign exchange markets function inefficiently, because traders could earn profits if they accounted for such unused information.

FOREIGN EXCHANGE MARKET EFFICIENCY

The efficient-markets hypothesis has three key implications. First, it indicates that there should be a definite relationship between the market price of or return on a bond and traders' expectation of the market price or return. Second, it implies that some factors are likely to cause greater movements in prices or returns than others. Finally, the efficient-markets hypothesis has an important prediction about efforts by traders to earn higher-than-average rates of return.

If foreign exchange markets are efficient, it follows that returns on internationally traded bonds should reflect all information possessed by those who trade these bonds. To evaluate whether foreign exchange markets are efficient, therefore, we must consider how savers' expectations of future exchange-rate movements influence the returns on internationally traded bonds.

Note that the two international interest parity conditions discussed above provide two reasons that the interest rate for a U.S. bond might be higher than the interest rate on an otherwise identical British bond. One reason, provided by the *covered* interest parity condition, is the presence of a forward premium in the forward exchange market, so that the differential between the U.S. interest rate and the U.K. interest rate is equal to

$$R_{US} - R_{UK} = (F - S)/S.$$

The other reason is the one implied by the *uncovered* interest parity condition:

$$R_{US} - R_{UK} = \%\Delta S^{e}.$$

This condition indicates that, in the absence of a risk premium, the amount by which the U.S. interest rate exceeds the U.K. interest rate should be the expected rate of depreciation of the dollar relative to the pound.

The Condition for Foreign Exchange Market Efficiency

The only way that both of these interest parity conditions are satisfied is if the right-hand terms in both are equal, or if

$$(F - S)/S = \%\Delta S^e.$$

This relationship states that the forward premium (or discount) for the pound relative to the dollar is equal to the rate at which the dollar is expected to depreciate (appreciate) relative to the pound in the spot foreign exchange market. Let's denote the expected future spot exchange rate at the time that a forward currency contract settles as S^e. It follows that the expected rate of dollar depreciation during the term of the contract, $\%\Delta S^e$, is equal to the expected change in the spot exchange rate, $S^e - S$, divided by the current spot exchange rate, S. Thus, $\%\Delta S^e = (S^e - S)/S$. If both covered and uncovered interest parity hold true, then

$$(F - S)/S = (S^e - S)/S,$$

or

$$F = S^e.$$

If both interest parity conditions are satisfied in the marketplace, the forward exchange rate is equal to the anticipated spot exchange rate at the time of settlement of the forward currency contract.

If this last equality is not satisfied, so that the forward exchange rate differs from the expected future spot exchange rate, then financial market traders perceive an arbitrage opportunity. In an *efficient market,* of course, such opportunities should be very fleeting. Market expectations and prices should adjust speedily to eliminate the potential for arbitrage profits. Thus, **foreign exchange market efficiency** exists when the forward exchange rate is a good predictor—often called an "unbiased predictor"—of the future spot exchange rate, meaning that on average the forward exchange rate turns out to equal the future spot exchange rate. When the foreign exchange market is efficient, therefore, forward exchange rates should adjust to the point at which the forward premium is equal to the expected rate of currency depreciation. Under the rational expectations hypothesis, the expected rate of currency depreciation should be the rational forecast of the rate of depreciation, or the forecast of depreciation based on all available information and an understanding of how exchange rates are determined.

Foreign exchange market efficiency
A situation in which the equilibrium spot and forward exchange adjust to reflect all available information, in which case the forward premium is equal to the expected rate of currency depreciation plus any risk premium. This, in turn, implies that the forward exchange rate on average predicts the expected future spot exchange rate.

Another way of thinking about the foreign exchange market efficiency condition is to relate it back to the efficient market theory. This theory broadly states that the price of a financial asset should reflect all available information. The foreign exchange market efficiency condition is analogous. It states that the forward and spot exchange rates, which are the spot and forward prices of a nation's currency, should take into account rational forecasts of the extent to which the nation's currency will depreciate. As a result, the premium or discount relating the forward and spot exchange rates should reflect all available information.

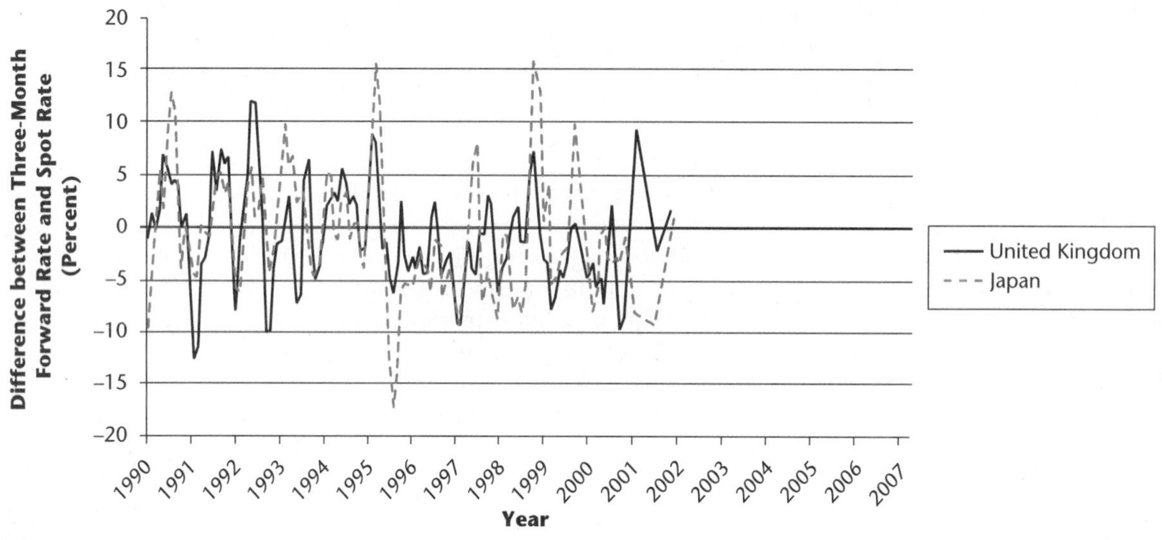

Figure 8-3

Forward and Spot Exchange-Rate Differentials

This figure plots the difference between the U.S. dollar three-month forward exchange rate and the actual U.S. dollar spot exchange rate that prevailed three months later for the United Kingdom and Japan. There are consistently substantial differences between the forward exchange rate and spot exchange rate at the settlement date of forward contracts.

Source: *International Financial Statistics,* International Monetary Fund.

Evidence on Foreign Exchange Market Efficiency

There is considerable evidence that covered interest parity generally holds in the markets for currencies of developed economies. The evidence on uncovered interest parity and, consequently, of foreign exchange market efficiency, is more mixed. For instance, consider Figure 8-3, which plots the percentage difference between three-month forward exchange rates and the spot exchange rates three months later for the U.S. dollar and British pound and for the U.S. dollar and Japanese yen. As you can see, the forward exchange rate often underestimates or overestimates the realized spot exchange rate.

Of course, foreign exchange efficiency relates the forward exchange rate to the *expected* future spot exchange rate. If the rational expectations hypothesis is correct, then the expected rate of depreciation should reflect a rational *forecast.* Consequently, studies of foreign exchange market efficiency entail trying to determine if exchange rate *expectations* are formed rationally. Trying to determine statistically whether foreign exchange market efficiency and rational expectations both hold at the same time is a difficult proposition. This is especially true if a risk premium widens the differential between national interest rates. Then economists must disentangle the relative contributions of the risk premium and potential expectational errors as factors causing potential deviations from foreign exchange market efficiency. Most studies indicate that risk premiums are important but are divided on whether foreign exchange markets are truly efficient.

Fundamental Issue 5

What is foreign exchange market efficiency?

According to the efficient-markets hypothesis, the market return on or price of a financial asset should reflect all available information in that market. This is so because the demand for and supply of an asset, such as a bond or a foreign exchange contract, will take into account rationally formed expectations of future prices of the asset. Traders form these expectations, in turn, in light of all information in their possession. Foreign exchange markets are efficient if savers cannot persistently earn higher returns by shifting holdings of bonds across national borders. Foreign exchange market efficiency requires that the forward premium, or the difference between the forward and spot exchange rates divided by the spot exchange rate, be equal to the expected rate of currency depreciation. This efficiency condition holds if both the covered and uncovered interest parity conditions are satisfied.

Revisiting Global Integration of the Real and Financial Sectors

As we discussed in Chapter 1, most economists believe that international financial markets are becoming more integrated. One reason that the concept of foreign exchange market efficiency is of practical interest is that efficiency of foreign exchange markets indicates that national markets more broadly are integrated.

The covered and uncovered interest parity conditions, however, relate *nominal* interest rate differentials to spot and forward exchange rates and expected spot exchange rates. Over shorter-term horizons when changes in inflation may be relatively small, the effects of different national inflation rates may have little effect on saving flows. Nevertheless, saving decisions are more likely to respond to overall price changes over longer time horizons. Thus, over longer intervals savers' decisions about financial-bond allocations are likely to be motivated by *real* interest rate differentials instead of *nominal* differentials.

REAL INTEREST RATE PARITY

To this point, we have only discussed interest rates in *current-dollar* terms. There is a problem with this, however. Inflation can erode the value of interest received when a bond matures. Any individual must take this into account when evaluating how much to save, either domestically or internationally.

The Real Interest Rate

For instance, suppose that a U.S. saver can earn a stated current-dollar, or **nominal interest rate** of 7 percent on each dollar that he allocates to a one-year bond. Suppose, also, that the saver expects that the inflation rate will be $\%\Delta P^e =$ 3 percent during the coming year. Such inflation will reduce the amount of goods and services that his interest return will permit him to purchase.

Nominal interest rate *A rate of return in current-dollar terms that does not reflect anticipated inflation.*

That is, though he earns positive interest on the bond, the saver anticipates that inflation will eat away at that interest at the rate of 4 percent. Hence, the **real interest rate** that this saver anticipates, or his expected inflation-adjusted interest rate, is *approximately* equal to

Real interest rate
The anticipated rate of return from holding a bond after taking into account the extent to which inflation is expected to reduce the amount of goods and services that this return could be used to buy.

$$r = R - \%\Delta P^e.$$

In this example, therefore the real interest rate is equal to 7 percent – 3 percent, or 4 percent. In terms of what the savings can buy, this saver anticipates earning only 4 percent on his one-year bond.

Combining Relative Purchasing Power Parity and Uncovered Interest Parity: Real Interest Parity

If savers anticipate that relative purchasing power parity will hold, then it implies that the difference between expected rates of inflation in the two countries should equal the expected rate of depreciation:

$$\%\Delta P^e - \%\Delta P^{*e} = \%\Delta S^e.$$

Remember that if uncovered interest parity holds, and if there is no risk premium, then it also will be the case that

$$R - R^{*} = \%\Delta S^{e},$$

so that the differential between any two nations' interest rates equals the expected rate of currency depreciation. If we put these two equations together, we get

$$\%\Delta P^e - \%\Delta P^{*e} = R - R^*.$$

Finally, we can rearrange this equation to obtain the following relationship:

$$R - \%\Delta P^e = R^* - \%\Delta P^{*e}.$$

This says that if both relative purchasing power parity and uncovered interest parity hold true, then the real interest rate in one country, $r = R - \%\Delta P^e$, equals the real interest rate in the other country, $r^* = R^* - \%\Delta P^{*e}$.

This is called the **real interest parity** condition, under which real interest returns on equivalent bonds of two nations are equal. Given the way we have obtained it, real interest parity is a condition that requires both relative purchasing power parity and uncovered interest parity to hold.

Real interest parity
An equality between two nations' real interest rates that arises if both uncovered interest parity and relative purchasing power parity are satisfied.

REAL INTEREST PARITY AS AN INDICATOR OF INTERNATIONAL INTEGRATION

Remember that uncovered interest parity is more likely to hold if financial markets are more integrated, so that savers can take advantage of opportunities for uncov-

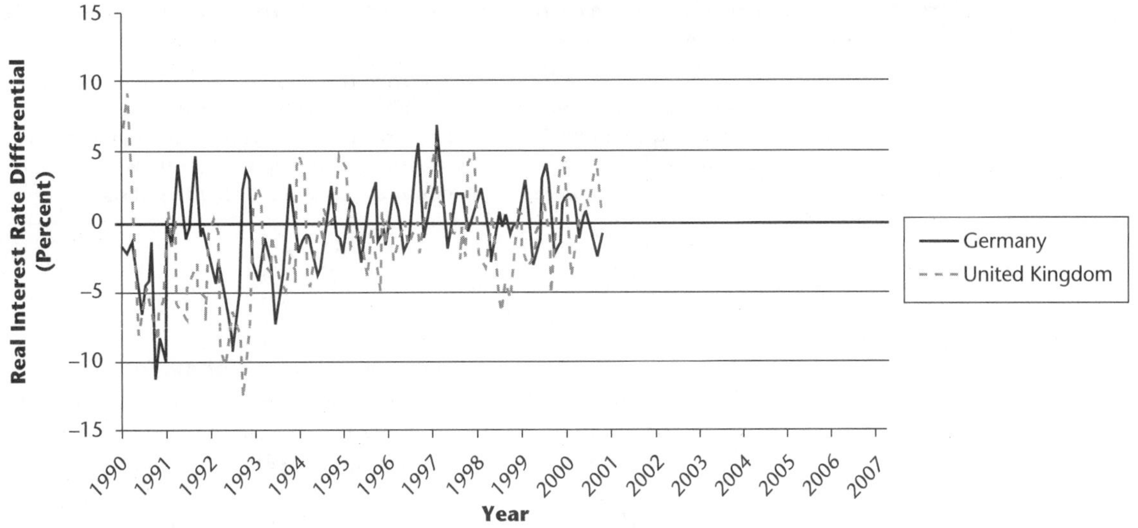

Figure 8-4

Real Interest Rate Differentials

Real interest rate differentials often persist, implying that real interest parity typically does not hold.

Source: *International Financial Statistics,* International Monetary Fund.

ered interest arbitrage. At the same time, relative purchasing power parity is more likely to hold if markets for goods and services are also more open to arbitrage.

It follows that if real interest parity holds true, then international financial and goods markets are likely to be integrated. To get a picture of whether real interest parity is likely to hold for the United States, Germany, and the United Kingdom, consider Figure 8-4, which plots differentials in real interest rates for U.S. versus German three-month treasury bills and U.S. versus U.K. treasury bills. These differentials use real interest rates calculated as the nominal treasury bill rate minus the actual inflation rate. Of course, real interest parity is based on real interest rates calculated using *expected* inflation rates, so Figure 8-4 can only provide a rough idea of whether real interest parity may hold for these nations.

Note that there were persistent negative real interest rate differentials in the early 1990s, followed by persistent positive differentials between real interest rates. These persistent differentials tend to cast doubt on the notion that international markets are fully integrated. In general, more sophisticated statistical tests of real interest parity tend to conclude that real interest differentials exist, even for the most developed, open economies. Nevertheless, work by Richard Marston of the University of Pennsylvania has shown that real interest differentials among these economies tend to be relatively small. This provides some indication that some national markets are fairly highly integrated.

6 **Fundamental Issue**

Under what conditions does real interest parity hold, and why is it a useful indicator of international integration?

If real interest rates in two nations are equal, then real interest parity is satisfied. For real interest parity to hold true, conditions of both uncovered interest parity and relative purchasing power parity must be satisfied simultaneously. If this is the case, then there is a high degree of integration of both financial markets and goods markets for the two nations. Hence, economists use real interest parity as an indicator of international integration.

CHAPTER SUMMARY

1) **Implications of Absolute Purchasing Power Parity for the Value of the Real Exchange Rate:** The real exchange rate equals the nominal rate of exchange of two nations' currencies times the ratio of the overall price levels for the two nations. Thus, the real exchange rate adjusts a nominal rate of exchange of national currencies for changes in the nations' price levels, thereby providing a measure of the purchasing power of domestic goods and services in exchange for foreign goods and services. According to the law of one price, the exchange-rate-adjusted price of a tradable good in one nation should equal the price of that good in another nation. Absolute purchasing power parity extends the law of one price by relating overall measures of the price levels, such as consumer price indexes, of two countries to the nominal exchange rate. According to absolute PPP, the nominal exchange rate equals the ratio of two nations' price levels. This implies that under absolute PPP the real exchange rate is always equal to 1.
2) **Relative Purchasing Power Parity and Its Usefulness as a Guide to Movements in Exchange Rates:** If relative purchasing power parity holds true for two countries, then the proportionate change in the nominal rate of exchange of the two countries' currencies equals the difference between the two countries' inflation rates. Relative PPP allows for the possibility that residents of different countries may consume various baskets of goods and services, so many economists prefer to apply relative PPP, rather than absolute PPP, when evaluating the relationship between national price levels and exchange rates. There is, nonetheless, considerable evidence indicating that even relative PPP is, at best, a long-run guide to understanding how exchange rates are determined.
3) **Covered and Uncovered Interest Parity:** If savers hedge international holdings of bonds by buying forward currency contracts, then they can earn arbitrage profits if the interest rate in one nation is different from the sum of another nation's interest rate and the forward premium. Their efforts to earn covered arbitrage profits by shifting funds between nations result in adjustments of national interest rates and exchanges rates toward values consistent with equality of the interest rate in one nation with the other nation's interest rate plus the forward premium, which is the covered interest parity condition. If savers engaged in unhedged currency transactions to finance purchases of bonds that are identical in all respects other than the fact that they are denominated in different nations' currencies, then the interest rates on these

bonds may be related through the uncovered interest parity condition. According to this condition, the difference in interest rates will equal the expected rate of currency depreciation.

4) **The Distinction between Adaptive and Rational Expectations:** An expectation that is formed adaptively is based only on past information. A rational expectation is formed using all available past and current information and relying on an understanding of how markets determine prices.
5) **The Efficient-Markets Hypothesis and Foreign Exchange Market Efficiency:** The efficient-markets hypothesis indicates that the market price of a financial asset should reflect all available information in that market. It should also reflect rational expectations about the price of the asset on the part of those who wish to buy and sell the asset. The foreign exchange market efficiency condition stems from combining covered interest parity with uncovered interest parity. It states that the forward premium, which is the difference between the forward and spot exchange rates divided by the spot exchange rate, should be equal to the expected rate of currency depreciation. This implies that the forward exchange rate should, on average, predict the future spot exchange rate in efficient foreign exchange markets. Combining uncovered interest parity with relative purchasing power parity also indicates that real interest parity, or equality of national real interest rates, should hold true if international financial and goods markets are integrated.
6) **Conditions for Real Interest Parity, and Why It Is a Useful Indicator of International Integration:** Real interest parity exists for two nations when their real interest rates are equal. Both the uncovered interest parity and relative purchasing power parity conditions must simultaneously be satisfied for real interest parity to hold true, thereby implying a high degree of integration of the nations' markets for financial assets and for goods and services. Consequently, economists regard real interest parity is a key indicator of international integration.

QUESTIONS AND PROBLEMS

1) Suppose the Swiss franc price of a dollar was 1.5341 Sfr/$ in 1990 and 1.6322 Sfr/$ in 2003. The price index for Switzerland (1990 = 100) was 118.11 in 2003, and the price index for the United States (1990 = 100) was 121.86 in 2003. What was the real exchange rate for the Swiss franc in 2003? Does absolute PPP hold? How can you tell?
2) Using the data provided in question 1, if absolute PPP is assumed to hold, is the dollar overvalued or undervalued, relative to the Swiss franc in 2003? Considering this information, would you expect the dollar to appreciate or depreciate? By what percentage?
3) Using the data provided in question 1, was the dollar overvalued or undervalued in 2003 according to relative PPP? Considering this information would you expect the dollar to appreciate or depreciate, and by how much (in percentage terms)?

4) When economists examine exchange-rate and price-level data available over periods as long as a century, they typically find that real exchange rates can vary considerably from year to year but can be relatively stable in the long run. What does this imply about relative purchasing power parity over long- versus short-run horizons?
5) Suppose that spot and forward exchange rates are measured in units of domestic currency per unit of foreign currency. There is a positive forward premium for the domestic currency. If covered interest parity holds, what should be true of the difference between the interest rate on a domestic bond and the interest rate on a foreign bond with the same risk and maturity characteristics?
6) What is the difference between covered and uncovered interest arbitrage?
7) Explain how the covered interest parity and uncovered interest parity conditions differ.
8) Could the covered interest parity condition be met if the uncovered interest parity condition is not also satisfied? Why or why not?
9) Suppose that foreign exchange markets are known to be efficient. The current spot exchange rate is 1.08 dollars per euro, and the current forward exchange rate is 1.11 dollars per euro. Do foreign exchange market traders anticipate that the euro will appreciate or depreciate relative to the dollar in the future?
10) Other things being equal, in a world of highly integrated financial markets but less integrated markets for goods and services, is real interest parity more or less likely to hold true, as compared with covered interest parity? Explain.

ONLINE APPLICATION

Internet URLs: http://www.oecd.org//std/nadata.htm *and* http://www.federalreserve.gov/releases/H10/hist

Titles: **Purchasing Power Parities—Organization for Economic Cooperation and Development** and **Exchange Rates—Board of Governors of the Federal Reserve System**

Navigation: To obtain data on exchange rates consistent with purchasing power parity, first go to the home page of the OECD (http://www.oecd.org). Click on "Statistics Portal," then "Frequently Requested Statistics," and then "Purchasing Power Parities." Click on "Statistics Online," and then click on "Purchasing Power Parities for OECD Countries." Print this document. Next, go to the Federal Reserve Board's home page (http://www.federalreserve.gov), and click on "Economic Research and Data." Then click on "Statistics: Releases and Historical Data," and under the H.10 under "Weekly Releases," click on "Historical Bilateral Rates."

Application: Use the reports at each Web site to apply the purchasing power parity doctrine to real-world data.

1) The first set of columns in the OECD table gives the currency-per-U.S.-dollar exchange rates that would be consistent with purchasing power parity for various OECD countries. The Federal Reserve Board provides data on actual ex-

change rates for a number of countries. Select a nation in the OECD's purchasing-power-parity table, and compare the exchange rates predicted by PPP for a selected year in the table with its *actual* exchange rates in the Federal Reserve's H.10 release. During the year you selected, did PPP indicate that this nation's currency was over- or undervalued?

2) Look over the nation's exchange rates in the Federal Reserve's H.10 release for all five years in the OECD table. In your view, were the actual exchange rates for the country you have selected even "roughly" consistent with PPP over this five-year period?

For Group Study and Analysis: Assign questions 1 and 2 to several groups, each of which examines the data for a different country. Have each group report its conclusions. Discuss possible reasons that PPP might have been a better approach to understanding exchange-rate determination for some countries but not for others.

REFERENCES AND RECOMMENDED READINGS

Cumby, Robert E. "Forecasting Exchange Rates and Relative Prices with the Hamburger Standard: Is What You Want What You Get with McParity?" NBER Working Paper, *5675* (July 1996).

Engel, Charles, and John Rogers. "Deviations from Purchasing Power Parity: Causes and Welfare Costs." International Finance Discussion Paper No. 666, Board of Governors of the Federal Reserve System, May 2000.

Frankel, Jeffrey, and Andrew Rose. "A Panel Project on Purchasing Power Parity: Mean Reversion within and between Countries." *Journal of International Economics* 40 (2) (May 1996): 209–224.

Lothian, James, and Mark Taylor. "Real Exchange Rate Behavior: The Recent Float from the Perspective of the Past Two Centuries." *Journal of Political Economy* 104 (3) (June 1996): 488–509.

MacDonald, Ronald, and Mark Taylor. "Exchange Rate Economics: A Survey." *IMF Staff Papers* 39 (March 1996): 1–47.

Marston, Richard. *International Financial Integration.* Cambridge: Cambridge University Press, 1995.

O'Connell, Paul. "The Overvaluation of Purchasing Power Parity." *Journal of International Economics* 44 (1) (February 1998): 1–19.

Pakko, Michael, and Patricia Pollard. "For Here or to Go? Purchasing Power Parity and the Big Mac." *Federal Reserve Bank of St. Louis Review,* 78 (1) (January/February 1996): 3–22.

Rogoff, Kenneth. "The Purchasing Power Parity Puzzle." *Journal of Economic Literature* 34 (3) (June 1995): 647–668.

Taylor, Mark. "The Economics of Exchange Rates." *Journal of Economic Literature* 33 (1) (March 1995): 13–47.

Taylor, Mark. "Covered Interest Parity: A High-Frequency, High-Quality Data Study." *Economica* 54 (November 1987): 429–438.

CHAPTER NINE

Global Money and Banking—Where Central Banks Fit into the World Economy

Fundamental Issues

1. **What are the responsibilities of the world's central banks?**
2. **What are the primary instruments of monetary policy available to central banks, and how do monetary policy actions affect market interest rates?**
3. **How do economists measure a nation's aggregate output and price level?**
4. **How are the equilibrium levels of aggregate output and prices determined, and how do central bank actions altering the quantity of money or exchange rates influence equilibrium real output and the price level?**
5. **How do central banks intervene in foreign exchange markets?**
6. **How effective are foreign exchange interventions?**

The Bank of England has had many detractors since it came into existence more than 300 years ago. For example, the economist David Ricardo (1772–1823) once observed that "the House of Commons did not withdraw its confidence from the Bank from any doubt of its wealth or integrity, but from a conviction of its total ignorance of political economy." From the very beginning, the Bank of England was a servant of the government. This became obvious in 1844 when it was divided into two departments—the Issue Department and the Banking Department. The former was strictly regulated by the British Treasury and was given the authority to issue bank notes covered by government securities. The Banking Department was simply the bank for the government and the repository of British monetary reserves. When the government took over actual ownership in 1946, there was no further question about who called the shots.

When Tony Blair of the Labour Party was elected head of the British government in the mid-1990s, he vowed that the government would make the Bank of England independent. On May 6, 1997, the British government followed through. Almost immediately, estimates of the expected annual inflation rate fell by almost a third of a percentage point, and within two weeks these estimates fell by nearly another third of a percentage point. The Bank of England now has so-called "instrument independence," in the sense that it is free to pursue its policy goals without interference from outside political pressures.

The reaction to this structural change in the United Kingdom illustrates how central banks can be perceived as important institutions within national economies. A select few central banking institutions—notably the Federal Reserve, the European Central Bank, and the Bank of Japan—can engage in policymaking activities that affect the global economy. In this chapter, you will learn about the functions and policies of these institutions.

The Role of Central Banks

The first central banking institution was established in 1668. It is the Swedish Sveriges Riksbank, which before 1867 was called the Risens Standers Bank. The Swedish parliament granted a special commission the authority to manage the Sveriges Riksbank. Initially, the Riksbank did not issue money, but by 1701 the government had granted the Riksbank the power to issue "transfer notes" that basically functioned as a form of currency. In 1789 the Riskdag established a National Debt Office that formally issued Swedish government currency. Finally, in 1897, the Riksbank Act made this institution the only legal issuer of Swedish currency.

Learn more about the history of the Riksbank at http://www.riksbank.com.

The world's second central bank, which was established in 1694, became better known. It was the Bank of England. The British parliament authorized the Bank of England to issue currency notes redeemable in silver. These notes then circulated alongside notes issued by the government and private companies. The Riksbank and Bank of England were the only central banks until 1800, and the total number of central banks remained a single digit until 1873. As you can see in Figure 9-1 on page 262, the number of central banks around the globe increased significantly during the latter part of the nineteenth century and the twentieth century. A portion of this growth stemmed from the establishment of central banks by former colonial states that achieved independence and developed their own currencies.

The most recently established central bank is also one of the most important. In January 1999, the central banks of eleven European nations—Austria, Belgium,

Figure 9-1

The Number of Central Banking Institutions, 1670–Present

There was considerable growth in the number of central banks during the twentieth century.

Source: Forrest Capie, Charles Goodhart, and Norbert Schnadt, "The Development of Central Banking," in Capie, et al., *The Future of Central Banking: The Tercentenary Symposium of the Bank of England* Cambridge, U.K.: Cambridge University Press, 1994, pp. 1–231.

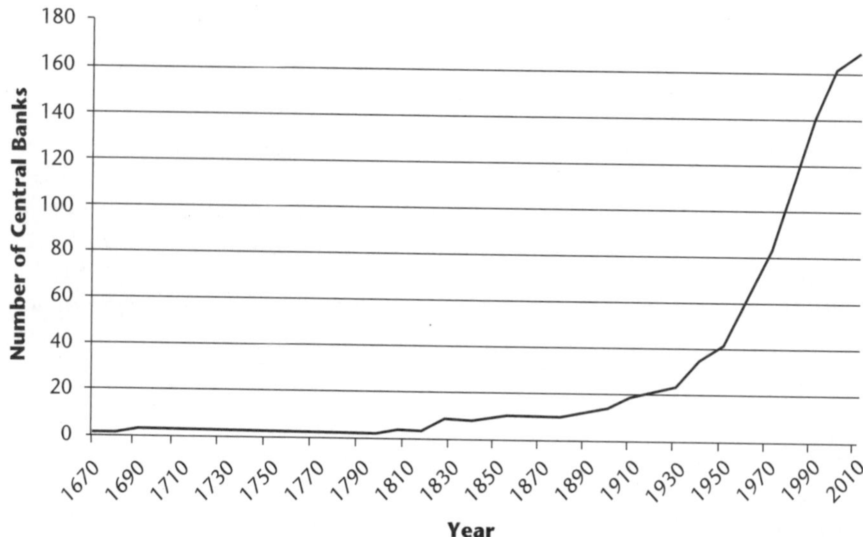

Finland, France, Germany, Ireland, Italy, Luxembourg, the Netherlands, Portugal, and Spain—formed the *European System of Central Banks* (ESCB). The six-member executive board for this system is based at the *European Central Bank (ECB),* the hub of the ESCB located in Frankfurt, Germany. All final operating and policy decisions for the system, however, must be approved by an eighteen-member governing council composed of the executive board in Frankfurt and the governors of the twelve national central banks (Greece is now a member nation). Thus, each member nation plays a role in determining the policies of the ECB.

CENTRAL BANKS AS GOVERNMENT BANKS

Governments often argue that they "need" central banks. For instance, a primary motivation for the founding of the Bank of England in 1694 was the desire for the bank to raise government funds to finance one of Britain's wars with France. In like manner, a justification that the French government gave for establishing the Banques de France in 1800 was to better manage the nation's public debt that had ballooned as France and Britain continued their military buildups.

Even in countries where providing financial services to governments has not been the key justification for a central bank, central banks typically have become the main governmental banking institution. For example, in the United States there had been long-standing opposition to central banks, but after the founding of the Federal Reserve System in 1913, the U.S. Treasury quickly began to rely on Federal Reserve banks as providers of depository services.

Central Banks as Government Depositories

National governments may hold unused funds on deposit at a single central bank office or in various regional branch offices of central banks.

For instance, the U.S. Treasury holds deposits at each of the twelve Federal Reserve banks. These regional banks clear checks drawn on those accounts. They also accept deposits of fees and taxes paid by U.S. residents and firms. Furthermore, they make payments at the direction of the U.S. Treasury, just as a private bank makes payments on behalf of a private customer.

Central Banks as Fiscal Agents

Central banks typically operate as **fiscal agents** for national governments, meaning that they issue, service, and redeem government debts. Treasury departments or finance ministries issue securities such as bills, notes, and bonds to cover shortfalls between tax receipts and expenditures on goods and services. In nations with highly developed financial markets, such as the United States, Japan, and nations of the European Union, treasury departments or finance ministries issue these securities at auctions. In their role as fiscal agents, central banks often review, tabulate, and summarize bids to purchase the securities, issue securities to successful bidders, and process the purchasers' payments to the government.

Fiscal agent
A term describing a central bank's role as an agent of its government's finance ministry or treasury department, in which the central bank issues, services, and redeems debts on the government's behalf.

In emerging nations with less developed financial markets, central banks may play more direct roles. They may effectively act as investment banks for their governments by lining up private individuals or firms willing to purchase new government security issues. In nations with particularly thin secondary securities markets, central banks even purchase the securities directly from government treasury departments or finance ministries. To help broaden the markets for government securities, central banks in some countries, such as South Korea, have even imposed regulations requiring private banks to purchase government bills, notes, and bonds. Economists say that such rules make private banks *captive buyers* of government debt.

CENTRAL BANKS AS BANKERS' BANKS

Although the immediate rationale for the 1694 founding of the Bank of England was a government desire to improve its ability to finance wartime expenditures, another justification that the British Parliament provided for creating the Bank was a perceived need for a government-related institution that would stabilize London financial markets and limit periodic fluctuations in the availability of currency and credit throughout England.

Do Banks "Need" a Central Bank?

In later years, governments of other nations offered similar rationales for the establishment of central banks. Many proponents of these institutions, in fact, have contended that private banks *need* a central bank. The key rationale for such a "need" is the idea that financial markets are subject to *externalities,* or situations in which transactions among individuals or firms can spill over to affect others.

According to this view, central banking institutions perform socially useful roles in supervising and regulating the processes and systems through which individuals, firms, and banks exchange payments. Hence, private banks "need" a central bank to keep systems payment systems operating smoothly on a day-to-day basis and to repair any breakdowns in these systems as they may occur.

Lenders of Last Resort

Lender of last resort
A central banking function in which the central bank stands willing to lend to any temporarily illiquid but otherwise solvent banking institution to prevent its illiquid position from leading to a general loss of confidence in that institution.

The most dramatic sort of financial breakdown is a *systemic* failure, in which large numbers of banking institutions fail. The classic example of this type of systemic failure is a *bank run,* in which large numbers of bank customers lose confidence in the ability of banks to maintain their asset values and, hence, anticipate depletion of the banks' net worth. As a result, customers seek to liquidate their deposits. This actually does push large numbers of banks into insolvency.

In principle, a central bank can keep bank runs from occurring by serving as the financial system's **lender of last resort** that stands ready to lend to any temporarily illiquid but otherwise solvent bank. By lending funds when necessary, the central bank might prevent such illiquidity from leading to a general loss of confidence that can lead to a system-wide "run on the bank."

CENTRAL BANKS AS MONETARY POLICYMAKERS

Visit the European Central Bank at http://www.ecb.int.

Most central banks devote the bulk of their resources, including the time and effort of their employees, to the tasks of providing services to their nations' governments and banking institutions. Nevertheless, the bulk of media attention on central bankers focuses on deciphering the complex issues involved in their monetary policymaking function. (At the European Central Bank, an additional complication of monetary policymaking is that central bank officials speak different languages; see *Policy Notebook: Monetary Policy Goes Multilingual in Europe*.)

CENTRAL BANK BALANCE SHEET ASSETS AND LIABILITIES

The best place to begin any examination of the functions of a central bank is its balance sheet, which is a tabulation of the central bank's assets, liabilities, and net worth. Table 9-1 on page 266 displays consolidated balance sheets of the three major central banks of the world—the U.S. Federal Reserve, the Bank of Japan, and the European Central Bank (ECB). The table displays dollar, yen, and euro amounts and percentages relative to total assets and to total liabilities and capital (net worth). Because nominal values of central bank assets, liabilities, and net worth change considerably over time while proportionate allocations tend to remain stable, you should concentrate most attention on the percentages in Table 9-1.

Central Bank Assets

Examination of Table 9-1 shows that the balance sheets of the Federal Reserve, the Bank of Japan, and the European Central Bank share some common features. They hold some analogous assets, and among these are securities issued by their nations' governments, which account for at least three-fourths of the assets of the Federal Reserve and the Bank of Japan. Government securities account for a smaller proportion of assets at the European Central Bank.

POLICY *Notebook*

POLICY MANAGEMENT

Monetary Policy Goes Multilingual in Europe

Many reports by economists at the U.S. Federal Reserve System are stamped "Confidential" or "Highly Confidential" in the upper-right-hand corner of the cover page. This label indicates that the economists' writings cannot be distributed or quoted publicly. At the European Central Bank (ECB), including a "Highly Confidential" label could require attaching a separate cover page to the report. This is because there would have to be labels in all languages spoken by residents of nations that are part of the European Monetary Union.

Although most discussions by the eighteen-member governing board of the ECB take place in English, translators stand ready at all meetings in case debate becomes so heated that governors lapse into their native tongues. The translators, who operate out of the ECB's language-services department, also spend considerable time translating both internal documents and reports intended for external distribution. One member of the language-services department is a "terminologist" who specializes in figuring out what to do with a word such as "vigilance," which to an English-speaking central banker is most often used to refer to in the context of being on the watch for inflation. The Italian version of the word, however, refers specifically to banking supervision. In Finnish, the right version for "vigilance" depends on the position of the word in a sentence. In Greek, the word is impossible to translate unless the context of its use is clearly specified.

During its first year of operation, the ECB's language-services department had a staff of twenty people. By 2000, however, these employees were overwhelmed by the demands on their time for oral and written translations. During that year, the ECB doubled the staff of this department and created another separate department of "legal-linguistic specialists" who work full time to prepare ECB legal documents for distribution in all of the European Monetary Union's various native languages.

For Critical Analysis:
Under what circumstances could linguistic miscommunications actually result in monetary policy mistakes?

The remaining assets of the central banks include various types of securities, loans, and certificates of ownership. The Federal Reserve, for instance, lends to private banks via the *discount-window* facilities of the Federal Reserve banks. Banks, in turn, must pay an interest charge, called the **discount rate**, to obtain loans from the Federal Reserve. Panel (a) of Table 9-1 indicates that the dollar amount of discount-window lending and proportionate Federal Reserve asset allocation to such lending is very small in comparison with the Bank of Japan and the European Central Bank. Panels (b) and (c) show that purchases and sales of private securities such as commercial paper and central bank lending to banks and other financial institutions are much more conspicuous central banking functions in

Discount rate
The interest rate that the Federal Reserve charges on discount window loans that it extends to depository institutions.

Table 9-1 **The Consolidated Balance Sheets of the Federal Reserve System, the European Central Bank, and the Bank of Japan**

(a) The Federal Reserve System ($ Billions, as of February 28, 2002)

Assets			Liabilities and Capital		
Asset	**Dollar Amount**	**Percent of Total Assets**	**Liability**	**Dollar Amount**	**Percent or Total Liabilities and Equity**
U.S. Treasury Securities	$567.6	86.4%	Federal Reserve Notes	$606.3	92.2%
			Bank Reserve Deposits	20.9	3.2%
Loans to Depository Institutions	0.1	—	U.S. Treasury Deposits	5.8	0.9%
Gold & SDR Certifictes	13.2	2.0%	Deferred Credit Items	6.2	1.0%
Foreign Currency Assets	14.2	2.2%	Other Liabilities	2.7	0.4%
Cash Items in Process of Collection	5.3	0.8%	Total Liabilities	641.9	97.7%
Other Assets	56.9	8.6%	Equity Capital	15.4	2.3%
Total Assets	$657.3	100.0%	Total Liabilities & Capital	$657.3	100.0%

Source: Data from *Federal Reserve Bulletin,* May 2002, Board of Governors of the Federal Reserve System.

(b) The European System of Central Banks (ESCB) (Billions of Euros, as of March 22, 2002)

Assets			Liabilities and Capital		
Asset	**Euro Amount**	**Percent of Total Assets**	**Liability**	**Euro Amount**	**Percent of Total Liabilities and Capital**
Domestic Securities and Bills	€98.0	12.5%	Currency Notes	€280.2	35.8%
Direct Loans to Private Banks	170.6	21.8%	Bank Reserve Deposits	133.9	17.1%
Other Loans and Securities	5.3	0.7%	Government Deposits	57.1	7.4%
Gold and SDR Certifictes	126.8	16.2%	Other Liabilities	247.3	31.6%
Foreign Currencies and Net Claims on Other Central Banks	269.9	34.5%	Total Liabilities	718.5	91.9%
			Equity Capital and Reserves	63.3	8.1%
Other Assets	111.3	14.3%	Total Liabilities & Capital	€781.8	100.0%
Total Assets	€781.8	100.0%			

Source: Data from European Central Bank, *Monthly Report,* April 2002.

(c) The Bank of Japan (Billions of Yen, as of May 31, 2002)

Assets			Liabilities and Capital		
Asset	**Yen Amount**	**Percent of Total Assets**	**Liability**	**Yen Amount**	**Percent of Total Liabilities and Capital**
Japanese Government Securities	¥ 85,112	66.5%	Currency Notes	¥ 66,797	52.2%
Loans	915	0.7%	Bank Reserve Deposits	14,975	6.1%
Gold	446	0.4%	Government Deposits	7,716	11.7%
Bills Purchased and Discounted	26,585	20.8%	Other Liabilities	35,742	27.9%
Foreign Currency Assets	4,207	3.3%	Total Liabilities	125,230	97.9%
Other Assets	10,680	8.3%	Equity Capital	2,715	2.1%
Total Assets	¥127,945	100.0%	Total Liabilities & Capital	¥127,947	100.0%

Source: Data from Bank of Japan, June 2002.

Japan and the European Monetary Union. At these and all other central banks, the sum of domestic securities and loans held as assets are called **domestic credit.**

Domestic credit
Total domestic securities and loans held as assets by a central bank.

All three central banks maintain holdings of assets denominated in the currencies of other nations. These are foreign-currency-denominated securities and deposits. As we have noted in earlier chapters and later discuss in greater detail, a key reason that central banks hold such securities and deposits is so that they can trade the assets when they wish to try to change the values of their nations' currencies in foreign exchange markets.

The *gold certificates* on the Federal Reserve's balance sheet remain from the days in which the gold standard was in force. During that period, the U.S. Treasury Department sold gold to the Federal Reserve in exchange for money. The U.S. Treasury issued gold certificates to the Federal Reserve to indicate the Federal Reserve's ownership of the gold that the Treasury continued to hold in reserve. The *Special Drawing Rights (SDR) certificates* listed in the table are assets issued by the International Monetary Fund (IMF) as a type of international currency intended to compensate for the declining role of gold as a basis for the world's currency system. The U.S. Treasury financed U.S. SDR shares with the IMF by issuing a fixed dollar amount of SDR certificates to the Federal Reserve. The Bank of Japan and the European Central Bank also hold gold and SDR certificates, though in smaller absolute quantities. The amount of SDRs held by the Bank of Japan is subsumed in the "other assets" categories of panels (b) and (c).

Central Bank Liabilities

At least three-fourths of each central bank's total liabilities and equity capital is composed of *currency notes* (known as "Federal Reserve notes" in the United States). Accountants designate currency notes as liabilities to indicate that the central banks "owe" holders of the notes something in exchange. For instance, if you had sought to redeem a $1 Federal Reserve note at a Federal Reserve bank before the early 1930s, you could have received gold in exchange. Now, however, you would receive a new $1 Federal Reserve note. Likewise, if you turned in yen- or euro-denominated notes to the Bank of Japan or European Central Bank, you also would receive new yen notes or euro notes in exchange. So in what sense are these notes really liabilities? The answer is that if the United States, Japanese, or European Monetary Union governments were to close down their central banks, they would be liable to holders of their notes for the dollar, yen, or euro value of goods and services as of the time of the closures.

Visit the Bank of Japan at http://www.boj.or.jp/en.

Another important liability of the three central banks is bank reserve deposits. Private banks may hold some of these deposits to meet legal requirements established by the central banks. In addition, however, they also hold a portion of these deposits as *excess* reserves to help facilitate check clearing and transactions with the central bank and other private banks, including transfers of funds that they may lend to one another in markets for very short-term loans among banks. These loans have large denominations and typically have maturities between one day and one week.

Table 9-1 indicates that a common type of deposit liability at all three central banks is government deposits. The U.S. Treasury, Japanese Ministry of Finance, and German Ministry of Finance draw on these deposit funds to make payments such as purchases of goods and services or tax refunds.

Central Banks and Money

Today, most of us take money for granted. Money performs four key functions: It is a medium of exchange, a store of value, a unit of account, and a standard of deferred payment.

The fundamental function of money is as a *medium of exchange.* This means that people who trade goods, services, or financial assets are willing to accept money in exchange for these items. Money also serves as a *store of value,* meaning that an individual can set money aside today with an intent to purchase items at a later time. Meanwhile, money retains value that the individual can apply to those future purchases. In addition, money functions as a *unit of account,* because people maintain their financial accounts by using money to value goods, services, and financial assets, and they quote prices of goods, services, and financial assets in terms of money. Finally, money serves as a *standard of deferred payment,* which means that people agree to loan contracts that call for future repayments in terms of money.

The measures of money that central banks tabulate are sums of various groupings of financial assets. For this reason, central banks refer to them as **monetary aggregates.** Each of these monetary aggregates differs according to the liquidity of the assets that are included or excluded.

Monetary aggregate *A grouping of assets sufficiently liquid to be defined as a measure of money.*

The Monetary Base

To understand how central banks can influence the quantity of money in circulation, we can take a look at their balance sheets. The reason is that the very narrowest measure of money is the **monetary base,** which economists sometimes call *high-powered money.* This is the amount of money produced directly by a central bank and thereby excludes forms of money, such as checkable or debitable accounts, created by private banks.

Monetary base *Central bank holdings of domestic securities and loans plus foreign exchange reserves, or the sum of currency and bank reserves.*

The monetary base for any nation is the sum of *currency*—paper notes and coins—held outside the government, the central bank, and private banking institutions plus *total reserves* of private banks—funds that private banks hold either as deposits with central banks or as cash in their vaults. The sources of these funds are the central banks themselves. As you can see in Table 9-1, the sums of currency and reserves that private banks hold with the Federal Reserve, the European Central Bank, and the Bank of Japan make up more than half of these central banks' total liabilities.

Broader Monetary Aggregates

A broader definition of money, a monetary aggregate that most central banks call **M1,** is designed to measure funds that are immediately spendable by all individuals and firms within a nation. There are two fundamental components of M1: currency

M1 *Currency plus transactions deposits.*

Table 9-2 Components of M2

M1	Currency, transactions deposits, and travelers' checks make up the broad category generally known as money.
Savings deposits and *money market deposit accounts* at depository institutions	Savings deposits are interest-bearing deposits without set maturities, and money market deposit accounts are savings accounts that permit limited checking privileges.
Small-denomination time deposits at depository institutions	Time deposits have set maturities, meaning that the holder must keep the funds on deposit for a fixed length of time to be guaranteed a negotiated interest return. Small-denomination time deposits have denominations less than $100,000.
Funds held by individuals, brokers, and dealers in *money market mutual funds*	These are mutual funds that specialize in holding money market securities.
Overnight repurchase agreements at depository institutions and *overnight Eurocurrency deposits* held by domestic residents (other than depository institutions) at foreign branches of domestic depository institutions	A repurchase agreement is a contract to sell financial assets, such as government bonds, with a promise to repurchase them at a later time, typically at a slightly higher price, and an *overnight* repurchase agreement permits the original holder to get access to funds for one day. Overnight Eurocurrency deposits are one-day, home-currency denominated deposits in foreign depository institutions and in foreign branches of domestic depository institutions. Despite the name *Eurocurrency,* such deposits might, for instance, be in Japanese or Australian branches of domestic banks.

and *transactions deposits* held at depository institutions. These include checking accounts, accounts from which automatic debits can be made, and so on. The currency component of M1 is the same as that used to compute the monetary base.

Another important monetary aggregate is an even broader measure that most central banks refer to as **M2.** Table 9-2 shows how most central banks tabulate this even broader measure of the quantity of money in circulation. As you can see, M2 is equal to M1 plus several other assets that people cannot directly spend but that are easily convertible to cash.

M2
M1 plus savings and small time deposits, overnight Eurocurrencies and repurchase agreements, and balances of individual and broker-dealer money market mutual funds.

Because a nation's monetary base depends on the size of its central bank's balance sheet, actions of the central bank directly determine the monetary base. Central banks cannot directly control broader monetary aggregates such as M1 and M2, but they can influence them by varying the amounts of their assets and liabilities. In this way, central banks conduct monetary policy.

Fundamental Issue

What are the responsibilities of the world's central banks?

Central banks are the main depository institutions for national governments, which in many countries are the owners of central banking institutions. Central banks typically serve as fiscal agents operating the systems through which governments issue debt instruments and make interest and principal payments, and by promoting broader markets for government debt instruments. Central banks also provide banking services for private banking institutions and function as lenders of last resort, providing liquidity in the event of systemic failures such as bank runs. Finally, central banks influence measures of the quantity of money in circulation, such as the monetary base, M1, or M2, by adjusting the sizes of their own balance sheets. The primary assets of central banks are government securities, loans to private banking institutions, and foreign-currency-denominated securities and deposits. Key central bank liabilities are currency notes and reserve deposits of private banking institutions, which constitute a nation's monetary base.

Banking, Money, and Interest Rates

There is good reason that the media often pay close attention to the monetary policy actions of central banks. In a number of economic environments, central banks can considerably affect a nation's level of interest rates, the exchange value of its currency, its price level, and, potentially, its volume of real economic activity.

INSTRUMENTS OF MONETARY POLICY

Central banks, of course, do not set a nation's price level. Nor do they directly add to a nation's real output, aside from the services that they provide to governments and private banks. Nevertheless, they have access to a number of *policy instruments,* which for central banks are financial variables that they can control, either directly or indirectly. By altering available policy instruments, a central bank can bring about variations in market interest rates, thereby changing the volumes of money and credit in its nation's economy and generating changes in the value of its nation's currency. Such financial-market effects can then, in turn, induce changes in the level of a country's economic activity.

Interest Rates on Central Bank Advances

Traditionally, a key central bank policy instrument has been the interest rate charged on *advances,* or loans, to private banks. As we noted earlier, in the United States the Federal Reserve's discount rate is the interest rate on U.S. central bank advances. In contrast to some other central banks, the discount rate is the *only* rate on advances that the Federal Reserve sets. Since 2002, the Federal Reserve has set the discount rate 1 percentage point above another market interest rate, called the *federal funds rate,* which is the market interest rate in the U.S. interbank funds market known as the *federal funds market.*

The European Central Bank establishes *two* interest rates on central bank advances. One of these rates is a discount rate slightly below prevailing interbank funds rates. The ECB established credit quotas for all private banks in the European Monetary Union. Because the discount rate is lower than market interest rates, banks typically borrow up to these limits. Consequently, the volumes of loans that these central banks make to private banks is relatively larger than in the United States and Japan.

The other interest rate on central bank advances with the European Monetary Union is traditionally called the **Lombard rate,** but the ECB formally calls it the *marginal interest rate.* This is an interest rate on advances that these nations' central banks set above current market interest rates. Banks can borrow at this penalty rate whenever they unexpectedly find themselves illiquid. Because EMU banks can finance a known amount of daily funds borrowings at the below-market discount rate and cover unanticipated credit requirements at the above-market Lombard rate, the market interest rate in the EMU interbank funds market tends to vary between these two central bank rates. Consequently, when it establishes values for the discount and Lombard rates, the ECB essentially places lower and upper limits on daily interest-rate variations.

Lombard rate
The specific name given to the interest rate on central bank advances that some central banks, such as the European Central Bank, set above current market interest rates.

The Bank of Japan also advances credit to private banks. The Bank of Japan sets its discount rate below the current interbank funds rate. It does not restrict access to credit at this rate, so the loans it extends to private banks account for a larger portion of its assets (about 10 percent, as shown in Table 9-1 on page 266). In contrast to the ECB, however, the Bank of Japan does not establish fixed credit quotas for private banks. Instead, it engages in discretionary rationing of discount-window credit on a daily basis, in order to limit the amount of borrowing, by private bankers.

Open-Market Operations

A second fundamental type of monetary policy instrument available to many central banks is **open-market operations.** This term refers to central bank purchases or sales of government or private securities. Most central banking institutions that engage in open-market operations, such as the U.S. Federal Reserve, buy or sell only government securities. Some, such as the Federal Reserve, buy securities in secondary markets, rather than purchasing them directly from the government.

Open-market operations
Central bank purchases or sales of government or private securities.

At the Federal Reserve, voting members of the *Federal Open Market Committee (FOMC)*—the seven Federal Reserve Board governors and five Federal Reserve bank presidents—set the overall strategy of open-market operations at meetings that take place every six to eight weeks. A document called the *FOMC Directive* outlines the FOMC's policy objectives, establishes short-term federal funds rate goals, and lays out specific target ranges for monetary aggregates. The Federal Reserve Bank of New York's *Trading Desk* then implements the Directive from day to day during the weeks between FOMC meetings.

When a central bank purchases a security, it typically makes payment to the prior owner by crediting the owner's deposit account at a banking institution. When the bank receives the funds, its reserves increase. The Trading Desk often uses outright purchases or sales when it wishes to permanently change the aggregate level of bank reserves. In contrast, it typically uses repurchase agreements when its main goal is to keep the current level of reserves from changing for some external reason. Nevertheless, the Trading Desk can substitute repurchase agreement transactions for outright purchases or sales to change the overall reserve level by continuously mismatching repurchase-agreement transactions as needed.

Because the European Central Bank is able to use its discount rate–Lombard rate system for advances to constrain market interest rates from day to day, it does not conduct open-market operations each day. Instead, it offers a set of repurchase agreements at a regular weekly auction. This enables the European Central Bank to maintain a desired level of bank reserves from week to week.

At the Bank of Japan, most open-market operations involve the purchase or sale of *privately issued* financial instruments, including commercial bills and paper and bank certificates of deposit. In the past, this has allowed the Bank of Japan to try to directly influence a variety of market interest rates. Since the late 1980s, however, the Bank of Japan has aimed its open-market operations primarily at influencing the Japanese interbank funds rate.

Open-market operations are much less common in less developed and emerging economies. The reason for this is simple: These nations do not have well developed markets for government securities and other short-term instruments. This makes it difficult for central banks in these countries to find a critical mass of banks and other institutions that regularly trade securities on a daily or weekly basis.

Reserve Requirements

Reserve requirements *Central bank regulations requiring private banks to hold specified fractions of transactions and term deposits either as vault cash or as funds on deposit at the central bank.*

In years past, an important instrument of monetary policy has been **reserve requirements.** These are rules specifying portions of transactions (checking) and term (time and savings) deposits that private banks must hold either as vault cash or as funds on deposit at the central bank.

Today, however, reserve requirements are less important instruments of monetary policy. Certainly, central banks rarely change reserve requirements in an effort to exert direct effects on the quantities of money and credit or on the levels of market interest rates. A key rationale that today's central banks offer for reserve requirements is that they may help ensure that private banks are sufficiently liquid to be able to make rapid, day-to-day reserve adjustments in response to unexpected events. To assist banks in this endeavor, most central banks assess reserve requirements on an *average* basis: Banks must meet their reserve requirements, but they need do so only on average over a period of one or two weeks.

Interest-Rate Regulations and Direct Credit Controls

In a number of nations, and especially in those with less developed financial markets, central banks traditionally have used more blunt means of influencing the quantities of money and credit. In East Asia, for instance, central banks commonly place restrictions on interest rates that private banks may pay their depositors. They sometimes use these limits as monetary policy instruments. For example, raising the allowable interest rate that banks may pay on deposits potentially can induce individuals and firms to hold more deposits, thereby increasing the amount of deposits, including those that circulate as money.

In nations such as China and Russia, central banks also use *direct credit controls,* which are explicit quantity constraints on how much credit banks and other financial institutions may extend to individuals and firms. If central banks in these nations wish to contract the growth of money and credit, perhaps in an effort to contain inflation, then they tighten credit constraints. If the central banks wish to induce higher growth in money and credit, perhaps to encourage increased near-term economic growth, then they loosen the controls somewhat.

MONETARY POLICY AND MARKET INTEREST RATES

A key channel through which a central bank's monetary policy actions affect economic activity is by altering market interest rates and thereby influencing the willingness of individuals and firms to borrow and spend at any given price level. Thus, it is important to understand how monetary policy actions influence market interest rates.

The Money Multiplier

A nation's level of interest rates adjusts to maintain equilibrium in the market for money. Central banks determine the overall supply of money in circulation—measured via a monetary aggregate such as M1 or M2, by varying the size of the monetary base. For instance, in the United States, when the Federal Reserve Bank of New York's trading desk executes a purchase of U.S. government securities, it wires funds to the account of a private bank from which it purchases the securities. This is the means by which the Fed begins the process of new money creation.

It is only the start of this process, however. For instance, if the Trading Desk were to purchase $1 million in government securities from a securities dealer who were to have the Fed wire the funds to its checking deposit account in a private bank based in Chicago, the Fed would respond by applying a $1 million credit to that bank's reserve account at the Federal Reserve Bank of Chicago. The private bank then would earmark these funds for the dealer's deposit account with the private bank. The Fed only requires private banks to impose a 10 percent reserve requirement on the bulk of U.S. checking deposits, and so the private Chicago bank would be able to lend $900,000 of the funds that it receives via the security dealer's deposit. If the Chicago bank were to make a loan to a construction company based in Louisville, Kentucky, and if the company were to place the funds in its checking account at a Louisville bank, then this bank would have $900,000 in new cash reserves. Of these, it could lend as much as $810,000, or 90 percent of the $900,000 additional funds now deposited. This ultimately would expand deposits at yet another bank, either in Louisville or elsewhere.

Consequently, the Fed's $1 million security purchase in our example would cause the total quantity of money in circulation to increase by an amount much greater than $1 million. The Chicago security dealer's checking deposits would increase by $1 million, the Louisville construction company's checking deposits would rise by $900,000, and some other loan recipient's checking deposits would rise by $810,000. This process would continue until the Fed's security purchase had an ultimate *multiplier effect* on the total quantity of checking deposits included in the nation's money stock.

To determine the size of the multiplier effect in our example, let's denote the amount of checking deposits at private banks as D, and let's call the total amount of cash reserves of these banks R. Finally, let's denote the Fed's ratio for determining required reserve holdings q. Hence, if banks were to hold no more cash reserves than the Fed required them to hold, total reserves in the banking system would be $R = q \times D$, and any change in reserves owing to a change in checking deposits at banks would be equal to $\Delta R = q \times \Delta$, where the "$\Delta$" symbol denotes a change in a quantity. We can rearrange this relationship, however, to find a change in checking deposits owing to a change in reserves induced by a Fed purchase of securities. To do so, we simply solve for ΔD by dividing both sides by q, which yields:

$$\Delta D = (1/q) \times \Delta R.$$

In our example of a Fed security purchase that causes an initial bank reserve expansion of \$1 million with a required reserve ratio of 10 percent, ΔR would equal \$1 million, and $1/q$ would equal $1/(0.1) = 10$. Therefore, ΔD would equal \$1 million $\times$ 10, or \$10 million, and so the Fed's \$1 million security purchase ultimately would cause the quantity of money in circulation to rise by a multiple amount of \$10 million. The ratio $1/q = 10$ would be a "money multiplier."

Realistically, the final multiplier effect of a Fed security purchase is smaller than this amount. A key reason is that people hold some money in the form of currency. Hence, if the Chicago securities dealer and Louisville construction company in our example had chosen to convert some of the funds they received into currency rather than depositing all the funds into checking accounts at their banks, then each of their banks would have had fewer funds available to lend. This would have reduced the extent of the deposit multiplier process. Another factor that typically depresses the size of the deposit multiplier effect is bank holdings of reserves over and above those that are required. To the extent that banks might hold such *excess reserves,* they would have fewer reserves available to lend at each stage of the multiplier process.

The Supply of Money

Of course, monetary aggregates such as M1 and M2 include a number of different types of deposits. They also include currency issued by the central bank. Central banks may also establish different required reserve ratios for separate types of deposits. Nevertheless, a multiplier relationship continues to exist even when we take into account both currency and various types of deposits.

Specifically, the quantity of money supplied by the central bank must be equal to a money multiplier times the monetary base. As in the simplest case illustrated above, the value of the money multiplier varies inversely with the required reserve ratio. The central bank can then influence the quantity of money by changing the size of its balance sheet, either by varying the quantity of currency it issues or, more likely, varying its policy instruments to alter the quantity of reserves in the banking system.

Money Demand, the Equilibrium Interest Rate, and the Effects of Monetary Policy Actions

People naturally hold money to engage in transactions. That is, they desire to have liquidity available to be able to purchase goods and services when they wish to do so. But they also hold money as an alternative to holding other financial assets. There is a relatively low risk to holding money, but most forms of money pay zero or very low interest rates. Hence, by holding money, people incur an opportunity cost equal to the market interest rate that they could have earned by holding a financial asset such as a Treasury security. Consequently, people typically choose to hold less money as the market interest rate increases or to hold more money as the interest rate declines.

This means that the market interest rate must adjust as necessary to make people willing to hold the quantity of money placed in circulation through actions of a central bank. When people are satisfied holding the amount of money outstanding, then the interest rate is at its equilibrium level.

Now consider what happens if the central bank increases the quantity of money, perhaps by engaging in an open-market purchase or reducing an interest rate on advances to induce banks to increase bank reserves and the monetary base. Through the money multiplier effect, this action raises the overall level of liquidity in the economy. At the previous equilibrium interest rate, people would not desire to hold newly produced money. They would seek to shift funds to interest-bearing assets. This overabundance of liquidity would tend to push the market interest rate downward. (To examine how the market interest rate is determined and how central bank policy actions influence the interest rate, see on the next page *Visualizing Global Economic Issues: Influencing the Equilibrium Interest Rate.*)

Fundamental Issue 2

What are the primary instruments of monetary policy available to central banks, and how do monetary policy actions affect market interest rates?

By determining values for their policy instruments, which may include interest rates on central bank advances, open-market operations, reserve requirements, and interest-rate and credit restrictions, central banks are able to influence interbank funds rates and hence bank reserves and the monetary base. The money multiplier determines the size of the effect on the quantity of money caused by a change in the monetary base. The equilibrium interest rate is the rate of interest at which people are satisfied holding the quantity of money supplied through policies of the central bank. A central bank action that increases the quantity of money raises the amount of total liquidity in the economy, thereby generating a reduction in the equilibrium interest rate.

Money, Prices, and Exchange Rates

Economists have long sought to understand how changes in the quantity of money in circulation—as well as variations in other factors such as government spending, taxes, exchange rates, labor productivity, and aggregate wages—may influence economic activity and the overall level of prices of goods and services.

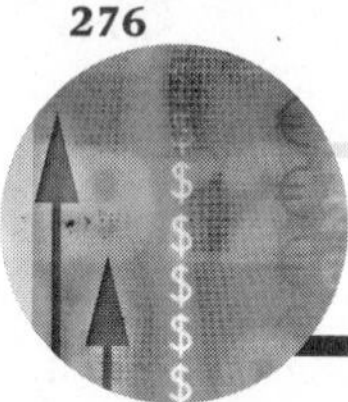

Visualizing Global Economic Issues

Influencing the Equilibrium Interest Rate

To evaluate the effects of monetary policy actions on the market interest rate, take a look at Figure 9-2. In both panels of the figure, the downward-sloping curve depicts the total *demand for money* in the economy. The money demand curve slopes downward because as the interest rate rises, the opportunity cost of holding money that pays a low or no rate of interest increases, inducing people to cut back on their money holdings. The vertical curve in both panels is the economy's *supply of money,* which the central bank influences by varying the monetary base or, if it wishes, by changing the required reserve ratio.

In panel (a), the crossing point of the two schedules depict a situation in which all individuals in the economy are satisfied holding the nominal money stock supplied by the central bank. Consequently, at this single point the quantity of money demanded by the public is equal to the quantity of money supplied via efforts of the central bank. Therefore, the interest adjusts to achieve this equilibrium point, and R_1 is the *equilibrium* interest rate.

Panel (b) shows the adjustment process following a central bank policy action that expands the quantity of money in circulation. An open-market purchase or reduction in the interest rate on central bank advances pushes up the monetary base, thereby increasing the quantity of money in circulation by a multiple amount. Hence, the money supply curve shifts rightward. The quantity of money supplied by the central bank increases from the initial amount M_1 to a larger quantity M_2 at any given interest rate. Thus, there is an excess quantity of money supplied at the initial equilibrium interest rate R_1, and the interest rate must fall to a new equilibrium level, R_2.

For Critical Analysis:
How would a central bank go about trying to push up the equilibrium interest rate?

NATIONAL INCOME AND PRICE DEFLATORS

To determine how various factors relate to a nation's overall economic performance, economists must first have reliable measures of economic activity. The most important of these is *gross domestic product*.

Measuring Economic Activity: National Income and Product

Gross domestic product (GDP) *The value, tabulated using market prices, of all final goods and services produced within a country's borders during a given period.*

The primary measure of economic activity during a given interval is the total value, computed using current market prices, of the output of *final* goods and services produced within a nation's borders during that period. This is called the economy's **gross domestic product (GDP).**

Businesses earn revenues on the output that they sell to consumers, other businesses, and the government. These revenues flow to the individuals who provide *factors of production* to businesses, which use the factors to produce the goods and services that they sell. Factors of production include labor, land, capital, and

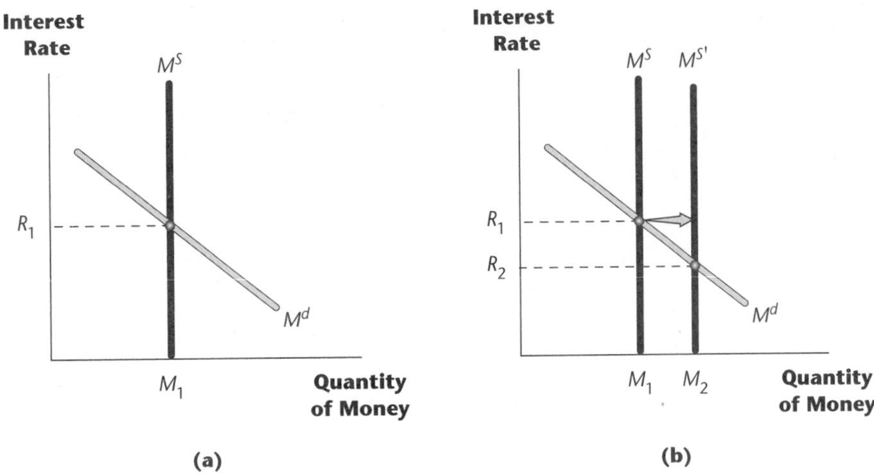

Figure 9-2

The Equilibrium Interest Rate and Monetary Policy

As the interest rate rises, the opportunity cost of holding money increases, inducing people to cut back on their money holdings. Hence, the money demand curve slopes downward. The money supply curve is vertical, and the central bank influences the position of the money supply curve by varying the monetary base or changing the required reserve ratio. Panel (a) depicts a single point where all individuals in the economy are satisfied holding the nominal money stock supplied by the central bank at the equilibrium interest rate R_1. *Panel (b) illustrates the adjustment process following an open-market purchase or reduction in the interest rate on central bank advances. Either action pushes up the monetary base, thereby increasing the quantity of money in circulation by a multiple amount and shifting the money supply curve rightward as the quantity of money supplied increases from* M_1 *to* M_2. *There is an excess quantity of money supplied at the initial equilibrium interest rate* R_1, *so the interest rate declines to a new equilibrium rate* R_2.

entrepreneurship. The earnings of the individuals who supply these factors of production are wages and salaries, rents, interest and dividends, and profits. Adding together all these receipts for all individuals in the economy yields the total income earnings of all individuals, or *national income.*

This means that, ultimately, the total value of output that businesses produced becomes the combined income of all individuals. Consequently, abstracting from minor accounting details distinguishing the government's two measures in the U.S. income and product accounting procedures, *national income and GDP must be identical.* This means that for all intents and purposes, GDP also is a good measure of the total income receipts of all individuals.

Real versus Nominal National Income

As shown in Figure 9-3 on page 278, U.S. GDP has persistently increased over time. It has done so for two reasons. One reason is that the economy has grown, meaning

Figure 9-3

U.S. Gross Domestic Product

The dollar value of newly produced goods and services within U.S. borders has increased each year because actual production has risen and because the price level has increased.

Sources: *Economic Report of the President,* 2002, and *Economic Indicators,* various issues.

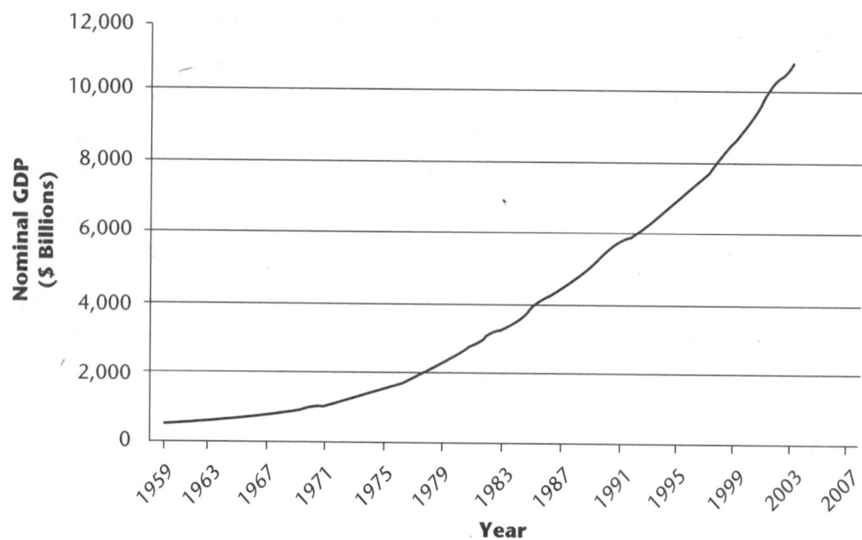

that businesses have expanded their resources and found ways to increase their production of goods and services. Another reason, however, is that prices have risen over time. Such overall price increases, or inflation, have increased the *measured value* of income and output in the economy. This means that you cannot necessarily look at Figure 9-3 and conclude that the actual production of goods and services consistently has increased in the United States. Some portion of the general rise in GDP occurred simply because prices rose over time as well. This means that using GDP as a measure of actual productive activity in the economy would lead to an overstatement of the true volume of such activity when inflation occurs.

To see why this distinction must be made, think about a situation in which an employer were to double the wages that you receive for providing labor services. This would increase your measured income. But if the overall prices that you have to pay to purchase goods and services also were to double, then you really would be no better off. Likewise, if total national income as measured by GDP were to double simply because prices increased by a factor of two, then the total volume of economic activity really would not have changed.

Real gross domestic product (real GDP) *A price-adjusted measure of aggregate output, or nominal GDP divided by the GDP price deflator.*

To avoid this problem, economists use an adjusted measure of GDP, called **real gross domestic product.** This measure of the total production of final output accounts for the effects of price changes and thereby reflects more accurately the economy's true volume of productive activity. Because the flow of final product ultimately makes its way to individuals as a flow of total national income, real GDP also is a measure of *real national income,* or the amount of total income that individuals truly receive, net of artificial increases resulting from inflation.

To distinguish real GDP from the unadjusted GDP measure, economists refer to unadjusted GDP as **nominal gross domestic product,** or GDP "in name only," because it has been measured in current dollar terms with no adjustment for effects of price changes. Likewise, they refer to unadjusted national income as *nominal national income,* or simply *nominal income.*

Nominal gross domestic product (nominal GDP) *The value of final production of goods and services calculated in current dollar terms with no adjustment for effects of price changes.*

The Price Level

Because real income measures the economy's true volume of production, multiplying real income by a measure of the overall level of prices would yield the value of real income measured in current prices, which is nominal income. That is, if y denotes real income and P is a measure of the overall price level, then total nominal income, denoted Y, is equal to $Y = y \times P$.

Because economists measure real income using real GDP and nominal income using nominal GDP, the factor P is called the **GDP price deflator,** or simply the "GDP deflator." It is called a "deflator" because the expression for nominal income, $Y = y \times P$, can be rearranged to obtain $y = Y / P$. That is, real income y is equal to nominal income Y adjusted by dividing by, or "deflating" by, the factor P. For instance, suppose that nominal GDP, Y, is equal to $10 trillion but that the value of the GDP deflator, P, is equal to 2. Then computing real GDP would entail deflating the $10 trillion figure for nominal GDP by a factor of one-half. Dividing $10 trillion by 2 yields a $5 trillion figure for real GDP. Panel (a) of Figure 9-4 on the following page depicts the GDP deflator for the United States since 1959.

GDP price deflator *A flexible-weight measure of the overall price level; equal to nominal GDP divided by real GDP.*

Panel (b) of Figure 9-4 plots both real and nominal GDP. Note that in 1996 nominal and real GDP are equal because 1996 is the **base year** in which $P = 1$ so that $Y = y$. Clearly, adjusting for price changes has a significant effect on how to interpret GDP numbers. This is why it is so important to use the GDP deflator to convert nominal GDP into real GDP. Only the latter measure can really provide information about the actual volume of economic activity.

Base year *A reference year for price-level comparisons, which is a year in which nominal GDP is equal to real GDP, so that the GDP deflator's value is equal to one.*

Fundamental Issue

How do economists measure a nation's aggregate output and price level?

Economists measure a country's total output using gross domestic product (GDP), which is the market value of all final goods and services produced during a given period. Nominal GDP is the total value of newly produced goods and services computed using the prices at which they sold during the year they were produced. In contrast, real GDP is the value of final goods and services after adjusting for the effects of year-to-year price changes. The basic approach to calculating real GDP is to divide nominal GDP by the GDP deflator, which is a key measure of the level of prices relative to prices for a base year.

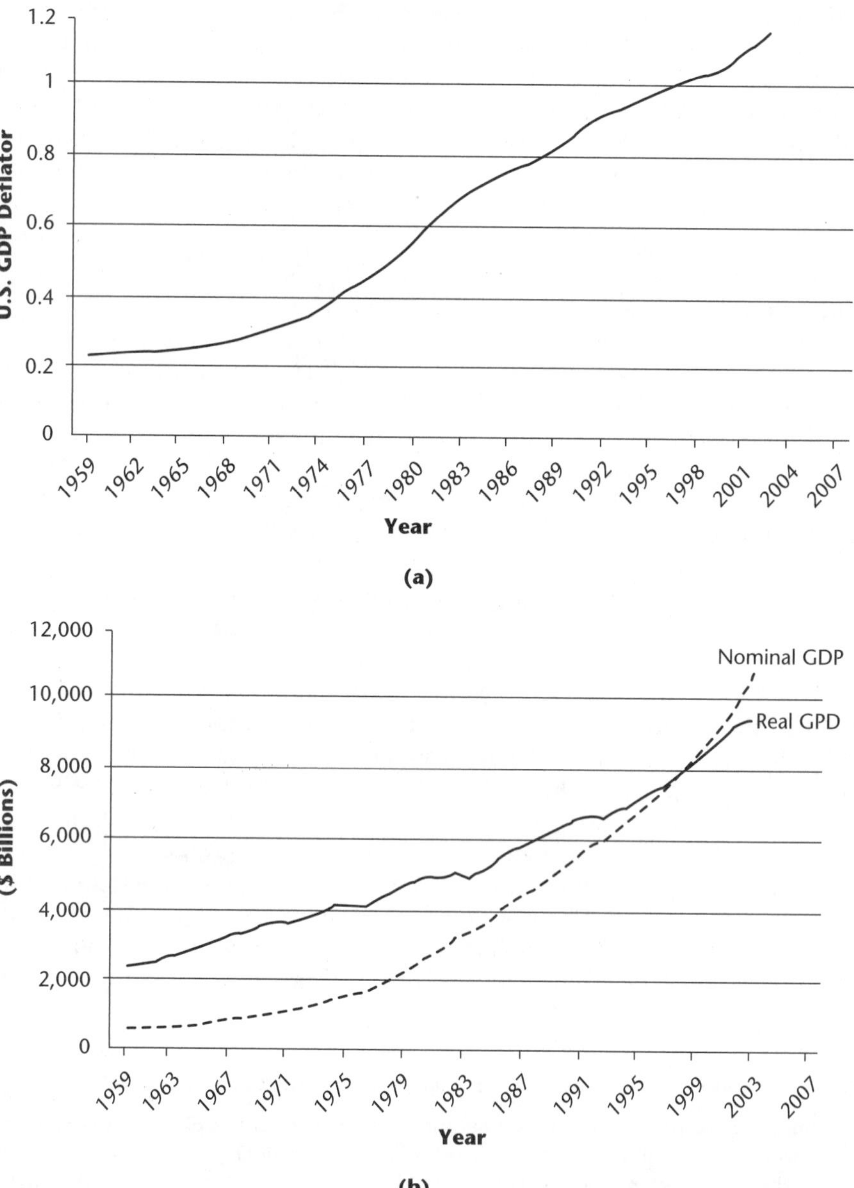

Figure 9-4

The GDP Deflator and Real and Nominal GDP in the United States since 1959

Panel (a) shows annual values of the U.S. GDP deflator. Panel (b) displays U.S. nominal GDP (the same chart as Figure 9-3 on page 278) and U.S. real GDP. As panel (b) indicates, because real GDP accounts for the effects of price changes, it exhibits less growth from year to year.

Sources: *Economic Report of the President*, 2002, and *Economic Indicators*, various issues.

AGGREGATE DEMAND, AGGREGATE SUPPLY, AND WHERE EXCHANGE RATES FIT IN

How do central bank policy actions affect a nation's income and prices? What role does the exchange rate play in this process? To address these questions, let's first consider how a nation's total output of goods and services and its price level are determined.

The Equilibrium Price Level and Equilibrium Real Output

A nation's price level adjusts to ensure that total desired spending on domestic output of goods and services by all domestic and foreign residents equals aggregate output produced by the nation's industries. When this condition is satisfied, the equilibrium price level is determined within the nation.

The total output of goods and services produced at this price level, in turn, is the equilibrium output for the economy. The real value of this output within a given interval is the measured volume of real GDP for the nation's economy. (For a graphical depiction of this process, see on pages 282–283 *Visualizing Global Economic Issues: Aggregate Demand, Aggregate Supply, and Equilibrium Output and the Price Level.*)

Monetary Policy, the Exchange Rate, and Equilibrium Output and Prices

In open economies, central banks can try to influence real output and the price level by altering the quantity of money in circulation or by bringing about a change in the exchange rate. Below we contemplate how a central bank might be able to generate changes in the exchange rate. For now, let's concentrate on determining how a central banks can affect its nation's real output and price level, assuming that it can alter the exchange rate.

To try to bring about an increase in the real output of domestic firms, a central bank could attempt to induce people to increase their total desired spending on output. One way to do this would be by expanding the quantity of money in circulation. As already discussed, this causes the market interest rate to fall. As a result, borrowing costs decline, which encourages people to increase their spending. Another way to generate increased desired spending on goods and services is for the central bank to push down the value of the nation's currency relative to other currencies. This makes domestic goods less expensive to foreign residents and makes foreign goods more expensive to domestic residents, thereby inducing an increase in export spending and a reduction in import spending. Both factors contribute to an increase in total desired expenditures on domestic output.

Naturally, firms will not produce the additional output that people want to purchase unless the price level increases. In the short run, when at least some input prices do not adjust in equal proportion to an increase in the prices of goods and services, firms will respond to a higher price level by increasing production. In this way, central banks can affect real GDP. (See on pages 284–285 a diagrammatic explanation in *Visualizing Global Economic Issues: Monetary Policy, Aggregate Demand, and Equilibrium Output and Prices.*)

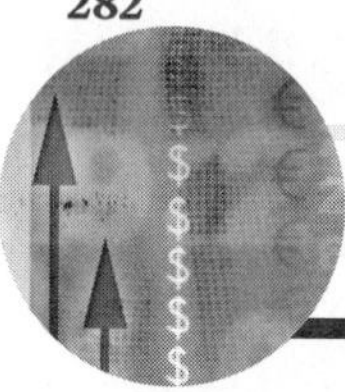

Visualizing Global Economic Issues

Aggregate Demand, Aggregate Supply, and Equilibrium Output and the Price Level

Figure 9-5 illustrates the determination of a nation's equilibrium real output and price level. The downward-sloping relationship between the price level P and the amount of real output y is the *aggregate demand (AD) curve,* which depicts the various combinations of price levels, P, and corresponding levels of real output of goods and services, y, which people at home and abroad are willing to purchase. Three factors lie behind the downward slope of the aggregate demand curve. First, a rise in the price level reduces the real quantity of money in circulation, thereby inducing domestic residents to cut back on their purchases of real output. Second, there is a fall in real liquidity in the economy caused by a price-level increase. As a result, there is an excess quantity of real liquidity demanded, and market interest rates tend to rise, thereby giving domestic residents an incentive to reduce expenditures financed by borrowing. Third, an increase in the prices of domestically produced goods and services makes them more expensive to residents of other nations. Hence, foreign purchases of exports decline, thereby contributing to an overall reduction in spending on domestically produced output.

The upward-sloping relationship is the *aggregate supply (AS) curve,* which depicts the levels of aggregate real output that all domestic businesses are willing and able to produce, y, at various levels of prices, P. If the prices of all factors of production and goods and services were to adjust speedily and in equal proportion to a rise in the price level, then firms' costs would rise as rapidly as their revenues following the price-level increase, and the aggregate supply curve would be vertical. This would be true only over a long-run horizon, however. In the short run, many prices are "sticky," meaning that input prices do not change very much or very quickly in response to changes in demand conditions. Thus, as the price level increases, so does the willingness of firms to produce output of goods and services. The aggregate supply curve thereby slopes upward in the short run.

The figure displays the determination of the equilibrium price level, denoted P_1, which corresponds to the point where the aggregate demand curve crosses the aggregate supply curve. At this level of

Fundamental Issue

How are the equilibrium levels of aggregate output and prices determined, and how do central bank actions altering the quantity of money or exchange rates influence equilibrium real output and the price level?

In equilibrium, total desired spending on a nation's goods and services equals the value of aggregate output production within the nation's borders. A nation's price level adjusts to ensure this equality. If a nation's central bank engages in a policy action that reduces the market interest rate or reduces the value of the nation's currency, then total desired spending increases, which causes an increase in the price level and, at least in the short run, an increase in real aggregate output.

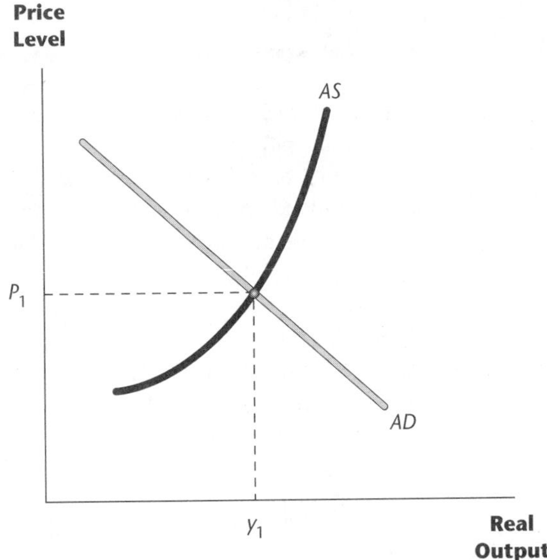

Figure 9-5

Aggregate Demand, Aggregate Supply, and Equilibrium

The downward-sloping aggregate demand (AD) curve shows combinations of price levels, P, and corresponding levels of real output of goods and services, y, which people at home and abroad are willing to purchase. The aggregate supply (AS) curve depicts the levels of aggregate real output, y, that all domestic firms are willing and able to produce at various levels of prices, P. This diagram depicts the aggregate supply curve that applies in the short run, when many prices are "sticky." In this situation, input prices do not change very much or very quickly in response to changes in demand conditions, so that firms are willing to increase their output as the price level increases. Consequently, the short-run aggregate supply curve slopes upward. At the equilibrium price level P_1*, residents of this nation are satisfied purchasing the total amount of real final output,* y_1*, that firms produce given the available quantities of factors of production.*

prices, residents of this nation are satisfied purchasing the total amount of real final output that businesses produce, given the available quantities of factors of production. If the price level were greater than P_1, residents would be unwilling to buy all the output that could be produced with available resources. Thus, the price level would fall back toward P_1. In contrast, if the price level were below P_1, the nation's residents would desire to purchase a greater volume of aggregate output than businesses could produce, given the available factors of production. They would bid against each other to try to purchase desired quantities of goods and services, and the general level of prices would rise toward P_1.

For Critical Analysis:
Is it likely that changes in aggregate demand can affect a nation's real output in the long run?

Foreign Exchange Market Interventions

Central banks, of course, recognize that variations in exchange rates can influence total desired spending on domestic output and, therefore, equilibrium real GDP and prices. This gives central banks an incentive to engage in foreign exchange interventions in efforts to alter, smooth, or peg exchange rates. They seek to influence exchange rates by purchasing or selling financial assets denominated in foreign currencies.

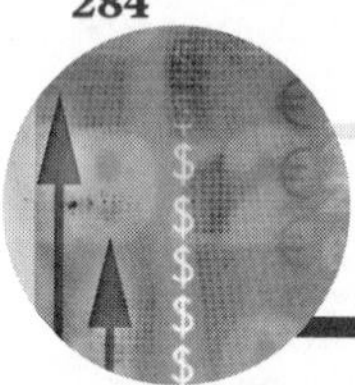

Visualizing Global Economic Issues

Monetary Policy, Aggregate Demand, and Equilibrium Output and Prices

Any factor contributing to higher total expenditures on goods and services causes an increase in aggregate demand, which corresponds to a rightward shift in the aggregate demand curve shown in Figure 9-6. One way that a central bank can generate a rise in total spending is by bringing about an increase in the quantity of money in circulation. Another is by intervening in foreign exchange markets by buying foreign assets. This can generate a fall in the value of the domestic currency relative to the currencies of trading partners, which makes domestic goods and services less expensive to foreign residents and thereby boosts their spending on export goods.

As shown in the figure, at the initial equilibrium price level P_1, total desired expenditures on goods and services exceed the real value of output produced by firms. People bid up the prices of goods and services, so the equilibrium price level increases to P_2. In the short run, firms' input costs do not rise in equal proportion, so the increase in the price level gives them an incentive to increase their production. Hence, equilibrium real output increases following an expansion of the quantity of money or a fall in the value of the nation's currency.

For Critical Analysis:
How would an increase in the value of the nation's currency affect equilibrium real output and the equilibrium price level?

MECHANICS OF FOREIGN EXCHANGE INTERVENTIONS

Now that you have learned about the balance-sheet compositions, structures, and functions of central banks and about how their activities can influence national economic performances, we can consider how these institutions conduct foreign exchange market interventions in an effort to influence exchange rates.

Leaning with or against the Wind

Leaning with the wind
Central bank interventions to support or speed along the current trend in the market exchange value of its nation's currency.

Leaning against the wind
Central bank interventions to halt or reverse the current trend in the market exchange value of its nation's currency.

A central bank intervenes either on its own account or on behalf of its national government in an effort to influence the value of its nation's currency in the foreign exchange market. If a central bank intervenes to support or speed along the current trend in the value of its nation's currency in the foreign exchange market, then economists say that its interventions **lean with the wind.**

In contrast, economists say that central bank interventions intended to halt or reverse a recent trend in the value of its nation's currency **lean against the wind.** Most often, central banks lean against the wind solely to halt, at least temporarily, sharp swings in market exchange rates. Consequently, a key rationale for many instances of leaning against the wind is simply to reduce volatility in exchange rates. Central banks do not necessarily lean against the wind with an aim to bring about long-term reversals in the trend value of their currencies, although

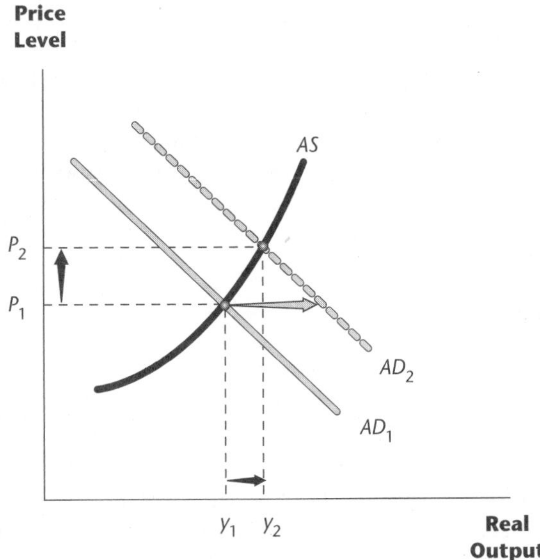

Figure 9-6

The Effects of an Expansionary Monetary Policy Action on Equilibrium Output and Prices

A central bank can bring about a rise in total spending by increasing the quantity of money in circulation or by engaging in foreign exchange market interventions that reduce the value of the domestic currency, thereby making domestic goods and services less expensive to foreign residents and inducing them to increase spending on export goods. Either action causes aggregate demand to increase from AD_1 to AD_2, so at the initial equilibrium price level P_1, total desired expenditures on goods and services are greater than the real value of output produced by firms. The prices of goods and services are bid upward, so the equilibrium price level increases to P_2. Firms' input costs do not rise in equal proportion in the short run. Consequently, equilibrium real output increases following an expansion of the quantity of money or a fall in the value of the nation's currency.

in some instances this might be an ultimate goal of a central bank or finance ministry upon whose behalf the central bank conducts a policy of leaning against the wind.

Financing Interventions

If central banks intervene in foreign exchange markets on their own behalf, then they do so using their own reserves of assets denominated in foreign currencies. Many central banks have "war chests" of foreign currency reserves in the event they desire to conduct interventions on their own account. In like manner, governments often maintain reserves of foreign-currency-denominated assets.

In the United States, the U.S. Treasury has primary responsibility for initiating foreign exchange interventions. Consequently, the Treasury often determines the timing and extent of U.S. interventions, even though the Federal Reserve conducts these interventions on the Treasury's behalf. The U.S. Treasury's position is that it has the legal authority to order the Federal Reserve to use its own foreign exchange reserves as well as those of the Treasury, and in the past the Federal Reserve has conducted Treasury interventions using its own reserves as well as those of the Treasury. Recently, this has become a source of tension within the Federal Reserve System, as some Federal Reserve officials have openly questioned this "subservience" of the Federal Reserve to the Treasury.

Nonetheless, the U.S. government maintains a separate *Exchange Stabilization Fund (ESF)* that it can use to finance its interventions when Federal Reserve foreign exchange reserves are not involved. If ESF officials intervene in support of the dollar's value by selling assets denominated in foreign currencies, they initially deposit the dollars obtained in the transaction in a Treasury deposit at the Federal Reserve. The Treasury Department then issues a nonmarketable security to the ESF, which purchases the Treasury security from its account with the Federal Reserve, which credits the Treasury's deposit account. To ensure that this sequence of transactions has no ultimate effect on the Federal Reserve's balance sheet, and hence on the monetary base, the Treasury then withdraws these funds from its deposit account at the Federal Reserve and redeposits them at private banks.

STERILIZATION OF INTERVENTIONS

Sterilization
A central bank policy of altering domestic credit in an equal and opposite direction relative to any variation in foreign exchange reserves so as to prevent the monetary base from changing.

A central bank **sterilizes** foreign exchange interventions when it buys or sells domestic assets in sufficient quantities to prevent the interventions from influencing the domestic money stock. As we noted earlier in this chapter, a key money measure is the *monetary base,* which we can view as either the sum of domestic credit plus foreign exchange reserves or as the sum of domestic currency and bank reserves. Thus, sterilization of the sale of foreign exchange reserves requires an equal-sized expansion of domestic credit, perhaps via a central bank open-market purchase, that would maintain an unchanged monetary base.

The mechanics of U.S. foreign exchange interventions entail accounting entries that lead to nearly immediate and complete sterilization. The European Central Bank and Bank of Japan also follow policies intended to ensure at least long-term sterilization of interventions.

Many other countries officially espouse a policy of sterilizing foreign exchange interventions, but in practice most find it difficult to fully offset the effects of the resulting changes in net foreign assets. Thus, many interventions by central banks around the world are at least partly nonsterilized, so that interventions cause changes in relative quantities of national moneys in circulation. It is through this channel, as we shall discuss in more detail in the following chapters, that many economists think that interventions actually may influence market exchange rates. As you will learn in the following chapters, nonsterilized interventions can, at least in principle, lead to a number of adjustments in national economies.

Indeed, a number of economists believe that *only* nonsterilized interventions can affect exchange rates. If central banks are able to sterilize interventions, they argue, then interventions really just amount to changes in the currency compositions of domestic and foreign assets that individuals and firms around the world regard as essentially perfect substitutes. Hence, changes in the relative supplies of these assets can have no effects on foreign exchange market equilibrium.

How do central banks intervene in foreign exchange markets?

Fundamental Issue 5

Central banks typically intervene in the spot market for foreign exchange, using swap transactions primarily to adjust the currency compositions of their portfolios of foreign exchange reserves. If a central bank intervenes to support the current trend in the value of its currency, then it leans with the wind. If it intervenes in an effort to halt or reverse the current trend in the value of its currency, then it leans against the wind. Both central banks and government finance ministries can intervene in foreign exchange markets. Although some nations seek to ensure that their interventions are sterilized, many others do not sterilize interventions fully.

Do Interventions Matter?

If sterilized interventions have no effects, then the implication would be that interventions would be redundant policies. After all, any central bank can vary the amount of money it places in circulation relative to other world currencies through purely domestic policy actions, such as varying interest rates on advances or engaging in open-market operations, that alter the monetary base. Consequently, an important issue for international monetary economists is whether foreign exchange interventions can and do have independent short- and long-term effects on market exchange rates.

GAUGING THE SHORT-TERM EFFECTS OF INTERVENTIONS

Most economists believe that sterilized foreign exchange interventions can, at least in theory, have at most two types of immediate effects on exchange rates. They call one of these the **portfolio balance effect:** If the exchange rate is viewed as the relative price of imperfectly substitutable assets such as bonds, then changes in government or central bank holdings of bonds and other assets denominated in various currencies can influence exchange rates by affecting the equilibrium prices at which traders are willing to hold these assets. For example, if an intervention reduces the supply of domestic assets relative to foreign assets held by individuals and firms, then the expected return on domestic assets must fall to induce individuals and firms to readjust their portfolios. A reduction in the anticipated rate of return on domestic assets, in turn, requires an appreciation of the domestic currency. Hence, a finance ministry or central bank purchase of domestic currency can, through the portfolio balance effect, cause the value of the domestic currency to rise.

Portfolio balance effect *An exchange rate adjustment resulting from changes in government or central bank holdings of foreign-currency-denominated financial instruments that influence the equilibrium prices of the instruments.*

The other possible effect is an intervention **announcement effect,** in which foreign exchange interventions may provide traders with previously unknown information that alters their willingness to demand or supply currencies in the foreign exchange markets. The announcement effect can exist, therefore, only if a

Announcement effect *A change in private market interest rates or exchange rates that results from an anticipation of near-term changes in market conditions signaled by a central bank policy action.*

government or central bank intervention clearly reveals some kind of inside information that traders did not have prior to the intervention. For instance, a central bank that plans to conduct a future anti-inflation policy by contracting its money stock may reveal this intention by leaning against the wind in the face of a recent downward trend in the value of its nation's currency. If currency traders believe this message provided by the central bank's intervention, then they will expect a future appreciation and will increase their holdings of the currency. This concerted action by currency traders then causes an actual currency appreciation. Thus, the announcement effect of the intervention, like the portfolio balance effect, induces a rise in the value of the domestic currency.

A major study of foreign exchange market interventions during the 1980s and early 1990s by Kathryn Dominguez of Harvard University and Jeffrey Frankel of the University of California at Berkeley found evidence that both effects were at work during that period, especially in the latter part of the 1980s when many of the world's governments conducted sizable interventions. Dominguez and Frankel found that during this interval, in which central banks coordinated several interventions, the *announcements* of the interventions actually had larger effects on exchange rates than the actual magnitudes of the interventions themselves. This, in their view, provides strong evidence of announcement effects in interventions. Particularly in the case of coordinated interventions during the late 1980s, traders seem to have viewed interventions as signals of government and central bank commitments to future policy changes and reacted by altering their desired holdings of domestic and foreign assets. The result was changes in market exchange rates, at least in the short run.

CAN EVEN COORDINATED INTERVENTIONS WORK IN THE LONG RUN?

As we discussed in Chapter 7, one of the most significant episodes of coordinated currency interventions took place beginning in 1985. In September of that year, at the Plaza Hotel in New York, the finance ministers and central banks of G5 nations announced that "in view of the present and prospective change in fundamentals, some orderly appreciation of the main nondollar currencies against the dollar is desirable. We stand ready to cooperate more closely to encourage this when to do so would be helpful." The Plaza Agreement was followed in 1987 by a reaffirmation of the Plaza principles at the Louvre Palace in Paris called the Louvre Accord. Much official rhetoric since these policy agreements has indicated that the G5 nations believed they largely accomplished their objective of stabilizing exchange rates at "desired" levels.

Some economists, however, believe this is an overstatement. Among these doubters are Michael Bordo of Rutgers University and Anna Schwartz of the National Bureau of Economic Research. In their view, central bank interventions really did not accomplish much except to distort exchange markets and to subject central banks to excessive risks of loss.

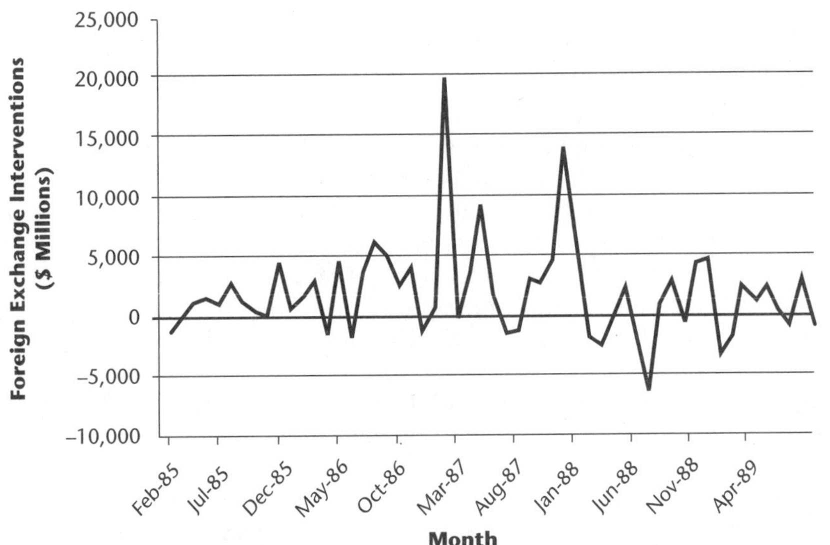

Figure 9-7

Combined U.S., German, and Japanese Interventions, February 1985 to August 1989

The total dollar amount of the foreign exchange interventions by these nations during the late 1980s varied considerably from month to month.

Source: Michael Bordo and Anna Schwartz, "What Has Foreign Exchange Market Intervention Since the Plaza Agreement Accomplished?" *Open Economies Review,* 2 (1) (1991): 39–64.

The Extent of Foreign Exchange Interventions in the Late 1980s

In support of this argument, Bordo and Schwartz conducted a study in which they tabulated data on the foreign exchange interventions coordinated by the United States, Germany, and Japan between early 1985 and late 1989. Figure 9-7 displays their estimates of the combined dollar amounts of interventions by central banks and finance ministries during that period.

Bordo and Schwartz reached two conclusions from their analysis of these interventions. First, the interventions were sporadic and highly variable, which potentially may have *added to,* instead of reducing, foreign exchange market volatility and uncertainty. These variable—and therefore often unexpected—central bank exchange market interventions likely caused individuals and firms to experience unintended wealth transfers. In addition, the increased risk of such transfers probably induced many traders to undertake more efforts to hedge against the risks of unexpected central bank interventions. This, as we discussed in Chapter 6, can be an effective, yet costly, activity.

Second, interventions during the late 1980s were very small in size relative to total trading in foreign exchange markets. Bordo and Schwartz note, for instance, that in April 1989 total foreign exchange trading amounted to $129 *billion* per day, yet the Fed purchased only $100 *million* in marks and yen in that entire month, on a single day. In fact, Fed purchases of marks and yen for all of 1989 amounted to about $17.7 billion, or the equivalent of less than 14 percent of the amount of an average day's trading in April of that year. Given the meager relative size of foreign exchange trading by even a coalition of the world's largest central banks during the 1985-1989 period, Bordo and Schwartz question the likelihood that central bank exchange market interventions can really have *long-lasting* effects on exchange rates.

Are the Direct Costs of Foreign Exchange Interventions Worth the Benefits?
In addition, Bordo and Schwartz argue that efforts by central banks to manipulate exchange rates have significant direct costs. Financing interventions requires expenditures of foreign exchange reserves, which either directly or indirectly (via ownership shares in central banks) are assets of national governments. During the late 1980s, Bordo and Schwartz argue, governments that participated in the coordinated effort to reduce the dollar's value exposed their governments, and hence their taxpaying citizens, to risks of sizable foreign exchange losses.

For instance, they point out that while the Federal Reserve and Treasury combined for more than $1 billion in realized gains from foreign exchange transactions in 1985 through 1989, the Netherlands lost 600 million Dutch guilders on dollar interventions in 1986 and 1987, and Germany reportedly lost 9 billion deutsche marks in the fourth quarter of 1987 alone. Bordo and Schwartz question the wisdom of central bank and finance ministry gambles with such large stakes given their limited abilities to achieve exchange rate goals.

Although Bordo and Schwartz make a strong case that the experience of the late 1980s indicates that central banks cannot manipulate exchange rates over long time horizons, many economists join Dominguez and Frankel in arguing that foreign exchange interventions can and do influence exchange rates from time to time. They contend that looking at the gains and losses from foreign exchange interventions by any single nation is misleading, because coordinated actions by several central banks are likely to have the most pronounced effects on exchange rates. They also argue that the announced willingness of central banks to influence exchange rates commonly can cause self-fulfilling prophecies: If traders believe that central banks can influence exchange rates and expect them to do so, then the traders themselves will act on their expectations in ways that push exchange rates in the directions central bankers desire. The coordinated interventions of the late 1980s, they point out, were unambiguously associated with an interval in which the value of the dollar declined. This decline, they note, continued even beyond the active period of interventions, potentially implying longer-term effects.

Efforts to manipulate exchange rates through foreign exchange interventions have been more muted since the 1980s. This may be because nations have less desire to influence exchange rates or because they have been unable to reach agreement on how to do so. Or it may be, as we shall discuss in Chapter 14, that modern central bankers and finance ministers have recognized the limits on their abilities to lean against the wind in today's foreign exchange markets. Before we reach that point, however, in the intervening chapters that follow you will need to learn much more about how policy actions of government finance ministries and central banks influence economic activity.

How effective are foreign exchange interventions?

Fundamental Issue 6

Economists are divided about the answer to this question, depending in part on whether one has in mind short-run or long-run effects on interventions. Most economists believe that nonsterilized interventions can have direct, short-run effects on exchange rates by changing relative quantities of currencies in circulation. Some economists also contend that sterilized interventions can alter exchange rates through portfolio balance effects or announcement effects. There is evidence that these latter effects mattered, at least in the short run, during the period of widespread foreign exchange interventions in the 1980s. There also is evidence, however, that even coordinated interventions had relatively small effects, may have added to exchange rate volatility, or may have caused taxpayer losses owing to greater currency risks incurred by governments and central banks.

CHAPTER SUMMARY

1) **Responsibilities of the World's Central Banks:** Central banks are depositories for funds held by national governments. They act as fiscal agents by operating the systems through which governments issue debt instruments, making interest and principal payments to those who hold government debt, and developing markets for government debt instruments. Central banks perform financial services for private banks and operate as lenders of last resort by providing liquidity to stem bank runs or other systemic banking problems. Furthermore, central banks vary policy instruments, such as interest rates on central bank advances, open-market operations, reserve requirements, and interest-rate and credit restrictions, to affect interbank funds rates and total bank reserves. This allows them to determine the monetary base. The monetary base is composed of currency notes and reserve deposits of private banks, which are key central bank liabilities. Important central bank assets are government securities, loans to private banks, and reserves of foreign currencies.
2) **Primary Central Bank Instruments of Monetary Policy, and How Monetary Policy Actions Affect Market Interest Rates:** Monetary policy instruments available to central banks include interest rates on central bank advances, open-market operations, reserve requirements, and interest-rate and credit restrictions. Central banks can alter these instruments to affect interbank funds rates, bank reserves, the monetary base, and, through the money multiplier, the quantity of money. At the equilibrium interest rate, a nation's residents are satisfied holding the quantity of money in circulation. A central bank action that increases the quantity of money raises the amount of total liquidity in the economy, thereby bringing about a decline in the equilibrium interest rate.
3) **How Economists Measure a Nation's Aggregate Output and Price Level:** Gross domestic product (GDP), which is the market value of all final goods and services produced during a given period, is the primary measure of a nation's total output. Nominal GDP is the total value of newly produced

goods and services computed using the prices at which they sold during the year they were produced, while real GDP is the value of final goods and services after adjusting for the effects of year-to-year price changes. Real GDP equals nominal GDP divided by the GDP deflator, which is a fundamental measure of the current price level relative to the price level in a base year.

4) **How Equilibrium Levels of Aggregate Output and Prices Are Determined, and How Central Bank Actions Altering the Quantity of Money or Exchange Rates Influence Equilibrium Real Output and the Price Level:** At a nation's equilibrium price level, total desired spending on the country's goods and services equals the value of aggregate output production within the nation's borders. If a nation's central bank engages in a policy action that reduces the market interest rate, thereby inducing an increase in desired investment expenditures, or reduces the value of the nation's currency, thereby generating a rise in export spending, then total desired spending rises. This brings about an increase in the price level and, at least in the short run, an increase in real aggregate output.
5) **How Central Banks Intervene in Foreign Exchange Markets:** Central banks typically intervene by buying or selling currencies in spot foreign exchange markets. Leaning with the wind refers to central bank interventions to support the current trend in the value of its currency, while leaning against the wind refers to interventions intended to halt or reverse the current trend in the value of its currency. Central banks and finance ministries both intervene in foreign exchange markets, though institutional frameworks governing the mechanisms for interventions and the extent to which they are sterilized varies from nation to nation.
6) **The Effectiveness of Foreign Exchange Interventions:** Many economists have concluded that nonsterilized interventions can influence market exchange rates by changing relative quantities of money supplied. Some also argue that sterilized interventions can alter exchange rates via portfolio balance effects or announcement effects. Evidence from the experience with interventions in the 1980s indicates that these latter effects were present, but there is also evidence from these episodes that even coordinated interventions may have had limited exchange-rate effects or could have contributed to greater exchange-rate variability and taxpayer losses in some nations.

QUESTIONS AND PROBLEMS

1) In your view, what is the single most important role of a central bank? Could a central bank perform this role without performing its other roles?
2) Can a central bank directly "control" the size of the monetary base? Why or why not?
3) Could a central bank conduct monetary policy solely by varying an interest rate on advances?

4) Why is it that a nation's real GDP, instead of its nominal GDP, is a better measure of overall economic activity?
5) What are some possible problems with using real GDP to gauge the "welfare" of a nation's residents?
6) What factors are likely to strengthen the price and output effects of a central bank policy action that increases the quantity of money in circulation?
7) What factors are likely to strengthen the price and output effects of a central bank policy action that reduces the value of a nation's currency?
8) Under what circumstances does the quantity of money in circulation within a nation change when its central bank conducts foreign exchange interventions?
9) Suppose that a nation's central bank does not use open-market operations to conduct monetary policy. How could the central bank vary the interest rate(s) that it charges on its advances to try to sterilize a foreign exchange intervention intended to raise the value of its nation's currency?
10) True or false? Even though most central banks conduct foreign exchange interventions in the spot market, there is no reason that forward market interventions would not be equally effective. Take a stand, and support your answer.

ONLINE APPLICATION

Internet URL: http://www.frbsf.org/system/fedsystem/monpol/index.html

Title: **How the Federal Reserve Conducts U.S. Monetary Policy**

Navigation: Begin at the home page of the Federal Reserve Bank of San Francisco (http://www.frbsf.org). Click on "Educational Resources," and under "Publications" click on "U.S. Monetary Policy: An Instruction."

Application: Click on and read the answers to the questions, and answer the following questions:

1) According to the discussion, for which monetary policy instruments does the Federal Open Market Committee (FOMC) establish guidelines? What group of individuals within the Federal Reserve System follows FOMC guidelines in conducting day-to-day U.S. monetary policy operations?
2) Based on the discussion, what Federal Reserve policymakers determine the remaining instruments of monetary policy? Do these policymakers have any say in FOMC deliberations as well?

For Group Study and Analysis: Assign groups of students to explore the conduct of monetary policy in specific sets of nations, perhaps based on geographic location. Have each group explore central bank Web sites available through links available at the home page of the Bank for International Settlements (http://www.bis.org). Convene the class, and have each group report on its findings. Are there similarities within the sets of nations? What types of differences exist?

REFERENCES AND RECOMMENDED READINGS

Bordo, Michael, and Anna Schwartz. "What Has Foreign Exchange Market Intervention Since the Plaza Agreement Accomplished?" *Open Economies Review* 2 (1) (1991): 39–64.

Broaddus, J. Alfred, and Marvin Goodfriend. "Foreign Exchange Operations and the Federal Reserve." Federal Reserve Bank of Richmond *Economic Review* 82 (Winter 1996): 1–19.

Capie, Forrest; Charles Goodhart, Stanley Fischer, and Norbert Schnadt. *The Future of Central Banking: The Tercentenary Symposium of the Bank of England.* Cambridge, U.K.: Cambridge University Press, 1994.

Dominguez, Kathryn, and Jeffrey Frankel. *Does Foreign Exchange Intervention Work?* Washington, D.C.: Institute for International Economics, 1993.

Giuseppi, John. *The Bank of England: A History from Its Foundation in 1694.* London: Evans Brothers Ltd., 1966.

Goodhart, Charles. *The Evolution of Central Banks.* Cambridge, Mass.: MIT Press, 1988.

Lewis, Karen. "Are Foreign Exchange Intervention and Monetary Policy Related, and Does It Matter?" *Journal of Business* 68 (1995):185–214.

Schwartz, Anna. "From Obscurity to Notoriety: A Biography of the Exchange Stabilization Fund." *Journal of Money, Credit, and Banking* 29 (May 1997): 135–153.

Smith, Vera. *The Rationale of Central Banking and the Free Banking Alternative* 1936; Indianapolis: Liberty Press, reprinted in 1990.

UNIT FOUR

Contemporary Global Economic Issues and Policies

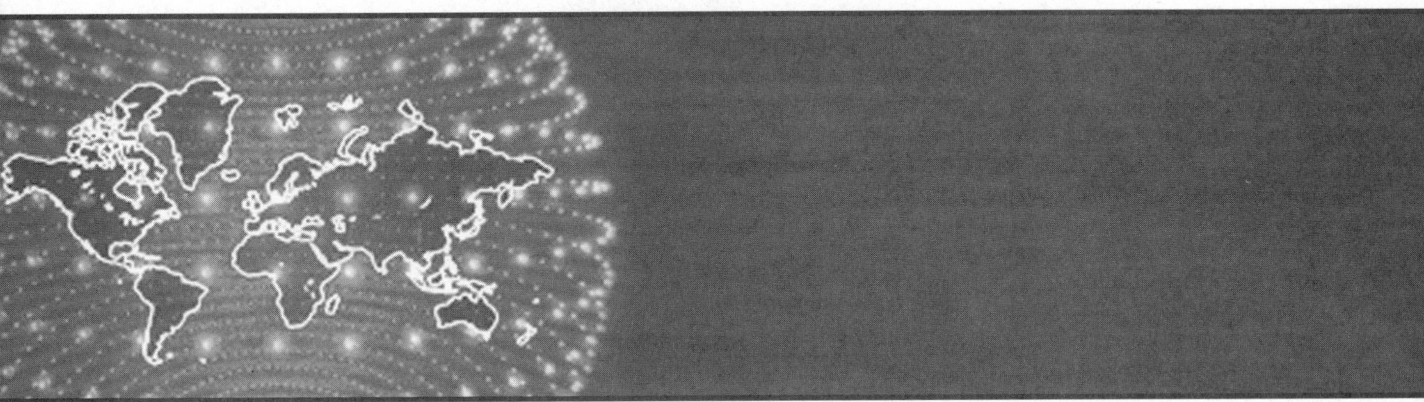

CHAPTER TEN

Can Globalization Lift All Boats?

Fundamental Issues

1. **What factors influence the demand for a nation's labor resources?**
2. **How are market wage rates determined, and how can increased international trade affect the wages earned by a nation's workers?**
3. **What are the implications of the factor proportions approach to international trade for how trade affects workers' earnings?**
4. **Why do labor and capital resources often flow across national borders?**
5. **How does greater openness to international trade affect wages and economic growth in developing nations?**
6. **What are the pros and cons of increased capital flows to developing nations?**

Traditionally, a linguistics degree has been among the least marketable of academic credentials. Because linguists have customarily labored to understand the nuances of languages spoken by peoples residing mostly in developing nations, their average earnings are on the low end relative to most professions. Jobs, when they were available—mostly for Ph.D. linguists in U.S. academia—typically paid at most a little over $35,000 per year.

How times have changed. In recent years, dozens of technology startups have begun commercializing linguistics research. Suddenly, many linguists have their pick of jobs as "lexicographers," "vocabulary engineers," and "vocabulary resource managers." For linguists with doctoral degrees, starting salaries now average around $60,000 (not including stock options). For those with more training and experience, annual salaries often exceed $100,000.

Two factors have accounted for this upsurge in the demand for linguists. First, linguistics experts help businesses improve their electronic commerce efforts by building so-called natural-language processing systems that can respond to typed requests for information transmitted over the Internet. Using databases that linguists develop, these systems can distinguish among multiple word meanings, relate words by concept, and narrow the scope of a search by asking questions of the site visitor.

In addition, a number of dot-coms, such as America Online, Amazon.com, and eBay.com, have made expanding into developing and emerging economies top business priorities. Thus, having the ability to distinguish between shades of meaning in, say, basic Brazilian Portuguese versus Brazilian Amazon dialects now has a market value that it did not have before.

In 1980, developing nations accounted for just over a tenth of world trade. Today their share of global trade is about one-third. The relationship between trade and development has always been an important topic for policymakers and, naturally, the residents of developing nations. Now it is also a topic of increasing relevance to multinational companies—and for workers who do not possess skills that these companies require to succeed in today's globalized economy. In this chapter, you will learn about a number of issues concerning how international trade affects workers' earnings in both developed and developing nations.

International Trade and Wages

A controversial aspect of international trade is its effect on the earnings accruing to the owners of a nation's factors of production, which you learned in Chapter 3 are resources used to produce goods and services. A fundamental factor of production in every nation is labor. The return that workers earn from providing their labor services is the wage rate that they earn. A longstanding issue is the extent to which international trade affects the overall level of workers' wages and the distribution of wages across different categories of workers.

THE ALLEGED "TRADE THREAT" FROM DEVELOPING NATIONS

For many U.S. workers, the 1990s and early 2000s were a time of higher inflation-adjusted earnings, increased fringe benefits, and (for a time) soaring values of stocks. U.S. residents did not share equally in these gains, however, and some have argued that rising international trade with developing nations is the reason.

Rising U.S. Earnings Inequality

Since the 1970s, the inflation-adjusted pay of male workers among the upper 10 percent from the top of the U.S. income distribution has risen by nearly 10 percent, but the inflation-adjusted compensation received by those 10 percent from the bottom has fallen by more than 20 percent. Female workers 10 percent from the bottom of the U.S. income distribution have done a little better than their male counterparts; their earnings have risen by just under 5 percent. Women in the top 10 percent have done considerably better, however. These high-income women have seen their earnings increase by nearly 30 percent.

Some politicians and union leaders have blamed greater U.S. earnings inequality on international trade. In the early 1970s, they note, only a sixth of U.S. imports of manufactured goods came from emerging economies. Today the proportion is about one-third. There must be a simple line of causation, they claim. Extrapolating from these data, they conclude that to keep from losing his job to foreign workers, the pay of an "average Joe" is falling. The "average Jane," they contend, has barely been holding her own in the face of this same competition from abroad.

Is International Trade the Culprit?

Take a look at Figure 10-1. Panel (a) shows the current shares of U.S. trade with the world's nations. Canada and Mexico are the top U.S. trading partners, followed by Japan, the United Kingdom, Germany, France, the Netherlands, and other developed nations. As you can see, developing and emerging countries other than Mexico currently account for more than one-fourth of U.S. trade. Together with Mexico, developing and emerging nations as a whole account for about 40 percent of U.S. exports and imports.

Panel (b) indicates that in recent decades there has been an increase in the share of products that U.S. residents buy from developing nations. Panel (b) also shows that the wages of manufacturing workers residing in other nations, including developing and emerging countries, have increased relative to the earnings of U.S. manufacturing workers.

One interpretation of the data displayed in Figure 10-1 is that some politicians and union leaders are correct: By purchasing more goods from developing and emerging nations, U.S. consumers end up reducing the wages of U.S. workers relative to low-wage workers in those countries. Thus, goes the argument, U.S. workers are losing out from freer trade, and the United States should put up barriers against imports from developing and emerging nations.

As you learned in earlier chapters, however, the story is not nearly this simple. The whole point of free trade is that it induces nations to specialize in producing goods for which they have a comparative advantage. Thus, when trade barriers are removed—as many of them were in the United States during the 1970s and 1980s—resources naturally shift into those industries. Resources shift away from industries producing goods for which a nation, such as the United States, does not have a comparative advantage.

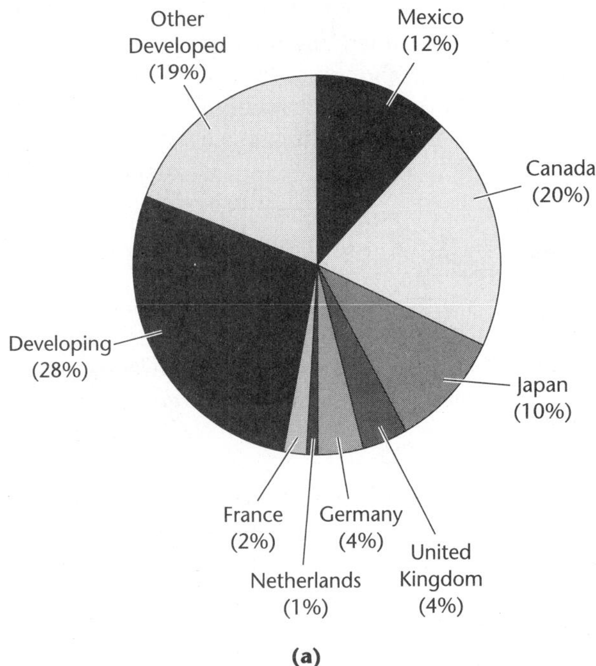

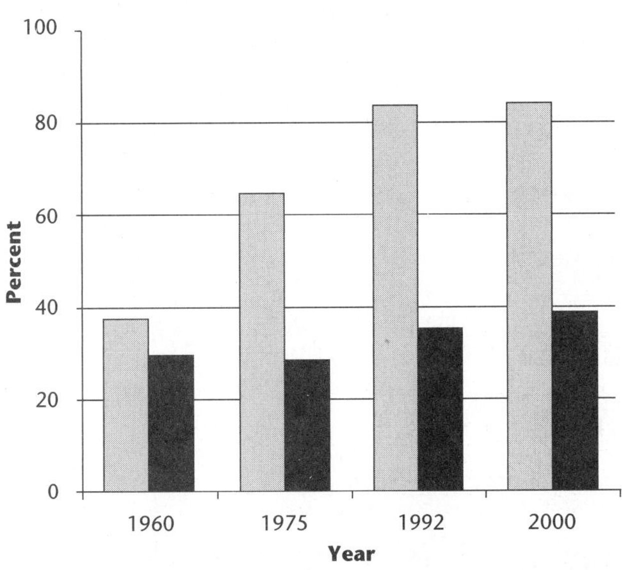

Figure 10-1

Shares of U.S. Trade and Wages of Manufacturing Workers as a Percentage of Wages of U.S. Manufacturing Workers

Panel (a) displays shares of U.S. trade for major trading partners of the United States. Panel (b) shows that in recent years wages earned by workers in manufacturing industries in nations that trade with the United States have increased relative to wages of U.S. manufacturing workers, and at the same time U.S. trade with developing nations has increased.

Sources: International Monetary Fund, *Direction of Trade Statistics* and U.S. Department of Commerce.

How does international trade affect the market wages earned by workers in the United States, or, for that matter, any nation? Does international trade really have anything to do with the changing distribution of earnings in the United States? How does it affect wages and distributions of earnings in other countries, including developing and emerging nations? Let's try to answer each of these questions in turn.

WAGES AND INTERNATIONAL TRADE

Before contemplating how international trade affects wages, it is helpful to take a look at the extent to which wages differ across countries. In addition, a prerequisite to evaluating the effects of international trade on wage patterns is developing a framework for understanding the fundamental determinants of wage rates.

International Wage Differences

Figure 10-2 displays index measures of the hourly rates of compensation that manufacturing companies in selected nations have paid their employees since 1975, where a value of 100 is equivalent to the U.S. hourly manufacturing compensation rate. The U.S. Bureau of Labor Statistics tabulates these indexes, which take into account pay for time worked, other indirect pay such as bonuses and holiday and vacation compensation, benefits, and labor taxes imposed on companies.

To develop the indexes in Figure 10-2, government statisticians calculate local hourly compensation levels in terms of local currencies. For purposes of compari-

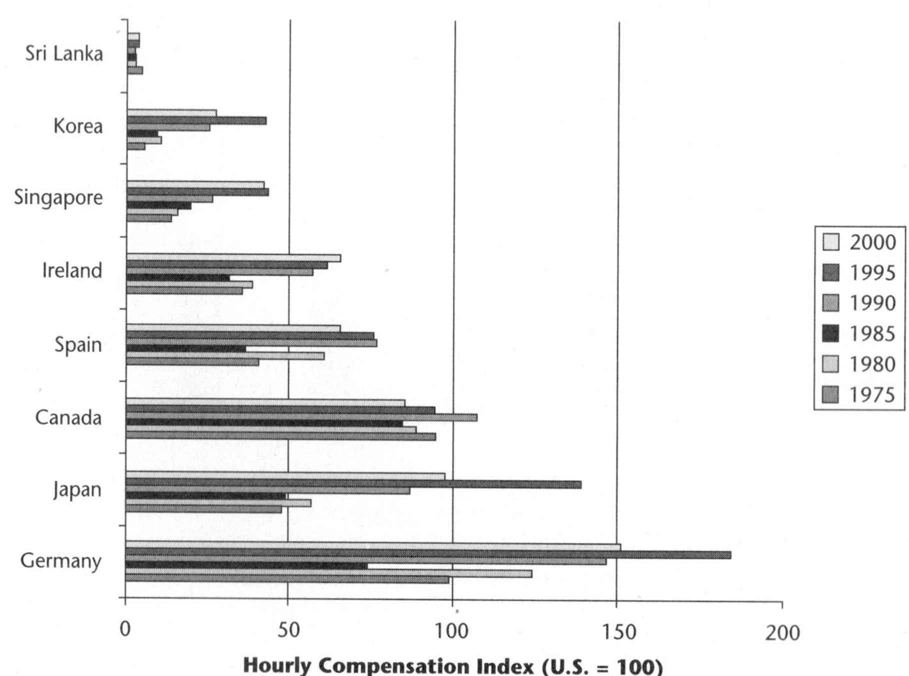

Figure 10-2

Indexes of Hourly Compensation Costs in Manufacturing for Selected Nations

This figure shows index measures of the hourly rates of compensation at manufacturers, where a value of 100 is equivalent to the U.S. hourly manufacturing compensation rate. These measures do not take into account price differences across nations, but they indicate significant differences in labor compensation, nonetheless.

Sources: U.S. Bureau of Labor Statistics.

son to U.S. compensation levels, the statisticians then convert the compensation levels into U.S. dollar amounts using prevailing rates of exchange relative to the dollar. Consequently, these hourly compensation indexes reflect several sources of direct and indirect income that workers receive, and they also take into account changes in the rates at which national currencies exchange.

It is important to recognize that the hourly compensation index values do not take into account price differences across nations. They fail to tell us very much, therefore, about the *purchasing power* of workers' wages. In addition, the indexes only apply to manufacturing workers' compensation. Thus, they are *not* necessarily representative of compensation levels of all workers in the indicated nations relative to all workers in the United States.

Nevertheless, the hourly compensation indexes displayed in Figure 10-2 clearly indicate that there have been large differences in hourly wages and benefits paid to manufacturing workers in the indicated nations. Perhaps not surprisingly, Canadian manufacturing workers have earned compensation levels very close to those of workers in U.S. manufacturing. German manufacturing workers' compensation levels have often exceeded U.S. levels in recent years. The hourly compensation of manufacturing workers in the other countries, and in particular Sri Lanka, has remained well below the compensation received by U.S. manufacturing workers.

Figure 10-2 has two other interesting implications. First, there has been persistence in the compensation differences for the selected countries. Workers' earnings in Sri Lanka have lagged well behind the levels received by workers in Korea and Singapore, whose earnings have consistently trailed the earnings of workers in Ireland and Spain. Workers in these last two countries, in turn, have tended to receive lower hourly rates of compensation than those of Canadian and German workers.

Second, since 1990 manufacturing workers in all seven nations, and especially in Japan, have earned noticeable higher hourly rates of compensation relative to the U.S. level. From the perspective of these countries, their manufacturing workers are catching up with U.S. workers. From the perspective of the United States, of course, this implies that as compared with past years, U.S. manufacturing workers are earning lower rates of compensation relative to workers residing in other nations.

See the latest international wage comparisons at the Web site of the Bureau of Labor Statistics at http://stats.bls.gov.

The Marginal Revenue Product of Labor

It is a challenge to explain why compensation differences among nations might change even as broad compensation patterns persist. It is likewise difficult to determine what role, if any, that international trade plays in influencing the compensation that workers receive for their labor.

The main type of compensation is wage payments. Wages are determined in markets for labor. Economists can measure units of labor in one of three ways. One is in terms of hours worked by a given number of people. The second is to measure the number of people employed. The third is to measure units of labor as a combination of the other two measures that economists call "person-hours."

Suppose that you are a manager of a company—say, a firm that provides online travel services—that is considering how many units of labor (hours, people, or person-hours) to hire. All of the company's other factors of production—land, capital, entrepreneurship, and the like—are fixed. In addition, suppose that your company's goal is to maximize its profits. If you think about this situation for a while, you will probably come up with a fundamental question that you must answer in order to decide how many units of labor to employ: How much revenue will be generated by each unit of labor that the company might hire, and how much will hiring each unit of labor affect the company's overall costs of production? Answering this question, after all, will determine the effect that your hiring decision will have on the company's profits.

Marginal revenue product of labor
The additional revenue generated by employing an additional unit of labor; also equal to marginal revenue times the marginal product of labor.

Marginal product of labor
The additional output generated by employing the next unit of labor.

Economists call the increase in revenue generated from hiring an additional unit of labor the **marginal revenue product of labor.** Table 10-1 illustrates how economists calculate the marginal revenue product of labor. If you were the manager of the fictitious U.S. company facing the situation illustrated in the table, then reading across the second row of the table indicates that hiring the first unit of labor (column 1) would yield ten units of output of services (column 2). Here, we define a unit of output as the sale of a standard travel package. This would also be the first labor unit's **marginal product of labor,** or the additional output produced by that additional unit of labor (column 3).

Marginal revenue
The additional revenue a firm earns from selling an additional unit of output.

If the company can sell each unit of its output at a price of $50 per unit (column 4), then the total revenues forthcoming from selling ten units of output are $500 (column 5). We assume that every company's product is perfectly substitutable with those of others, and that each company's output is sufficiently small relative to total industry production so that no one company can influence the product price. Because each unit sells for the same price, the company's **marginal revenue**—the addition to total revenues from selling an additional unit of output—is $50 per unit (column 6). Finally, the marginal revenue product of labor (column 7) is the additional revenue generated by hiring the first unit of labor. In column 5, total revenues rose from $0 to $500, so the marginal revenue product of the first unit of labor is $500 per unit of labor. In addition, however, we can calculate the marginal revenue product in column 7 by multiplying marginal product (column 3) by marginal revenue (column 6). For the first unit of labor, this entails multiplying ten units of output per unit of labor times $50 per unit of output, which yields $500 per unit of labor shown in column 7. This, again, is the marginal revenue product of labor. Hence, we can always calculate the marginal revenue product of labor by multiplying a company's marginal product of labor by its marginal revenue.

Law of diminishing marginal returns
An economic law stating that when more and more units of a factor of production such as labor are added to fixed amounts of other productive factors, the additional output for each new unit employed eventually declines.

The remaining rows of Table 10-1 provide analogous calculations for the second, third, fourth, fifth, and sixth units of labor that your company might hire. Note that column 2 indicates that as the company hires each additional unit of labor, its output naturally increases. As column 3 shows, however, the *additional* output per unit of labor hired *declines.* Thus, the marginal product of labor falls as the company hires more workers. This is consistent with a general rule that economists call the **law of diminishing marginal returns:** When more and more

Table 10-1 Calculating the Marginal Revenue Product of Labor

Quantity of Labor (1)	Output (2)	Marginal Product (3)	Product Price (4)	Total Revenues (5)	Marginal Revenue (6)	Marginal Revenue Product (7)
0	0	—	$50	$0	—	—
1	10	10	$50	$500	$50	$500
2	19	9	$50	$950	$50	$450
3	27	8	$50	$1,350	$50	$400
4	34	7	$50	$1,700	$50	$350
5	40	6	$50	$2,000	$50	$300
6	45	5	$50	$2,250	$50	$250

units of a factor of production such as labor are added to fixed amounts of other productive factors, the additional output for each new unit employed eventually tends to decline. In our example, marginal product rises from zero units of output per unit of labor to ten units of output per unit of labor in column 3. Then the marginal product of labor declines immediately if the company employs additional workers.

Because the product price is the same for each unit of output that the company sells ($50 per unit in column 4) no matter how many units it sells, its marginal revenue is equal to that same amount per unit (column 6). By definition, marginal revenue product is marginal product multiplied by marginal revenue. Marginal revenue is the same no matter how many workers the company hires, but the marginal product of labor declines as the company hires more workers. Consequently, the company's marginal revenue product of labor declines as it hires more workers.

The Derived Demand for Labor

Now let's think about the management decision you must make: You must decide how many units of labor to hire. Now you know how your hiring decision will affect your company's revenues. To make your decision, you must also know the wage rate that you must pay to hire each unit of labor.

Let's suppose that units of labor are measured as one week of work by each individual you might hire. In addition, let's suppose that the prevailing wage rate paid by all other companies in your industry is $400 per week. Now take a look back at Table 10-1. You might consider hiring four individuals at this wage rate, but the problem is that the fourth person you would hire would only generate an additional $350 in revenues for the company (see the fifth line of column 7). This means that the fourth worker hired would generate a net *loss* of $50, meaning that hiring the fourth worker would reduce your company's profits by $50.

You might, therefore, contemplate hiring only two workers. The second worker would generate $450 additional revenues for your company each week (the fourth line of column 7), and the company would expend only $400 in weekly wages. Thus, it would definitely make sense to hire the second worker, because the company's profits would be increased by $50.

Hence, the company's profits increase with additional hiring, and it makes sense to consider hiring *one more worker beyond the second worker.* Employing a third worker generates $400 in additional revenues (the fifth line of column 7), which just covers the $400 wage expense that the company incurs. At the point where the company hires the third worker, therefore, it has exhausted all possibilities for adding to its profit. This means that hiring the third worker maximizes the company's profits. Thus, we reach the following conclusion:

A profit-maximizing firm hires workers up to the point where the marginal product of labor is equal to the wage rate that it pays the next worker hired.

Suppose that you were just about to offer positions to the first three workers, but then you learn from another manager that the wage rate paid by other companies in your industry has risen to $450 per week. The marginal revenue product of the third worker you would have hired is still only $400, so now you must reconsider your decision. Hiring the third worker would entail losing $50 in profits on net. Indeed, the potential for adding to the company's profits are now used up when you hire the second worker, whose marginal revenue product of $450 per week just covers the $450 weekly wage payment.

A rise in the wage rate that a company must pay to attract workers induces the company to reduce its employment of labor. It decides how much to cut back on hiring by equalizing the new, higher wage with the marginal revenue product of labor. Thus, a company's marginal revenue product is its guide to determining how many workers to hire—that is, it determines the company's demand for labor.

As Table 10-1 indicates, a company's marginal revenue product of labor depends on its marginal product of labor and on the price at which it sells its product. The price of its product, in turn, depends on conditions in the marketplace for the good or service that it sells. For this reason, economists say that a company's demand for labor is *derived* from conditions in the market for its product. Hence, labor demand is a derived demand. (It also follows that a graph of the company's marginal revenue product at each quantity of labor must be its labor demand curve; see *Visualizing Global Economic Issues: The Labor Demand Curve.*)

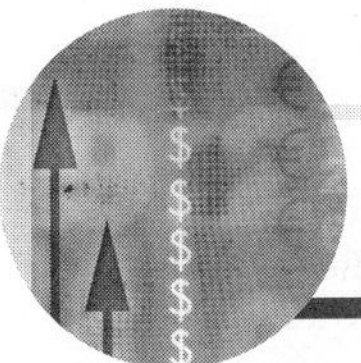

Visualizing Global Economic Issues

The Labor Demand Curve

We can use a graph to examine a company's demand for labor by graphing the U.S. online travel service company's marginal revenue product at each quantity of labor that it might hire. Figure 10-3 displays the marginal revenue product corresponding to each possible quantity of labor tabulated in Table 10-1. The resulting downward-sloping schedule is the *marginal revenue product curve* for this fictitious company.

As you can see, when the wage rate paid by this company is $400, we can read down from the marginal revenue product curve to see that the profit-maximizing quantity of labor hired by the company is three workers. If the wage rate rises to $450, the company maximizes profits by reducing employment to two workers. Hence, the rise in the wage rate results in an upward movement along the marginal revenue product schedule and a decline in the quantity of labor demanded by the company. This means that the marginal revenue product curve is also the company's *labor demand curve* that depicts the amount of labor hired at any given wage rate.

For Critical Analysis:
A change in the wage rate results in a movement along a company's labor demand curve. What would happen if an improvement in technology were to raise the marginal product of labor at every given quantity of labor that the company might hire?

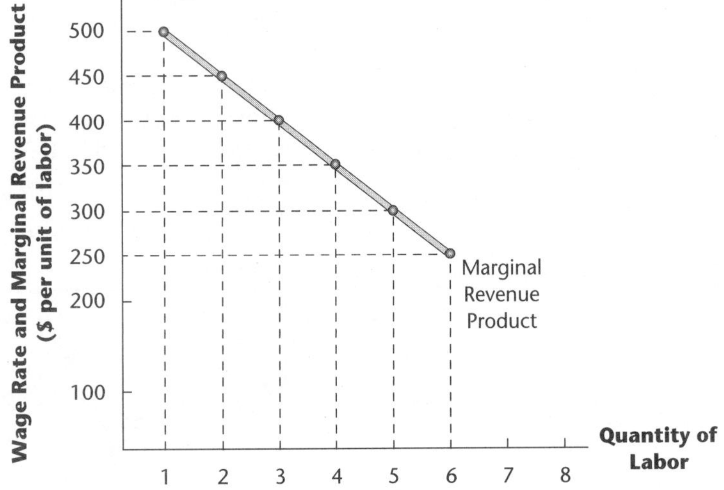

Figure 10-3

The Labor Demand Curve

Plotting the marginal revenue product values in Table 10-1 yields a downward-sloping marginal revenue product curve. As the wage rate increases, a profit-maximizing firm reduces employment to the point where the new wage equals a higher marginal revenue product, which induces the firm to cut back on employment of labor. Consequently, the marginal revenue product curve is the firm's labor demand curve.

What factors influence the demand for a nation's labor resources?

A profit-maximizing firm hires labor to the point at which the marginal revenue product of labor, the additional revenues generated by hiring the next unit of labor, equals the wage rate. The marginal revenue product of labor equals marginal revenue (the additional revenue earned from selling an additional unit of output) times the marginal product of labor (the additional output that an additional unit of labor can produce). Hence, both the product price and the marginal product of labor determine the quantity of labor that companies wish to hire within a nation's labor market. In addition, so do wage levels in that country.

The Market Wage Rate

Market wage rate
The wage rate at which the quantity of labor supplied by all workers in a labor market is equal to the total quantity of labor demanded by firms in that market.

The wage rate is the price that companies must pay to hire labor to produce goods and services. It is also the price that sellers of labor—in this case, U.S. workers such as those employed by the U.S. online travel service operator—receive when they supply their labor services. The **market wage rate** is the wage rate at which workers are willing to supply the total amount of labor that all companies wish to hire at that particular wage. Hence, at the market wage rate, the quantity of labor supplied by all workers equals the quantity of labor demanded by all companies in the market for labor.

Table 10-2 illustrates the determination of the market wage rate. The first column of the table displays various possible weekly wages. The second column gives the total quantity of labor demanded by all firms in the market at each wage rate. Each of these quantities is simply the sum of the quantity of labor demanded by all companies, including the fictitious online travel service operator we just examined. The third column of Table 10-2 tabulates the quantity of labor that all workers in the market are willing and able to supply at each possible wage rate.

Suppose that initially the wage rate is equal to $450 per week. As you saw in Table 10-1, at this wage rate the U.S. online travel service operator is willing to

Table 10-2 Determining the Market Wage Rate

Weekly Wage Rate	Quantity of Labor Demanded by Firms	Quantity of Labor Supplied by Workers
$550	4,000	13,000
$500	6,000	12,000
$450	8,000	11,000
$400	**10,000**	**10,000**
$350	12,000	9,000
$300	14,000	8,000
$250	16,000	7,000

hire two workers. Table 10-2 indicates that this company and others together are willing to hire 8,000 workers. There are 11,000 people, however, who are willing to work at this weekly wage. Thus, 3,000 people are unemployed at this wage. To obtain employment, some of these people will offer to work for a lower wage, so the wage rate will begin to decline toward $400. At this wage rate, the quantity of labor by all firms in the market demanded equals the quantity of labor supplied by all workers. Hence, $400 per week is the market wage rate.

Now let's think about what will happen if there is a decrease in the price of products sold by companies that hire these workers. Recall that the marginal revenue product is equal to marginal product times marginal revenue. In the case of the online travel service operator, marginal revenue is always equal to the price of the standard travel package it sells. If this price falls below the initial level of $50 (see Table 10-1 on page 303), then marginal revenue product will decrease at every given quantity of labor that the company might hire. Thus, the company's demand for labor will decline; it will now desire to hire fewer workers at any given weekly wage rate. This would be true for all companies in the marketplace as well, following a decrease in the price of the products that they sell.

Table 10-3 illustrates the effect that a fall in the product price has on the market wage rate. As compared with the second column of Table 10-2, in the second column of Table 10-3 you can see that following the price decrease all companies now wish to hire 3,000 fewer workers *at any given wage rate* than they did before. At the previous equilibrium weekly wage rate of $400, therefore, companies will desire to reduce their employment of labor by 3,000 workers. Many workers, however, will choose to work for a lower weekly wage rather than lose their jobs. As a result, the wage rate will begin to fall in the marketplace, toward a new market wage rate of $350 per hour, at which the total quantity of labor demanded by

Table 10-3 Determining the Market Wage Rate

Weekly Wage Rate	Quantity of Labor Demanded by Firms	Quantity of Labor Supplied by Workers
$550	1,000	13,000
$500	3,000	12,000
$450	5,000	11,000
$400	7,000	10,000
$350	**9,000**	**9,000**
$300	11,000	8,000
$250	13,000	7,000

firms and supplied by workers equals 9,000. Hence, the fall in the price of companies' products causes both a decline in the market wage rate and a decrease in the total quantity of labor employed.

What might cause a decline in the product price received by companies, such as the U.S. online travel service operator, that hire workers in this market for labor? There are several possibilities. Consumers of travel services and related products may have reduced the quantities that they purchase at any price, and this decline in the demand for companies' products may thereby have induced the decline in the price of these products. Alternatively, there may have been an increase in the supply of these products that brought about the price reduction. For instance, new online travel service companies might have entered the market for these products.

Some of these online travel service operators might be based in countries outside the United States. Naturally, U.S. travelers who purchase the services provided by such foreign travel firms import these services. Other things being equal, we can conclude that by importing the services of foreign online travel service companies, U.S. consumers contribute to a fall in the price of travel services. This price decline, in turn, brings about a decline in the demand for labor services provided by U.S. workers. As a result, both the market wage rate paid to workers and the number of workers employed in this U.S. labor market decline. In this way, increased openness to international trade can bring about reduced U.S. wages and lower U.S. employment. (To see a graphical depiction of how these effects take place, see on pages 309–310 *Visualizing Global Economic Issues: The Wage and Employment Effects of Increased Competition from Abroad.*)

The Complicated Relationship between International Trade and Market Wages

In the example we just considered, increased international trade led to lower U.S. wages and employment. The reason was that trade took the form of imports that led U.S. residents to substitute away from U.S.-produced products in favor of products from abroad. The resulting decline in the product price reduced the marginal revenue product of labor, causing U.S. companies to reduce their demand for labor.

Of course, greater openness to international trade can also induce more U.S. companies to export goods and services abroad. As more domestic firms enter foreign markets, the demand for U.S. workers rises at any given wage rate. This tends to push the market wage *upward* in labor markets in which these firms compete for labor. In addition, employment *rises* in these labor markets.

Consequently, we can conclude that increased international trade must have conflicting overall effects on U.S. wages and employment. If we imagine that all other things are constant, then greater openness to imports tends to depress domestic wages and employment. An increased propensity to export goods and services tends to raise domestic wages and employment, however.

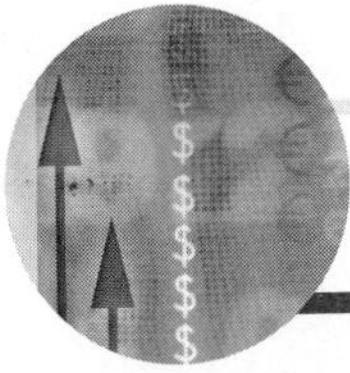

Visualizing Global Economic Issues

The Wage and Employment Effects of Increased Competition from Abroad

In the example illustrated in Tables 10-2 and 10-3, increased competition from foreign travel service companies caused a decline in the wage and employment of U.S. workers. To see these effects graphically, take a look at Figure 10-4. Panel (a) displays the demand for and supply of domestically provided travel services. The initial price earned by domestic travel service operators is a $50 fee charged for each standard travel package they sell. Panel (b) shows the domestic demand for travel services offered by foreign-based suppliers and the supply of services by these companies, which initially cross at the same $50 price. Finally, panel (c) displays the U.S. market for labor used in the production and sale of U.S. travel services. At the initial product price of $50, the quantity of labor demanded at each possible wage rate is taken from Table 10-2 on page 306, as is the quantity of labor supplied at each wage rate. Hence, the initial market wage rate is the $400 weekly wage shown in Table 10-2.

If more foreign travel service companies successfully market their products to U.S. consumers, perhaps by establishing online presences the U.S. travelers can access, then the supply of foreign travel services increases in panel (b). This results in a decline in the price of foreign-provided travel services, to $40 per standard travel package. As U.S. travelers who surf the Web for the best travel deals substitute away from services provided by U.S. travel service companies, the demand for domestically provided travel services declines, as shown in panel (b). Hence, the U.S. price of a standard travel package also declines to $40.

As noted earlier, the fall in product price reduces the marginal revenue product of labor for U.S. companies at any given weekly wage. Thus, these companies' total demand for labor declines, as depicted in panel (c). The result is a fall in the market wage rate, from $400 to $350, and a reduction in employment in this U.S. labor market, from 10,000 workers to 9,000 workers. Thus, increased international trade in travel services can reduce wages and employment among workers in the U.S. travel service industry.

For Critical Analysis:
If the U.S. workers who lose their jobs with online travel service companies are successful in offering their services to online retail companies located in the United States, what is likely to happen to the wages of workers in that industry? What is likely to happen to total employment in this online retail industry?

continued

continued from page 310

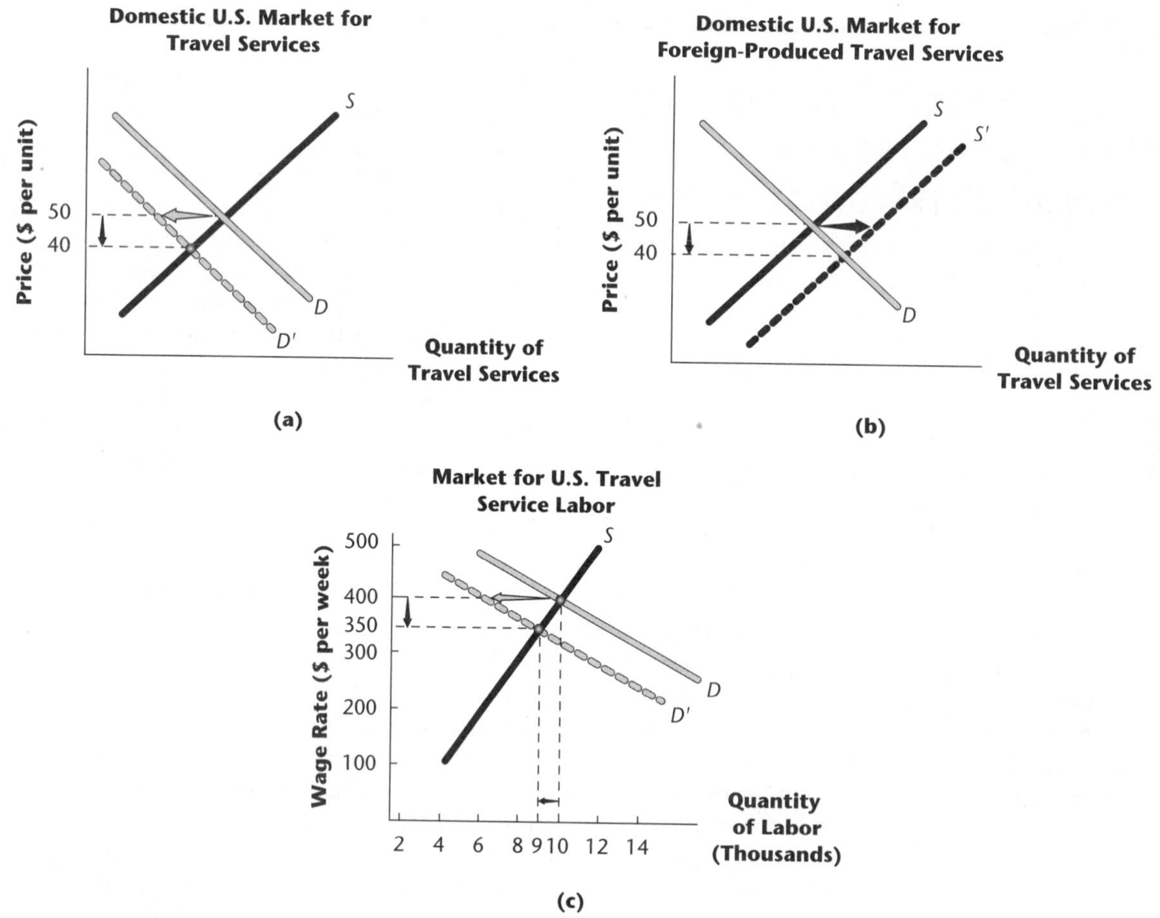

Domestic U.S. Market for Travel Services

Price ($ per unit)

50

40

S

D

D'

Quantity of Travel Services

(a)

Domestic U.S. Market for Foreign-Produced Travel Services

Price ($ per unit)

50

40

S

S'

D

Quantity of Travel Services

(b)

Market for U.S. Travel Service Labor

Wage Rate ($ per week)

500

400

350

300

200

100

S

D

D'

2 4 6 8 9 10 12 14

Quantity of Labor (Thousands)

(c)

Figure 10-4

The Labor-Market Effects of a Decline in Product Price Induced by Increased International Trade

When more foreign travel service companies successfully enter the domestic U.S. market for travel services, there is an increase in the supply of foreign travel services, as shown in panel (b). The price of foreign-provided travel services declines from $50 to $40, so in panel (a), U.S. travelers substitute away from services provided by U.S. travel service companies, and the demand for domestically provided travel services declines. As a result, there is a fall in the U.S. price of a standard travel package, from $50 to $40, so that in panel (c) the marginal revenue product of labor declines at U.S. companies, which implies a fall in the demand for labor in the United States. The U.S. domestic market wage falls to $350 from $400, and employment in the U.S. labor market falls from 10,000 workers to 9,000 workers. Hence, increased international trade in travel services causes a decline in wages and employment in the U.S. travel service industry.

How are market wage rates determined, and how can increased international trade affect the wages earned by a nation's workers?

Fundamental Issue 2

At the market wage rate, companies are willing to hire all the workers who are willing and able to work at that wage rate. On the one hand, increased openness to foreign imports reduces the product price earned by domestic firms, so the domestic marginal revenue product of labor declines. This results in a reduction in these companies' total demand for labor, which causes the market wage and employment at these firms to fall. On the other hand, when exports of domestic companies rise, the total demand for labor by these firms increases, which pushes up wages and employment at these companies. On net, therefore, if quantities of other factors of production are unchanged, increased international trade can either raise or reduce average wages and employment levels within a country.

Labor and Capital Mobility

The "other-things-are-constant" assumption plays an important role in leading to the conclusion that importing goods and services tends to depress wages and employment in affected industries while industries that export goods and services tend to experience higher wages and employment. All other things are not really constant, however. The extent to which labor is mobile, both within a country's borders and across its borders, also affects the wage and employment effects of increased international trade. In addition, the United States is a big country, so adjustments in its product and labor markets can spill back into world markets. Finally, flows of other factors of production, particularly capital, also affect conditions in national labor markets.

LABOR MOBILITY WITHIN NATIONS, INTERNATIONAL TRADE, AND THE DISTRIBUTION OF EARNINGS

Let's consider a situation in which labor does not move across national borders but is completely mobile among industries within national borders. Nevertheless, for now we shall abstract from spillover effects caused by the large size of the United States. Initially, we shall also assume that factors of production other than labor, including capital, are fixed within each nation that engages in trade.

Factor Proportions and Trade

Suppose that producers located in two countries, the United States and China, produce two products: computer software and toys. Each country's producers have access to the same technologies for producing these goods, and companies in both nations require two key factors of production to produce the goods: skilled labor and unskilled labor. Because we assume that within each country both types of labor are perfectly mobile between the computer software and toy industries, both industries within each country compete in the same marketplaces for skilled and unskilled workers. In each nation, therefore, market wages earned by skilled workers are the same in both industries, and wages earned by unskilled workers are the same in both industries.

Furthermore, we assume that in both nations the market wage of skilled workers is higher than the market wage of unskilled workers. In addition, we suppose that in the absence of trade, U.S. skilled workers earn a higher market wage than Chinese skilled workers. U.S. unskilled workers also earn a higher market wage than Chinese unskilled workers.

We also suppose that relative product demands are the same in both countries. That is, residents of both the United States and China desire to consume computer software in the same proportion to their consumption of toys.

In both nations the best available technology requires using relatively more skilled labor than unskilled labor to produce computer software as compared with producing toys. Producing toys requires relatively more unskilled labor than skilled labor. Thus, the production of computer software is relatively *skilled-labor-intensive* relative to toy production. This is equivalent to saying that toy production is relatively *unskilled-labor-intensive* relative to the production of computer software.

There are many more workers in China than there are in the United States. This difference between the two nations is not important to the economic argument that follows, however. The crucial respect in which the two nations differ is that relative to China, a higher proportion of U.S. workers are skilled workers. Consequently, *factor proportions,* which you learned in Chapter 3 are the ratios of quantities of available factors of production, differ in the two nations. What this immediately implies is that the ratio of skilled workers to unskilled workers is higher in the United States, while the ratio of unskilled workers to skilled workers is higher in China. Given the conditions we have imposed on the situation both countries face, this means that the United States has a comparative advantage in producing skilled-labor-intensive computer software. China, by way of contrast, has a comparative advantage in producing unskilled-labor-intensive toys.

Thus, in this situation the United States gains by exporting to China the good in which it has a relative abundance of the factor of production, skilled labor, that must be used more intensively, which is computer software. China gains by exporting toys to the United States, because it has a relative abundance of the unskilled labor required more intensively in the production of toys.

Factor Proportions and Wages of the Skilled and Unskilled

Now let's contemplate how opening U.S. and Chinese borders to this flow of trade is likely to affect the wages earned by workers in both nations. As you learned earlier, when U.S. residents import more of a good such as toys, the domestic market price of toys declines. This reduces the marginal revenue product of labor at U.S. toy companies, and toy producers' demand for labor—most of which is unskilled labor—declines. At the same time, when U.S. companies export more of a good such as computer software, their demand for labor increases. In our example, most of the increased labor demand in the U.S. computer software industry is for skilled workers. Thus, the predominant effects within the United States following the opening of a trade flow with China are a net decline in the demand for unskilled U.S. workers and a net increase in the demand for skilled U.S. workers.

By way of contrast, in China higher imports of U.S.-manufactured computer software reduce the price of computer software in China, which causes the marginal revenue product of labor at Chinese software companies to decline. Thus, there is a fall in the demand for labor—most of which is skilled labor—on the part of Chinese software companies. Chinese toy producers' demand for labor rises, however. Most of this increase in labor demand is for unskilled workers. Hence, the main effects in China after it engages in trade with the United States are a net decline in the demand for skilled Chinese workers and a net increase in the demand for unskilled Chinese workers.

This reasoning leads to three important conclusions that we can draw from a situation in which countries have different factor proportions for skilled and unskilled labor:

1) **International trade will tend to cause the relative wages of U.S. and Chinese workers possessing similar skills to converge.** Because skilled labor is relatively more abundant in the United States as compared with China, before trade between the two countries took place the wages of skilled workers in the United States would have been relatively closer to those of unskilled workers. In contrast, in China, where skilled workers are relatively less abundant, the differential between the wage rate for skilled workers and the wage rate for unskilled workers initially would have been relatively higher. Hence, the market wage of skilled workers *relative* to the market wage of unskilled workers would have been lower in the United States than in China before the two nations began to engage in trade.

   After trade begins, however, there is a net increase in the demand for skilled workers in the United States and a net decrease in the demand for skilled workers in China. At the same time, the advent of trade brings about a net decline in the demand for unskilled workers in the United States and a net increase in the demand for unskilled workers in China. As a result, the market wage earned by skilled U.S. workers will begin to rise relative to the market wage earned by unskilled U.S. workers, and the market wage earned by skilled Chinese workers will start to fall relative to the market wage earned by unskilled Chinese workers. Hence, opening up trade between the nations causes a tendency toward cross-country convergence of the wages of skilled workers relative to unskilled workers.

2) **From the perspective of unskilled workers in China, trade with the United States helps them to "gain ground" relative to skilled Chinese workers.** Exporting toys to the United States and importing U.S.-produced computer software raises the wages of unskilled Chinese workers relative to skilled Chinese workers. Consequently, in China the distribution of earnings among unskilled and skilled workers will tend to even out somewhat after trade with the United States commences.

3) **From the perspective of unskilled workers in the United States, trade with China causes them to "lose ground" relative to skilled U.S. workers.** Exporting computer software to China and importing Chinese-manufactured toys raises the wages of skilled U.S. workers relative to unskilled U.S. workers. In the United States, therefore, the differential between the earnings of skilled workers and unskilled workers will tend to widen following the opening of the two nations' borders to trade.

It is important to keep in mind that these conclusions do not mean that either the United States or China loses, on net, from trade. Because the United States has a comparative advantage in computer software production while China has a comparative advantage in producing toys, both countries experience overall gains from trade. Nevertheless, relative wages earned by skilled and unskilled workers change *within* both countries. As a result, the distribution of earnings must adjust in each nation. It is only in a *relative* sense that workers in each country might feel that they have "gained" or "lost" ground. Nevertheless, skilled Chinese workers will rightfully conclude that they do not gain as much as unskilled workers from trade with the United States. Unskilled workers in the United States also will correctly determine that they have not benefited as much as skilled U.S. workers have from trade with China. (Sometimes, however, governments feel obliged to require unemployed domestic workers to compete with unskilled workers abroad; see *Policy Notebook: How Much Training Do People Really Need to Pick Asparagus in Germany?*)

Taking into Account "Big-Country" Spillover Effects

Throughout our discussion of how differing factor proportions can influence the effects that international trade has on wages, we maintained the reasonable assumption that workers are immobile between China and the United States. In addition, however, we have assumed that neither China nor the United States is sufficiently large that changes in its wage structure can affect the relative prices of both skilled-labor-intensive goods (such as computer software) and unskilled-labor-intensive goods (such as toys). This means we have assumed that the relative demands for both goods in the United States and China are unaffected by changing wages in the two countries.

This, it turns out, is probably not a realistic assumption. U.S. residents make more than one-fourth of the world's total expenditures on output. A change in the U.S. wage structure can affect total U.S. spending and thereby alter the relative mix of spending on both types of products. This, in turn, feeds back to influence the wage structures in the two countries. James Harrigan, a staff economist at the Federal Reserve's Board of Governors, has found evidence that this feedback effect is sufficiently important that the net effect of increased U.S. trade with China and other nations on the U.S. earnings distribution has been very small.

Explaining the Changing U.S. Earnings Distribution

As shown in Figure 10-5 on page 316, however, the ratio of U.S. college graduates' average wage to the average wage of U.S. high school graduates has increased

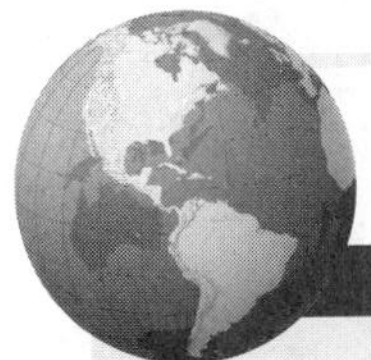

POLICY *Notebook*

POLICY MANAGEMENT

How Much Training Do People Really Need to Pick Asparagus in Germany?

Asparagus is a popular vegetable in Germany; nearly every restaurant features a special asparagus menu including such items as asparagus sandwiches, asparagus with schnitzel, and asparagus-filled tortelloni. The average German household consumes nearly 5 pounds of asparagus each year.

A Source of Extra Income for Poles

German farmers hire many foreign workers to pick asparagus from their fields. Each year, about 25,000 residents of neighboring Poland take "vacations" from their regular jobs and travel to Germany to pick asparagus. The reason is that many Poles can earn higher wages picking asparagus than they can in their regular jobs.

For instance, truck drivers who make just over the equivalent of $200 per month in Poland can earn more than four times as much picking asparagus in Germany. A number of the Polish residents who make the trek across the border during asparagus season are schoolteachers who earn much lower wages writing on chalkboards in Poland than they can earn by using calloused hands to break the thick stalks of German asparagus plants.

Training Germans to Pick Asparagus

Even as the annual asparagus parades wound their way through the streets of Berlin year after year during the 1990s, the unemployment rate in Germany exceeded double digits. The nationwide German unemployment rate continues to hover close to 10 percent, and in eastern Germany it is nearly 18 percent. Nevertheless, unemployed German workers spurned work picking asparagus, because earnings from picking asparagus amounted to little more than their government unemployment checks—hardly enough to compensate for sore backs and calloused hands.

Since 1998, however, the German government established a new quota: at most, 85 percent of asparagus pickers can be foreign residents. It also ordered some unemployed German workers to seek jobs as asparagus pickers or face losing a portion of their regular unemployment compensation.

By 2000, these policies had spawned a new industry. Government-supported temporary agricultural-help agencies set up fast-track seminars in the art of asparagus picking all over Germany. In these seminars, trainees learn how to loosen the soil around asparagus stalks that have just poked through the soil, how to plunge a special shoehorn-shaped hoe into the dirt, and how to clip the asparagus stalk at its base. Many trainees, however, admit that they hope to fail the course.

For Critical Analysis:
How might the factor proportions approach be modified to account for differences in the extent to which nations' governments provide unemployment compensation to domestic workers?

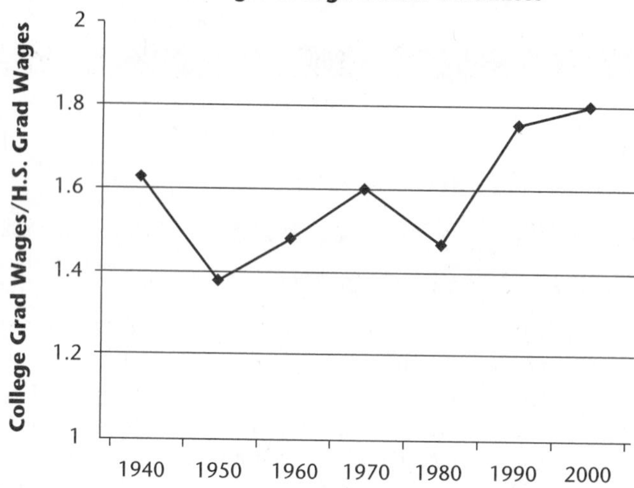

Figure 10-5

The Ratio of the Average Wage of U.S. College Graduates to the Average Wage of U.S. High School Graduates

The ratio of college graduates' average wages to the average wages of high school graduates declines after World War II before rising over the next two decades and then falling off slightly between 1970 and 1980. Since 1980, however, this ratio has risen noticeably.

Source: Lawrence Katz, "Technological Change, Computerization, and the Wage Structure," in *Understanding the Digital Economy,* Erik Brynjolfsson and Brian Kahin, eds., Cambridge, Mass.: MIT Press, 2000, 217–246; authors' estimate for 2000.

considerably, from nearly 1.5 in 1980 to close to 1.8 in 2000. Hence, the earnings of a typical college graduate relative to the earnings of a typical high school graduate rose by 20 percent. This means that if a high school graduate at a typical company earned $40,000 in 1980, a college graduate at the same company was likely to earn $60,000 that year. If a high school graduate at the same company earned the $40,000 in 2000, however, a college graduate was likely to earn $72,000.

As discussed in Chapter 1, U.S. trade with other nations increased considerably after 1980. Nevertheless, as noted above, the "big-country" effect that the United States has on relative prices of goods and the mix of product consumption tends to reduce the effect that international trade otherwise might have on the U.S. wage structure. If international trade is not the main explanation for a widened differential between the wages of college graduates and high school graduates in the United States, then what factor does account for this change?

So far, most economists have concluded that workers with more skills are earning relatively more simply because the worldwide demand for skilled-labor-intensive products, such as computer software, has increased. Thus, U.S. industries that specialize in producing skilled-labor-intensive products have benefited, as have their employees, which are the skilled U.S. workers who manufacture these products. Thus, even if international trade had not increased since 1980, the relative shift in preferences toward skilled-labor-intensive products probably would have widened the differential between the earnings of skilled and unskilled U.S. workers.

If this conclusion is correct, it has an important implication for the United States: U.S. residents undoubtedly have experienced gains from trade as the extent of international trade has risen. Overall, increased U.S. trade with other nations has benefited both skilled and unskilled workers in the United States. It is likely that the earnings of less-skilled workers have not advanced as much as those of higher-skilled workers because higher-skilled workers have been producing lots of products that people want to buy, and not because U.S. residents engage in more trade with other nations. (It is possible that increased U.S. trade with other nations has *narrowed* the gap between the earnings of male and female workers; see on pages 318–319 *Management Notebook: Is the United States Importing Gender Earnings Equality?*)

Fundamental Issue 3

What are the implications of the factor proportions approach to international trade for how trade affects workers' earnings?

The factor proportions approach emphasizes how differences in relative proportions of factors of production can account for comparative advantages and flows of trade between nations. This approach predicts that a nation with a relatively high proportion of skilled workers will tend to export skilled-labor-intensive goods and import unskilled-labor-intensive goods from a country with a relatively high proportion of unskilled workers. In the latter country with a high proportion of unskilled workers, increased trade tends to narrow the wage difference between skilled and unskilled workers. In the former country with a high proportion of skilled workers, greater trade tends to widen this wage differential.

INTERNATIONAL TRADE AND LABOR AND CAPITAL FLOWS

Whether they are high-skilled or low-skilled, workers do not produce goods and services in a vacuum. The companies that employ them make use of other factors of production, including entrepreneurship, land, and capital. Taking into account the role of capital is especially important when assessing the effects of international trade.

The Market for Capital

The demand for capital, like the demand for labor, is a *derived demand.* Firms decide how much capital to utilize by equating the price of capital with the **marginal revenue product of capital,** the additional revenue generated by utilizing an additional unit of capital. By definition, the marginal revenue product of capital equals the firm's marginal revenue times the **marginal product of capital,** which is the additional output forthcoming from utilization of an additional unit of capital. A change in either the price that the firm must pay to obtain capital or the firm's product price that alters the marginal revenue product of

Marginal revenue product of capital *The additional revenue generated by using an additional unit of capital.*

Marginal product of capital *The additional output generated by using an additional unit of capital.*

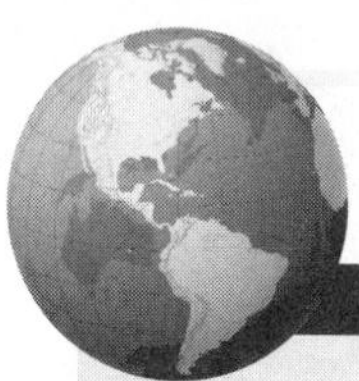

MANAGEMENT *Notebook*

POLICY MANAGEMENT

Is the United States Importing Gender Earnings Equality?

In 1957, the University of Chicago economist and Nobel laureate Gary Becker developed the hypothesis that increased globalization helps women and minorities. The basis of Becker's argument was that trade barriers protect domestic industries from foreign competition and thereby make it easier for managers of protected companies to engage in discriminatory practices. Because owners and managers of protected industries are more assured that they will earn relatively high profits, Becker argued, it is easier for them to rationalize the higher costs they incur by hiring "favored" groups, such as white males, instead of women or members of minority groups. Increased openness to international trade, he concluded, would force employers to reduce discrimination against these latter individuals.

One key implication of Becker's theory is that domestic profit pressures caused by increased exposure to import competition should lead domestic employers to bid the wages of female employees closer to men's wages. Sandra Black of the Federal Reserve Bank of New York and Elizabeth Brainerd of Williams College examined the relationship between U.S. imports and the so-called *gender gap,* which is the gap between female and male earnings. As you can see in Figure 10-6, a rise in the ratio of the wages of female workers relative to those of male workers has accompanied increased U.S. openness to imports. Black and Brainerd verify with statistical methods that there is indeed a relationship between imports and the gender gap. In a sense, therefore, the United States may really be importing greater wage equality between men and women.

For Critical Analysis:
Does a reduction in the gender gap necessarily imply that male and female U.S. workers experience overall wage gains as a result of increased international trade?

capital will induce the firm to change the extent to which it utilizes capital as a factor of production.

The price of capital adjusts to bring about equality between the total quantity of capital demanded by firms that utilize capital and the total quantity of capital supplied by capital-producing firms. Just as international trade can affect market wages in domestic labor markets, changes in cross-border flows of trade can influence the market price of capital.

Applying the Factor Proportions Approach to Allocations of Labor and Capital

As a first step toward evaluating how international trade affects conditions in domestic markets for capital, economists often apply the factor proportions ap-

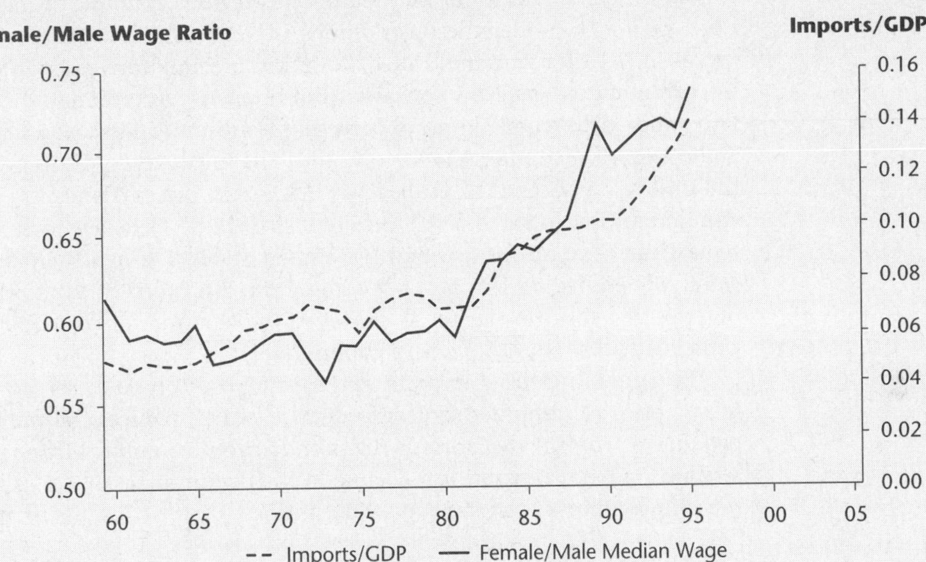

Figure 10-6

The Labor-Market Effects of a Decline in Product Price Induced by Increased International Trade

As U.S. imports have risen relative to U.S. GDP, the ratio of females' wages to males' wages has also increased.

Source: Sandra Black and Elizabeth Brainerd, "Importing Equality? The Effects of Increased Competition on the Gender Wage Gap," Working Paper, Federal Reserve Bank of New York, March 1999.

proach. Consider again a possible trading relationship between the United States and China. Let's maintain the same assumptions as before: full labor mobility across industries within nations, labor immobility between nations, technology that requires identical factor proportions in both countries, and an absence of big-country effects that might alter fixed and identical relative demands for the products manufactured in each nation.

Now, however, suppose that the two goods that both nations produce are computer servers (the devices that link individual computers to computer networks) and textiles (cloth and other materials used to manufacture clothing). In addition, the two factors of production available in each nation are labor and capital. Computer servers are capital-intensive goods, while textiles are labor-intensive goods. Naturally, we shall assume that China has an abundance of labor relative to capital. In contrast, in the United States there is an abundance of capital relative to labor. This means that in the absence of trade, the price of labor—the wage rate—is relatively lower in China as compared with the United States. The price of capital in China, however, is high relative to the price of capital in the United States.

By the same reasoning we used in our previous example of the factor proportions approach, under these conditions China has a comparative advantage in producing textiles, and the United States has a comparative advantage in producing computer servers. Now consider what happens, according to the factor proportions approach, when China exports textiles to the United States and the United States exports computer servers to China. The importation of Chinese textiles into the United States tends to push down U.S. textile prices. Hence, the marginal revenue product of labor at U.S. labor-intensive textile firms declines, which tends to reduce the demand for labor in the United States. On net, therefore, the market wage rate earned by U.S. labor declines. As U.S. exports of capital-intensive computer servers to China increase, however, the demand for capital increases in the United States, so the U.S. price of capital rises.

In China, increased imports of U.S.-produced computer servers cause the domestic price of computer servers to decline, which reduces the marginal revenue product of capital at Chinese firms that produce capital-intensive computer servers. On net, the result is a decline in the demand for capital in China, so that the Chinese market price of capital declines.

Exporting Capital: Foreign Direct Investment

What happens if there are barriers to U.S. trade with China? Such barriers might be overt impediments such as tariffs, quotas, and the like. Distance and associated shipping costs might also discourage trading certain goods and services.

In the face of such trade barriers, it might pay for the companies located in the country with a relative abundance of capital—in this situation, the United States—to export capital to China. By building factories to produce capital-intensive goods such as computer servers in China, the U.S. companies would engage in *foreign direct investment* (see Chapter 1).

By moving capital into China for use in producing capital-intensive goods for sale there instead of exporting U.S.-produced goods to China, the U.S. companies would circumvent the barriers to direct trade in those goods. Essentially, the U.S. companies would substitute exports of capital for exports of capital-intensive goods.

Exporting Labor: Emigration and Immigration, Legal and Illegal

Barriers to trade between the United States and China also could limit Chinese exports of labor-intensive goods such as textiles to the United States. Because this raises the relative wage that workers can earn in the United States, it provides an incentive for the owners of Chinese labor services—Chinese workers themselves—to move to the United States. In the absence of Chinese limitations on emigration and U.S. restraints on immigration from China, therefore, such a movement of labor resources from China to the United States effectively could substitute for exports of labor-intensive Chinese goods to the United States.

As panel (a) of Figure 10-7 on page 322 shows, the number of U.S. immigrants during the 1991–2000 period surpassed those of the decades with the previous record immigration levels, 1981–1990 and 1901–1910. These figures should be interpreted with some care. After all, there were only about 92 million people in the United States in 1910, so the nearly 9 million immigrants into the United States during the ten preceding years constituted nearly 10 percent of the population at that time. By way of contrast, the nearly 12 million immigrants during the 1991–2000 period make up only about 4 percent of today's U.S. population of nearly 280 million people. Yet, the recent increase in U.S. immigration is significant.

Panel (b) indicates that there has been a shift, relative to earlier decades, in U.S. immigrants' points of origin. In the 1950s, most U.S. immigrants arrived from Europe and Canada. Today, most hail from countries in Asia and Latin America. Undoubtedly, by keeping U.S. wages relatively high, trade barriers that inhibit U.S. imports of labor-intensive goods provide one of the many incentives that motivate people to emigrate from their home countries to the United States. As shown in panel (c), an increasing portion of today's U.S. immigrants are less likely, relative to native U.S. residents, to have attained a high school degree. Hence, many U.S. immigrants today seek higher wages for unskilled labor that the United States has in relatively less abundance, as compared with nations in Asia and Latin America.

Limitations of the Factor Proportions Approach

The factor proportions approach helps to explain patterns of trade and cross-country flows of capital and labor. It does a particularly good job of explaining **inter-industry trade,** which is the cross-border exchange of completely different goods and services, such as Chinese purchases of computer software and hardware and U.S. purchases of Chinese toys and textiles. The reason is that the factor proportions approach identifies why comparative advantages in producing dissimilar goods and services might arise from differences in relative factor abundances across nations.

Inter-industry trade *International trade of completely distinguishable goods and services.*

It is important to recognize, however, that the factor proportions approach has some limitations. The approach is not well suited, for instance, to explaining **intra-industry trade,** which is cross-border trade in similar goods or services, such as U.S. exports of Cadillac autos to Germany and U.S. imports of Mercedes autos from Germany. Explaining intra-industry trade flows and their implications often requires examining situations in which companies have some ability to determine the prices of their products independently from the actions of other producers. The basic factor proportions approach, by way of contrast, relies on the assumption that each company is highly limited by its small relative size and by the close substitutability of its products for those of other firms. As a result, trying to vary its price from those of its competitors is inconsistent with maximizing its profits. We will revisit this issue in much greater detail in Chapter 11.

Intra-industry trade *International trade of goods or services that are closely substitutable.*

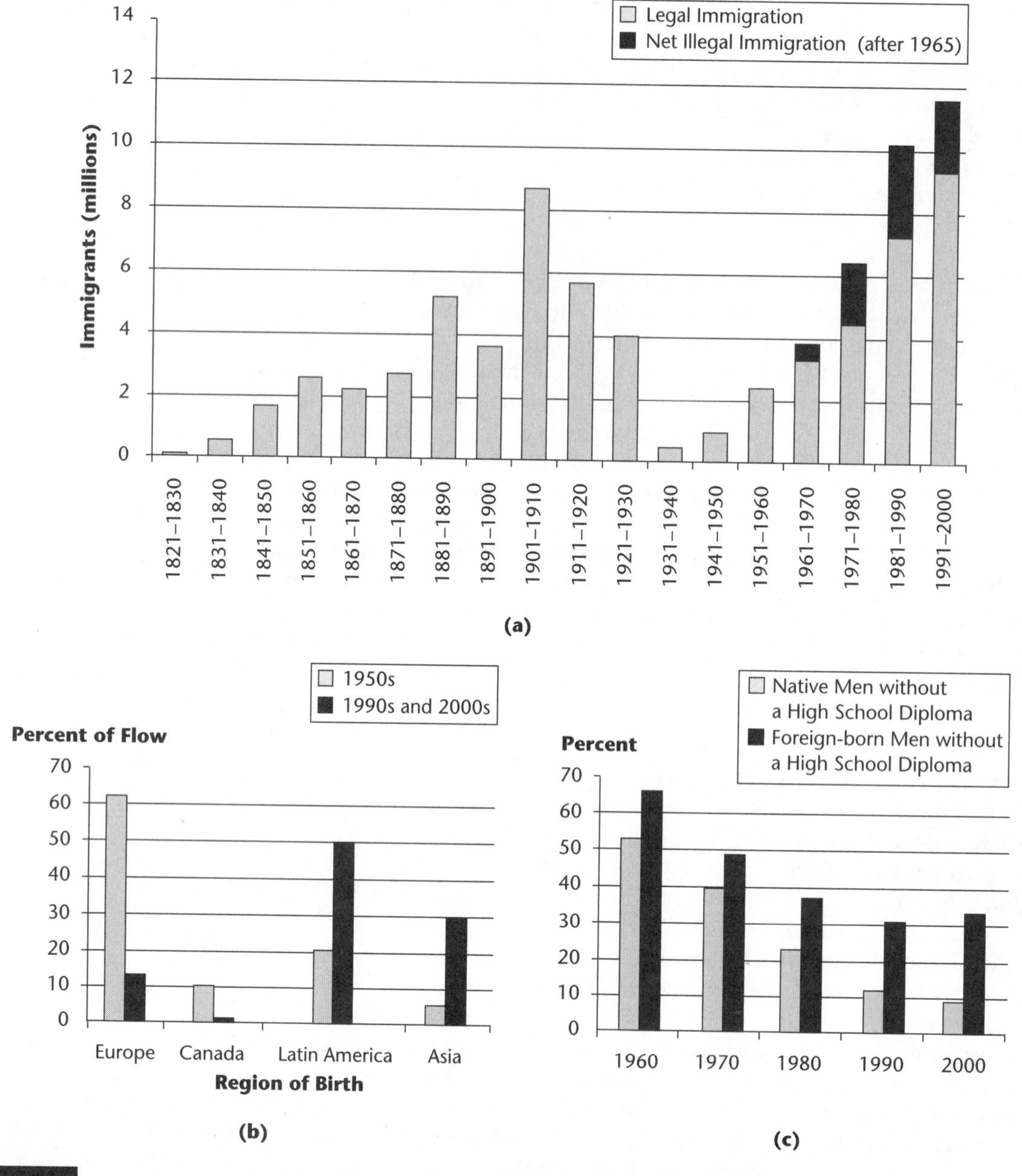

Figure 10-7

Immigration into the United States

Panel (a) shows the numbers of immigrants entering the United States during each decade since 1821–1830. The numbers of immigrants have noticeably increased during recent decades. As panel (b) indicates, recently there has been a pronounced shift in the origins of immigrants. In the 1950s, most U.S. immigrants were from Europe and Canada; today most come from Latin America and Asia. Finally, panel (c) shows that relative to native U.S. residents, U.S. immigrants are increasingly likely not to have graduated from high school.

Source: Pia Orrenius and Alan Viard, "The Second Great Migration: Economic and Policy Implications," Federal Reserve Bank of Dallas *Southwest Economy*, May/June 2000, 1–8; and authors' estimates.

Fundamental Issue 4

Why do labor and capital resources often flow across national borders?

Applying the factor proportions approach to trade in labor-intensive and capital-intensive goods indicates that countries with relatively large proportions of capital resources tend to export capital-intensive goods and to import labor-intensive goods from countries with relatively large proportions of labor resources. If there are natural or government-erected trade barriers, however, residents of relatively capital-abundant countries tend to export capital by engaging in foreign direct investment. Residents of relatively labor-abundant countries, by way of contrast, may immigrate to capital-intensive countries where they can earn relatively higher wages.

International Trade and Economic Development

Economists who specialize in *development economics* study the factors that influence a nation's economic growth and development. In the 1950s, development economists noticed an important byproduct of wage increases accruing to residents of developing nations that experienced significant growth: As workers' inflation-adjusted wages rose, so did their productivity. A key reason this occurred was that before development took place, many workers in these countries were malnourished. Naturally, earning higher wages enabled these individuals to purchase wider varieties of foods, so that they could eat more balanced meals and build stronger bodies and minds. As a result, they become more productive workers.

TRADE AND WAGES IN DEVELOPING NATIONS

As we noted at the outset of this chapter, developing nations account for a much larger portion of total world trade than they did in years past. You have learned in this chapter that greater openness to international trade has conflicting effects on workers' wages but generally bestows gains from trade upon the residents of nations that exchange goods and services. To consider how international trade affects the economies of developing nations, let's start by examining the extent of trade by these nations and the implications of increased trade openness for their residents'.

Developing Nations and World Trade

Figure 10-8 on the following page shows the distributions of the world's population and international trade among six regions of the world. As you can see, the generally most developed regions of North America and Europe together contain only about 13 percent of the world's population but account for roughly two-thirds of global trade. Asia, which contains a mix of industrialized, emerging, and developing national economies, contains more than half of the world's people. Nevertheless, Asian nations account for only a fourth of global trade. Africa has almost a fifth of the world's population but accounts for less than 2 percent of total international trade.

ON THE WEB

Track the international trade of all nations and various world regions by going to http://www.wto.org, clicking on "Resources," and then clicking on "Statistics."

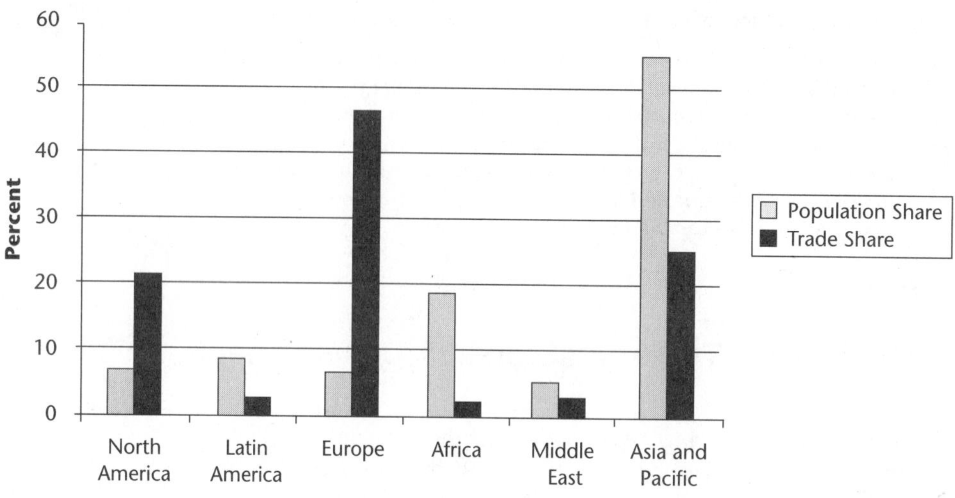

Figure 10-8

Population and Trade Shares of Selected World Regions

The regions of the world that account for the largest shares of the world's population tend to account for much smaller shares of total world trade.

Sources: World Bank, *World Development Indicators,* and International Monetary Fund, *Direction of Trade Statistics.*

The dramatic disparity in trade is also revealed if we divide total trade flows by population to determine per capita trade volumes. In terms of U.S. dollars, the annual per capita trade flow in developing nations is typically less than $75 per year. That is, the average resident of a developing nation exports and imports a total of about $75 in goods and services. In the United States, by way of contrast, the annual per capita trade flow normally exceeds $8,000 a year.

These comparisons indicate just how unbalanced international trade is in relation to the distribution of the world's population. You have learned that there are gains from trade and potentially even wage enhancements that can result from greater openness to trade (depending, of course, on how countervailing wage effects net out). Undoubtedly, residents of the United States and other developed nations experience the bulk of these benefits, because they engage in the bulk of the world's trade. (There is also a significant disparity in Internet access around the world; see on pages 326–327 *Online Globalization: The Global Digital Divide.*)

Wages, Comparative Advantage, and Development

Compared with developed nations, developing nations currently have relatively higher factor proportions of resources such as oil and minerals. It is not surprising, therefore, that developing nations account for more than half of the world's exports of fuels and mining products.

In addition, developing countries have relatively abundant labor resources. Developing nations cannot take advantage of this particular relative factor abun-

Table 10-4 **Unit Labor Costs in Selected Developing Countries**

(Ratio of wages per employee to value added per employee, divided by the U.S. level)

Source: United Nations Trade and Development Report.

Economy	Footwear	Textiles	Clothing	Metal Products	Wood Products	Rubber Products	Plastic Products	Electrical Machinery
Egypt	NA	1.50	0.50	0.85	0.48	1.50	1.23	0.93
India	0.99	1.01	0.49	0.97	0.91	0.88	0.88	0.85
Indonesia	0.85	0.47	0.95	0.55	0.53	0.72	0.64	0.76
Kenya	1.13	1.61	1.17	0.91	1.20	0.61	0.63	0.55
Malaysia	1.08	0.73	1.42	0.83	0.85	0.76	0.92	0.97
Mexico	1.62	0.96	1.20	0.76	0.76	0.96	0.83	0.83
Philippines	1.36	0.69	1.12	0.79	0.90	0.71	0.69	0.84
Thailand	1.23	0.87	1.70	0.71	0.57	0.56	0.83	0.65
Turkey	0.69	0.42	0.38	0.46	0.96	0.57	0.34	0.51
Zimbabwe	0.95	0.56	1.26	0.99	0.73	0.74	1.36	1.05

NA: Not available

dance throughout all sectors of their domestic economies, however. To see why, take a look at Table 10-4. It displays ratios of unit labor costs to value added per employee (relative to the U.S. level) for various industries within selected developing nations. A relatively low value of this ratio within a given industry indicates that a nation is more likely to have a comparative advantage in competing within that industry.

As you can see, possessing a relative abundance of labor does not necessarily give a developing nation a comparative advantage, even within relatively labor-intensive industries such as footwear, textiles, and clothing. Some developing nations naturally will have more success than others in their efforts to transform a relative abundance of labor into a comparative advantage. According to the factor proportions approach, this also means that wages are likely to rise more speedily in some less-developed nations than others. To the extent that international trade contributes to the developing world's economic growth, which economists commonly measure using the annual rate of increase in a nation's per capita income, the pace of growth is likely to be unevenly distributed among developing nations.

Online Globalization

The Global Digital Divide

There is considerable evidence that some groups in the United States have more access to the Internet than others. This propensity for some groups to have greater Internet access has come to be known as a *digital divide.* Because there are a number of ways to categorize people, several possible digital divides might conceivably exist.

Explaining the Digital Divide

Most studies indicate that income is a key criterion determining whether a U.S. resident has Internet access. A recent report by the Commerce Department, for instance, found that the highest-income U.S. residents were twenty times more likely to be online than people at the lowest income threshold. Thus, there is evidence of an income-based digital divide in the United States. Undoubtedly, the expense of purchasing hardware and software is daunting for lower-income individuals, as are the monthly fees to Internet service providers. By way of contrast, such expenses constitute much smaller portions of total expenditures by higher-income people.

At one time, there was a widespread concern about the possible existence of racial and ethnic digital divides. Although these concerns still exist, recent research indicates that because race and ethnicity are often correlated with income, perceived racial and ethnic digital divides in Internet access probably reflect the income-based division separating Internet users from nonusers.

Gradually, the Rest of the World Is Also Going Online

A more dramatic type of digital divide is apparent in Figure 10-9(a), which displays the physical populations of selected regions as percentages of the world's

Figure 10-9

Physical and Online Population Distributions and Internet Access Prices for Selected Regions and Nations

Panel (a) indicates that the vast majority of people with Internet access reside in the developed nations in North America, Europe, and Asia. As shown in panel (b), the price of Internet access varies considerably across nations.

Sources: Organization for Economic Cooperation and Development and International Telecommunications Union.

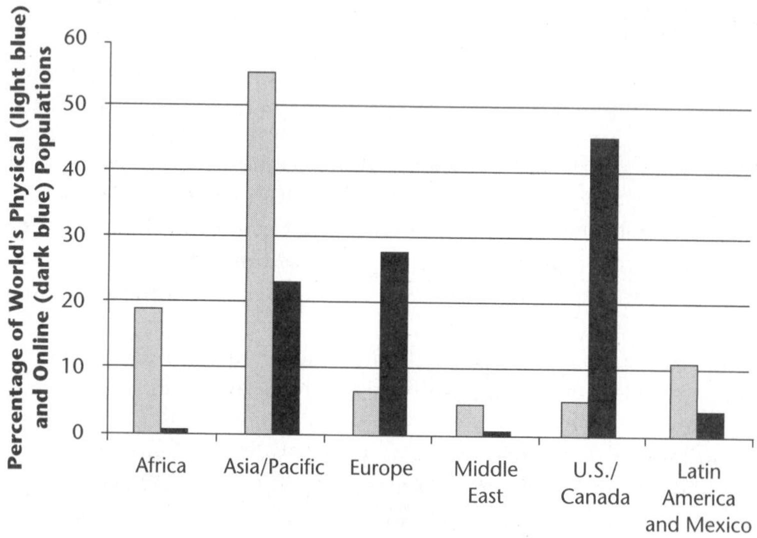

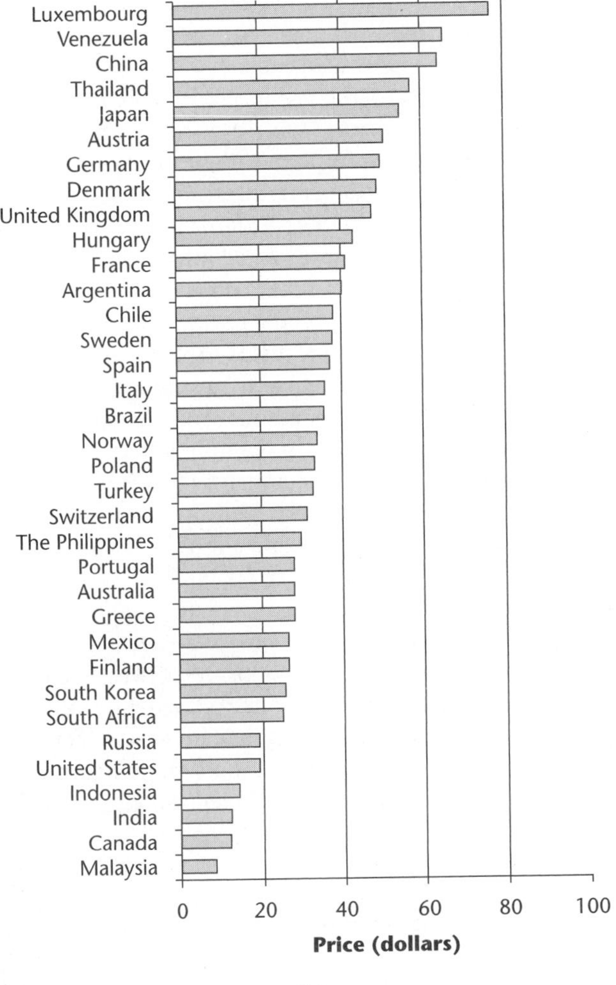

(b)

population and the online populations of the same regions as percentages of the world's population with online access. Currently, 44 percent of people with access to the Internet reside in the United States and Canada. Those two wealthy North American countries and Europe together contain slightly less than three-fourths of the world's online population. Developed portions of Asia contain most of the rest.

As panel (b) shows, Internet access prices vary considerably across nations. There is no apparent separation between access prices in developed and developing nations, however. The residents of some developing nations face relatively high access prices, but so do those of several developed nations. A much bigger problem for most people in less-developed regions of the world—those with less wealth and lower incomes—is simply a lack of *access* to basic telecommunications services, let alone to the Internet.

Make no mistake about it, however; overall Internet connectivity is proceeding rapidly. Media pundits often marvel at the significant expansion of Internet access among the U.S. population, which continues at an annual pace close to 15 percent. But more astounding annual growth rates can be found in Europe and South America, where growth of the online populations slightly exceeds 100 percent. Moveover, in Africa, the online population growth rate is about 135 percent, and the Asia/Pacific region has the fastest growth of online access, at 155 percent. Currently more than 300 million people worldwide have regular access to the Internet.

For Critical Analysis:
If smaller portions of the developing world have Internet access, how can rates of growth of Internet access in these countries be so high?

STIMULATING GROWTH: OPENNESS OR PROTECTIONISM?

Should a developing nation that seeks greater growth encourage or discourage trade with other countries? On the one hand, promoting such trade could permit a nation to specialize in production of goods and services that its industries can produce most efficiently. On the other hand, inhibiting trade might protect fledgling industries from foreign competition and permit them to grow more quickly.

In years past, and even today, some economists have contended that protectionism promotes economic growth. The basis of this argument is the idea that pure competition might not be the best market structure to promote economic growth. Instead, proponents of protectionism favor the view that the centralization of resources among a few home businesses might permit them to grow more rapidly. In addition, protection for foreign competition can, they argue, keep new home industries from failing prematurely in the face of short-term profit fluctuations that might occur if they were exposed to variations in world prices.

ON THE WEB

Take a look at the U.S. State Department's reports on other nations' trade practices at http://www.state.gov/www/issues/economic/trade_reports.

Nevertheless, today most economists who study economic growth tend to believe that greater openness to trade is the best way to promote growth. Developing nations benefit by gaining access to new knowledge and ideas that are diffused around the globe more rapidly when technologies can move across national borders freely, they argue. Furthermore, more developing economies may experience higher rates of economic growth if their own industries have access to a larger market. Home industries that are protected by trade barriers such as tariffs or quotas can become isolated from world technological progress. Former communist countries and a number of developing nations in Latin America and elsewhere experienced this problem in years past.

Economists continue to debate this issue. Currently, however, those who promote openness have some strong evidence favoring their view. As Figure 10-10 shows, there seems to be some evidence of an inverse relationship between economic growth and the level of trade barriers in a nation. So far, experience indicates that greater openness is more conducive to higher economic growth. (Openness can also improve a nation's health by widening the flow of new medical knowledge in developing nations; see on page 330 *Online Globalization: Online Medical Services in Bangladesh.*)

5 Fundamental Issue

How does greater openness to international trade affect wages and economic growth in developing nations?

Developing countries have become increasingly open to international trade, and together these nations now account for about one-third of total global trade flows. Because developing countries tend to be relatively labor-abundant, increased trade with more capital-abundant developed nations is likely to raise the wages of workers in developing countries, thereby pushing up their per capita incomes. Comparative advantages in producing labor-intensive goods vary across developing nations, however, so not all developing countries are likely to share equally in economic growth generated by increased international trade.

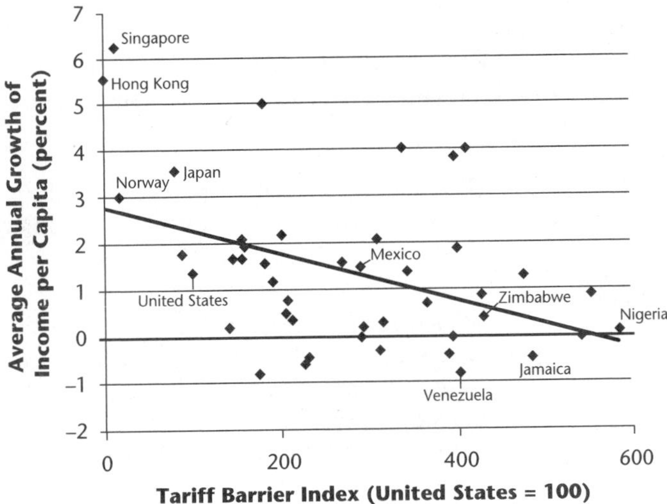

Figure 10-10

Trade Barriers versus Economic Growth

Governments of nations with closed economies use trade barriers to prevent imports from entering the country and sometimes keep exports from leaving the country. Such protectionism closes off such nations to new technologies and other sources of economic growth. The data appear to favor the view that more nearly closed economies experience lower rates of growth, all other things held constant.

Source: World Bank, *World Development Indicators* and *Competitiveness Indicators,* 2002.

CAPITAL FLOWS AND DEVELOPING NATIONS

Both labor and capital are fundamental resources required for economic growth. As you have seen, a developing nation with a low proportion of capital relative to labor typically ends up exporting labor-intensive products and importing capital-intensive products. Alternatively, residents of the nation can import capital and manufacture capital-intensive goods on their own.

Are Capital Inflows "Bad" for Developing Nations?

As we discuss in greater detail in Chapter 14, in recent years a number of developing nations—for instance, Mexico in 1994, Malaysia, Indonesia, and Thailand in 1998, Brazil in 1999, and Argentina in 2002—have been "burned" by sudden shifts in international capital flows. During such episodes, many domestic industries that had counted on foreign capital to provide the underpinning for planned expansions have faced sudden halts in capital flows. The consequences have been severe economic shocks and significant contractions in per capita incomes.

Online Globalization

Online Medical Services in Bangladesh

Until the late 1990s, most medical schools in Bangladesh were fortunate to own a single computer. The country's top medical school, Dhaka Medical School, could afford current subscriptions to only one or two medical journals at a time. Consequently, doctors were in the dark about the latest medical developments in treating serious illnesses and injuries.

Medinet to the Rescue

A few years ago, however, health-care professionals in Bangladesh established Medinet, a non-profit online medical-information network. Medinet began with two digital phones. System operators downloaded medical information from the Web on a regular basis. They placed data in a central computer system, from which they produced paper reports that six offices regularly distributed to seventeen organizational users, including the nation's medical schools, and sixty individual users.

Today, a growing number of Bangladesh medical schools have access to electronic mail. A doctor trying to determine the best way to treat a particular condition can send an e-mail request to Medinet, which assists the doctor in electronically retrieving articles concerning the latest treatment techniques.

A Virtual Training Ground

Gradually, medical schools in Bangladesh have used basic e-mail access to develop a network built around the Medinet system. Today, Medinet serves as the center for the distribution of national public health information.

It also has become a major resource for training new physicians. Six up-to-date medical courses are accessible on the Medinet system, and more than 200 medical students have used these courses to supplement their training.

For Critical Analysis:

What would happen to the dissemination of new medical knowledge if every medical practitioner could get access to the latest articles on medicine without paying for the information? (*Hint:* Why do scientific and professional journals charge subscription fees to libraries and to individual subscribers?)

ON THE WEB

Learn more about Medinet at http://www.angelfire.com/ak/medinet.

Panel (a) of Figure 10-11 shows total net flow of private capital to developing nations, as well as the components of that flow, since 1975. Private capital flows were relatively small and stable until the late 1980s. Then they grew considerably and became more variable by the mid-1990s. A sharp decline occurred in 1997 and 1998. Since then, capital flows to developing nations have increased once more.

In panel (b) of Figure 10-11, you can see the consequences of the sharp decline in the flow of private capital to developing nations in 1997 and 1998. Russia and Asian nations experienced significant declines in income growth. So did Latin American and Central and Eastern European nations, although income declines in these countries were less pronounced.

In Figure 10-12 on page 332, you can see why Asian countries were hit particularly hard by the sudden downturn in international capital flows to developing countries. In years past, the main destinations of foreign capital flows were Latin

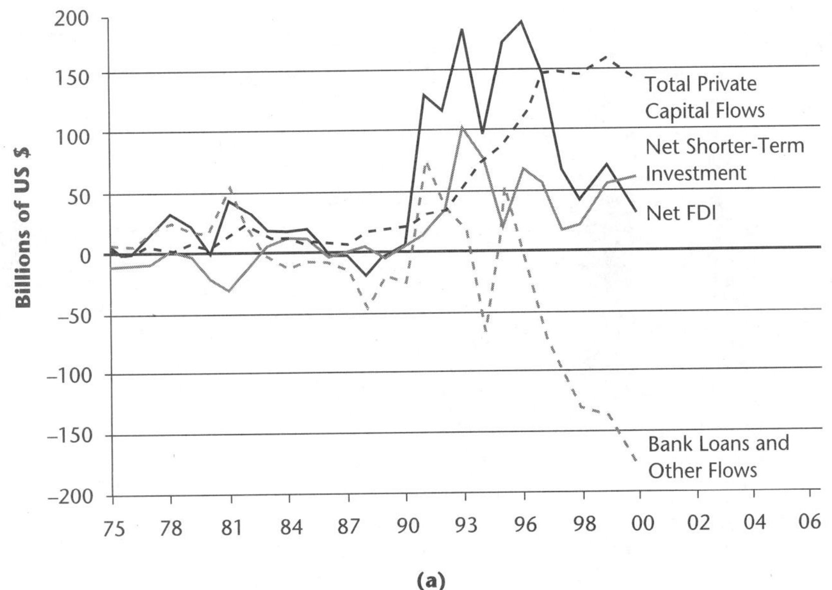

(a)

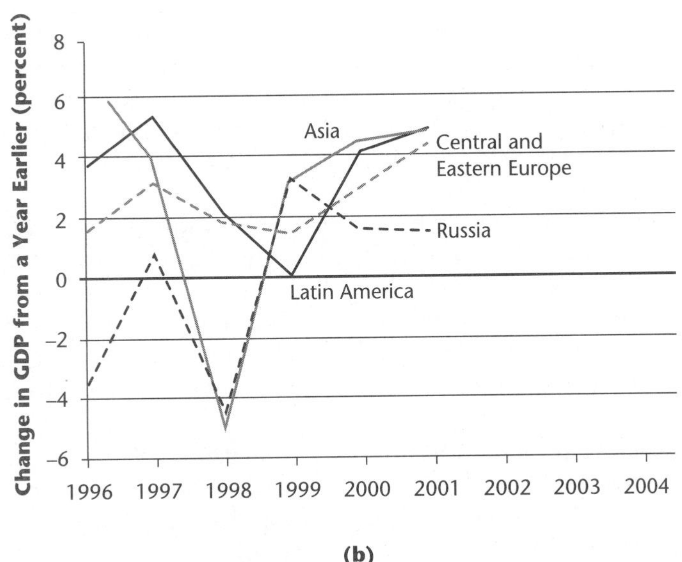

(b)

Figure 10-11

Private Capital Flows and National Income Growth in Developing Nations

Panel (a) displays total private capital flows to developing nations since 1975 and the sources of these flows. Although foreign direct investment in developing nations increased steadily after the mid-1980s, other sources of private capital flows to these countries have been more variable. As shown in panel (b), the drop-off in total private capital flows in the late 1990s was associated with flat or declining annual GDP growth in the world's developing regions.

Source: International Monetary Fund.

American and Caribbean countries. East Asian and Pacific nations' share of these flows has risen considerably in recent years. This increased reliance on foreign capital exposed Asian countries to the risk of major financial disturbances in the event of sudden disruptions of international capital flows.

During and immediately after the "Asian crisis" of 1997 to 1998, some economists, and even more politicians and policymakers, began to argue that developing nations would be better off if they were to spurn imports of foreign capital. In the end, they did not do this (one significant exception was Malaysia, which

Figure 10-12

Shares of Foreign Direct Investment in Developing Regions

The East Asia/Pacific share of foreign direct investment to developing nations has risen considerably during the past three decades.

Source: United Nations, *Trade and Development Report.*

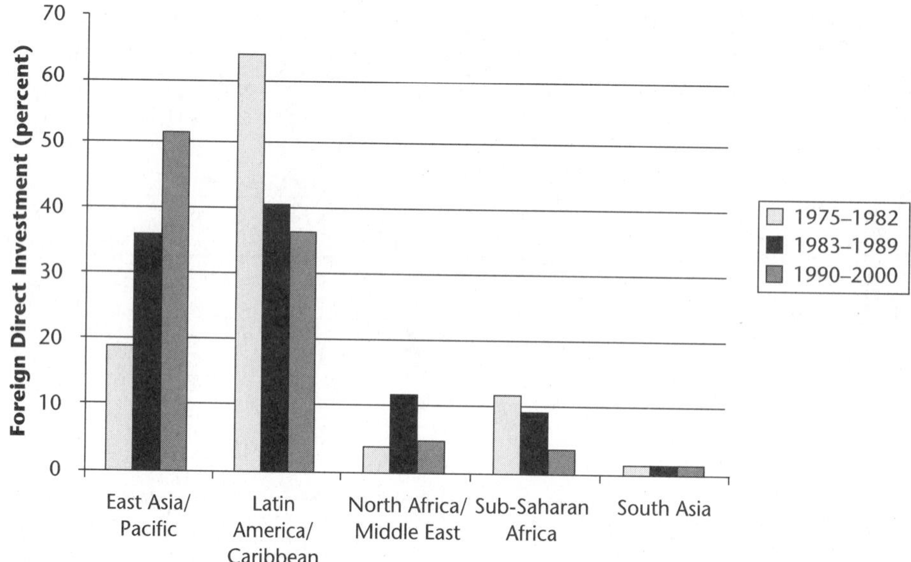

placed controls on cross-border capital flows for several months). Nevertheless, several tried to find ways to smooth the effects of the variability in capital flows depicted in panel (a) of Figure 10-11. A few Asian governments even resorted to intervening in national stock markets by dedicating tax revenues raised from their nations' residents to domestic capital investment intended to replace lost foreign capital.

These efforts were little more than band-aids, however. As you have learned in this chapter, only two changes could ultimately turn around the Asian crisis: Increased international trade with developing nations mainly exporting labor-intensive goods and importing capital-intensive goods or a renewed inflow of foreign capital. In fact, both changes gradually took place, which in recent years has helped bring about gradual economic recoveries in many developing countries.

Developing-Nation Indebtedness: Burden or a Key to Growth?

There are two basic ways that developing nations with an underabundance of capital resources and relatively low national income levels can acquire capital resources from abroad. One is to finance the acquisition of capital by borrowing from abroad. The other is to permit foreign direct investment.

There are three problems with borrowing abroad. One is that interest payments on the debt obligations are transfers from domestic residents to foreign residents who own these obligations. Another is that foreign borrowers may place conditions on loans that effectively transfer some control over resource-allocation decisions away from domestic residents. A third problem is depicted in panel (a) of Figure 10-11: Foreign shorter-term investment and loans can be highly volatile.

Panel (a) of Figure 10-11 shows that foreign direct investment typically has been a much more stable source of capital inflows. Foreign owners of capital resources nonetheless earn all returns on those resources that are not reinvested domestically. In addition, foreign owners typically have considerable say in how capital resources are directed within the domestic economy.

Nevertheless, there is widespread agreement among development economists that sustained capital accumulation is a fundamental prerequisite to achieving and maintaining persistent economic growth within developing countries. For now, most developing nations have cast their lot with the long-term benefits that they perceive will emerge from foreign capital inflows. These nations appear willing to accept the near-term burdens and risks that accompany large but volatile cross-border flows of capital.

Fundamental Issue 6

What are the pros and cons of increased capital flows to developing nations?

Economists have found that capital accumulation contributes to persistent economic growth. Consequently, flows of foreign capital to developing nations, which typically have relatively underabundant capital resources, have contributed to growth of their economies. The downside of reliance on foreign capital inflows is that developing nations must borrow from abroad or permit foreign direct investment. Both methods entail transfers of domestic returns on capital to foreign residents. Borrowing can entail some loss of control over the management of capital projects, and foreign direct investment nearly always does. Although foreign direct investment flows have usually been relatively stable, flows of capital financed through borrowing can be volatile and thereby can contribute to economic instability.

CHAPTER SUMMARY

1) **Factors That Influence the Demand for a Nation's Labor Resources:** Companies maximize their profits by hiring workers to the point where the marginal revenue product of the last worker hired, the additional revenues generated by hiring the next worker, equals the wage rate the worker earns. The marginal revenue product of labor equals marginal revenue (the additional revenue earned from selling an additional unit of output) times the marginal product of labor (the additional output that an additional unit of labor can produce). Consequently, the price that domestic companies earn from selling their product, the marginal product of labor, and wage rates influence how many workers that companies hire in a country's labor markets.
2) **How Market Wage Rates Are Determined, and How Greater International Trade Can Affect Wages Earned by a Nation's Workers:** The market wage rate is the wage rate at which firms in a labor market are willing to hire all the workers who are willing and able to work at that wage rate. Greater openness to foreign imports reduces the product price earned by domestic firms, which causes the domestic marginal revenue product of labor

to fall, thereby reducing the demand for labor. Thus, the market wage and employment at affected firms decline. An increase in exports of domestic companies, however, causes an increase in the total demand for labor by exporting firms. Consequently, wages and employment increase at these companies. On net, therefore, if other factors of production are fixed, increased international trade can either raise or reduce a nation's overall wage and employment levels.

3) **Implications of the Factor Proportions Approach to International Trade for How Trade Affects Workers' Earnings:** The factor proportions approach emphasizes how differences in relative proportions of factors of production can account for comparative advantages and flows of trade between nations. This approach predicts that a nation with a relatively high proportion of skilled workers will tend to export skilled-labor-intensive goods and import unskilled-labor-intensive goods from a country with a relatively high proportion of unskilled workers. In the latter country with a high proportion of unskilled workers, increased trade tends to narrow the wage difference between skilled and unskilled workers. In the former country with a high proportion of skilled workers, greater trade tends to widen this wage differential.
4) **Why Labor and Capital Resources Flow Across National Borders:** The factor proportions approach to trade in labor-intensive and capital-intensive goods predicts that countries with relatively abundant capital resources tend to export capital-intensive goods and to import labor-intensive goods from countries with relatively abundant labor resources. The presence of significant trade barriers tends to induce residents of relatively capital-abundant countries to export capital by engaging in foreign direct investment in relatively labor-abundant nations. In contrast, residents of relatively labor-abundant countries may seek higher relative wages by becoming immigrants of capital-intensive countries.
5) **How Greater Openness to International Trade Affects Wages and Economic Growth in Developing Nations:** Since the 1980s, the share of global international trade accounted for by developing countries has increased from 10 percent to more than one-third. Developing countries generally have relatively high proportions of labor resources. Hence, increased trade with developed nations that have higher proportions of capital resources is likely to raise the wages of workers in developing countries. As a result, international trade is likely to contribute to higher per capita incomes in developing countries. Nevertheless, because comparative advantages of developing nations differ, increased international trade is likely to make unequal contributions to the economic growth rates of developing countries.
6) **The Pros and Cons of Increased Capital Flows to Developing Nations:** There is considerable evidence that capital accumulation contributes to economic growth. Thus, flows of foreign capital to relatively labor-abundant developing nations have helped boost the growth of these nations'

economies. Increasing foreign capital inflows requires either borrowing from abroad or attracting foreign direct investment, which has the drawback of transferring domestic returns on capital to foreign residents. Permitting foreign direct investment sacrifices local control over the management of capital resources, and in some instances lenders also have some control over how capital resources are directed. In recent years, flows of foreign direct investment have been relatively stable, but flows of capital financed through borrowing have been much more variable.

QUESTIONS AND PROBLEMS

1) Fill in parts (a) through (l) in the table below, which applies to a domestic firm's weekly employment and production situation. Draw a rough graph of the labor demand curve for this firm. Suppose that at the current domestic market price and marginal revenue, the market wage rises from $280 per week to $320 per week. How does the firm's employment change?

Quantity of Labor (1)	Output (2)	Marginal Product (3)	Product Price (4)	Total Revenues (5)	Marginal Revenue (6)	Marginal Revenue Product (7)
0	0	—	$40	$0	—	—
1	8	(a)	$40	$320	$40	(g)
2	15	(b)	$40	$600	$40	(h)
3	21	(c)	$40	$840	$40	(i)
4	26	(d)	$40	$1,040	$40	(j)
5	30	(e)	$40	$1,200	$40	(k)
6	33	(f)	$40	$1,320	$40	(l)

2) An influx of foreign competition causes the domestic market price and marginal revenue faced by the firm to decline to $30 per unit. On a separate sheet of paper, completely redo the table from question 1. Draw a graph of the firm's new labor demand curve. How does increased foreign competition affect the firm's demand for labor?

3) Consider the table below, which applies to a domestic labor market, and answer the questions that follow.

Weekly Wage Rate	Quantity of Labor Demanded by Firms	Quantity of Labor Supplied by Workers
$500	8,000	26,000
$450	12,000	24,000
$400	16,000	22,000
$350	20,000	20,000
$300	24,000	18,000
$250	28,000	16,000
$200	30,000	14,000

(a) What is the current equilibrium quantity of labor? What is the current market wage rate?
(b) Suppose that two events occur: (i) Opportunities to work abroad induce 4,000 domestic residents to move to foreign labor markets, irrespective of domestic wages; and (ii) increased demand for the products of domestic firms induce them to offer to hire 2,000 more workers each week at any given domestic wage rate. What is the new equilibrium quantity of labor? What is the new market wage rate?

4) Consider the table below, which applies to a domestic labor market, and answer the questions that follow.

Weekly Wage Rate	Quantity of Labor Demanded by Firms	Quantity of Labor Supplied by Workers
$700	4,000	13,000
$650	6,000	12,000
$600	8,000	11,000
$550	10,000	10,000
$500	12,000	9,000
$450	14,000	8,000
$400	16,000	7,000

(a) What is the current equilibrium quantity of labor? What is the current market wage rate?

(b) Suppose that two events occur: (i) An influx of immigration results in an increase in the quantity of labor supplied to the domestic labor market equal to 2,000 units of labor per week; and (ii) increased foreign rivalry for the products of domestic firms induces a decrease in demand for domestic output, causing domestic firms to cut back on employment by 1,000 per week at any given wage rate. What is the new equilibrium quantity of labor? What is the new market wage rate?

5) Explain in your own words why a bilateral agreement with another country that opens a nation's borders to both imports from and exports to that country might not necessarily reduce the domestic nation's employment of labor.

6) Northsea and Eastcoast are neighboring countries with border posts that effectively prevent workers from crossing their border. Both have industries that use the same technologies to produce computers and brooms using skilled labor and unskilled labor, and both types of labor are perfectly mobile between the computer and broom industries. Computer production intensively uses skilled workers, and broom production intensively uses unskilled workers. Industries within each nation compete in the same markets for skilled and unskilled workers. Market wages earned by skilled workers are the same in both industries, and wages earned by unskilled workers are the same in both industries. In both nations, the market wages of skilled workers is higher than the market wage of unskilled workers, but in the absence of trade Northsea's skilled workers earn a higher market wage than skilled workers in Eastcoast. Northsea's unskilled workers also earn a higher market wage than unskilled workers in Eastcoast. Residents of both countries wish to consume computers in the same proportion to their consumption of brooms.

(a) What can you say about relative factor proportions in Northsea and Eastcoast?

(b) Which nation has a comparative advantage in broom production? In computer production? If trade occurs between the two countries, which directions will trade flow?

(c) What happens to the demand for skilled workers in each nation? To the demand for unskilled workers in each nation? What directions do wages of skilled and unskilled workers move in each nation?

7) Reconsider the situation described in question 6 if the first sentence of the question is changed to "Northsea and Eastcoast are neighboring countries that permit workers to cross their border freely." Which type of worker will tend to move to (or commute to) Northsea? To Eastcoast? Will Northsea and Eastcoast necessarily desire to engage in trade of computers and brooms? Explain.

8) Southshore is a developed nation with a relative abundance of capital, and Landsend is a neighboring, less-developed nation with a relative abundance of labor. Both countries produce capital- and labor-intensive products using the same technologies. Southshore currently prevents immigration from Landsend. Landsend's government prevents inflows of capital and restrains

trade with Southshore. Landsend's government is contemplating opening its border with Southshore to flows of capital and trade. Discuss the issues that Landsend's government faces in reaching a decision.

9) Suppose that in the situation described in question 8, Landsend's government decides to permit free trade but maintains restraints on capital flows in an effort to protect capital owners. Will this protectionist effort necessarily succeed in preventing lower returns on capital in Landsend? Explain your reasoning.
10) Reconsider the situation described in question 8. Suppose now that Landsend's government decides to permit capital flows but maintains restraints on trade. At the same time, Southshore decides to allow immigration from Landsend. Assuming that owners of capital and labor can freely relocate their resources, is either group necessarily harmed by Landsend's trade restraints? Explain your reasoning.

ONLINE APPLICATION

Internet URL: http://www.wto.org/english/res_e/statis_e/statis_e.htm

Title: **World Trade Organization Trade Statistics**

Navigation: Go to the WTO's home page (http://www.wto.org). Click on "Resources," and then click on "Statistics."

Application: Perform the indicated operations and answer the accompanying questions.

1) Under "Historical series" click on "Merchandise Trade and Selected Economies by Region." Using the "value" measure of trade, which regions of the world have recently experienced the greatest growth in international trade flows? The least growth? In which regions has growth in international trade been most variable? Least variable?
2) Using the "volume" measure of trade, which regions of the world have recently experienced the greatest growth in international trade flows? The least growth? In which regions has growth in international trade been most variable? Least variable? Does it matter which measure of trade—value versus volume—is used? If so, why?

For Group Study and Analysis: Separate the class into three groups, and assign each group to examine the sets of trade statistics in the reports on "Leading Exporters and Importers." When intra-EU trade is included, what nations are the leading importers and exporters? What happens to this list when intra-EU trade is excluded? Why? Does the list of top exporters and importers change noticeably when commercial services are considered? Which developing nations rank highest in these listings?

REFERENCES AND RECOMMENDED READINGS

Black, Sandra, and Elizabeth Brainerd. "Importing Equality? The Effects of Increased Competition on the Gender Wage Gap." Working Paper, Federal Reserve Bank of New York, March 1999.

Destler, I. M., and Peter Balint. *The New Politics of American Trade: Trade, Labor, and the Environment*. Policy Analyses in International Economics, No. 58, Institute for International Economics, October 1999.

Fishlow, Albert, and Karen Parker, eds. *Growing Apart: The Causes and Consequences of Global Wage Inequality*. New York: Council on Foreign Relations, 1999.

Golub, Stephen. "Does Trade with Low-Wage Countries Hurt American Workers?" *Business Review,* Federal Reserve Bank of Philadelphia (March/April 1998): 3–15.

Harrigan, James. "International Trade and American Wages in General Equilibrium, 1967–1995." In Robert Feenstra, ed. *The Impact of International Trade on Wages*. Chicago: University of Chicago Press, 2000.

Katz, Lawrence. "Technological Change, Computerization, and the Wage Structure." In Erik Brynjolfsson and Brian Kahin, eds. *Understanding the Digital Economy*. Cambridge, Mass.: MIT Press, 2000, pp. 217–246.

Kletzer, Lori. "Trade and Job Loss in U.S. Manufacturing, 1979–1994." In Robert Feenstra, ed. *The Impact of International Trade on Wages*. Chicago: University of Chicago Press, 2000.

Krueger, Anne. *Trade Policies and Developing Nations*. Washington, D.C.: Brookings Institution, 1995.

Moreno, Ramon. "What Explains Capital Flows?" Federal Reserve Bank of San Francisco *Economic Letter,* No. 2000–22 (July 21, 2000).

Orrenius, Pia, and Alan Viard. "The Second Great Migration: Economic and Policy Implications." Federal Reserve Bank of Dallas *Southwest Economy* (May/June 2000): 1–8.

Watal, Jayashree. "Developing Countries' Interests in a `Development Round.'" In Jeffrey Schott, ed. *The WTO After Seattle*. Washington, D.C.: Institute for International Economics, 2000.

CHAPTER ELEVEN

Industrial Structure and Trade in the Global Economy—Businesses without Borders

Fundamental Issues

1. **How do economies of scale help to explain a nation's specialization in inter-industry trade?**
2. **How do economies of scale and product variety provide an explanation for intra-industry trade?**
3. **In what way can foreign direct investment affect international trading patterns?**
4. **What are alternative industry structures, and how does industry structure matter in the global economy?**
5. **Why do companies engage in cross-border mergers and acquisitions, and how do international market linkages complicate measuring the degree to which a few large firms may dominate markets?**
6. **How do governments regulate international merger and acquisition activities?**

In 2000, the now-defunct telecommunications firm Worldcom, which in 1998 had acquired the long-distance phone company MCI, decided to purchase another U.S. long distance carrier, Sprint. A key reason was that Sprint was at the forefront of efforts to integrate telephone communications with Internet-based data services. The U.S. Justice Department, however, objected to the proposed acquisition, arguing that the planned combination would make the U.S. market for long distance phone service "too concentrated." Within days, Worldcom had abandoned the planned acquisition. Shortly thereafter, Sprint had a new suitor. It was the European telecommunications giant, the part-German-government-owned Deutsche Telecom.

That same year, customers and competitors of Time–Warner, Inc. and America Online raised concerns when the two media and Internet giants announced their intentions to merge, and U.S. regulators held up the planned combination following months of investigations. A few weeks later, NTT Communications Corporation, a subsidiary of Japan's state-controlled Nippon Telephone and Telegraph, offered to purchase a large U.S. Internet Service Provider, Verio, Inc. Following speedy consideration by a special Treasury Department-led task force, the U.S. government approved the NTT-Verio combination.

Some observers decried what they perceived to be unwarranted U.S. government intrusions to slow or even halt U.S. media-Internet-telecommunications consolidations even as it was permitting foreign forays into U.S. Internet and telecommunications markets. Others objected to both domestic and foreign combinations of big media, Internet, and telecommunications firms. They argued that these firms already were "too large," and that further combinations would weaken competition in media, Internet, and telecommunications markets. In addition, they worried that the German and Japanese firms seeking to buy U.S. companies might eventually gain an "upper hand" in worldwide competition within these markets, to the ultimate detriment of U.S. consumers' welfare.

Why might companies within a market desire to engage in mergers and acquisitions? How does the number of sellers affect the degree of competition within a market? What "market" should one consider when trying to answer these questions? In this chapter we shall address these and other issues concerning the global implications of industry structure.

Industrial Organization and International Integration

Industrial organization is the study of the structures of and interactions among firms and markets. Traditionally, industrial organization economists focused their attention on firm and market structures within nations. Today, however, they must also take into account international issues. Likewise, economists who study international trade increasingly must consider the importance of industry structure as a factor influencing trade flows.

Industrial organization *The study of the structures of and interactions among firms and markets.*

One of several reasons that industrial organization has become an international subject is the significant growth of *intra-industry trade.* The traditional theory of international trade that we first discussed in Chapter 2 and the factor proportions approach to international trade that we examined in Chapter 3 and applied to labor-market issues in Chapter 10 both emphasize *inter-industry trade,* or international trade in different goods and services. As you learned in Chapter 10, intra-industry trade primarily entails the international exchange of goods or services that are close substitutes. Examples include automobiles, computers, beer, financial services, and the like that flow across a nation's borders as both exports *and* imports. Another aspect of intra-industry trade is the cross-border exchange of component parts or services at various stages of production prior to completion of a final product, such as when a U.S. auto manufacturer transports parts to an assembly plant based in Mexico and then exports completed vehicles back to the United States.

ECONOMIES OF SCALE AND INTERNATIONAL TRADE

Before we consider the role of industry structure in explaining intra-industry trade, let's take a look at an important way that industry structure can influence inter-industry trade. In earlier chapters, you learned that inter-industry trade occurs because it allows residents of two countries to take advantage of comparative or absolute advantages that they possess. As a result, they can experience gains from trade. One factor that can help explain the process by which this occurs through the actions of producers is *economies of scale.* As we shall see shortly, this concept is also important in understanding why intra-industry trade occurs.

Economies of Scale

Long-run average cost *The ratio of a firm's total production cost to its output when the firm has sufficient time to vary the quantities of all factors of production.*

A key factor influencing the optimal size, or *scale,* of a company is its **long-run average cost,** which is the ratio of its total production cost to its output when it is able to adjust quantities of all factors of production, including capital as well as land, labor, and entrepreneurship. Typically, firms are able to adjust their capital over a relatively long period, the *long run,* which stretches from months to years. For most firms, over relatively small ranges of output long-run average cost usually declines as they expand their ability to produce additional units of a product. When this happens, a firm experiences **economies of scale,** which arise any time that an increase in the amount of output that a firm produces leads to a decrease in its long-run average cost.

Economies of scale *A reduction in long-run average cost induced by an increase in a firm's output.*

Economies of scale may arise because of specialization: When a firm's scale of operations increases, its opportunities to specialize in the use of factors of production also increase. For instance, a larger firm may be able to reduce its long-run average cost by dividing its existing work force into separate units that focus on specific aspects of its production process. In addition, a company may be able to take advantage of physical processes that permit it to produce more output with proportionately fewer inputs. For example, consider a company that ships liquids such as chemicals or other fluid products. It can gain from using larger storage containers, because the volume of containers, which helps determine the company's shipping capacity, rises more than proportionately with the surface area of the containers, which helps determine how much steel or plastic must be used in container construction.

Diseconomies of scale *An increase in long-run average cost caused by an increase in a firm's output.*

Economies of scale normally are not unbounded, however. As a company continues to enlarge the scale of its operations, it encounters factors that can result in **diseconomies of scale,** or increases in long-run average cost generated by increases in its output. This occurs, for instance, when layers of supervision increase as a company's scale of operations increase, so that the costs of compiling information and maintaining communication grow more than proportionately with the size of the firm.

Minimum Efficient Scale and International Trade

A typical company finds that as it increases its size, initially it experiences economies of scale. As it raises its scale of operations further, however, it eventually begins to experience higher long-run average costs and diseconomies of scale. The scale of operations at which economies of scale end and diseconomies of scale set in is the firm's **minimum efficient scale.** This is the firm size at which the company minimizes its long-run average cost. When all firms in a given industry have achieved their minimum efficient scale, then the industry itself operates at the minimum efficient scale for that industry.

Minimum efficient scale *The size at which a firm or industry minimizes its long-run average cost over a time frame in which quantities of all factors of production may be adjusted.*

An industry limited to producing and selling only within a single nation's borders may be unable to attain its minimum efficient scale. Taken alone, this can help to reinforce why a nation might gain a comparative advantage in producing a particular good or service. The U.S. aircraft industry, for instance, may be able to achieve its minimum efficient scale at lower longer-run average cost, as compared with aircraft industries in many other countries. Thus, the U.S. aircraft industry may have the capability to expand output beyond quantities that U.S. residents wish to consume and export additional jets, turboprop planes, and helicopters to other countries at a lower per-unit cost. Indeed, this is likely to be a reason that the U.S. aircraft industry produces a large portion of the world's aircraft and that a number of nations do not even produce aircraft. (For more details on how this might occur, see on pages 344–345 *Visualizing Global Economic Issues: International Trade and Economies of Scale*.)

It turns out, however, that economies of scale can also help to explain why nations with industries producing *similar* but slightly different products may experience international trade involving the products of those industries. This explanation relies on combining the idea of economies of scale with the possibility that competition might exist among firms in different countries that sell closely related, yet slightly different, products. Let's next consider why this is so.

Fundamental Issue 1

How do economies of scale help to explain a nation's specialization in inter-industry trade?

A firm or an industry experiences economies of scale when long-run average cost declines as total output expands through greater usage of all factors of production. At the minimum efficient scale of a firm or industry, long-run average cost is minimized. Any further increase in output would push up long-run average cost and thereby result in diseconomies of scale. Opening national borders to international trade helps give a cost advantage to countries with firms that already have experienced economies of scale. The industry in this nation can more speedily use this opportunity to expand to the minimum efficient scale for output of the good or service produced by that industry.

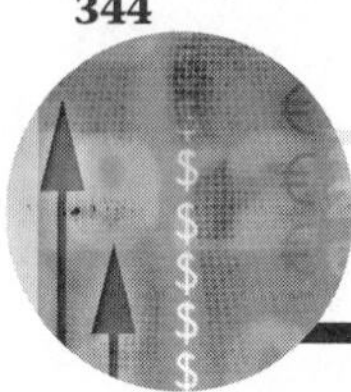

Visualizing Global Economic Issues

International Trade and Economies of Scale

To think about how economies of scale might induce countries to specialize in producing particular goods or services, take a look at Figure 11-1. It depicts a possible *long-run average cost (LRAC) curve* for any given national aircraft industry, under the assumption that all countries have access to the same aircraft-producing technologies.

Let's suppose that in the absence of trade, two countries, the United States and Israel, have aircraft industries that produce propeller planes, jets, and helicopter craft for domestic consumption. The demand for aircraft within the U.S. aircraft market, however, is much greater than demand within the Israeli market. Hence, in the absence of trade, U.S. aircraft production initially is Q_{US} at point *US* along the long-run average cost curve. Israeli aircraft production is Q_I at point *I*, so in the absence of trade Israeli manufacturers operate at a cost disadvantage relative to U.S. producers, simply because their scale of operations is lower.

Now suppose that the two nations initiate open trade. Even though Israel's aircraft manufacturers have access to the same technology, U.S. producers immediately operate with a cost advantage over Israeli producers. Furthermore, by expanding their production, U.S. companies can reach the minimum efficient scale (MES) for aircraft production at point *MES.* U.S. aircraft manufacturers then could produce Q_{MES} units. They could continue to sell many of these units domestically, but they could export the remainder to other nations such as Israel. In the end, the United States would develop a specialization in producing aircraft, and Israel ultimately might import most of its aircraft from the United States.

For Critical Analysis:
Who would lose if barriers to trade prevented U.S. companies from exporting aircraft to Israel and other nations? Who would gain? (*Hint:* In this situation, U.S. and Israeli aircraft production levels would remain at Q_{US} and Q_I in Figure 11-1.)

PRODUCT VARIETY, IMPERFECT COMPETITION, AND INTRA-INDUSTRY TRADE

The previous discussion shows how economies of scale help create a comparative advantage that leads to inter-industry trade. Because intra-industry trade by definition entails exchanges of similar goods and services, however, gains from trade do not arise from comparative advantage or absolute advantage. Instead, gains from intra-industry trade stem from cost efficiencies that producers experience and from the effects of an expanded *product variety* that intra-industry trade offers to consumers.

Common experience indicates that many industries located in different countries produce goods and services that are easily distinguishable but nonetheless are relatively close substitutes for each other. Examples include German and U.S. beers, Swedish and Japanese automobiles, Swiss and Italian wristwatches, British and Caribbean financial services, and the like. By engaging in intra-industry

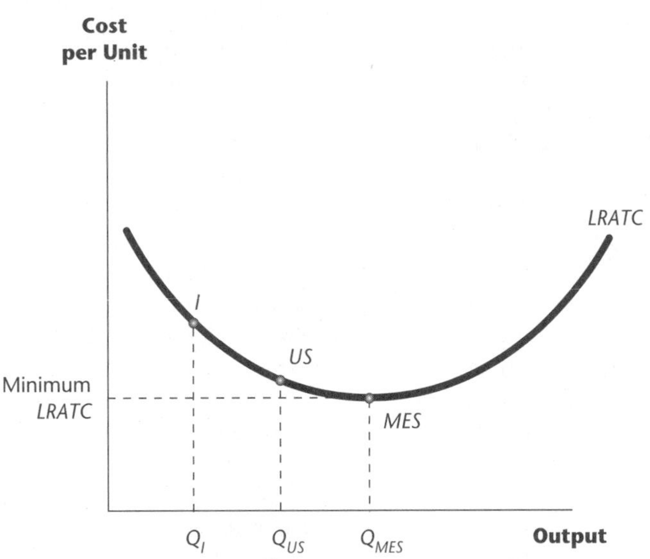

Figure 11-1

A Hypothetical Long-Run Average Cost Curve for an Aircraft Industry

*Groups of aircraft manufacturers located in the United States and Israel produce essentially the same products using the same technology. Hence, they face the same long-run average total cost (*LRATC*) curve. Because the demand for the products of firms in the U.S.-based aircraft industry is greater relative to the demand for products of firms in the Israel-based aircraft industry, however, U.S. output is higher, at point* US*, than Israeli output, at point* I*. In the absence of trade, therefore, Israeli aircraft manufacturers operate at a cost disadvantage relative to U.S. firms. Hence, U.S. firms have a cost advantage over Israeli firms if international aircraft trade takes place, and U.S. firms are better positioned to expand toward the minimum efficient scale (*MES*).*

trade, residents of these and other nations clearly are able to consume a broader variety of products.

A Theory of Imperfect Competition

In addition, the existence of intra-industry trade allows the companies that produce these products to market their goods and services to more consumers. Because the companies sell products that are not identical yet are substitutable, they are said to be *imperfectly competitive* firms. Consumers can distinguish among companies' products, which gives each individual firm the ability to set prices different from the average price charged by other firms in the industry. By way of contrast, any single *perfectly competitive* firm that sells products identical to those of other firms has no incentive to set a price that differs from the market price, because setting a price above the market price induces its customers to buy the identical product from other firms, and setting a price below the market price reduces the firm's profits.

Economies of scale and imperfect competition with its variety of similar products provide an explanation for why nations often experience intra-industry trade. To think about why this is so, consider a situation in which **monopolistic competition** prevails. In this situation, there are many firms, each of which has an output level that is relatively small compared with total industry output. In addition, it is easy for firms to enter or leave the industry. Nevertheless, firms produce similar but not identical products. Each is able to set the price of its own product, but the demand for its product depends on the availability of the close substitutes produced by other firms in the industry.

Monopolistic competition
An industry structure with a relatively large number of firms, easy entry or exit, and similar but not identical firm products.

In the short run, a firm in a monopolistically competitive industry can earn a *positive economic profit,* which means that its total revenue can exceed the opportunity cost of being part of that industry instead of another industry. Positive economic profits, however, encourage other firms to enter the industry. As they enter and capture some of the existing firm's customers, the demand for its product declines, and its economic profit declines toward zero. In the long run, therefore, the total revenue earned by a firm in a monopolistically competitive industry just covers the opportunity cost of remaining in the industry. (To learn how to use graphs to examine the behavior of a monopolistically competitive firm in both the short run and long run, see on pages 347–348 *Visualizing Global Economic Issues: Monopolistic Competition in the Short Run and in the Long Run.*)

Monopolistic Competition, Economies of Scale, and Intra-Industry Trade

Now consider what happens when monopolistically competitive firms in two nations are able to export their products across their nations' borders. In the domestic country, a typical domestic firm experiences an increase in the demand for its product because foreign residents can now purchase it. By itself, this tends to encourage the firm to expand its output.

At the same time, however, foreign firms are able to sell their products to domestic residents, so the demand for the typical domestic firm's product begins to decline somewhat. This induces the domestic firm to cut back slightly on its production, although the net effect of open trade is an increase in its output. In addition, because domestic residents can choose among a wider variety of products, the quantity of the domestic firm's product that they desire to consume becomes more sensitive to changes in the price that the domestic firm charges. This encourages the domestic firm to keep its price low.

In fact, in the long run the domestic firm responds to open trade by cutting its price somewhat. The reason is that expanding its output allows the domestic firm to experience economies of scale. Its average production cost falls as it increases its output. Because the firm produces more efficiently, keeping its price low to retain its customers in the face of greater competition from abroad is also consistent with its efforts to maximize profit. Nevertheless, in the long run the maximum economic profit that each domestic firm earns remains equal to zero.

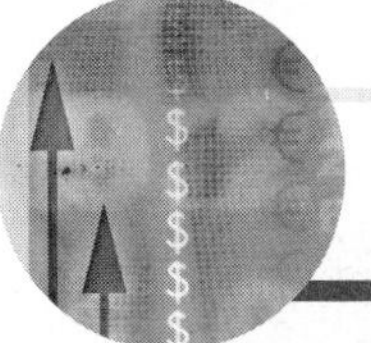

Visualizing Global Economic Issues

Monopolistic Competition in the Short Run and in the Long Run

Because a monopolistically competitive firm sells a product that is at least slightly different from the products of all other firms, there is a unique customer demand for its product. Panel (a) of Figure 11-2 displays a representative demand curve faced by such a firm. The demand curve, which shows the price that the firm's customers are willing and able to pay for each quantity it sells, slopes downward. Thus, if the firm wishes to sell an additional unit of its product, it must reduce the price that it charges. One effect of a price reduction is an increase in the quantity of its product that its customers desire to consume at the lower price, and this effect tends to raise the firm's revenues. Another effect of a price cut, however, is a reduction in revenues on the fewer units it could have sold at a higher price.

Marginal Revenue and Marginal Cost

Together, the two effects of a price reduction imply that at any quantity the firm sells, its *marginal revenue*—the additional revenue it earns from selling an additional unit of its product—is always less than the price it charges. Hence, the firm's *marginal revenue curve,* which shows the marginal revenue it can earn at each quantity it sells, lies below the demand curve.

Panel (b) shows a possible short-run situation that this firm might face when it takes into account its production costs as well as the demand for its product and its implied marginal revenue curve. To simplify a little, we assume that it can always vary all factors of production, so that its long-run average cost curve applies. The other cost curve shown in panel (b) is the firm's *marginal cost curve.* It shows, for each possible rate of output, the additional cost that the firm will incur if it produces one more unit of output, which is its **marginal cost.**

Short- and Long-Run Equilibrium under Monopolistic Competition

To maximize its economic profit—total revenue less all costs, including the opportunity cost of being in this business instead of some other business—the firm produces to the point at which marginal revenue equals marginal cost. This is point *S,* where the marginal revenue and marginal cost curves cross. Consequently, in the short-run situation shown in panel (b), the firm's profit-maximizing output rate is Q_S. If it were to produce less output, marginal revenue would exceed marginal cost, so the firm could add to its profits by producing more units. If it were to raise its output above Q_S, however, then marginal cost would rise above marginal revenue, and the firm's profit would begin to fall. This is why Q_S is the output rate that maximizes the firm's profit. The firm charges the price P_S that the demand curve indicates its customers are willing to pay for this amount of output. The average cost of producing Q_S units is AC_S. The firm's total profit, therefore, equals ($P_S - AC_S$), which is the height of the shaded rectangle, times Q_S, which is the base of the rectangle. Thus, the shaded rectangle depicts a positive **economic profit** for the firm.

In a monopolistically competitive industry, it is easy for new firms to enter the industry. The fact that the firm depicted in panel (b) earns a positive economic profit is a signal that revenues in this industry are more than sufficient to cover the opportunity cost of being in this industry instead of another one. In the long run, therefore, additional firms will enter the industry. Panel (c) shows what happens at the previously existing firm in panels (a) and (b) following the entry of new firms. First, the demand for this firm's product will decline, because some of its customers will buy similar goods from other firms. Thus, the demand curve shifts leftward. Second, because the entry of new firms means that more substitute products are available, the demand for this

continued

continued from page 347

firm's product becomes more *elastic.* That is, a given proportionate price increase will induce a larger proportionate decrease in the quantity of the firm's product that customers wish to purchase. Because the firm's marginal revenue curve stems from its demand curve, it also shifts leftward and becomes more elastic. The firm's costs are unaffected by entry of new firms, so the result is a decline in the firm's economic profits to zero in the long run. As panel (c) indicates, this occurs when the firm's demand curve shifts to a point of tangency with the long-run average cost curve at point *L.* At this point, the economic profit of firm falls to zero. It produces a lower rate of output, Q_L, at a lower price, P_L, and the total revenue it earns just covers the opportunity cost of being part of this industry. This removes the incentive for any more firms to enter the industry.

For Critical Analysis:
What would happen if so many new firms initially entered the industry that the firm's demand curve were to "overshoot" point *L,* so that the firm finds itself operating at a loss (a negative economic profit)?

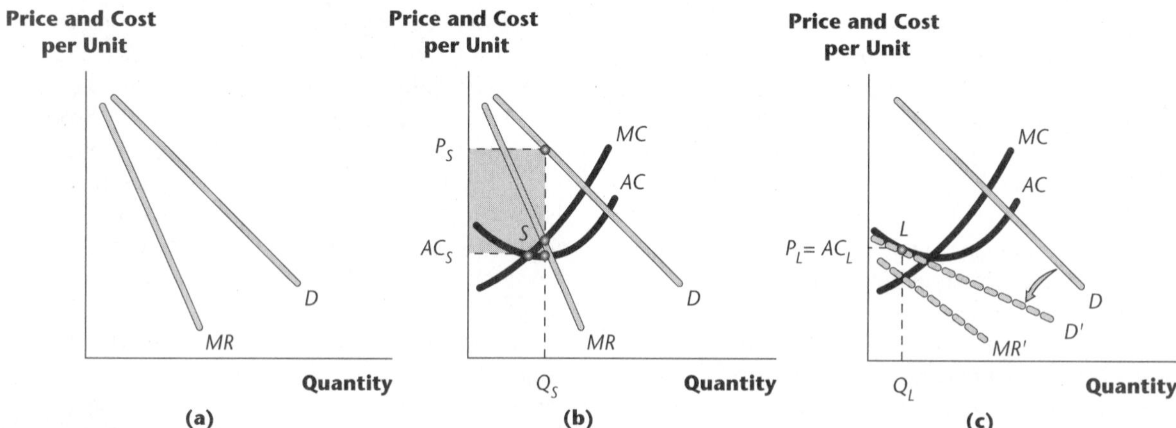

Figure 11-2

Demand, Production, and Pricing at a Monopolistically Competitive Firm

Panel (a) shows demand and marginal revenue curves for the product of a monopolistically competitive firm. Marginal revenue, or the additional revenue earned from selling an additional unit, is always less than the price the firm charges. In panel (b), the firm maximizes its economic profit in the short run by producing to the point where marginal revenue equals marginal cost, at point S, where it produces output Q_S and charges a price P_S, thereby earning maximum profit equal to $(P_S - AC_S) \times Q_S$. In the long run, additional firms enter the industry when this and other firms earn positive economic profits. In panel (c), entry causes the demand for this firm's product to decline, because some of its customers will buy similar goods from other firms, and to become more elastic, so that a given proportionate price increase induces a larger proportionate decrease in the quantity of the firm's product that consumers desire to purchase. In the long run, the firm's economic profits equal zero at point L where the demand curve is tangent to the firm's long-run average cost curve. The firm's total revenues just cover the opportunity cost of being part of this industry, so there is no incentive for more firms to enter the industry.

Marginal cost
The additional cost that the firm incurs from producing an additional unit of output.

Economic profit
Total revenue minus explicit and implicit opportunity costs.

Hence, intra-industry trade broadens the range of products from which consumers can choose. The opportunity to export their products encourages domestic firms to increase their production. They experience economies of scale as they push up their output, which enables them to reduce their prices in the face of competition from foreign imports. On net, therefore, domestic residents are able to consume more industry output at lower prices. So can foreign residents, where these effects are the same. Thus, both domestic and foreign residents experience gains from intra-industry trade. (For more details on how these gains arise, see on pages 350–351 *Visualizing Global Economic Issues: Intra-Industry Trade with Monopolistically Competitive Firms.*)

Fundamental Issue

How do economies of scale and product variety provide an explanation for intra-industry trade?

Today a significant portion of international trade is intra-industry trade. When consumers can readily distinguish among the products of different firms and firms in the industry can easily enter or leave the industry, then monopolistic competition prevails. In the long run, firms enter or leave the industry until revenue just covers the opportunity cost of being in that industry instead of some other industry. In the presence of international trade, each firm tends to expand its output to reduce its long-run average cost, which permits charging a lower price to help retain customers in the face of greater intra-industry competition from firms in other countries.

Foreign Direct Investment and Trade Patterns

An important factor contributing to the growth of intra-industry trade has been foreign direct investment. Most foreign direct investment occurs through the actions of multinational corporations with operations spanning two or more countries.

TYPES OF FOREIGN DIRECT INVESTMENT

When engaging in foreign direct investment, multinational firms must decide where to invest, what production techniques to use and what kinds of facilities to establish, whether to buy or lease existing facilities or construct new facilities, and whether to bring in local partners. Most fundamentally for the resulting pattern of trade, they must determine whether to engage in *horizontal* or *vertical* foreign direct investment.

Horizontal Investment

A multinational firm may undertake **horizontal foreign direct investment,** in which a foreign subsidiary of the firm produces goods or services similar to those produced in the firm's home country. Horizontal subsidiaries tend to produce for national or regional markets. Generally speaking, it involves

Horizontal foreign direct investment
Establishment of a foreign subsidiary of a multinational firm that produces a good or service that is similar to the one the firm produces in its home country.

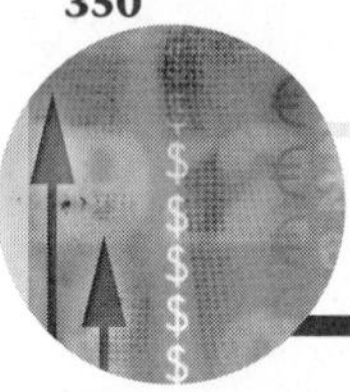

Visualizing Global Economic Issues

Intra-Industry Trade with Monopolistically Competitive Firms

To see how intra-industry trade tends to affect production and pricing decisions at monopolistically competitive firms, take a look at Figure 11-3. The figure depicts an initial long-run situation, at point *N*, for a domestic company before any intra-industry trade occurs. To maximize its profit, the firm produces to the point at which marginal revenue cost equals marginal revenue. In this "no-trade" situation, the firm produces Q_N units, charges the price P_N, and earns an economic profit equal to zero. Thus, its total revenue just covers the opportunity cost of being in this industry.

Now think about what happens when intra-industry international trade takes place. When the firm is able to export some of its output for sale to residents of other nations, the demand for its product starts to rise. At the same time, however, companies in other countries are able to sell competing products domestically. This tends to reduce the demand for the domestic firm's product somewhat and, simultaneously, to cause the demand for its product to become more elastic. As a result, the domestic firm ends up in a new long-run, "trade" situation such as the one shown by point *T*. On net, it produces and sells more output, Q_T. In addition, because there is a downward movement along the firm's long-run average cost curve, the firm experiences economies of scale. Its long-run average cost is lower, so the firm operates more efficiently and thus produces more output to sell at a lower per-unit price, P_T. Thus, the firm's domestic *and* foreign customers gain from intra-industry trade.

For Critical Analysis:
This firm earns an economic profit equal to zero in the long run without or with intra-industry trade, so what is its incentive to export its product? (*Hint:* What would happen if the firm chooses not to export but faces increased competition from foreign firms that do choose to engage in intra-industry trade?)

multinational firms based in industrialized nations that establish subsidiaries in other industrialized nations.

Vertical Investment

Vertical foreign direct investment *Establishment of a foreign subsidiary of a multinational firm that produces components that are assembled elsewhere or uses components produced elsewhere to assemble the firm's final product.*

A multinational firm may alternatively engage in **vertical foreign direct investment.** In this case, a foreign subsidiary produces components to be assembled elsewhere or uses components produced elsewhere to complete assembly of a final product. In most circumstances, vertical investment involves multinational firms based in industrialized nations, which establish subsidiaries in less developed countries.

Distributing production facilities across two or more countries allows a firm to take advantage of national differences in the costs of factors of production. For instance, a U.S. multinational company may establish facilities for designing and manufacturing components of its final product in the United States, thereby tak-

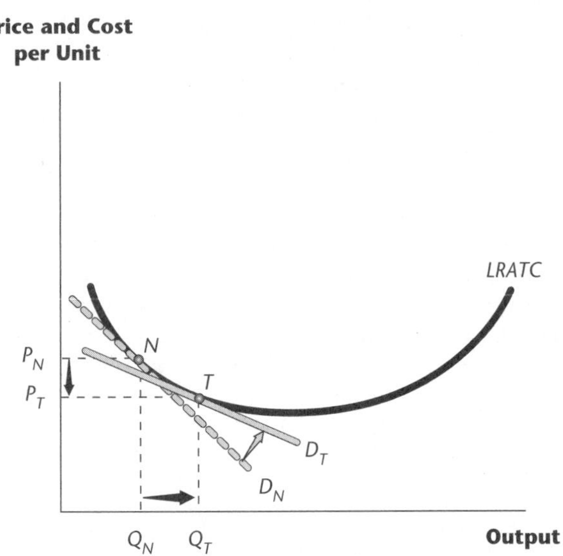

Figure 11-3

The Effects of Intra-Industry Trade under Monopolistic Competition

The initial long-run equilibrium for this monopolistically competitive firm in the absence of international trade is at point N, where the firm earns zero economic profits producing Q_N units that it sells at a price of P_N. When intra-industry international trade takes place, the firm experiences an increase in the demand for its product from foreign residents. At the same time, however, companies located abroad are able to sell their products domestically, which tends to reduce demand somewhat. The availability of more substitute products from abroad also makes the demand for the domestic firm's product more elastic. This results in a new long-run equilibrium with intra-industry trade at point T, at which the firm produces more output, Q_T, at a lower long-run average total cost that it sells at a lower price, P_T.

ing advantage of relatively low costs of capital resources in that relatively capital-abundant country. It then may set up an assembly facility in a relatively labor-abundant nation, such as Mexico, so that it can keep its wage costs relatively low.

TRADE EFFECTS OF FOREIGN DIRECT INVESTMENT

Horizontal investment provides an inflow of capital to the nation where it occurs. It usually does not, however, contribute substantially to that country's flow of international trade. The reason is that multinational companies tend to create parallel facilities in other nations primarily as a means of avoiding barriers to trade with those nations. Thus, the firms tend to sell most of their horizontal subsidiaries' production within the nations where the goods or services are manufactured.

By way of contrast, because multinational companies engaging in vertical investment must transfer components from facilities in one nation, such as the

United States, to another, such as Mexico, their actions create flows of intra-industry trade. Consequently, recently surging growth in vertical investment has been a major contributor to measured increases in international trade. (For one example of how vertical foreign direct investment has affected measured trade flows, see *Management Notebook: Is Production Sharing Making Mexico a "Trampoline" for U.S. Products?*)

3 Fundamental Issue

In what way can foreign direct investment affect international trading patterns?

Horizontal foreign direct investment involves a company's establishment of international facilities that produce goods or services that are similar to those produced in its home country. Although the growth of horizontal foreign direct investment has helped push up worldwide capital flows, it has not had a significant effect on international trade. By way of contrast, vertical foreign direct investment, which entails spreading a company's production processes across different nations, can induce significant increases in measured trade flows when companies transfer components from one nation to another for final assembly. This has helped generate the recent rise in intra-industry trade.

Globalization and Industry Structure

In a monopolistically competitive industry, consumers gain from intra-industry trade both because they can consume a greater variety of products and because increased international competition induces producers to increase production and cut prices. Thus, imperfect competition can help explain why intra-industry trade takes place. This is not the only way in which imperfect competition plays an important role in the global trading system, however. It has effects in other ways as well.

BARRIERS TO ENTRY

Not every imperfectly competitive industry contains monopolistically competitive firms that can easily enter or leave the industry. Many industries, both within nations and around the globe, contain only a few firms. Within some countries, a nationwide industry comprises a single firm. Let's now consider such industries and their implications for world trade.

Barriers to entry *Any factors inhibiting entrepreneurs from instantaneously founding a new firm.*

Industries with relatively small numbers of firms exist because of **barriers to entry,** which are factors that prevent entrepreneurs from immediately creating a new firm. There are four basic types of entry barriers. One is the presence of significant economies of scale. If companies in an industry find that increasing the scale of their operations continues to reduce long-run average cost up to relatively large output rates, then it may be that only a few firms can achieve minimum efficient scale within a marketplace.

Another barrier to entry is exclusive ownership of a relatively large portion of a key resource used to produce a good or service. For example, for a number of years a diamond firm called De Beers owned mines containing a large portion of

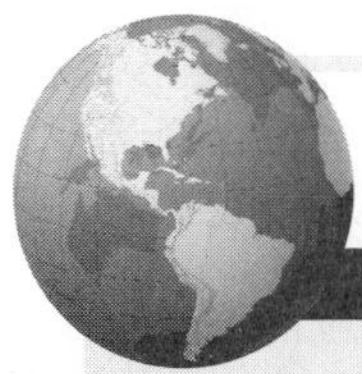

MANAGEMENT *Notebook*

POLICY MANAGEMENT

Is Production Sharing Making Mexico a "Trampoline" for U.S. Products?

In 1999, the United States ran a $15 billion trade deficit with Mexico. In 2000, this deficit grew to more than $20 billion. U.S. opponents of the North American Free Trade Agreement—and more generally, those who oppose all U.S. trade—commonly seize on such statistics to document how the U.S. residents "lose out" from international trade.

Production Sharing

Hidden in these bilateral trade deficit figures, however, is the fact that large portions of the components of imported Mexican goods originate in the United States. Large quantities of U.S.-originated components also make their way into final products assembled in Mexico for shipment to other nations. For instance, an estimated 70 percent of all components of computer products manufactured in Mexico for sale to points around the globe had a U.S. origin.

What lies behind this pattern of trade is *production sharing,* in which multinational firms located in the United States shift part of their production processes to Mexico. In a U.S. company's financial reports, the final sales from production sharing appear on a line item called "foreign affiliate sales."

The Trampoline Effect

Each year, an International Business Machines factory in Mexico exports final products valued at nearly $3 billion to the United States and close to $1 billion in products to other nations. Because about 70 percent of the components of Mexican-assembled computer products originate in the United States, this means that this IBM Mexican plant essentially functions as a "trampoline" for hundreds of millions of dollars in U.S.-manufactured components.

This story repeats itself at other U.S. multinational firms that engage in production sharing with Mexican affiliates. All told, in 2000 U.S. multinational firms sent more than $40 billion of components to Mexico for final assembly. This was more than Mexico's entire trade surplus with the United States for 1999 and 2000 combined. For the most part, the U.S. trade deficit with Mexico arises because assembly of components adds considerable market value. After all, a final product, such as an automobile, is much more useful to a buyer than the individual components, such as steering wheels, axles, and transmissions.

Mexico is not the only nation in which these foreign affiliate sales function in part as a conduit for distributing U.S.-manufactured components to other countries. For instance, about 40 percent of U.S. companies' affiliate sales in the Netherlands and Switzerland involve items that are re-exported to other nations after final assembly in those nations. Since 1995, exports by foreign affiliates of U.S. multinationals in Mexico, the Netherlands, Switzerland, and elsewhere have more than tripled.

For Critical Analysis:

How could a large and increasing U.S. trade deficit with Mexico be good news for the U.S. economy?

the world's uncut diamonds. This permitted De Beers to dominate the world's diamond market until the 1990s, when other diamond discoveries took place and new mining firms began to actively participate in the market for uncut diamonds.

A third barrier to entry can arise from differences among products that help explain monopolistic competition. In some instances, it may be possible that a company has a **first-mover advantage** meaning that during its time as the only firm in the market it takes advantage of relatively low marketing costs to establish a long-term entry barrier by identifying its product as the *industry* product. It took a number of years, for example, before later entrants to the copy machine industry were able to overcome the tendency of many people to think of copying pages as "Xeroxing" them.

First-mover advantage
A barrier to entry arising from the ability of the initial firm in an industry to develop marketing advantage by identifying its own product as the industry product.

Fourth, governments can erect barriers to entry by sanctioning government-sponsored firms or by establishing licensing requirements for an industry and then restricting the number of licenses. (Comparing the experiences of the Internet-service-provider industries of Morocco and Tunisia helps illustrate what a difference government-erected entry barriers can make; see *Online Globalization: Mobile in Morocco.*)

ALTERNATIVE FORMS OF IMPERFECT COMPETITION

Under perfect competition, there are many firms and many consumers, firms produce indistinguishable products, and it is easy for firms to enter or leave the industry. Monopolistic competition is a form of imperfect competition that arises because each firm's product can be distinguished from those of other firms. Otherwise, however, a monopolistically competitive firm also has many firms and many consumers, and firms can accomplish industry entry or exit at trivial cost. The existence of barriers to entry makes the entry of new firms difficult in the short run and much more costly in the long run. This naturally tends to limit the number of firms in the industry.

Oligopoly

Economists use the term **oligopoly** to describe an industry structure in which only a few firms supply the bulk of the industry's output. Most of the world's output of automobiles, for instance, is produced by a handful of companies: General Motors, Ford Motor Company, DaimlerChrysler, Toyota, and Honda.

Oligopoly
An industry structure in which a few firms are the predominant suppliers of the total output of an industry, so that their pricing and production decisions are interdependent.

In contrast to perfectly competitive or monopolistically competitive firms, firms in an oligopolistic industry practice *strategic pricing.* When they set their prices and quantities, they recognize that their decisions will affect the decisions of their rivals in the marketplace. Economists call this *oligopolistic interdependence,* and there are many theories of the price- and quantity-setting strategies that a few interdependent firms may adopt.

Monopoly

One special case of strategic pricing is cooperative decision making within an oligopolistic industry. In principle, by working together a few firms can establish a

Online Globalization

Mobile in Morocco

Half of the residents of Morocco do not have access to electricity or running water. Four-fifths of its villages do not have paved roads. Traditional phone lines serve only about 6 percent of the country's population. Nevertheless, more than 85 percent of Morocco's population of just over 28 million people has access to mobile phones. Today, many of these people also have wireless access to the Internet. They are served by hundreds of Internet service providers (ISPs).

Privatization to the Rescue

Even though Tunisia was the first country in northern Africa to offer Internet access, it still only has two ISPs. Tunisia's population is less than one-third of Morocco's, but this population difference alone cannot explain the big difference in the number of ISPs.

The main reason that Morocco is so far ahead in wireless phone and Internet service is that in 1999 it turned to the private sector. The Moroccan government was looking for ways to raise funds. It decided to auction off government-owned telecommunication companies to private bidders. Then it began selling licenses to other telecommunication startup companies. Before long, wireless telecommunication was suddenly a much more competitive business in Morocco.

A Regional Web Hub?

Bypassing traditional phone lines has allowed Morocco to leapfrog old telephone technologies that would have required years for the country's residents to develop. Because Morocco is so much more advanced in telecommunications than its neighbors, it may well become a regional hub for Internet-based commerce. Already, several Moroccan-based satellite networks are in operation, and there is discussion of bypassing traditional television service via the wireless Web.

For Critical Analysis:

In Tunisia, the two existing Internet service providers are both closely connected to the national government. What might Tunisia learn from Morocco's experience?

---

cartel and restrain their output, coordinate their pricing decisions, and maximize their joint profit. Essentially, they then act as a **monopoly**, or single producer in a marketplace. True monopoly situations are relatively rare. Nevertheless, traditionally, local telephone, water, and energy services often are provided by government-regulated monopolies. Cartels that mimic a monopoly are perhaps even more rare. The reason is that each cartel member typically has an incentive to cheat on a cartel agreement by expanding its production above limits established by the cartel. Thus, most cartels fail to act as a single monopoly producer for long.

Monopoly
An industry that consists of a single firm.

The effective operation of a cooperative cartel or of a true monopoly tends to reduce consumer welfare. The reason is that a profit-maximizing monopolist faces the entire demand for the industry's product. By reducing production and pushing up the product price relative to the levels that perfectly competitive firms would choose, a monopoly reduces consumer surplus. (To see how we can use a diagram to illustrate these adverse welfare effects of monopoly, see on pages 356–357 *Visualizing Global Economic Issues: The Welfare Effects of Monopoly*.)

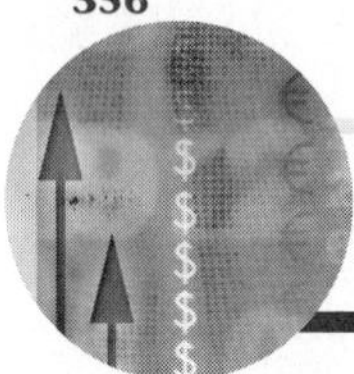

Visualizing Global Economic Issues

The Welfare Effects of Monopoly

To see why an unregulated monopoly can reduce consumer welfare, take a look at Figure 11-4. It displays a market demand curve that is faced either by a perfectly competitive or monopolistic industry. As a simplification, let's assume that under perfect competition the market supply curve is perfectly elastic, which is the situation if the marginal cost of each firm in the industry is constant and identical. This automatically implies that marginal cost and average cost are equal. Under perfect competition, the market price, P_{PC}, is equal to marginal cost, and total industry output is equal the quantity demanded at this price, which is Q_{PC}. Consumer surplus, therefore, is given by the large shaded triangle in the diagram.

If this industry is monopolistic, however, then the single firm faces the market demand curve and the indicated marginal revenue curve. To maximize its profit, the monopoly produces to the point at which marginal revenue equals marginal cost. Hence, the monopoly produces the quantity Q_M. It then charges the price that consumers are willing to pay, which is P_M. Consumer surplus thereby shrinks to the dashed triangle above this monopoly price. Hence, consumer welfare is lower under monopoly.

Monopolistic competition and oligopoly are more common types of industry structures than monopoly. Comparing the welfare implications of these structures directly with perfectly competition is a little more complicated, but under nearly all circumstances the same basic conclusion follows: Imperfectly competitive industries typically yield lower consumer welfare than perfectly competitive industries.

For Critical Analysis:
Does the monopoly capture the entire amount of the "lost" consumer surplus in the form of profit?

Market Structure and the Prices of Imports: Dumping Revisited
Recall from Chapter 4 that an important type of import penalty that nations impose are antidumping duties. Under international law, a company engages in *dumping* if it sells its product abroad at a price that is either below the price that it charges in its home country or below its per-unit production cost.

You have learned that under imperfect competition, it is commonplace for firms to charge prices higher than the market price in perfectly competitive industries. Now think about what is likely to happen if a perfectly competitive industry within a domestic nation suddenly confronts import competition from an imperfectly competitive industry located in a foreign country that protects its industries from international competition. Suppose that both industries have the same pro-

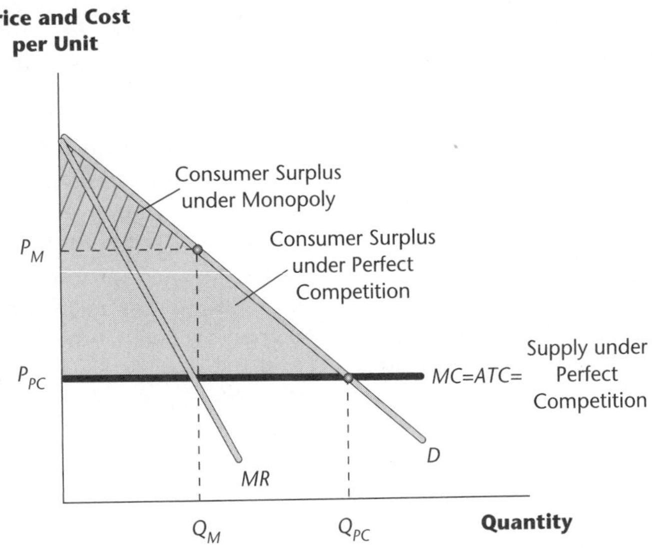

Figure 11-4

Comparing Monopoly with Perfect Competition with Constant Marginal Cost

The market demand curve in this diagram applies whether the industry is perfectly competitive or monopolistic. Marginal cost is constant, and hence also equals average cost, and is identical for each firm in the industry. Under perfect competition, therefore, the market supply curve is perfectly elastic. The market price, P_{PC}, is equal to marginal cost. Total industry output equals the quantity demanded at this price, Q_{PC}, and consumer surplus is the large shaded triangle in the diagram. If this industry is monopolistic, then the single firm faces the market demand curve and the corresponding downward-sloping marginal revenue curve. To maximize its profit, the monopoly produces to the point at which marginal revenue equals marginal cost. It produces the quantity Q_M and charges the price P_M, so consumer surplus declines to the dashed triangle above this monopoly price. Thus, consumer welfare is lower under monopoly, as compared with perfect competition.

duction costs. Because foreign firms are imperfectly competitive, the price that they charge in their home country typically will be higher than the market price charged by perfectly competitive firms in the domestic country. The foreign firms, however, will only be able to sell their products in the domestic market at the lower domestic market price. Once they do, they automatically will engage in dumping as defined by international law, even though increased domestic import competition will benefit domestic consumers. (To learn how to use diagrams to examine why the logic of antidumping rules is problematic, see on pages 358–359 *Visualizing Global Economic Issues: Foreign Monopoly and Dumping in a Domestic Market—Who Gains, and Who Loses?*)

ON THE WEB

For a review of antidumping actions in the United States and around the world, examine a survey provided by the Congressional Budget Office at http://www.cbo.gov/showdoc.cfm?index=439&sequence=0&from=1.

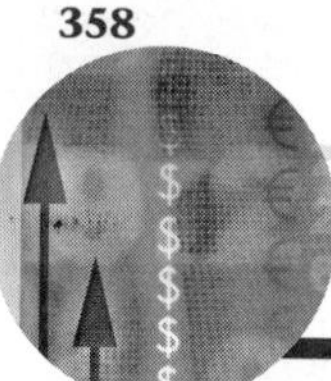

Visualizing Global Economic Issues

Foreign Monopoly and Dumping in a Domestic Market—Who Gains, and Who Loses?

To see why the logic of antidumping rules is problematic, take a look at Figure 11-5. Panel (a) displays a situation in which companies within a domestic industry are perfectly competitive and sell their output at the market price P_D^1. Panel (b) depicts the situation of a relatively large foreign monopoly that is protected from both home and international competition. In the foreign country, therefore, the foreign monopoly charges the price P_F^1 that foreign residents are willing to pay.

Suppose that the domestic market is opened to trade but the foreign monopoly remains protected from international competition. As long as the domestic price exceeds the foreign firm's average production cost, the foreign firm can expand its profits by producing a higher output rate and selling additional units to domestic residents. Thus, the domestic supply curve shifts rightward in panel (a) by the amount of these foreign exports, which are assumed to be significant relative to total output in the domestic market. This pushes down the domestic price somewhat, to P_D^2. Although total domestic purchases increases to Q_D^2, the amount of output supplied by domestic firms declines to Q_D'. Hence, the foreign firm exports the amount $Q_D^2 - Q_D'$ to the domestic market, so its total production rises from Q_F^1 to $Q_F^2 = Q_F^1 + (Q_D^2 - Q_D')$. As shown in panel (b), the foreign firm continues to sell Q_F^1 units to foreign residents at the price P_F^1. Now, however, it generates additional profit by selling $Q_D^2 - Q_D'$ units to domestic residents at the new domestic market price P_D^2.

Because the foreign firm sells its product in the domestic country at the price P_D^2 that is below the price P_F^1 that it charges foreign residents, thereby earning this additional profit, the foreign firm has engaged in dumping. Domestic firms typically claim to have "lost" revenue equal to the sum of the areas labeled *A, B,* and *C* in panel (a). The area *A* is domestic revenue lost solely because of the market price reduction. The area *B* is revenue that the foreign firm receives from selling its output in the domestic market at the new market price, and the area labeled *C* constitutes a transfer of revenue previously earned by domestic firms to the foreign firm. All three of these amounts, however, would normally constitute revenue losses for domestic firms as a result of opening the domestic market to foreign competition. Domestic consumers, of course, gain from the increased competition, because they are able to purchase more units of the good at a lower price.

Nevertheless, under World Trade Organization rules, the domestic country can impose an antidumping penalty on the foreign firm equal to the amount imported times the difference between the foreign market price P_F^1 and the domestic market price P_D^2. This is the area *E* in panel (b). The size of area *E,* the antidumping penalty, could be as large, or possibly even larger, than the additional profit that would induce the foreign firm to export additional output to the domestic country in the first place. It is for this reason that most economists regard antidumping rules as protectionist policies aimed primarily at restricting imports and protecting domestic firms from international competition.

For Critical Analysis:
Sometimes companies charge that foreign firms sell some of their output in domestic markets at a price below their average production costs. Are there ever any circumstances in which this could be either a short-run or a long-run profit-maximizing strategy for these foreign firms?

Domestic Market

Price

P_D^1
P_D^2
A
C B
S
S'
D
Quantity
Q_D' Q_D^2
Q_D^1

(a)

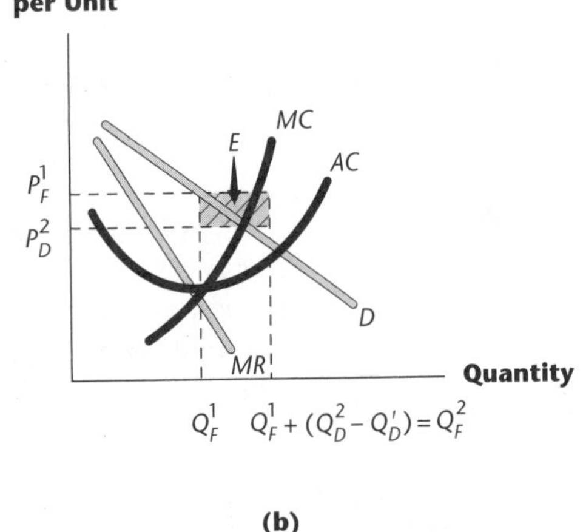

(b)

Figure 11-5

Domestic Dumping by a Foreign Monopoly

In panel (a), firms in a domestic industry are perfectly competitive and sell their output at the market price P_D^1. In panel (b), a relatively large foreign monopoly that is protected from both home and international competition charges the price P_F^1. If the domestic market is opened to trade, then the foreign firm exports $Q_D^2 - Q_D'$ to the domestic market, so its total production rises from Q_F^1 to $Q_F^2 = Q_F^1 + (Q_D^2 - Q_D')$ in panel (b). The domestic supply curve to shifts to the right in panel (a), which causes the domestic price to P_D^2 and total output sold domestically increase to Q_D^2. The amount of output supplied by domestic firms declines to Q_D'. The foreign price P_F^1 exceeds the domestic price P_D^2, so the foreign firm has engaged in dumping. The area A in panel (a) is domestic revenue lost solely because of the market price reduction, the area B is revenue that the foreign firm receives from selling its output in the domestic market at the new market price, and the area labeled C is a transfer of revenue previously earned by domestic firms to the foreign firm. Area E in panel (b) equals the amount imported times the difference between the foreign market price P_F^1 and the domestic market price P_D^2, which is the potential antidumping penalty under current world trade rules.

4 Fundamental Issue

What are alternative industry structures, and how does industry structure matter in the global economy?

Under perfect competition, many firms produce indistinguishable products and can enter or leave the industry with ease. Monopolistically competitive industries also have many firms and easy entry or exit, but each firm's product is easy to distinguish from the products of other firms. Oligopoly is an imperfectly competitive industry structure that is characterized by barriers to entry that reduce the number of firms. In the extreme case of monopoly, there is one single firm in the market. As compared with perfect competition, monopoly leads to a reduction in industry output and an increase in the product price, which lead to lower consumer welfare, either within nations or across nations. Differences in market structures across countries complicate evaluating the effects of trade policies such as antidumping penalties.

Evaluating the Competitive Implications of Industry Structure

Many companies located in different nations have sought to combine their operations within the past several years. In some cases, the companies involved in these proposed combinations have been very large. Let's think about why such companies might wish to merge, and let's also think about the possible consequences of combining companies across national borders.

ON THE WEB

For a comprehensive review of global merger and acquisition issues, go to http://www.unctad.org/en/docs/wir99ove.en.pdf.

MOTIVATIONS FOR CROSS-BORDER MERGERS AND ACQUISITIONS

In recent years there has been a burst of cross-border activity in corporate mergers and acquisitions. For instance, Daimler-Benz of Germany merged with Chrysler Corporation of the United States, and the French media giant Vivendi acquired the North American company Seagram, Inc. and then sold it to another French firm. In addition, Deutsche Bank of Germany acquired the U.S. bank Bankers' Trust, and the French carmaker Renault acquired portions of the assets of Samsung Motors of Korea.

Traditional Justifications for Combining Companies

Traditionally, there are two essential reasons that companies wish to engage in mergers and acquisitions. One is to combine the resources of firms to assist in achieving economies of scale within a single new company. The resulting cost efficiencies enhance the overall performance of the combined entities.

The other traditional rationale for mergers and acquisitions is that a combined firm may be able to earn higher revenues. Realizing economies of scale from the consolidation of the operations of two or more firms leads to expanded production within the new firm, which may increase total revenue at the combined entity. In addition, consolidating operations through a merger or acquisition may give the newly combined company greater power to push up product prices, thereby enhancing revenue.

Corporate Governance in Cross-Border Mergers and Acquisitions

Interestingly, in some recent cross-border mergers and acquisitions, another objective appears to have been to alter the nature of *corporate governance,* which is the legal and institutional framework under which companies operate. In some countries, such as the United States, *public companies* are commonplace, and ownership shares are widely distributed among national residents. In others, such as Germany, *private companies* owned by an inside group of partners are more common, and ownership of public companies is often more narrowly distributed among a limited set of wealthy individuals.

In recent years a consensus has emerged among many management experts that publicly owned companies with widely dispersed owners tend to react more flexibly to changes in the marketplace. This conclusion does not rule out the potential for some private companies to outperform public companies. Nevertheless, it has caused many residents of countries where private companies or more narrowly held public companies predominate to contemplate changing the structures of their companies. One speedy way for companies to do this is through mergers with or acquisitions of public companies located in countries where there are numerous shareholders. A number of observers believe that this desire to develop a broader public structure helps explain why Daimler-Benz merged with Chrysler, why Deutsche Bank acquired Banker's Trust, and why Deutsche Telecom has sought to acquire U.S. telecommunications companies.

ASSESSING MARKET CONCENTRATION AND ITS EFFECTS

Do larger firms that compete with fewer rivals necessarily behave in ways that significantly reduce consumer welfare? Unfortunately, there is no consensus about the answer to this question. One fundamental reason is that economists do not agree about just how large firms must be relative to the rest of the market before they can exert effects on market prices. Another reason, however, is that competition from international sources can complicate efforts to define a "market."

Measuring Market Concentration

Traditionally, economists have sought to measure whether a few firms account for a large portion of industry output using **concentration ratios,** which are the portions of total industry sales accounted for by the largest few firms. The most commonly examined concentration ratio is the four-firm concentration ratio, or the percentage of total sales at the top four firms in the market.

Concentration ratio
The share of total industry sales by the top few firms.

An obvious problem with concentration ratios is that they can fail to reflect important differences among structures of different industries. For example, suppose that the top four firms in two different markets each have a 20 percent share within each market, so that the four-firm concentration ratio for each industry is 80 percent. In one of the markets, however, there might be just one more firm, so that rivalry within the market is limited to a total of five firms. In the other market, there might be ten more firms equally sharing the remaining 20 percent of industry sales and attempting to actively compete with the top four companies.

Partly in response to this and other perceived problems with simple concentration ratios, beginning in the early 1980s the U.S. Department of Justice and Federal Trade Commission began emphasizing a different concentration measure. This measure, called the **Herfindahl–Hirschman index,** is the sum of the squared market shares for all firms in an industry. For the example of a five-firm industry with a 20 percent market share at each firm, this would yield a Herfindahl–Hirschman-index value of 2,000. For the case of the industry in which the top four firms have 20 percent market shares while ten others each have a 2 percent share, the value would be 1,640. The lower index value for the latter industry would thereby reflect its greater potential for more broad-based competition among a relatively large set of producers.

Herfindahl–Hirschman index
The sum of the squares of the market shares of each firm in an industry.

Naturally, how high a concentration ratio or Herfindahl–Hirschman-index value must be to indicate that individual firms are likely to have significant power to affect market prices is a judgment call. Even more problematic, however, is that concentration ratios or Herfindahl–Hirschman-index values have meaning only if they are calculated using correctly defined markets. For instance, one might find that the four-firm concentration ratio for the cable-modem Internet-access industry is very high in many areas. Indeed, in most areas where cable modem service is available there are likely to be fewer than five providers of cable-modem Internet access, so a four-firm concentration ratio of 100 percent is likely to be common. Most economists would agree, however, that this ratio would be meaningless, because the **relevant market**—the true economic marketplace taking into account the availability of all products that directly constrain product prices for individual producers—surely includes other providers of Internet access, such as traditional phone-dial-up providers, providers of Internet direct service lines, and satellite-service providers.

Relevant market
The true economic marketplace taking into account the availability of all products that directly constrain product prices for individual producers.

Defining Markets: Where Does Geography Fit In?

Because they complicate determining the scope of the relevant market, cross-border mergers and acquisitions add an additional challenge to evaluating the degree of market competition. In nations with borders open to international trade, the availability of close international substitutes for domestically produced goods and services can help restrain the pricing power of domestic sellers. Applying concentration measures only to domestic markets could therefore be misleading.

The presence of significant international competition can complicate government policies regarding mergers. Consider, for instance, the recent experience of the Canadian banking industry. For all its massive geographic size, Canada's population is slightly smaller than California's. The nation has four dominant, Toronto-based banking institutions—the Royal Bank of Canada, the Bank of Montreal, the Toronto-Dominion Bank, and the Canadian Imperial Bank of Commerce—which serve as depositories for two-thirds of all funds in Canadian banks. Recently, these four institutions proposed merging into two, with Royal Bank of Canada set to merge with the Bank of Montreal and the Toronto-Dominion Bank poised to merge with the Canadian Imperial Bank of Commerce. The four institutions wanted to consolidate to assist in fending off competition from big U.S.

banks. They also wanted to embark on an effort to compete more successfully in the United States, thereby geographically diversifying their operations.

The Canadian government disallowed both merger requests, however, ruling that the "relevant banking market" was Canada alone. For the banks that had proposed to merge, this was a serious blow to their long-range plans regarding their ability to compete effectively in the *international* banking markets that they felt were most relevant.

Fundamental Issue 5

Why do companies engage in cross-border mergers and acquisitions, and how do international market linkages complicate measuring the degree to which a few large firms may dominate markets?

Common justifications for cross-border mergers are that combining the operations of previously independent companies can reduce average costs for the new entity and that a gain in pricing power can allow the merged firm to earn higher revenues than two firms could have earned alone. In some instances, companies have engaged in cross-border mergers in an effort to alter the nature of corporate governance. To gauge the extent to which market concentration may influence the pricing power of firms, economists use concentration ratios, or the portion of sales by the top firms in the market, and the Herfindahl–Hirchman index, or the sum of squares of the market shares of all firms. Interpreting these concentration measures is problematic, especially in light of difficulties in defining the relevant market for calculating either measure.

Antitrust in an Evolving Global System

Governments seek to influence the extent of market competition using **antitrust laws.** These legal statutes are aimed at ensuring that consumers and producers experience benefits of market competition within the context of broader national economic policies.

Antitrust laws
Statutes designed to achieve benefits of competition for consumers and producers.

THE GOALS OF ANTITRUST LAWS

In years past, countries have concentrated on enforcing antitrust laws within national borders. As relevant markets have expanded to include foreign firms, however, antitrust policy has increasingly become a global issue.

Traditionally, a fundamental goal of antitrust laws has been to limit the pricing power available to firms. Because cartels have an incentive to enrich participating firms at the expense of consumer welfare and economic efficiency, many antitrust laws explicitly prohibit efforts by combinations of firms to restrain market competition. Indeed, most national antitrust laws make it a crime even to try to form a monopoly.

It is also common for antitrust laws to restrict **price discrimination.** One type of price discrimination entails charging different consumers different prices for identical goods. Another involves charging the same consumer different prices

Price discrimination
Charging different consumers different prices for identical goods or services, or charging the same consumer different prices for the same good or service depending on number of units that the consumer purchases.

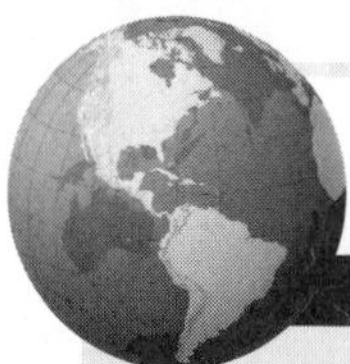

POLICY *Notebook*

POLICY MANAGEMENT

That Price Is Too Low!—Wal-Mart Meets German Antitrust Policy

In 1997, Wal-Mart entered the highly regulated German grocery market, and today the U.S. based retailer operates about 100 stores in Germany. Soon, the company was surpassing its rivals in sales of basic items, such as flour, milk, and sugar. Within three years the company's share of sales within the German hypermarket grocery market—an industry composed of large stores selling food and nonfood items at discount prices—was nearly 11 percent.

In the fall of 2000, however, German antitrust authorities ordered Wal-Mart to raise its prices, claiming that the company was exploiting its size and market share to sell food products below cost on a continuing basis. The authorities admitted that Wal-Mart's lower prices benefited consumers, but they concluded that it also caused undue harm to Wal-Mart's smaller German competitors. Threatened with a fine of nearly $500,000, Wal-Mart raised its prices. Nevertheless, it promised to test the limits of its ability to compete on the basis of price. The company also continued to push for allowing its stores to remain open until 10:00 P.M. on weekdays, two hours later than the closing times mandated by German regulators.

For Critical Analysis:
German authorities argued that in the long run, consumers would be hurt if Wal-Mart's lower prices drove rival firms from the grocery market. Evaluate this reasoning.

Predatory pricing
A situation in which a firm sets artificially low prices intended to induce competitors to leave the industry and to dissuade potential rivals from entering the industry.

Industrial policies
Government policies intended to promote the development of specific national industries.

for the same good, depending on the number of units that the consumer purchases. Many nations also prohibit efforts to engage in so-called **predatory pricing,** in which firms are alleged to reduce their prices to drive competitors out of business and dissuade potential rivals from entering the marketplace. Antitrust laws seeking to restrain price discrimination and predatory pricing often generate controversy, because it is not unusual for enforcement of these laws to raise market prices. (See *Policy Notebook: That Price Is Too Low!—Wal-Mart Meets German Antitrust Policy.*)

In some nations the balancing act between protecting consumers and promoting the interests of producers is complicated by **industrial policies.** These are government policies that aim to actively promote the development of specific industries. For instance, in 2000 the Japanese government decided that a key national goal was for Japan to have the world's foremost Internet infrastructure by 2005. This obliged the government to establish a regulatory framework consistent with attaining global leadership for its mobile phone and broadband-Internet industries. Industrial policies such as this can become entangled with antitrust enforcement to the benefit of producers, because by pursuing these policies governments often facilitate interactions among competing firms. This can lay the groundwork for implicit governmental sanctioning of cartel arrangements.

ON THE WEB

To learn more about antitrust policies in various nations, go to the U.S. Department of Justice's worldwide antitrust links at http://www.usdoj.gov/atr/contact/otheratr.htm.

ANTITRUST ENFORCEMENT ACROSS NATIONAL BOUNDARIES

How should national antitrust authorities define the relevant market if AT&T decides that it wishes to merge with British Telecommunications, or if Germany's Deutsche Telecom wants to acquire Sprint? What should they have done if America Online and Time–Warner, each of which had a global presence in markets for Internet access, instant messaging, cable communications, and entertainment, wished to merge? How should they have reacted when Time–Warner simultaneously attempted to merge with EMI, one of the world's largest recorded-music companies?

These are not just rhetorical questions, as U.S. and E.U. antitrust authorities learned in 2000 and 2001 when all these issues surfaced. The emergence of cross-border markets for many goods and services has increasingly made antitrust policy a global undertaking.

Clashing Goals of Antitrust Enforcement

In the late 1990s, when U.S. authorities approved the acquisitions of Chrysler by Daimler-Benz and Banker's Trust by Deutche Bank, they did so after careful study of relevant markets in automobiles and banking. The relevant market for each industry, U.S. regulators determined, had become sufficiently globally based that these combinations would not have anticompetitive consequences for U.S. consumers.

In 2000, however, EU antitrust authorities ruled against a proposed combination of Time–Warner and EMI, which it had appeared the U.S. antitrust authorities were on the way to approving. A year later, EU policymakers decided against approving another planned merger—in this case, one that U.S. regulators had already endorsed—between two large multinational corporations, General Electric and Honeywell International. These cases highlight a significant problem for antitrust enforcement across national borders: conflicting objectives of national antitrust policies.

In the United States, the overriding goal of merger policies is to protect the interests of consumers. This is also a formal objective of EU antitrust efforts. In the EU, however, there is also a requirement that policymakers must reject any merger that "creates or strengthens a dominant position as a result of which effective competition would be significantly impeded." This additional clause currently creates a tension between U.S. and EU policymaking. In the United States, increasing dominance of a market by a single firm raises the concern of antitrust authorities, but U.S. authorities will remain passive if they determine that greater market dominance arises from factors such as exceptional management and greater cost efficiencies that ultimately benefit consumers by reducing prices. By way of contrast, under EU rules antitrust authorities are obliged to block any merger that increases the dominance of any producer, irrespective of what factors motivate its preeminence in the marketplace.

Will Antitrust Go Global?

The EU's scuttling of the proposed General Electric–Honeywell merger raised concerns in the United States, where during the late 1990s antitrust authorities had given the green light to several mergers between U.S. and EU firms and to acquisitions of U.S. firms by EU companies. Some U.S. critics argued that the European Union's leadership was using antitrust policy as a weapon of protectionism. The real aim of EU antitrust policies, they claimed, was to prevent U.S. firms from broadening their competitive positions within Europe even as European companies were acquiring U.S. firms.

In the summer of 2001, EU antitrust authorities responded to these criticisms by resolving to strengthen bilateral cooperation with U.S. regulators in an effort to reduce the risk of future policy disagreements. EU and U.S. policymakers increased the extent of existing interactions among staff lawyers and economists. They also broadened the scope of discussions of methods for harmonizing their approaches to evaluating and enforcing policies governing proposed cross-border mergers and acquisitions.

The initiation of these bilateral efforts encouraged some antitrust experts to propose widening the scope of interactions to a multilateral discussion of appropriate antitrust goals, rules, and enforcement mechanisms. So far, however, multilateral cooperation among the world's antitrust authorities remains a goal rather than a reality.

6 **Fundamental Issue**

How do governments regulate international merger and acquisition activities?

Governments often authorize antitrust authorities with the power to determine whether proposed cross-border mergers and acquisitions will affect the pricing power of firms. Antitrust authorities commonly enforce rules limiting price discrimination or prohibiting predatory pricing. In some nations, antitrust enforcement is complicated by national industrial policies, which aim to promote particular domestic industries. Recently conflicting objectives of antitrust policies in the United States and the European Union have led to inconsistent decisions about proposed mergers among companies based in those regions of the world. This has led to proposals for coordinated policymaking among U.S. and EU antitrust authorities when firms propose cross-border mergers or acquisitions, but so far, this idea has not advanced beyond the stage of general discussions.

CHAPTER SUMMARY

1) **How Economies of Scale Help to Explain a Nation's Specialization in Inter-Industry Trade:** Economies of scale arise for a firm or an industry whenever long-run average cost falls as increased usage of all factors of production expands total output. Long-run average cost is minimized at the minimum efficient scale of a firm or industry, beyond which any additional rise in output would increase long-run average cost. Countries containing firms that have already experienced economies of scale will have lower average

production costs than firms in other countries when international trade is permitted. Thus, these countries are more readily able to specialize in producing the good or service of that particular industry.

2) **How Economies of Scale and Product Variety Assist in Explaining Intra-Industry Trade:** Under conditions of monopolistic competition, firms produce a variety of easily distinguishable yet similar products, and it is easy for firms to enter or leave the industry whenever revenue rises above or falls below the opportunity cost of being in that industry instead of another. Opening borders to international trade induces a typical monopolistically competitive firm to raise its output. It experiences economies of scale, so it can reduce the price of its product to attract customers in the face of increased intra-industry competition from firms abroad. Horizontal foreign direct investment has contributed to higher global capital flows, but the main way that foreign direct investment has added to intra-industry trade is through vertical investment. Multinational companies that undertake vertical investment transport product components across national borders, and these flows are counted in international trade statistics.

3) **How Foreign Direct Investment Affects International Trading Patterns:** Companies that establish facilities abroad that produce goods or services similar to products of facilities located in its home country engage in horizontal foreign direct investment. In contrast, companies placing facilities that handle products at various stages of production in different nations engage in vertical foreign direct investment. Increased horizontal foreign direct investment has boosted global capital flows but has had relatively small effects on international trade. Greater vertical foreign direct investment can bring about sizable increases in intra-industry trade as firms transfer product components between nations.

4) **Alternative Industry Structures, and How Industry Structure Matters in the Global Economy:** Under perfect competition, many firms produce indistinguishable products, and they can enter or leave the industry with ease. Monopolistically competitive industries also have many firms and easy entry or exit, but each firm's product is easy to distinguish from the products of other firms. Oligopoly is an imperfectly competitive industry structure that is characterized by barriers to entry that reduce the number of firms. In the extreme case of monopoly there is a single firm in the market. As compared with perfect competition, monopoly leads to a reduction in industry output and an increase in the product price, which lead to lower consumer welfare. Differences in national industry structures can complicate evaluating the effects of trade policies such as antidumping penalties.

5) **Why Companies Desire to Merge across Borders, and How International Market Linkages Complicate Measuring the Market Concentration:** One traditional rationale for cross-border mergers is that the new entity may be able to operate at lower average cost than the previously separate companies. Another is that the combination may be able to take advantage of greater pricing power and earn higher revenues than two firms could

have earned alone. Companies may also engage in international mergers to take advantage of cross-country differences in the structure of corporate governance. One way that economists attempt to measure the degree of market concentration is via concentration ratios, which is the percentage of total industry sales by top firms. Another is the Herfindahl–Hirschman index, which is the sum of squares of the market shares of all firms. Using either measure requires subjective judgments, and correctly defining the relevant market for applying the measures can be difficult.

6) **How Governments Regulate International Merger and Acquisition Activities:** Typically, national governments give antitrust officials the authority to decide if proposed cross-border mergers or acquisitions are appropriate. The effect of mergers and acquisitions on domestic prices is usually the main focus of antitrust policies, but in many nations antitrust authorities also enforce laws restraining price discrimination, forbidding predatory pricing, or enforcing industrial policies that seek to support specific domestic industries. In the early 2000s, differing U.S. and EU antitrust goals caused antitrust authorities for the two regions to reach conflicting conclusions regarding proposed mergers among multinational firms. This has led to preliminary discussions of possible coordination of U.S. and EU antitrust policies.

QUESTIONS AND PROBLEMS

1) Some economists have argued that the U.S. e-commerce firms such as eBay.com and Amazon.com have a comparative advantage over Internet-based rivals located abroad, which the U.S. companies derive from their ability to offer differentiated products in relatively greater volumes at relatively lower average cost as they expand the long-run scale of their operations. Without taking a stand on whether this argument may be "correct," use appropriate diagrams to explain why this might be a viable hypothesis for the currently dominant position of many U.S. firms in cross-border Internet-based trade.
2) Suppose that the market for U.S. e-commerce services such as those discussed in question 1 is monopolistically competitive. In addition, however, suppose that experience proves that e-commerce firms located in the United States and elsewhere have essentially identical long-run average costs, which initially decline but eventually increase as firms expand their scale of operations. Assume that short-run and long-run costs at a typical U.S. e-commerce firm are identical, and explain how the demand faced by the firm is likely to be affected if foreign e-commerce firms begin offering products to U.S. consumers even as the U.S. firm broadens its capability to market its products to residents of other nations via the Internet. What are the effects on the U.S. firm's rate of production and on the price it charges for its product?

3) Previously, a domestic market containing monopolistically competitive firms was open to foreign competition. Domestic firms have succeeded, however, in convincing their government to close the nation's borders to foreign competition. As a result, foreign nations have responded by prohibiting the sale of the products of domestic firms within their borders as well. Evaluate the effects of these domestic and foreign policy actions on the production and pricing decisions of a domestic producer.
4) In your own words, distinguish horizontal foreign direct investment from vertical foreign direct investment.
5) A nation has experienced a large increase in foreign direct investment, and measured capital inflows have increased dramatically. So far, however, the country's trade flows have not changed. Provide a possible explanation.
6) Recently, a nation opened its borders to movements of all goods and services, including factors of production. Its government has observed jumps in the rates of growth in measured imports and exports far in excess of increases that could have resulted from greater purchases of final goods and services by consumers at home and abroad. Speculate about other factors that might have contributed to this nation's significant increases in measured imports and exports.
7) In the global market for a good, for a number of years there have been only a few producers, each of which produces an indistinguishable product. What type of market structure is this? What factors could explain this structure?
8) A domestic industry has been able to prove that a foreign producer engaged in dumping. The foreign producer's counterargument is that it has charged higher prices in its home market simply because this is its profit-maximizing strategy in its home market where barriers to entry have given it monopoly pricing power, whereas it faces considerable competition in the domestic market and hence charges a lower price for its product in that market. Explain why this might be a reasonable economic argument yet do little to fend off the imposition of antidumping penalties under current international antidumping rules.
9) Consider on the following page the fictitious sales data for domestic and foreign firms, and answer the questions that follow.
   (a) Domestic producers 1 through 6 and foreign firms 7 through 11 produce similar but distinguishable products. Currently, antitrust authorities define the relevant market to include both domestic and foreign firms. Calculate the four-firm concentration ratios and Herfindahl–Hirschman indexes under this definition of the relevant market.
   (b) Now suppose that antitrust authorities determine that the relevant market includes only domestic producers. Recalculate the market shares and squared market shares implied by the table under this definition of the relevant market, and use these data to calculate four-firm concentration ratio and Herfindahl–Hirschman indexes.
10) What do your answers to question 9 reveal about the importance to antitrust policy of correctly determining the relevant market for a product? Explain.

Domestic Sales of Domestic Firms				Domestic Sales of Foreign Firms			
Firm	Sales	%	%^{2}	Firm	Sales	%	%^{2}
1	750	7.5	56.25	7	4,200	42.0	1764.00
2	50	0.5	0.25	8	2,000	20.0	400.00
3	50	0.5	0.25	9	1,950	19.5	380.25
4	50	0.5	0.25	10	450	4.5	20.25
5	50	0.5	0.25	11	400	4.0	16.00
6	50	0.5	0.25		9,000		
	1,000						

Table Key:
Sales are in millions of units of the national currency
% denotes percentage of domestic and foreign share of total domestic sales, rounded to the nearest tenth of one percentage point
%^{2} denotes squared percentage of market share of sales, rounded to the nearest whole number

ONLINE APPLICATION

Internet URL: http://www.usdoj.gov/atr/icpac/finalreport.htm

Title: **Final Report of the International Competition Policy Advisory Committee**

Navigation: Go to the home page of the Antitrust Division of the U.S. Department of Justice (http://www.usdoj.gov/atr/). Then click on "Public Documents," and next click on "International Competition Policy Advisory Committee" and "ICPAC Final Report."

Application: Perform the indicated operations, and answer the questions.

1) Click on "Chapter 3—Multijurisdictional Mergers: Rationalizing the Merger Review Process Through Targeted Reform." Take a look at Box 3-A, which gives information about the "merger challenge rate" in selected countries and regions. Suppose that a multinational corporation considering acquiring a firm within these nations regarded the challenge rates of its antitrust authorities as measures of the probability that national policymakers would dispute a proposed acquisition. In which area would the multinational corporation regard its chances of running into difficulties in acquiring a firm to be highest? Lowest?

2) Now consider Box 3-B, which gives approximate dollar values of worldwide sales for a proposed combination of companies that trigger a requirement for firms to provide notification of planned mergers or acquisitions to antitrust authorities within selected countries. How might these notification requirements influence the choice of a foreign firm seeking to expand globally by finding a merger partner or an acquisition target?

For Group Study and Analysis: Assign the above chapter as a reading for the entire class. Then divide the class into three fictitious "countries," denoted *A*, *B*, and *C*. Antitrust goals of each country are as follows: *A*—maximize consumer welfare; *B*—minimize the dominance of any one firm; and *C*—protect domestic industries from foreign competition. Have each group draft a one-paragraph "policy guideline" for judging mergers and acquisitions within its country. Reconvene the class, and compare the guidelines developed by each group. Discuss why differing objectives may help explain significant national differences in antitrust rules and their enforcement.

REFERENCES AND RECOMMENDED READINGS

Braithwaite, John, and Peter Drahos. *Global Business Regulation*. Cambridge, U.K.: Cambridge University Press, 2000.

Carlton, Dennis, and Jeffrey Perloff. *Modern Industrial Organization*. Reading, Mass.: Addison-Wesley-Longman, 1999.

Evenett, Simon, Alexander Lehmann, and Benn Steil, eds. *Antitrust Goes Global*. London: Blackwell, 2000.

Graham, Edward, and J. David Richardson. *Competition Policies for the Global Economy*. Policy Analysis in International Economics No. 51, Washington, D.C.: Institute for International Economics, November 1997.

Klitgaard, Thomas, and Karen Schiele. "Free versus Fair Trade: The Dumping Issue." *Current Issues in Economics and Finance*. Federal Reserve Bank of New York 4 (3) (August 1998).

Morici, Peter. *Antitrust in the Global Trading System*. Economic Strategy Institute, 2000.

Ruffin, Roy. "The Nature and Significance of Intra-Industry Trade." Federal Reserve Bank of Dallas *Economic and Financial Review* (4th Quarter 1999):2–9.

CHAPTER TWELVE

The Public Sector in the Global Economy

Fundamental Issues

1. **In what ways do government regulators seek to safeguard the interests of consumers?**
2. **How do the world's governments protect rights to intellectual property?**
3. **What are international externalities and global public goods, and what can national governments or multinational institutions do about them?**
4. **How can the world's nations protect the global environment?**
5. **How does increased globalization complicate the efforts of governments to finance their activities?**

The rural area surrounding the small town of Clanton, Alabama, is best known for the peaches that are grown in dozens of groves and sold in local grocery outlets and fruit stands. Recently, however, the town became the center of an investigation by the U.S. Food and Drug Administration. The FDA suspected that a "men's clinic" in Clanton, which had emerged as a center for online marketing and distribution of the prescription drug Viagra, was engaged in illegal activities. The clinic's owners insisted that their operations were legitimate. They claimed that customers who wished to order the medication were linked to a Web site hosted by a computer in Australia. There, customers filled out virtual forms detailing their medical history, providing legal consent, and authorizing payment. These forms then were transmitted to an office in Clanton, which forwarded the medical information to a computer network operated by a group of doctors in Romania, who, in turn, issued prescriptions electronically to a pharmacy in West Virginia, a state that recognizes foreign prescriptions. The Clanton men's clinic then distributed the pills that the Romanian doctors prescribed for the U.S. residents who placed the orders.

Ultimately, the government concluded that this arrangement violated the law and convinced a court to shut it down. Nevertheless, this sort of circuitous—literally round-the-globe—procedure for obtaining a prescription medication from Romanian physicians instead of U.S. doctors is just the tip of the iceberg. Companies worldwide are testing the limits of their ability to use the Internet to circumvent national and international regulations. To critics, such activities constitute blatant attempts to violate laws designed to safeguard consumers from potentially harmful products and to protect reputable firms from cutthroat competition by unscrupulous upstarts. To defenders, many of these companies are simply harnessing borderless Internet connections to bypass intrusive and unnecessary restrictions that they argue are designed mainly to protect many of the world's established producers from competition.

Should the U.S. government get involved in determining whether an Alabama company can take advantage of a West Virginia law that permits Romanian doctors to compete with physicians based in the United States while giving the company a competitive niche in distributing a prescription medication? These kinds of questions are becoming increasingly common in the world economy. In this chapter, we explore, among other things, how globalization is affecting the scope of regulations intended to safeguard consumers. More broadly, we consider the general role of the public sector in the world economy.

Protecting Consumer and Producer Interests in the Global Economy

Traditionally, a fundamental reason that governments have existed has been to provide a coordinated system of safeguarding the interests of their citizens. Thus, for many years governments have protected producer rights to returns on inventions. More recently, governments have also sought to protect consumers from the potentially unscrupulous actions of producers.

PROTECTING CONSUMERS—IS THERE COMMON GROUND?

"Consumer beware" was once the operative phrase in business-to-consumer exchanges. Today, however, many national governments require companies to meet specified minimal standards in their dealings with customers. For instance, in 2000 the U.S. Federal Trade Commission (FTC) assessed monetary penalties on several Internet sellers because they failed to ship goods that they had promised to customers in time for Christmas. Such actions would have been unheard of in most nations a few decades ago.

The Rationale for Consumer Protection

Asymmetric information
One party's possession of information in an economic transaction that the other party to the transaction does not possess.

Adverse selection
The tendency for manufacturers of the lowest-quality products to have the greatest incentive to misrepresent the attributes of those products.

Moral hazard
The potential for a buyer or seller to behave differently after an economic transaction than what was agreed to before the transaction.

Why do governments get involved in consumer protection? The main argument favoring government intervention in business–consumer interactions is the problem of **asymmetric information,** or the possession of information by one party to a transaction that is not possessed by the other party. One way in which asymmetric-information difficulties arise is through **adverse selection,** which refers to the likelihood that businesses that manufacture particularly poor-quality products are the ones that have the greatest incentive to misrepresent their attributes in an effort to sell them. To help generate sales, some businesses also succumb to the temptation to misrepresent the customer services they will provide after a sale takes place. The possibility that a seller may act in such an "immoral" (from a consumer's perspective) manner after a sale occurs is an example of **moral hazard,** which refers to the potential for either a borrower or seller to alter behavior in an undesirable way following an economic transaction.

These asymmetric-information problems provide a rationale for government agencies such as the Federal Trade commission (FTC) to provide consumer protection services. These agencies act both as a "consumer watchdog," in an effort to minimize the adverse selection problem, and as an "industry policeman," with the goal of combating the moral hazard problem. (Other nations, such as those of the European Union, have their own industry policemen, and sometimes it is hard to tell if their regulations are designed to protect consumers or producers; see *Online Globalization: Are Privacy Protection and Online Protectionism Synonyms in the European Union?*)

Differing Views about Government's Role in Safeguarding Consumers

Governmental interventions aimed at protecting consumers are most common in developed nations in North America, Europe, and, to a lesser extent, Asia. They are much less commonplace in other locales. Even within developed countries, there is not complete agreement on the proper scope of consumer protection laws and enforcement.

For example, European regulators commonly require companies to keep all information they have about consumers confidential. Companies can only reveal such information to other firms if consumers explicitly request that they do so. By way of contrast, information sharing among companies has been commonplace in the United States for years. U.S. companies often sell lists of customer names, addresses, phone numbers, and e-mail addresses. Recent legal changes have restricted the ability of U.S. companies to continue some of these practices, but U.S. rules continue to be much less restrictive than those in place in Europe. Undoubtedly during the coming years consumer protection will emerge as another area of

Online Globalization

Are Privacy Protection and Online Protectionism Synonyms in the European Union?

Various U.S. regulations are designed to *restrict* the use of consumer data that companies obtain from Internet interactions with customers. The goal of U.S. regulations is to allow firms to make limited use of information they collect about their customers while providing certain consumer privacy protections. In the European Union (EU), by way of contrast, privacy rules *forbid* the transferral of online consumer data. In the EU, a consumer's right to privacy is absolute.

The EU Data Privacy Directive

The EU implemented its online personal-privacy rules in October 1998 when it adopted a set of guidelines known collectively as the *Data Protection Directive.* Under the EU Data Protection Directive, before a company can transfer any data it has obtained about a customer to any other firm, it must obtain the customer's written permission. Online permission will not suffice.

EU regulations apply to both offline and online interactions among individuals and companies, but they have especially important implications for ongoing efforts by U.S. Web firms to do business in Europe. The reason is that EU rules require U.S. companies to develop separate systems for their online dealings with customers in both parts of the world.

Online Protectionism in the European Union?

To satisfy EU rules, U.S. companies doing business with EU consumers essentially have had to develop a separate "track" for EU marketing, sales, and customer service. For instance, U.S. firms have had to develop European advertising efforts that satisfy EU guidelines. U.S. firms also must use separate "European contracts," which are legally enforceable promises to European consumers that they will not share data with other companies. By way of contrast, fledgling European online firms do not face a requirement to expend resources on separate marketing, sales, and customer-service tracks for EU and U.S. consumers.

Some U.S. critics have contended that privacy protection in Europe may really be a protectionist policy intended to increase the height of barriers to entry by foreign firms. In the view of these critics, privacy protection laws in Europe may have more to do with discouraging U.S.-based Internet sellers from entering the European electronic marketplace than they do with protecting the privacy of European residents. According to this contention, European governments realize that U.S. Internet sellers have a first-mover advantage in marketing to European residents. By slowing up U.S. firms and raising their costs, critics allege, the European Union hopes to give European companies a chance to catch up.

For Critical Analysis:

Which residents of Europe gain or lose if the costs of meeting the Data Protection Directive discourage a significant number of U.S. firms from offering to sell their products online in Europe?

controversy within multilateral trade negotiations. (For an example of disagreement about whether a U.S. regulation is designed to safeguard U.S. consumers or to protect U.S. producers, see on the next page *Management Notebook: The U.S. Drug-Import Ban—Protecting Consumers from Inferior Medicines or Pharmaceuticals Firms from Foreign Competition?*)

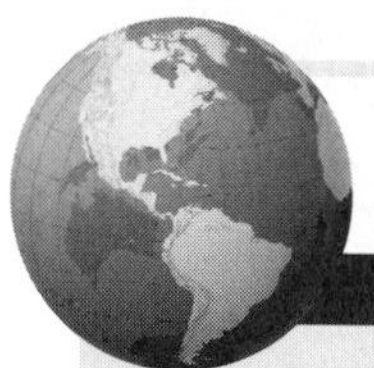

MANAGEMENT *Notebook*

POLICY MANAGEMENT

The U.S. Drug-Import Ban—Protecting Consumers from Inferior Medicines or Pharmaceuticals Firms from Foreign Competition?

In 1988, the U.S. Congress enacted legislation barring the sale of imported pharmaceuticals. The law exempted only U.S. companies, which were authorized to reimport drugs they originally had manufactured for export back into the United States.

Rationalizing an Import Ban: Safeguarding U.S. Consumers

When Congress passed this law, the rationale was that import restrictions on drugs were necessary to safeguard U.S. consumers. Promoters of the law argued that the import ban would protect U.S. residents from substandard foreign products.

The concern in Congress was that foreign importers might seek to sell counterfeit, inferior, or even expired medications. Within the United States, the chief pharmaceuticals regulator, the FDA, has the power to police domestic producers in an effort to minimize the potential for consumers to be harmed. Its regulatory powers naturally do not extend beyond U.S. borders. Congress did, however, give the FDA the power to enforce the ban on imported drugs.

Voluntary Supervision by the FDA?

In 1999 and 2000, however, U.S. pharmaceuticals prices surged. Several studies found that drug prices in Canada and other nations with fewer import restrictions were much lower than the prices that prevailed in the United States. A number of economists pointed out that while the 1988 import ban might be protecting consumers from a few bad foreign medications, it also appeared to be doing a good job of protecting domestic drug manufacturers from global competition.

In the summer of 2000, the U.S. House of Representatives passed a bill barring the FDA from enforcing the 1988 import ban. Senate supporters added an amendment designed to ensure that consumers are not victimized by impure or fraudulent medications by requiring foreign companies to sell pharmaceuticals in the United States to voluntarily subject themselves to FDA inspections and testing. U.S. drug companies successfully engaged in heavy lobbying to stop passage of a final bill, and to date Congress has not lifted the ban on drug imports.

For Critical Analysis:

Why is it likely to be difficult to balance the gains from consumer protection with gains from trade?

The advent of international trade conducted via the Internet has further complicated the regulatory landscape. For instance, in 2000 a French judge ruled that the Internet auction firm eBay had violated French laws prohibiting trade of Nazi-related goods when it permitted someone to auction World War II-era Nazi artifacts using the eBay Web site. This raised the specter that Web-based firms might eventually have to find a way to design Web sites that anyone in any nation can access while satisfying consumer protection statutes in scores of different countries. Already, some observers are calling for multilateral discussions of minimum global standards for online consumers.

Fundamental Issue

In what ways do government regulators seek to safeguard the interests of consumers?

Because firms often have more information than consumers about the quality of their products and customer service, there are potential asymmetric-information problems. One problem that can result is adverse selection, or the potential for low-quality products to be offered for sale. Another is moral hazard, or the possibility that one party to an exchange may undertake actions that another party deems undesirable after the exchange has already been arranged or taken place. To address these problems, governments may enact regulations establishing minimal standards for quality or service, and they may establish agencies to enforce those standards.

SAFEGUARDING INTELLECTUAL PROPERTY RIGHTS

By inventing new products, implementing new production processes, and organizing new ways of marketing, selling, and delivering goods and services, scientists, engineers, and businesspeople contribute to economic development and growth. To encourage the efforts of these individuals, governments often enact systems of **intellectual property rights,** which are legal rules governing the ownership of creative ideas. Today one of the major issues arising in regional and multilateral trade discussions is concern over how to develop an appropriate framework for the international regulation of intellectual property rights.

Intellectual property rights
Laws granting ownership of creative ideas, typically in the form of a copyright, trademark, or patent.

There are three ways that governments ensure rights to intellectual property. One is by issuing **copyrights,** which grant authors exclusive privileges to reproduce, distribute, perform, or display creative works. Copyrights cover works such as articles, stories and novels, computer programs, audio recordings, and cinematographic films. Governments also protect intellectual property by establishing rules governing **trademarks.** These are words or symbols that companies use to identify their goods or services and distinguish them from the goods or services produced by other firms. **Patents** are legal documents granting an inventor the exclusive right to make, use, and sell an invention for a specified number of years.

Copyright
An author's legal title to the sole right to reproduce, distribute, perform, or display creative works, including articles, books, software, and audio and video recordings.

Trademark
A company's legal title to a word or symbol that identifies its product and distinguishes it from the products of other firms.

Patent
An inventor's legal title to the sole right to manufacture, utilize, and market an invention for a specific period.

The Pros and Cons of Protecting Rights to Intellectual Property

Currently, many nations abide by international standards for intellectual property rights established by a multilateral agreement called the *Agreement on Trade-Related Aspects of Intellectual Property Rights,* or *TRIPS.* Nations that do not currently meet these standards—mainly the least-developed nations of the world—have agreed to meet them by January 2006. TRIPS establishes a fifty-year minimum standard for copyright protection, common rules governing international trademark protections, and a minimum term of patent protection of twenty years.

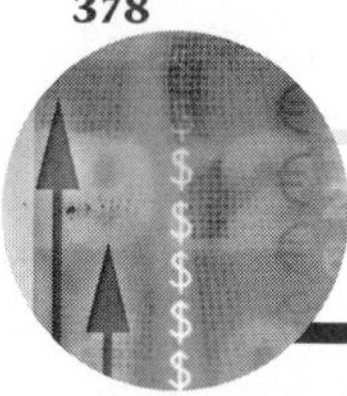

Visualizing Global Economic Issues

The Trade-Off in Patent Protection

To see why there is a social trade-off associated with intellectual property rights, take a look back at Figure 11-4 on page 357. Once a product is available, consumer surplus is greatest if the many perfectly competitive producers have the unhindered right to imitate the product and sell essentially perfect substitutes under their own company names. As a result, the price of the product is equal to marginal cost across the industry, and the quantity produced equals the quantity demanded at this price.

This perfectly competitive result arises, however, only if the product is available for free imitation. The perfectly competitive outcome entails zero economic profits, so there is no inducement for an inventor to incur a potentially sizable up-front cost of developing the product in the first place. As a result, failure to provide intellectual property rights could lead to a complete loss of the large shaded consumer surplus triangle in Figure 11-4.

Granting complete intellectual property rights effectively gives the owner of a patent the power to set a monopoly price for the product. This shrinks consumer surplus to the dashed triangle shown in Figure 11-4. The economic profit earned by the patent's owner is a transfer from society to the inventor. Thus, the trade-off associated with patent protection is that granting a patent induces an inventor to make a product available but reduces consumer welfare relative to the perfectly competitive welfare level.

For Critical Analysis:
If the inventor who receives a patent lives in another country, then what area in the figure constitutes an international resource transfer resulting from granting global patent protection to that inventor?

ON THE WEB

What are the latest developments in U.S. copyright rules regarding digital copies? Find out by going to http://www.loc.gov/copyright and clicking on "Digital Transmissions."

Society faces a trade-off in granting intellectual property rights. The rationale for granting international property rights is that in the absence of such rights, there would be less incentive for inventors and innovators to develop new products and technologies. If people are free to imitate the creative ideas of others, then society gains from the speedy diffusion of products and processes that results. Competition among firms in industries using these ideas, however, leads to zero economic profits. Hence, there is no return beyond covering the opportunity cost of being in the industry to compensate inventors for the time and effort they invested in developing the new product or process. If governments grant patents to an investor, however, then the inventor can charge a monopoly price to those who would like to use the new product or process, which reduces consumer welfare. (To see this trade-off on a diagram, see *Visualizing Global Economic Issues: The Trade-Off in Patent Protection.*)

Who Gains and Who Loses from Strengthened Intellectual Property Rights?

In recent years more nations have agreed to enact protections of intellectual property rights. Panel (a) of Figure 12-1 displays significant increases in the numbers of

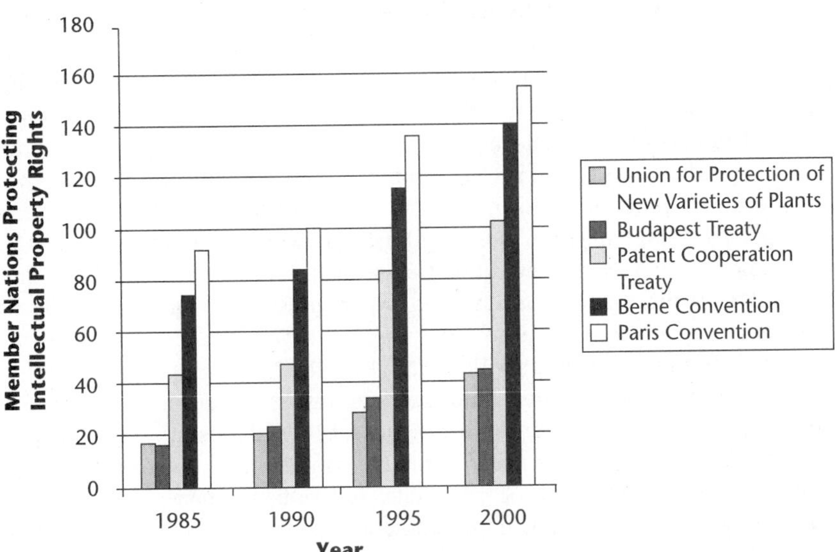

(a)

(b)

Figure 12-1

Increased International Protection of Intellectual Property Rights and the Immediate Winners and Losers

As panel (a) indicates, there has been a significant increase in the numbers of nations that are members of treaties or conventions protecting intellectual property rights. Panel (b) shows that the immediate gains from these arrangements go to developed nations that own the largest numbers of patents, copyrights, and trademarks.

Source: Keith Maskus, *Intellectual Property Rights in the Global Economy,* Washington, D.C.: Institute for International Economics, August 2000.

nations participating in various international conventions for assuring common standards for the protection of international property rights.

Increased protection of intellectual property rights naturally has immediate benefits for current owners of intellectual property. For those who wish to incorporate new ideas and processes into their businesses, however, strengthening intellectual property rights is likely to push up business expenses by forcing them to make payments to owners of copyrights, trademarks, and patents. (Banking and international trade processes are recent areas where patents to computer processes have threatened to increase business expenses; see *Online Globalization: Does the U.S. Patent and Trademark Office Know What It's Doing?*)

ON THE WEB

What are the various e-commerce programs of the U.S. Patent and Trademark Office? To find out, go to http://www.uspto.gov, click on "Activities & Education," and then click on "eBusiness Center."

Currently most owners of intellectual property reside in the United States and Western Europe. As shown in panel (b) of Figure 12-1, this means that residents located in these regions are most likely to realize immediate gains from the growing globalization of intellectual property rights. Residents of other regions, most of which are less developed, experience immediate losses.

Nearly all of the recent additions to the memberships of international conventions for protecting intellectual property rights have been developing nations, however. Some of these nations undoubtedly felt pressured by U.S. threats of trade retaliation if they did not join these conventions. Presumably, a number of these nations have also decided that it is in their best interest to incur losses in the present in return for potentially significant gains, in the form of greater development and higher economic growth, in future years.

Circumventing Intellectual Property Rights: Parallel Imports

In spite of the general trend toward greater worldwide protection of rights to intellectual property, some who engage in international trade continue to find ways to avoid paying owners of copyrights, trademarks, and patents. One issue that has received particular attention in recent years is **parallel imports,** sometimes known as *gray-market imports,* which are goods or services brought into a country without authorization of the owner of a copyright, trademark, or patent after initially being legitimately placed into circulation in some other locale.

Parallel imports
Gray-market imports, or goods and services brought into a country without authorization after initially being permitted to be sold elsewhere.

For instance, an authorized Canadian distributor of U.S.-manufactured software might sell software in Canada at a wholesale price below the retail price in Mexico. The Canadian dealer could then profit from transferring the software to Mexico. The Canadian firm thereby would contribute to the flow of parallel imports.

So far, the multilateral TRIPS agreement leaves addressing the issue of parallel imports to national governments. Some TRIPS member nations have pushed hard for tougher multilateral standards and enforcement mechanisms, and this issue promises to be an important item on the agendas for future multilateral trade negotiations.

Online Globalization

Does the U.S. Patent and Trademark Office Know What It's Doing?

In July 2000, the U.S. Patent and Trademark Office issued a patent to a new system for managing banking payments, thereby giving patent owners the rights to collect payments from every bank that used the system. There was a problem, however. The newly patented technology had been in place at banks for years. Within short order, the Patent Office agreed to participate in an emergency meeting with representatives of the American Banker's Association, the National Automated Clearinghouse Association, and other banking groups. It was time, the Patent Office agreed, for patent examiners to get some lessons in banking.

This sort of thing wasn't supposed to happen. Just four months earlier, the Patent Office had embarked on a series of changes intended to improve the review process for applications for patents relating to computerized business methods. It had added a new layer of review and doubled the number of applications receiving an automatic final screening by the most highly experienced patent examiners.

Nevertheless, in August 2000 a small Virginia company called DE Technology began warning other firms that it would soon be demanding a fee equal to 0.3 percent of the value of every cross-border trade deal arranged using computers. After all, DE Technology had just received a letter from the U.S. Patent Office indicating that it would soon obtain a broad patent covering "a process for carrying out an international transaction . . . using computer-to-computer communication." If DE Technologies did receive the patent, and if courts interpreted it as applying as broadly as the company claimed, nearly everyone using computer-to-computer links to arrange international trade would have to pay DE Technologies. Based on current computer-processed international trade transactions and the patent rate DE Technologies indicated it planned to charge, the company would stand to earn hundreds of millions of dollars in patent fees each year.

DE Technology's primary owner had applied for the patent in the early 1990s. In the meantime, businesses all over the world were already engaged in computer-to-computer trade processes. Forwarders of international freight had implemented a number of computer-based processes for streamlining international trade shipments. An active market for computer software for these processes also had developed. The use of computers for processing trade was taken for granted.

For Critical Analysis:

Analysts' estimates of the patent royalties that DE Technologies might receive were based on total trade processed using computer links in the absence of payment of fees to DE Technologies. Why did some economists argue that these estimates probably were too high? (Hint: Remember the law of demand: An increase in the price of any item reduces the quantity demanded.)

How do the world's governments protect rights to intellectual property?

To encourage the efforts of inventors and innovators, governments typically establish intellectual property rights, or legal rules that determine the ownership of creative ideas. For creative works such as articles, stories and novels, computer programs, audio recordings, and movies, governments grant copyrights, or exclusive privileges to reproduce, distribute, perform, or display such works. Governments establish rules for trademarks, which are words or symbols that companies use to differentiate their products from those of other firms. They also issue patents, which grant an inventor the exclusive right to make, use, and sell an invention for a specified number of years.

Dealing with Market Failures—Should Regulators Go Global?

Market failure
Inability of unhindered private market processes to produce outcomes that are consistent with economic efficiency, individual freedom, and other broader social goals.

Even under perfect competition, too few or too many resources can sometimes go to certain economic activities. Such situations are **market failures** that prevent the attainment of economic efficiency, individual freedom, and other potential social goals. Traditionally, many economists argued that addressing market failures requires active intervention by national governments. Today, a growing number of economists contend that market failures have international consequences that may require actions by supranational, *global* authorities.

ARE MARKET EXTERNALITIES BOUNDED BY BORDERS?

Economic efficiency results only when individuals know the true opportunity costs of their decisions. In some circumstances, the price that someone actually pays for a good or service can be higher or lower than the opportunity cost that society as a whole incurs. In other circumstances, it is possible that private markets will fail to provide goods that would benefit nearly everyone. Such situations can arise domestically. It is possible that they can also span national borders.

Market Spillovers and Their International Consequences

Consider the plight of Hungarian and Yugoslav fisherman whose livelihood depends on their daily catch from the Tisza River, a tributary of the Danube River. In early 2000, 100,000 tons of cyanide-laden sludge byproducts from Romanian gold mining operations washed down the river. Within days, more than 100 tons of dead fish floated downstream in both Hungary and Yugoslavia.

Cyanide is a substance that naturally arises when gold producers separate the shiny metal from other ores. Romanian gold producers must do something with the cyanide, so they normally place it in temporary storage in tanks of water before draining it off for safe disposal. In the meantime, they ship their final product, pure gold, to gold dealers who market the gold to industrial users, jewelry wholesalers, and the like. Fishermen in Hungary and Yugoslavia experienced an **externality,** which is an economic consequence of activity within a market, such as the production of gold, which spills over to affect third parties not directly involved in that market, such as those fishermen.

Externality
A spillover effect influencing the welfare of third parties not involved in transactions within a marketplace.

Most consumers of Romanian gold probably had no idea that cyanide could pollute rivers in Eastern Europe. From their perspective, therefore, the price that they paid in early 2000 had nothing to do with the production of cyanide. The literal spillover effect that Hungarian and Yugoslav fishermen experienced dramatically illustrates how the market price of a product such as gold may fail to reflect the broader social costs relating to its production. Because the market price of Romanian gold was lower than the price that society as a whole had to pay for this metal, production of this good entailed a *negative externality.* From society's perspective, too many resources were allocated to gold production at the private market price of gold. Furthermore, this was true beyond Romania's borders, so there was an **international externality** in which spillover effects from market activities within one country affect third parties located in other nations.

International externality
A spillover effect arising from market activities in one nation that influences the welfare of third parties in another country.

In some situations, private markets can underallocate resources to the production of a good or service. For instance, inoculating the residents of several developing nations with vaccines might prevent the spread of diseases to other developing and developed nations, thereby improving the quality of life for residents of all nations. The private market price of vaccinations in the developing nations may be too low, however, to induce potential producers of such services to offer them in the quantity that would benefit society. Under such circumstances, there is a *positive externality.* Positive externalities may occur either domestically or, as in this example, internationally.

A Possible Role for Government: Correcting Externalities

Because private market activities do not take into account externalities, it is possible that government action could help to induce producers and consumers in markets that create externalities to take them into account. In the case of a negative externality such as cyanide pollution, a multinational authority might impose and enforce minimum standards for safe storage of cyanide, limitations on cyanide production—and, as a consequence, gold production—or taxation on producers of goods such as gold that yield cyanide as a byproduct. (Sometimes national authorities attempt to tackle perceived international externalities; see on the next page *Online Globalization: A French Judge Combats an International Externality.*)

When there is a positive externality such as disease-reducing vaccinations, a multinational authority might provide the service directly, subsidize private producers of vaccines and inoculation services, or undertake policies aimed at increasing the demand for the vaccines and inoculation services. (Learn how using demand-supply diagrams to examine how such policies might help to correct negative and positive externalities on pages 386–387 *Visualizing Global Economic Issues: Correcting International Externalities via Multilateral Interventions.*)

How does the U.S. government use regulations to try to protect the environment? Find out at http://es.epa.gov/oeca.

Are There Global Public Goods?

Most goods and services are *private goods* that can be consumed by only one individual at a time. Individuals can simultaneously consume a number of goods and services, such as the entertainment services provided by a band or orchestra concert. Among these goods and services, there are a few that also cannot be provided

Online Globalization

A French Judge Combats an International Externality

In April 2000, several groups filed a joint lawsuit in a French court against Yahoo.com. They argued that Yahoo.com's willingness to host auctions of Nazi artifacts amounted to a "banalizing of Nazism" and violated French laws prohibiting selling or displaying any items that might incite racism. The groups asked for judicial relief in the form of a ban on Yahoo.com's ability to offer auctions of Nazi artifacts on any Web site that French residents might visit.

Making Yahoo Pay

Yahoo.com's response to the lawsuit contended that since the company did not permit exchange of Nazi artifacts on its French auction site, it violated no French laws. The company contended that French residents who found displays of these artifacts offensive should simply choose not to visit the U.S. auction site where it permitted such auctions to take place.

On May 22, 2000, however, a French judge concurred with the groups that had filed the lawsuit. The judge appointed a panel of experts to determine the technical feasibility of preventing French Web users from accessing Yahoo.com's U.S. auction site. After the panel provided its conclusions in November 2000, the judge ordered the company to incur the costs of implementing a special filtering system. This system would identify French visitors to Yahoo.com's auction site using their Internet protocol addresses and prohibit them from accessing the site. Failure to abide by the order within 90 days, the judge declared, would result in a fine of $13,000 per day.

Shortly thereafter, eBay.com announced that it would no longer permit trading of Nazi artifacts via its on-line auction site, and several other firms announced similar policies. Hence, forcing Yahoo.com to incur the cost of cleaning up the perceived negative externality induced other firms to voluntarily cut back on the provision of certain services.

The Issue of Regulatory Jurisdiction

This situation revealed two problems relating to international externalities. First, in this situation the "historical memorabilia" of some residents of one nation was an "offensive artifact" to some residents of another nation. Unlike air or water pollution, which anyone surely agrees are negative international externalities, the Nazi artifacts are visual pollution to some but not to others. A few U.S. residents who purchased such items online contended that even though they detested Nazi ideas, they were interested in the historical significance of certain Nazi artifacts.

Second, the situation highlighted the problem of determining what countries have regulatory jurisdiction to address online international externalities, which know no boundaries. When Amazon.com received complaints about its willingness to sell Adolf Hitler's radical book, *Mein Kampf,* it responded by refusing to sell the book for shipment to a German address. If a ruling similar to that of the French judge had applied in the case of Hitler's book, Amazon.com would have had to filter the book's availability from view by German consumers. Undoubtedly, governments of many nations would like to restrain Amazon.com and other Internet booksellers from offering to sell certain books. A dictator, for instance, might desire to prevent residents of his or her nation from being able to view a book containing writings about freedom and democracy by Thomas Jefferson or James Madison. If more governments follow the example established by this French judge, operating costs for firms selling items online to residents of multiple nations could rise dramatically in coming years.

For Critical Analysis:

How might a government go about determining that a negative international externality exists and should be corrected?

to some consumers without others being able to derive benefits from them. In addition, some have the property that, once provided, additional people can consume the goods or services at no additional cost. Furthermore, it is difficult, if not impossible, to deny the benefits of these goods or services to an individual who fails to pay for it. A good or service that satisfies these criteria is a **public good.**

Public good
Any good or service that can be consumed by many people at the same time, cannot be consumed by one individual without others also consuming it at no extra cost, and cannot be withheld from a person who has not contributed to funding its production.

Public Goods in a Global Economy

Although most economists agree that there are public goods, it is often difficult to find widespread agreement about specific examples. For instance, one of the most commonly proposed examples of a public good is a lighthouse. Arguably, the services of a lighthouse can be used by several seafarers at the same time, and once a lighthouse is in place additional ship navigators can use it at no additional cost. In the thirteenth century, however, the French King Louis IX erected a 105-foot tower with a dual purpose. In addition to serving as a lighthouse, it also was a lookout point to spot ships sailing close enough to view its light. Speedy ships of the king's navy would then prevent the masters of these ships from escaping payment for the lighthouse's service. Thus, this French king found a way to try to ensure that everyone paid for the service they received from his lighthouse.

Nevertheless, several goods and services often appear on lists of national or regional public goods. These include national or regional defense, forest fire suppression, groundwater pollution cleanup, flood control, and animal disease control. Some people like to include parks, rivers, waterways, highways, and even the Internet, although most economists classify these as "impure" public goods because it is possible to prevent people who do not pay from using them. There are also a number of goods and services that often appear on lists of **global public goods** that arguably benefit people worldwide, including ocean pollution cleanup, weather forecasting, protection of the world's ozone layer, and disease eradication. Lists of global public goods also differ from person to person. Some observers include items such as world satellite orbits, continental and oceanic ship and air transport corridors, and allocations of bands of the electromagnetic spectrum, although it is also possible to prevent people from using these goods if they do not pay for them.

Global public good
A good or service that yields benefits to a number of the world's people simultaneously, cannot provide benefits to one person without others around the world deriving benefits at no additional cost, and cannot be withheld from a person who has failed to contribute to its provision.

It is important to distinguish public goods from goods and services that government entities sometimes choose to provide. For instance, some observers classify health care as a national, regional, or even global public good. From an economist's standpoint, however, it is incorrect to classify health care as a public good, because it is a simple matter to deny access to health care when people will not or cannot pay for the care. Nevertheless, many national governments around the world either partially or fully fund health care. Some even provide relatively large amounts of health care services directly. In these countries, health care has been deemed a **merit good** that societies have determined they wish to promote through government intervention in the marketplace. Thus, national governments have chosen to provide health care alongside or instead of privately produced care.

Merit good
A good or service that residents of a nation determine, typically through a political process, to be socially desirable.

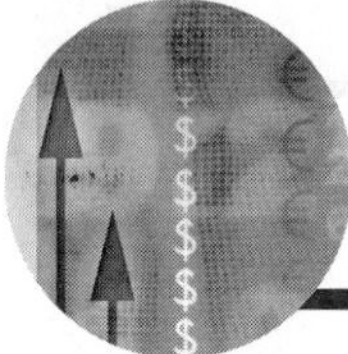

Visualizing Global Economic Issues

Correcting International Externalities via Multilateral Interventions

To think about how a multinational authority developed by coordinated efforts of several nations might address international cyanide pollution by gold producers, consider panel (a) of Figure 12-2. If gold producers and consumers are oblivious to the social costs caused by cyanide byproducts of gold production, then the private market price of gold is P_1, and the quantity of gold produced and consumed is Q_1. If the world's gold producers took into account additional social costs caused by cyanide pollution, however, they would incur these costs and be willing to produce any given quantity of gold, only at a higher price. Thus, the market supply curve would shift upward, from S_1 to S_2. As a result, gold consumers around the world would pay the higher market price P_2, and gold manufacturers would produce Q_2 units of gold.

To bring about this socially preferable outcome, a multinational authority might contemplate policies that limit production of cyanide-producing activities, such as gold production. In principle, one approach might be to place limits on international trade in gold to reduce overall world gold production to the socially preferred level. Most economists, however, doubt that a multinational authority would be able to successfully fine-tune such quantity-focused policies to produce exactly the socially preferred production level. Consequently, economists traditionally have advocated imposing taxes on producers of goods and services that yield negative externalities. If a multinational authority could determine the per-unit amount of the social cost resulting from the polluting effects of gold production, then it might require gold producers to incur these costs. This would have the effect of shifting the market supply curve by exactly the amount shown in panel (a) of Figure 12-2, thereby pushing up the private market price and inducing a cutback in gold production that would reduce cyanide pollution. Alternatively, the authority might induce the same outcome by imposing or requiring national governments to impose a per-unit tax equal to this cost. The authority or national governments could then use the tax revenues to fund pollution cleanup or prevention activities.

Panel (b) shows how a multinational authority might deal with a positive externality. In this situation, only consumers in the locale of this marketplace who are willing and able to be inoculated against disease benefit from vaccines, so D_1 is the market demand curve. People elsewhere would also benefit from more widespread inoculations, however, so society as a whole would prefer for the demand curve to be D_2. Then the market price would rise from P_1 to P_2, which would induce private producers to supply more vaccines, and the total number of inoculations would increase from Q_1 to Q_2.

Free-rider problem
The potential for an individual to try to avoid contributing funds to pay for provision of a public good because he or she presumes that others will do so.

The Free-Rider Problem

Even though what constitutes a true global public good is often in the eye of the beholder, a common feature of any public good is the **free-rider problem.** This problem arises when individuals presume that others will pay for public goods so that, individually, they can escape from paying for their portion without reducing production of the public good.

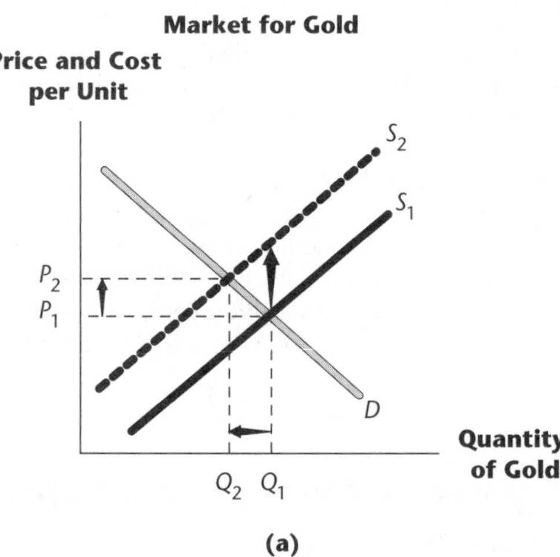

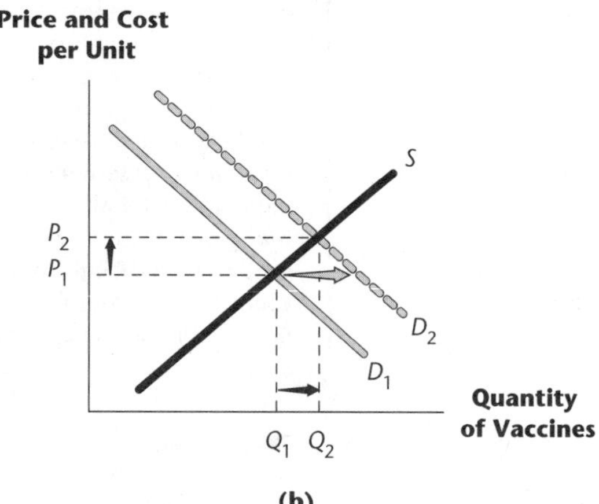

Figure 12-2

Policies to Correct Negative and Positive Externalities

Panel (a) shows that if gold producers and consumers ignore the social costs caused by cyanide byproducts of gold production, the private market price of gold is P_1*, and the quantity of gold produced and consumed is* Q_1*. If the world's gold producers take into account additional social costs caused by cyanide pollution, the market supply curve shifts upward, from* S_1 *to* S_2*, gold consumers around the world pay the higher market price* P_2*, and gold manufacturers produce* Q_2 *units of gold. Panel (b) displays a situation in which* D_1 *is the market demand curve for vaccines when only consumers willing and able to be inoculated against disease benefit from the production and sale of vaccines. Because people elsewhere would also benefit from more widespread inoculations, society prefers for the demand curve to be* D_2*, so that the market price rises to* P_2*, producers supply more vaccines, and the total number of inoculations rises to* Q_2*.*

To push the quantity of administered vaccinations up to Q_2, a multinational authority might administer the vaccinations directly. Alternatively, it might offer subsidies to private suppliers to push the effective price that private suppliers receive up to P_2. Another option would be to offer subsidies directly to consumers to give them a greater incentive to be inoculated.

For Critical Analysis:
Why do economists tend to prefer price-based approaches to government interventions in markets over efforts to force producers to provide specific quantities?

Naturally, if a sufficiently large number of people attempt to be *free riders,* it may prove difficult to fund provision of the public good. This is a key reason that most tax systems are compulsory. It is also a reason that taxation is a hotly debated subject everywhere in the world. After all, if a country's citizens disagree about which goods or services to classify as public goods or merit goods, then they are unlikely to agree about how many taxes they should contribute to fund the provision of these goods or services.

Fundamental Issue

What are international externalities and global public goods, and what can national governments or multinational institutions do about them?

International externalities are spillover effects from market activities in one country that affect the well being of third parties in other countries. A global public good can be consumed by many of the world's people simultaneously, cannot be provided to one person without others around the world deriving benefits at no additional cost, and cannot be withheld from a person who has failed to contribute to its provision. To correct negative international externalities such as cross-border environmental pollution, governments or multinational authorities can attempt to limit production or trade of the good or service that generates the externality, require producers to incur the costs of the externality, or tax producers. Although some observers perceive the world's environment to be a public good, there is no consensus concerning appropriate international trade policies to promote preservation of the environment.

Protecting the Global Environment—A Multinational Problem with Multilateral Solutions?

Externalities can affect the world's environment. Some people even view the world's overall environment as a global public good. Certainly, many parts of the world's environment are **common property,** which is a nonexclusive resource that is owned by everyone and thus not by any single individual. For instance, everyone shares the world's atmosphere, but no individual owns any of it. When no one owns a particular resource, no one has any incentive (aside from conscience, perhaps) to consider misuse of the resource.

Common property
A nonexclusive resource owned by everyone and therefore by no single individual.

PUBLIC GOOD ASPECTS OF THE GLOBAL ENVIRONMENT

Even though a significant portion of the earth's surface is privately owned, individuals or companies may still use these resources in ways that create negative externalities by degrading and polluting the environment. One way of addressing this problem might be for governments to turn many currently private lands into public lands, perhaps by purchasing or even confiscating private property. Under this perspective, the world's resources are a global public good. Hence, there is a need for concerted governmental efforts to ensure a pristine environment.

Problems with Viewing "the" World Environment as a Public Good

Nation's governments have not always proven to be effective managers of their countries' environments. Undoubtedly, former residents of the defunct Soviet Union who still dwell near the barren and ruined lands around and within the boundaries of the formerly pristine Aral Sea can attest to the potential for governmental failures in environmental protection.

In addition, in most nations the ability to own private property is a fundamental human freedom. Hence, while many governments often purchase and set aside public lands, most do not confiscate lands for the purpose of environmental protection.

Furthermore, many features of the world's environment do not even come close to satisfying the definition of a global public good. Some arguably are not even national or regional public goods. For instance, it is relatively easy to exclude people from deriving whatever benefits are available from most tracts of land. In addition, fences and walls can keep out people who refuse to pay for the uses of land. While certain uses of land certainly can create externalities for people in other locations, the world's land does not satisfy the criteria for classification as a global public good.

The World's Atmosphere and Oceans as Global Public Goods

Other features of the world's environment come closer, however, to satisfying the criteria for categorization as global public goods. The Earth's atmosphere and its bodies of water top the list. In principle, it is possible to exclude certain people from using the air at a certain location on or above the Earth's surface, but from a practical standpoint this would be hard to arrange using a market mechanism.

Likewise, most of the world's oceans and a number of its rivers appear to meet the global public goods criteria. It is possible to use police powers to prevent certain individuals from swimming, boating, or shipping across a particular region of an ocean, and countries with coastlines often place legal limits on these activities to a certain distance outward from their shores. Any efforts to develop private approaches to excluding these activities on the high seas, however, are likely to prove infeasible. Naturally, the water within an ocean flows from place to place, so even assigning property rights to portions of an ocean would be a problematic undertaking.

Both the atmosphere and the oceans are classic examples of common property. No one individual "owns" any given portion of the Earth's atmosphere any more than any other individual "owns" any region of one of the Earth's oceans. This helps to explain why there has been greater success in reaching multilateral agreement concerning efforts to protect the world's air and waters as compared with its lands.

ALTERNATIVE APPROACHES TO SOLVING THE WORLD'S ENVIRONMENTAL PROBLEMS

Most attempts to improve the global environment have focused on treating misuse of the private property within the global environment as a negative externality instead of viewing the entire environment as a public good. Thus, most environmental protection efforts focus on regulating the *uses* of private property.

An Economic Perspective on Combating World Pollution

Nations have experimented with many approaches to protecting the environment from pollution. For instance, countries may require owners to file *environmental impact statements* before embarking on activities that may destroy wetlands, damage animal habitats, or kill members of endangered species. Many have enacted rules requiring companies to incur significant costs to avoid generating pollution. Some have implemented schemes for taxing polluters.

A significant issue, however, is determining the appropriate goal for national or international environmental protection efforts. Some of the world's citizens and policymakers contend that the goal of reducing pollution, also called *pollution abatement,* should be the eventual elimination of *all* pollution. Most economists argue, however, that the complete elimination of pollution is not *necessarily* best for society. The reason is that society experiences costs as well as benefits from engaging in pollution abatement efforts.

Nearly everyone agrees that efforts to keep the environment clean are beneficial. Every extra bit of additional water cleanliness, for instance, raises overall social welfare. How *much* each additional unit of water cleanliness raises social welfare depends, however, on how polluted the environment already is. Suppose, for instance, that according to a physical standard of measurement the maximum degree of water cleanliness is 100 percent. If a lake bordering several nations is only 62 percent clean, then an 8-percentage-point increase in water cleanliness is likely to raise welfare by a greater magnitude than will an 8-percentage-point increase in water cleanliness when the water is already 91 percent clean. Water that is only 62 percent clean may be barely drinkable, and an additional 8 percentage points of cleanliness may be improve the water quality sufficiently for people to consume it. By way of contrast, a lake that is already at the 91 percent threshold of cleanliness is already usable in many contexts, so a number of people may not even notice a cleanliness increase of 8 percentage points.

Combating pollution is a costly endeavor. Furthermore, the per-unit cost of reducing pollution tends to vary with the quality of the environment. For example, a lake that is only 62 percent clean may receive pollution from a number of sources, from careless dumping at nearby production facilities to excessive plankton buildup caused by heat emanating from those facilities. Reducing or eliminating careless dumping is likely to be a relatively inexpensive form of pollution abatement that can bring about, say an 8-percentage-point increase in water quality. When the same lake is already at the 91 percent cleanliness level, however, raising water cleanliness by 8 percentage points may require reducing the transmission of heat. This, in turn, may necessitate considerable reconfiguring of production processes, which is likely to be a very expensive endeavor.

As society brings about additional increases in water cleanliness, therefore, the additional benefit from pollution abatement efforts declines at the same time that the cost of additional pollution abatement rises. This means that attaining perfectly clean water is not likely to be the best outcome for society. It could well be in the best interest of society to aim for, say, 90 percent cleanliness in a lake bordering several nations. (To consider how economists envision the determination of society's optimal level of environment, see on pages 392–393 *Visualizing Global Economic Issues: Determining How Much to Reduce Pollution.*)

Multilateral Efforts to Reduce Global Pollution

Of course, in many parts of the world the immediate goal of many residents has been simply to find ways to reduce pollution below existing levels that they feel are too high. Only as pollution levels have started to fall have some nations begun the process of determining exactly how low they wish to push pollution levels.

Until recently, the bulk of pollution-abatement efforts have taken place *within* nations. Today, however, a variety of environmentally directed *nongovernment organizations*—private international groups that pursue special interests including global environmental protection—are pushing for global efforts to coordinate environmental protection efforts.

Some of these efforts have paid dividends for the organizations. Many of the world's nations have entered into international treaties establishing minimal national pollution standards and worldwide rules for use of shared environmental resources. Current estimates indicate that there are about 500 international agreements that relate to environmental regulations. Table 12-1 lists some of the most important multilateral agreements. In some cases, nations signing these treaties have conducted detailed studies of costs and benefits of pollution abatement before agreeing to national and global targets for antipollution efforts. Nevertheless, many recent efforts to establish multilateral environmental rules have been focused on the realm of international trade arrangements.

International Trade and the Environment

At present, however, beyond agreement that environmental protection is important, nongovernment organizations have failed to reach a consensus in their

Table 12-1 Key International Environmental Agreements

Agreement	Year
Convention for the Regulation of Whaling	1946
Convention on the Prevention of Marine Pollution	1972
Convention on International Trade in Endangered Species	1973
Convention for the Prevention of Pollution from Ships	1973
Convention on Long-Range Transboundary Air Pollution	1979
Vienna Convention for the Protection of the Ozone Layer	1985
Basle Convention on the Control of Transboundary Movements of Hazardous Wastes and Their Disposal	1989
Framework Convention on Climate Change	1992
Convention on Biological Diversity	1992
International Convention to Combat Desertification	1994
Kyoto Climate Change Convention	1997

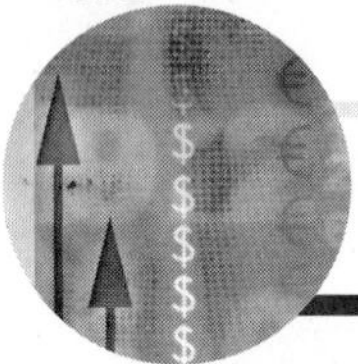

Visualizing Global Economic Issues

Determining How Much to Reduce Pollution

Economists call the additional benefit that society gains from a given increase in water cleanliness the *marginal social benefit of pollution abatement.* The benefit that society derives from raising cleanliness of a body of water by any given amount is lower at a 91 percent cleanliness level than it is at a 62 percent level of cleanliness. This implies that the marginal social benefit curve for society depicted in Figure 12-3 slopes downward. As overall water cleanliness increases, the extra benefit that society receives from an additional unit of water cleanliness declines.

By way of contrast, the additional cost that society incurs to achieve a given increase in cleanliness, which economists call the *marginal social cost of pollution abatement,* increases at higher overall cleanliness levels. Thus, the marginal social cost curve shown in Figure 12-3 is upward sloping.

Now suppose that the degree of overall cleanliness of this body of water is equal to 75 percent. As you can see, at this overall level of water cleanliness the marginal social benefit of pollution abatement is higher than the marginal social cost of pollution abatement. Hence, society experiences a net gain from further efforts to improve water quality. If the overall level of cleanliness of this body of water is equal to 90 percent, however, marginal social cost exceeds marginal social benefit, so society devotes too much effort to pollution abatement. By this line of reasoning, the socially optimal degree of water cleanliness, C^*, is 83 percent, at which the marginal social benefit of pollution abatement is just equal to the marginal social cost of pollution abatement. Note that the optimal extent of water cleanliness is almost never likely to be as high as 100 percent. Social welfare typically is at its highest with at least some amount of water pollution.

For Critical Analysis:
What factors are likely to affect how close C^* is to 100 percent in Figure 12-3?

environmental policy recommendations. Some environmentally focused non-government organizations, for instance, view international trade as an environmental threat. The foundation for this view is that foreign direct investment and other capital flows from developed nations to developing nations will contribute to degradation of virgin lands that now exist primarily in developing nations.

There are four basic reasons that some nongovernmental organizations oppose international trade:

1) By increasing the breadth of the world marketplace, international trade worsens the scope for global market failures that harm the environment.

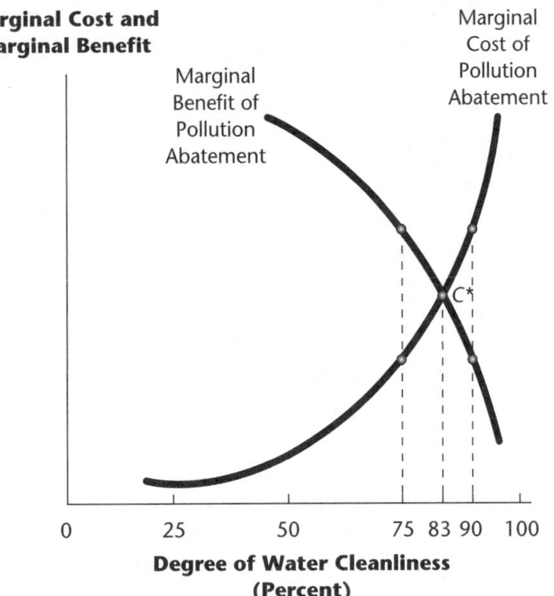

Figure 12-3

Determining the Socially Optimal Degree of Water Cleanliness

The additional benefit that society gains from a given increase in water cleanliness, or the marginal social benefit of pollution abatement, falls as overall water cleanliness increases, so that the marginal social benefit slopes downward. In contrast, the additional cost that society incurs to achieve a given increase in cleanliness, or the marginal social cost of pollution abatement, increases at higher overall cleanliness levels, so the marginal social cost curve slopes upward. If the degree of overall cleanliness of this body of water is 75 percent, then the marginal social benefit of pollution abatement exceeds the marginal social cost of pollution abatement, so society experiences a net gain from further efforts to improve water quality. If the overall level of cleanliness of this body of water is equal to 90 percent, however, marginal social cost exceeds marginal social benefit, so society allocates too many resources to pollution abatement. The socially optimal degree of water cleanliness is 83 percent, at which the marginal social benefit of pollution abatement is just equal to the marginal social cost of pollution abatement.

2) Greater international trade erodes regulatory standards as governments loosen regulations to assist domestic industries in response to heightened international competition.
3) Increased economic growth ultimately is unsustainable, and growth-enhancing international trade only speeds the pace at which the world's resources will be exhausted.
4) Multilateral trade agreements and institutions tend to focus on economic aspects of trade without giving due consideration for trade's environmental effects.

Thus, those who view international trade as an environmental menace perceive the resulting market failures to be insurmountable and the economic growth that trade promotes to be counterproductive. Consequently, nongovernment organizations continue to lobby and protest against further efforts to expand global trade. A few groups even desire to reverse the recent growth of trade flows.

By way of contrast, some nongovernment organizations view increased international trade as a potential long-term boon to the world's environment. Their position is based on the following arguments:

1) Gains from trade help raise living standards in developing nations, and evidence indicates that environmental protection efforts increase with higher per capita incomes.
2) Opening the markets of developing countries encourages industries within these nations to operate in more efficient ways that are less environmentally harmful; in addition, multinational companies that engage in foreign direct investment in developing nations apply the most advanced pollution-control techniques, which help reduce environmental degradation in the developing world.
3) Increased international trade and investment will speed the pace of innovation, which will permit sustainable growth of the global economy.
4) Multilateral trade agreements and institutions provide forums for facilitating coordinated international efforts to protect the environment.

These views, of course, stand in sharp contradiction to the perceptions of those who view international trade as a factor contributing to worldwide environmental peril. Economic arguments can be advanced to support both sets of views. For this reason, the desirable scope for environmental protection within regional and multilateral trade agreements and regulations will have to be sorted out within the political arena.

Nearly everyone agrees that environmental protection is a multinational problem. Given the broad gap in perspectives about how international linkages via foreign trade and investment affect the environment, however, it seems unlikely that multilateral policy solutions will emerge quickly. Nonetheless, discussions about multilateral approaches to environmental protection are likely to dominate the international stage for years to come.

4 **Fundamental Issue**

How can the world's nations protect the global environment?

Most nations engage in unilateral efforts to protect the environment through pollution-abatement policies that attempt to address the negative externalities generated by environmental pollution. To combat environmental externalities that span national borders, governments or multinational authorities can attempt to develop quantitative limits based on perceived marginal benefits and marginal costs of combating the externalities. Currently, multilateral efforts to protect the environment are governed by treaties specifying mutually agreeable environmental goals. Some environmentally focused nongovernment organizations contend that trade with developed nations will contribute to degradation of the environments of developing nations, but others argue trade-induced factors such as increases in living standards or technological improvements will enhance the efforts of developing nations to improve their environments.

Funding the Public Sector—Globalization and International Tax Competition

Regulating businesses, providing public goods and merit goods, and attempting to correct externalities are costly activities for national governments and multinational institutions to perform. Hence, they must have sources of funds. Determining how to fund these public-sector activities can be a difficult problem.

THE GROWING INTERNATIONAL RIVALRY FOR TAX REVENUES

To generate the revenues to fund their activities, national governments typically rely on domestic taxes and user fees, tariffs, and other miscellaneous revenue sources. Taxation of domestic residents is the most important source of revenues for the governments of most countries. National governments typically levy taxes on individual and corporate incomes, business sales, and/or household and business consumption.

In the past, domestic considerations have guided governments in structuring their tax systems. Increasingly, however, globalization has caused international considerations to impinge on domestic tax policies.

Determining Total Tax Revenues: The Static View

Most tax systems entail multiplying a **tax rate,** which is a fraction determining the amount of taxes owed the government, times a **tax base,** which is an economic quantity, such as labor earnings, consumption spending, or capital income, subject to taxation. Figure 12-4 on the next page displays average tax rates on labor, consumption, and capital in the EU, Japan, and the United States.

Tax rate
A fraction of a tax base an individual or company is legally required to transmit to the government.

Tax base
The value of goods, services, incomes, or wealth subject to taxation.

In a personal-income-tax system, an individual determines total income taxes owed by multiplying the appropriate income tax rate by total income subject to taxation, which is the tax base. In a corporate-income-tax system, a firm calculates the total taxes it owes on its net income by multiplying the corporate income tax rate by its total net income, or the tax base for this tax system. In a U.S.-style sales-tax system, a firm determines total sales taxes to transmit to the government by multiplying the sales tax rate by a tax base that equals the firm's total taxable sales.

For many tax systems, therefore, the total tax revenues that a government collects equals the tax rate multiplied by the tax base. A good example is a proportional income-tax system. If the income-tax rate is a fraction t and the tax base B is total income subject to taxation, then the government's total income-tax revenues equal $T = t \times B$. That is, tax collections of the government are a fixed proportion, t, of the tax base. This equation provides the foundation for understanding alternative perspectives about how tax revenues, the tax rate, and the tax base are related.

One of these perspectives is called the *static view.* According to this approach, if a nation's tax base B declines, then maintaining the same amount of tax revenues T requires the nation's government to increase the tax rate t. That is, a

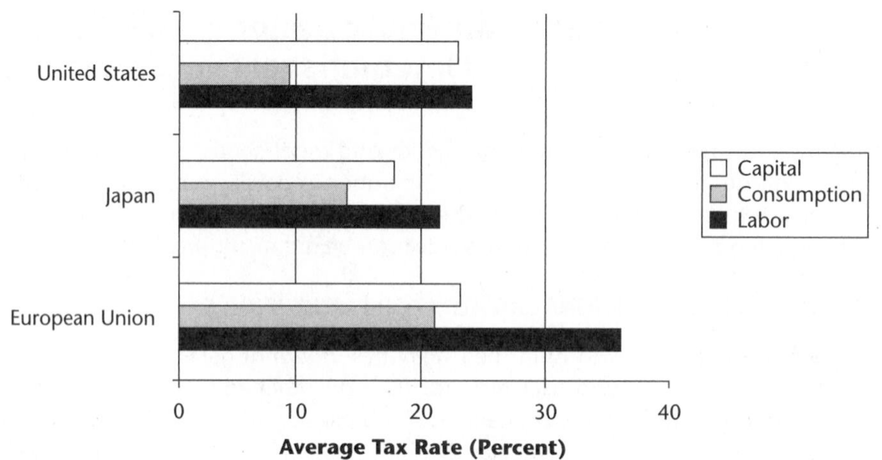

Figure 12-4

Average Tax Rates in the European Union, Japan, and the United States

Among these developed regions of the world, tax rates on consumption spending and labor income are highest in the European Union. Tax rates on capital are slightly lower in Japan and comparable in the United States and the European Union.

Source: Carlos Martinez-Mongay, "ECFIN's Effect Tax Rates: Properties and Comparisons with Other Tax Indicators," Economic Paper No. 146, Directorate for Economic and Financial Affairs, European Commission, October 2000.

nation's government can respond to a fall in the tax base by raising its rate of taxation. This action will keep tax revenues from declining further. (See on pages 398–399 *Visualizing Global Economic Issues: The Static Prescription for Dealing with a Shrinking Tax Base.*)

Determining Total Tax Revenues: The Dynamic View

There is a problem with the static view of the relationship between the tax rate and actual tax collections. The problem is that it ignores the incentives that taxpayers face to respond to a higher tax rate by finding ways to avoid contributing to the national tax base.

In the case of income-tax systems, for instance, domestic residents could find ways to earn incomes in other nations. Likewise, in a sales-tax system domestic residents could begin buying more products abroad. The *dynamic view* of the relationship between tax rates and tax revenues takes such incentives into account.

According to the dynamic view, trying to maintain tax revenues at a goal level by raising the tax rate as the tax base declines is likely to be a self-defeating policy. The reason is that an even-higher tax rate will generate an even-smaller tax base. In a highly globalized economy, a nation's residents can find a way to generate incomes, sales, or other taxable activities in other nations, thereby depressing the domestic tax base and domestic tax revenues. Raising tax rates in the face of a declining tax base will only worsen the problem faced by a national government. (See on page 400 *Visualizing Global Economic Issues: The Dynamic View's Bad News for Efforts to Attain a Tax-Revenue Goal with a Declining Tax Base.*)

As the tax base declines even more following an increase in the domestic tax rate, the domestic government's tax revenues once again will begin to fall below its tax-revenue goal. If cutting public spending to match the government's lower revenues is not regarded as a feasible option, then if it can only act alone, the domestic government has only three choices:

1) *Increase the tax rate again.* This action would essentially duplicate the steps recommended by the static view. As the dynamic view makes clear, however, this is likely to lead to a further reduction in the domestic tax base.
2) *Increase tax rates within a different domestic tax system in an effort to raise revenues from a different tax base.* Of course, the same problem of a shrinking tax base in another system may result if lower tax rates apply in other nations. For instance, if the domestic government responds to a fall in domestic income by raising the tax rate on firms' sales, then domestic residents may begin purchasing substitute products in nations with lower sales-tax rates.
3) *Broaden the tax base.* For instance, in an income-tax system, a national government could begin taxing the earnings its residents receive in other nations, thereby removing the incentive to shift earnings abroad. Naturally, this might induce at least some residents to end their residency in the domestic nation as a way to avoid the broadened tax base.

In principle, governments could opt for any or all of these choices. If other nations assess tax rates that are lower than tax rates in the domestic nation, however, these various actions at best will slow the shrinkage of the domestic tax base.

GLOBALIZATION AND TAX COMPETITION

The dynamic view on the effects of higher domestic tax rates illustrates why nations with relatively high tax rates are likely to observe shrinking tax bases and lower tax revenues. Higher personal-income-tax rates, for instance, tend to induce individuals to earn incomes abroad, and higher sales-tax or corporate-income-tax rates give firms an incentive to attempt to offer their products for sale in other countries.

Naturally, the converse is also true: A nation with relatively low tax rates tends to experience a relatively higher tax base. This is one reason why nations' governments sometimes engage in **tax competition,** reducing their tax rates below those prevailing in other countries in an effort to induce individuals and businesses to engage in taxable activities within their borders instead. By reducing their tax rates, nations actually might be able to broaden their tax bases sufficiently to generate net *increases* in their tax revenues. (See on page 401 *Management Notebook: Fighting Over Capital Flows in the European Union.*)

ON THE WEB

What are alternative views on the effects of international tax competition? For readings on this issue, visit http://www.worldbank.org/publicsector/tax/intertaxcompetition.htm.

Tax competition
Reducing tax rates below those of other regions in an effort to induce individuals and businesses to engage in taxable activities in that region.

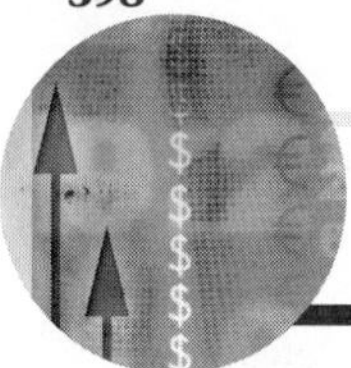

Visualizing Global Economic Issues

The Static Prescription for Dealing with a Shrinking Tax Base

To contemplate the static view's tax-policy prescriptions on a diagram, take a look at panel (a) of Figure 12-5, which depicts the equation for a nation's tax revenues, $T = t \times B$ as a straight line extending from the origin. The equation implies that a change in tax revenues, ΔT, which is measured along the vertical axis in the diagram, equals the tax rate t times a change in the tax base, ΔB, which is measured along the horizontal axis. Hence, $\Delta T = t \times \Delta B$. Rearranging this equation yields $t = \Delta T / \Delta B$. The slope of the *tax schedule* graphed in panel (a), therefore, or the "rise" divided by the "run," is the tax rate t.

Panel (b) of Figure 12-5 illustrates a situation in which a national government desires to collect a total amount of taxes equal to T^*. This tax-revenue goal may be an amount of funding required to build hospitals or provide various social services.

If the tax base is equal to B_1, the government achieves a tax-revenue goal T^* at point A by establishing a tax rate equal to t_1. Setting this tax rate ensures that the tax schedule crosses point A, thereby achieving the desired level of tax collections T^* given the tax base B_1.

Now suppose that the nation's tax base declines, perhaps because residents of this and other nations can earn incomes (in the case of an income tax) or purchase substitute goods (in the case of a sales tax) outside this country at a lower rate of taxation. This implies a lower tax base equal to B_2 at point C, and tax collections fall below the tax-revenue goal T^*, to the quantity T_2.

According to the static view of taxation, the domestic government can respond to this situation by raising the tax rate. As shown in panel (b), a sufficient increase in the tax rate, to t_2, raises the slope of the tax function. At the lower tax base, B_2, this higher tax rate yields tax collections equal to T^*, at point D. Thus, increasing the tax rate can allow the government to attain its tax revenue objective even though it faces a smaller tax base.

For Critical Analysis:
If a nation experiences considerable economic growth that results in an increase in its income-tax base, what does the static view indicate its government should it do to maintain its tax revenues at a level equal to its tax-revenue goal? Why might a government be tempted to do nothing?

Fighting Tax Competition: International Coordination among Taxing Authorities

There are two basic perspectives on the increased international tax competition that has accompanied globalization. From one point of view, tax competition is harmful. According to this perspective, because national governments realize that their tax bases will shrink if they maintain relatively high tax rates, some portion of residents will attempt to become free riders by reducing their contributions to their nations' tax bases. To avoid inducing declines in national tax bases, governments will establish lower tax rates than they otherwise would. This, in turn, restrains the ability of national governments to earn revenues high enough to maintain socially desirable spending programs.

Those who view tax competition as harmful typically favor international coordination of tax policies. A number of governments in industrialized nations with well-developed tax bases promote tax coordination. Since the formation of

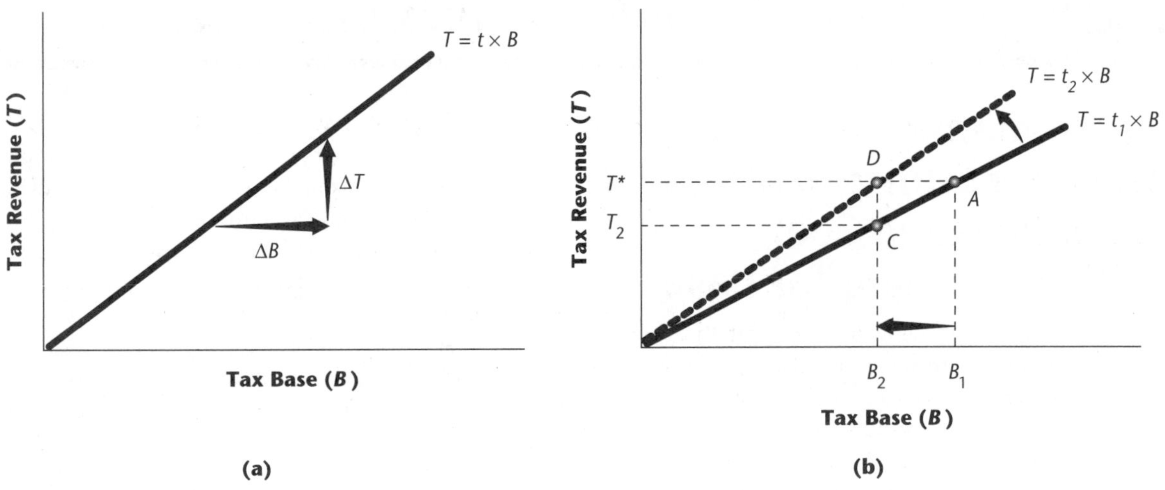

Figure 12-5

The Tax Schedule and Attaining a National Tax-Revenue Goal by Adjusting the Tax Rate

Panel (a) shows the tax schedule, which is a graph of the equation $T = t \times B$, *where* T *is the government's tax revenues,* B *is the tax base, and* t *is the tax rate. The tax rate is the slope of the tax schedule, which is the "rise,"* ΔT, *divided by the "run,"* ΔB. *Panel (b) displays a situation in which initially the tax base is equal to* B_1, *and the government can achieve a tax revenue objective* T^* *at point* A *by setting a tax rate equal to* t_1. *If tax base falls to* B_2 *at point* C *because residents of this and other nations shift economic activity to nations with lower rates of taxation, then the government's tax collections fall to* T_2. *From a static perspective on the relationship between the tax rate and tax revenues, the government can respond to this situation by raising the sales-tax rate* t_2, *which raises the slope of the tax function and pushes tax collections back up to* T^* *at point* D.

the European Monetary Union in 1999, for example, member nations have developed mechanisms for coordinating certain aspects of their tax systems.

Some nations have even coordinated efforts to try to force other countries to join their tax-coordination schemes. In 2001, the thirty member nations of the Organization for Economic Cooperation and Development (OECD), which includes the United States, Japan, Canada, and major European nations, signed a "Memorandum of Understanding" requiring OECD nations to "blacklist" nations with "harmful tax regimes." Specifically, countries that the OECD determined had set tax rates sufficiently low to "unfairly erode the tax bases of other countries and distort the location of capital and services" would be targeted for various sanctions, such as imposing withholding taxes on payments of residents of harmful tax regimes, denying foreign tax credits for taxes paid to their governments, and perhaps even adopting overt trade sanctions. Interestingly, the tax systems of

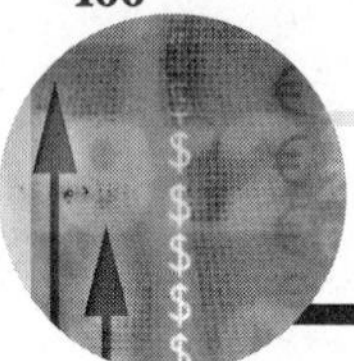

Visualizing Global Economic Issues

The Dynamic View's Bad News for Efforts to Attain a Tax-Revenue Goal with a Declining Tax Base

To understand why those who subscribe to the dynamic view of the relationship between the tax rate, the tax base, and tax revenues are pessimistic about the ability to maintain tax revenues in the face of a declining tax base, consider Figure 12-6. As in panel (b) of Figure 12-4, Figure 12-6 shows a decline in the tax base, to B_2 at point *C*, and a resulting fall in tax revenues to T_2, which is below the tax-revenue goal T^*.

The static view prescribes dealing with this situation by raising the tax rate to t_2, thereby increasing and pushing tax revenues back up to T^*, at point *D*. The problem with this analysis, however, is that it ignores the *dynamic* responses of individuals and firms to the higher tax rate in a globalized economy. Many domestic residents will respond to the new, higher domestic tax rate by moving taxable activities abroad, where lower tax rates exist. This will further lower the domestic tax base, to a level such as B_3 at point *E* in Figure 12-6. Consequently, the domestic government will still be unable to achieve its tax-revenue goal. Indeed, in the example illustrated in the figure, total tax collections fall even *farther* below the tax-revenue goal.

For Critical Analysis:
Within the context of the dynamic view, is it possible that the domestic government could actually push up its tax collections by *reducing* its tax rate?

Figure 12-6

The Dynamic View of the Relationship between the Tax Rate and Tax Revenues

From a dynamic perspective the concluding situation Figure 12-5(b) cannot be the conclusion to a government's efforts to maintain its tax revenues after a decline in the tax base. If the government responds to a fall in the tax base to B_2 *and a resulting fall in tax revenues to* T_2 *below the tax-revenue goal* T^* *by raising the tax rate to* t_2*, then tax revenues do not necessarily rise back to* T^* *at point* D. *The reason is that in a globalized economy, a number of domestic residents will respond to this increase in the tax rate by moving taxable activities to countries with lower tax rates. This will further reduce the domestic tax base, to a level such as* B_3 *at point* E, *and it is possible that total domestic tax collections will fall even farther, to* T_3.

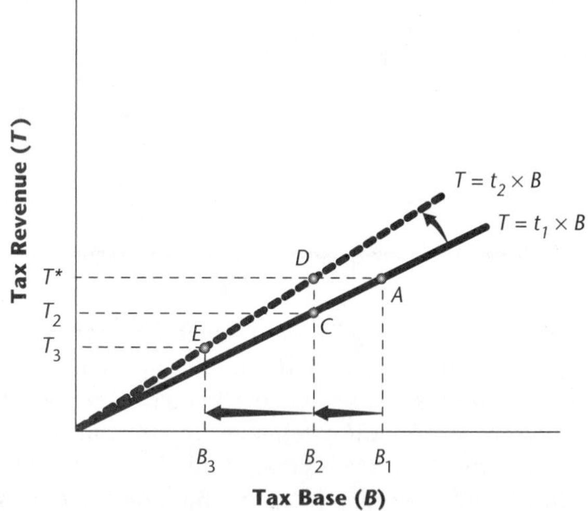

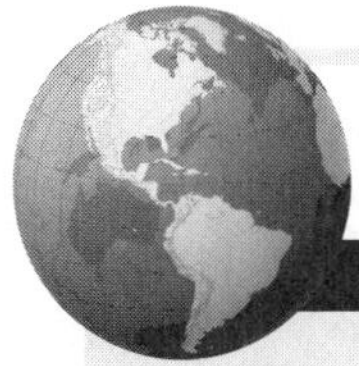

MANAGEMENT *Notebook*

POLICY MANAGEMENT

Fighting Over Capital Flows in the European Union

As indicated in Figure 12-4 on page 396, the average tax rate on capital in the European Union is currently about 23 percent. EU governments use revenues received from imposing taxes on capital income to help finance a broad array of social programs.

When entrepreneurs are considering starting a new business or when existing businesspeople are assessing where to construct a new facility, what they care about are *marginal* tax rates. These are the tax rates that they will face on earnings generated by the *next additional* unit of capital. Joeri Gorter and Ashok Parikh of the Netherlands Bureau for Economic Policy Analysis have estimated marginal tax rates on capital in EU nations, and their estimates are reported in Figure 12-7.

Gorter and Parikh's estimates indicate that if managers are otherwise equally inclined to consider capital investments in any given EU country, taking into account marginal tax rates on their investment will push them toward considering such relatively low-tax locales as Greece and Ireland. Managers are less likely to consider France and Germany, which have the highest marginal tax rates on capital.

This has important implications for flows of foreign direct investment within Europe. Gorter and Parikh find that each one-percentage-point reduction in the marginal tax rate on capital relative to the EU average tax rate tends to increase any given EU nation's flow of foreign direct investment by about 4 percent.

For Critical Analysis:
Based on the estimates of Gorter and Parikh and assuming all other factors are equal, which EU nations would you predict are most likely to experience the largest capital inflows?

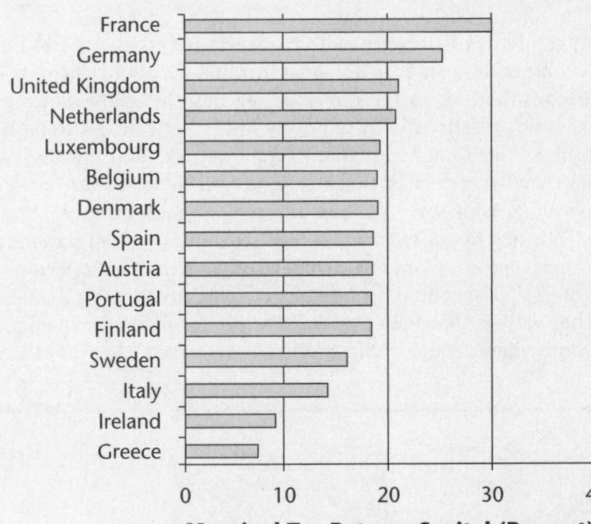

Figure 12-7

Marginal Tax Rates on Capital in the European Union

Marginal tax rates are the additional taxes that a businessperson must pay on income derived from the next unit of capital. Within the European Union, marginal tax rates vary considerably, from just under 7 percent in Greece to just over 30 percent in France.

Source: Joeri Gorter and Ashok Parikh, "How Mobile Is Capital within the European Union?" Research Memorandum No. 172, Netherlands Bureau for Economic Policy Analysis, The Hague, November 2000.

OECD nations Luxembourg, Switzerland, the United Kingdom, and the United States all qualified as harmful tax regimes under the OECD's definition, but the OECD nations aimed their coordinated tax sanctions—which they softened somewhat in 2002—only against non-OECD members. (Coordinating taxation policies regarding Internet transactions has recently emerged as an international policy issue; see *Online Globalization: Should U.S. Internet Sellers Have to Collect Taxes on Behalf of European Governments?*)

Tax Coordination or Tax Cartels?

Another perspective views tax competition as a positive side-effect of the process of globalization. Proponents of this contrary view contend that by depressing tax rates and thereby restraining overall tax revenues, international tax competition induces national governments to be more efficient in their provision of government services and more frugal in their other various types of public expenditures. In addition, they contend, tax competition helps governments resist the temptation to assess high tax rates on growth-promoting activities relating to saving and investment.

Value-added taxes (VAT) *Taxes applied to each stage of production in which value is added to a good or service.*

According to those who promote this perspective, citizens should resist efforts by their governments to coordinate tax policies. Such activities, they argue, effectively amount to attempts to establish international *tax cartels* among participating national governments intent on establishing uniformly high rates of taxation on the world's residents. Not surprisingly, critics of tax coordination were particularly disapproving of a 2002 UN proposal to move toward worldwide coordination of tax policies and potentially even the creation of a global taxation authority.

5 Fundamental Issue

How does increased globalization complicate the efforts of governments to finance their activities?

In a highly globalized economy, residents of a country with a government that imposes relatively high tax rates assessed on a tax base such as personal income, corporate income, or business sales can reduce their contributions to the domestic tax base by shifting income-earning or sales-producing activities to nations with relatively lower tax rates. Although a government with relatively high tax rates might be able to maintain its tax collections by further increasing tax rates, another byproduct of these actions is likely to be further erosion of national tax bases. Governments of some nations also may engage in international tax competition by setting relatively low tax rates to encourage residents of other nations to relocate economic activities to their nations. From one perspective, international tax competition harms broader social interests by encouraging free riders to shift economic activities to lower-tax nations, but another view is that tax competition encourages governments to be more efficient and discourages them from setting high tax rates that can retard economic growth.

Online Globalization

Should U.S. Internet Sellers Have to Collect Taxes on Behalf of European Governments?

In April 2000, the Advisory Commission on Electronic Commerce that the U.S. Congress had established to review various e-commerce issues recommended a five-year extension of an existing moratorium on subjecting Internet sales to taxes. Congress hastened to enact that recommendation into law. This U.S. action has not, however, stopped other countries from pursuing efforts to tax electronic commerce. Because U.S. companies lead the way in e-commerce, they are the starting point for international efforts to tax Internet sales.

The European Union's Online Tax Proposal

Nations of the European Union (EU) rely heavily on **value-added taxes (VATs)** to provide revenues to fund government expenditures. Unlike sales taxes, which are assessed solely on the final sales price in a transaction, a VAT is applied to each stage of production in which value is added to a good or service, including final assembly or the provision of a final service to a consumer.

In July 2000, the EU's Executive Commission proposed requiring U.S. companies with annual sales on Internet-downloadable products within EU nations exceeding $96,000 to register in at least one EU nation. Companies selling downloadable goods and services, including software, videos, music, and computer games within the EU would have to collect a VAT of 15 to 25 percent for payment to that nation's government.

Are EU Governments Needy or Simply Greedy?

The EU's Executive Commission offered two rationales for their proposal. First, EU online sellers must collect a VAT on each downloadable product that they sell. If U.S. companies are able to sell downloadable products tax-free while EU companies are not, then U.S. companies will have an "unfair advantage" over their European rivals. Second, EU governments undertake considerable social spending, and they need the revenues.

U.S. firms blasted the EU proposal. The U.S. government's response was more diplomatic and muted. Nevertheless, a Treasury undersecretary noted that it appeared that at least some of the tax rates that the EU was proposing to use were higher than the tax rates that EU governments charge on the same products when sold offline. Some economists speculated that the EU planned to charge higher online taxes to push up the effective price of the online products predominantly sold by U.S. firms—thereby effectively placing a tariff on EU imports of downloadable U.S. products.

By 2002, the EU proposal had become a "plan" with an additional wrinkle. Whereas EU companies would charge residents of EU nations a flat tax on online purchases based on the headquarters location of the Internet seller, under the EU online taxation plan U.S. companies will have to charge taxes based on where the EU resident is located. Thus, the EU plan imposes a greater administrative burden on U.S. Internet sellers, which would have to determine the country of residence of each EU buyer before calculating the applicable tax.

Clearly, the broad issue of how to deal with different national approaches to taxing online commerce is unlikely to go away soon. Just recently, for instance, China announced that it also will be taxing e-commerce transactions, and it is already exploring ways to tax the sales of both domestic and foreign firms.

For Critical Analysis:

Should a sales tax or a VAT apply based on the location of the seller or on the location of the buyer? Why does it matter?

CHAPTER SUMMARY

1) **Ways That Government Regulators Seek to Safeguard the Interests of Consumers:** A situation of asymmetric information arises when one party to an exchange has information not possessed by another party to the exchange. This can result in adverse selection, or the potential for sellers to offer low-quality products to customers. In addition, moral hazard, or the possibility that one party to an exchange may undertake actions that another party deems undesirable after the exchange has already been arranged or taken place, can arise. In an effort to protect consumers from losses that might arise from these asymmetric-information problems, national governments may enact regulations establishing minimal standards for quality or service. Governments also may establish agencies to enforce those standards.
2) **How the World's Governments Protect Rights to Intellectual Property:** Governments attempt to encourage firms to engage in invention and innovation by establishing intellectual property rights, which are legal rules assigning ownership to creative ideas. Governments award copyrights to creators of works such as articles, stories, novels, computer programs, audio recordings, and movies, giving those individuals or firms exclusive privileges to reproduce, distribute, perform, or display such works. They provide a means for firms to register words or symbols, known as trademarks, which firms use to distinguish their goods or services from those of other firms. Governments also grant patents that give an inventor the exclusive legal right to make, use, and sell an invention for a specified number of years.
3) **International Externalities and Global Public Goods, and What National Governments or Multinational Institutions Can Do about Them:** International externalities are welfare spillovers that activities in one nation's marketplace can exert on third parties in other countries. A global public good bestows benefits on many people around the world at the same time, cannot be provided to one individual without others being able to benefit at zero cost, and cannot be deprived from an individual who has failed to contribute to producing the good. Governments or multinational authorities that wish to correct negative international externalities such as cross-border environmental pollution can attempt to limit production or trade of the good or service that generates the externality, require producers to incur the costs of the externality, or tax producers. Although some observers perceive the world's environment to be a public good, at present there is no consensus concerning appropriate international trade policies to promote preservation of the environment.
4) **How the World's Nations Seek to Protect the Global Environment:** At present, global efforts to protect the world's environment are coordinated through treaties that commit nations to pursuing pollution-abatement policies aimed at quantitative limits on pollution. National governments or multinational authorities can attempt to develop quantitative limits based on per-

ceived marginal benefits and marginal costs of combating the externalities. Although some nongovernment organizations that press environmental issues contend that that international trade promotes capital flows that degrade environments of developing nations, others contend that trade improves living standards, promotes technological improvements and environment-friendly innovations, and provides a forum for making pollution abatement a feature of international trade agreements.

5) **How Increased Globalization Complicates Governments' Efforts to Finance Their Activities:** Increased globalization makes it easier for residents of a country with relatively high tax rates to shift their taxable economic activities abroad, thereby reducing the domestic tax base. It is possible that a government with relatively high tax rates might be able to maintain its tax collections by further increases in tax rates. Nevertheless, further increases in tax rates are likely to generate additional declines in the nation's tax bases. Some nations' governments engage in international tax competition by establishing relatively low tax rates to induce other countries' residents to relocate economic activities within their borders. On one hand, international tax competition can be harmful to society by encouraging free riders to shift economic activities to lower-tax nations. On the other hand, tax competition encourages governments to be more efficient and to establish lower tax rates that promote economic growth.

QUESTIONS AND PROBLEMS

1) Discuss the key rationales for governmental regulation reviewed in this chapter. Why do you suppose that national governments may disagree about the appropriate scope of consumer-protection regulations?
2) A source of conflict in international trade is a potential trade-off between free trade and a desire to protect domestic residents from potentially harmful products, such as substandard drugs. Briefly outline one way that nations might cooperatively deal with this problem within the context of online trade in pharmaceuticals.
3) Recently ministers of justice of nations of the European Union approved a law that subjects anyone selling goods or services on the Internet to the laws of each of the fifteen EU member nations. How might this law discourage foreign competition even if it was not intended to be protectionist legislation?
4) In the early 2000s, Congress considered legislation to make it illegal for U.S. residents to import a number of goods, such as perfumes, shampoos, and wristwatches, unless the products had appropriate safety labels. The proposed law immediately drew harsh reaction from online discount retailers, which charged this law was a trade quota in disguise that would damage their businesses. In what way might this law have the same effect as an explicit quota on international trade?

5) If a national government chose to limit itself to issuing only patents, copyrights, or trademarks in the electronic marketplace, which form of intellectual-property-right protection do you believe it should choose to enforce? Support your position.
6) What are the advantages and disadvantages for developing nations of enforcing international standards for protecting intellectual property rights?
7) What features of the definition of a global public good make it difficult to identify very many items that everyone can agree are global public goods?
8) The U.S. government has established a pollution-abatement policy in which firms can buy or sell rights to pollute up to a legally mandated pollution limit. Discuss the pros and cons of a multilateral extension of this policy to the rest of the world.
9) Why might some environmentally oriented nongovernment organizations regard a "marginal-benefit-equals-marginal-cost" standard for pollution abatement as undesirable?
10) What nations of the world do you think are most likely to favor fighting "harmful tax competition" by establishing international organizations to coordinate tax policies and pressing efforts to induce all the world's nations to join those organizations? What nations do you suppose are least likely to wish to join such organizations? Why?

ONLINE APPLICATION

Internet URL: http://www.ciesin.org/TG/PI/TRADE/tradhmpg.html

Title: **Trade Policy and Global Environmental Change**

Navigation: Go to the home page of Columbia University's Center for International Earth Science Information Network (http://www.ciesin.org). Then click on "Browse by Subject" and click on "Thematic Guidelines on Political Institutions." Finally, click on "Trade Policy and Global Environmental Change."

Application: Perform the indicated operations, and answer the accompanying questions.

1) Click on "Trade and the Environment: Conflicts and Opportunities," and read the article. Why might residents of developing nations be less likely, as compared with residents of developed nations, to be concerned about global externality and public-good aspects of environmental issues? Which of the mechanisms for addressing environmental problems in developing nations that the article discusses do you believe has the greatest potential for success? Why?
2) Back up to the "Trade Policy and Global Environmental Change" page, click on "Harmonization, Trade, and the Environment," and read the article. With respect to environmental issues, what does the author mean by "harmoniza-

tion"? Of the advantages and disadvantages of harmonization that the author discusses, which do you regard as most important? On net, do you believe harmonization is a good or bad idea? Use economic arguments based on what you have learned in this chapter to justify your position.

For Group Study and Analysis: Divide the class into two groups, and have each group draft a list of proposed guidelines for determining what activities constitute international environmental externalities, what features of the environment (if any) should be regarded as global public goods, and multinational mechanisms for addressing international environmental problems.

REFERENCES AND RECOMMENDED READINGS

Braithwaite, John, and Peter Drahos. *Global Business Regulation.* Cambridge, U.K.: Cambridge University Press, 2000.

Destler, I. M., and Peter Balint. "The New Politics of American Trade: Trade, Labor, and the Environment." *Policy Analysis in International Economics,* No. 58, Washington, D.C.: Institute for International Economics, October 1999.

European Policy Forum. *Tax Competition: Broadening the Debate.* June 2000.

Gorter, Joeri, and Ashok Parikh. "How Mobile Is Capital within the European Union?" Research Memorandum No. 172, Netherlands Bureau for Economic Policy Analysis, The Hague, November 2000.

Horner, Frances. "The OECD, Tax Competition, and the Future of Tax Reform." *Directorate for Financial, Fiscal, and Enterprise Affairs, Organization for Economic Cooperation and Development* (January 2000).

Janeba, Eckhard, and John Wilson. "Tax Competition and Trade Protection." National Bureau of Economic Research Working Paper No. 7402, October 1999.

Kaul, Inge, Isabelle Grunberg, and Marc Stern, eds. *Global Public Goods.* New York: Oxford University Press, 1999.

Maskus, Keith. *Intellectual Property Rights in the Global Economy.* Washington, D.C.: Institute for International Economics, August 2000.

Rosen, Harvey. *Public Finance.* 5th ed. New York: McGraw-Hill, 1999.

World Trade Organization. *Trade and Environment.* Switzerland: WTO Publications, 1999.

CHAPTER THIRTEEN

Rules versus Discretion—Can Policymakers Stick to Their Promises?

Fundamental Issues

1. **What are the ultimate goals of policymakers in open economies?**
2. **What are the main problems with discretionary policymaking?**
3. **Why is policy credibility a crucial factor in maintaining low inflation, and how might nations attain policy credibility?**
4. **What is structural interdependence, and how can it lead nations to cooperate or to coordinate their policies?**
5. **What are the benefits and costs of international policy coordination?**
6. **Could nations gain from adopting a common currency?**

In November 18, 1994, a Wall Street Journal *headline stated, "Mexico Posts Surprisingly Solid Growth, As Turnaround in Economy Advances." A figure accompanying the article showed recent Mexican GDP growth of nearly 5 percent per year and was entitled "On the Move." On December 21, however, the Mexican government unexpectedly devalued the peso, and the peso's value relative to the dollar plummeted by nearly 13 percent. During the next week following the devaluation, U.S. residents who held peso-denominated financial assets lost more than one third of the dollar value of their holdings. Mexican residents also experienced significant losses. Economists estimated that the total cost of bailing out Mexican banks that failed during the crisis was about 15 percent of the nation's output of goods and services during a typical year. In addition, the annual Mexican inflation rate shot up from 7 percent in 1994 to 35 percent in 1995 and again in 1996.*

Today, however, the Bank of Mexico, the nation's central bank, possesses more than $40 billion in foreign currency reserves. The peso–dollar exchange rate has been stable since late 1998, and the inflation rate is once again below double digits, at about 9 percent. One Wall Street economist recently went so far as to call the peso Latin America's "flight-to-quality" currency—a currency that investors were likely to desire to hold as store of value in the event of a crisis elsewhere within Latin America.

What accounted for this turnaround of fortunes for the Mexican peso? Many economists credited efforts by the Bank of Mexico to reestablish credibility as a central bank committed to containing inflation. These economists argued that by proving to both domestic residents and international investors that it would not engage in short-term efforts to artificially stimulate economic activity via bursts of inflation, the Bank of Mexico had succeeded in providing a renewed foundation for long-term economic stability.

In this chapter, you will examine the arguments in favor of discretionary policy, both monetary and fiscal, as well as those in favor of rules—no discretionary policy. In addition, you will learn about how nations with fixed exchange rates can try to make their policies credible.

Policy Goals in Open Economies

In Unit 3, we discussed how various international financial and monetary policies can influence the ebbs and flows of economic activity within nations. You learned that central bank actions influence interest rates and exchange rates, thereby influencing total desired expenditures on domestic goods and service, real output, and the price level. Recognizing that their actions can affect a nation's economic performance, central banks often contemplate adopting policy strategies with an explicit intention to achieve specific national economic goals.

You have not yet encountered other tough questions, however. What should international financial and monetary policymakers do? What goals should they seek to achieve? How should they go about pursuing those goals? In this chapter, you will learn that even if there might be widespread agreement concerning the appropriate *objectives* of policymaking in the realm of international trade and finance, the best way to *implement* policy still might not be apparent.

In this chapter, we will begin by examining the factors that determine the **ultimate goals,** or final objectives, of policymakers who face global economic issues. Then we will devote the bulk of the remainder of the chapter to contemplating how policymakers might go about trying to pursue these goals.

Ultimate goals
The final objectives of national economic policies.

Table 13-1 The Costs of Inflation and Inflation Variability

Type of Cost	Cause
Resources expended to economize on money holdings (more trips to banks, etc.)	Rising prices associated with inflation
Costs of changing price lists and printing menus and catalogs	Individual product/service price increases associated with inflation
Redistribution of real incomes from individuals to the government	Inflation that pushes people into higher, nonindexed nominal tax brackets
Reductions in investment, capital accumulation, and economic growth	Inflation variability that complicates business planning
Slowed pace of introduction of new and better products	Volatile price changes that reduce the efficiency of private markets
Redistribution of resources from creditors to debtors	Unexpected inflation that reduces the real values of debts

INTERNAL GOALS

One aim of central banks could be to achieve *internal goals,* which relate to purely domestic policy objectives. Although a central bank might seek to achieve a number of internal goals, three objectives typically top the list of potential internal goals:

1) *Inflation Objectives.* As Table 13-1 indicates, there are a number of costs associated with high and variable inflation. In light of these inflation costs, there is good justification for a central bank to try to maintain low (or even no) inflation. In addition, there is a strong rationale for limiting year-to-year variability in inflation rates.
2) *Output Goals.* Another potential ultimate goal of economic policy might be to lay a foundation of financial-market and monetary stability that promotes the highest feasible growth of real GDP. In addition, central banks could strive to prevent sharp swings in real GDP. Pursuing these policy goals regarding national output might help to limit cyclical fluctuations within a nation's economy.
3) *Employment Goals.* Labor is a key factor of production, and in a democratic republic workers also account for the bulk of voters. Consequently, central bank policymakers are likely to feel pressures to pursue policies that aim to prevent significant variability in worker unemployment rates and that might spur greater growth in real output and employment.

EXTERNAL GOALS

In addition to purely domestic, internal goals, a nation's central bank might also be concerned about international payment flows. Thus, central bank policymakers may desire to achieve *external goals,* or the attainment of objectives for international flows of goods, services, income, and assets or for the relative values of their national currencies.

Why would a nation's residents desire for central-bank policymakers to pursue external objectives? One reason is that international factors help determine domestic outcomes in open economies. If residents of a nation engage in significant volumes of trade with other nations, international considerations may affect a nation's ability to achieve its output, employment, and inflation objectives. Consequently, internal and external objectives may go hand in hand. Another reason, however, is that a number of a nation's citizens may have immediate interests in the international sectors of their nation's economies. They may perceive that international variables themselves—such as the nation's trade balance—should be ultimate policy goals.

International Objectives and Domestic Goals

As we discussed in Chapter 9, two factors that play a role in determining a country's aggregate desired expenditures are export expenditures on the nation's output of goods and services by residents of other nations and import spending by its own residents on foreign-produced goods and services. An increase in export expenditures increases aggregate desired expenditures, whereas a rise in import spending reduces the fraction of disposable income available for consumption of domestically produced output. Therefore, both of these international factors influence the equilibrium level of real income.

It follows that a central bank typically must consider the volumes of export and import expenditures when contemplating appropriate policy strategies. At a minimum, a central bank must account for the real-income effects of trade-related expenditures that are unrelated to purely domestic influences. More broadly, however, a central bank may reach the conclusion that achieving its internal goals may require careful attention to international factors. For example, a central bank may seek to achieve balanced international trade as part of a general strategy intended to achieve its domestic inflation, output, and employment objectives.

External Balance for Its Own Sake

Central banks in most countries, however, typically regard external objectives as a set of goals that are separable from its internal balance objectives. Workers and business owners in industries that export large portions of their output often push their governments to enact policies that promote exports. At the same time, workers and business owners in industries that rely on domestic sales of their output may pressure government and central bank officials to pursue policies that restrain imports. Persistent efforts by both of these interest groups could induce a nation's policymakers to seek trade-balance *surpluses* as external balance objectives.

History is replete with examples of nations that have sought to achieve persistent trade surpluses. For example, in the seventeenth and eighteenth centuries successive generations of British citizens advocated a national policy of **mercantilism.** The view of this school of thought is that inflows of payments relating to international commerce and trade are a primary source of a nation's wealth. During this period, therefore, British mercantilists advocated policy actions designed to promote exports and to hinder imports. A fundamental difficulty with mercantilist thought, of course, is that if *all* countries simultaneously try to attain trade surpluses through import limitations, international commerce likely would be stymied. Realization of this self-defeating aspect of mercantilism led to its decline in the nineteenth century. Mercantilist thought supports the goals of special interest groups in any open economy, however, so these groups still use mercantilist arguments today in an effort to pressure policymakers to maintain balanced trade, if not trade surpluses.

Mercantilism
A view that a primary determinant of a nation's wealth is international trade and commerce, so that a nation can gain by enacting policies that spur exports while limiting imports.

The interests of exporters and importers also may make exchange-rate objectives part of the mix of external balance goals. On the one hand, a reduction in the exchange value of a nation's currency effectively makes domestically produced goods less expensive to foreign residents. Thus, if export industries form a predominant political interest group, a country's central bank also may face pressures to reduce the value of its currency. On the other hand, an increase in a currency's exchange value reduces the effective price that domestic residents pay for foreign-produced goods. Consequently, if importers have considerable political clout, a central bank may be lobbied to push up the value of the nation's currency.

Fundamental Issue

What are the ultimate goals of policymakers in open economies?

Ultimate goals of the national economic policymakers are the final objectives of their policy strategies and actions. There are two categories of economic goals that policymakers often pursue. One consists of internal objectives, which are ultimate goals for national real income, employment, and inflation. The other consists of external balance objectives, which are objectives for the trade balance and other components of the balance of payments.

Rules versus Discretion in Economic Policymaking

In their pursuit of ultimate policy goals, national economic policymakers often engage in **discretionary policymaking,** or undertaking policy responses on an *ad hoc* basis in the presence of perceived "needs" to counteract socially undesirable economic booms or busts. In spite of this predisposition among policymakers to use their discretion, many economists have argued that society could benefit if national policymakers would instead adopt a **policy rule.** This is a policy strategy to which a central bank or government would *bind* or *commit* itself, thereby following that strategy no matter what events might take place.

Discretionary policymaking
The act of responding to economic events as they occur, rather than in ways it might previously have planned in the absence of those events.

Policy rule
A commitment to a fixed strategy no matter what happens to other economic variables.

TIME LAGS AND RULES VERSUS DISCRETION

A fundamental problem faced by a policymaker in any nation is the existence of **policy time lags.** These are intervals between the need for a policy action and the ultimate effects of that action on an economic variable. Any policymaker faces three types of constraints on its ability to make the best policy choices that it can as quickly as such choices should be made:

Policy time lags
Time intervals between the need for a countercyclical monetary policy action and the ultimate effects of that action on an economic variable.

1) At any given point in time, policymakers face limited information, particularly in the presence of time lags, about current events.
2) Policymakers are fallible human beings who face constraints on their abilities to recognize and respond appropriately to changing circumstances, particularly in light of lags in their recognition of varying circumstances.
3) Policymakers are constrained by their lack of certainty about the actual effects, and timing of those effects, of policies that they may enact.

Together, these constraints can slow policymakers' responses to episodes or incidents that may require speedy attention if policymakers really wish to make a positive contribution to attainment of their goals. Consequently, they can greatly complicate efforts to engage in discretionary policymaking.

National economic policymakers such as central bank officials who determine monetary policies and exchange rate policies face three types of policy time lags. These are the *recognition lag,* the *response lag,* and the *transmission lag.* Let's discuss each in turn before considering their broader consequences.

The Recognition Lag

A key problem that the policymakers confront as they pursue their ultimate inflation, output, employment, and balance of payments objectives is limited current information. Although government statisticians often can estimate nominal GDP data on a weekly basis, at best they typically can compile data on real GDP, the unemployment rate, the price level, and international transactions only on a monthly basis. Nevertheless, government statisticians often must revise these monthly computations as they discover measurement or calculation errors. As a result, policymakers cannot always place complete faith in the accuracy of initial values for these economic goal variables.

Near-term data uncertainties complicate the lives of policymakers. To see why, suppose that a nation's inflation rate were to embark on a sizable increase owing to an unexpected rise in aggregate demand caused by an unexpected rise in incomes abroad that has boosted foreign purchases of domestic goods and services. Other things unchanged, an appropriate central bank response would be to cut back on the growth rate of the money stock. This would help to curtail the rise in aggregate demand and to alleviate resulting upward price pressures. In light of data limitations that the central bank faces, however, officials might not realize that inflation had started to rise until a number of weeks had passed.

The time between the need for a policy action and the recognition of that need is called the **recognition lag.** As in the situation just described, the recognition

Recognition lag
The interval that passes between the need for a countercyclical policy action and the recognition of this need by a policymaker.

lag could be a matter of a few weeks. Other factors, however, can lengthen this policy time lag. For instance, even if central bank officials notice a rise in the inflation rate, it might take them awhile to ascertain its causes, particularly in a highly open economy. Some officials might speculate that recent but temporary upticks in the prices of imported goods might have been responsible, indicating no need for the central bank to take action. Misleading signals such as this might hold up central bank action to contain inflation for several additional weeks. Consequently, the recognition lag could easily increase from a few weeks to a few months. This is true for both monetary policy and for government policies regarding public expenditures and taxation.

The Response Lag

Response lag
The interval between the recognition of a need for a countercyclical policy action and the actual implementation of the policy action.

Even after policymakers reach the conclusion that altered economic circumstances require a policy change, it may take some time for them to decide on the appropriate action to take. The **response lag** is the time between recognition of the need for a change in economic policy and the actual implementation of that change.

At most central banks, the response lag for monetary policy should never be more than a few weeks, because this is the typical interlude between formal meetings of central bank officials in most nations. In fact, the response lag for monetary policy is often shorter than this because officials within most central banks communicate daily. A factor that could contribute to a lengthening of the monetary policy response lag, however, is a lack of consensus among central bank officials concerning the best policy to implement. Some officials, for example, might believe that a swift, significant response is needed in response to a perceived rise in the inflation rate. Other officials, in contrast, might argue for a more gradual, measured response to an observed increase in the price level. Such disagreements among central bank officials could lead to delays in central bank policy actions, which could lengthen the monetary policy response lag significantly.

The response lag is often even longer for policies regarding government spending and taxation. In most nations, an executive officer such as a prime minister or president and a majority of one or more legislatures must reach agreement on changes in the national budget intended to address a given situation. This can be a laborious task that can take many months. Indeed, political gridlock can inhibit government policy actions for years. Consequently, the policy response lag for public-spending and tax policies typically is much longer than the average response lag of monetary policy.

The Transmission Lag

Transmission lag
Time that elapses between the implementation of an intended countercyclical policy and its ultimate effects on an economic variable.

It takes time for a fiscal or monetary policy action to transmit its effects to overall economic activity. The time that passes before an implemented policy action fully exerts effects on the national or global economy is the **transmission lag.** In Chapter 9, we envisioned the effects of a particular policy action on real income or the price level without regard to the time that it takes for such effects actually to occur. In fact, it can take months or even years for the effects of policy actions to be transmitted to ultimate policy goal variables. Current estimates indicate, for instance, that the average length of the monetary policy transmission lag is just over twelve months. For monetary policy, therefore, combining the recognition, response, and transmission lags leads one to conclude that the time elapsing between the initial need for a monetary policy action and that action's final effects on the economy could easily stretch to well over a year. Given the longer response lags that are common in implementing changes in public expenditures and taxation—sometimes several years—time lags for these forms of economic policy could be even longer.

This raises the possibility that well-intentioned discretionary policymaking can actually be *destablizing* in many instances. For example, a policy action aimed at restraining the growth of aggregate demand to contain inflation detected several months back could begin to exert its effects just as the economy is entering a downturn, thereby contributing to an even larger economic contraction. Policy time lags, therefore, weaken the case for discretionary economic policymaking while strengthening the case for policy rules.

IS POLICY DISCRETION UNAVOIDABLE?

Even economists who promote policy discretion agree that the existence of policy time lags poses a significant problem for discretionary policymaking. There is another argument against policy discretion, however, that hinges neither on policy time lags nor on the pursuit of self-interest by policymakers. This alternative view is consistent with policymakers having up-to-date information, responding quickly to that information, and influencing the economy immediately. Its key implication is that discretionary policymaking unambiguously makes society worse off, as compared with staying the course with a policy rule, in one important respect: Policy discretion tends to push up a nation's average inflation rate.

Few policymakers would ever claim that they desire positive average inflation rates. Nevertheless, during the past several decades most nations in the world have experienced inflation. Figure 13-1 on the following page displays annual inflation rates since the mid-1980s for several diverse nations. In recent years, economists have applied *game theory*—the theory of strategic interactions among individuals or institutions—to try to understand why inflation is so pervasive throughout these and other national economies.

Policy Goals and the Inflation-Output Trade-Off

A key feature of the game theory approach to explaining persistent inflation is the assumption that an ultimate objective of a nation's economic policymakers is to attain a target output level that is equal to the **capacity output** for the economy. This is the real output that firms could produce if labor and other productive factors were employed to their utmost. Typically the capacity output level is higher than the output level that a nation's economy tends to produce in the long run. On reason for this is that income taxation in the form of assessments on wages and salaries induce workers to supply fewer labor services than they would have otherwise. As a consequence, the total output of firms tends to be lower than the capacity level. Another reason is government regulations, such as restrictions

Capacity output
The real output that the economy could produce if all resources were used to their utmost.

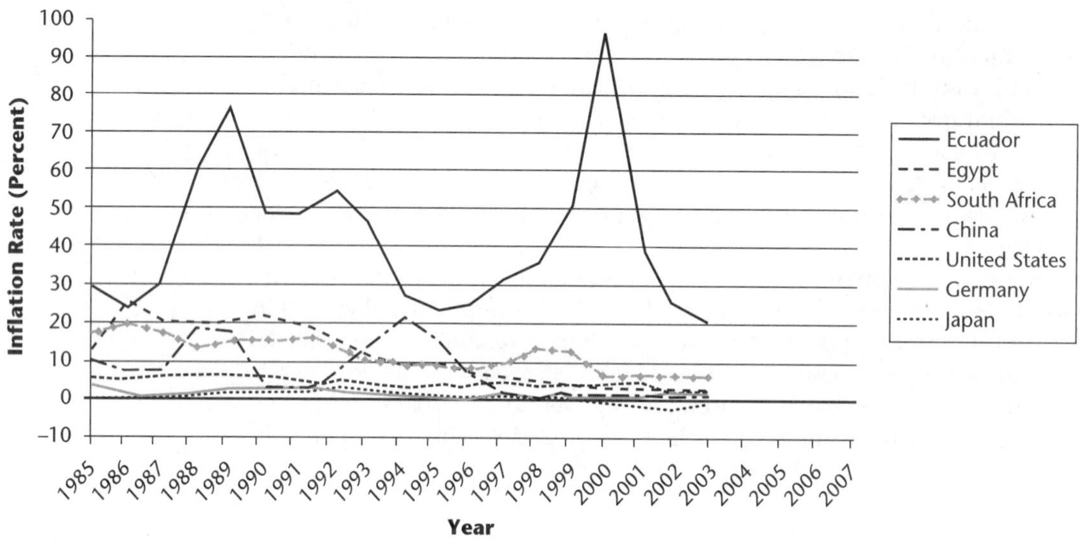

Figure 13-1

Inflation in Selected Nations

Since the mid-1980s, consumer price inflation rates in the United States, Germany, and Japan have been well below those in most other nations. Nevertheless, all nations typically have experienced positive inflation in nearly every year.

Source: International Monetary Fund, *World Outlook,* various issues; IMF and authors' estimates for 2001 and 2002.

on entry into various industries, such as licensing requirements, which restrain production of goods and services by those industries.

Another fundamental assumption is that a policymaker prefers to keep down inflation. As you learned in Chapter 9, however, in the short run increases in a nation's output are possible only if the price level increases. Thus, a policymaker faces a trade-off between a goal of pushing national output closer to the capacity output level and an objective of restraining inflation. Each policymaker will place its own weights on these conflicting objectives and determine how much inflation is acceptable relative to the corresponding increase in output that might be attainable via an expansion of aggregate demand.

Credibility and the Inflation Bias of Discretionary Economic Policy

Now let's consider the interplay between a nation's economic policymakers and its residents envisioned by the game theory approach. The policymaker can conduct discretionary policy actions and would like to raise output toward the capacity level while restraining inflation. Depending on how much weight the policymaker places on these conflicting goals, the policymaker is likely to "split the difference" by enacting policies that raise output *toward* the capacity output level.

Consider, however, how the nation's residents are likely to behave if they recognize the policymaker's goals. They will realize that the policymaker will be tempted to increase real output at the expense of greater inflation, thereby reducing the real spending power of their wages. Hence, workers will seek wage increases *in anticipation* of a policy action that increases aggregate demand. Wage increases raise firms' costs, so firms will reduce their production at any given price level. On net, the nation's aggregate output will not change, but the price level will unambiguously rise. By pursuing its output and inflation goals in a discretionary manner, the policymaker would cause inflation to occur. That is, there would be an **inflation bias,** or a tendency for the nation to experience positive average inflation year after year.

Inflation bias
Tendency for the economy to experience continuing inflation as a result of discretionary monetary policy that takes place because of the time inconsistency problem of monetary policy.

What if the policymaker promised not to try to raise aggregate demand in spite of its well-known preference for higher national output? There are two possible answers. One is that the nation's residents might not believe the policymaker really would honor such a commitment. If they did not, but the policymaker did in fact stand by its promise, then wage increases obtained by workers in anticipation of a policy-induced aggregate-demand expansion that failed to materialize would generate both a reduction in output and a higher price level. Because workers realize that the policymaker certainly would not want these events to occur, it would be even harder for them to believe the policymaker's promise not to increase aggregate demand through an expansionary policy action. Indeed, this would give the policymaker added incentive to raise aggregate demand, making it unlikely that this particular possibility will arise as a typical outcome in a discretionary interaction between a national policymaker and a country's residents.

The other possibility is that the nation's residents might find a policymaker's promise to abide by a commitment not to engage in policy actions to raise aggregate demand *credible,* or believable. If so, then workers would not seek higher wages, and the economy would not experience a higher price level. Under such a committed policy rule, there would be no tendency for inflation to occur. (To see a diagrammatic exposition of how discretionary economic policymaking generates a tendency toward inflation, see on pages 418–419 *Visualizing Global Economic Issues: The Inflation Bias of Discretionary Policy.*)

Fundamental Issue 2

What are the main problems with discretionary policymaking?

Economists generally agree that the potential for discretionary policymaking to succeed in stabilizing economic activity is limited by three types of policy time lags: (1) the recognition lag, or the time between the need for a policy action and a policymaker's realization of the need; (2) the response lag, or the interval between recognition of the need for an action and actual implementation of a policy change; and (3) the transmission lag, or the time from implementation of a policy action and the action's ultimate effects on the economy. All told, these lags can sum to well over a year in duration and can cause a well-meaning discretionary policymaker to engage in actions that ultimately destabilize the economy. Another problem is that if a nation's policymaker has the discretion to try to raise real output toward its capacity level, thereby bringing about an increase in output that requires policies intended to raise aggregate demand and push up the price level. This induces a nation's residents to negotiate higher wages, thereby reducing aggregate supply and causing output to fall in the absence of higher aggregate demand. Consequently, the policymaker in fact raises aggregate demand as the nation's residents anticipated, resulting in an inflation bias.

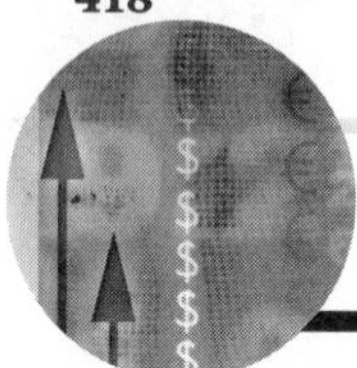

Visualizing Global Economic Issues

The Inflation Bias of Discretionary Policy

A diagrammatic explanation of the game theory approach to understanding the relationship between discretionary policy and inflation appears in Figure 13-2. It displays an initial aggregate demand-aggregate supply equilibrium point *A,* at an equilibrium price level P_1 and an equilibrium level of output y_1. The output level y^* is the economy's *capacity output.* A national economic policymaker has two objectives that are known to all of the nation's residents. One is to push output toward the capacity level y^*. The other is to minimize inflation.

In the short run, the policymaker can only influence output by engaging in policies that alter the position of the aggregate demand schedule. An increase in aggregate demand from AD_1 to AD_2 in Figure 13-2 causes a rightward movement along the short-run aggregate supply schedule, thereby raising real output toward the target y^* at point *B.* How much the policymaker is willing to expand aggregate demand would depend on the weight that the policymaker places on its output objective relative to its aim to keep inflation as low as possible.

Evaluating Alternative Strategies of the Policymaker and the Nation's Residents

Figure 13-2 depicts four *potential* outcomes that might emerge from the interaction between the nation's residents—who determine wages and thereby firms' costs and the position of the aggregate supply schedule—and the policymaker, who determines the position of the aggregate demand schedule. The four potential outcomes of this interaction are points *A, B,* C, and *D.* Let's consider each in turn.

Because the policymaker wishes to push real output toward the capacity output level y^* while keeping inflation as low as possible, Point *B* might represent a compromise outcome: Real output would rise *toward* the capacity target at the cost of permitting *some* inflation.

At point *B,* the price level would be higher, which erodes the real value of the wages workers would earn from laboring more hours and producing additional output. The nation's residents know the policymaker's incentives, however, so they will bargain for higher wages in an effort to maintain the real value of their earnings, which, in turn, increases firms' costs and shifts the aggregate supply schedule leftward, from AS_1 to AS_2. The result is point *C* in Figure 13-2. Point *C* is consistent with the strategy of the nation's residents, because at this point they have maintained their real wage earnings by pushing up their wages to compensate for higher prices. In addition, point *C* is consistent with the policymaker's intent to raise aggregate demand to try to raise output while keeping inflation low (even though, after the fact, the policymaker would not succeed in its effort). Consequently, in contrast to point *B,* point *C* is a possible equilibrium in the policy game.

At point *C,* the policymaker fails to expand real output. Suppose that the policymaker recognizes that it cannot really raise output and commits itself to leaving that aggregate demand schedule at the position AD_1. Such a commitment would constitute a policy *rule* in which the policymaker avoids responding to the incentive that it otherwise has to try to raise real output in the short run. If the nation's residents did *not* believe that the central bank could follow through on such a commitment, however, they would still raise their price expectation and negotiate an increase in the contract wage. This would cause the aggregate supply schedule to shift from AS_1 to AS_2, resulting in point *D.* This point would be inconsistent with the policymaker's strategy, because at this point inflation occurs and real output falls even *farther* below the capacity objective. Hence, point *D* could not be an equilibrium point in the policy game.

There is one point that could, under a special circumstance, arise in the policy game. This is point *A*. *If* the central bank could commit to maintaining the aggregate demand schedule at AD_1, and *if* the nation's residents could be induced to believe that the central bank would honor that commitment, then point *A* would be maintained as the final equilibrium point. There would be no inflation.

Credibility and the Inflation Bias

Economists call point *A* the *commitment policy equilibrium.* If the policymaker cannot credibly commit to abstaining from inflation, however, point *A* cannot arise, because then the nation's residents will bargain for higher wages. The policymaker knows this and thereby must raise aggregate demand to avoid both lower output and higher inflation at point *D*. Point *C*, therefore, is the *discretionary policy equilibrium* that results when the policymaker cannot commit to a rule. The difference between the new price level P_2 at point *C* and the initial price level P_1 at point *A* is the *inflation bias* arising from discretionary monetary policy.

Clearly, the determinant of whether inflation arises in the policy game is whether the policymaker can credibly commit not to engage in inflationary policymaking. A nation with a policymaker possessing significant credibility is more likely to experience an equilibrium at or close to point *A*, whereas a national policymaker lacking credibility is more likely to experience a sizable inflation bias.

For Critical Analysis:
How could a policymaker who currently lacks policy credibility go about developing it?

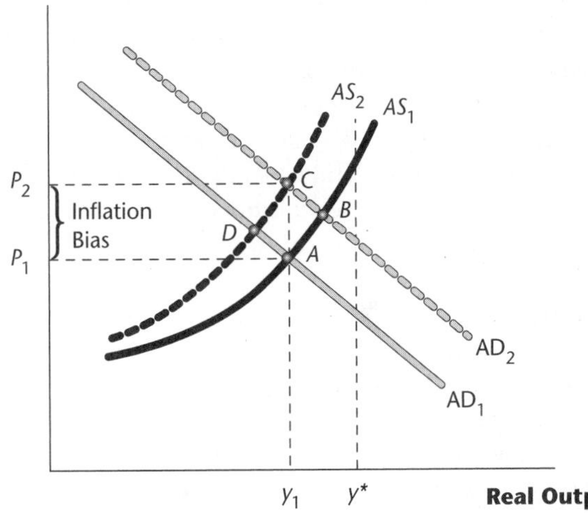

Figure 13-2

The Inflation Bias of Discretionary Monetary Policy

If the current equilibrium for the economy is point A, and if the policymaker's goals are to raise output toward the capacity output level y but to keep inflation low, then typically a policymaker's temptation is to split the difference between these conflicting objectives by inducing a rise in aggregate demand, to point B. But if workers realize that the policymaker has an incentive to permit prices to rise, they will bargain for higher contract wages, thereby raising labor costs for businesses and shifting the aggregate supply schedule leftward. This means that if the policymaker ignores the temptation to induce a rise in aggregate demand, the results are higher prices and lower real output at point D. The policymaker will feel pressure to avoid this outcome by raising aggregate demand as workers expect. The final equilibrium in the absence of policymaker credibility not to increase inflation, therefore, is at point C, with unchanged real output but a higher price level. A noninflationary equilibrium in which the policymaker maintains a commitment to zero inflation at point A could result only if the policymaker's commitment were credible.*

ESTABLISHING POLICY CREDIBILITY

Policy credibility
Believability of a commitment by a central bank or governmental authority to follow specific policy rules.

The reasoning that leads to the conclusion that policy discretion creates an inflation bias indicates that the key determinant of how much inflation actually occurs is **policy credibility,** which is believability of a policymaker's willingness and ability to commit to a low-inflation policy rule. If a policymaker were willing and able to follow through on such a commitment, then workers and firms could believe that it might stick to its rule. The economy would remain at its long-run output level without experiencing inflation. But if a nation's workers and firms doubt a policymaker's willingness to honor a commitment, or if they feel that the policymaker is willing but unable to do so, then this lack of policy credibility would lead to an inflation bias.

Time Inconsistency and the Inflation Bias

Time inconsistency problem
Policy problem that can result if a policymaker has the ability, at a future time, to alter its strategy in a way that is inconsistent both with the desires and strategies of private individuals and with its own initially announced intentions.

Policy credibility is difficult to achieve in the setting that we have described. This is because of the **time inconsistency problem:** Although commitment to a policy rule yields zero inflation, such a commitment is inconsistent with the strategies of a nation's residents if the policymaker can alter its strategy at a later time. In our example, the policymaker could renege on a commitment to zero inflation and expand aggregate demand, which would benefit the policymaker but not the nation's workers. This induces workers to protect themselves by bargaining for higher wages, thereby forcing even a policymaker that might otherwise prefer to stick to a rule to expand aggregate demand to avoid a decline in national output.

An inflation bias, therefore, results from the time inconsistency problem and a lack of policy credibility. The inflation bias of discretionary policy is a third reason—along with the potential for discretionary policy to be destabilizing in the presence of time lags and for policymakers to pursue their own narrow self interests—that many economists argue that society should find ways to dissuade policymakers from engaging in discretionary actions and to encourage them to find ways to make policy rules credible.

Possible Solutions to the Credibility Problem

In light of the twin dangers that monetary policy may be both destabilizing and prone to produce an inflationary bias, what could be done to induce a central bank to adopt a fixed rule for its policymaking? In addition, what could be done to make such a commitment to a rule credible? It turns out that several potential solutions exist: as described here.

1) *Constitutional Limitations on Monetary Policy.* One possibility would be to change a nation's constitution. A number of economists, such as Milton Friedman of the Hoover Institution at Stanford University, have advocated amending national constitutions to place clear limits on the discretion of monetary policymakers. Some critics of governmental involvement in banking and monetary systems would go even farther. They would make it illegal for governments to have anything to do with money creation, leaving such matters to private markets. Essentially, these critics of the *status quo* believe that gov-

ernments will always conduct discretionary policies unless their monetary powers are sharply contained, if not eliminated.

2) *Credibility through Reputation.* So far constitutional limitations on monetary policy have not advanced beyond the stage of proposals. In the absence of such radical institutional changes, how could a central bank itself make its commitments to low inflation more credible?

    One possibility is for a central bank to establish and maintain a reputation as a "tough inflation fighter." To understand how a central bank could do this, recall that if a central bank sticks to a promise not to raise aggregate demand in pursuit of short-term output gains but is not believed by workers who seek higher wages that raise business costs, then the result will be higher inflation and reduced output. If the central bank cares only about the present, it would never want this to happen. But if the central bank wants to establish a future reputation as an inflation fighter, then it might be willing to let the economy experience both lower output and inflation. Henceforth, its promises not to increase aggregate demand might then be credible.

3) *The "Conservative" Central Banker.* Obtaining a reputation for being a "tough inflation fighter" is difficult unless there really is some toughness on the inside as well as on the outside. The discretionary theory of inflation outlined above indicates that one key factor influencing the central bank's inflationary bias is how much it dislikes inflation relative to how much it wishes to try to expand real GDP. There is nothing that a central bank actually can do to increase real GDP in the long run, and so society would be better off with a central banker who would be less willing to try to increase aggregate demand. Consequently, appointing such a **conservative central banker,** or an individual who dislikes inflation more than the average member of society, might be one way to reduce the extent of the Fed's inflation bias. (A central banker who especially dislikes inflation has less relative concern about unemployment, but unemployment insurance might also make an "average" central banker less worried about unemployment relative to inflation; see on the next page *Policy Notebook: Can Unemployment Insurance Substitute for a Conservative Central Banker?*)

Conservative central banker
A central bank official who dislikes inflation more than an average citizen in society and who thereby is less willing to induce discretionary increases in the quantity of money in an effort to achieve short-run increases in real output.

4) *An Independent Central Bank.* The idea behind establishing central banker contracts is that contracts would make central bank officials more *accountable* for their performances. Using central banker contracts would not, however, rule out granting central bank officials considerable *independence* to central bankers to conduct monetary policy as they see fit, while continuing to hold them responsible if inflation gets out of hand.

    Indeed, many economists argue that central bank independence might be the key to maintaining low inflation rates. After all, a conservative central banker cannot establish a reputation as a tough inflation fighter if he or she is hamstrung by legal requirements to try to achieve other objectives as well, such as a low unemployment rate or a high growth rate for real output. Furthermore, even if a central banker contract holds an official accountable for a nation's inflation performance, achieving the required performance may be

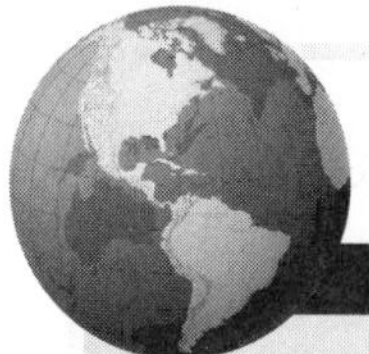

POLICY *Notebook*

POLICY MANAGEMENT

Can Unemployment Insurance Substitute for a Conservative Central Banker?

By definition, as compared with an average member of society, a conservative central banker is more concerned with keeping inflation low than with maintaining low unemployment. This relatively smaller worry about the unemployment effects of monetary policy actions is what causes a conservative central banker to aim for smaller increases in aggregate demand over time. The result is a lower inflation bias.

According to Rafael Di Tella of Harvard University and Robert MacCulloch of the London School of Economics, a nation's government may be able to bring about essentially the same outcome without necessarily finding conservative central bankers. A way to do this, the authors argue, is to establish relatively generous unemployment insurance programs. If a central banker knows that workers who may become unemployed as a result of tough monetary policy actions will be protected by such programs, then the central banker will have less concern about the unemployment effects of policy actions, relative to the effects on inflation. Thus, the central banker will be able to concentrate more on the inflationary effects of its policy choices, thereby behaving as though he or she is a conservative central banker.

Figure 13-3 plots inflation rates of various nations on the vertical axis and index measures of levels of those nations' unemployment insurance benefits on the horizontal axis. Note countries with relatively meager unemployment compensation levels, such as Greece and Portugal, have higher inflation rates than nations with relatively more generous unemployment insurance programs, such as Belgium and France. Consistent with the authors' hypothesis, the figure indicates a generally inverse relationship between unemployment insurance benefits and the inflation rate. The authors have verified this relationship with more sophisticated statistical analysis that also takes into account factors such as the duration of unemployment benefits.

For Critical Analysis:
What are the pros and cons of seeking to reduce inflation by establishing a generous program of unemployment insurance instead of trying to identify and appoint conservative central bankers?

difficult unless the official has sufficient independence to pursue this objective in the most efficient manner.

Central bank independence has two dimensions. One of these is *political independence,* or the lack of influence of the government and other outside individuals or groups on the process by which a central bank reaches decisions. Another dimension of a central bank's independence is *economic independence,* or the ability to control its own budget or to resist efforts by the government to induce the central bank to make loans to the government or to pro-

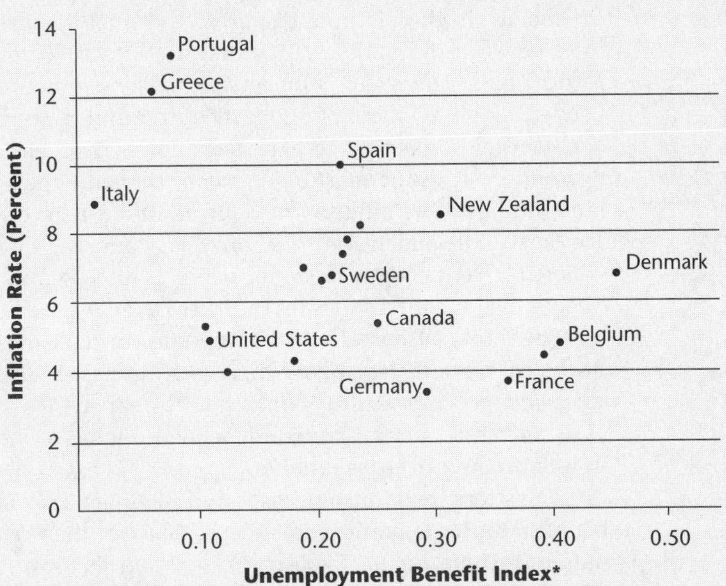

Figure 13-3

Inflation Rates and Unemployment Benefit Levels in Selected Nations

Countries with lower overall levels of unemployment benefits tend to have higher inflation than countries with higher unemployment insurance compensation. This is consistent with the hypothesis that in nations with relatively generous unemployment insurance programs, central bankers feel more comfortable concentrating on containing inflation, because they know that unemployed workers will not fare as badly because of contractionary policies.

Source: Rafael Di Tella and Robert MacCulloch, "Unemployment Benefits as a Substitute for a Conservative Central Banker," Harvard Business School and London School of Economics, May 2000.

vide other forms of direct support to government policies. Hence, we can reach the following conclusion:

A truly independent central bank would be both politically and economically independent. Political independence would permit the central bank to conduct the policies that it believes to be best in the long run, without the influence of short-term political pressures. Economic independence would give the central bank the budgetary freedom to conduct these policies.

Strong evidence that central bank independence is related to good inflation performance has been provided by the Harvard University economists Alberto Alesina and Lawrence Summers. This evidence is summarized in Figure 13-4. In each panel, an index of central bank independence is measured along the horizontal axis of the diagram. An increase in this index indicates that a nation's central bank is more politically and/or economically independent. In the diagram displayed in panel (a), average annual inflation rates between the middle 1950s and the late 1980s are measured along the vertical axis. The result is an *inverse relationship* between central bank independence and average inflation, meaning that countries with more independent central banks tend to experience lower average inflation. Note that the two nations with the most independent central banks, Germany and Switzerland, had average inflation rates of around 3 percent. The two nations with the least independent central banks, in contrast, which were New Zealand (before a recent change in status, which is discussed shortly) and Spain, experienced average inflation rates that were over twice as great.

Panel (b) of Figure 13-4 measures the variance of inflation along the vertical axis. Nevertheless, again there is an inverse relationship: Countries with more independent central banks tend to experience less inflation volatility. Thus, increased central bank independence tends to yield more price stability as well as lower average inflation.

The strong relationships displayed in Figure 13-4 have convinced a number of countries to grant more independence to their central banks. Recent examples include Japan, Mexico, France, and Pakistan. The evidence also led Western European nations to grant the European Central Bank considerable independence from national governments.

Central banker contract
A legally binding agreement between a government and a central banking official that holds the official responsible for a nation's inflation performance.

5) *Contracts for Central Bankers?* During the past few years, another idea for addressing the inflation bias has emerged. This is to enforce explicit **central banker contracts,** which would be legally binding agreements between governments and central banking officials. One example is the contract adopted in New Zealand's 1989 Reserve Bank Act, which holds central bank officials directly responsible for any failure to achieve price stability. If New Zealand's top central banking official fails to meet clearly specified inflation targets, then under the terms of the contract this individual is subject to immediate dismissal.

In principle, a contract also could contain a carrot as well as a stick, however. For example, one way to induce a central banking official to keep inflation low would be to reward the individual with a higher salary in exchange for better inflation performance. It might seem that this would entail paying such a person a bonus for doing the job that he or she is supposed to be doing. Nevertheless, proponents of such payment schemes point out that salary bonuses would compensate central bankers for fighting political pressures favoring inflationary monetary policies.

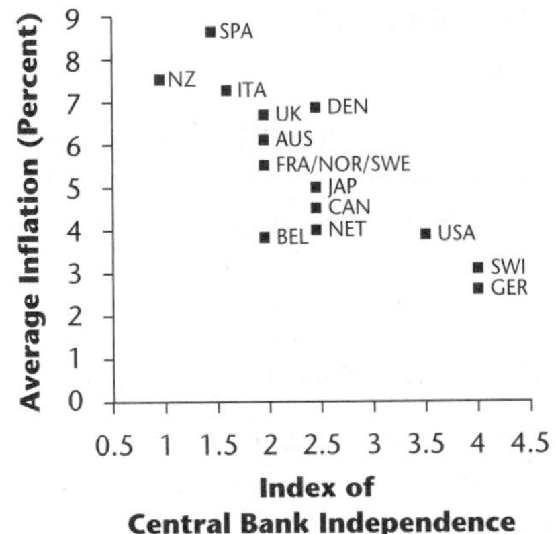

(a)

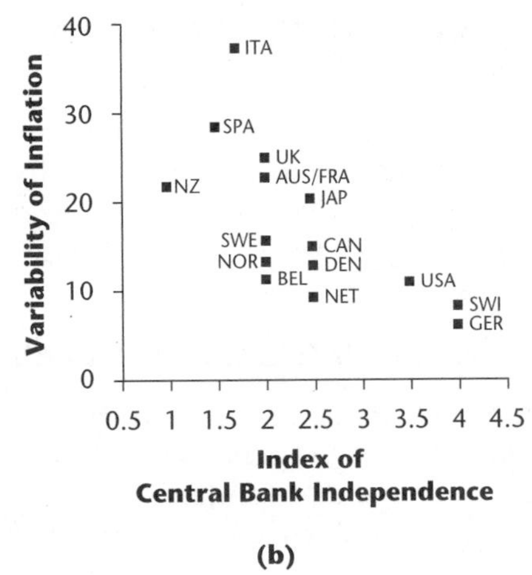

(b)

Figure 13-4

Central Bank Independence, Average Inflation, and Inflation Variability

As shown in panel (a), nations with more independent central banks, such as Germany, Switzerland, and the United States, have lower average inflation rates as compared with countries with less independent central banks. Panel (b) shows that nations with more independent central banks also have less variable rates of inflation.

Source: Alberto Alesina and Lawrence Summers, "Central Bank Independence and Macroeconomic Performance," *Journal of Money, Credit, and Banking* (May 1993), pp. 151–162.

Key:

AUS:	Austria	FRA:	France	NET:	Netherlands	SWE:	Sweden
BEL:	Belgium	GER:	Germany	NOR:	Norway	SWI:	Switzerland
CAN:	Canada	ITA:	Italy	NZ:	New Zealand	UK:	United Kingdom
DEN:	Denmark	JAP:	Japan	SPA:	Spain	US:	United States

ON THE WEB

What are the current policy responsibilities of the Governor of the Reserve Bank of New Zealand under the terms of the Reserve Bank Act? You can review the most recent agreement between the New Zealand Treasurer and its Reserve Bank governor by going to the Reserve Bank of New Zealand's home page at http://www.rbnz.govt.nz and clicking on "Policy Targets Agreement."

Fundamental Issue 3

Why is policy credibility a crucial factor in maintaining low inflation, and how might nations attain policy credibility?

The time inconsistency problem encountered in discretionary policymaking yields an inflation bias, which a nation can reduce or avoid only if it can find a way to make a credible commitment to low inflation. Central bankers can gain credibility by permitting output to fall in the near term as a way to convince workers of their commitment to low future inflation. Governments might also appoint conservative central banking officials who are known to have a distaste for inflation and grant sufficient independence to permit them to contain the inflation bias. Alternatively, governments might establish contracts requiring central bank officials to attain a national inflation goal.

Policymaking in an Interdependent World

Globalization causes more countries to share common interests. International transactions in goods, services, and financial assets connect an increasing number of countries, giving their residents a greater incentive to consider jointly determining national economic policy actions.

STRUCTURAL INTERDEPENDENCE AND INTERNATIONAL POLICY EXTERNALITIES

In today's world, in which countries citizens trade significant amounts of goods and services and exchange sizable volumes of financial instruments across national boundaries, national economies are structurally interdependent. This means nations' economic systems—their markets for goods and services, financial markets, and payment systems—are interlinked.

Consequences of Structural Interdependence

Structural interdependence *A situation in which interconnectedness of national markets for goods, services, and financial assets causes events in one nation to affect the economies of other nations.*

An important consequence of **structural interdependence** is that events that benefit or harm the interests of one country may also have a bearing on the interests of citizens of another nation. This means that collective actions that a nation's citizens undertake in their own interest may spill over to influence the welfare of other countries' residents. As discussed in Chapter 12, economists refer to such spillover effects as *externalities,* or costs experienced by one individual or group as a result of actions by another individual or group in a separate location or market.

You learned in Chapter 12 that an *international externality* may arise if the actions of residents in one nation affect the economic performance of another nation. In some situations, there are negative international externalities, in which events in one country have adverse consequences in another. It is also possible, however, that the collective actions of one nation's residents may improve the economic performance in another country, so that there is a positive international externality.

International Policy Externalities

A nation's political system typically charges individual leaders, groups of representatives or delegates, or government agencies with conducting economic policies on behalf of the nation's citizens. As we have discussed in the preceding chapters, such policies can alter the choices of private residents and businesses, thereby influencing a country's overall economic performance.

International policy externalities *Spillover benefits or costs that policy actions within one nation have for the economies of other nations.*

Locomotive effect *A stimulus to economic activity in one nation generated by an increase in economic activity in another country.*

If national economies are structurally interdependent, then **international policy externalities,** or benefits or costs of policy effects that spill over onto other nations, may result. For instance, various trade policies discussed in Chapter 4 cause negative international policy externalities, or *beggar-thy-neighbor effects.* Such policies may accomplish domestic objectives but bring about worsened economic performance within other nations. Positive international policy externalities can also occur, however. Economists often call these **locomotive effects** that arise when a policy-induced effect on the domestic economy generates an improvement in economic performance in another country.

National policymakers recognize that their policy actions may affect other countries. They also realize that decisions by foreign policymakers may influence economic performance at home. This gives policymakers an incentive to engage in **strategic policymaking**, meaning that they develop a plan for achieving objectives for their own nation, taking into account the extent to which their nation is structurally linked to others and courses of action that other nations' policymakers may pursue. Recognition that positive and negative externalities may result from policies that policymakers undertake also may induce them to band together to minimize the negative consequences of their individual policy choices and to enhance the positive spillovers that might result.

Strategic policymaking *The formulation of national policies in light of the structural linkages among nations and the ways in which policymakers in other nations make decisions.*

ACCOUNTING FOR INTERDEPENDENCE: INTERNATIONAL POLICY COOPERATION AND COORDINATION

There are two ways that nations might try to work together to achieve their economic performance objectives.

ON THE WEB

Learn more about the activities of the finance ministers of the G7 and G8 at http://www.g7.utoronto.ca/g7/finance.

International Policy Cooperation

The first of these is through **international policy cooperation.** This refers to the formal establishment of institutions and processes through which national policymakers can collaborate on their national goals, provide information about specific approaches they intend to follow in implementing policies, and share information and data about their countries' economic performances.

International policy cooperation *The development of institutions and procedures through which central banks share data and inform one another about their policy objectives and strategies.*

An example of an institutional arrangement that facilitates international policy cooperation is the *Group of Seven (G7).* This is a collection of seven nations—Canada, France, Germany, Italy, Japan, the United Kingdom, and the United States—whose chief economic policy officials meet on a regular basis. At these meetings, G7 officials discuss their broad policy objectives and plans, as well as more specific economic issues of concern to the member nations. Later, the G7 has included Russia in its discussions. Then it became known as the G8.

Another example is the *Bank for International Settlements (BIS),* which is based in Basel, Switzerland. This institution functions as a trustee for various international loan agreements and serves as an agent in miscellaneous foreign exchange markets for many of the world's central banks. Private U.S. banks, including Citibank and J. P. Morgan, participated with governments of the Group of Ten (G10) nations—the G7 plus Belgium, the Netherlands, and Sweden—in developing the BIS beginning in 1930. Indeed, many private banks continue to own shares of ownership in the BIS. Its original task was to supervise the settlement of financial claims among European nations that related to terms of the World War I Armistice. After World War II, the BIS became a central agent for clearing payments among nations participating in the European Recovery Program designed to rebuild the economies of countries recovering from the ravages of that war. Ultimately, the BIS developed into a clearinghouse for information of central banks of the G10 plus the Bank of Switzerland, the Swiss central bank. Economic staff members of the BIS organize periodic briefings for top G10 central banking officials and coordinate conferences for staff economists of policy making agencies of the G10 nations.

International Policy Coordination

International policy coordination *The joint determination of monetary policies by a group of central banks for the intended combined benefit of the nations they represent.*

The Bank for International Settlements facilitated one instance of **international policy coordination,** which refers to the joint determination of national economic policies for the mutual benefit of a group of countries. In 1988, central banks and other banking regulators of the G10 nations adopted the *Basel Agreement,* which established common risk-based bank capital adequacy standards—minimum levels of owner backing of banks' assets, adjusted for the riskiness of those assets—for private banking institutions incorporated within those countries.

By coordinating their banking policies, the G10 nations sought to address the international policy externalities that naturally can arise from the widespread competitive interactions of their countries' banks. For instance, if only one of the G10 countries had adopted tough capital standards for its banking system, its banks would have been placed at a competitive disadvantage in international financial markets, because its banks would have needed to back their assets with larger volumes of private capital. Likewise, if one nation had failed to adopt the Basel standards, its nations' banks could have grabbed larger shares of lending around the world. Coordination of the imposition of capital requirements ensured that neither of these policy externalities arose.

Proponents of international policy coordination argue that nations can gain considerably from broad-based policy coordination. Rather than just coordinating their policies from time to time, as in the 1988 Basel Agreement on bank capital standards, these observers contend that nations should make policy coordination a day-to-day process. Indeed, many argue that countries could reap considerable gains from coordinating *all* their economic policies, including those aimed at broad output and inflation objectives.

4 **Fundamental Issue**

What is structural interdependence, and how can it lead nations to cooperate or to coordinate their policies?

When national economies are linked together, then they are structurally interdependent. As a result, policy actions in one country can have spillover effects, or international policy externalities, that influence economic performance in other nations. International policy externalities are said to be positive if they improve other countries' economic performances. They are negative if they worsen those nations' prospects. To enhance the potential for positive policy externalities, or to reduce the likelihood of negative externalities, nations may choose to cooperate by sharing information about economic data and policy objectives. They also may choose to coordinate their policymaking by determining policy actions that are in their joint interest.

The Pros and Cons of International Policy Coordination

In principle, nations potentially can benefit from working together in pursuit of their national economic goals. Hence, there are several general arguments in favor of international policy coordination. In addition, there are some strong reasons to question whether policy coordination is always beneficial.

POTENTIAL BENEFITS OF INTERNATIONAL POLICY COORDINATION

Proponents of international policy coordination typically offer three fundamental rationales:

1) *Internalizing International Policy Externalities.* The act of coordinating policies for the mutual benefit of a group of countries effectively requires the nations' policymakers to behave as if their countries were a single entity. Thus, international policy coordination *internalizes* the externalities that individually formulated nation policies otherwise would tend to produce. Imagine, for instance, what would happen if each of the fifty states of the United States were to make all policy decisions without regard to their effects on the other states. By coordinating the entire nation's policies through a federal government, the citizens of the fifty states minimize the potential for negative policy spillovers that would result from noncoordinated policy making.

   Likewise, the Basel Agreement on bank capital regulation reflected a recognition of potential negative competitive consequences for national banking systems of separate national restrictions on bank management. The agreement may have permitted G10 nations to avoid adverse outcomes arising from negative policy externalities.

2) *Getting the Most Out of a Limited Number of Policy Instruments.* It also is possible that international coordination can permit national policymakers to achieve a larger number of goals with the limited policy instruments they possess. As a simple example, suppose that two nations' central banks each have the same two goals: to achieve an increase in equilibrium domestic output and to minimize exchange rate variability. Each, therefore, has an incentive to increase its money stocks, because doing so pushes up aggregate demand in each nation while preventing one nation's money stock from changing relative to the other's and thereby preventing an exchange rate change.

   This is an intentionally simplified example, but it illustrates the basic point. If national policymakers have few policy instruments but related goals, then by working together to determine the appropriate settings of their policy instruments, the policymakers potentially could come closer to achieving their multiple objectives. Coordination thereby might be mutually beneficial.

3) *Gaining Support from Abroad.* The third rationale for international policy coordination is that policymakers in various countries might gain additional strength to withstand domestic political pressures by banding together with other policymakers. When faced with internal pressures to enact policies that might provide short-term gains at the expense of long-term social costs, policymakers could use their commitment to international coordination agreements as a justification for holding the line against such actions.

   For example, suppose that a Chilean government facing a difficult election were to call upon the Bank of Chile to engage in inflationary policies intended to spur the Chilean economy during the months before the election. If the Bank of Chile could argue that such a policy would violate an accord to coordinate its policies with other central banks, thereby damaging Chile's credibility with those central banks and more broadly in world financial markets, then the Bank of Chile might be able to withstand the government's pressures.

POTENTIAL DRAWBACKS OF INTERNATIONAL POLICY COORDINATION

International policy coordination is not a free lunch. There are at least four possible drawbacks:

Sovereignty *The supremacy of a nation's citizens to control the resources within its geographic borders.*

1) *Policy Coordination May Entail National Sacrifice.* Ultimately, what defines any nation is its **sovereignty,** or the supremacy of its citizens' own control of the resources within their country's geographic borders. If international policy coordination is to achieve benefits for a nation, its citizens and leaders must be amenable to giving up some degree of sovereignty. They must be willing to pursue *international* objectives along with purely domestic goals.

   For instance, suppose that on January 1, 2007, a group of nations were to agree that their relative currency values must be fixed beginning March 1 of that year. At the end of February, however, one of the nations determines that it could gain by devaluing its currency relative to the currencies of the other countries in the group. Nevertheless, to abide by the policy coordination agreement, the nation's leaders would have to sacrifice the nation's discretion to pursue its own self-interest by devaluing its currency.
2) *Other Countries May Not Be Trustworthy.* This last example illustrates a fundamental problem with international policy coordination, which is that there typically are incentives for countries that enter into coordination agreements to cheat. To see why this is so, consider Figure 13-5. Each cell in the figure gives hypothetical values, in "welfare units," of the citizens of two countries, denoted *A* and *B*, when their countries do or do not coordinate their policies. In the upper-left-hand cell of Figure 13-5, we see that if country *A* and country *B*

	Country B Does Not Coordinate	Country B Coordinates
Country A Does Not Coordinate	Country A Welfare = 75 Country B Welfare = 75 Total Welfare = 150	Country A Welfare = 150 Country B Welfare = 25 Total Welfare = 175
Country A Coordinates	Country A Welfare = 25 Country B Welfare = 150 Total Welfare = 175	Country A Welfare = 100 Country B Welfare = 100 Total Welfare = 200

Figure 13-5

Hypothetical Welfare Levels for Two Nations with and without Policy Coordination

If policymakers in two nations fail to coordinate their policies, then their combined welfare is 150 units. If both work together to coordinate policy actions, however, their total welfare is 200 units. The difficulty is that if either nation "cheats" and fails to coordinate as promised, it can raise its own welfare to 150 units, which yields only 25 units of welfare for the other nation that honors the coordination agreement.

conduct independent, noncoordinated policies, each derives a welfare level of 75 units. In contrast, if both nations coordinate their policy making, then the lower-right-hand cell indicates that they both attain welfare levels of 100 units. Thus, policy coordination is beneficial for both countries.

Nevertheless, the potential for each country to gain from cheating could still result in a failure to coordinate policies. Country *A*'s policymakers know that country *A*'s welfare can be raised to 150 units if country *A* fails to follow through on a coordination agreement with country *B* while country *B*'s policymakers continue to honor the agreement. Consequently, there is an incentive for the policymakers in country *A* to renege on the deal to achieve higher national welfare. As a result, as indicated in the upper-right-hand cell of Figure 13-5, country *B*'s welfare declines to 25 units. Hence, country *A* gains, but only at country *B*'s expense. At the same time, country *B*'s policymakers face the same temptation to cheat and pursue a beggar-thy-neighbor policy, as the lower-left-hand cell of the figure shows.

Clearly, in this example the combined welfare of both nations' citizens is highest, at 200 units, if policymakers in the two nations follow through and coordinate their policies. Yet each nation has an incentive to renege in favor of a beggar-thy-neighbor policy that yields a lower welfare level of 175 units. If *both* countries cheat simultaneously, however, then total welfare is at its lowest, at 150 units. Nevertheless, each individual country might feel that it is better off than it would be if it were to stick with the agreement, only to be cheated by the other nation's policymakers.

This example illustrates a key problem of international policy coordination. Agreements to coordinate national policies can work only if all participants trust each other. Hence, each nation's commitment to an international policy coordination arrangement must be *credible* to other participating nations. In the absence of such credibility, each nation would recognize that it is worse off by agreeing to coordinate and exposing its citizens to the adverse effects caused by other nations' cheating.

3) *Other Policymakers Could Be Incompetent.* The potential for deception and cheating is not the only factor that can cause individual nations to lose from agreeing to coordinate their policies with those of other countries. Another problem that a nation encounters when it sacrifices some sovereignty in hopes of reaping gains from coordination is the possibility that other nations' policymakers may lack competence to pursue the best common policy. That is, to be willing to cede some of its policy making sovereignty to another country, a nation must be confident in two things. The nation must have confidence that policymakers in the other country will honor the coordination agreement. The nation also must believe that the other nation's policymakers have the ability to do their jobs effectively.

There is also the possibility that policymakers of coordinating nations may have conflicting outlooks on the appropriate policies for all nations to pursue jointly, even if the policymakers otherwise trust themselves to honor their agreements and to competently implement policy actions. Such conflicts may arise because of different policymaker preferences concerning, say, how much relative weight to place on real output versus inflation objectives. Alternatively, policymakers might not agree about the best way to implement a coordination agreement. For example, if Germany and the United Kingdom were to agree to coordinate their policies, but the Bundesbank's economic staff believed strongly in targeting money growth rates while the Bank of England economic staff believed just as strongly in targeting nominal interest rates, then such a technical argument concerning policy implementation might still cause a coordination agreement to break down.

4) *"Successful" Coordination Can Sometimes Be Counterproductive.* Even if nations agree to coordinate, stick to their agreement, and determine their policies taking joint welfare into account, there is still the possibility that in the end their residents could be worse off.

Suppose, for instance, that two nations experience positive international monetary policy externalities. If either nation's central bank increases the quantity of its currency in circulation, there are two effects. One is an increase in home aggregate demand. Another is a locomotive effect as the resulting increase in residents' incomes induces them to purchase goods and services from the other nation's residents, which pushes up their incomes and desired consumption levels, thereby generating an increase in aggregate demand within that nation.

In addition, suppose that the central banks of the two countries both face the problem of time inconsistency and low policy credibility. The residents of their countries know that both policymakers thereby have an incentive to try to raise national output levels by expanding their money stocks and pushing up aggregate demand. In the absence of policy coordination, there will be an increase in aggregate demand in each country following a monetary expansion and a simultaneous reduction in aggregate production as workers negotiate higher wages in anticipation of higher inflation. The result is an inflation bias in each country.

Now think about what happens if the nations' central banks succeed in coordinating their monetary policies. Each central bank will then take into account not only the incentive it faces to push up output at home, but also the other central bank's incentive to try to boost output in the other nation. As a consequence, each central bank will tend to raise its money stock even more than it would have in the absence of policy coordination. Residents of both nations will realize this and expect even more inflation, so they will bargain for larger wage boosts when their central banks coordinate their policies. Thus, the inflation bias in each country will be greater with coordinated monetary policies than it would have been if the central banks had chosen not to coordinate. In both nations, residents will have to bear higher inflation costs.

Fundamental Issue 5

What are the benefits and costs of international policy coordination?

The most significant gain that might arise from policy coordination is the internalization of international policy externalities, meaning that working together toward joint goals could permit national policymakers to minimize the ill effects of negative externalities or improve the prospect for benefits of positive externalities. It also is possible that policy coordination might increase the number of policy instruments that could be aimed at policymakers' objectives. In addition, the establishment of formal policy coordination agreements or institutions could assist a policymaker's efforts to resist domestic political pressures to enact short-sighted policies with potentially harmful long-term effects. One difficulty with entering into policy coordination agreements is that nations must give up at least some measure of national sovereignty to implement such agreements. In addition, they must trust each other, both to pursue promised policy actions and to do so in a competent manner. Yet there typically will be an incentive for one nation to cheat on a policy coordination agreement in the pursuit of gains at another country's expense, and there is always the possibility that one nation's policymakers will fail to pursue policies that another nation believes to be appropriate. Finally, international policy coordination can, if policymakers' credibility levels are low within their own countries, lead to higher average inflation rates.

Optimal Currency Areas and Monetary Unions

As we have discussed, if a nation chooses to enter into an international policy coordination arrangement, it must give up at least some degree of national sovereignty. Would there be any gain from taking another step and giving up its own currency in favor of a currency common to it and others in a coalition of policy-coordinating nations? That is, should a nation join a formal **monetary union,** a grouping of nation-states that agree to use a single currency? To contemplate this issue, we must consider the theory of *optimal currency areas.*

Monetary union
A set of countries that choose to use a common currency.

OPTIMAL CURRENCY AREAS

In 1991, nations of the European Union negotiated a treaty in the Netherlands' city of Maastricht. The treaty authorized establishment of a European Central Bank to issue the euro as a circulating currency beginning in 2002. Initially, eleven nations—Austria, Belgium, Finland, France, Germany, Ireland, Italy, Luxembourg, the Netherlands, Portugal, and Spain—participated in the *European Monetary Union (EMU)* that adopted this new currency. Greece joined shortly thereafter.

Throughout the process, many skeptical economists continued to question whether the EMU could last. They based their arguments on an economic theory developed more than thirty years ago by Robert Mundell of Columbia University. This is the **theory of optimal currency areas,** which is an analytical approach to determining the extent of a geographic area whose residents would be better off by fixing their exchange rates or even by using a common currency.

Theory of optimal currency areas
An approach to determining the size of a geographic area within which residents' welfare is greater if their governments fix exchange rates or adopt a common currency.

The Theory of Optimal Currency Areas

Financial newspapers such as the *Wall Street Journal* or the *Financial Times* publish daily listings of exchange rates for more than fifty national currencies. These are not complete exchange rate listings because these newspapers list only the currencies with large trading volumes in the foreign exchange markets.

Why are there so many different national currencies? Why do residents of all fifty states of the United States use the same currency, even though states such as California and New York have higher volumes of GDP than most nations of the world? Will all nations within the European Union truly benefit from following the example of the fifty U.S. states? Should all of Europe be part of the EMU? The theory of optimal currency areas seeks to address these issues.

The Advantage of Separate Currencies and a Floating Exchange Rate

To understand the essential features of the theory of optimal currency areas, let's consider two hypothetical regions. People in one region, which we shall call region *X*, specialize in producing pastries. Residents of the other region, denoted region *Y*, manufacture exercise equipment. In both regions, wages and prices are inflexible in the short run. Initially, both regions experience balanced trade.

Suppose that residents of one region cannot seek employment in the other region, perhaps because of language or cultural barriers, or because governments of one or both of the regions have established restrictions preventing region *X* residents who are employed in pastry production from moving to region *Y* to make exercise equipment, and *vice versa*. Nevertheless, residents of the two regions face no restrictions on their ability to purchase both regions' goods.

Finally, let's suppose that each region has its own currency. The exchange rate for these currencies can either float in the foreign exchange market, or regional policymakers can fix the exchange rate.

Consider now what happens if residents of both regions become more health conscious. As a result, they cut back on their purchases of high-cholesterol pastries manufactured in region *X* and increase their demand for the exercise equipment produced in region *Y*. Region *Y* begins to run a trade surplus, and its output and employment increases. In contrast, region *X* begins to experience a trade deficit, and its output and employment decline.

If the rate of exchange between the regions' currencies is fixed, then the assumed short-run stickiness of wage and prices causes unemployment to persist for some time in region *X* following the changes in consumers' tastes. In the long run, of course, the price of the exercise equipment manufactured in region *Y* increases, and the price of the pastries made in region *X* decline, leading to an ultimate rebalancing of trade between the two regions. Until this long-run adjustment occurs, however, region *X* can experience a significant unemployment problem.

If the exchange rate is flexible, however, then the trade surplus in region *Y* and trade deficit in region *X* induces a speedy depreciation in the value of region *X*'s currency relative to the currency of region *Y*. This causes an immediate fall in the effective price of pastries from region *X* as perceived by residents of region *Y* and a rapid increase in the effective price of region *Y*'s exercise equipment faced by residents of region X. As a result, trade between the two regions is balanced much more rapidly with a floating exchange rate, and the unemployment problem in region X is much more short-lived.

This example illustrates a situation in which two regions gain from using separate currencies with relative values that adjust freely in the foreign exchange market. Fixing the rate of exchange between the currencies, or taking the further step of adopting a single currency, would prevent the exchange rate from serving as a means of short-run adjustment to changes in relative demands for the regions' goods. This exposes the regions to the potential for chronic payments imbalances and unemployment problems.

Certainly, with separate currencies and a market-determined exchange rate, residents of both nations face foreign exchange risks arising from exchange rate movements and costs of converting one currency to another when they wish to purchase another region's goods. Nonetheless, adopting individual currencies and a floating exchange rate protects the regions from unemployment dangers that arise from language, cultural, or legal barriers to worker migration.

When Could Nations Benefit from Using a Single Currency?

Now suppose that the conditions that have led to past constraints on worker migration break down. As a result, residents of region X can move freely to region Y to work, and *vice versa*. Let's further suppose that shortly following this development, there is another fall in the demand for the fattening pastries manufactured in region X and a rise in the demand for region Y's exercise equipment.

The immediate results, again, are a trade surplus, higher output, and higher employment in region Y and a trade deficit, lower output, and lower employment in region X. Consequently, some residents of region X find themselves without work. Now, however, these unemployed residents of region X can migrate—or perhaps even commute—to newly available jobs in region Y. Thus, region X unemployment is at worst a temporary phenomenon. Indeed, unemployment for both regions together is minimized in the face of such changes in the relative demands for their products.

In this example, there is no reason that the rates of exchange between the two regions cannot be fixed, thereby permitting residents of both regions to avoid foreign exchange risks. Indeed, economists would conclude that the two regions together constitute an **optimal currency area**, or a geographical area within which fixed exchange rates may be maintained without slowing regional adjustments to changing regional circumstances. Furthermore, within such an optimal currency area, separate regions find it beneficial to adopt a *common currency* if the cost of converting currencies for regional trade exceeds any perceived gain from having separate currencies. If, for example, the residents of regions A and B continue to perceive sizable benefits from using separate currencies even though no barriers otherwise separate their regions, then they might wish to continue to incur currency conversion costs that arise when they trade goods. But if currency conversion costs are sufficiently large relative to the potential benefits of maintaining separate regional currencies, then the residents of the two regions that

Optimal currency area
A geographic area within which labor is sufficiently mobile to permit speedy adjustments to payment imbalances and regional unemployment to permit exchange rates to be fixed and a common currency to be adopted.

constitute an optimal currency area might gain, on net, from adopting a single, common currency.

IS EUROPE AN OPTIMAL CURRENCY AREA?

The Maastricht Treaty for European Monetary Union requires a country wishing to join the EMU to have a national budget deficit no larger than 3 percent of GDP, total government debt no greater than 60 percent of GDP, an inflation rate no higher than one and one half percentage points higher than the average of the three best-performing EMU member nations, and long-term interest rates no higher than two points above the same benchmark. Some European nations, such as Sweden, have embraced pursuing these goals and joining the EMU. Others, such as Denmark and the United Kingdom, have been more hesitant. (See *Policy Notebook: The United Kingdom Studies Hard for What Turns Out to Be a Practice Exam.*)

Undoubtedly, residents of Denmark and the United Kingdom are concerned about losing their currencies, the krona and the pound, which have long been symbols of national sovereignty. Another reason that some Danish and British doubters offer for their hesitancy to join the EMU is uncertainty about whether all the EU nations truly constitute an optimal currency area. Research by Barry Eichengreen of the University of California at Berkeley has compared measures of labor mobility in Western Europe with those of other countries with single currencies. His evidence indicates that, as compared with other nations made up of separate states and regions, such as the United States and Canada, labor is much less mobile across the borders of the nations of Western Europe. This implies that the full European Union is not necessarily an optimal currency area.

Of course, the euro is a reality, irrespective of the concerns of skeptical economists. Furthermore, there are indications that the EMU will continue to expand in the coming years. Today the world is witnessing a fascinating real-world experiment, in which several nations may implement a common currency even though they fail to satisfy fundamental conditions for an optimal currency area.

6 Fundamental Issue

Could nations gain from adopting a common currency?

Countries qualify as an optimal currency area, or a geographic area in which movements of workers among regions alleviate unemployment and payments imbalances without the need for exchange rate adjustment, if labor is highly mobile across national boundaries. In such an environment, nations could save their residents from incurring foreign exchange risks and currency conversion costs by joining a monetary union with a common currency. Currently, it is unclear that European nations satisfy the conditions of an optimal currency area, but so far this has failed to hinder the formation and potential expansion of the European Monetary Union.

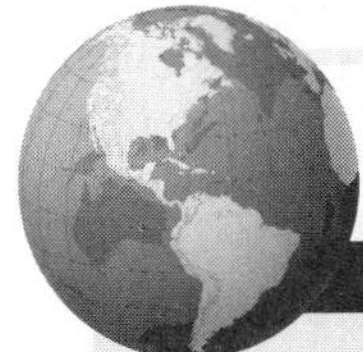

POLICY *Notebook*

POLICY MANAGEMENT

The United Kingdom Studies Hard for What Turns Out to Be a Practice Exam

In 1997, the government of the United Kingdom developed five "economic tests" that it said it would use to determine whether the nation was ready to join the European Monetary Union (EMU). Based on the country's experience following the 1999 formation of the EMU, the government would evaluate whether (1) the British inflation rate would fall to a level closer to the EMU average, (2) British capital investment would grow at a steady pace, (3) employment growth in the United Kingdom would remain stable, (4) London would maintain its status as a world financial center, and (5) the British economy would withstand economic shocks.

By the summer of 2000, Britain's inflation rate had fallen to an annualized rate of 0.5 percent, well below of the EMU average inflation rate of nearly 2 percent. Domestic capital investment in the United Kingdom had remained steady, and the British unemployment rate stood at 4.7 percent, well below the average EMU unemployment rate. London's financial markets were thriving. The only unknown, given the lack of significant economic turbulence, was whether the United Kingdom could weather unexpected economic shocks that it might face if it were part of the euro zone.

Nevertheless, opinion polls consistently indicated that a large majority of the British public remained opposed to joining the EMU. As the time for the next British parliamentary election approached, the government reinterpreted the five tests. It would not be sufficient for the five tests to be met, the government decided. In addition, there would have to be strong evidence of "sustainability" and "durability" of the nation's ability to satisfy the five conditions. The government was careful, however, not to specify just how long the nation would have to meet the five tests before it could consider officially becoming a part of the euro zone. The United Kingdom had passed the test for EMU membership, yet the nation remained outside the EMU.

For Critical Analysis:
What factors might explain the hesitancy of the United Kingdom to join the European Monetary Union?

CHAPTER SUMMARY

1) **The Ultimate Goals of Policymakers in Open Economies:** Government fiscal authorities and central banks typically pursue two sets of economic goals. One set is internal balance objectives, which are goals for national real income, employment, and inflation. The other is external balance objectives, which are goals for the trade balance, other components of the balance of payments, and exchange rates.

2) **The Main Problems of Discretionary Policymaking:** One key difficulty with discretionary policymaking concerns policy time lags, which are the intervals separating a need for a policy action and the action's eventual effects on the economy. The recognition lag is the time between the need for a policy action and the policymaker's realization of the need, and the response lag is the interval between recognition of the need for an action and actual implementation of a policy change. Finally, the transmission lag is the time from implementation of a policy action and the action's ultimate effects on the economy. Together, these three policy time lags can cause a discretionary policymaker that reacts to changing circumstances to undertake a policy action that is destabilizing. A second problem is that when workers and firms know that a policymaker has an incentive to try to push real output toward its capacity level via increases in aggregate demand, they are likely to doubt the sincerity of a policymaker's commitment to restrain inflation and negotiate higher wages. This reduces aggregate supply and causes real output to decline in the absence of higher aggregate demand. To avoid this outcome, the policymaker must raise aggregate demand. The result is an inflation bias.
3) **Why Policy Credibility Is a Crucial Factor in Maintaining Low Inflation, and How Nations Might Attain Policy Credibility:** One possible approach to trying to establish policy credibility would be to make it unlawful for central banks to permit inflation in excess of a certain rate. Central banks can also gain credibility by establishing reputations as inflation fighters and permitting real output to decline in the short run in the face of people's doubts about commitments to policy rules. To reduce the likelihood that central banks would pursue inflationary policies, governments could appoint conservative central banking officials who are known to dislike inflation. The ability of a central bank to exhibit such demonstrations of its commitment, however, would require that it be sufficiently independent from political influences. Governments might also sign central bank officials to contracts that base their continued employment or their salaries on a nation's inflation outcomes.
4) **Structural Interdependence, and How It Can Lead Nations to Cooperate or to Coordinate Their Policies:** National economies are structurally interdependent if one country's economy responds to events affecting the performance of another. In such situations, international policy externalities can exist, meaning that policy actions in one country can have spillover effects on the economies of other nations. Positive international policy externalities exert beneficial spillover effects on other nations' economic performances, whereas negative international policy externalities contribute to a worsening of those nations' economic performances. To enhance positive externalities or mitigate negative externalities, nations may cooperate by establishing institutional structures for sharing data or for collaborating on national goals. They also may decide to coordinate their policies by determining policy actions that are best for their common good.

5) **The Benefits and Costs of International Policy Coordination:** A key advantage of international policy coordination is that it can internalize international policy externalities, so that jointly pursuing national objectives might allow economic policymakers to limit the adverse consequences of negative externalities or to enhance the beneficial aspects of positive externalities. International policy coordination might increase the number of policy instruments that policymakers can direct toward attainment of their ultimate goals. Furthermore, participating in formal policy-coordination agreements could help domestic policymakers resist domestic pressures to engage in policies that might yield short-term internal political benefits but undesirable longer-term outcomes. A fundamental drawback associated with international policy coordination is the potential loss of national policymaking sovereignty. National policymakers must also trust that their counterparts will actually pursue promised policy objectives and that they will do so in a competent manner. Nevertheless, there usually is an incentive for policymakers to cheat on a coordination agreement, and policymakers may disagree about the most appropriate mix of policy actions to implement. In addition, if central banks have imperfect antiinflation credibility, then coordinating their monetary policies can increase the inflation bias arising from discretionary monetary policymaking.
6) **The Possibility that Nations Could Gain from Adopting a Common Currency:** Nations lie inside an optimal currency area if there is sufficient mobility of workers across national boundaries to alleviate unemployment and payments imbalances without the need for exchange rate adjustment. Countries in an optimal currency area could, in principle, eliminate foreign exchange risks and currency conversion costs faced by their residents if they were to form a monetary union with a common currency. Current evidence indicates that the formation of the European Monetary Union has continued apace even though Europe as a whole probably does not constitute an optimal currency area.

QUESTIONS AND PROBLEMS

1) Consider a situation in which all nations of the world pursue mercantilism as a single ultimate goal, and explain why no nations are likely to succeed in attaining its objective.
2) List and define the three types of policy time lags. Which do you think is likely to be *least* problematical for monetary policy? Which do you think is likely to be the *greatest* problem for monetary policy? For government policies regarding public spending and taxation? Explain your reasoning.
3) Why can the time inconsistency problem lead to an inflation bias in policymaking? How does appointing a conservative central banker potentially reduce the inflation bias?

4) Evaluate the following statement: "A real strength of performance contracts for central bankers is that they give central bankers policy discretion while subjecting them to a societal rule."
5) Explain the distinction between political and economic independence of central banks. Are both necessary for central banks truly to be independent to conduct antiinflationary monetary policies?
6) During the years preceding establishment of the European Central Bank, leaders of Germany and France argued about whether it should be overseen by a committee of political leaders. French leaders supported establishment of such a group to ensure that political leaders could steer the European Central Bank toward policies consistent with higher economic growth for Europe. German leaders successfully opposed the idea, which they argued would lead to higher European inflation. In light of what you have learned in this chapter, which country's leaders do you think were correct? Explain your reasoning.
7) Explain the difference between international policy cooperation and international policy coordination. Which do you believe is most common today?
8) Summarize the potential advantages of coordinating national economic policies. Of these, which do you think is most important? Explain.
9) Discuss the likely disadvantages of international policy coordination. Which do you believe to be the greatest disadvantage? Take a stand, and justify your position.
10) As noted in this chapter, there is not strong evidence that all the nations of Europe constitute an optimal currency area in the conventional sense. Yet many countries outside the EMU continue to express interest in joining it. Can you think of any other arguments that leaders of these nations might give to support their goal of becoming part of the EMU? Explain.

ONLINE APPLICATION

Internet URL: http://www.ecb.int

Title: **About the European Central Bank**

Navigation: Begin at the above home page, and click on "About the ECB"

Application: Perform the indicated operations, and answer the accompanying questions.

1) Click on "EN" next to "Constitution of the ESCB: History—Three Stages Towards EMU," and read the article. In what ways is policymaking within the European System of Central Banks different from policymaking under the old European Monetary System?
2) Back up to "About the ECB," and click on "EN" next to "Organization of the European System of Central Banks." Read the article. What aspects of the ESCB's structure promote policy credibility?

For Group Study and Analysis: Divide the class into groups. At the page titled "Organization of the European System of Central Banks," each group can click on "National Central Banks (NCBs)" to get to links to the central banks of the European Union. Have each group explore Web sites of the central banks that are currently in the ESCB. What are the roles of the individual national central banks within the ESCB? Within their domestic economic and financial systems?

REFERENCES AND RECOMMENDED READINGS

Bank for International Settlements. *Overview of the New Basel Capital Accord.* Basel Committee on Banking Supervision, January 2001.

Bayoumi, Tamin, and Barry Eichengreen. *One Money or Many? Analyzing the Prospects for Monetary Unification in Various Parts of the World.* Princeton Studies in International Finance, International Finance Section, Princeton University, 1994.

Di Tella, Rafael, and Robert MacCulloch. "Unemployment Benefits as a Substitute for a Conservative Central Banker." Harvard Business School and London School of Economics, May 2000.

Eichengreen, Barry. "Is Europe an Optimum Currency Area?" CEPR Discussion Paper No. 478, November 1990.

von Furstenberg, George, and Joseph Daniels. *Economic Summit Declarations 1975–1989: Examining the Written Record of Cooperation.* Princeton Studies in International Finance, International Finance Section, Princeton University, 1992.

Humpage, Owen. "A Hitchhiker's Guide to International Policy Coordination." Federal Reserve Bank of Cleveland *Economic Review* (Quarter 1, 1990), 2–14.

Kokotsis, Ella, and Joseph Daniels. "G8 Summits and Compliance." In Michael Hodges, John Kirton, and Joseph Daniels, eds. *The G8 Role in the New Millennium.* Aldershot, U.K.: Ashgate Publishing Ltd., 1999.

Mundell, Robert. "A Theory of Optimal Currency Areas." *American Economic Review,* 51 (1961), 657–665.

Rogoff, Kenneth. "Can International Monetary Policy Coordination Be Counterproductive?" *Journal of International Economics,* 18 (May 1985), 199–217.

Treaty on European Union. Maastricht, The Netherlands, 1992.

CHAPTER FOURTEEN

Dealing with Financial Crises—Does the World Need a New International Financial Architecture?

Fundamental Issues

1. **How have recent developments in global capital markets differed across regions?**
2. **What are some of the problems pervasive to financial markets, and what is a financial crisis?**
3. **What is the difference between portfolio capital flows and foreign direct investment, and what role did these types of capital flows play in recent financial crises?**
4. **What are the main activities of the International Monetary Fund and the World Bank?**
5. **What aspects of IMF and World Bank policymaking have proved controversial in recent years?**
6. **What changes in the international financial architecture have economists proposed in recent years?**

In the early 2000s, trading volumes in East Asian government bond markets grew tremendously. Within a four-year period, the volume of government bond issues tripled. In spite of this growth, total government debt in the region remained relatively small, amounting to less than 20 percent of regional GDP. In the United States and Europe, government debt now totals approximately one-half of GDP. Policymakers in East Asia are hoping the bond market will continue to grow and benefit the economies in the region.

Back in 1997, however, there was miniscule bond trading in East Asia. Many policymakers in the region have concluded that this contributed to the financial crisis that began that year. Because governments and corporations issued relatively few bonds, most borrowing took place through the nations' unstable banking systems. Bonds also provide important information to borrowers and lenders. Traders often use yields on government bonds, for example, to judge appropriate yields on relatively riskier private-sector bonds. In addition, a vibrant bond market is important for savers' long-term planning. Without bonds, savers can choose between only bank deposits and equities. Likewise, insurance and pension organizations are limited in how they can invest premiums.

Nations such as Hong Kong and Singapore are so eager to develop these markets that in some cases they have issued government bonds and reinvested the proceeds even when they had no need to borrow in the first place. Other nations, such as Thailand, have issued large amounts of government bonds to finance deficits that ballooned during the financial crisis. Whether these efforts will further encourage the development of a corporate bond market remains to be seen.

How important are international capital flows for economic development? What role did international capital flows play in recent financial crises? How should national policymakers and international institutions respond to financial crises? In this chapter you will examine how different types of global capital flows affect the stability and growth of a nation's economy and considers the role of capital flows in recent financial crises. In addition, this chapter discusses efforts by multinational institutions such as the International Monetary Fund and the World Bank to prevent, predict, and respond to such crises. You will also consider recent proposals for restructuring or redirecting the activities of these institutions.

International Capital Flows

The 1994 Mexican financial crisis represented the first of a new type of crisis. In contrast to previous crises, which tended to evolve slowly in response to accumulated trade deficits, the Mexican crisis unwound quickly as a result of rapid capital flight. This new crisis was much deeper than policymakers expected. Although Mexico's fortunes have improved considerably, a number of Mexican financial institutions, companies, and individuals are still trying to recover from the crisis's aftermath.

International financial architecture
The international institutions, governmental and nongovernmental organizations, and policies that govern activity in the international monetary and financial markets.

Financial crises that took place in East Asia, Central Europe, Russia, Turkey, and South America in the years since the Mexican meltdown have induced policymakers and economists around the world to reconsider the **international financial architecture.** This includes the international institutions, national policies and regulatory agencies, and international agreements that govern activity in the international monetary and financial markets. Whether the world's nations should alter the shape of the international financial architecture and, if so, what types of reforms should be adopted, are among the most important global policy issues of the 2000s.

EXPLAINING THE DIRECTION OF CAPITAL FLOWS

Since the collapse of the Bretton Woods system, the most important feature of the international financial system has been the increased volume of financial flows between nations. As you learned in Chapter 1, in recent years there has been dramatic growth of the volume of transactions in the international capital markets. To understand the nature of this recent upswing, it is important to account for differences between the capital flows experienced by developed countries and emerging economies. It is also crucial to distinguish between foreign direct investment (FDI) and shorter-term capital flows.

Foreign Direct Investment and Developed Nations

Growth in FDI is one of the most important developments in the evolution of global capital markets. FDI is the acquisition of foreign financial assets that results in an ownership share of 10 percent or more. Hence, an FDI inflow is an acquisition of domestic financial assets that result in an ownership share of 10 percent or more of a domestic entity by a foreign resident. An FDI outflow is an acquisition of foreign financial assets that results in an ownership share of 10 percent or more of a foreign entity by a domestic resident.

Chapter 1 showed that, in spite of recent financial crises, since the latter half of the 1980s, growth in world FDI has greatly surpassed the growth of world exports. These flows—indeed much of long-term capital flows—tend to be concentrated among the developed nations, however. Table 14-1 provides the geographical distribution of FDI inflows discussed in Chapter 1. The table shows that, on average, 60 percent of FDI inflows go to the developed nations. In the years immediately following the major emerging-economy financial crises of 1995 and 1998, FDI inflows to the developed economies spiked upward as FDI inflows to the emerging economies declined. By the end of the 1990s, however, more than 70 percent of FDI inflows went to the developed economies.

The Concentration of Cross-Border Mergers and Acquisitions

Cross-border mergers and acquisitions
The combining of firms located in different nations in which one firm absorbs the assets and liabilities of another firm (merger) or purchases the assets and liabilities of another firm (acquisition).

As discussed in Chapter 11, cross-border mergers and acquisitions (M&A), which are the combining of firms in different nations, are another prominent feature of the global monetary and financial markets. Cross-border M&A activity is the driving force behind the recent surge in FDI within the developed economies. **Cross-border mergers and acquisitions** are the combining of firms in different nations. A merger occurs when a firm absorbs the assets and liabilities of another firm. An acquisition occurs when a firm purchases the assets and liabilities of another firm. Changes in national tax codes, relaxation of business regulations and labor laws, and a changing shareholder culture spurred a dramatic increase in cross-border M&A deals. As shown in Figure 14-1, after the mid-1990s M&A inflows increased to more than $900 billion annually. During the same interval, M&A outflows also increased considerably, rising to more than $1 trillion annually.

Consistent with the geographical pattern of FDI, M&A activity is concentrated among developed nations—the United States, Japan, and the European Union.

Table 14-1 Geographical Distribution of Foreign Direct Investment, Percent of Total Inflows

FDI inflows are highly concentrated in the developed nations. On average, more than 60 percent of FDI inflows go to the developed nations. FDI inflows to the developing nations fell following the Mexican financial crisis of later 1994 and the East Asian crisis of 1997.

Source: United Nations *World Investment Report,* various issues United Nations Conference on Trade and Development *FDI Statistics,* and authors' estimates.

	1995	1996	1997	1998	1999	2000
Developed Nations	63.4	58.8	58.9	71.5	77.2	79.1
European Union	35.1	30.4	27.2	35.7	43.6	48.1
Other European Nations	1.8	1.8	1.9	1.2	1.5	1.7
North America	20.7	23.9	26.0	32.6	29.8	27.1
Other Developed Nations	5.7	2.8	3.8	2.0	2.3	2.2
Developing Nations	32.3	37.7	37.2	25.8	20.7	18.9
Transitional Nations	4.3	3.5	4.0	2.7	2.2	2.0

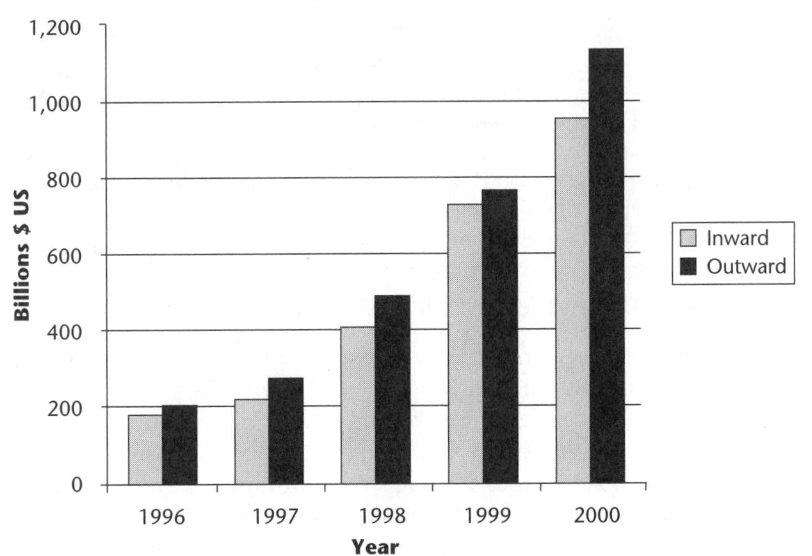

Figure 14-1

Cross-Border Merger and Acquisition Inflows and Outflows

Cross-border mergers and acquisitions are the driving force behind recent increases in FDI. During the period shown in the figure, cross-border mergers and acquisition inflows increased by more than 300 percent and outflows by more than 200 percent.

Source: United Nations *2000 World Investment Report,* and authors' estimates.

ON THE WEB

For data on FDI, M&A, and capital flows, visit the home page of the Organization for Economic Cooperation and Development at http://www.oecd.org.

According to data gathered by the Organization for Economic Cooperation and Development, European companies were the leading purchasers in merger and acquisition deals. In 2000, the United Kingdom completed more mergers and acquisitions than any other nation, accounting for 30 percent of global M&A activity that year. During the late 1990s and early 2000s, the United States, by contrast, attracted more M&A deals than any other nation, capturing more than a third of global M&A purchases.

Private Capital Flows to the Emerging Economies

Chapter 1 detailed another important development in the recent evolution of global capital markets: the growth of private capital flows to the emerging economies. In Chapter 10 you learned that the emerging economies in the Western Hemisphere, such as Mexico, Brazil and Argentina, experienced significant private capital inflows during the early 1990s. A large portion of this capital inflow, however, was shorter-term investment instead of FDI. The 1994–1995 financial crisis that struck the region resulted in a precipitous decrease in private capital, but capital inflows eventually recovered by 1996.

Beginning in the early 1990s through 1995, the volume of capital flows to Asian emerging nations more than doubled, increasing by more than $100 billion. Many economists believe that the systems of financial intermediaries in these nations were overwhelmed by such large capital inflows, partially explaining the crises that occurred in East Asia in 1997 and Russia in 1998. These capital flows dropped sharply during the crises years of 1997 and 1998.

What is important to remember is that in all of these cases, nations relied heavily on portfolio capital and other forms of development aid—that is, short-term capital flows—as opposed to longer-term FDI flows.

1 Fundamental Issue

How have recent developments in global capital markets differed across regions?

Two important developments in the global capital markets are the growth of cross-border mergers and acquisitions and foreign direct investment (FDI) among developed nations and surging private capital flows to emerging economies. Normally, FDI has been concentrated among the United States, Japan, and the European Union, where the rise of cross-border mergers and acquisitions has recently contributed to FDI within these regions. Since the early 1990s, private capital flows to emerging economies have also increased significantly. Capital flows to these nations average more than $150 billion per year.

CAPITAL ALLOCATIONS AND ECONOMIC GROWTH

In Chapter 10 you learned that most development economists believe that sustained capital accumulation is a fundamental prerequisite to achieving and maintaining persistent economic growth within developing countries. These advocates of *capital-market liberalization*—allowing relatively open issuance and competition in stock and bond markets—argue that unhindered capital movements allow savings to flow to their most productive use, resulting in a more efficient allocation of scare resources. Those projects that yield high returns reward savers, who are, in fact, financial speculators, for the risk they have assumed. In this way, markets direct resources in the most efficient pattern, resulting in development of real resources and higher productivity. Savers, therefore, assume the risks in cross-border financial transactions and provide essential liquidity to a nation's economy.

How Capital Inflows Can Smooth Domestic Business Cycles

With access to foreign direct investment and portfolio capital provided by foreign savers, domestic households and businesses then might expand their lending and borrowing activities abroad. This allows domestic businesses and consumers to continue to spend and invest during domestic economic downturns. They repay foreign savers during periods of economic growth. In this way, foreign capital inflows can help to offset domestic business cycles, providing greater stability to the domestic economy.

Hence, domestic savers can diversify internationally and reduce their exposure to domestic economic shocks. These positive aspects of foreign capital inflows allow domestic savers to enjoy higher risk-adjusted rates of return, spurring even higher levels of saving and investment activity. In turn, increased saving and investment induce additional economic growth.

How Capital Inflows Can Contribute to Long-Term Development

For developing nations, access to global capital in the form of foreign direct investment and portfolio capital inflows considerably reduces the cost of financing investment projects. This permits domestic firms and individuals to undertake more investment projects, which contributes to the development of real resources. In the long run, this translates into higher standards of living and higher rates of economic growth. Additionally, private savings from abroad may substitute for uncertain development aid from foreign governments that often comes with inefficiency costs associated with bureaucratic red tape and constraints.

For emerging economies, **financial-sector development**—the development and strengthening of financial institutions, payment systems, and regulatory agencies—is necessary to attract global capital and promote domestic saving. Economic theory indicates, however, that financial-sector development may either increase or decrease saving. As just discussed, financial-sector development can improve the allocation of domestic and foreign savings flows. Nevertheless, wider availability of the various hedging instruments, such as those described in Chapter 6, potentially reduces precautionary saving. In addition, improvements in household credit markets may allow agents to borrow more than they might have otherwise to engage in current consumption or to initiate projects that previously might have been deemed unworthy of financial support. Hence, if financial-sector development induces lower total *net* saving—saving less borrowing—economic growth could actually suffer.

Financial sector development
The strengthening and growth of a nation's financial sector institutions, payments systems, and regulatory agencies.

In general, economists have two opposing points of view of the contribution of the financial sector to long-run economic development. Some economists argue that the development of real resources, including physical resources such as plant and equipment, and the development of technology and human capital are the crucial determinates of long-run economic performance. According to this view, the financial sector does not play an important role in the long run.

An alternative view is that the development of the financial sector induces changes in economic fundamentals. The financial sector can attract foreign capital and affect private agents' long-run saving and borrowing decisions, and, therefore, long-run investment strategies. In this way, development of the financial sector influences long-run economic performance.

Why financial development evolves differently across nations is still somewhat unclear. Recent research on the casual relationship between financial development and real sector growth, however, tends to support the second view above. This research concludes that financial development does indeed affect economic growth by promoting savings and directing funds to the most productive investment projects.

CAPITAL MISALLOCATIONS AND THEIR CONSEQUENCES

In spite of the arguments for capital-market liberalization, *financial market imperfections* and *policy-created distortions* may cause a nation's financial system to fall short in contributing to its economic development.

Financial Market Imperfections

Many economists believe that asymmetric information—the fact that one party in a financial transaction, such as a borrower, often possesses information not available to another party, such as a lender—is pervasive to financial markets. Asymmetric information can bring about an inefficient distribution of capital through resulting problems of adverse selection, herding behavior, and moral hazard.

Adverse selection, another type of market imperfection that affects financial markets, is the potential for those who want funds for unworthy projects to be the most likely to want to borrow. Both market imperfections were discussed in Chapter 12. Adverse selection can make savers less willing to lend to or hold instruments, including lending to or holding debt instruments of those seeking to finance high-quality projects. Additionally, poor information may result in herding behavior. *Herding behavior* occurs when savers who lack full information base their decisions on the behavior of others who they think are better informed. In a global context, herding behavior can be a catalyst for *contagion,* the spread of financial instability to regional levels. Herding behavior can also lead to a reduction of asset prices or currency values that greatly exceed what would be warranted.

Another potential problem that may affect financial markets is *moral hazard,* or the potential for a borrower to engage in much riskier behavior after issuing a debt instrument. For instance, moral hazard may arise when a domestic government implicitly or explicitly guarantees that a firm or bank will not be allowed to fail. Knowing that it will not be allowed to fail, the firm may engage in higher-risk projects in search for higher returns. International organizations, such as the International Monetary Fund, have also been accused of creating moral hazard in much the same way, by standing ready to bail out sovereign nations facing liquidity crises. The argument goes that if the sovereign government knows the IMF is willing to loan it funds when it runs out of foreign reserves, the government will not conduct its policies in a manner prescribed by its exchange rate arrangement.

Policy-Created Distortions

Capital flows may also respond to policy-created distortions, leading to an inefficient and capricious allocation of capital. A **policy-created distortion** results when a government policy leads a market to produce a level of output that is different from the desired level of output, or economically efficient level of output. Microeconomic policies (e.g., tariffs on imports and subsidies to specific industries) protect producers in those industries from foreign competition. This type of protection is typically offered to industries that are not competitive in global markets. Yet by protecting the industry, these policy measures result in a different level of output and higher economic profits than would be experienced in a competitive environment. In turn, these higher profits attract capital flows into the protected industry and away from other, perhaps more productive, industries. Differential national taxation policies, trade restrictions, and macroeconomic policies are but a few policy-created distortions that can lead to a misallocation of capital.

Policy-created distortion
When a government policy results in a market producing a level of output that is different from the economically efficient level of output, causing a less than optimal allocation of an economy's scarce resources.

In addition, differing national regulations of financial transactions may generate *regulatory arbitrage,* or when domestic institutions locate abroad or conduct certain types of operations abroad in order to avoid domestic regulation and supervision. This diminishes the regulatory abilities of governments and exposes domestic intermediaries to the very types of risk that regulators seek to minimize.

Although these distortions result from domestic economic policies, they should be viewed in an international context as well. In principle, the absence of international cooperation and coordination can bring about a potential "race to the bottom," or a movement toward the regulatory and tax environment of the least stringent nation. The possible role of multinational policy cooperation and coordination in reducing this possibility is discussed later in this chapter.

Financial Instability and Financial Crises

When market imperfections and policy-created distortion are severe, they may result in **financial instability,** a situation in which the financial sector is unable to allocate funds to the most productive projects. Severe financial instability can trigger a **financial crisis,** or complete breakdown in the functioning of financial markets. A financial crisis typically involves a banking crisis, a currency crisis, and a foreign debt crisis. A key policy objective of all nations, therefore, is to reduce the potential for the types of problems described thus far, creating a stable financial environment.

Financial instability
When a nation's financial sector is no longer able to allocate funds to the most productive projects.

Financial crisis
A situation that arises when financial instability becomes so severe that the nation's financial system is unable to function. A financial crisis typically involves a banking crisis, a currency crisis, and a foreign debt crisis.

WHERE DO FINANCIAL INTERMEDIARIES FIT IN?

There are several ways in which *financial intermediaries*—the institutions that channel funds from savers to those who ultimately make capital investments—can contribute to financial stability and spur greater economic growth. One key function of financial intermediaries is to funnel savings to borrowers with minimum inefficiencies. The process of intermediation can be costly and, therefore, absorbs a fraction of each dollar of saving being channeled to a borrower. An efficient intermediary absorbs a smaller fraction of each dollar and can channel a greater portion of each dollar of saving on to the borrower. As a result, a greater portion of the nation's saving is invested, spurring greater economic growth. Reducing reserve requirements, a central bank policy instrument discussed in Chapter 9, and unnecessary and costly regulations may improve the efficiency of a nation's financial intermediaries.

Another way that financial intermediaries reduce inefficiencies is by making it possible for many people to pool their funds together. This increases the amount of total savings managed by a single authority. Such centralization can yield economies of scale that reduce average fund-management costs below the levels that savers would incur if they were to manage their savings alone. In this way, intermediaries may increase the amount of savings ultimately invested by reducing unnecessary costs.

An efficient system of financial intermediaries may also reduce the degree of information asymmetries, thereby improving capital allocations and enhancing financial-market stability. By specializing in the assessment of the quality of debt instruments and continuously monitoring the performance of firms that issue these instruments, financial intermediaries are able to reduce the extent of information imperfections.

In addition, intermediaries provide a means for savers to pool risks. If savers are unable to pool risks, they will only invest in the most liquid projects. More productive but less liquid projects are not financed, resulting in lower potential economic growth.

Hence, intermediaries perform a multifaceted role. Relying on their informational capabilities, they evaluate investment projects, determine those with the highest potential return, and induce savers to invest in higher-risk but more profitable projects by providing a means of sharing risks at reduced average costs. Because of their important role in allocating capital, the supervision and regulation of financial intermediaries is a key element of various proposals for the reform of the international financial architecture discussed later in this chapter.

2 Fundamental Issue

What are some of the problems pervasive to financial markets, and what is a financial crisis?

Several problems are particularly pervasive to financial markets. One type of financial market failure is asymmetric information, or the fact that borrowers and lenders often possess different information. Asymmetric information may result in problems of adverse selection, herding behavior, and moral hazard. Policy distortions, such as differential taxation and regulation, may also result in a less than optimal allocation of capital. When financial market imperfections and policy distortions are severe, they may result in financial instability and a financial crisis. A financial crisis is when financial instability becomes so severe that the nation's financial system no longer functions, and usually involves a banking crisis, a currency crisis, and a foreign debt crisis. Efficient financial intermediaries reduce the impact of financial market imperfections, thereby encouraging more saving and financing more investment projects.

Capital Flows and International Financial Crises

Recent research by economists indicates that capital-market liberalization generally leads to improvements in capital allocations and further development of a nation's financial sector. Nearly every nation that liberalized its capital markets during the last three decades has experienced some type of financial crisis, however. How have international capital flows contributed to recent financial crises? (For more information on capital-market liberalization, the role of foreign capital flows, and capital controls, see on the next page *Policy Notebook: Is Capital-Market Liberalization the Right Policy?*)

ARE ALL CAPITAL FLOWS EQUAL?

Although capital-market liberalization and access to global capital may reduce the cost of investment projects and spur economic growth, the resulting collective debt obligations may destabilize the economy. The maturity structure of a nation's public and private foreign debt is one important aspect. Attracting both short-term and long-term debt allows for a diversified portfolio of debt instruments, a manageable repayment structure and, therefore, a more stable portfolio of debt.

Because governments, firms, and households have different borrowing needs, and because investment projects have different time horizons, it is important that a nation's financial sector attract both short-term investment flows and long-term foreign direct investment capital. Economists consider **portfolio investment** as the purchase of financial instruments that results in less than a 10 percent ownership share. Portfolio capital flows tend to have a shorter term to maturity and lower borrowing costs, and typically they are viewed as a means of generating near-term income. On the other hand, FDI is a long-term investment strategy in which the source of funds establishes financial control. Because portfolio capital and foreign direct investment represent different investment strategies, have different maturity structures, and different borrowing costs, they are not equivalent in terms of their potential short-run and long-run consequences.

Portfolio investment
The acquisition of foreign financial assets that results in less than a 10 percent ownership share in the entity.

Portfolio Capital Flows

Portfolio capital deals, which are short-term in nature, are easier to arrange, have lower borrowing costs, and do not require a firm to relinquish financial control to a foreign entity. Over time, portfolio capital inflows may improve capital allocations within a nation and help a nation's financial sector develop. Because portfolio capital is a nonownership and relatively liquid form of investment, however, portfolio capital flows can reverse direction quickly. Portfolio capital flight out of a developing country can leave its fragile financial sector short of much needed liquidity, generating financial instability. This can trigger a financial crisis that can threaten both the solvency of a nation's financial intermediaries and the viability of its exchange-rate regime.

POLICY *Notebook*

POLICY MANAGEMENT

Is Capital-Market Liberalization the Right Policy?

For some developing nations, capital-market liberalization can be a mixed blessing. In 1999 alone, more than $80 billion of foreign capital flowed into developing economies. Representing less than 1 percent of world output and approximately 3 percent of developing nations' output, these funds allow developing countries to finance trade and investment opportunities that otherwise would be impossible. A portion of these funds, however, can flow out of a nation just as quickly as they flow in, putting severe strains on a nation's financial system and affecting the exchange value of the nation's currency.

As a result, some nations have put into place restrictions on capital flows in order to prevent "hot" capital flows. During the 1990s, Chile, for example, placed a number of constraints on foreign capital flows that included restrictions on borrowing from abroad. Some economists think these capital controls contributed to Chile's solid macroeconomic and exchange value performance. Others, though, see the capital controls as a hindrance to optimal capital allocation and the reason for a stagnant stock market. They credit Chile's economic performance to appropriate macroeconomic policymaking.

Regardless of the perceived benefits of these restrictions, Chile now faces greater competition from other South American nations for foreign capital than it did in the past, and it now finds foreign capital more difficult to attract. As a result, in the presidential election of 2000 both the Socialist and conservative candidates pledged to end the nation's remaining capital restrictions.

Russia, by way of contrast, is considering implementing new controls on capital outflows. False invoicing has led to considerable capital flight from the nation. False invoicing occurs when a company writes a fraudulent invoice for imports to transfer money abroad. To curtail this practice, the Russian government has proposed a tax on all transfers of money abroad, including those to pay for imports.

Is capital-market liberalization the right policy, or should countries continue to restrict capital flows? John Williamson of the World Bank and Molly Mahar of the Federal Reserve Bank of San Francisco studied the economic performance of thirty-four nations that undertook some degree of capital-market liberalization. The authors find that only two nations, the United Kingdom and Singapore, were spared systemic economic crises following liberalization. Nonetheless, they conclude that financial liberalization has, in general, led to more efficient allocations of capital and deepening of the nations' financial markets. They conclude that capital-market liberalization offers real gains but also carries risk, and they suggest that nations focus on effective regulation and supervision of their financial sector while gradually liberalizing their capital markets.

For Critical Analysis:
As a policymaker in a developing or emerging economy, what types of capital flows would you encourage? What policy actions would you take to encourage the desired capital flows?

Foreign Direct Investment

By way of contrast, FDI is a relatively illiquid ownership form of investment that can have a stabilizing effect on a nation's economy. As noted earlier, FDI most often occurs when multinational firms establish foreign affiliates or enter into strategic alliances with foreign firms. In doing so, they seek long-term commitments. As multinational firms become entrenched in foreign nations, they establish valuable relationships and networks with customers and suppliers. One would not therefore expect multinational firms engaging in FDI to enter and exit foreign nations with much frequency. It is the potential for long-lasting commitments and corporate entrenchment that makes FDI a stabilizing influence on a nation's economy. These long-term arrangements, however, are more difficult to arrange and result in some degree of foreign ownership of domestic firms.

Hence, portfolio capital and direct investment offer different positive and negative features. Because capital flows are not all equal, it is important for a nation's financial sector to create an environment that attracts both long-term and short-tem capital. In this way, capital allocations are improved, spurring real sector and financial sector development while minimizing financial instability.

THE ROLE OF CAPITAL FLOWS IN RECENT CRISIS EPISODES

The 1994–1995 Mexican financial crisis illustrates well the consequences of relying too heavily on portfolio capital flows. As explained in the opening of Chapter 13, Mexico experienced a dramatic increase in private capital inflows during the early and mid-1990s. Portfolio capital accounted for a large portion of these inflows. The combination of political instability in Mexico and rising interest rates in developing nations sparked an outflow of portfolio capital during 1994 and 1995. In 1995 alone there was an outflow of $68.3 million from the emerging economies of the Western Hemisphere, representing a 112 percent decline in private capital inflows and resulting in an overall negative net portfolio flow for the region. These capital outflows put considerable downward pressure on the exchange values of the currencies of most nations in the region, and a complete collapse of the crawling-peg arrangement in Mexico.

During the mid-1990s, the distribution of private capital flows to the emerging economies of Asia, such as Thailand, Malaysia, Indonesia, and Korea, were similar to that of Mexico during the early 1990s. Although the region was able to attract a greater proportion of FDI prior to the 1997 financial crisis, it still relied heavily on portfolio capital and other forms of short-term lending. When the value of the Thai baht collapsed in the fall of 1997, it triggered an outflow of capital from the region in a manner similar to that of the Mexican crisis. In 1998 and then again in 2002 capital outflows and their consequences returned to the western hemisphere as the Brazilian real plummeted because of capital outflows.

The lesson learned from the experiences of these two regions in the late 1990s and early 2000s is that excessive reliance on portfolio capital flows can be destabilizing. It is important to note, however, that outflows of foreign portfolio capital were not the root cause of these financial crises. Foreign capital outflows were a symptom, triggered by a loss of confidence in the nation's macroeconomic and microeconomic policies, its political stability, and the soundness of its financial markets and real productive and manufacturing sectors.

Foreign Direct Investment as a Stabilizing Element

Because FDI is a stabilizing element, many nations strive to create an environment that attracts FDI. Table 14-1 (on page 445), however, indicates that FDI is concentrated among the developed countries. An important policy issue for emerging economies, therefore, is how to attract FDI and minimize the reliance on portfolio capital flows in financing investment projects.

In considering policy approaches to achieve this goal, former U.S. Secretary of Labor Robert Reich argues that nations should pay less attention to the nationality of multinational corporations. He says that they should consider instead the positive impact that the act of locating production or distribution operations of a foreign firm within a country can have on the country's employment and income. He contends that multinational firms invest in foreign markets because they perceive advantages to doing so: skilled workforces, good distribution networks, developed supply chains, access to finance, and so on. A country that invests in education, research, training, and infrastructure, therefore, can expect to continually attract FDI, enabling it to maintain high levels of employment and income. In this way, a nation could create a virtuous spiral of growth and investment, whereby domestic investment and FDI continually reinforce one another.

Following the international financial crises of the 1990s, academics, private agencies, and international policy groups generated a large body of policy recommendations for nations to improve the mix of capital inflows. A sampling of these proposals is provided later in this chapter.

Is There a Role for Capital Controls?

Some economists believe that countries cannot limit their efforts to attracting FDI. They contend that emerging nations should actively take steps to reduce their level of reliance on portfolio capital flows. Economists favoring greater government intervention often advocate attempting to control short-term portfolio flows in an effort to pace the gradual liberalization of financial markets.

Most economists are skeptical of controls on capital flows, however. Sebastian Edwards of the University of California in Los Angeles studied the effect of Chile's capital controls on the composition of that country's capital flows and its macroeconomic stability. One important conclusion that he reaches is that regardless of the type and extent of legislation imposed, the private sector eventually finds ways of getting around the restrictions. Edwards argues that controls on capital *outflows* should be avoided, as they are particularly ineffective in this regard.

Controls on capital *inflows* may prove to be effective in the short run and slow the pace of short-term inflows and lengthen the maturity of foreign debt. By lengthening the maturity of debt, they give policymakers an opportunity to liberalize capital markets and allow the financial sector to develop. In the case of Chile, for example, controls on capital inflows resulted in a decline of short-term capital inflows, as a percentage of overall capital inflows, from more than 95 percent in 1988 to less than 3 percent in 1997.

Edwards concludes, however, that capital controls be used as a *temporary stop-gap* measure. He argues that policymakers should eventually remove capital controls as they create additional borrowing costs. As discussed earlier, Chile is removing the last of its capital controls because they have increased the cost of capital significantly. Once the financial sector is developed, complete capital-market liberalization can improve capital allocations, spurring real economic development.

Fundamental Issue 3

What is the difference between portfolio capital flows and foreign direct investment, and what role did these capital flows play in recent financial crises?

Because portfolio capital inflows constitute a nonownership, income-generating form of investment, these flows tend to be shorter-term and more liquid than FDI. An excessive reliance on portfolio capital flows for financing investment project, therefore, can be destabilizing. By way of contrast, FDI represents a long-term financial control strategy and, therefore, may have a stabilizing effect for the economy. An excessive reliance on portfolio capital flows appears to be one of the factors that contributed to the recent financial crises in the emerging economies.

Financial Crises and Multilateral Policymaking

In the past, many nations have sought to develop a stable financial system capable of channeling steady and diversified sources of funds from domestic and foreign savers. Despite these efforts, however, a number of countries have experienced financial crises. Furthermore, crises that have begun in some countries have sometimes cascaded through the global financial system to exert effects on other nations, as was the case in the Asian crisis of 1997 and 1998.

In recognition of the possible inability of individual countries to prevent crises and of the potential for crises to spread internationally, many of the world's nations have developed multinational institutions intended to engender multilateral policy cooperation and coordination. These institutions aim both to limit the likelihood of crises and to contain crises when they occur.

THE CURRENT MULTILATERAL STRUCTURE

There are two supranational organizations at the center of current multilateral efforts to prevent and stem international financial crises. These are the International Monetary Fund and the World Bank.

The International Monetary Fund

As discussed in Chapter 7, the International Monetary Fund (IMF) is a multinational organization that promotes international monetary cooperation, exchange arrangements, and economic growth and that provides temporary financial assistance to

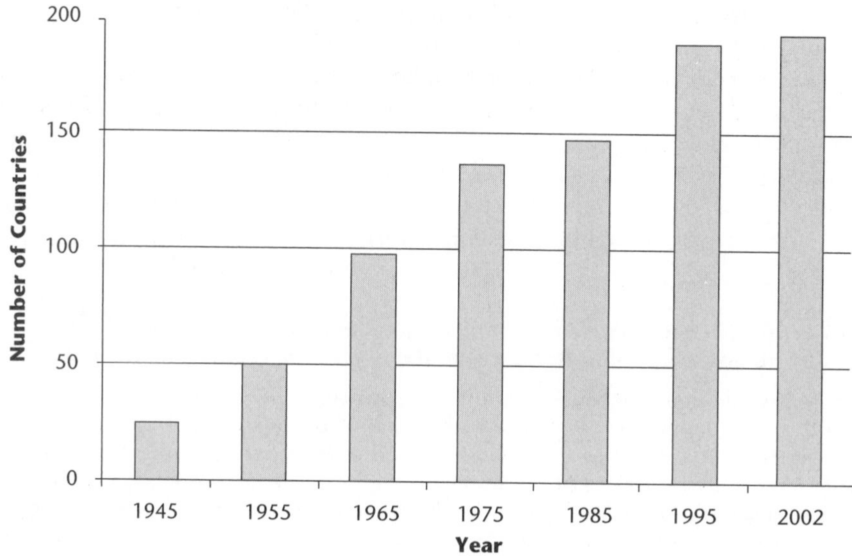

Figure 14-2

Growth in IMF Membership

The number of member nations in the International Monetary Fund is now about six times larger than it was when the organization was founded.

Source: International Monetary Fund.

nations experiencing balance-of-payments difficulties. Figure 14-2 charts the growth of IMF membership since the founding of the organization in July 1944. Currently, the IMF has 182 member nations.

When a country joins the IMF, it deposits funds to an account called its **quota subscription.** These funds, which are measured in terms of **special drawing rights,** a composite currency of the IMF, form a pool from which the IMF can draw to lend to members. Figure 14-3 displays current quota subscriptions for selected IMF member nations.

Quota subscription *The pool of funds deposited by IMF member nations that IMF managers can use for loans to member nations experiencing financial difficulties.*

Special drawing right *A composite currency of the International Monetary Fund in which the value is based on a weighted average of the currencies of five member nations.*

The IMF sets each nation's quota subscription based on its real national income. The quota subscription determines how much a member can borrow from the IMF under the organization's standard credit arrangements. It also determines the member's share of voting power within the IMF. The U.S. quota subscription, for instance, is just over 17 percent of the total funds provided by all member nations, so this is the IMF voting share held by the United States.

When the IMF considers providing financial support to a member country in the way of short-term loans, it normally imposes specific limitations on the actions of that country's government. This IMF policy, called **conditionality,** requires countries to cooperate with the IMF in establishing plans for the nation's financial policies. Sometimes the IMF will not extend assistance to a nation unless it takes certain actions before receiving the loan. As part of broader satisfaction of conditionality requirements, the IMF may only request a general commitment to aim policies in a certain direction, known as *low conditionality.* In this case, the IMF is said to have a *policy understanding* with the nation. Alternatively, the IMF may impose *high conditionality.* Then it requires a nation to aim for specific, quantifiable targets, called *performance criteria.* Failure to meet these targets can lead to suspension of IMF loan disbursements.

Conditionality *The set of limitations on the range of allowable actions of government of a country that is a recipient of IMF loans.*

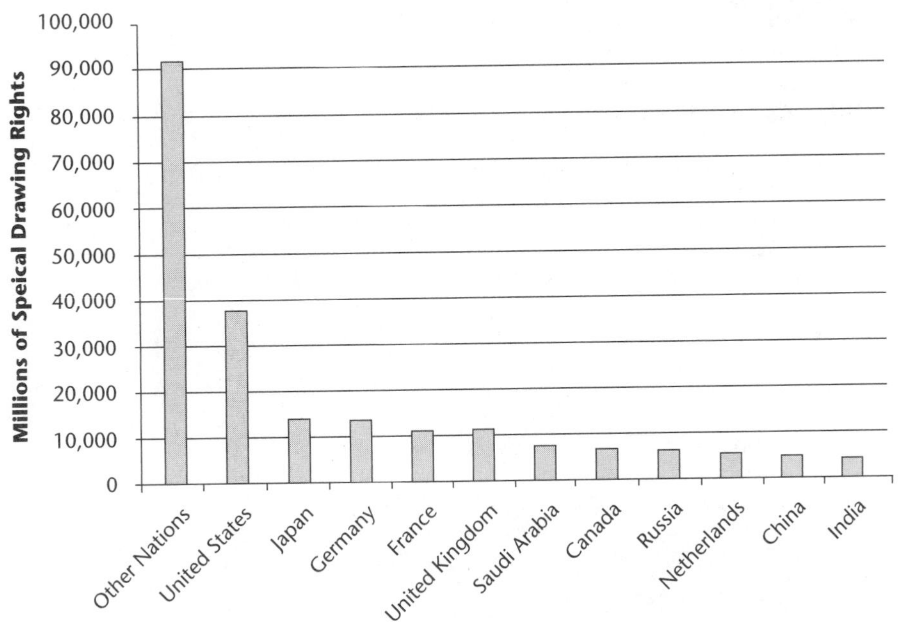

Figure 14-3

IMF Quota Subscriptions

The quota subscription of each member nations in the IMF, which is denominated in special drawing rights, depends on the nation's real national income. A country's quota subscription determines its share of voting power within the IMF and how much it is eligible to borrow under standard IMF credit arrangements.

Source: International Monetary Fund.

Table 14-2 lists the main funding programs offered by the IMF. Originally, the IMF's primary function was to provide so-called standby arrangements and short-term credits, and it continues to offer these types of assistance through *regular IMF facilities.* The end of the gold standard in the early 1970s reduced the need for short-term adjustment credit, however, and the IMF adapted by expanding other lending programs. One of these is *concessionary assistance,* which the IMF offers to poor and heavily indebted countries, either as long-term loans intended to support growth-promoting projects or as short- or long-term assistance aimed at helped countries experiencing problems in repaying existing debts. The other is *other financing facilities.* Under these funding programs, the IMF seeks to assist any qualifying member experiencing an unusual fluctuation in exports or imports, a loss of confidence in its own financial system, or spillover effects from financial crises originating elsewhere.

The World Bank

The other key supranational institution that provides support to nations experiencing financial problems is the World Bank. This institution, which also was created during the 1944 Bretton Woods conference, is more narrowly specialized than the IMF. The World Bank makes loans solely to about 100 developing nations with an aim toward reducing poverty and improving living standards. It estimates that within its client nations, about 3 billion people live on less than $2 per day, about 40,000 die of preventable diseases each day, and more than 100 million never attend schools of any type.

Table 14-2 IMF Financing Facilities

Source: International Monetary Fund.

Regular IMF Facilities	
Stand-by Arrangements (SBA)	Intended to assist in situations requiring temporary or cyclical adjustments. Arrangements are typically for 12 to 18 months and are phased in on a quarterly basis, with releases of funds contingent on meeting performance criteria and periodic program reviews.
External Fund Facility (EFF)	Designed to provide assistance for adjustment to problems arising from structural macroeconomic problems for periods up to three years.
Concessional Assistance	
Poverty Reduction and Growth Facility (PRGF)	Provides financial assistance for supporting long-term structural programs intended to foster increased economic growth via 10-year loans.
Heavily Indebted Poor Countries (HIPC) Initiative	Provides financial assistance to countries experiencing difficulties in repaying large bilateral and multilateral external debts.
Other Financing Facilities	
Conpensatory Financing Facility (CFF)	Intended to assist members experiencing difficulties arising from temporary export declines or increased expenses in importing foodstuffs.
Supplemental Reserve Facility (SRF)	Designed to assist members experiencing sudden and disruptive adjustment problems arising from a loss of market confidence.
Contingent Credit Lines (CCL)	Designed to assist members affected by contagion effects of financial crises originating elsewhere.

In contrast to the IMF, the World Bank has always specialized in relatively long-term loans used to fund long-term development and growth. Its initial objective was to provide assistance to countries in the post-World War II rebuilding period. In the 1960s it refocused its mission by broadening its scope to encompass global antipoverty efforts.

Whereas nations' governments commonly use IMF loans to supplement their overall budgetary resources, countries typically seek loans from the World Bank to fund specific projects, such as improved irrigation systems, better hospitals, and the like. Nevertheless, in recent years some of the World Bank's programs have

Table 14-3 World Bank Institutions

Source: World Bank.

International Development Association	On behalf of 161 member countries, specializes in funding loans aimed toward poverty reduction in developing nations.
International Bank for Reconstruction and Development	On behalf of 182 member nations, provides loans and other forms of development assistance to middle-income countries and the more creditworthy developing nations.
International Finance Corporation	On behalf of 174 member nations, promotes private-sector investment in developing countries by committing its own funds, brokering loans from private sources, and offering advice to private firms.
Multinational Investment Guarantee Agency	On behalf of 153 member countries, promotes foreign direct investment in developing nations by offering political risk insurance to lenders and investors.
International Center for Settlement of Investment Disputes	On behalf of 132 member nations, provides conciliation and arbitration facilities for settling investment disputes arising between foreign investors and developing countries.

overlapped with IMF efforts to finance longer-term structural adjustments and debt refinancing activities within heavily indebted nations.

The World Bank actually is composed of five separate institutions, which are listed and described in Table 14-3. These institutions lend to both governments and private firms. They also provide advice and assistance in various aspects of development finance, including resolving disputes that may arise between foreign investors and developing countries. The world's wealthiest countries fund most of its activities, although the World Bank also raises some of its funds in international capital markets.

Fundamental Issue 4

What are the main activities of the International Monetary Fund and the World Bank?

The International Monetary Fund and World Bank are multinational economic organizations consisting of more than 180 member nations. One of the IMF's broad objectives is to encourage economic growth by facilitating international monetary cooperation and effective exchange arrangements. Another fundamental IMF goal is to hinder or combat international financial crises by providing temporary and longer-term financial assistance to nations experiencing balance-of-payments difficulties. The World Bank also seeks to promote economic growth, but it does so primarily via longer-term loans to support investment projects within the world's less-developed nations.

EVALUATING THE STATUS QUO

The experiences with crises in the 1990s engendered a number of economists and policymakers to offer proposals for restructuring the IMF and the World Bank. Before examining these proposals, it is important to consider the current policies of these institutions.

Ex Ante versus *Ex Post* Conditionality at the IMF

Like any other lender, the IMF encounters two key problems, which were described earlier in this chapter: adverse selection and moral hazard.

The IMF's policy of imposing conditionality terms on borrowers seeks to address the moral hazard problem. Most observers, however, agree that there are at least two weaknesses in the IMF's approach. First, IMF officials do not publicly announce the terms of the institution's lending agreements with specific nations. This means that it is solely up to the IMF to monitor whether borrower nations are wisely using funds donated by other countries. Often, private investors can discern that a country has failed to abide by its agreement with the IMF only when the IMF undertakes an action such as withholding a scheduled loan installment. Swift adverse market reactions following such IMF moves can place borrower nations in even worse financial straits, making it even more difficult for the borrower to meet the terms of its original agreement with the IMF. Thus, the IMF's policy of keeping loan agreements secret can undermine its efforts to protect members' funds from misuse.

Second, it is common for IMF officials to initially place only very general conditions on the loans they extend. They tend to switch to high conditionality only after a borrower nation has already enacted policies that violate the original low-conditionality arrangement. By that point, of course, the IMF has already failed to avoid the moral hazard problem.

Critics argue that IMF secrecy and its tendency to impose high conditionality only when pressed to, effectively amounts to firm conditionality only on an *ex post*, or after-the-fact, basis. They contend that this after-the-fact, discretionary approach to establishing conditions under which the IMF lends, which they call ***ex post* conditionality,** undermines the IMF's credibility both with actual borrowers *and* with prospective borrowers. This lack of credibility, they argue, increases the likelihood for moral hazard problems while also widening the scope of the adverse selection problem by attracting borrower nations that are most likely to try to take advantage of vague conditions of a policy of low conditionality.

***Ex post* conditionality** *The imposition of IMF lending conditions after a loan has already been granted.*

To reduce the extent of both problems, IMF critics have long suggested the use of ***ex ante* conditionality,** or conditions for IMF loans that are publicly known in advance. They have also pushed for imposing a few straightforward conditions, so that it is easy for everyone to monitor whether borrower nations have complied. To date, however, the IMF has maintained its generally secretive and discretionary lending policies.

***Ex ante* conditionality** *The imposition of IMF lending conditions before the IMF grants the loan.*

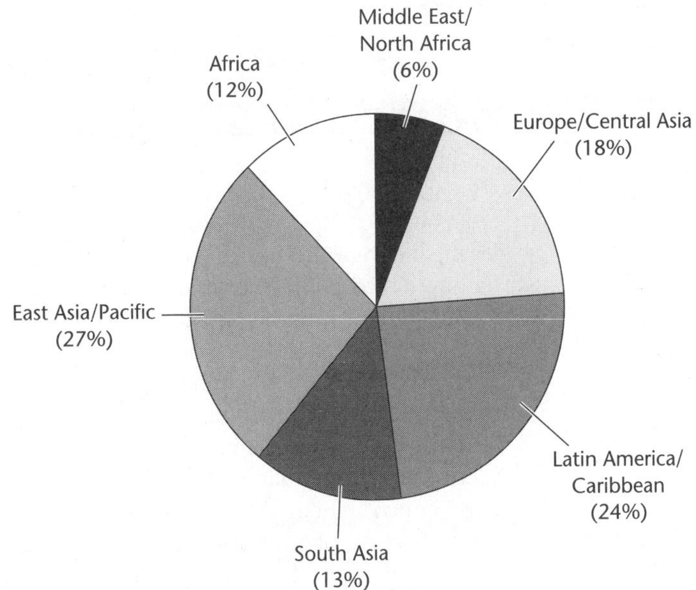

Figure 14-4

The Distribution of World Bank Lending

Even though Africa has the world's poorest nations, it has received only 12 percent of total World Bank loans since 1990.

Source: World Bank.

Searching for a Mission at the World Bank

The World Bank currently extends more than $15 billion annually in lending assistance to developing nations. In some nations, particularly in Africa, attracting private investment has proved difficult. Consequently, the World Bank has been a key source of credit for these nations. All the same, as Figure 14-4 indicates, only about 12 percent of lending by the World Bank since 1990 has been directed to African countries.

Even though more than $150 billion in private capital flows into developing nations each year, the World Bank continues to make many of its loans to nations that have little trouble attracting private funds. For instance, in the late 1990s, when foreign investors sought to finance the construction of China's largest thermal power plant, makers of the power plant turned them away because they were able to get a loan from the World Bank at more favorable terms.

Although the World Bank's official mission is to lend to people in developing nations with projects that cannot attract private capital, the development agency increasingly competes with private investors. In such competitions, the institution typically wins out over private lenders by offering loans at below-market rates. Critics of such loans argue that they distort the market for private capital and encourage the kind of inefficient investment that contributed to East Asia's economic woes in the late 1990s. They also contend that countries such as China are inappropriate recipients of development assistance. After all, China has foreign currency reserves exceeding $150 billion, and it has persistently run an annual current account

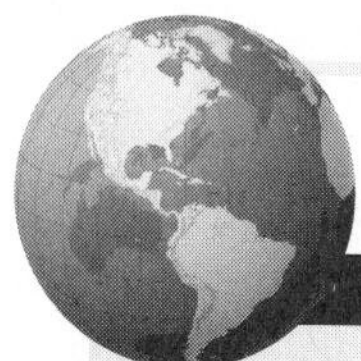

POLICY *Notebook*

POLICY MANAGEMENT

Is the European Bank for Reconstruction and Development Promoting Corruption in Russia?

The International Monetary Fund and the World Bank are *global* multinational institutions. Countries in some parts of the world have also established *regional* multinational institutions that provide development loans and, therefore, perform functions analogous to those of the IMF and World Bank. One example is the European Bank for Reconstruction and Development (EBRD). The EBRD has 59 member nations. The European Union contributes about 60 percent of the EBRD's funding, and France, Germany, Italy, and the United Kingdom individually contribute almost 9 percent each. Canada, Japan, Russia, and the United States are also contributors.

These nations created the EBRD in 1991 to "promote private and entrepreneurial initiative in the Central and Eastern European countries committed to applying the principles of multiparty democracy pluralism, and market economics." They authorized the EBRD to lend up to 60 percent of its funds to private companies and up to 40 percent to national governments.

In the early 1990s, the EBRD directed nearly $2 billion in loans to Russia. Today many of those funds are gone. Most Russian companies that received loans failed, and the EBRD had to conduct expensive legal battles to recover some its funds that were directed to fraudulent or illegal activities.

Undeterred, the EBRD has indicated that it plans to lend more than $1 billion in new funds to Russian companies in the early 2000s. What remains to be seen is whether this lending program will be any more successful in contributing to Russia's economic development. Critics of the EBRD contend that its loans actually *deter* economic development in Russia by making it easier for Russian companies to avoid structural changes that would promote market efficiency, such as adopting internationally recognized accounting principles, conducting regular audits, and ending ties to organized crime. Indeed, one of the EBRD's biggest problems during the 1990s was that many Russian borrowers siphoned borrowed funds to offshore companies owned by individuals who were hard to identify given the companies' sloppy bookkeeping. Some economists suspect that the bulk of the funds that the EBRD directed to Russian during the 1990s actually ended up in other countries.

For Critical Analysis:
What actions could the EBRD take to ensure that the funds it lends to Russian companies are used only to develop Russian resources?

surplus in the tens of billions of dollars. As a result, China is a net exporter of capital. Nevertheless, China typically borrows between $2 billion and $3 billion from the World Bank each year. (Some critics of such policies of multinational institutions contend that their lending can actually *hinder* economic development even in nations that have trouble attracting foreign capital; see *Policy Notebook: Is the European Bank for Reconstruction and Development Promoting Corruption in Russia?*)

An important constraint that the World Bank faces is pressure from nations that are net donors to its lending pool to maintain a significant revenue stream of its own, thereby reducing the donors' risks of loss. Projects in developing nations that are most likely to maintain stable and reasonably high returns are also the ones that are most likely to attract the interest of private investors. By way of contrast, projects in the poorest and most needy countries are least likely to yield steady payoffs for the World Bank.

ON THE WEB

Learn more about the EBRD at http://www.ebrd.com.

Fundamental Issue 5

What aspects of IMF and World Bank policymaking have proved controversial in recent years?

The IMF has received criticism for failing to publicize conditions it places on loans to member countries. Critics have also questioned the IMF's tendency to make such conditions very general and hard to measure. Both aspects of IMF policymaking, they argue, increase the potential for moral hazard by making it easier for borrowers to commit IMF funds to riskier projects. Although the World Bank directs a significant portion of its financial assistance to the world's poorest countries, it also makes a large amount of loans in countries that receive significant private capital inflows. In some of these nations, critics argue, the World Bank makes financial markets less efficient by offering loans at below-market interest rates.

Does the International Financial Architecture Need a Redesign?

Multinational institutions have confronted two types of criticisms in recent years. One set of critics believes that these institutions are correctly designed and structured but contends nevertheless that these institutions could do a much better job of heading off financial crises before they occur. Another group, however, criticizes the operations of, and in some cases even the existence of, multinational financial institutions. According to this latter group, at a minimum the international financial architecture requires some retuning, and it may even require a redesign.

CAN POLICYMAKERS PREDICT INTERNATIONAL FINANCIAL CRISES?

To be able to limit, or even prevent, international financial crises, policymakers must have a good idea about their underlying causes. In fact, however, there are differing perspectives concerning the main causes of crises. Let's consider each in turn to discuss what guidance they provide about factors that might help national and supranational authorities determine when they should intervene to try to reduce the likelihood of a crisis.

Economic Imbalances and International Financial Crises

The traditional view of financial crises focuses on **economic fundamentals,** which are underlying factors such as the nation's current and likely future economic prospects and its monetary and fiscal policies. According to this view, an

Economic fundamentals *Basic factors determining a nation's current exchange rate, such as the country's current and likely future economic policies and performance.*

inconsistency between the value of the exchange rate corresponding to a nation's economic fundamentals and an officially targeted exchange rate value can engender a financial crisis. If foreign exchange traders perceive that the official value of a nation's currency is higher than its true value in private foreign exchange markets based on economic fundamentals, then there naturally will be a tendency for traders to sell their holdings of assets denominated in that currency to avoid losses. By unloading these assets, traders who are averse to risk will reduce their losses if it should happen that the government or central bank run out of foreign currency reserves used to purchase the currency and maintain the official exchange rate.

Furthermore, speculators may seek to profit from their anticipations of an imminent exhaustion of official foreign exchange reserves by selling assets denominated in the nation's currency in an effort to push the government or central bank into giving up on supporting the exchange rate at its officially targeted level. At the same time they can bet on a collapse of the official exchange rate via positions they take in markets for futures, options, and swaps. This type of behavior is called a **speculative attack** on a nation's official exchange rate.

Speculative attack
A concerted effort by financial-market speculators to profit from anticipations of a depletion of official foreign exchange reserves via sales of assets denominated in the nation's currency intended to induce abandonment of an exchange rate target that will yield them profits in derivative markets.

If a speculative attack is successful, then speculators potentially can earn significant profits from taking these positions. They can do this by effectively selling foreign-currency-denominated assets at the high official prices via arrangements to buy them in derivatives markets at lower prices more nearly consistent with underlying economic fundamentals. Of course, speculators can, and sometimes do, lose these kinds of bets, so speculative attacks do not necessarily succeed. Nevertheless, if the official exchange rate is sufficiently misaligned with the exchange rate such that it would be consistent with economic fundamentals, the probability that a speculative attack will succeed increases.

Self-Fulfilling Expectations and Contagion Effects

A second perspective focuses on the potential role of *self-fulfilling anticipations* and contagion effects that can bring about an international financial crisis even when underlying economic fundamentals are consistent with an officially pegged exchange rate or when governments and central banks otherwise have sufficient foreign exchange reserves, given a slight misalignment of the government's exchange-rate target. According to this view, all that is needed to induce a speculative attack is a relatively widespread perception by traders that a nation's policymakers face relatively high internal costs, perhaps because of resulting political difficulties, from maintaining the official exchange rate.

Suppose, for instance, that currency speculators perceive a lack of resolve on the part of policymakers. They might then attempt to profit from their anticipation that policymakers will give in and devalue a currency rather than accept higher interest rates or other changes that may have negative economic spillovers. If a sufficient number of speculators develop anticipations that government authorities in a nation lack the will to accept such spillovers, then large sales of assets denominated in the nation's currency can occur. This can induce other risk-averse traders to sell their foreign-currency-denominated assets as well in an effort to avoid losses. Essentially, according to this alternative view a speculative attack takes place simply because of expectations that it will be successful, but not necessarily because of underlying problems with economic fundamentals.

Structural Moral Hazard Problems

Finally, a third perspective focuses on flaws within the structure of a nation's financial system as the major factors that lay the groundwork for a crisis situation. From this view, crisis conditions exist when governmental policies create a situation of rampant *moral hazard problems.* For instance, a nation's government might require its banks to make loans to specific firms or industries, and because these firms and industries know that they will receive credit no matter how they use the funds, they commit them to risky undertakings. Many observers of the financial crises in Malaysia and Indonesia during the late 1990s have argued that such moral hazard problems existed in those nations. Ultimately, the risks taken on by those who receive government-directed credit generate actual losses and failures, these observers conclude, which sets off a crisis situation.

Others who emphasize the potential for moral hazard problems to generate financial crises also contend that the policies of multinational institutions such as the IMF and the World Bank also can contribute to financial crises. On the one hand, they argue, when such institutions provide credit for industries and governments at prices below the market price of credit in the recipient nations, this tends to push down standards of creditworthiness in those countries. The reason, goes this argument, is that in their quest to earn profits, private lenders who are unable to compete for borrowers at the below-market rates charged by the IMF and the World Bank lower their credit standards and make loans to less creditworthy borrowers. On the other hand, because governments know that they can apply for IMF and World Bank assistance if overextension of credit to unworthy borrowers leads to widespread financial failures, they have little incentive to rein in risky lending within their financial systems.

Crisis Prediction and Early Warning Systems

Each of these perspectives indicates different factors that might help in predicting financial crises. According to the view that emphasizes the importance of imbalances in economic fundamentals, variables such as exports, imports, foreign exchange reserves, real income, monetary aggregates, exchange rates, and interest rates might all be useful indicators of the potential for a crisis. For instance, if a country's trade balance quickly worsens and its foreign exchange reserves rapidly decline, then a crisis may be in the offing.

The perspective emphasizing moral hazard problems, however, indicates that such changes in economic fundamentals are likely to occur when a crisis is already in progress. Hence, variations in economic fundamentals will not necessarily help predict crises far enough in advance to help prevent them. The view that self-fulfilling expectations can induce crises offers an even more pessimistic view about the usefulness of economic fundamentals as crises indicators. According to this view, it may be difficult to find a close relation between fundamentals and crises, because crises may sometimes take place without a previous significant change in fundamentals.

Before considering what factors aid in predicting financial crises, it would be helpful if economists agreed about what constitutes a crisis. There are, however, different views on how to determine that a crisis has occurred. Jeffrey Frankel of Harvard University and Andrew Rose of the University of California at Berkeley, for instance, propose that a crisis definitely exists when a nation's currency experiences a nominal depreciation of at least 25 percent within a year that follows a depreciation of at least 10 percent the previous year. Most economists, however, have considered more flexible index measures of speculative pressures that take into account exchange rate changes and variations in foreign exchange reserves. They consider a crisis to have occurred when such an index exceeds a threshold that depends on the normal, historical pattern of variation that the index has exhibited in prior years.

Financial crisis indicator
An economic variable that normally moves in a specific direction and by a certain relative amount in advance of a financial crisis, thereby helping to predict a coming crisis.

In such studies, economists seek to determine whether they can identify any economic variables that serve as **financial crisis indicators,** or factors that typically precede such crises and thereby aid in predicting them. One such study is by Morris Goldstein of the Institute for International Economics, Graciela Kaminsky of George Washington University, and Carmen Reinhart of the University of Maryland. One type of indicator that these authors consider is ratings of the countries' debts, such as credit ratings by Moody's and other credit rating bureaus. These ratings might reflect moral hazard problems. In addition, however, they evaluate a large set of potential "leading indicators" of financial crises that includes exchange rates, interest rates, national income levels, quantities of money in circulation, and the like. Such variables, naturally, reflect economic fundamentals that the traditional view of financial crises predicts should play important roles, and these variables also provide important information that traders use to form expectations.

These authors find that credit ratings do not help predict financial crises. This could be because moral hazard problems are not a key causal factor in crises, but it is also possible that rating agencies such as Moody's do not have sufficient information to accurately assess the scope of moral hazard and its implications for the true creditworthiness of international borrowers. The authors find that several economic fundamentals together tend to do a better job of predicting financial crises than any single indicator.

Early warning system
A mechanism that multinational institutions might use to track financial crisis indicators to determine that a crisis is on the horizon, thereby permitting a rapid response to head off the crisis.

The objective of studies searching for financial crisis indicators is to develop an **early warning system,** or a mechanism for monitoring financial and economic data for signals of trouble that might eventually evolve into a crisis. The idea is that if a multinational institution could develop an effective early warning system, it would receive sufficient warning to intervene speedily and head off a crisis before it occurs.

There is some optimism inside and outside the International Monetary Fund and World Bank that economists may ultimately develop a reliable early warning system. Many economists remain skeptical, however. Some doubt that any single view of the causes of international financial crises—shifts in economic fundamentals, speculation driven by self-fulfilling expectations, or moral hazard problems caused by inadequate conditions on domestic or multinational loans—can single-handedly "explain" every crisis. Thus, these skeptics doubt that any early warning system based on a limited set of indicators is likely to improve the capability of multinational institutions to react quickly enough to prevent them from occurring. (Other economists suggest that policymakers might have more success predicting crises by relying on market-based indicators; see on pages 468–469 *Management Notebook: Do Financial Markets Predict Financial Crises?*)

RETHINKING ECONOMIC INSTITUTIONS AND POLICIES

The strongest critics of multinational institutions contend that there is little evidence that these institutions have developed the capability to head off financial crises before they occur. Indeed, a number of critics contend that multinational institutions themselves can contribute to the likelihood of international financial crises. Accordingly, these critics argue, the world's nations should consider making fundamental reforms in the structure of these institutions.

Rethinking Long-Term Development Lending

Not all lending by supranational institutions is related to crisis situations. As discussed earlier, both the IMF and the World Bank also make longer-term loans intended to foster growing standards of living in many of the world's poorer nations.

Since the early 1990s, one of the main themes of development economics has been that markets work better at promoting growth when a developing nation has more effective institutions, such as basic property rights, well-run legal systems, and uncorrupt government agencies. Considerable evidence indicates that countries where property rights are not well enforced, the rule of law is weak, and governments are corrupt tend to grow more slowly, even if they otherwise permit markets to function without regulatory hindrances.

This implies that a top priority of supranational organizations dedicated to higher standards of living in developing nations should be finding ways to improve those nations' fundamental institutions. At the most basic level, economists emphasize the paramount importance of putting in place basic market foundations, such as property and contract rights. This requires constructing credible legal systems to enforce laws and setting up the kinds of institutions that are likely to lead to better national policies, perhaps including establishment of independent central banks and transparent budget processes for fiscal authorities.

Furthermore, bringing about structural reforms consistent with achieving a higher long-term growth rate requires nations to develop strategies for making reforms last. This requires building a consensus for reform and sometimes may entail compensating those who lose when reform is enacted.

A key issue is what, if anything, a supranational institution such as the World Bank can do to promote pro-growth institutional improvements within developing nations. From one standpoint, there is little that the IMF and World Bank can do.

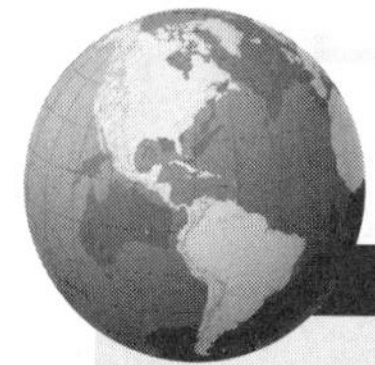

MANAGEMENT *Notebook*

POLICY MANAGEMENT

Do Financial Markets Predict Financial Crises?

In principle, policymakers could try to use a number of alternative indicators to predict financial crises. Some economists, however, believe that policymakers are fooling themselves if they think they are likely to do a better job of crisis prediction than private individuals and firms who stand to lose wealth if a crisis occurs. Because people and companies participating in financial markets have a strong incentive to monitor events in countries that are susceptible to crises, these economists argue, policymakers should look to market-based indicators when trying to anticipate financial crises.

As one example of a possible crisis indicator, consider J.P. Morgan's *emerging market bond index (EMBI) spread.* This is a measure of the differential between a weighted average of interest rates on bonds issued in emerging economies and the average yield on U.S. Treasury Securities. Panel (a) of Figure 14-5 shows how the EMBI spread varied during the

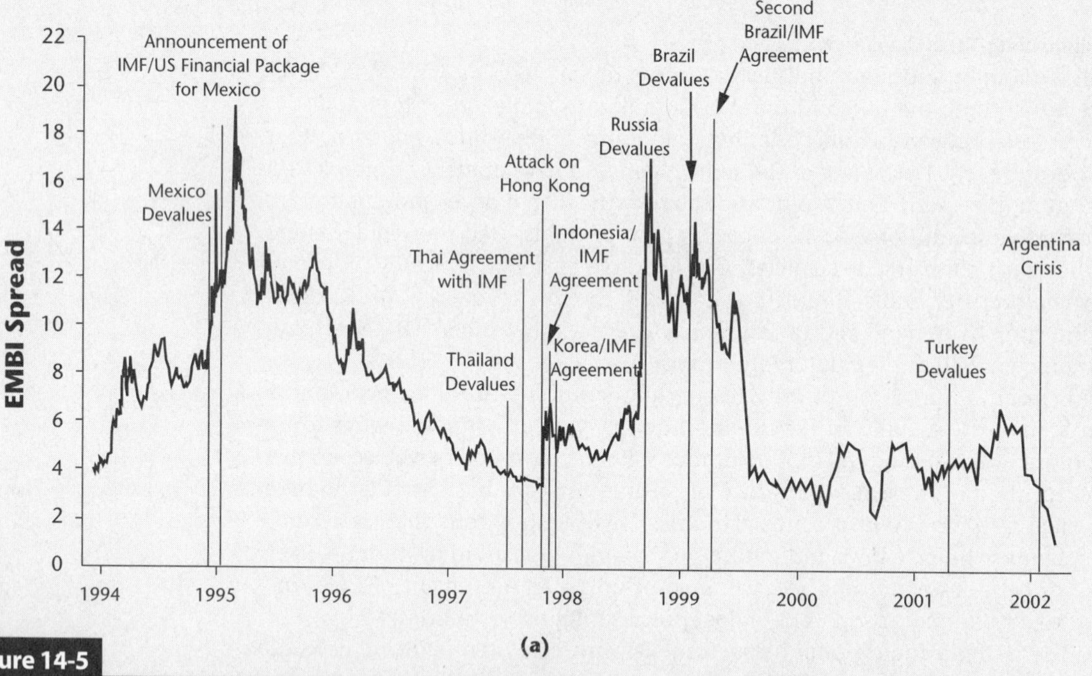

Figure 14-5

The Emerging Market Bond Index (EMBI) Spread and Private Capital Flows During the 1990s

Panel (a) shows that the EMBI spread increased prior to the Mexican crisis, the Russian crisis, and the Brazilian crisis. In addition, panel (b) shows that there is an apparent inverse relationship between the EMBI spread and global capital flows and that especially pronounced changes in the EMBI spread are associated with rapid changes in international flows of private capital that can contribute to financial crises. For this reason, some observers view the EMBI spread as a possible market-based indicator of financial crises.

1994–1999 interval that encompassed financial crises in Mexico, Southeast Asia, Russia, and Brazil. Economists who argue in favor of the EMBI spread as a potential crisis indicator note that it rose in the weeks leading up to the Mexican crisis, the Russian crisis, and the Brazilian crisis.

Critics of this argument, of course, point to the fact that the EMBI spread was falling prior to the first stages of the Asian crisis in Thailand and Hong Kong. Nevertheless, those who promote this market-based indicator argue that relative movements in bond rates in emerging economies and developed countries such as the United States typically bring about swings in private capital flows that can trigger a financial crisis. As panel (b) in Figure 14-5 indicates, there is a strong inverse relationship between the EMBI spread and global capital flows. Particularly sharp changes in the EMBI spread appear to be associated with rapid changes in international flows of private capital that can contribute to financial crises.

For Critical Analysis:
Does the fact that the EMBI spread clearly failed to predict the start of the Asian crisis necessarily mean that it is not a useful crisis indicator?

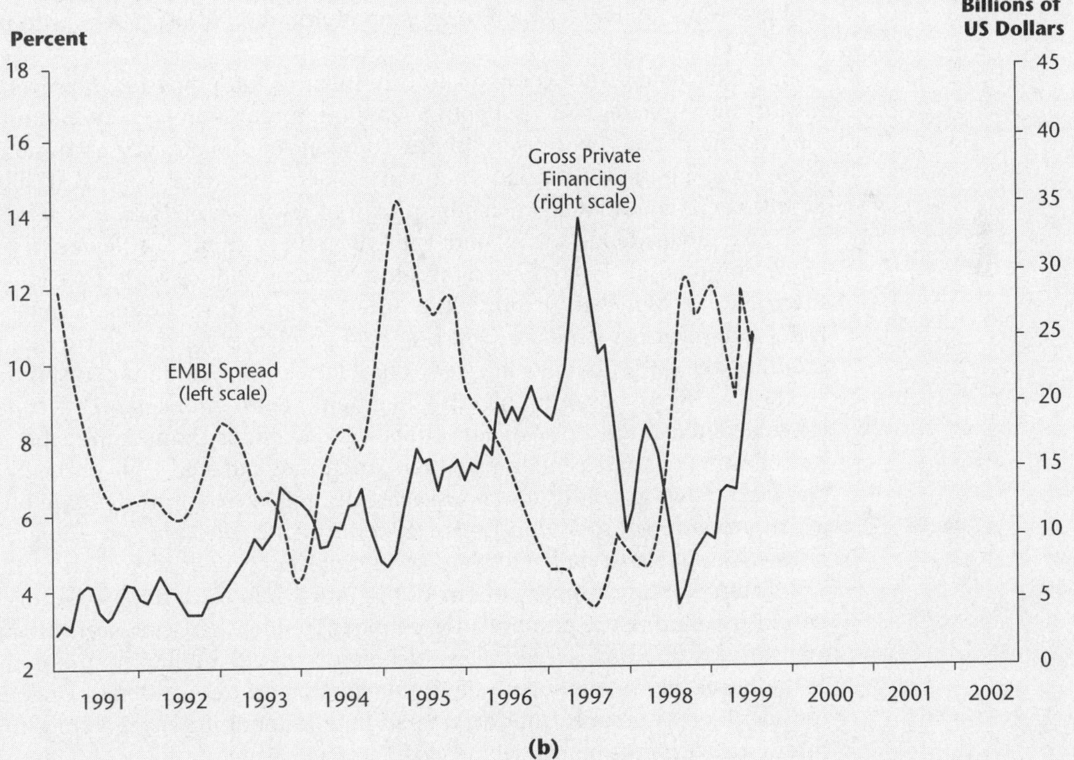

(b)

Source: International Monetary Fund.

After all, the shapes of national institutions are largely political matters for the people of developing nations to decide.

Nevertheless, a number of economists have suggested that the IMF and World Bank should adopt strict policies against countries with institutional structures that fail to promote individual property rights, law enforcement, and anticorruption efforts. This would, they argue, give countries an incentive to shape up their institutional structures.

Other economists, in contrast, advocate direct financial assistance to governments attempting to implement such institutional reforms. Funds put to such use, they argue, could compensate those who lose power as a result of reform efforts and could help fund infrastructures required to make reforms work. Those proposing this more active role for supranational lenders contend that the result could be much larger long-term returns for borrower nations and donor nations alike—as compared with the piecemeal payoffs from such projects as dams, power plants, and bridges.

Alternative Institutional Structures for Limiting Financial Crises

Most proposals for altering the international financial architecture focus on multinational policymaking related to financial crises. A few of these are summarized in Table 14-4. They range from relatively minor changes in existing institutions and procedures to replacement of existing multinational institutions with new institutions.

Several features are common to a number of the proposals, however. These include more frequent and in-depth releases of information both by multinational lenders and national borrowers, improved financial and accounting standards for those receiving funds from multinational lenders, increased use of both high and *ex ante* conditionality for IMF lending, and, in several proposals, increased efforts to induce private lenders to extend credit. Beyond these areas of common ground, however, proposals typically diverge sharply. Some call for more oversight of the International Monetary Fund, while others suggest a wholesale change in the IMF's management structure. Still other proposals would, if adopted, entail dismantling the IMF and replacing it with new forms of multinational institutions.

So far, few proposals for altering the international financial architecture have led to actual change. The IMF has adopted some minor changes in its procedures for collecting and releasing information, and it has stiffened some of the financial and accounting standards that borrowers must follow to obtain credit. In addition, a U.S. proposal led to establishment of confirmed credit lines (see Table 14-2 on page 458), but to this date relatively few nations have made use of this facility.

Naturally, the member nations of the IMF would have to agree to the adoption of more dramatic proposals for change. To date there has been little movement in this direction. Nevertheless, debate on the desirability of minor changes in the status quo versus potentially significant departures continues. Undoubtedly consideration of proposals for an altered international financial architecture will continue to generate global debate in the years to come.

Table 14-4 A Sampling of Proposals to Restructure the International Financial Architecture

Source: Barry Eichengreen, *Toward a New International Financial Architecture.* Washington, D.C.: Institute for International Economics: 1999, Appendix A.

National Proposals	**Description**
Canada Proposal for Emergency Standstill Clause	Under this proposal, countries would establish rules for restricting capital outflows that threaten international financial stability.
France Proposal for an IMF Council Composed of National Finance Ministers	The proposal would upgrade an "Interim Committee" of national finance ministers to the status of the ultimate governing and decision-making body for the International Monetary Fund.
United Kingdom Proposal for a Standing Committee for Global Financial Regulation	This proposed committee would encompass the IMF, World Bank, and Bank for International Settlements and would establish and implement international standards for financial regulation and economic policymaking.
Private Proposals	
Calomiris-Meltzer Proposals for Strict International Lending Rules	Although these economists' proposals are different in certain respects, they share the idea that current multinational institutions might be replaced with a single institution that makes only short-term loans to illiquid countries.
Garten's Proposal for a Global Central Bank	This proposal envisions a new multinational institution overseen by the G-7 and rotating emerging-economy members that would engage in open-market operations using funds raised from members and international taxes.
Soros's Proposal for an International Investor Insurance Agency	Under this proposal, nations would create a public corporation that would insure investors against debt defaults up to a specified ceiling level.
International Proposals	
IMF Proposal for Internal Reforms	This proposal entails, among other things, requiring borrowers to provide more in-depth financial information, to adopt better accounting standards, and to release more IMF data and information to the public.
G-7 Proposals for a Larger Role for Private-Sector Lenders	This proposal extends the IMF proposal by calling for greater private-sector involvement in providing funds to distressed nations and providing incentives for private lenders to be willing to participate.
G-22 Proposals for Greater Accountability, Stronger Financial Systems, and Crisis Containment	Under this proposal, the IMF would be required to prepare a "Transparency Report" for each nation receiving an IMF loan. Nations requesting loans would have to follow common financial and accounting principles, and international loan contracts would contain flexible-payment provisions simplifying loan renegotiations in the event that crises take place.

6 **Fundamental Issue**

What changes in the international financial architecture have economists proposed in recent years?

Many critics of the IMF and the World Bank have argued that they should develop early warning systems to aid in predicting and perhaps even preventing international financial crises. A fundamental problem that these institutions face in such efforts, however, is that there is little agreement about why crises occur and, hence, about what indicators should be used to try to predict crises. A common theme of existing proposals for altering the international financial architecture is to enforce stronger conditions on the long-term and short-term loans that multinational institutions extend to borrowers. Many proposals also entail more publicity of the internal operations and lending policies of the International Monetary Fund and the World Bank. Some proposals, however, argue for changing the management structure of the IMF and World Bank, supplementing these institutions with additional multinational institutions, or even replacing them with new multinational institutions that would follow different procedures or pursue different objectives.

CHAPTER SUMMARY

1) **Regional Differences in Global Capital Market Developments:** The growth of foreign direct investment among the developed economies and the growth of private capital flows to the emerging economies are two of the most important developments taking place in the global capital markets. Over the last decade, private capital flows to the emerging economies averaged more than $100 billion annually. In spite of this remarkable growth, FDI has been concentrated among the triad countries of the United States, Japan, and the European Union. Mergers and acquisitions are the driving force of the recent surge in FDI, and are also concentrated in the triad countries.
2) **Problems Pervasive to Financial Markets, and Financial Crises:** One type of problem pervasive to financial markets is asymmetric information, or when borrowers and lenders possess different information. Asymmetric information may lead to problems of adverse selection, herding behavior, and moral hazard. Policy distortions, such as differential taxation and regulatory policies, are another type of problem. If these problems are severe, they may result in financial instability and a financial crisis. A financial crisis is when financial instability is so severe that the nation's financial system no longer functions. A financial crisis usually involves a banking crisis, a currency crisis, and a foreign debt crisis.
3) **The Difference between Portfolio Capital Flows and Foreign Direct Investment and the Role of These Capital Flows in Recent Financial Crises.** Portfolio capital flows are a nonownership form of investment and tend to have short-term maturities. FDI represents an ownership strategy and tends to be long-term in maturity. Recent financial crises demonstrate that an

excessive reliance on portfolio capital flows can destabilize an economy. FDI, on the other hand, might have a stabilizing influence on an economy.

4) **The Main Activities of the International Monetary Fund and the World Bank:** The IMF and World Bank are multinational economic organizations that are owned and operated by more than 180 of the world's nations. The IMF exists to promote global economic growth by encouraging international monetary cooperation and effective exchange arrangements and to limit the scope for international financial crises by providing temporary and longer-term financial assistance to nations experiencing balance-of-payments difficulties. Like the IMF, the World Bank's function is to encourage economic growth, but the World Bank seeks to fulfill this duty mainly by extending relatively long-term loans to fund investment projects by governments or firms located in the least-developed nations of the world.

5) **Aspects of IMF and World Bank Policymaking That Have Been Controversial in Recent Years:** Although the IMF can place strong and measurable conditions on its loans to member countries, it often fails to do so. The IMF also does not release complete information about the conditions it places on loans. It is arguable that these aspects of IMF policymaking make it easier for borrowers to use IMF funds for unworthy projects, thereby increasing the scope of the moral hazard problem in international financial markets. The World Bank provides a significant percentage of the credit available to the world's poorest countries, but it also extends large numbers of loans to governments and private companies located in countries that receive relatively large volumes of private capital inflows. It is possible that by offering loans to these governments and companies at interest rates below private market levels, the World Bank contributes to less-efficient financial markets in those nations.

6) **Changes in the International Financial Architecture Proposed by Economists in Recent Years:** A number of economists have favored greater IMF and World Bank efforts to head off crises by developing early warning systems that would permit them to predict and more rapidly respond to international financial crises. Nevertheless, skeptics doubt that such efforts will bear fruit in light of general disagreement among economists about why crises occur and, therefore, about what indicators the IMF or World Bank might use to attempt to predict crises. A number of proposals for redesigning the international financial architecture include adding and enforcing stricter and more measurable conditions for borrowers to meet before receiving long-term and short-term loans from the IMF and World Bank. Another common feature of many proposals is the release of more public information about the internal operations and lending policies of these institutions. A few proposals suggest more dramatic changes, such as new management structures for the IMF and World Bank, adding additional multinational institutions to supplement their activities, or replacing existing multinational institutions with new institutions that would operate differently or aim to achieve different objectives.

QUESTIONS AND PROBLEMS

1) This chapter provides the tools needed to understand the events that took place in Mexico in 1994. At that time, Mexico pegged the value of the peso to the U.S. dollar. Explain how the Federal Reserve's interest rate increases affected the value of the peso. Explain how the Bank of Mexico had to respond to maintain the currency peg.
2) List three benefits of portfolio capital and three benefits of foreign direct investment. Give one negative aspect of each. Explain why it is undesirable to rely on portfolio capital only. Explain why it is undesirable to rely on FDI only.
3) Suppose a nation has a pegged exchange rate system and you are the nation's chief central banker. Construct a supply and demand diagram of the spot exchange market for the domestic currency. Explain, using the diagram, how the central bank must react to portfolio capital inflows and outflows so as to maintain the currency peg.
4) Explain how allowing foreign banks to enter and compete in the domestic financial sector might improve capital market allocations. Explain how, in general, competition among financial intermediaries is important to financial stability.
5) Explain how savers and borrowers might benefit from regulation of a nation's financial intermediaries. Does regulation impose costs? How do these costs affect long-run economic development?
6) In the early 1990s, on the heels of a major political restructuring of central and eastern European nations, the IMF granted billions of dollars in loans to Russia. Russia ended up partially defaulting on the loans, rescheduling loan payments, and applying for yet more IMF loans. Then in the late 1990s, in the midst of the fallout from the Asian financial crisis, the IMF granted billions of dollars in additional loans to Russia. Once again, Russia defaulted on loan repayments, postponed many of its payments, and applied for additional IMF funding. Discuss possible reasons for this repetition of IMF-Russian interactions during the 1990s, and offer two proposals for how the IMF and Russia might avoid yet another repetition in the 2000s. Explain why you believe your proposals might be successful in this regard.
7) Some observers have responded to harsh criticisms of World Bank policies in the 1990s by arguing that the World Bank's net-donor members have saddled it with conflicting goals by requiring it to maintain a significant revenue stream of its own. Do you agree that the World Bank confronts conflicting objectives? If not, why not? If so, which of the allegedly conflicting goals do you think should take precedence?
8) Construct a table with three columns that lists each of the views on the causes of international financial crises in the left-hand column. In the second column of the table, list at least one possible financial crisis indicator corresponding to each view that might be tracked in an IMF early warning system for predicting financial crises. In the third column, propose how to evaluate

whether each potential indicator you have proposed actually helps predict a crisis. Does this exercise help explain why economists have a hard time constructing reliable early warning systems?

9) Table 14-4 on page 471 lists a plan by Jeffrey Garten to establish a global central bank monitored by the G7 nations and rotating developing nations. Credit lines from national governments and/or revenues from taxes would fund the global bank. This central bank would be authorized to use these funds to conduct purchases and sales of securities issued in the financial markets of member nations in order to generate additional revenue. Identify the strengths and weaknesses that you see in this proposal.
10) Should multinational institutions lend funds at interest rates below, equivalent to, or above private-market interest rates? Take a stand, and support your position.

ONLINE APPLICATION

Internet URL: http://www.g7.utoronto.ca

Title: **G8 Information Centre**

Navigation: Go directly to the above URL for the home page of the *G8 Information Centre*. Scroll down to "Summits, Meetings & Documents of G7 and G8" and click on "Summits: Delegations and Documents. Click on *Köln, Germany."* View the G7 Finance Ministers' report on strengthening the international financial architecture by clicking on "Report of G7 Finance Ministers to the Köln Economic Summit."

Application: Perform the following operations, and answer the following questions.

1) What are the six fundamental reforms recommended by the Finance Ministers?
2) Provide, in your own words, a two to three sentence rationale for each of the six items above.

For Group Study and Analysis: Discuss the reforms and try to identify what reforms have been taken since the Köln Summit. Discuss whether national governments, international institutions, private organizations, or some combination of these initiated the reforms you identified. Discuss what remains to be done.

REFERENCES AND RECOMMENDED READINGS

Aghion, Philippe, Philippe Bacchetta, and Abhijit Banerjee. "Capital Markets and the Instability of Open Economies." Centre for Economic Policy Research, Discussion Paper No. 2083 (March 1999).

Berg, Andrew, and Catherine Pattillo. "The Challenge of Predicting Economic Crises." *International Monetary Fund Economic Issues* 22 (July 1999).

Choe, Hyuk, Bong-Chan Kho, and René Stulz. "Do Foreign Investors Destabilize Stock Markets? The Korean Experience in 1997." *Journal of Financial Economics* 54 (1999): 227–264.

Council on Foreign Relations Task Force. "The Future of the International Financial Architecture." *Foreign Affairs* 78 (6) (1999): 169–184.

Eichengreen, Barry. *Toward a New International Financial Architecture.* Washington, D.C.: Institute for International Economics, 1999.

Eichengreen, Barry, Michael Mussa, Giovanni Dell' Ariccia, enrica Detragiache, Gian Maria Milesi-Ferretti, and Andrew Tweedie. "Liberalizing Capital Movements: Some Analytical Issues." *International Monetary Fund Economic Issues,* 17 (1999).

Fischer, Stanley. "Reforming the International Financial System." *The Economic Journal* 109 (459) (1999): F557–F576.

Frankel, Jeffrey, and Andrew Rose. "Currency Crashes in Emerging Markets: An Empirical Treatment." *Journal of International Economics* 41 (1996): 351–366.

Goldstein, Morris, Graciela Kaminsky, and Carmen Reinhart. *Assessing Financial Vulnerability: An Early Warning System for Emerging Markets.* Washington, D.C.: Institute for International Economics: 2000.

International Monetary Fund. *External Evaluation of IMF Surveillance: Report by a Group of Independent Experts,* September 1999.

Meltzer, Allan. "What's Wrong with the IMF? What Would Be Better?" *Independent Review,* Hoover Institution (Fall 1999).

Mishkin, Fredic, S. "Global Financial Instability: Framework, Events, Issues." Journal of Economic Perspectives, 13 (4) (Fall 1999): 3–20.

Obstfeld, Maurice. "The Global Capital Market: Benefactor or Menace?" *Journal of Economic Perspectives* 12 (4) (1998): 9–30.

Vaubel, Roland. "The Political Economy of the IMF: A Public Choice Analysis." In Doug Bandow and Ian Vasquez, ed. *Perpetuating Poverty: The World Bank, the IMF, and the Developing World.* Washington, D.C.: Cato Institute: 1994.

White, William. "What Have We Learned from Recent Financial Crises and Policy Responses?" Working Paper No. 84, Bank for International Settlements, January 2000.

Williamson, John, and Molly Mahar. "A Survey of Financial Liberalization," *Essays in International Finance, No. 211.* International Finance Section, Princeton University (1998).

Glossary

A

absolute advantage The ability of a nation's residents to produce a good or service at lower cost, measured in resources required to produce the good or service, or, alternatively, the ability to produce more output from given inputs of resources, as compared with other nations.

absolute quota A quantitative restriction that limits the amount of a product that can enter a country during a specified time period.

adaptive expectations Expectations that are based only on information from the past.

***ad valorem* tariff** A tariff calculated as a percentage of the value of the good or service.

adverse selection The tendency for manufacturers of the lowest-quality products to have the greatest incentive to misrepresent the attributes of those products.

American option An option in which the holder may buy or sell an amount of a currency any time before or including the date at which the contract expires.

announcement effect A change in private market interest rates or exchange rates that results from an anticipation of near-term changes in market conditions signaled by a central bank policy action.

antitrust laws Statutes designed to achieve benefits of competition for consumers and producers.

arbitrage Buying an item in one market to sell at a higher price in another market.

asymmetric information One party's possession of information in an economic transaction that the other party to the transaction does not possess.

autarky A no-trade situation.

B

backward shifted The amount of a tax that producers pay in the form of lower revenue per unit.

balance of payments A system of accounts that measures transaction of goods, services, income, and financial assets between domestic residents, businesses, and governments and the rest of the world during a specific time period.

Bank for International Settlements (BIS) An institution based in Basle, Switzerland, which serves as an agent for central banks and a center of economic cooperation among the largest industrialized nations.

barriers to entry Any factors inhibiting entrepreneurs from instantaneously founding a new firm.

base year A reference year for price-level comparisons, which is a year in which nominal GDP is equal to real GDP, so that the GDP deflator's value is equal to one.

beggar-thy-neighbor policy A policy action that benefits one nation's economy but worsens economic performance in another nation.

C

call option An options contract giving the owner the right to purchase an amount of a currency at a specific rate of exchange.

capacity output The real output that the economy could produce if all resources were used to their utmost.

capital The physical equipment and buildings used to produce goods and services.

capital account A tabulation of the flows of financial assets between domestic private residents and businesses and foreign private residents and businesses.

central banker contract A legally binding agreement between a government and a central banking official that holds the official responsible for a nation's inflation performance.

combination tariff A tariff that combines an *ad valorem* tariff and a specific tariff.

common market A trading arrangement under which member nations remove all barriers to trade among their group, erect common barriers to trade with other countries outside the group, and permit unhindered movements of factors of production within the group.

common property A nonexclusive resource owned by everyone and therefore by no single individual.

comparative advantage The ability of a nation's residents to produce an additional unit of a good or service at a lower opportunity cost relative to other nations.

concentration ratio The share of total industry sales by the top few firms.

conditionality The set of limitations on the range of allowable actions of government of a country that is a recipient of IMF loans.

conservative central banker A central bank official who dislikes inflation more than an average citizen in society and who thereby is less willing to induce discretionary increases in the quantity of money in an effort to achieve short-run increases in real output.

consumer price index (CPI) A weighted sum of prices of goods and services that a typical consumer purchases each year.

consumer surplus The benefit that consumers receive from the existence of a market price. Consumer surplus is measured as the difference between what consumers are willing and able to pay for a good or service and the market price.

consumption possibilities All possible combinations of goods and services that a nation's residents can consume.

contract manufacturing A production strategy in which one organization hires another organization to manufacture a good under the hiring firm's name and to the hiring firm's specifications.

convertibility The ability to freely exchange a currency for a reserve commodity or reserve currency.

copyright An author's legal title to the sole right to reproduce, distribute, perform, or display creative works, including articles, books, software, and audio and video recordings.

countervailing duty (CVD) A tax on imported goods and services designed to offset the domestic price effect of foreign export policies.

covered exposure A foreign exchange risk that has been completely eliminated with a hedging instrument.

covered interest parity A prediction that the interest rate on one nation's bond should approximately equal the interest rate on a similar bond in another nation plus the forward premium, or the difference between forward exchange rate and the spot exchange rate divided by the forward exchange rate.

crawling band A range of exchange values that combines features of a crawling peg with the flexibility of an exchange-rate band.

crawling peg An exchange rate system in which a country pegs its currency to the currency of another nation but allows the parity value to change at regular time intervals.

credit entry A positive entry in the balance of payments that records a transaction resulting in a payment to a domestic resident from abroad.

cross-border mergers and acquisitions The combining of firms located in different nations in which one firm absorbs the assets and liabilities of another firm (merger) or purchases the assets and liabilities of another firm (acquisition).

currency-basket peg An exchange-rate system in which a country pegs its currency to the weighted average value of a basket, or selected number of currencies.

currency board An independent monetary authority that substitutes for a central bank. The currency board pegs the value of the domestic currency, and changes in the foreign reserve holdings of the currency board determine the level of the domestic money stock.

currency futures An agreement to deliver to another party a standardized quantity of a specific nation's currency at a designated future date.

currency option A contract granting the right to buy or sell a given amount of a nation's currency at a certain price within a given period or on a specific date.

currency swap An exchange of payment flows denominated in different currencies.

current account Measures the flow of goods, services, income, and transfers or gifts between domestic residents, businesses, and governments and the rest of the world.

customs union A trading arrangement that entails eliminating barriers to trade among participating nations and common barriers to trade with other countries outside the group.

D

deadweight loss A loss of consumer or producer surplus that is not transferred to any other party and that represents a decline in economic efficiency.

debit entry A negative entry in the balance of payments that records a transaction resulting in a payment abroad by a domestic resident.

demand The relationship between the prices that consumers are willing and able to pay for various quantities of a good or service for a given time period, all other things constant.

devalue A situation in which a nation with a pegged exchange rate arrangement changes the pegged, or parity, value of its currency so that it takes a greater number of domestic currency units to purchase one unit of the foreign currency.

discount rate The interest rate that the Federal Reserve charges on discount window loans that it extends to depository institutions.

discretionary policymaking The act of responding to economic events as they occur, rather than in ways it might previously have planned in the absence of those events.

diseconomies of scale An increase in long-run average cost caused by an increase in a firm's output.

dollarization A system in which the currency of another nation circulates as the sole legal tender.

dollar-standard exchange-rate system An exchange rate system in which a country pegs the value of its currency to the U.S. dollar and freely exchanges the domestic currency for the dollar at the pegged rate.

domestic credit Total domestic securities and loans held as assets by a central bank.

dumping A situation in which a firm sells its output to foreign consumers at a price that is less than what the firm charges its domestic consumers, or when a foreign firm prices its exports below their cost of product.

E

early warning system A mechanism that multinational institutions might use to track financial crisis indicators to determine that a crisis is on the horizon, thereby permitting a rapid response to head off the crisis.

economic efficiency A condition when scarce resources are allocated in a most productive, least-cost pattern.

economic exposure The risk that changes in exchange values might alter today's value of a firm's future income streams.

economic fundamentals Basic factors determining a nation's current exchange rate, such as the country's current and likely future economic policies and performance.

economic growth Occurrence when a nation experiences an increase in available resources or a technological advance and the nation's production possibilities expands.

economic integration The extent and strength of real-sector and financial-sector linkages among national economies.

economic profit Total revenue minus explicit and implicit opportunity costs.

economic union A trading arrangement that commits participating nations to remove all barriers to trade among their group, to abide by common restrictions on trade with other countries outside the group, to allow unhindered movements of factors of production within the group, and to closely coordinate all economic policies with other participants.

economies of scale A reduction in long-run average cost induced by an increase in a firm's output.

effective exchange rate A weighted-average measure of the value of a currency relative to two or more currencies.

efficient-markets hypothesis A theory that stems from application of the rational expectations hypothesis to financial markets, which states that equilibrium prices of and returns on bonds should reflect all past and current information plus traders' understanding of how market prices and returns are determined.

European option An option in which the holder may buy or sell an amount of a currency only on the day that the contract expires.

***ex ante* conditionality** The imposition of IMF lending conditions before the IMF grants the loan.

excess quantity demanded The amount by which quantity demanded exceeds quantity supplied at a given price.

excess quantity supplied The amount by which quantity supplied exceeds quantity demanded at a given price.

exchange rate Expresses the value of one currency relative to another currency as the number of units of one currency required to purchase one unit of the other currency.

exchange-rate band A range of exchange values, with an upper and lower limit within which the exchange value of the domestic currency can fluctuate.

exchange-rate system A set of rules that determine the international value of a currency.

exercise price The price at which the holder of an option has the right to buy or sell a financial instrument; also known as the strike price.

export subsidy A payment by a government to a domestic firm for exporting its goods or services.

***ex post* conditionality** The imposition of IMF lending conditions after a loan has already been granted.

externality A spillover effect influencing the welfare of third parties not involved in transactions within a marketplace.

F

factor price equalization theorem A theorem indicating that under the assumptions of the factor proportions model, uninterrupted trade will bring about equalization of goods prices and factor prices across nations.

factors of production The resources firms utilize to produce goods and services.

financial crisis A situation that arises when financial instability becomes so severe that the nation's financial system is unable to function. A financial crisis typically involves a banking crisis, a currency crisis, and a foreign debt crisis.

financial crisis indicator An economic variable that normally moves in a specific direction and by a certain relative amount in advance of a financial crisis, thereby helping to predict a coming crisis.

financial instability When a nation's financial sector is no longer able to allocate funds to the most productive projects.

financial sector A designation for the portion of the economy in which people trade financial assets.

financial sector development The strengthening and growth of a nation's financial sector institutions, payments systems, and regulatory agencies.

first-best trade policy A trade policy that deals directly with the problem that policymakers seek to remedy.

first-mover advantage A barrier to entry arising from the ability of the initial firm in an industry to develop marketing advantage by identifying its own product as the industry product.

fiscal agent A term describing a central bank's role as an agent of its government's finance ministry or treasury department, in which the central bank issues, services, and redeems debts on the government's behalf.

flexible exchange-rate system An exchange rate system whereby a nation allows market forces to determine the international value of its currency.

foreign-currency-denominated financial instrument A financial asset, such as a bond, a stock, or a bank deposit, whose value is denominated in the currency of another nation.

foreign direct investment The acquisition of assets that involves a long-term relationship and controlling interest of 10 percent or greater in an enterprise located in another economy.

foreign exchange derivative instruments Currency instruments with a return that is linked to, or derived from, the returns of other financial instruments.

foreign exchange market A system of private banks, foreign exchange brokers, and central banks through which households, firms, and governments buy and sell national currencies.

foreign exchange market efficiency A situation in which the equilibrium spot and forward exchange adjust to reflect all available information, in which case the forward premium is equal to the expected rate of currency depreciation plus any risk premium. This, in turn, implies that the forward exchange rate on average predicts the expected future spot exchange rate.

foreign exchange risk The risk that the value of a future receipt or obligation will change due to variations in foreign exchange rates.

forward exchange market A market for contracts that ensures the future delivery of and payment for a foreign currency at a specified exchange rate.

forward premium or discount The difference between the forward exchange rate and the spot exchange rate expressed as a percentage of the spot exchange rate.

forward shifted The portion of a tax that consumers pay in the form of a higher price per unit.

free-rider problem The potential for an individual to try to avoid contributing funds to pay for provision of a public good because he or she presumes that others will do so.

free trade area A trading arrangement that removes all barriers to trade among participating nations but that allows each nation to retain its own restrictions on trade with countries outside the free trade area.

G

gains from trade Additional goods and services that a nation's residents can consume, over and above the amounts that they could have produced within their own borders, as a consequence of trade with residents of other nations.

GDP price deflator A flexible-weight measure of the overall price level; equal to nominal GDP divided by real GDP.

General Agreement on Tariffs and Trade (GATT) An international agreement among more than 140 nations about rules governing cross-border trade in goods.

General Agreement on Trade in Services (GATS) An international agreement among more than 130 nations about rules under which services are traded internationally.

global public good A good or service that yields benefits to a number of the world's people simultaneously, cannot provide benefits to one person without others around the world deriving benefits at no additional cost, and cannot be withheld from a person who has failed to contribute to its provision.

globalization The increasing interconnectedness of peoples and societies and the interdependence of economies, governments, and environments.

gross domestic product (GDP) The value, tabulated using market prices, of all final goods and services produced within a country's borders during a given period.

Group of Eight (G8) The nations of France, Germany, Japan, the United Kingdom, the United States, Canada, Italy, and Russia.

Group of Five (G5) The nations of France, Germany, Japan, the United Kingdom, the United States.

Group of Seven (G7) The nations of France, Germany, Japan, the United Kingdom, the United States, Canada and Italy.

Group of Ten (G10) The nations of France, Germany, Japan, the United Kingdom, the United States, Canada, Italy, Belgium, the Netherlands, and Sweden.

Heckscher–Ohlin theorem A theorem stating that a relatively labor-abundant nation will export a relatively labor-intensive good, while a relatively capital-abundant nation will export a relatively capital-intensive good.

hedging The act of offsetting or eliminating risk exposure.

Herfindahl–Hirschman index The sum of the squares of the market shares of each firm in an industry.

horizontal foreign direct investment Establishment of a foreign subsidiary of a multinational firm that produces a good or service that is similar to the one the firm produces in its home country.

human capital The knowledge and skills that workers possess.

import quota A policy that restricts the quantity of imports.

industrial organization The study of the structures of and interactions among firms and markets.

industrial policies Government policies intended to promote the development of specific national industries.

inflation bias Tendency for the economy to experience continuing inflation as a result of discretionary monetary policy that takes place because of the time inconsistency problem of monetary policy.

intellectual property rights Laws granting ownership of creative ideas, typically in the form of a copyright, trademark, or patent.

inter-industry trade International trade of completely distinguishable goods and services.

international externality A spillover effect arising from market activities in one nation that influences the welfare of third parties in another country.

international financial architecture The international institutions, governmental and nongovernmental organizations, and policies that govern activity in the international monetary and financial markets.

International Monetary Fund A supranational organization whose major responsibility is to lend reserves to member nations experiencing a shortage.

international policy cooperation The development of institutions and procedures through which central banks share data and inform one another about their policy objectives and strategies.

international policy coordination The joint determination of monetary policies by a group of central banks for the intended combined benefit of the nations they represent.

international policy externalities Spillover benefits or costs that policy actions within one nation have for the economies of other nations.

intra-industry trade International trade of goods or services that are closely substitutable.

J

Jamaica Accords A meeting of the member nations of the IMF, occurring in January 1976, amending the constitution of the IMF to allow, among other things, each member nation to determine its own exchange-rate system.

L

large country A large country's market share is sufficiently large that the production and consumption decisions of its residents affect the global prices of goods and services.

law of demand An economic law that states that there is an inverse, or negative, relationship between the price that consumers are willing and able to pay and the quantities that they desire to purchase.

law of diminishing marginal returns An economic law stating that when more and more units of a factor of production such as labor are added to fixed amounts of other productive factors, the additional output for each new unit employed eventually declines.

law of supply An economic law that states that there is a positive or direct relationship between the prices producers receive and the quantities that they are willing to supply to the market.

leaning against the wind Central bank interventions to halt or reverse the current trend in the market exchange value of its nation's currency.

leaning with the wind Central bank interventions to support or speed along the current trend in the market exchange value of its nation's currency.

lender of last resort A central banking function in which the central bank stands willing to lend to any temporarily illiquid but otherwise solvent banking institution to prevent its illiquid position from leading to a general loss of confidence in that institution.

Leontief paradox A finding by Wassily Leontief that contradicted the Heckscher–Ohlin theorem, in that it indicated that imports of the United States, a relatively capital abundant nation, were relatively more capital intensive than the exports of the United States.

locomotive effect A stimulus to economic activity in one nation generated by an increase in economic activity in another country.

Lombard rate The specific name given to the interest rate on central bank advances that some central banks, such as the European Central Bank, set above current market interest rates.

long-run average cost The ratio of a firm's total production cost to its output when the firm has sufficient time to vary the quantities of all factors of production.

Louvre Accord A meeting of the central bankers and finance ministers of the G7 nations, less Italy, that took place in February 1987. The participants announced that the exchange value of the dollar had fallen to a level consistent with "economic fundamentals" and that the central banks would intervene in the foreign exchange market only to ensure stability of exchange rates.

M

M1 Currency plus transactions deposits.

M2 M1 plus savings and small time deposits, overnight Eurocurrencies and repurchase agreements, and balances of individual and broker-dealer money market mutual funds.

magnification principle A position of the Stolper–Samuelson theorem which implies that the change in the price of a factor is greater than the change in the price of the good that uses the factor relatively intensively in its production process.

managed or dirty float An exchange rate system in which a nation allows the international value of its currency to be primarily determined by market forces but intervenes from time to time to stabilize its currency.

marginal cost The additional cost that the firm incurs from producing an additional unit of output.

marginal product of capital The additional output generated by using an additional unit of capital.

marginal product of labor The additional output generated by employing the next unit of labor.

marginal revenue The additional revenue a firm earns from selling an additional unit of output.

marginal revenue product of capital The additional revenue generated by using an additional unit of capital.

marginal revenue product of labor The additional revenue generated by employing an additional unit of labor; also equal to marginal revenue times the marginal product of labor.

market clearing or equilibrium price The price at which quantity supplied equals quantity demanded. The equilibrium price is referred to as a market-clearing price, because neither an excess quantity demanded nor an excess quantity supplied exists at this price.

market demand A curve that illustrates the prices that consumers are willing and able to pay for various quantities of a good or service for a given time period, all other things constant. Because of the negative relationship between price and quantity demanded, the demand curve slopes downward.

market failure Inability of unhindered private market processes to produce outcomes that are consistent with economic efficiency, individual freedom, and other broader social goals.

market price The price determined by the interactions of all consumers and producers in the marketplace.

market supply A curve that illustrates the prices that producers are willing to accept for various quantities of a good or service they supply to the market for a given time period, all other things constant. Because of the positive relationship between price and quantity supplied, the supply curve slopes upward.

market wage rate The wage rate at which the quantity of labor supplied by all workers in a labor market is equal to the total quantity of labor demanded by firms in that market.

mercantilism A view that a primary determinant of a nation's wealth is international trade and commerce, so that a nation can gain by enacting policies that spur exports while limiting imports.

merit good A good or service that residents of a nation determine, typically through a political process, to be socially desirable.

minimum efficient scale The size at which a firm or industry minimizes its long-run average cost over a time frame in which quantities of all factors of production may be adjusted.

monetary aggregate A grouping of assets sufficiently liquid to be defined as a measure of money.

monetary base Central bank holdings of domestic securities and loans plus foreign exchange reserves, or the sum of currency and bank reserves.

monetary order A set of laws and regulations that establishes the framework within which individuals conduct and settle transactions.

monetary union A set of countries that choose to use a common currency.

monopolistic competition An industry structure with a relatively large number of firms, easy entry or exit, and similar but not identical firm products.

monopoly An industry that consists of a single firm.

moral hazard The potential for a buyer or seller to behave differently after an economic transaction than what was agreed to before the transaction.

most favored nation (MFN) A country that receives reductions in trade barriers to promote open international trade.

multilateralism An approach to achieving freer international trade via a wide interplay among many of the world's nations, with an aim toward inducing each country to treat others equally in trading arrangements.

N

nominal exchange rate A bilateral exchange rate that is unadjusted for changes in the two nations' price levels.

nominal gross domestic product (nominal GDP) The value of final production of goods and services calculated in current dollar terms with no adjustment for effects of price changes.

nominal interest rate A rate of return in current-dollar terms that does not reflect anticipated inflation.

non-tariff barriers Instruments other than import tariffs that restrict international trade.

O

official settlements balance A balance-of-payments account that tabulates transactions of reserve assets by official government agencies.

oligopoly An industry structure in which a few firms are the predominant suppliers of the total output of an industry, so that their pricing and production decisions are interdependent.

open-market operations Central bank purchases or sales of government or private securities.

opportunity cost The highest-valued, next-best alternative that must be sacrificed to obtain an item.

optimal currency area A geographic area within which labor is sufficiently mobile to permit speedy adjustments to payment imbalances and regional unemployment to permit exchange rates to be fixed and a common currency to be adopted.

outsourcing A strategy in which one organization hires another organization to complete a particular stage of the production process.

overvalued currency A currency in which the current market-determined value is higher than the value predicted by an economic theory or model.

P

parallel imports Gray-market imports, or goods and services brought into a country without authorization after initially being permitted to be sold elsewhere.

patent An inventor's legal title to the sole right to manufacture, utilize, and market an invention for a specific period.

pegged exchange-rate system An exchange rate system in which a country pegs the international value of the domestic currency to the currency of another nation.

Plaza Agreement A meeting of the central bankers and finance ministers of the G5 nations that took place at the Plaza Hotel in New York in September 1985. The participants announced that the exchange value of the dollar was too strong and that the nations would coordinate their intervention actions in order to drive down the value of the dollar.

policy-created distortion When a government policy results in a market producing a level of output that is different from the economically efficient level of output, causing a less than optimal allocation of an economy's scarce resources.

policy credibility Believability of a commitment by a central bank or governmental authority to follow specific policy rules.

policy rule A commitment to a fixed strategy no matter what happens to other economic variables.

policy time lags Time intervals between the need for a countercyclical monetary policy action and the ultimate effects of that action on an economic variable.

portfolio balance effect An exchange rate adjustment resulting from changes in government or central bank holdings of foreign-currency-denominated financial instruments that influence the equilibrium prices of the instruments.

portfolio investment The acquisition of foreign financial assets that results in less than a 10 percent ownership share in the entity.

predatory pricing A situation in which a firm sets artificially low prices intended to induce competitors to leave the industry and to dissuade potential rivals from entering the industry.

preferential trade arrangement A trading arrangement in which a nation grants partial trade preferences to one or more trading partners.

price discrimination Charging different consumers different prices for identical goods or services, or charging the same consumer different prices for the same good or service depending on number of units that the consumer purchases.

producer surplus The benefit that producers receive from the existence of a market price. Producer surplus is measured as the difference between the price that producers are willing to accept to supply a particular quantity and the market price.

production possibilities All possible combinations of total output of goods and services that residents of a nation can produce given currently available technology and resources.

public good Any good or service that can be consumed by many people at the same time, cannot be consumed by one individual without others also consuming it at no extra cost, and cannot be withheld from a person who has not contributed to funding its production.

purchasing power parity (PPP) A proposition that the price of a good or service in one nation should be the same as the exchange-rate-adjusted price of the same good or service in another nation.

put option An options contract giving the owner the right to sell an amount of a currency at a specific rate of exchange.

Q

quota rent A portion of the loss of consumer surplus caused by an import quota that is transferred to the foreign supplier as additional profits.

quota subscription The pool of funds deposited by IMF member nations that IMF managers can use for loans to member nations experiencing financial difficulties.

R

rational expectations hypothesis The idea that individuals form expectations based on all available past and current information and on a basic understanding of how markets function.

real exchange rate A bilateral exchange rate that has been adjusted for price changes that occurred in the two nations.

real gross domestic product (real GDP) A price-adjusted measure of aggregate output, or nominal GDP divided by the GDP price deflator.

real interest parity An equality between two nations' real interest rates that arises if both uncovered interest parity and relative purchasing power parity are satisfied.

real interest rate The anticipated rate of return from holding a bond after taking into account the extent to which inflation is expected to reduce the amount of goods and services that this return could be used to buy.

real sector A designation for the portion of the economy engaged in the production and sale of goods and services.

recognition lag The interval that passes between the need for a countercyclical policy action and the recognition of this need by a policymaker.

redistributive effects of trade Altered allocations of incomes among a nation's residents as a result of changes in international trade flows.

regionalism Establishment of trading agreements among geographic groupings of nations.

relatively capital-abundant nation In a two-country setting, the nation endowed with more capital units per labor unit than the other nation.

relatively capital-intensive good In a two-good setting, the good with a production process requiring more capital per labor unit than the other good.

relatively labor-abundant nation In a two-country setting, the nation endowed with more labor units per capital unit than the other nation.

relatively labor-intensive good In a two-good setting, the good with a production process requiring more labor per capital unit than the other good.

relevant market The true economic marketplace taking into account the availability of all products that directly constrain product prices for individual producers.

reserve currency The currency commonly used to settle international debts and to express the exchange value of other nation's currencies.

reserve requirements Central bank regulations requiring private banks to hold specified fractions of transactions and term deposits either as vault cash or as funds on deposit at the central bank.

response lag The interval between the recognition of a need for a countercyclical policy action and the actual implementation of the policy action.

revalue A situation in which a nation with a pegged exchange-rate system changes the pegged, or parity, value of its currency so that it takes a smaller number of domestic currency units to purchase one unit of the foreign currency.

rules of origin Regulations governing conditions under which products are eligible for trading preferences under trade agreements.

Rybczynski theorem The theory that if a nation experiences an increase in the amount of a resource, it will produce more of the good that uses the resource relatively intensively in its production process and produce less of the other good.

S

second-best trade policy A trade policy that deals indirectly with a problem that policymakers seek to remedy.

small country A country so small its consumption and production decisions do not affect the international price, so that its residents take the international price as a given.

sovereignty The supremacy of a nation's citizens to control the resources within its geographic borders.

special drawing right A composite currency of the International Monetary Fund in which the value is based on a weighted average of the currencies of five member nations.

specific tariff A tariff specified as an amount of money per unit of the good sold.

speculative attack A concerted effort by financial-market speculators to profit from anticipations of a depletion of official foreign exchange reserves via sales of assets denominated in the nation's currency intended to induce abandonment of an exchange rate target that will yield them profits in derivative markets.

spot market A market for immediate purchase and delivery of currencies.

sterilization A central bank policy of altering domestic credit in an equal and opposite direction relative to any variation in foreign exchange reserves so as to prevent the monetary base from changing.

Stolper–Samuelson theorem Theory that, in the context of the factor proportions model, free trade raises the earnings of the nation's relatively abundant factors and lowers the earnings of the relatively scarce factors.

strategic policymaking The formulation of national policies in light of the structural linkages among nations and the ways in which policymakers in other nations make decisions.

structural interdependence A situation in which interconnectedness of national markets for goods, services, and financial assets causes events in one nation to affect the economies of other nations.

supply The relationship between the prices of a good or service and the quantities supplied to the market by producers within a given time period, all other things constant.

T

tariff A tax on imported goods and services.

tariff-rate quota A quota that allows a specified quantity of a good to enter the country at a reduced tariff rate. Any quantity above that amount is subject to a higher tariff rate.

tax base The value of goods, services, incomes, or wealth subject to taxation.

tax competition Reducing tax rates below those of other regions in an effort to induce individuals and businesses to engage in taxable activities in that region.

tax rate A fraction of a tax base an individual or company is legally required to transmit to the government.

theory of optimal currency areas An approach to determining the size of a geographic area within which residents' welfare is greater if their governments fix exchange rates or adopt a common currency.

time inconsistency problem Policy problem that can result if a policymaker has the ability, at a future time, to alter its strategy in a way that is inconsistent both with the desires and strategies of private individuals and with its own initially announced intentions.

trade concentration ratio The sum of bilateral trade shares within a regional trading bloc divided by the region's share of world trade.

trade creation An additional amount of international trade resulting from trade preferences that a nation grants to a trading partner.

trade deflection The movement of goods or components of goods from a country outside a trading arrangement to one within such an arrangement so that the seller can benefit from trading preferences within the arrangement.

trade diversion A shift in international trade caused by one nation giving trade preferences to another, which can cause trade with a third country to decline.

trademark A company's legal title to a word or symbol that identifies its product and distinguishes it from the products of other firms.

trade share One nation's flow of international trade as a percentage of a regional or global trade total.

transaction exposure The risk that the revenues or costs associated with a transaction expressed in terms of the domestic currency may change due to variations in exchange rates.

translation exposure Foreign exchange risk resulting from the conversion of a firm's foreign-currency-denominated assets and liabilities into the domestic currency value.

transmission lag Time that elapses between the implementation of an intended countercyclical policy and its ultimate effects on an economic variable.

U

ultimate goals The final objectives of national economic policies.

uncovered interest parity A relationship between interest rates on bonds that are similar in all respects other than the fact that they are denominated in different nations' currencies. According to this condition, which applies to a situation in which an individual engages in unhedged currency trades to fund bond purchases abroad, the interest rate on the bond denominated in the currency that holders anticipate will depreciate must exceed the interest rate on the other bond by the rate at which the currency is expected to depreciate.

undervalued currency A currency in which the current market-determined value is lower than that predicted by an economic theory or model.

V

value added The revenue received by a producer less the cost of the intermediate good it purchased.

value-added taxes (VAT) Taxes applied to each stage of production in which value is added to a good or service.

vertical foreign direct investment Establishment of a foreign subsidiary of a multinational firm that produces components that are assembled elsewhere or uses components produced elsewhere to assemble the firm's final product.

voluntary export restraint (VER) An agreement between policymakers and producers in two nations to restrict the exports of a good from one nation to the other.

W

World Bank A sister institution of the International Monetary Fund that is more narrowly specialized in making loans to about 100 developing nations in an effort to promote their long-term development and growth.

World Trade Organization A multinational organization that oversees multilateral trade negotiations and adjudicates trade disputes that arise under multilateral trade agreements formed under the GATT and the GATS.

Index

A

B

C

D

E

F

G

H

I

J

K

L

M

N

O

P

Q

R

S

T

U

V

W

Y

Z

GREENLAND
ICELAND
CANADA
IRELAND
ATLANTIC OCEAN
U.S.A.
Canary Islands
MEXICO
THE BAHAMAS
WESTERN SAHARA
CUBA
DOM. REP.
JAMAICA
HAITI
BELIZE
HONDURAS
SENEGAL
GUATEMALA
EL SALVADOR
NICARAGUA
GAMBIA
PANAMA
COSTA RICA
VENEZUELA
GUYANA
FRENCH GUIANA
SURINAME
COLOMBIA
ECUADOR
PACIFIC OCEAN
PERU
BRAZIL
BOLIVIA
PARAGUAY
CHILE
ARGENTINA
URUGUAY
FALKLAND ISLANDS
SOUTH GEORGIA ISLAND